EXCEPTIONAL CHILDREN
IN TODAY'S SCHOOLS
Second Edition

Edward L. Meyen
University of Kansas

LOVE PUBLISHING COMPANY®
Denver, Colorado 80222

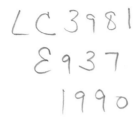
Cover photo location: Vail Public Library, Vail, Colorado

Statue of boy credit: Titled "The need to know" by Hollis Williford, Williford Arts Ltd.,
Loveland, Colorado

Cover photo credit: Jo Culbertson Design

Page 2 poem credit: "For Johanna" by Karen Kenyon, © Copyright 1974,
Meredith Corp. All rights reserved. Reprinted from *Ladies
Home Journal* magazine with permission of the author.

Chapter 16 credit: "*Challenge Projects for the Gifted Reader* © 1989.
Used with permission by Houghton Mifflin Company"

Chapter 16 credit: "Come to Think of It, Elbows Don't Look Much Like Elbows Either
by Dale Mazer. Reprinted by permission of *The Wall Street Journal*,
© Dow Jones & Company, Inc. (1989).
All Rights Reserved Worldwide."

Library of Congress Catalog Card Number 90-60835

Copyright © 1990 Love Publishing Company
Printed in the U.S.A.
ISBN 0-89108-213-1

Contents

Preface

American schools are in the midst of a major reform movement. Business and industry, concerned about the quality of the workforce, emphasize that people who enter the world of work must be prepared as problem-solvers and be capable of life-long learning. Policy makers are calling for the restructuring of schools and alternative approaches to the preparation of teachers. Parents and citizens generally share in their desire for more effective schools and in their concern for the burden that taxpayers must shoulder if significant changes are to occur. Within these broad and pervasive concerns are problems that focus on diversity in the classroom. It is here that children from multicultural backgrounds and those with disabilities and special talents share common needs. They challenge the abilities of teachers to accommodate their varying learning styles. Their education histories add to the teaching challenge in the classroom. Both groups require understanding, sensitivity, and a particular approach to pedagogy if qualitative changes in education are to be implemented successfully.

This book will introduce you to the special needs of exceptional children and youth, to their abilities and talents, and to the ways in which educational programs evolve in the schools in response to their changing needs. Particular attention has been given to selecting contributing authors who are experienced in teaching introductory courses and who are sensitive to the special qualities and needs of exceptional children and youth. Of equal importance has been the commitment to present new information and to ensure that contemporary issues are addressed.

The book begins with a chapter by Stuart Schwartz and Paul Sindelar, which reminds the readers of the humanistic qualities of students with special needs—their importance as individuals. It also points to the educator's obligation to understand them as learners and as individuals who should not be described by lists of characteristics or attributes, but, rather, by the values they hold and the talents they possess. In reading this chapter you will be forced to think about your personal perspectives on life as you temporarily assume the role of an individual who must cope with the demands of life often experienced by exceptional children and youth. This chapter is designed to provide you a humanistic frame of reference as you read the text and continue your study of students with special needs.

Introductory texts must be responsive to the changing conditions surrounding the lives and education of exceptional children and youth. It is not enough to provide readers a resource that summarizes the conditions which result in disabilities, outlines evolving public policies, and describes how schools and communities organize themselves to provide educational and related services to students with special needs. It is important to provide insights about the emerging models of service and about national events that can be expected either to affect who is considered exceptional or bring about changes in needed services. Introductory books also should cause readers to speculate on the future and their personal responsibilities as they assume professional roles.

This is the second edition of *Exceptional Children In Today's Schools*. In some ways it is an update in that it remains comprehensive, with chapters on each area of exceptionality, the organization of schools, legal issues, families, and early childhood education. And it is designed as a resource for the beginning student. But in many ways it is also a new book because it differs from the first edition in several ways. In addition to the focus on values and humanistic qualities in the first chapter, the book contains three chapters that have not been included typically in introductory texts. The chapter by Donna Lehr on "Special Health Needs of Today's Exceptional Children" addresses the subject of children born with the effects of drugs, AIDS, and similar contemporary issues. These conditions recently have increased the population of children who will grow up having special needs and whom the schools must be prepared to serve. The chapter by Marlene Pugach and Caren Wesson, on approaches to collaboration among professionals in providing support to special needs students in the schools, discusses the latest ideas on how professionals, through teaming, can best assist students with special needs in realizing their abilities and in meeting demands of schooling. The final chapter by Judy Smith-Davis places the education of exceptional children and youth in the larger context of society and challenges the reader to think about the future.

Texts, particularly those designed as introductory books, must meet varied expectations. Beginning students want an authoritative reference that is comprehensive and informative. They also want the content presented in an interesting style. Most expect to be challenged, but some hope for learning without effort. Through the collective efforts of the authors and editor we have attempted to focus on our perceptions of what beginning students in the study of exceptional children and youth expect from a good text. We respect your intellect, the knowledge you have acquired from other courses, and the insights you have gained from your personal experiences in working with children and youth. Above all, we acknowledge your capacity to go beyond this book in your search for information and your commitment to let inquiry and curiosity guide you as your career evolves.

Edward L. Meyen, 1990

Acknowledgments

Introductory books on exceptional children and youth pose a special challenge to authors. The content must be comprehensive, current, and sensitive to the interests of beginning students. The book must provide an overview, but at the same time treat each subject in enough depth to ensure the reader's readiness for subsequent courses in the field. This edition was a team effort, with care taken to select authors who are experienced in teaching introductory courses and knowledgeable about their speciality areas. I wish to express my appreciation to the authors for sharing their talent and insights and for their willingness to work within a book design based upon responses to the first edition and suggestions from students and professors of introductory courses.

Acknowledgment must also go to the researchers, educators, parents, policy makers, and to exceptional children and youth who have contributed to the changing of attitudes, expansion of knowledge, and the formulation of public policies that have influenced the futures of special students. Through their collective efforts, progress is being made in providing appropriate education for all students and the study of exceptional children and youth has taken on new meaning. Just as it is impossible to thank each advocacy group, it is not feasible to identify the many contributors to the literature whose views become part of the language of the profession or sources of ideas, or those whose anecdotes have found their way into the book.

As is always true in projects of this nature, there are individuals who make very special contributions and without whose help the book would not have survived the early draft stages. Appreciation is expressed to Stan Love, the publisher, and his staff for their concern for quality and personal interest in the book. Special mention is due Jeannette Johnson for her assistance in preparing the manuscript and to Cheryl Harrod for her help on the glossary. And to Jane Sorensen, who for a dozen years has kept me organized through projects of this nature, I remain indebted.

To my family—thanks again!

E.L.M.

1

Introducing Today's Exceptional Children

Stuart E. Schwartz
Paul T. Sindelar
University of Florida

FOR JOHANNA
By Karen Kenyon

Will you see the butterfly
  better because you won't
  wonder where he came from?

Will the flowers be brighter
  because you won't have to
  know their names?

Will you be able to trust
  completely in today because
  you will have no worries about
  tomorrow?

And will the world be a better place
  because of you?
Because you will not learn to hate,
  and you will not make war.
And you will not hold life to its promises,
  because it didn't give you any.

And you will be a part of everything,
  you will be the butterfly,
  you will be the flower.
And I will let you be all of this in me.

*Poem by mother of
mentally retarded infant girl.*

Understanding exceptional children and adolescents is difficult, especially for those of us who have never had the opportunity to experience disabilities. People who have had a broken leg or a serious but temporary illness have some idea of the effects of being exceptional, but they also knew at the time that their problem was not permanent. Having a full understanding of what an exceptionality is, how it "feels," and what its impact is on individuals and their families is critical for people who in their careers plan to work with exceptional individuals.

Aspiring airline pilots study their aircraft and the passengers who will be served. Future police officers review police tactics and laws as well as the people with whom they will be working. So must future special education teachers and other future professionals in related fields in which exceptional people are involved. Those who are entering special education must not only learn curriculum, instructional technology, and laws and legislation affecting the education of exceptional individuals; they must become totally familiar with these exceptional persons. It would not be sufficient for professionals simply to know definitions that explain what certain exceptionalities are. Nor would it be adequate for them to know merely how to identify these individuals, place them properly in special education programs, evaluate their progress, and write excellent reports describing that progress.

To be a true professional in a field such as special education or the many related areas that serve exceptional persons (such as physical therapy, art therapy, and speech therapy) requires knowledge of the exceptional person inside and out, backward and forward, thoroughly and comfortably. This chapter and book will greatly enhance your understanding of people who are commonly labeled as mentally retarded, gifted and talented, learning disabled, deaf, blind, physically disabled, emotionally disturbed, multiply handicapped, or speech/language impaired.

Activity 1, page 13, gives you a chance to understand the feelings of a handicapped child in a classroom.

You may associate exceptionality with school-age persons. We hear about learning disabled children, gifted and talented learners, mentally impaired children, and Jerry's kids. But what happens to these children at adulthood? What evidence do we see every day to remind us that exceptional people are around? Much of it has become so familiar that we accept it as part of our everyday world.

For example, most of us recognize that ramps leading into buildings provide access to people in wheelchairs. But what about curb cuts? Do you recognize their role in enabling persons in wheelchairs to move from streets to sidewalks, and from sidewalks to streets, without bone-jarring bumps? Adapted toilet facilities and modified machinery and equipment also enable persons with disabilities to function at work in a normalized fashion.

The same point may be made about braille labels on elevators and office doors. They enable blind persons to use certain facilities and find certain locations that previously required sight. Nature trails along which rope guides lead from exhibit to exhibit enhance the entertainment opportunities of blind persons as close captioned television broadcasts do for deaf and hearing impaired people.

Handicapped parking spaces and assistance at self-service filling stations provide disabled drivers greater opportunity to move around their communities. Like all drivers, they must understand and heed the caution sign warning of a deaf child in the neighborhood.

People with exceptionalities do not disappear in adulthood. In fact, so many have become so much a part of our lives that we have lost conscious sight of the ways in which our world has been adapted to their great advantage, and ours. This chapter is designed to assist you in taking a fresh look at persons, both children and adults, who are labeled as exceptional. Old stereotypes will be thrown aside, myths and misconceptions will be reviewed, differences and similarities between exceptional and nonexceptional people will be analyzed, and other avenues will be followed to aid you in discovering what really is within the person whose name is Exceptional.

EXCEPTIONALVILLE

Imagine yourself in a very busy airport after a particularly exhausting day. Although drowsy and partially dozing, you have been keeping one ear open listening for your flight home to be called. But you are so sleepy.

Ah, your flight's number has been called, which takes you dashing through the airport's corridor toward your aircraft. Rushing on board you wonder if you are really on the right plane. Did you hear the correct gate number? Of course, you must be on the right plane as the flight attendant would not have boarded you otherwise. Back to a deep sleep you go as the plane whisks you off to your destination.

The flight attendant is rousing you. You are finally there, and you bounce down the plane's off ramp only to discover that you must be in the wrong city. But being the brave soul that you are, you decide to explore your new environment prior to catching another flight. But the people here are very different. They are all more than 15 feet tall, and they communicate with hand gestures. Rushing to call home to let your family know that you are okay, you face your first difficulty. You cannot reach the telephone. Your next stop is the bathroom, but another crisis awaits. You cannot reach the toilet easily—it is so high! Hungry after that long flight? Just try to reach the tall counter to buy a hot dog! Exhausted running through the airport? But you cannot even climb into one of the chairs in the lobby!

Maybe one of these tall people will help you. Just ask; they look pleasant enough. But your voice is the first one you have heard, and these tall people just stare at you when you speak—they do not understand you. This is the first time you realize that it seems that everyone is looking at you. Why even some of the tall children are staring at you and laughing. Some of the adults are looking at you with pity in their eyes. Others shy away and do whatever they can to not look at you or not be near you.

Apparently they are very uncomfortable with someone who is so different—you! Why are they avoiding you? Laughing at you? Pitying you? Why you are really the same as they are in most ways. Are you not?

What is that noise? A loud voice is being repeated. Your flight number is being called. Awakening you realize that your flight has not yet left but that you had better end this dream and rush to catch that flight home.

Has this "dream" given you a different perspective by suggesting how those individuals who are exceptional may view you and their surroundings? If you were a visitor to Exceptionalville, you would have gained a better understanding of what it really is like to be different from the norm. If you have been ill for an extended period of time or if you have had a broken limb, you have gained an insight into the world of handicaps. But it is impossible for a nondisabled person to know truly what the world of handicaps is all about. If you wear the label of nondisabled, it may be difficult for you to understand the frustrations, worries, hopes, anguish, pains, and joys of being handicapped.

Hopes and Concerns

Think of a 6-year-old child who is facing the first day of school. That child must be excited about the new experience, frightened by the new situation and people, hopeful of making new friends, and eager to learn and participate in all of the school activities. In addition to all of these emotions and expectations, the child who is disabled must also face additional burdens. This special child must recognize that some of the other children will notice and call attention to the disability. The child will be affected by disability labels when being grouped for learning activities and when interacting with peers. Imagine what this child must be thinking when leaving the rather protective home to go to school.

A similar situation faces exceptional adolescents. This is the time when attention turns to such things as dating and sexual development, career entry, further educational opportunities, and physical appearance. These areas of concern are shared by both disabled and nondisabled youths. But those with disabilities have these concerns and many more. The effects of the exceptionality on social opportunities are a major consideration. Getting and keeping a job are hampered by misconceptions and negative attitudes. Entry into colleges may be limited due to disability and the need for support services (such as a tutor-notetaker for a deaf student and the availability of reading assignments on audiotape for blind students). Teens also consider physical appearance to have great importance, and students with disabilities are no exception. While the nondisabled student may be worried about a blemish, a disabled student may be fearful of peer reactions to a wheelchair or an artificial limb.

It is not easy being a child or an adolescent. And it is definitely not easy being a child or an adolescent with an exceptionality. As you work with exceptional children and youth, remember that they usually have all of the hopes and concerns that others have and then many more. By keeping this in mind, you will be better prepared to understand and work with handicapped children and adults.

In Exceptionalville you were really the exceptional person, and it would have helped for those people to realize that you really were not so different. Now it is your turn to learn that exceptional people are not so different either.

EXCEPTIONALITY

An exceptional person is simply a person who is different from the norm. (Later in this book you will have the opportunity to study about specific groups of different individuals. In this section we consider exceptionalities in general.) Being different from the norm does not imply that exceptional individuals are different in many or most respects; it merely implies that in one or some ways they are different. Exceptional people may learn more rapidly, run faster, have difficulty reading, behave erratically, rely on a different language than most people use, have a health problem, have difficulty with walking, or not see well. Although different, exceptional people are like nonexceptional people in most ways. They enjoy a good joke, desire to succeed in life, work for a living, watch TV or read good books, look forward to vacations, and enjoy relationships with others. A list of similarities would far exceed a list of differences. Try developing those lists—you will see!

Exceptional people differ in ways that either help or hinder their daily lives. On the one hand, those who are thought to be gifted or unusually talented may exceed others in such creative abilities as musical composition or performing. Or they may enjoy extra income and prestige from their ability to develop new vaccines to eradicate disease or new materials to be used in the space program. On the other hand, the disability may cause a difficulty or handicap for the individual.

The Difference Between Handicap and Disability

Most people think of the words *handicap* and *disability* as synonymous. Nevertheless, they have two distinct meanings that apply to persons who are exceptional. A disability usually refers to the condition the exceptional individual has, such as a missing limb, a learning disorder, or a speech difficulty. The disability may present minor or major problems for the person. Those problems may occur in learning, communication, social interactions, and employment and are actually the handicaps caused by the disability. Therefore handicaps are usually temporary or solvable problems created by the interaction between individuals and their environment.

Thus, a person without an arm has a disability but is only handicapped to the extent that he or she is unable to do certain tasks that require two arms. When the person uses a different method or a prosthetic device such as an artificial limb to accomplish a particular task, the handicap is erased or reduced even though the disability remains. Likewise, an individual who has a learning disability may have trouble doing mathematical computations. But when that person learns how to use an electronic calculator, the handicap caused by the learning disability is mitigated or ended. It is clear that a disability presents certain handicaps, and a major goal for disabled persons and for those who live and professionally interact with them is the reduction and elimination of the handicaps caused by the disabilities.

In analyzing the phenomenon of exceptionality, you must recognize that although some exceptionalities are obvious, others are hidden. The person who has epilepsy, the individual with a criminal record, the adult who reads on a second-grade level, and the mildly retarded person are exceptional in ways that are not easily detectable and therefore not known to others. People with hidden exceptionalities may or may not choose to let others know. Either strategy, depending on the attitudes of others, may cause specific expectations and behaviors.

Expectations and Behaviors

For instance, when people know that certain individuals have a particular disability, they may assist them, avoid them, or have lower expectations for them. Individuals who decide to enter a professional field that deals with exceptional people fit into the first category. Professionals who desire to work with handicapped individuals usually are more than willing and eager to work with persons with difficulties and are challenged by trying to find methods and strategies to reduce or overcome handicaps.

Others may shun exceptional individuals due to fears, myths, prejudice, or ignorance. Have you ever taken conscious steps to avoid a person with a severe disability? Because you are reading this book, you are probably a person with positive attitudes about others with disabilities; imagine what persons without your positive attitudes feel when seeing or discovering that a person is disabled. For the sake of "science," conduct your own survey by portraying a disabled person while shopping. Clerks may avoid you. People may walk away from you. Others may stare. Some people may get up and move to tables farther away when you are seated for lunch near them. People with hidden exceptionalities may tend to keep their secrets to avoid this type of unnecessary harassment and prejudice. People with visible disabilities have no choice but to help others reduce their fears, myths, and ignorance.

Still others may actually have lower expectations of disabled people. This would be true with those who are in careers related to handicapped persons and with those who are not. Imagine the reactions of those with less interest and understanding. Employers would make decisions not to hire disabled persons because of incorrect negative expectations associated with the label. Parents of disabled children would tend to treat them as children forever and not nurture them toward maturity. Special education teachers would likewise tend to interact with their students in ways that would not encourage emotional growth and independence. It behooves all of us to remember and remind others that avoidance and lowered expectations of exceptional individuals are extremely detrimental, prejudicial, ignorant, and totally unfair.

Labeling

The phenomenon of labeling, whether of a hidden or visible disability or whether of a severe or mild disability, is probably one of the most significant causes of difficulties for disabled people because labels create expectations in others. Imagine if we believed, and told everyone of our belief, that people who wear white socks were smelly, unable to learn, rude, dangerous, and dishonest. If we truly believed this were true and promoted this belief, manufacturers of white socks would soon be out of business. But when there are false beliefs about people who have other labels, such as deaf, physically disabled, gifted, or blind, the persons who own those labels cannot throw them out and stop buying them the way people who own white socks can.

Try wearing a sign (your own label) that says, "I am different," for a full day. You will see how differently you are treated. Imagine what it would be like if the sign were there permanently. You would quickly appreciate and probably hate the white socks phenomenon.

Activity 2, page 13, gives you a hands-on opportunity to experience the negative effects of labeling.

Labels create expectations in others. Try being different.

Labels also incorrectly suggest inappropriate behaviors toward people with exceptionalities. Some persons believe that it is necessary to shout at people in wheelchairs because they think that wheelchair users cannot hear. Others think that they cannot say, "Hi, it's nice to see you today" to a blind person. Those persons must think it improper to use such words as look, see, beautiful, pretty, and lovely with blind people, even though these words are part of our everyday language and blind people use them freely in conversations with others. Some individuals may incorrectly think that all gifted children are socially awkward and therefore may not invite them to parties. This, of course, may cause social awkwardness. Still others may avoid mentally retarded or mentally handicapped persons out of fear for their personal safety. These people do not realize that mentally handicapped people are usually kind, gentle, caring individuals who have no desire to ever harm another.

Labels play an important role in helping to assign youngsters to specific learning environments and therapy programs. Beyond that, "white socks" just do not seem to have any relevance or purpose. Professionals in special education and related areas can do much for exceptional individuals by merely convincing others that labels explain nothing. We should all be encouraging everyone to interact with persons who are disabled in a natural, normal way without prejudice, misconceptions, and incorrect expectations.

SIGNIFICANT INFLUENCES

To understand exceptional people, consider the environment in which they live, their age, the type and severity of the difference, public attitudes toward disabled persons, and the types and quality of intervention programs that have been available and utilized. These factors all play significant roles in how successful exceptional individuals are in childhood and adult adjustment.

Environment

A caring and supportive family environment is vital for all children. Children who are different share that need, and it may even be more critical for them to receive love and support. When children are recognized as intellectually gifted, their families often support enriched educational programs and offer additional growth and challenging learning opportunities at home. Children who are gifted but whose talents are not nurtured, however, may underachieve due to lack of motivation. They may even fail purposely to gain family and peer acceptance in an environment in which achievement is not valued.

Children who have learning or behavior problems likewise need supportive family environments. Parents who work with their children's teachers to provide a consistent family structure that supports school goals and behavioral expectations play a vital role in their children's development and improvements. Imagine how a learning disordered child would react in a family in which school failure is constantly ridiculed. Then recognize how that same student would fare if praised for small steps of achievement that were identified and jointly supported by family members and special education teachers.

Another example of the critical nature of the family environment is the parents' attitude toward independence. Those individuals whose parents accept that even handicapped children become adolescents and adults and therefore need some freedom to explore, learn independently, and take risks will probably achieve higher and faster than if they are raised in an overly protective family. When adolescents and young adults are treated like children and not given opportunities to mature and move toward independence, they may never become independently functioning adults. Too often disabled adolescents are treated like children by well-intentioned families when they really need the chance to become independent adults.

Age

Age is also an important factor to consider in understanding the phenomenon of exceptionality. The needs of all people, handicapped or not, differ with age. Just as nondisabled newborns need nurturing and care, so do disabled infants. Just as normally developing children need appropriate educational programs to ensure maximum achievement, so do children with disabilities. Just as adolescents need attention to careers and the effects of puberty, so do their disabled peers. When thinking of and attending to exceptional people, keep in mind all of the "normal" needs of their age group, and recognize that they have all of these needs in addition to those caused by the exceptionality.

Type and Level of Difference

The type of exceptionality and the level of difference, such as hard of hearing versus deafness, also are significant issues. The major categories of exceptionality—speech and language disorders, intellectual differences (in both directions), learning and behavior problems, physical disabilities, health impairments, and sensory difficulties—and their levels of severity are all related to different sets of expectations and characteristics and different problems and advantages.

Public Attitudes

The attitude of the public toward exceptional people seems to be improving, especially toward those persons with sensory impairments, speech and language difficulties, or learning disorders and those who are mildly rather than severely handicapped. Yet much work remains to be done to demonstrate to the public at large that exceptional persons are simply people with differences. Exceptional people themselves, university special education instructors, and professional persons in special education and related fields can do much to enhance the image of exceptional persons.

Disabled persons must strive to become visible in our everyday world and by example demonstrate that they are as normal as others. A public relations program that sells disabled people as normal, contributing, taxpaying members of society may do much to improve the public's image of disabled persons. Public speaking opportunities with local civic groups and with elementary and secondary school classes, for example, can be very effective in educating people about the contributions being made on a daily basis by many disabled Americans. That many disabled persons live independent or semi-independent adult lives deserves recognition. The effort that goes into their training and the savings that result to the public coffers are appreciated by far too few. The neighbors, shopkeepers, and persons who interact with these people in their everyday routines quickly understand that disability does not mean abnormality or inability. Whatever can be done by disabled citizens to promote these positive images and remove old stereotypes (such as blind people and physically disabled people begging) will help exceptional people.

Activity 3, page 14, provides you with an exercise that will enable you to recognize some of the frustrations wheelchair-bound people experience and some of the successes they achieve.

Teacher educators likewise have a major obligation to improve the life chances of disabled persons. Those students who are attending colleges and universities throughout the country are the leaders of tomorrow. It is essential that our local, state, and national leaders develop positive images of disabled persons and recognize their abilities. Present college students are the future leaders who will influence the hiring of people, the provision of community services, decisions on bank loans, and so on, and they must attend to the needs of disabled persons in a fair and just manner. A course, such as that taught by this chapter's senior author at the University of Florida where annually more than 2,100 undergraduates, 97% of whom are not preparing for careers related to education, learn about exceptional people, should be offered at every college in our nation. This can be a major step undertaken by college professors of special education to improve the life chances of exceptional people.

A similar obligation likewise lies with those professionals who have decided to work directly with exceptional individuals. It is not sufficient for special education teachers, vocational rehabilitation counselors, art and music therapists, speech and language therapists, psychologists and counselors, recreation therapists, and others engaged in the business of special education merely to provide services. Professionals must carry the message of the achievements and successes of disabled people to the community via public speaking engagements, other public relations activities, and everyday conversations with friends and colleagues. A major difference can be made in our communities if service providers, college instructors, and exceptional persons themselves actively engage in such positive image-building activities.

Types and Quality of Intervention

The types and quality of intervention programs available to all exceptional persons also play a critical role in determining the life success of handicapped individuals. Where early intervention programs, community sign language classes, integrated community recreation programs, appropriate special education programs, solid vocational rehabilitation programs, and other types of services exist, exceptional persons will have better opportunities to learn and succeed. It is critical that disabled people, their families, and the professionals who work with them become knowledgeable of the latest trends and research results so that they can help their local agencies, government, and educational institutions achieve high grades in terms of the services and intervention programs provided.

Normalization, a principle advanced by Wolfensberger (1972), suggests that persons with disabilities should receive services and be included in activities that are as normal as possible. Advocates for handicapped persons and handicapped persons themselves should constantly strive for normalization as a way of life, as a general attitude, and as a golden rule to ensure that they receive all to which they are entitled and nothing less. The concept of normalization does not suggest that we should "hire the handicapped"; it merely points out that we should hire the person who is able to do the job regardless of individual differences. Thus, if we keep in mind the principle of normalization as we work with exceptional individuals, we will demand nothing more than what is needed for their success and accept nothing less. The doors behind which handicapped persons have been hidden in the past are now opening, and special educators and handicapped people must ensure that they remain open.

SUMMARY THOUGHTS

New laws, legislation, parent groups, mainstreaming, deinstitutionalization, and improving attitudes are currently contributing to higher success levels for exceptional youth and adults. We are at an exciting time in society when attitudes are improving and opportunities are emerging. As you read this book and study about exceptional persons, recognize your developing role and critical responsibility in ensuring that disabled persons succeed. That is their goal. And that must be yours as well.

REFERENCES

Wolfensberger, W. (1972). Will there always be an institution? II: The impact of new service models: Residential alternatives to institutions. *Mental Retardation, 33,* 1453–1460.

1

Purpose

☐ To assist you in understanding the specific needs and feelings of handicapped youths in the classroom situation.

Steps

1. Read the following passage.
2. Describe what the teacher did well and poorly.
3. Describe how Rudy must have felt during the reading lesson.
4. Describe what effects this experience may have had on the other children.

Passage

Rudy dreaded being called on to read aloud and knew Mrs. Weller almost always asked for and called on volunteers. But the last time she substituted she misread the seating chart and believing she was calling on James (who, in the seat behind Rudy, was waving his hand frantically) called on Rudy instead. She compounded her error by insisting that Rudy take the turn. The tittering began before Rudy found his place and grew more obvious with each misread word. The excruciating moments he spent struggling with the words ended with an explosion of laughter. Mrs. Weller's comment that Rudy had forgotten his thinking cap only made matters worse. As Mrs. Weller walked into the classroom today, Rudy put his head on his desk, started to feel ill, and prayed that Mrs. Weller would be careful with *her* reading of the seating chart.

Analysis

☐ Did you identify the need for teachers (and substitutes) to be sensitive to the skill levels of individuals and to the problems that may be caused by forcing students to perform poorly in front of their peers?

☐ Were you able to completely analyze the effects of Rudy's experiences on him and the other students?

2

Purpose

☐ To give you an opportunity to "wear" a label and recognize the effects that a label has on exceptional persons.

Steps

1. Make a sign that says, "I am different," and pin it prominently on your clothing. Wear the sign for the entire day.

2. Keep a list of the reactions of others to you and of your feelings whenever you noticed others looking at you.

Analysis

☐ What were the typical reactions of others? Were they curious? Rude? Pleasant? Did they avoid you?

☐ How did you feel throughout the day? Were you embarrassed? Did you wish you could take the sign off? Did you avoid going certain places?

Purpose

```
3
```

☐ To experience some of the frustrations and difficulties exceptional persons often face.

☐ To recognize the successes and abilities of exceptional persons.

Steps

1. Obtain a wheelchair and use it for a few hours one day. Before starting, decide that you will not use your legs at all during the time period.

2. During the time period, do at least two or three activities, such as going to your school's library to check out a book or to a local shopping area to buy or eat something.

3. When you are finished, make a list of all your frustrations and a list of all your successes.

Analysis

☐ Did you recognize difficulties and frustrations that you had not imagined before?

☐ Were you able to identify the many successes and abilities that persons who use wheelchairs have?

2

Educating Exceptional Children Today

Edward L. Meyen
University of Kansas

If you are reading this book for an introductory course in special education, you are probably a member of the first generation of high school graduates who attended elementary and secondary school with classmates who had disabilities or handicapping conditions. Or you are an educator whose career has been in schools where the mainstreaming of children and youth with disabilities was a routine practice. The exclusion from or segregation within school of classmates or students with physical, sensory, intellectual, or emotional disabilities or problems is foreign to your personal experience. Of course, you are aware of individuals in your community who are called "mentally retarded" and who live at home; you may know of a child with severe disabilities who has spent much of his or her life in and out of hospitals or special schools. But in general, your experiences have been different from those of previous generations of students enrolled in introductory special education courses. Your attitudes toward exceptional children and youth and your knowledge of them are likewise different. This book has been planned and written with you in mind.

The passage in 1975 of Public Law (PL) 94-142, the Education for All Handicapped Children Act, significantly changed the futures of young people with disabilities and handicapping conditions. Nevertheless, even after more than a decade of major initiatives to ensure all exceptional children and youth a quality education, much remains to be achieved. Their learning problems have not disappeared, many fail to achieve their potential, teachers often lack the necessary instructional tools, families must persevere to obtain needed services, and the transition to employment, independence, and a quality social life as adults continues for some to be their most significant challenge. Circumstances have changed, but progress is slow. This book will help you understand from an educational perspective the process of social change as it affects the development and quality of life of exceptional children and youth. The emphasis in this book will be on building a foundation for you in your studies of exceptional children and youth.

This book is introductory. Its purpose is fourfold: (1) to provide you with an overview of how schools organize themselves to deliver special education services, (2) to aid you in understanding how disabilities and handicapping conditions affect the lives and education of young people, (3) to further your development of healthy attitudes toward them and their families, and (4) to introduce you to the issues and trends that our system of education is addressing in its attempt to achieve educational equity for *all* students.

THE EVOLUTION OF SPECIAL EDUCATION

The earliest attempts to educate children with handicapping conditions did not take place in the public schools. In the 19th century, most such children were educated in private residential settings known as "institutions" or "asylums." The first of these, the American Asylum for the Deaf, was established in 1817 at West Hartford, Connecticut. The Perkins School for the Blind opened in Watertown, Massachusetts, in 1831. As public acceptance of residential programs grew, institutions for the mentally retarded came into being and by the 1880s were common in several states (Gearhart, 1980).

Special Education in the Public Schools

Public school classes for the mentally retarded, deaf, and blind did not gain any popularity until the early 1900s. Programs for the mentally retarded increased in 1916 with the revision of the Stanford-Binet Intelligence Scale; this revision made differentiation of students by ability levels possible. Schools could thus identify children considered mentally retarded or underachieving (performing at a level lower than tested ability).

Intelligence testing subsequently became quite popular and provided the impetus for many practices in the schools beyond setting admissions criteria for certain special education programs. Such testing later came under considerable scrutiny, and the fairness of such testing for some populations of learners was questioned. This questioning continues periodically, and intelligence tests are revised in response to such criticisms of their fairness. Nevertheless, they remain a major factor in the diagnosis and placement of exceptional children in special education programs.

Until the late 1950s, public school services to exceptional children were limited primarily to children identified as mildly mentally retarded, hearing or visually impaired, emotionally disturbed, or physically handicapped. These children were served in self-contained special education classes that were segregated from other students or that were in special schools. Many such children were excluded from attending school altogether, and several groups that today receive special services were attending schools that gave little attention to their special instructional needs.

No state or federal special financial assistance existed for school districts providing special education, and only a few states had established eligibility criteria to guide program organization. Instead, students with special needs were grouped by disability and, to the extent possible, by age. Their educational needs were defined largely by their characteristics and the obvious implications of their disabilities or handicapping conditions. As educational programs for these children became more prevalent, however, teachers began to receive special training, curricula were developed for special students, and program standards began to evolve. At the same time, districts became sensitive to the increased cost of providing special education programs, if for no other reason than the pupil-teacher ratio for special education was much smaller and added to the cost.

Government Subsidization of Special Education

States soon began to subsidize local districts that elected to provide special services as a way of stimulating the development of special education programs. To ensure accountability, states established eligibility criteria for access to special education services and for receipt of special state financial aid. In sparsely populated rural areas where a district might have only three or four children with similar special needs, several districts would join together so that they had a sufficient number of children to justify establishing a class. In some states, such as Iowa and Wisconsin, multicounty cooperative units were organized to create a sufficient population base to support the provision of comprehensive special education services. (Cooperative models are still an effective mechanism for delivering services to special needs students in rural areas.)

With the expansion of special education services came demands for specially trained teachers. Training programs began to expand; colleges and universities offered summer programs in teaching methods so that teachers could receive emergency certificates to teach in special education. The early emphasis of educational efforts was on preparing teachers for the rapidly expanding classes of children with mental retardation. Unfortunately, there were few teacher educators qualified to provide the necessary training. In response, in 1958 Congress passed PL 85-926, which provided funds to prepare teacher educators to train teachers of children with mental retardation. This landmark piece of legislation was later expanded to cover other categories of the disabled.

The passage of PL 85-926 set the stage for a series of significant bills and amendments during the next two decades that culminated in the passage in 1975 of PL 94-142, which declared that public schools must provide equal educational opportunity to all students with disabilities and handicapping conditions, including students with severe/profound handicaps. (Implementation of PL 94-142 began in 1978.) These two decades also saw the expansion of special education programs to include children with learning disabilities. These changes were accompanied by a philosophical shift among educators away from advocacy of separate programs and toward advocacy of integration of special needs students into regular classes. Special interest groups, including the movement among the disabled for equal rights, agitated at federal, state, and local levels for greater equality of opportunity and access. Later, federal legislation mandated that states must also provide services to special needs children from 3 to 5 years of age, which added another group to the family of exceptional children in the public schools. Public attention is currently focused on children with Acquired Immune Deficiency Syndrome (AIDS), abused and neglected children, and adjudicated youths as groups in need of special services. These groups may at some point also join those considered exceptional.

IDENTIFYING EXCEPTIONAL CHILDREN

The establishment in the 1950s of eligibility criteria for special education programs began the process of "defining" exceptional children and youth. This defining process shifted the focus from describing the child's characteristics to matching the child's needs with the features of special education programs. One consequence of this approach is that such definitions are meaningful to educators but are not necessarily useful to practitioners in other disciplines or to parents and the lay public.

Another consequence is that children are referred to by labels as if the labels are intrinsically meaningful.

The basis of the defining process is this:

A child becomes "diagnosed" as exceptional when he or she meets the eligibility criteria for participation in special education services. These criteria typically are set by state educational agencies. Thus for educational purposes, a group of children with special needs will not be considered exceptional until appropriate programs become available and eligibility criteria for entrance into these programs are established. In identifying exceptional children or in determining eligibility for special education services, the school district must consider the services and interventions needed to give the learner an appropriate education (see Table 2.1). If a student has a handicapping condition but is able to function effectively and without assistance in the regular education program, the child is not considered exceptional. If the impairment at some point leads to a need for special services, then the student

Table 2.1 Types of Exceptionalities and Service/Instructional Implications

Exceptionality	Special Service/Instructional Implications
Hearing impaired	• Special language and speech training • Low pupil-teacher ratios • Amplification equipment (e.g., hearing aid) • Acoustically treated classrooms • Special seating arrangements in regular class • Adapted or specialized assessment techniques • Interpreters
Visually impaired	• Reader service • Braille or other technology • Special materials (e.g., large print, audio-transcriptions) • Mobility training • Resource teacher or tutors when placed in regular classes
Physically handicapped	• Special equipment • Possible structural changes for access to facilities • Special instructional techniques because of secondary handicaps • Instruction aids (e.g., stand-up tables, page turners) • Adaptive physical education
Mentally retarded	• Curriculum modifications • Special instructional techniques • Cognitive testing • Early emphasis on vocational skills • A major concern for social development
Emotionally disturbed	• Mental health treatment services

is considered exceptional. Similarly, a student currently receiving services may at some point not need them; then the student would no longer be considered exceptional. (This focus on the educational implications of the child's condition differentiates the educational approach to the defining of exceptional from the medical perspective on disease; the latter approach emphasizes the identification of symptoms, diagnosis, the prescription of appropriate treatment.)

The primary focus on the instructional implications of a child's disability, rather than on the specific physical or behavioral characteristics of that disability, makes determination of exceptionality far from precise. If the student's need for special services or instructional interventions could be ignored and all the attention given to learning characteristics, educators would have a much easier job. But that could lead to the overidentification of children as exceptional. For example, some students with physical disabilities do not require special assistance and might be disadvantaged through special educational placements or the use of special services.

Table 2.1   *continued*

Exceptionality	Special Service/Instructional Implications
Emotionally disturbed	• Special educational and behavioral techniques • Counseling • Close school/family cooperation and intervention
Gifted and talented	• Curriculum modifications • Broadened experiences • Access to specialized instructional facilities • Emphasis on leadership development
Learning disabled	• Intense remediation • Varied performance in school-related skills • Close monitoring of academic progress • Specific problems difficult to diagnose • Performance problems frequently related to language
Speech disordered	• Impact primarily in communication • Emphasis on speech/language development • Frequently a secondary handicap • Individual and/or group therapy • Highest incidence among all exceptionalities • Assistance from specialists and regular and/or special teachers
Severely multiply handicapped	• Low pupil-teacher ratio • Early emphasis on self-help skills • Application of behavioral analysis techniques • Assistance in language development • Assistance in positioning • Frequent motoric problems • High incidence of secondary handicaps

Refining Eligibility Criteria

States have made significant progress in refining eligibility criteria for admission to special education programs and in developing regulations that ensure program quality. In addition to eligibility requirements, controls typically include caseloads, pupil-teacher ratios, and, in some cases, the quality of physical facilities or the availability of special equipment. The goal for the future is to develop ways of identifying children and youth with special needs and to provide for their needs appropriately without giving them labels such as mentally retarded, learning disabled, emotionally disturbed, or hearing impaired. In order for this to happen, schools will have to offer a broad array of services and instructional options to accommodate the full spectrum of student needs. As instruction becomes more individualized for all students, the visibility that accompanies being identified as exceptional and assigned to special services will be reduced. In essence, the features of special education will become the norm, and the stigma of receiving special services will disappear. In the interim, the trend away from terms that serve to label children and toward instructional descriptors continues. Instructional options that direct attention away from the student and toward the range of instructional interventions required to accommodate varied learner needs include:

☐ Accurate, in-depth assessment of learner strengths and weaknesses
☐ Attention to intensive remediation intervention by specially trained teachers, support personnel, and instructional aides
☐ A focus on instructional needs that require more time to remediate than routinely can be accomplished in regular instructional settings
☐ Precise instructional planning by teachers and support personnel
☐ The use of specially designed instructional materials and/or activities
☐ Modifications or adaptations in the organization and/or structure of the regular curriculum.

SPECIAL EDUCATION TERMS AND CONCEPTS

As is true in most fields of study, traditional terms take on different meanings in the course of time, and new terms are added to the nomenclature. Presently, at least four sets of terms warrant clarification: exceptional/handicapped, disability/handicap, categorical/noncategorical, and basic principles and definitions related to PL 94-142. The following definitions of these terms are used in this book.

Exceptional/Handicapped

Exceptional refers to the wide range of children with handicapping conditions and special abilities requiring instructional modifications and/or special education, including the gifted and the talented. *Handicapped* refers to the wide range of children with handicapping conditions requiring instructional modifications and/or special education but not including the gifted and the talented. Although educators have readily used these terms among themselves in program development, the public continues to interpret the terms differently. The general preference of the lay public is to use *exceptional* when referring to the gifted and the talented and *handicapped* when referring to individuals with known handicapping conditions. Thus, some confusion still exists in the use of these terms.

Disability/Handicap

Disability is often used to denote a specific condition such as a heart ailment, loss of a limb, or paralysis. More precisely, the term refers to the condition itself, not to its impact on the person. *Handicap* is increasingly used to describe the consequences of a disability. In other words, a person becomes handicapped if he or she is limited functionally by a disability. During the 1970s, the equal rights movement for the handicapped, as it gained momentum, focused considerable attention on differentiating between disability and handicap. Some individuals function effectively in spite of a disability, whereas others are unable to function effectively as a result of a disability. Thus, a disability may become a handicap for some but not for others.

Categorical/Noncategorical

Categorical refers to a specific type of exceptional child—for example, the mentally retarded, deaf, learning disabled, or emotionally disturbed. A type of exceptionality constitutes a category. When special education programs are organized to serve children by type of exceptionality, they are often referred to as categorical programs.

Noncategorical refers to programs that are based not on types of exceptionality but on instructional needs. Children with different handicapping conditions may have similar instructional needs in areas such as language, math, and reading. Noncategorical programs emphasize the common instructional needs rather than the cause (handicap) of the need. Such programs are sometimes referred to as *interrelated*.

Activity 1, page 45, allows you to understand the term *exceptional child* and to explore the perceptions other people have of this term.

Evidence suggests that exceptional students have many similar instructional needs and that giving primary attention to their exceptionality is somewhat artificial. In each there has been a trend toward placing more emphasis in teacher training on noncategorical approaches to preparing teachers of the handicapped. Nevertheless, there also are instructional needs that are unique or at least specific to each exceptionality. Although the trend is away from using categorical labels in identifying exceptional children, most states maintain eligibility requirements based on programs for children with certain characteristics. In allocating fiscal resources, much of the state and federal legislation also defines the needs of students by areas of exceptionality. Thus, the categorical orientation remains somewhat necessary for communication among professionals and for funding of programs.

PL 94-142 Principles and Definitions

Due process refers to specific due process procedures that districts must implement and make known to parents and guardians. The intent of these procedures is to ensure that discriminatory practices do not occur and that if they do occur, they can be challenged. Due process procedures are set by state and federal law and are highly detailed. They include but are not limited to the right to appeal, the right to cross-examine, and the right to be represented by counsel. Although the due process provision allows for impartial hearings when a parent or guardian is not satisfied with a child's program, the goals of all concerned should be to resolve the conflict cooperatively in the best interest of the student and to avoid time-consuming and costly litigation.

Free and appropriate education refers to the provision that school districts cannot exclude children from an appropriate education because of disability. Appropriateness includes an individualized educational program (IEP) and those related services required to meet the student's needs. Because appropriateness is difficult to assure, the IEP must be agreed to by parents and guardians and must be periodically evaluated.

Individualized educational program refers to a written plan describing the student's educational program. It includes a statement of the student's current performance, annual goals, short-term objectives, related services, and evaluation criteria. The IEP is a source of accountability in determining whether a student is receiving an appropriate education.

Least restrictive environment (LRE) refers to the provision that to the maximum extent appropriate, handicapped children in public and private facilities are to be educated with children who are not handicapped. This principle set the stage for what has become identified as *mainstreaming*—the placement of handicapped children in regular classes, with the appropriate instructional support offered the student and/or consulting assistance offered the teacher. Mainstreaming, as the term is popularly employed, is not synonymous with LRE, as there are levels of least restrictiveness depending on the nature of a child's disability. For example, placement in a self-contained special class may be least restrictive for a severely/profoundly handicapped child.

The U.S. Department of Education, through regulations to implement PL 94-142 has set forth specific definitions for groups considered to be handicapped within the context of the law. The term *gifted* was not included in the act and is therefore not in these regulations. Schools, however, do include the gifted in their special education programs. The primary change brought about by these regulations concerns autism. The term *autism,* which was originally included in the definition for "seriously emotionally disturbed," is now included in the definition for "other health impaired." These definitions influence the eligibility criteria for special education services established for state education agencies (see Table 2.2 for federal definitions).

THE ORGANIZATION OF SCHOOLS TO SERVE EXCEPTIONAL STUDENTS

The public schools always seem to be in a state of transition in how they organize themselves to deliver special education services to exceptional children. Not only are schools continually expanding the populations they serve, but new approaches to delivering services appear in the literature on a regular basis and influence how schools organize special education programs. Some of the influence is due to active research programs in special education; other modifications result from changes in state regulations or from federal mandates. Since the early 1970s, there has been a movement to mainstreaming. For the mildly handicapped, this typically takes the form of regular class placement. As a result of mainstreaming, self-contained special classes have become less popular, while the use of resource rooms and of consultants to assist regular class teachers in accommodating the instructional needs of exceptional students in their classrooms has increased. Severely/profoundly handicapped children who once were placed in separate facilities or not served at all are now placed in special classes in regular attendance centers and in some districts are integrated on a part-time basis in regular classes. Contractual agreements are evolving between school districts and health agencies to provide special education to infants and toddlers with disabilities. Within the schools, new roles emerge in response to district preferences about how exceptional children can be best served in their particular situations; more traditional roles remain as options because they have stood the test of time for specific circumstances.

Because student needs vary and local organizational structures differ in how they respond to students and community needs, no single assortment of services, arrangements, or roles is "right" for all situations. Each district has had to explore existing options and develop new ones, thereby creating a range of options that allows individual needs to be met. Although school districts may refer to these options by different names and may have various means for implementing them, a typical pattern of options is available through individual school districts or through several districts cooperating to provide them. These widely used service delivery options fall into 10 categories.

Regular Class

For a number of years, regular classes were not considered appropriate for handicapped students. Today, with skilled teachers and support services for both teacher and student, regular classes are a feasible option. Most exceptional students now receive a portion of their instruction from regular class teachers. The number of exceptional students placed full time in regular classes continues to grow as special materials become available and as teachers develop skills suited to the needs of exceptional children.

Consulting Teacher

These specialists provide consultation to teachers and other school personnel. Consulting teachers do not instruct or offer other direct services to students, although

Table 2.2   Federal Definitions of Handicapped Children

(a) As used in this part, the term "handicapped children" means those children evaluated in accordance with Regs. 300.530–.534 as being mentally retarded, hard of hearing, deaf, speech impaired, visually handicapped, seriously emotionally disturbed, orthopedically impaired, other health impaired, deaf-blind, multi-handicapped, or as having specific learning disabilities, who because of those impairments need special education and related services.

(b) The terms used in this definition are defined as follows:

   (1) "Deaf" means a hearing impairment which is so severe that the child is impaired in processing linguistic information through hearing, with or without amplification, which adversely affects educational performance.

   (2) "Deaf-blind" means concomitant hearing and visual impairments, the combination of which causes such severe communication and other developmental and educational problems that the child cannot be accommodated in special education programs solely for deaf or blind children.

   (3) "Hard of hearing" means a hearing impairment, whether permanent or fluctuating, which adversely affects a child's educational performance but which is not included under the definition of "deaf" in this section.

   (4) "Mentally retarded" means significantly subaverage general intellectual functioning existing concurrently with deficits in adaptive behavior and manifested during the developmental period, which adversely affects a child's educational performance.

   (5) "Multi-handicapped" means concomitant impairments (such as mentally retarded–blind, mentally retarded–orthopedically impaired, etc.), the combination of which causes such severe educational problems that they cannot be accommodated in special education programs solely for one of the impairments. The term does not include deaf-blind children.

   (6) "Orthopedically impaired" means a severe orthopedic impairment, which adversely affects a child's educational performance. The term includes impairments caused by congenital anomaly (e.g., clubfoot, absence of some member, etc.), impairments caused by disease (e.g., poliomyelitis, bone tuberculosis, etc.), and impairments from other causes (e.g., cerebral palsy, amputations, and fractures or burns which cause contractures).

   (7) "Other health impaired" means

      (i) having an autistic condition, which is manifested by severe communication and other developmental and educational problems; or

      (ii) having limited strength, vitality, or alertness, due to chronic or acute health problems such as a heart condition, tuberculosis, rheumatic fever, nephritis, asthma, sickle cell anemia, hemophilia, epilepsy, lead poisoning, leukemia, or diabetes, which adversely affects a child's educational performance.

these consultants may work with exceptional students when demonstrating a teaching technique or material to teachers. Most districts do not assign supervisory or administrative responsibilities to consulting teachers. Their major purpose is to give teachers access to resource people who are knowledgeable about instructional programming for exceptional students.

Consulting teachers have had previous experience and training as regular and special teachers, and districts employing these specialists have found them to be particularly helpful in maintaining exceptional students in regular classes. The new-

---

Table 2.2   *continued*

---

(8) "Seriously emotionally disturbed" is defined as follows:
   (i) The term means a condition exhibiting one or more of the following characteristics over a long period of time and to a marked degree, which adversely affects educational performance:
      (A) an inability to learn, which cannot be explained by intellectual, sensory, or health factors;
      (B) an inability to build or maintain satisfactory interpersonal relationships with peers and teachers;
      (C) inappropriate types of behavior or feelings under normal circumstances;
      (D) a general pervasive mood of unhappiness or depression; or
      (E) a tendency to develop physical symptoms or fears associated with personal or school problems.
   (ii) The term includes children who are schizophrenic. The term does not include children who are socially maladjusted, unless it is determined that they are seriously emotionally disturbed.
(9) "Specific learning disability" means a disorder in one or more of the basic psychological processes involved in understanding or in using language, spoken or written, which may manifest itself in an imperfect ability to listen, think, speak, read, write, spell, or to do mathematical calculations. The term includes such conditions as perceptual handicaps, brain injury, minimal brain dysfunction, dyslexia, and development aphasia. The term does not include children who have learning problems which are primarily the result of visual, hearing, or motor handicaps, of mental retardation, of emotional disturbance, or of environmental, cultural, or economic disadvantage.
(10) "Speech impaired" means a communication disorder such as stuttering, impaired articulation, a language impairment, or a voice impairment, which adversely affects a child's educational performance.
(11) "Visually handicapped" means a visual impairment which, even in correction, adversely affects a child's educational performance. The term includes both partially seeing and blind children.

Under separate legislation, the Gifted and Talented Children's Education Act of 1978, which later was incorporated into the Education Consolidation and Improvement Act, Congress defined gifted and talented children as "children, and whenever applicable, youth, who are identified at the preschool, elementary, or secondary level as possessing demonstrated or potential abilities that give evidence of high performance capability in areas such as intellectual, creative, specific academic, or leadership ability, or in the performing and visual arts, and who, by reason thereof, require services or activities not ordinarily provided by the school" (Sec. 902).

Source: From E. L. Meyen and T. M. Skrtic, 1988, *Exceptional Children and Youth: An Introduction*, pages 10–12, Denver: Love Publishing Co.

ness of this option accounts for the lack of a clear "job description," however. Consulting teachers, in addition to helping teachers resolve instructional problems specific to individual students, may assume leadership roles in curriculum development, program planning and evaluation, or organization of assessment programs and may help coordinate the implementation of IEPs.

Itinerant Teacher

Itinerant teachers provide services directly to exceptional students assigned to regular classes or other instructional settings. Itinerant teachers do not maintain separate classrooms but aid individual students who are having difficulties. For example, an itinerant teacher may help a student with a visual impairment develop braille writing skills, may prepare materials for the student, or may obtain audiotape material. The nature of the service depends on the individual's needs. The itinerant teacher may work with the exceptional student within the regular class or prepare materials for use by other students in the regular class. If the exceptional student requires more regular and sustained instruction, a resource teacher will likely enter the picture.

Resource Teacher/Resource Room

In most schools, the most common alternative to regular class placement is the resource room or resource teacher. The key element is not the room but the *role* of the teacher and the way in which the teacher delivers instruction. Typically, a student whose needs cannot be met fully in a regular class is assigned to a resource

Resource room teachers assist students with special learning needs.

teacher for supplemental instruction 1 or 2 hours each day. The resource teacher is usually assigned several students and works with five or six at a time. Each student's program is individually planned and is coordinated with the instruction the student is receiving in a regular class. Resource teachers most frequently assist students in reading and mathematics. At the secondary level, resource teachers may work with students in a number of subject areas. The goal is to improve the student's performance so that he or she can function effectively in a regular classroom setting. The intent is to use the resource teacher as a *resource,* not as a primary source of instruction.

Special Class

Special classes represent an option for students whose instructional needs cannot be met through placement in a regular class supplemented by other services. Most special classes are self-contained (consisting of several exceptional students with similar needs) for purposes of instruction. Sometimes students are assigned to a special class and receive additional services from a speech clinician or physical therapist. The special class teacher is usually responsible for the student's total curriculum. Although special classes are most frequently used at the elementary level for students with moderate to severe handicapping conditions, they are also used at the secondary level. Part-time placement in a special class is an additional instructional option. In this situation, a student may attend a regular class part time and also may receive the services of a resource teacher.

Homebound Instruction

Many handicapped students have physical or health problems that cause them to miss school from time to time. To minimize educational interruptions caused by a student's confinement at home, a special teacher is often employed to provide homebound instruction. The primary role of these teachers is to coordinate instruction with the student's regular teacher in order to help the student maintain progress in his or her school program. In unusual circumstances a student may have homebound instruction for an extended time, but the basic intent is to provide short-term help while the student is able to participate in the school setting.

Hospital School

Some hospitals that specialize in treating children with handicapping conditions also operate educational programs. These programs are typically offered in cooperation with the local school district and are designed to minimize the interruptions in schooling caused by a child's hospital stay. In some cases, a homebound teacher works with the student in the hospital.

In larger programs an instructional staff is assigned full time to the hospital, with primary responsibility for helping students with their schoolwork during their hospital confinements. A major feature of hospital school programs is the coordination of instruction with the student's teachers at school. Sometimes this is complicated because hospitals specializing in treatment of handicapped students often provide regional services and students must leave the home school district to receive medical treatment. When this happens, plans are made in advance to coordinate the educational program before the child is admitted to the hospital.

Transitional Programs

A number of service options have been developed to enhance the transition of students from special education to adulthood, including support systems designed to assist handicapped youths in acquiring and sustaining employment as well as postsecondary education opportunities. Examples of transition services include the following:

Adult activity center: a facility that provides instruction in daily living skills, training in work tasks, and recreation. The center usually serves clients who have moderate to severe handicapping conditions.

Enclaves: an approach to work involving groups of clients working together under supervision in business or industry.

Job coach: a person who provides one-on-one training to a client at a job site. The job coach also provides follow-up to determine the need for additional training.

Mobile work crews: an approach to work involving groups of clients working under supervision at different sites in a building or a community.

Supportive employment: an approach to work involving clients being integrated into community work settings, being paid, needing continued support, and probably receiving training from a job coach for varying periods of time.

Sheltered workshop: a facility designed for persons not able to work in competitive environments. The person typically receives training to perform specific work tasks that can be performed for pay under supervision in the sheltered workshop.

Day School

Special day schools are attendance centers designed exclusively for handicapped students. They may be operated by either public or private agencies. These schools offer an instructional program and special services but do not include residential care. A child may live at home, in a foster home, or in some other living situation while attending a day school. During the 1950s and 1960s, a number of school districts centralized programs for handicapped students in order to achieve a number sufficient to permit organization of classes by age and ability levels. A day school may be designated as an attendance center for handicapped students, in which case students are transported to that location. With the change toward least restrictive environments, however, most schools dispersed their special programs. Very few districts still operate special day schools, although privately supported day schools are still in existence.

Residential Center

Residential centers, both state and privately operated, offer 24-hour comprehensive care that includes education, recreation, special services, and medical treatment. As a result of the trend in recent years toward deinstitutionalization, state residential programs now primarily serve severely/profoundly handicapped individuals. Only students for whom the LRE is residential care are placed in these settings. If a local school district does not have sufficient resources to provide properly for the needs of a handicapped student, the district may decide that a residential facility offers the most appropriate placement for that individual.

INSTRUCTIONAL SUPPORT SERVICES

Many handicapped students need supporting services in order to participate in instructional programs. Implementation of the LRE approach has caused school districts to increase their instructional support services. The term *instructional* (rather than *special* or merely *support services*) illustrates the relationship between services and instruction. Without support services, many handicapped students would not profit from instruction or would be placed in more restrictive environments. For example, physical therapy may improve a student's motor skills, allowing greater mobility and participation in a wider range of educational opportunities. The seven types of personnel who most frequently provide these services also participate in program planning.

Speech-Language Pathologist (SLP)

The largest single group of students requiring special services consists of those with speech and language disorders. For many handicapped students, speech and language disorders are a secondary handicap; for others, speech and language problems constitute their only handicap. Speech-language pathologists (or clinicians) conduct individual and group therapy sessions as well as serve as consultants to classroom teachers. Historically, SLPs worked mostly with speech disorders—articulation problems, voice disorders, or stuttering—but since the late 1970s, language disorders have received increasing attention. This SLP role is still evolving, and SLP training has broadened somewhat to accommodate these new roles.

School Psychologist

The school psychologist's role continues to change. During the 1950s and 1960s, much of his or her time was spent in administering intelligence tests to determine eligibility of students for special class placement. Although extensive assessment services continue, the emphasis has been broadened to include criterion measures and many forms of nondiscriminatory tests. School psychologists now spend more time consulting with teachers in curriculum planning, conferring with parents, and coordinating team meetings. The basic role of the school psychologist has expanded from that of an evaluator to that of a resource person knowledgeable about student behavior, instruction, program development, and assessment.

Physical Therapist (PT)

With the recent development of public school programs for the severely/profoundly handicapped, the need for physical therapy has increased substantially. On the prescription of a physician, the PT provides treatment in the general area of motor performance and focuses on correction, development, and prevention.

Occupational Therapist (OT)

Occupational therapy comprises individual and group activities designed to enhance social, psychological, and cognitive development. Although it has been a major service in the general field of rehabilitation for a long time, occupational therapy has not been routinely provided by the public schools. Many handicapped students, however, require this service, and it is becoming an important component in comprehensive programming. Currently, OTs in the school system work primarily with early childhood programs for the handicapped and with programs for the severely/profoundly handicapped.

School Social Worker

With the current emphasis on placement programming conferences, the school social worker's role has taken on increased importance. Efforts are being made to train school social workers to become skilled in communication, casework, planning, and counseling. The functions of the school social worker have at times influenced the role of the school psychologist. In many schools, much of what can be described as casework has been assigned to school social workers. Their responsibility in serving students now goes far beyond the monitoring of truancy often identified with them in the past.

School Nurse

The school nurse has an important task in identifying handicapped children, especially those with sensory or health-related problems. Because many handicapped students are vulnerable to communicable diseases and have special health needs, the services of a school nurse are essential. These professionals also provide consultation in interpreting the needs of handicapped students to parents and teachers. In addition, the school nurse is sometimes involved in placement or program decisions affecting students with health-related needs.

Adaptive Physical Education Therapist and Music Therapist

Two additional developing support services are provided by the adaptive physical education therapist and the music therapist. PL 94-142 stimulated the growth of adaptive physical education by its requirement of physical education for handicapped students, many of whom are unable to take part in regular physical education programs. Colleges and universities have begun to develop training programs in this area, and inservice training is being directed toward practicing physical education instructors.

Music therapy has tended to be most popular in special day schools and residential centers, but it is receiving increased attention in public schools as a form of intervention for handicapped students. Music therapy is more than simply involving students in music activities; it is the use of music to teach students needed skills, to encourage positive attitudes toward learning, and to develop feelings of self-worth.

INSTRUCTIONAL PROGRAMMING FOR EXCEPTIONAL CHILDREN

One result of the PL 94-142 mandate requiring a free and appropriate public education for all students with disabilities is that extensive resources are required to assess students in order to develop IEPs. Without systematic identification procedures, students may not receive appropriate services, or they may be misdiagnosed. If the latter occurs, a student could be placed in an inappropriate program. Both circumstances are serious concerns to school districts.

The commitment of districts to serve all children with disabilities often places major demands on district financial resources. A study by the Robert Wood Johnson Foundation and the Commonwealth Fund (Butler & Palfrey, 1988) reported that the pressures on school districts to contain costs even as special education enrollments expand might undermine the progress that had been made toward providing all such students with the services they needed. There are two parts to this problem. One relates to the need to serve all children with disabilities, and the second pertains to how they are served. To date, the focus has been largely on direct services through special programs. Given the constraints of public resources and the competition for those resources, whether districts can continue to serve larger numbers of students through special programs is questionable. To do so will require the public to significantly increase its investment in public education.

One response to the growing number of students needing special education services is to restructure the process through which students are identified and to change the nature of services provided for some mildly handicapped students. It is reasonable to assume that the needs of some exceptional students may be accommodated through curriculum adjustments or additional support for their regular teacher(s). Preassessment or prereferral systems are being proposed as alternatives to the traditional screening and referral procedures used in identifying students for special education.

Referral

Historically, exceptional children were identified on the basis of referral from a regular class teacher once they began to encounter academic difficulties. Today, because of the growing number of preschool programs for children with disabilities and active Child Find programs (systematic communitywide initiatives to identify children with disabilities as early as possible), most children with disabilities have been identified or at least referred for evaluation before they encounter serious academic problems in the regular class. This is particularly true for children with visual, auditory, language, or motoric problems. It is less often true for students with mild learning handicaps. Typically, the latter group is still identified through screening or referral procedures.

By design, the referral process is simple and is intended to serve as a mechanism for bringing the suspected needs of the student to the attention of appropriate professionals without undue delay. Referral forms are standard across a district and include requests for the following information:

> Date of referral
> Name of person making the referral
> Parent's name, address, and phone number
> Student's current placement
> Reason for referral
> Examples of attempts to correct problem
> Responses of student to such efforts

Some districts include a checklist or ask for additional information at the time of referral, but in most cases such information is sought after further determination is made of the nature of the student's problem. Teachers should collect information and be prepared to provide additional data and clarification at any point. Teachers must also keep in mind that following a referral they may be asked to meet with the specialist(s) involved and to participate in conferences with parents. The teacher's responsibility in the evaluation process does not end with the referral.

Referrals can arise from sources other than teachers, of course. School personnel such as counselors, principals, and school nurses sometimes initiate referrals, as do community sources such as physicians, clergy, private schools, departments of public health, and social agencies. In some cases, parents request that their child be evaluated, which has the effect of being a referral.

In addition to adhering to the referral procedures and making sure the information on the referral form is accurate and clearly communicated, the teacher must prepare the student for the referral. Once the teacher knows that the student will be evaluated or even interviewed, the student should be helped to understand what is taking place. If the student will be going to a different building or to an unfamiliar office, this should be thoroughly explained. Performance can be affected if a student is frightened or unduly concerned when entering a testing situation. If the student is bilingual or uses English as a second language, this must be taken into consideration in testing.

The student's parents should also be helped to understand the referral process and the reasons for the referral. Although parental permission is required before undertaking an actual evaluation, merely obtaining this permission is not enough. In the absence of additional information, it may only heighten parental concern. Effective communication between home and school is one way to help gain a total picture of the child's needs and to prevent disagreements and misunderstandings that too often lead to delays in needed services.

On referral, the information on the form is reviewed, and an appropriate specialist may be called on for involvement in the evaluation—psychologist, speech clinician, school nurse, or other expert, as the need suggests. Depending on the problem, the specialist may observe the student, review previous work samples, interview the teacher, or meet with the parents. The total evaluation generally involves a team that reviews previous test data and school performance and considers all the information gathered. These procedures are known to all staff members and should be communicated to parents and others involved in the evaluation.

Activity 2, page 45, lets you experience the referral process and gain new perceptions of this important area.

Prereferral

The initial referral is a critical step in the process leading to appropriate education for a child with a disability. If the referral does not occur at the earliest detection of a problem, opportunities for remediation may be missed or the problem may be allowed to become more serious. School districts, in their efforts to control enrollments in special education programs and to find means of controlling escalating costs, must guard against employing procedures that reduce the likelihood of a student receiving needed services in a timely manner as well as against overusing referrals. The prereferral process (often referred to as preassessment) is an evolving program that broadens the focus from a concern only with the child's needs to an emphasis on the teacher, classroom setting, curriculum and instructional variables. By viewing these as sources of support, preassessment reduces the need for special placements or related services.

According to Graden, Casey, and Christenson (1985), a prereferral intervention model is based on an indirect, consultative model of service delivery in which resources are directed at providing intervention assistance at the point of initial referral. They propose that the prereferral program be designed to prevent inappropriate placements in special education through increasing the skill and knowledge of regular classroom teachers, thereby preparing them to intervene effectively with diverse groups of students. The intent of prereferral is to provide indirect rather than direct services to the referred student, with an emphasis on intervention and teaching rather than on diagnosis and placement.

Models such as that described by Graden, Casey, and Christenson (1985) are offered as an alternative to the referral, evaluation, and placement process that has characterized most special education programs and as a way to encourage the use of existing resources. This model has six stages, of which four represent the prereferral process and two represent the formal referral, assessment, and decision-making process for special education eligibility (p. 379). The stages are (a) request for consultation, (b) consultation, (c) observation, (d) conference, (e) formal referral, and (f) formal program meeting. Educators anticipate that increasing numbers of students with mild handicaps will be served through models of this nature. This will reduce the need for formally placing students in special education programs that are more costly and may not be any more effective or as effective in enhancing students' educational performance.

The implementation of prereferral programs raises a major concern, however. There is a delicate balance between meeting the needs of students with disabilities in an effective and efficient manner and risking the withholding of needed services. A prereferral model has many advantages. It meets the principle of least restrictiveness and is less costly. Nevertheless, careful monitoring is necessary to ensure that the student is truly benefiting from remaining in the regular classroom with available supportive services. Maintaining the student in the regular class merely to reduce demands for additional services is not justifiable and is not the intent of a prereferral system.

Placement

Following referral, exhaustion of prereferral alternatives, and evaluation, three major decisions remain in providing an appropriate program: determination of eligibility for special education services, placement, and development of an IEP. Although these are independent decisions, they are related and generally involve input from the same team members. These decisions are typically made as part of the IEP conference.

Districts vary in their use of multidisciplinary teams in making the required decisions. Some districts hold separate meetings for specific aspects of the total process, and others incorporate the decision making in a single meeting. The Office of Special Education (OSE) addressed the question of separate versus all-inclusive meetings in a policy paper (*Federal Register,* 1980). The OSE position is that the issue of separate versus single meetings should be a state or local decision. If separate meetings are held, however, the placement decision must be made at the IEP conference with the parent(s) or surrogate parent(s) present. The OSE further recommends that if separate meetings are held, parents be included in the meeting on eligibility.

A major consideration in deciding whether meetings will be combined is the number of participants involved. The student's teacher, the person responsible for the evaluation, an administrator, the parent(s), and other appropriate specialist(s) are important contributors. Yet the number in attendance should be kept sufficiently small so that the parent does not feel overwhelmed. A disadvantage of separate meetings is that time delays result from trying to schedule several meetings. If the parent works, chances of scheduling one meeting at a convenient time are greater than trying to arrange two or three meetings.

If a district adopts the practice of combining eligibility, placement, and IEP decisions in one meeting, considerable advance preparation must be made. Good case management practices include:

☐ Maintaining communication with parents
☐ Coordinating evaluations
☐ Formulating interpretations of results so that they are easily understood
☐ Organizing supplemental information from appropriate sources (teachers, records, parents, etc.)
☐ Having available descriptive information on assumed appropriate alternatives and eligibility information regarding student performance
☐ Being prepared to present information and respond to inquiries from parents and other team members on questions related to eligibility, placement options, and program needs
☐ Conducting team meetings that are in the student's best interests and that allow for full participation
☐ If trial placement is to be considered, it should become an additional part of the evaluation and preparation for the development of an IEP. Districts should have written policies to govern trial procedures.

The Individualized Educational Program

The IEP serves as an accountability measure in determining the effectiveness of districts in meeting the requirements of PL 94-142. A review of an IEP and an assessment of how well the student is performing in his or her program allows judgments to be made on the appropriateness of the student's education. Much also can be learned about how a district is meeting its obligations to students with disabilities by reviewing its IEP process and actual IEPs.

IEP Decision Making

The IEP requirement does not dictate the use of particular teaching methodologies, nor does it even prescribe an instructional planning process, but it calls for specific instructional and related service decisions to be made within a time frame and with the full participation of relevant professionals and parents. The teacher's role is central to the IEP decision-making process. Prior to PL 94-142, the teacher tended

Communication with parents is essential in IEP decisions.

to make use of information available at the time the student was placed in his or her classroom and proceeded to work with the student in establishing a program according to the teacher's perceptions of the student's current performance level. This was often done without input from other specialists and with few expectations of accountability. Parents generally were not sensitive enough to the planning process or sufficiently aware of how instructional decisions were being made to exert much influence on the process. The situation has changed with PL 94-142. The process has been formalized and made public. Parents have been given a major role in decisions related to what is included in the IEP.

Features of the IEP

The federal government has been very specific in describing what should be included in the IEP and the conditions under which decisions should be made. Local districts have refined their procedures and forms as they have gained experience with the process. Some have incorporated features that allow IEPs to be computerized and integrated with evaluation data. The basic requirements of PL 94-142 state the following (*Federal Register,* 42(163) August 23, 1977):

Sec. 12a.346 Content of Individualized Education Program.

The Individualized Education Program for each child must include:

(a) A statement of the child's present levels of educational performance;

(b) A statement of annual goals, including short-term instructional objectives;

(c) A statement of the specific special education and related services to be provided to the child, and the extent to which the child will be able to participate in regular educational programs;

(d) The projected dates for initiation of services and the anticipated duration of services; and

(e) Appropriate objective criteria and evaluation procedures and schedules for determining, on at least an annual basis, whether the short-term instructional objectives are being achieved.

During the early implementation of IEP requirements, some districts encountered difficulties in meeting the intent of the requirements. These districts tended to view the requirements as procedures rather than as a process for improving instructional decisions and a focal point for team decisions. Because of these concerns, the OSE issued a policy paper on IEPs (*Federal Register,* 1980) to clarify the intent of the IEP. Table 2.3 includes part of that statement.

Table 2.3   Federal Intent of Individualized Educational Programs

---

The IEP provision in the Act and regulations has two main parts: (A) the IEP meeting(s)—at which parents and school personnel jointly make decisions about a handicapped child's "program," and (B) the IEP document itself—which is a written record of the decisions reached at the meeting. The overall IEP requirement, composed of these two parts, has a number of purposes and functions, as set out below:

1. The IEP meeting serves as a communication vehicle between parents and school personnel and enables them, as equal participants, to jointly decide upon what the child's needs are, what will be provided, and what the anticipated outcomes may be.

2. The IEP itself serves as the focal point for resolving any differences between the parents and the school; first through the meeting and second, if necessary, through the procedural protections that are available to the parents.

3. The IEP sets forth in writing a commitment of resources necessary to enable a handicapped child to receive needed special education and related services.

4. The IEP is a management tool that is used to insure that each handicapped child is provided special education and related services appropriate to his/her special learning needs.

5. The IEP is a compliance/monitoring document which may be used by monitoring personnel from each governmental level to determine whether a handicapped child is actually receiving the free appropriate public education agreed to by the parents and the school.

6. The IEP serves as an evaluation device for use in determining the extent of the child's progress toward meeting projected outcomes. [NOTE: The law does not require that teachers or other school personnel be held accountable if a handicapped child does not achieve the goals and objectives set forth in his or her IEP. See Section 121a.349 of PL 94-142.]

Source: Federal Register. Individualized education programs (IEP): OSE policy paper. Washington, DC: U.S. Education Department, Assistant Secretary for Special Education and Rehabilitation Services, Office of Special Education, May, 1980.

IEP Conference

The purpose of an IEP conference is not for school personnel to report to parents or guardians on the child's performance; rather, the IEP conference is intended as a planning session at which information is exchanged and decisions are made cooperatively. Even though prior to the conference representatives of the school have made preparations, preliminary meetings involving teachers and specialists have been held, and discussions with the parents or guardians have been carried out, the IEP is planned and agreed to during the conference. School districts have some latitude in determining who participates in each conference. Teams vary depending on the student involved. The law, however, does specify the primary participants (*Federal Register,* 42(163) August 23, 1977):

Sec. 121a.344 Participants in meetings.

(a) *General.* The public agency shall insure that each meeting includes the following participants:
   (1) A representative of the public agency, other than the child's teacher, who is qualified to provide, or supervise the provision of, special education.
   (2) The child's teacher.
   (3) One or both of the child's parents, subject to Sec. 121a.345.
   (4) The child, where appropriate.
   (5) Other individuals at the discretion of the parent or agency.
(b) *Evaluation personnel.* For a handicapped child who has been evaluated for the first time, the public agency shall insure:
   (1) That a member of the evaluation team participates in the meeting; or
   (2) That the representative of the public agency, the child's teacher, or some other person is present at the meeting who is knowledgeable about the evaluation procedures used with the child and is familiar with the results of the evaluation.

Whereas school personnel have had experience in conducting IEP meetings and may be skilled in conducting conferences, for parents or guardians the experience can be threatening. They may be intimidated by the number of people involved or uneasy because of prior interactions with representatives of the school. It is important to create an atmosphere in which accurate and sufficient information can be shared as a basis for decision making. Parents should be encouraged to share information and to ask questions. Voluntary expressions should be acknowledged and their questions answered. It is particularly important to establish or strengthen communication with parents during the IEP meeting. Parents play a major role in the child's learning. Teachers depend on parents to reinforce the child in his or her schoolwork. If communication between the school and the home is not good, the child is disadvantaged. The goal is to determine the child's needs, agree on an appropriate program, and set the stage for the child's receipt of special education services.

Activity 3, page 46, gives you a better understanding of the IEP conference with a hands on experience. You will learn from this activity what takes place and how to deal with it.

TECHNOLOGY APPLICATIONS

Fifteen years ago an introductory text on special education would have speculated on the applications of technology to the education of exceptional children and youth. Today the question is, What are the limits, if any, to the influence of technology on the lives of persons with disabilities? Advances in technology are far ahead of applications, and training of teachers, therapists, and parents to assist persons with disabilities in the use of technologies lags even further behind. Much, however, is being achieved, and the future holds great promise. For this reason, discussions on technology applications appear in each chapter on an area of exceptionality.

The range of technology applications for special education is growing with each new generation of technology. In describing applications to special education, Hutinger and Gentry (1986) included augmentative and adaptive devices to increase sensory input, enhance mobility, serve as physical prosthesis, and facilitate communication; instructional applications involving programmed instruction, tutorials, simulations, problem solving, drill and practice, and exploration and divergent activities; and management applications in instructional planning, scheduling, communication, data analysis, and telecommunications. They also suggested uses to stimulate motivation through the arousing of interest and reinforcement of responses.

Technology can greatly improve the quality of life for most individuals with disabilities. Some of the more dramatic benefits are in the areas of communicative devices and those that enhance mobility. Not only do these applications directly affect quality of life; they increase the individual's access to the environment, expanding the ability to gain maximally from opportunities such as education. It is in education, particularly for the mildly handicapped, that most of the attention has been focused relative to technology applications. Just as considerable progress has been made in regular education in applying technology to the teaching of academic skills, progress is being made in special education. Many of the applications are the same, and given an assessment of individual performance and close monitoring, much of the instructional software is applicable to all students. Nevertheless, exceptional students do present special needs and in turn require software that is specially designed or at least modified.

Semmel and Lieber (1986), through their research with mildly handicapped students and educational applications of microcomputers, found that grouping children to work together on problem-solving activities led to effective academic and social outcomes. Academic performance was facilitated when handicapped learners worked with a partner rather than alone. This is an important observation because there is often a tendency to perceive computer-assisted instructional (CAI) applications as individualized approaches to instruction that are performed individually. The intellectual limitations of many mildly handicapped students make following directions difficult, whereas in small groups peers can assist each other and approach the task in a cooperative manner. This increases the array of educational applications and software appropriate for use with special students.

Lack of Integration into Curriculum

One of the major problems being experienced in the instructional applications of technology in special education is the lack of attention to the integration of technology in the curriculum. Teachers tend to use technology in a somewhat sporadic manner for specific purposes without capitalizing on the opportunity for using technology systematically to teach defined elements of the curriculum in a coordinated manner. Panyan, Hummel, and Jackson (1988) proposed the development of a model measured by four indicators: (a) achievement on IEP or curriculum-referenced goals, (b) achievement under a variety of conditions and for extended periods, (c) integrated CAI activities, and (d) complementary decision-making processes by teachers and administrators. Until recently, the availability of good software and authoring systems was limited, or at least insufficient, which caused teachers to select individual options without much attention to the potential for integrating into the curriculum what was taught through CAI. As instructional applications of technology in special education are developed, it becomes both possible and necessary to eliminate isolated uses and to focus on the integration of technology into the curriculum.

SUMMARY THOUGHTS

Public policy on the education of children and youth with disabilities changed dramatically with passage of the Education for All Handicapped Children Act in 1975. Today it is common practice for children with disabilities, regardless of their severity, to be served by the public schools. Public responsibility is being extended downward to include 3- to 5-year-olds, and programming for infants and toddlers with disabilities is fast becoming public policy.

Individualized programming has become a routine way of ensuring the appropriateness of educational programs, and schools are giving special attention to the instructional needs of handicapped students in regular classrooms. Efforts are being made to improve assessment procedures and to improve instructional interventions. Defining exceptional children has moved from describing characteristics of the learner to a dual emphasis on learner characteristics and instructional alternatives. The intent is to match learner needs with instructional and service options. The once-popular special class is now one of several options, and most exceptional children are being served at least part time in regular classes. In making placement decisions, the first assumption is that the regular class provides an appropriate alternative, but placement in any setting must be clearly justified as being least restrictive and in the student's best interest.

Technology holds great promise as a source of powerful instructional interventions for special education and for improving the quality of life for all persons with disabilities. Advances in technology are ahead of educational applications, but progress is being made by developers in producing appropriate applications and by educators in integrating technology in the curriculum for special students.

REFERENCES

Butler, J.A., & Palfrey, J.S. (1988). *Serving handicapped children: A special report*, Princeton, NJ: Robert Wood Johnson.

Federal Register (Part IV), (August 1977), *42*(163).

Federal Register, Individualized education programs (IEP): OSE policy paper (1980, May). Washington, DC: U.S. Education Department, OSE.

Gearheart, B. R. (1980). *Special Education for the 80's.* St. Louis: Mosby.

Graden, J. L., Casey, A., & Christenson, S. L. (1985). Implementing a prereferral intervention system: Part I. The Model. *Exceptional Children, 51*(5), 377–384.

Hutinger, P. L., and Gentry, D. (1986). Microcomputer applications for young handicapped children: Report from the ACTT symposium. *Journal of the Division for Early Childhood, 10*(3), 2240–2246.

Panyan, M. V., Hummel, J., & Jackson, L. B. (1988). The integration of technology in the curriculum. *Journal of Special Education Technology, 9*(2), 109–119.

Semmel, M. I., & Lieber, J. A. (1986). Computer application in instruction. *Focus on Exceptional Children, 18*(9), 1–12.

ADDITIONAL READINGS

Algozzine, B., Morsink, C. V., & Algozzine, K. M. (1988). What's happening in self-contained special education classrooms. *Exceptional Children, 55*(3), 259–265.

Conoley, J. C., & Conoley, C. W. (1988). Useful theories in school-based consultation. *Remedial and Special Education, 9*(6), 14–20.

Cooney, J. (1988). Child abuse: A developmental perspective. *Counseling and Human Development, 20*(5), 1–10.

Johnson, L. J., Pugach, M. C., & Hammittee, D. J. (1988). Barriers to effective special education consultation. *Remedial and Special Education, 9*(6), 41–47.

Marston, D. (1987-1988). The effectiveness of special education: A time series of reading performance in regular and special education settings. *Journal of Special Education, 21*(4), 13–26.

Reynolds, M. C., Wang, M. C., & Walberg, H. J. (1987). The necessary restructuring of special and regular education. *Exceptional Children, 53*(5), 391–398.

Ryan, L. B., & Rucker, C. N. (1986). Computerized vs. noncomputerized individualized education programs: Teacher's attitudes, time and cost. *Journal of Special Education Technology, 8*(1), 5–12.

Will, M. C. (1986). Educating children with learning problems: A shared responsibility. *Exceptional Children, 52*(5), 411–415.

Ysseldyke, J. E., Thurlow, M. L., Christenson, S. L., & Weiss, J. (1987). Time allocated to instruction of mentally retarded, learning disabled, emotionally disturbed, and nonhandicapped elementary students. *Journal of Special Education, 21*(3), 43–55.

1

Purpose

☐ To acquaint students with the perceptions of exceptional children held by regular classroom teachers.

☐ To assist students in becoming familiar with how students with disabilities are accommodated in regular classes.

Steps

1. After reviewing the chapter write in your own words a definition of each exceptionality.
2. Contact an elementary, middle, or senior high school principal and request permission to interview three teachers.
3. During the interviews focus on three questions/comments.
   a. How do you accommodate exceptional children in your classroom?
   b. Describe the learning problems experienced by the exceptional students in your classroom.
   c. What is the major challenge presented to you as a teacher by each exceptional student in your class?

Analysis

☐ Compare the responses of teachers to your definitions.

☐ Identify any major discrepancy between your definition and the descriptions by teacher of the learning problems experienced by exceptional students and the challenges they present to teachers.

☐ Meet with other students and compare responses.

2

Purpose

☐ To familiarize you with the information essential to include on a referral form.

☐ To give you an opportunity to interact with teachers in gaining their perceptions of referral forms.

Steps

1. Make a list of the information you consider important to include on a referral form. You may want to obtain sample copies from a local district for review.
2. Confer with teachers on what they think should be included.
3. Design a referral form.

Analysis

☐ Submit your final form to teachers for review.

☐ Compare your form with those of your associates and with samples available from local districts.

☐ Experiment with the form. Fill it out and see how long it takes to complete.

3

Purpose

☐ To help you understand the various roles in an IEP conference.

☐ To cause you to analyze what takes place in an IEP conference.

Steps

1. Interview a parent and a professional who have participated in an IEP conference, if possible. Ascertain their perceptions of what occurred.

2. Make three lists including:
   — things that could be done to arrange the physical setting of the conference to have a positive effect.
   — kinds of information that should be shared during the conference.
   — suggestions that would be helpful to participants in maintaining an atmosphere conducive to making program decisions for a student.

3. Meet with other students or associates to discuss your lists and theirs.

4. Compile a final, comprehensive list.

Analysis

☐ Keep in mind that there are few set rules for participation in an IEP meeting and that individuals' perceptions vary in what is appropriate. Coming to understand others' perceptions is important. But you also must be comfortable with your personal perceptions and role. Don't change your list unless you are convinced that others' ideas fit your own.

☐ Keep in mind that parents are partners in the planning process and that they need to feel they are equals in the partnership.

3

The Legal Foundations Of Special Education

Edward L. Meyen
University of Kansas

The December 7, 1988, issue of *Education Week* (Volume VIII, Number 14) carried the headline "Rising Enrollment and Costs Threaten Special-Education Gains, Study Finds." The article discussed a recent report documenting the efforts of school districts to contain costs as the numbers of students requiring special services under PL 94-142 continue to increase. School administrators and policy makers know that the public policy of providing a free and appropriate education to all handicapped children is a costly obligation. They are equally sensitive to the fact that not providing a free and appropriate education to this important segment of our school population has a costly consequence. The American public is learning to live with this dilemma, but with some frustration. Public conscience supports equal rights for persons with disabilities as it does civil rights related to race or gender, but social change requires more than changes in attitudes, policies, and practices—it requires an economic investment. In the case of equal education for handicapped children, the costs are highly visible to the local taxpayer and state legislators.

WHO PAYS FOR SPECIAL EDUCATION?

Government subsidization of special education services grew out of a recognition at the state level of the additional costs incurred by local districts to maintain these services. Through the efforts of parents and educators, legislators became convinced that taxpayers at the community level should not have to pay the "excess" costs of educating handicapped students and that the state should take on those extra costs. Individual states established formulas for determining excess costs and procedures for reimbursing districts for them. As programs expanded, states continued to adhere to the concept of state aid for special education, but they began to reimburse districts for less than 100% of the excess costs. In other words, school districts, through local taxpayers, began to absorb a growing portion of the financial responsibility for educating handicapped children. Failure of states to fulfill their obligations evoked an assertive response from advocacy groups and educators, who lobbied state legislators for increased state aid for special education. This aid began in the 1950s and continues today. The difference today is that there is a third player and the stakes are higher. The federal government, as a consequence of passing PL 94-142, not only mandated a free and appropriate education for all handicapped children but made a commitment to assume a significant portion of the costs. After more than a decade, however, this commitment is yet to be honored. Yes, federal funds are provided to state and local educational agencies, but not at the level anticipated or needed. The *Tenth Annual Report to Congress on the Implementation of the Education of the Handicapped Act* (U.S. Department of Education, 1988) reported a total of $11,795,541,996 being expended by state, local, and federal educational agencies in the 1983-84 school year for the provision of special education and related services. Of this amount, only $1,795,541,996 came from federal sources.

Concerns about the costs of serving handicapped children under the requirements of PL 94-142 reflect neither a change in public attitudes nor second thoughts on the part of policy makers. They do reflect questions about how best to apportion the financial burden. Public education in this country is supported largely by local property taxes, which also serve as the source of revenue for most other public services. Taxpayers, without discriminating against any particular group of beneficiaries, are saying, "Enough is enough" and are exercising their options to limit taxes and, when possible, to reduce them. Schools are caught between the obligation to provide special education services and the inability to generate additional resources locally. This shifts the responsibility to the state and federal governments, where policies are made and options for revenue exist, albeit the stresses of budget deficits limit governmental options. Herein lies the dilemma of implementing a public policy that most people agree is important to our society both now and in the future but having to provide fiscal resources beyond what many taxpayers believe they can afford. In other words, the public feels handicapped children are entitled to services but may not be prepared to pay for them. In thinking about this dilemma, note that PL 94-142 was passed in the House of Representatives by a margin of 404 to 7 and in the Senate by a margin of 87 to 7. Clearly, there was overwhelming support for the public policies embedded in PL 94-142 when the legislation was passed. The subsequent votes for funding have been less supportive.

Meeting the Need for Resources

The implications of this issue are basic to the education of exceptional children and youth in today's schools. The way in which schools respond in the future to demands for the increased resources needed to educate exceptional students will influence the quality and appropriateness of special education and related services. There are several options, including increased state and federal investments. The prereferral systems being proposed in many states may prove to be successful, the Regular Education Initiative (REI) has potential, new interventions resulting in more effective instruction may evolve, and programming for infants and toddlers with disabilities could reduce the numbers of school-age students in special education. Of course, legislatures could redefine eligibility for special education and related services, thereby reducing the number of students whom districts are required to serve through special services. The latter is not a desirable alternative, but it is not inconsistent with the way governmental agencies have historically approached the identification of exceptional children and youth.

Whatever option is pursued by the schools as they struggle to meet the needs of exceptional children and youth, the probabilities are that the chosen option will be the result of serious reflection by legislative bodies. The advocacy movement that brought about the passage of PL 94-142 is even more sophisticated today. Advocacy organizations are no longer loose networks of parent groups; they are professional organizations with broad constituencies. They have professional staffs and members who not only are committed to educational equity for children and youth with disabilities but are experienced in the legislative process. Their credibility with legislators is a consequence of their long-term investment in learning how to use the legislative process. Their power rests on a 15-year history of public support and their linkages with a very large constituency base. Persons with disabilities have also established themselves as effective self-advocates, many of whom have benefited from PL 94-142 and are not likely to allow the requirements of the law to be diminished because of initiatives to reduce resources.

The Progress Made in Special Education

The evolutionary process of achieving a free and appropriate education continues. Compared to the status of special education prior to the 1970s, significant progress has been made. The history of a concerted effort in American education to provide programs for exceptional children and youth is only about 35 years old. States began to define their responsibilities as public policy in the 1950s. This is a relatively short period of time, given the magnitude of change that has occurred. Special education programs are not only more extensive today but are greatly improved in quality. At the same time, the intent of PL 94-142 has not yet been achieved, nor have the conditions essential to meet the goal of an appropriate education for all been fully defined or realized. But most children and youth with disabilities are being served, and individualized education programs are being planned through the collective efforts of professionals and parents or guardians.

Nondiscriminatory assessment methodologies are being refined, effective instructional interventions are evolving, due process has been established as a routine practice, and districts are employing accountability measures to ensure their compliance with state and federal statutes. Professionals and the lay public have accepted the importance of early intervention, and the government has mandated programs for 3- to 5-year-old children with disabilities. Public attention now has begun to focus on new groups of children and their special needs, such as children with AIDS and children with disabilities who come from culturally diverse backgrounds. Conversely, practices such as those that led to over-representation of children from minority groups in special education programs have been changed and are now being guarded against. This background of change opens the door for a new era. Much of what will occur in the next decade will be a response to the changing conditions brought about by the last two decades in the history of special education.

LEGISLATION

The Education for All Handicapped Children Act was passed in 1975. Why should it continue to receive so much attention in an introductory book on the education of exceptional children and youth in the 1990s? Or, for that matter, why should any legislation receive attention in a book on educational practices? The answer is simple: No other piece of legislation has impacted the public schools in the same way as has PL 94-142. In specifying educational practices and in broadening the clientele that the schools are responsible for serving, PL 94-142 is unique. It is unlikely that anyone, even policy analysts, could have predicted 30 years ago the mandate of a practice as specific as the IEP or the establishment of detailed procedures of due process. Nor could analysts have anticipated that subsequent amendments would be passed to extend the responsibilities of the schools to 3- and 4-year-olds, let alone to infants and toddlers. Special education has become, to a significant extent, a creation of legislation. This development is neither good nor bad, but it is important to remember that legislation is central to the study of special education and that many special education practices are not necessarily the result of what professional educators prefer. Instead, they are a mixture of what professionals propose, advocates request, and legislators are willing to support. The courts have also had an influence as they add their interpretations of what laws intend and mean.

> It is important to understand federal legislation. Activity 1, page 73, allows you to analyze, challenge, and understand federal legislation. Major legislative acts are discussed on the next pages of this text.

Major Legislative Acts

Between 1827 and the passage of PL 94-142 in 1975, 175 federal laws specific to the handicapped were enacted, 61 between March 1970 and March 1975 (Weintraub, Abeson, Ballard, & LaVor, 1976, pp. 103–111). They included the Education of the Handicapped Amendments of 1974(PL 93-380), the Education for All Handicapped Children Act of 1975(PL 94-142), and Section 504 of the Rehabilitation Act of 1973(PL 93-516). These were followed by the 1983 and 1986 amendments of the Education of the Handicapped Act. In contrast to human service legislation that had been enacted without provisions for enforcement, these acts had built-in safeguards to ensure implementation as well as the support of strong advocacy groups and a responsive public. This has not always been the case with legislation related to the handicapped. In discussing the enforcement implications of Section 504 and PL 94-142, Turnbull (1986) stated:

> The two laws cover all handicapped children without regard to where they live in the state (whether in the community or in an institution, for example) or which state or local agency serves them (whether a department of public education or a department of human resources, for example). There is no real escape from these Acts for state and local agencies dealing with handicapped children. The two Acts seal all the cracks in services and carry out policies of zero reject and nondiscrimination. (p. 20)

Many assume that PL 94-142 was an independent act. It actually was an amendment to PL 93-380, which was passed in 1974 to extend and amend the Elementary and Secondary Education Act of 1965. Although the latter two acts are significant to the history of education for the handicapped, from a public policy perspective PL 93-380 was the first act to address the concept of education for all:

> Sec. 801. Recognizing that the Nation's economic, political, and social security require a well-educated citizenry, the Congress (1) reaffirms, as a matter of high priority, the Nation's goal of equal educational opportunity, and (2) declares it to be the policy of the United States of America that every citizen is entitled to an education to meet his or her full potential without financial barriers.

Congress set 1978 as the deadline for implementation of PL 94-142 and during the interim required states to revise their statutes to comply. Some states had already revised old legislation in anticipation, but many had to initiate major new legislative processes so that policies and procedures would be compatible with new federal laws. Although PL 94-142 did not include the gifted, many states defined special education services to include services for gifted and talented students. This is why school programs typically include gifted students in special services, even though the law refers to the "handicapped" rather than the "exceptional."

Table 3.1 indicates that the principles of these three acts (PL 93-516, PL 93-380, and PL 94-142) and the requirements they set forth dictated a wide array of responses on the part of the public schools. For example, to implement PL 94-142, schools had to do more than identify all handicapped students and provide for their education at public expense; the law's rules and regulations were specific, detailed, and, as many administrators who supported the principles found, restrictive. Others, however, recognized that without specific regulation, school districts would differ greatly in how they implemented principles, and monitoring for compliance would be difficult if not impossible. Because the federal rules and regulations (*Federal Register,* August 23, 1977) called for the development of state and local plans on procedures for implementing the law, dissemination of the requirements occurred within a short time. The development of such plans served a useful purpose: State and local districts systematically reviewed the law and their own policies and procedures.

The importance of Section 504 of the Rehabilitation Act is often overlooked because of the attention PL 94-142 receives. Section 504 was originally applied primarily to employment, but in 1974 PL 93-516 amended Section 504 to cover a broader array of services for the handicapped. These amendments made Section 504 the basic source of enforcement for PL 94-142 and PL 93-380. The amendment defined a handicapped person as follows:

> any person who (A) has a physical or mental impairment which substantially limits one or more such person's major life activities, (B) has a record of such an impairment, or (C) is regarded as having an impairment.

With this amendment, educational services were covered by the nondiscriminatory provisions of Section 504.

Table 3.1   Educational Implications of Major Federal Legislation on Education of the Handicapped

Law	Date Passed	Implications	Comments
PL 93-516	1974	Amended Section 504 of the Rehabilitation Act of 1973 to cover a broader array of services for handicapped children and adults.	This was the first federal civil rights law to specifically protect the rights of handicapped children and adults.
		The nondiscrimination provisions of this law were almost identical to the nondiscrimination provisions related to race in Title VI of the Civil Rights Act of 1964 and to Title IX of the Education Amendments of 1972.	Section 504 provided one basis for enforcement of PL 94-142.
		Rules and regulations of Section 504 governing schools were similar to those for PL 94-142.	All special education personnel should be familiar with this legislation because of its broad implications for handicapped children and adults.
PL 93-380	1974	Extended and amended the Elementary and Secondary Act of 1965 to establish equal educational opportunity for all citizens as national policy.	This law will likely be considered in the future as a historical statement of public social policy.
		Section 613(A) set forth the due process procedures that became the basis for many of the provisions in PL 94-142.	
PL 94-142	1975	Amended PL 93-380.	This law is sometimes referred to as the "Bill of Rights for the Handicapped."
		1. Mandated a free and appropriate public education for all handicapped children and youth. Related services including speech pathology, audiology, psychological and counseling services, physical and occupational therapy, recreation, medical services (for diagnosis and evaluation only).	Rules and regulations were published in the *Federal Register*, August 1977. Gifted children were not included in the definition of handicapped, unless a gifted child was also handicapped.
		2. An IEP must be developed (in conference with parents present) and maintained for each handicapped student. The law set specific requirements on the contents of the IEP and the manner in which it was to be developed.	
		3. A special feature of PL 94-142 (and PL 93-380) was the principle of least restrictive environment, which stated that to the maximum extent appropriate, handicapped children, including children in public and private facilities, are to be educated with children who are not handicapped.	This revised the previous pattern of relying solely on the segregated special class as the primary placement for most handicapped students.
		4. Due process procedures included requirements such as the following: a. Parents are allowed to examine all records pertaining to the school's examination of their child. b. Parents may obtain evaluation from examiners independent of the school.	If due process procedures do not result in a program satisfactory to the parent or guardian, an impartial due process hearing must be provided as an option to the parent. Parents may also exercise the option of pursuing civil action through the

Table 3.1   *continued*

Law	Date Passed	Implications	Comments
		c. Surrogate parents must be appointed if parents or guardians of the child are not known or available or if the child is a ward of the state. d. Notice in written form and native language of the parent or guardian must be provided to the parent or guardian whenever the school proposes a change in the identification, evaluation, or educational placement of their handicapped child. e. A process must be provided through which parents are able to present complaints on any matter relating to identification, evaluation, or educational placement of their child. f. Protection is afforded against the use of discriminatory tests.	court judicial system after they have a due process hearing. Schools may require such hearings.
PL 98-199 Sec. 1419 and 1423	1983	Replaced the State Implementation Grants with the Early Childhood State Grant Program (from birth through age 5). The planning grants are of three types: needs assessment, plan development, and implementation to fund implementation and evaluation of state plans.	In 1984, 23 grants for the planning stage were awarded, 2 for development and 1 for implementation. Many states had, by 1983, begun to serve children with disabilities from 3–5 years of age. The group from birth through age 2 represents the population that is either not served or underserved.
Sec. 1402, 1424(a), and 1425		Addressed the transition from school to adulthood, allowing for programs to be developed and disseminated for postsecondary education, the delivery of transitional services, and the creation of a national clearinghouse on postsecondary education for the handicapped.	
PL 99-457 Sec. 671, 673, 676, 680, and 682	1986	Amended the Education of the Handicapped Act by establishing new federal discretionary programs to assist states to develop and implement a comprehensive, coordinated, interdisciplinary program of early intervention services for handicapped infants and toddlers and their families; strengthened incentives for states to serve all handicapped children ages 3–5; amended Part B evaluations; and amended and extended the authority for discretionary programs under Parts C through G.	Research supports the advantages of early intervention for infants and toddlers with disabilities. These amendments represented a significant change from the authorizations in the 1983 amendment in terms of services to young children with disabilities.

Source: From E. L. Meyen and T. M. Skrtic, 1988, *Exceptional Children and Youth: An Introduction,* pages 20-21, Denver, CO: Love Publishing Co.

Features of 1983 and 1986 Amendments

Two programs were not adequately addressed in PL 94-142. They were early intervention programs and programs to enhance the transition of students from school to employment. The Amendment to the Education of the Handicapped Act (PL 98-199) expanded services to include children beginning at birth and established transitional programs for young adults. In anticipation of the legislative amendments, several states initiated such programs prior to 1983.

Early Childhood Education

Although PL 94-142 did not mandate provision of services to handicapped infants and toddlers, Congress did authorize grants to state education agencies (SEAs) to extend special education and related services to handicapped children from 3 to 5 years of age. The Incentive Grant Program was intended to stimulate the development of preschool programs for children with disabilities and, in terms of growth, has been successful. The Incentive Grant Program was preceded by PL 90-538, the Handicapped Children's Early Education Assistance Act (HCEEAA), in 1968. The act was designed to support activities demonstrating the effectiveness of strategies to serve preschool handicapped children and their families. A major outcome was the development of models to guide the establishment of local programs.

Based in part on the success of the HCEEAA, Congress created the State Implementation Grant (SIG) program in 1976 to aid states in planning and coordinating comprehensive preschool service delivery systems. The National Association of State Directors of Special Education reported that the SIG program succeeded in assisting states to develop a capacity to initiate planning and in creating structures to enhance the provision of services statewide.

Out of this history of initiatives in the early education of children with disabilities emerged a legislative effort to amend PL 94-142. In 1983, PL 98-199 extended services to handicapped children beginning at birth. The *Seventh Annual Report to Congress on the Implementation of the Education of the Handicapped Act* (U.S. Department of Education, 1985), in summarizing studies on the effectiveness of preschool programs, reported that handicapped infants and preschool-age children who received early intervention showed significant improvement in development and learning.

The 1983 amendments to PL 94-142.   The 1983 amendment provided three types of early childhood grants for states: planning grants, development grants, and implementation grants. Each grant serves a particular purpose for a specified time. *Planning grants* provide support to SEAs in coordinating needs assessment studies and designs for the development of state plans. *Development grants* provide support for the development of comprehensive state plans. The emphasis is on interagency collaboration. *Implementation grants* provide support for the implementation and evaluation of comprehensive state plans for early education of handicapped children.

PL 98-199 stimulated the development of programs beginning at birth for children with disabilities but did not necessarily create new kinds of services. What did evolve between the 1983 and 1986 amendments, in addition to expanded services, were effective interagency collaborative arrangements. These arrangements grew out of the varied needs of infants and toddlers (from birth to age 2) with disabilities and to the lack of a single agency at the state and community levels responsible for this age group. The range of services required by handicapped infants is influenced greatly by the needs of parents. If parents are able to provide good care and to implement interventions learned through training programs, the need for programs outside the home is minimal. If both parents work, or if other circumstances prevent the family from providing the needed care and intervention, the child's development depends on services in the community.

PL 99-457 amended the Education of the Handicapped Act by (a) establishing new federal discretionary programs to assist states in developing and implementing a comprehensive, coordinated, interdisciplinary program of early intervention services for handicapped infants and toddlers and their families; (b) strengthening the incentives for states to serve all handicapped children aged 3 to 5; and (c) changing Part B evaluations and changing and extending the authority for the discretionary programs under Parts C through G.

The 1986 amendments to PL 94-142.   The 1986 amendments defined handicapped infants and toddlers as:

> individuals from birth to age two, inclusive, who need early intervention services because they are (1) experiencing developmental delays, as measured by appropriate diagnostic instruments and procedures, in one or more of the following areas: cognitive development, physical development, language and speech development, psychosocial development, or self-help skills, or (2) having a diagnosed physical or mental condition which has a high probability of resulting in development delay.

States may also serve infants and toddlers who are considered to be at risk and who are not otherwise covered by the general definition previously cited.

The 1986 amendments also repealed the incentive program of PL 94-142 and created a new preschool grant program that represented a national initiative:

> to provide federal financial assistance to states to: develop and implement a statewide, comprehensive, coordinated multidisciplinary interagency program of early intervention services for all handicapped infants and toddlers and their families; facilitate coordination of payments for early intervention services from various public and private sources; and enhance its capacity to provide quality early intervention services and expand and improve existing services.

The 1986 amendments also required an individualized family service plan for handicapped infants and toddlers. (At this age, family involvement in intervention is essential.) The individualized family service plan must:

1. Include a multidisciplinary assessment of needs
2. Include the identification of required services
3. Be in written form
4. Be reviewed at least every 6 months
5. Be developed within a reasonable time following the assessment

The written individualized family service plan must include:

1. Levels of development
2. Family strengths and needs
3. Expected major outcomes from infants and toddlers and families
4. Description of needed intervention services
5. Dates services are to be included
6. Name of case manager
7. Steps for transition to special education services if needed following intervention

Transition Programs

The capstone of special education programs is effective transition into the world of work. For most students without serious intellectual or communications problems, the transition has been achievable, but for groups such as those with serious learning disabilities, mental retardation, emotional disorders, or physical disabilities that seriously limit their mobility, gainful employment has often been an unmet goal. Although secondary level special education programs have evolved, they came much later than programs at the elementary level and were often not as well designed. Vocational rehabilitation services, while available to handicapped adults, initially focused on individuals with physical and sensory handicaps. Not until special education programs in secondary schools were developed did vocational rehabilitation services become accessible to other groups of young adults with disabilities. Because the emphasis has historically been on the elementary age group and because several groups of students with special needs have become eligible for special education in relatively recent years, programs intended to enhance transition from school to employment have not been developed sufficiently. This has been a serious concern to educators, parents, and policy makers.

Support for transition services.   Section 626 of Part C of the Education of the Handicapped Act, as amended by PL 98-199 in 1983, authorized what was described as the Secondary Education and Transitional Services for the Handicapped Youth Program. The amendment authorized support for projects that (a) assist in preparing handicapped youth for the transition from school to competitive and supportive employment, postsecondary education and training, and adult services, and (b) stimulate the development and improvement of secondary special education programs. A major requirement of successful transition programs is interagency collaboration. The schools can be successful in preparing an individual for employment, and the individual may obtain employment, but without a support system, he or she may not be able to hold a job. Cooperation among the employer, family, and community agencies is often required to ensure a successful transition from school to employment. Similar efforts are necessary in order for some graduates of special education programs to sustain employment.

Service options. Wehman, Moon, and McCarthy (1986) identified five options for transitional programs: (a) adult activity centers and sheltered workshops, (b) supported employment, (c) supported competitive employment, (d) enclaves in industry, and (e) mobile work crews. *Adult activity centers* provide recreation, instruction in daily living skills, and opportunities to develop work skills. In contrast, *sheltered workshops* provide work experiences for which clients are paid. Both tend to be segregated facilities that emphasize the buildings, not the staff. *Supported competitive employment* is not appropriate for all youths with severe handicaps, but it is a reasonable goal for most individuals with handicapping conditions. The foundations of supported employment are paid employment, integration into the community, necessity for ongoing support, and presence of severe disability. A job coach must be accessible for individualized one-to-one training and follow-up. Emphasis is on structured assistance in job placement and job site training (Wehman & Melia, 1985). *Enclaves* involve groups of disabled clients working under supervision in a business or industry. *Mobile work crews* perform (under supervision) at different locations within a building or community. Both provide employment to disabled individuals who have been unsuccessful in or excluded from other employment opportunities. Table 3.2 illustrates the range of services needed by students 16 and older as reported by public schools to the OSE. The figures reported in the table are conservative, but they do identify the types of services and the relative importance of each service to young adults in special education programs.

Certification of graduation. According to the *Tenth Annual Report to Congress* (U.S. Department of Education, 1988), a total of 213,623 handicapped youth between the ages of 16 and 21 were reported by states to have exited from school during the 1985-86 academic year. Of this group, 43% received high school diplomas and 17% received certificates of completion. The others left school without evidence of successfully completing a program. In a national study, Bodner, Mellard, and Clark (1987) found that about 60% of the states allowed local districts to set policy on the type of document to be awarded upon completion of a special education program. Seventeen states reported that state policy required a different type of certificate to be awarded to special education students if they had not met the regular graduation requirements. An additional fourteen states required the awarding of the same diploma whether the student met regular or alternative requirements.

Table 3.2 Types of Services Needed in 1986-87 by Students 16 Years of Age and Older Exiting the Educational System in 1985-86[a]

Service Type	Number	Percent
Counseling/guidance	73,889	14.1
Transportation	22,312	4.3
Technological aids	10,140	1.9
Interpreter services	2,974	.6
Reader services	8,282	1.6
Physical/mental restoration	14,556	2.8
Family services	29,769	5.7
Independent living	27,368	5.2
Maintenance	21,159	4.0
Residential living	11,585	2.2
Vocational training	82,719	15.8
Postemployment services	31,347	6.0
Transitional employment services	38,851	7.4
Vocational placement	73,903	14.1
Evaluation of vocational rehabilitation services	66,096	12.6
Other services	8,931	1.7
Total	523,881	100.00

[a]Data as of October 1, 1987.

Source: U.S. Department of Education (1988). Produced by ED/SEP Data Analysis System.

LOCAL, STATE, AND FEDERAL EDUCATIONAL AGENCIES

Because enforcement of the Education of the Handicapped Act involves federal and state monitoring, financial subsidy for special education programs is provided at the state and federal levels, and because of concerns that errors not be made in the identification and/or educational placement of exceptional children, responsibilities are clearly differentiated at the local, state, and federal levels of our educational system. Local districts are governed in their operation of special education programs by detailed regulations established at the state and federal levels. State laws tend to mirror federal statutes in their intent; thus, regulations are relatively uniform across states. For example, PL 94-142 and the 1983 and 1986 amendments provided the basis for most state statutes governing programs and services provided to exceptional children and youth. States do differ, however, in the language used to describe them. Table 3.3 lists the general responsibilities and functions of educational agencies and facilitates an understanding of how the needs of exceptional children and youth are met and why varied approaches to the delivery of services exist.

The Role of the Courts

Although landmark legislation such as PL 93-380, PL 94-142, and Section 504 of the Rehabilitation Act has been a primary force in bringing about equality for the

Table 3.3   Responsibilities of Education Agencies

Agency	Function
U.S. Department of Education Office of Special Education and Rehabilitative Services (OSERS) Office of Special Education Programs (OSEP)	• Serves as a resource to Congress in legislation • Enforces implementation of federal laws • Provides leadership in coordinating national responses toward meeting the needs of exceptional children and youth • Administers federal funds to state and local education agencies • Provides leadership in stimulating research and personnel training
State education agencies (SEAs)	• Establish rules and regulations for the approval of local educational programs serving exceptional children and youth • Serve as a resource to the state legislature on matters relating to exceptional children and youth • Provide leadership in developing and implementing comprehensive statewide plans to ensure equal educational opportunity for exceptional students • Serve as the major appeal source in disputes involving the education of exceptional children and youth • Serve in liaison role with other state agencies in coordinating the services to exceptional children and youth • Serve in liaison role with other state agencies in coordinating the services to exceptional students and their families • Monitor compliance of local districts in meeting state and federal requirements • Provide leadership to local districts in development of inservice training • Maintain data on numbers of exceptional children served and identified and on program expenditures
Local education agencies (LEAs)	• Provide appropriate educational programs and services for all exceptional children and youth • Implement programs in compliance with state and federal regulations • Conduct inservice training to assure that all educational personnel are effective in meeting the needs of exceptional students • Maintain due process procedures • Serve as liaison with community agencies in coordinating program for exceptional children and youth
Intermediate education units (IEUs)[a]	• May provide direct services to exceptional children and youth • Frequently offer support services to LEAs • Comply with state and federal regulations governing the education of exceptional children and youth • Often contract with LEAs to provide transportation for exceptional children and youth • Generally operate inservice training programs as part of an instructional materials center

[a]An IEU is an organizational structure between the local education agency and the state education agency. In several states IEUs are set up by county boundaries. Others encompass several counties. Other states ignore county lines and allow adjoining districts to organize as IEUs. Intermediate education units vary in the services they provide. Some have taxing powers; others obtain funds from SEAs and by contracting with LEAs.

handicapped, the courts have also had, and will continue to have, a significant influence on issues affecting the handicapped. Enactment of major legislation has usually been the consequence of the collective efforts of groups and organizations to address broad issues. Court cases, on the other hand, are often initiated by an individual, an agency, or a small group seeking clarification of special points of law. Sometimes a court decision will have a broad impact that was not immediately apparent or anticipated at the time the case was heard. The 1954 *Brown* v. *Topeka Board of Education* decision, which established the right of all children to an equal educational opportunity, was one such case. Although most of the early attention given to this decision centered on its implications for racial integration, it later became a primary reference in advocacy for the handicapped.

When legislation is passed, detailed regulations are written as guidelines for implementation. Nevertheless, legislation as complex and far-reaching as the Education for All Handicapped Children Act is difficult to translate into regulations that anticipate all possible eventualities. Consequently, the courts play an important role in interpreting law. The due process provisions of PL 94-142 have been helpful in resolving conflicts between families of handicapped children and educational agencies. But the courts have had to clarify and provide interpretation of the basic principles underlying the law.

Many of the court cases involving PL 94-142 have built on earlier cases that helped to clarify public policy and the constitutional rights of the handicapped. The summaries that follow describe cases that have had a major impact on the ways that schools seek to comply with legislation.

Hobson v. Hanson (1968)

This was the first major court case questioning placement practices related to special education students. Misuse of tests in the Washington, D.C. school district resulted in handicapped students, particularly those from minority groups, being placed in the lower track of the educational program. The court found the *track system* (grouping children on the basis of test scores) to be unconstitutional because it discriminated against blacks and poor children.

Diana v. State Board of Education (1970)

This suit challenged the cultural bias of standardized tests used to place students in classes for the mentally retarded. The case involved Diana, a student in Monterey County, California, and eight other Spanish-speaking children who were placed in special classes for mildly retarded students on the basis of intelligence tests given in English. The courts ordered that the children be reevaluated in their native language.

Mills v. Board of Education, the District of Columbia (1971)

A class-action suit (which is a suit that extends the findings to all others similarly situated) was filed on behalf of seven school-age children who were excluded from school because of their handicapping conditions. The reason for exclusion was the professed inability of the school to provide financially for their education. The decision set forth the principle that handicapped children should be provided a free and suitable education. The court did not accept the plea of lack of funds as a justifiable reason to exclude handicapped students from school.

Pennsylvania Association for Retarded Citizens (PARC) v. The Commonwealth of Pennsylvania (1971)

A landmark class action suit against the Commonwealth of Pennsylvania, this case resulted in a decision declaring the right of all handicapped children, including the mentally retarded, to a free and appropriate public education. The decision was based on constitutional and statutory principles.

Larry P. v. Riles (1972)

This case, also filed in California, was similar to *Diana* v. *State Board of Education* except that it applied to black children. The court made the schools responsible for proving that their testing measures were not discriminatory on the basis of race. The court mandated that tests take into consideration the cultural background of students with whom they are used.

Wyatt v. Stickney (1972)

Filed in Alabama on behalf of patients in state institutions, the decision declared that patients had the right to appropriate treatment (including educational standards) and placed the responsibility for provision of treatment on the state.

Le Banks v. Spears (1975)

This case was important to the concept of appropriate education for the handicapped. The court decreed that the plaintiffs were to be provided public education and that the education be "appropriate" to their capabilities or "suited to their needs."

Board of Education of the Hendrick Hudson Central School District v. Rowley (1982)

In clarifying the meaning of "free and appropriate education," the Supreme Court ruled that a school district satisfied the requirements of the Education for All Handicapped Children's Act if the district provided personalized instruction and services that were reasonably calculated to bring about educational benefits to the child and if all the act's procedural provisions were adhered to in formulating the child's Individualized Educational Program. The Court also ruled that services were to be provided at public expense.

Irving Independent School District v. *Tatro (1984)*

Some children require periodic catheterization throughout the day. The law, however, is not specific in defining catheterization as a related service. The Supreme Court ruled in *Irving Independent School District* v. *Tatro* that because catheterization could be provided by a school nurse or a trained layperson, it should be provided as a related service. The Court reasoned that catheterization was a health, not a medical, service. The Court therefore required schools to provide catheterization to a child if the child needed it in order to attend school.

Burlington School Committee v. *Department of Education (1985)*

This case involved a parent who, believing that his child's placement was inappropriate, enrolled his son in a private facility at his own expense. The parent later requested reimbursement. The district refused and filed suit. Yanok (1986), in describing the court's decision, stated, "If a handicapped student has been denied a public educational placement in the least restrictive environment, school officials are obligated to pay the costs of providing a proper private instructional program. However, parents who unilaterally alter their child's placement during the pendency of review proceedings do so at their own risk" (p. 53).

STATUS OF SPECIAL EDUCATION IN TODAY'S SCHOOLS

Assessing the effectiveness of special education programs is difficult, as the primary indicator—the appropriateness of education for the individual students served—is qualitative in nature. Although compliance by local districts with state and federal mandates is monitored and specific efforts are made to assure that IEPs are developed and implemented, what occurs in the classroom or in the delivery of related services is not easily evaluated. Nevertheless, the combination of reporting procedures, the filing of local and state plans, monitoring, parental involvement, the availability of due process, and continued efforts to prepare quality personnel produces conditions conducive to the improvement of quality. What is available are data on the progress of schools in the numbers of students identified and served, data about where they are served, and demographic data on the development of programs. These data allow us at least to infer the responsiveness of the schools in meeting the educational needs of special students.

Numbers Served

States have historically relied on estimates of incidence rates to assess the extent to which specific groups of exceptional children are being served. The lack of a central reporting system precluded the availability of accurate data prior to PL 94-142. Today states are required to report annually to the Office of Special Education and Rehabilitative Services (OSERS) the number of children receiving special education services. This does not answer the question of how many children and youth exist with specific handicapping conditions because variability still exists in how states define and group exceptional children for purposes of instruction. Furthermore, as changes occur in eligibility requirements, the numbers may increase or decrease. But the data are much improved over those available prior to passage of PL 94-142, and having access to data nationally and regionally is useful in planning and assessing progress.

The terms *prevalence* and *incidence* are frequently used in judgments on the number of students served by handicapping condition. Although the terms are often used synonymously, they have different meanings. Prevalence refers to the current number of exceptional children; incidence refers to the number of children who at some time in their lives might be considered exceptional. Incidence figures are higher and much more difficult to verify. This is particularly true in assessing the incidence of exceptional children and youth, as eligibility for services largely determines whether a child is exceptional or not. A student may receive special education services in the elementary grades but not at the secondary level. In other situations, a student may develop a need for special education services after having returned to the regular class for several years. Prevalence data are available, and from these data statisticians infer incidence rates. Even here caution must be exercised because factors such as funding formulas for state aid, the availability of personnel, or the philosophy of the district on placement in regular classes may cause districts to under- or overidentify the numbers of exceptional children.

An accurate account of the number of children served in special education must include data on students served both through the Education of the Handicapped Act and (EHA-B) and through the Education and Consolidation Improvement Act—State Operated Programs (ECIA). Both serve handicapped children and represent unduplicated counts. OSERS is required to submit an annual report to Congress accounting for the compliance of schools in providing special education services to handicapped children and youth.

Table 3.4 illustrates the growth in the number of students served in special education from the implementation of PL 94-142 in 1977-78 through the 1987-88 school year. In 1987-88, 4,494,280 children were served, a 1.6% increase over 1986-87 and the largest percentage increase since the 1980-81 school year. The nearly 4.5 million children served in 1986-87 represented 6.6% of the population between 3 and 21 years of age. According to OSERS, the high increase in the rate of gain could not be attributed to growth in a small number of states; rather, the majority of the states experienced increases, with only 14 states reporting that the same number or fewer handicapped children were being served. Table 3.5, which provides more detailed information, lists a series of handicapping conditions and the number of children served in each group. The largest group is the learning disabled, who comprised 47.0% of the students served, followed by the speech or language impaired, at 23.2%, and the mentally retarded, at 14.6%. In terms of rate of increase over the 1986-87 school year there was a 2.8% increase for the multihandicapped and a 2.0% increase for the learning disabled. Historically, the multihandicapped have been underserved. The increase suggests that progress is being made

Table 3.4   Number and Percentage Change in Number of Children Aged 3 through 21 Years Counted Under Chapter 1 of ECIA (SOP) and EHA-B from School Year 1976-77 to 1987-88

School Year	Percentage Change in Total Number Served from Previous Year	Total Served	EHA-B	ECIA (SOP)
1987-88	1.6	4,494,280	4,235,263	259,017
1986-87	1.2	4,421,601	4,166,692	254,909
1985-86	0.2	4,370,244	4,121,104	249,140
1984-85	0.5	4,362,968	4,113,312[a]	249,245
1983-84	1.0	4,341,390	4,094,108	247,291
1982-83	1.5	4,298,327	4,052,595	245,732
1981-82	1.3	4,233,282	3,990,346	242,936
1980-81	3.5	4,177,689	3,933,981	243,708
1979-80	3.0	4,036,219	3,802,475	233,744
1978-79	3.8	3,919,073	3,693,593	225,480
1977-78	1.8	3,777,286	3,554,554	222,732
1976-77	—	3,708,913	3,485,088	223,825

[a]Beginning in 1984-85, the number of handicapped children reported reflects revisions to State data received by the Office of Special Education Programs following the July 1 grant award date, and includes revisions received by October 1. Previous reports provided data as of the grant award date.

Source: From U.S. Department of Education, 1989, *Eleventh Annual Report to Congress on the Implementation of The Education of the Handicapped Act,* p. 3, Washington, DC: U.S. Government Printing Office.

in serving this group. In the area of learning disabilities, there is speculation that the increase is due to several factors: a desire not to stigmatize students with other labels such as mental retardation, action by the courts and legislators to reclassify children with mental retardation, and the desire to obtain supplemental services for handicapped children at a time when other sources of services are becoming less available (Singer & Butler, 1987).

Where Served

Where children are served becomes important in assessing the extent to which the principle of least restrictiveness is being achieved. OSERS collects data on the placement of students in nine different environments, including:

Regular classes (receive special education and related services for less than 21% of the school day)

Resource rooms (for at least 21% and no more than 60% of the school day)

Separate classes (for more than 60% of the school day)
Public separate school facilities
Private separate school facilities
Public residential facilities
Private residential facilities
Correctional facilities
Homebound or hospital environments

Each option represents a different level of restrictiveness based on the relationship of the placement to the integration of handicapped students with nonhandicapped students. Because least restrictiveness varies depending on the particular

Table 3.5   Students Served Under Chapter 1 of ECIA (SOP) and EHA-B by Handicapping Condition[a]

Handicapping Condition	EHA-B		ECIA (SOP)		Total	
	Number	Percent	Number	Percent	Number	Percent
Learning disabled	1,917,935	48.6	23,796	13.2	1,941,731	47.0
Speech or language impaired	946,904	24.0	9,236	5.1	956,140	23.2
Mentally retarded	539,717	13.7	61,571	34.1	601,288	14.6
Emotionally disturbed	336,992	8.5	37,738	20.9	374,730	9.1
Multihandicapped	63,046	1.6	16,086	8.9	79,132	1.9
Hard of hearing and deaf	40,324	1.0	16,613	9.2	56,937	1.4
Orthopedically impaired	41,084	1.0	6,325	3.5	47,409	1.1
Other health impaired	43,093	1.1	2,772	1.5	45,865	1.1
Visually handicapped	16,932	0.4	5,932	3.3	22,864	0.6
Deaf-blind	777	0.0	695	0.4	1,472	0.0
All conditions	3,946,804	100.0	180,764	100.0	4,127,568	100.0

[a]The figures represent children from 6 to 20 served under Chapter 1 of ECIA (SOP) and children from 6 to 21 years old served under EHA-B.

Source: From U.S. Department of Education, 1989, *Eleventh Annual Report to Congress on the Implementation of The Education of the Handicapped Act,* p. 15, Washington, DC: U.S. Government Printing Office.

needs of the individual student, all learning disabled or all hearing impaired students, for example, are not served in the same placement environment. OSERS reports that the majority of handicapped children and youth in the 1985-86 school year received special education and related services in settings with nonhandicapped students. More than 26% received special education primarily in regular classes; another 41% received special education and related services primarily in resource rooms; and an additional 24% received services within a regular education building. Table 3.6 illustrates the percentage of students served in each of the nine environments, reported by handicapping condition. Table 3.7 reports the same data by age level. A major shift occurred in the percentage of students placed in regular classes between the 6–11 and 12–17 age groups, with 35.88% of 6–11-year-olds being placed in regular classes and only 15.6% of the 12–17 age group served in regular classes. For the older groups, the shift is primarily to resource rooms, with

Table 3.6   Percent of Handicapped Children and Youth Served in Nine Educational Environments By Handicapping Condition During School Year 1985–1986

Handicapping Condition	Regular Class	Resource Room	Separate Class	Public Separate School Facility	Private Separate School Facility	Public Residential Facility	Private Residential Facility	Correctional Facility	Homebound/ Environment
Learning disabled	15.29	61.80	21.06	0.93	0.54	0.04	0.04	0.23	0.89
Speech or language impaired	66.26	25.55	5.54	0.87	1.46	0.06	0.02	0.04	0.19
Mentally retarded	3.06	25.29	55.81	10.12	1.90	2.78	0.35	0.27	0.41
Emotionally disturbed	8.85	33.78	35.86	8.81	4.51	1.81	2.36	1.68	2.33
Hard of hearing and deaf	18.72	21.02	34.62	9.47	3.84	10.53	1.06	0.12	0.59
Multihandi- capped	4.06	15.25	43.23	19.26	9.26	2.96	2.84	0.33	3.58
Orthopedically impaired	25.62	16.14	32.03	13.06	4.12	0.61	0.44	0.89	7.99
Other health impaired	25.86	18.79	25.77	5.26	2.54	3.06	0.77	0.19	17.74
Visually handi- capped	31.49	24.00	19.44	10.32	2.05	10.27	0.95	0.11	1.37
Deaf-blind	6.55	17.06	23.30	11.90	3.11	27.56	8.41	0.04	1.36
All conditions	26.26	41.30	24.40	3.79	1.64	0.97	0.37	0.31	0.79

Source: U.S. Department of Education (1988). *Tenth Annual Report to Congress on the Implementation of the Education of the Handicapped Act,* p. 30, Washington, DC: U.S. Government Printing Office.

Table 3.7   Number and Percent of all Handicapped Children and Youth Served in Nine Educational Environments by Age Group During School Year 1985-86

Environment	3-5 Years		6-11 Years		12-17 Years		18-21 Years	
	Number	Percent	Number	Percent	Number	Percent	Number	Percent
Regular class	109,431	36.89	726,586	35.88	277,424	15.60	21,908	9.66
Resource room	58,718	19.79	807,144	39.86	849,989	47.81	75,429	33.25
Separate class	78,487	25.46	408,345	20.16	500,315	28.14	72,601	32.01
Public separate school facility	22,797	7.68	40,955	2.02	71,870	4.04	28,451	12.54
Private separate school facility	18,577	6.26	22,199	1.10	23,784	1.34	6,507	2.87
Public residential facility	3,659	1.23	9,532	0.47	18,018	1.01	10,673	4.71
Private residential facility	330	0.11	3,420	0.17	9,567	0.54	2,487	1.10
Correction facility	38	0.01	197	0.01	7,948	0.45	5,073	2.24
Homebound/hospital	4,614	1.56	6,813	0.34	18,952	1.07	3,709	1.64

Source: U.S. Department of Education (1988). *Tenth Annual Report to Congress on the Implementation of the Education of the Handicapped Act,* p. 32, Washington, DC: U.S. Government Printing Office.

47.81%, and separate classes, with 28.14%. Only 9.66% of the 18–21 age group was served in regular classes, with 33.25% in resource rooms and 32.10% in separate classes. Students in the higher age group were more likely to be those with moderate or severe handicaps whose needs were more difficult to meet in regular classes.

SUMMARY THOUGHTS

If the past predicts the future, change will characterize the future of special education. The last two decades have brought about dramatic alterations in how and where exceptional children are educated. Some children who today are considered exceptional were not eligible for services as recently as 10 years ago. Children who today are placed in special education programs may not be eligible for the same services 5 years from now. Children with AIDS and those who are medically fragile may become dominant groups among those defined as exceptional in the 21st century. The regular classroom may truly become the instructional placement of preference for children and youth with disabilities. The investment of resources may shift from services for school-age children to programs for infants and toddlers with disabilities. The education of exceptional children and youth may emerge as a primary educational challenge together with the broader issue of how cultural diversity can best be accommodated in the classroom. The focus of public policy may shift from a concern for special populations and discrete age groups to an emphasis on life-span needs and a continuum-of-care philosophy. These are all possibilities. Each is a reasonable expectation; none is assured.

What can be predicted is that some issues will be addressed because they are already of such significance that they can no longer be ignored. Emerging needs and problems that were once beyond reasonable resolution will become addressable, whether because intervening problems have been solved or because someone has initiated efforts to incorporate the need or problem within the responsibilities of special education. Few, if any, would have predicted even 30 years ago that the severely handicapped would become the responsibility of the public schools or that local property taxes would be used to pay for private education of students with disabilities. It is very likely that the boundaries of special education will be broadened to include new groups and services. At the same time, there will probably be continuing initiatives to curb the escalating costs that districts incur for delivering special education services. What is not predictable is how these two forces will interact.

The beginning professional in special education will have an opportunity to participate in shaping the future boundaries of special education. Participation carries with it responsibility. To be a participant means more than being good at one's professional role—be it that of a teacher, administrator, school psychologist, school nurse, or other specialist. It means becoming a student of the larger context of social issues that surround public policy and disability. It involves understanding the dynamics of families, the economics of human services, the sociology of education, the cultural diversity in our communities, the organization of schools, the relationship between human rights and the implications of disability, the power of advocacy, and the legislative process. These are not topics that can be studied in an introductory course or that can be covered in a single text. They are, however, ones you will encounter in your professional reading and in your role as a special education professional.

REFERENCES

Bodner, J., Mellard, D., & Clark, G. M. (1987). *State graduation policies and program practices in high school special education programs: A national study.* Unpublished manuscript.

Butler, John A., & Palfrey, Judith S. (1988). *Serving handicapped children: a special report.* Princeton, NJ: Robert Wood Johnson.

Federal Register (Part IV), August 1977, *42*(163).

Singer, D., & Butler, J. A. (1987). The Education of All Handicapped Children Act: Schools as agents of social reform. *Harvard Educational Review, 57,* 125–152.

Turnbull, H. R. (1986). *Free appropriate public education: The law and children with disabilities.* Denver: Love Publishing.

U.S. Department of Education. (1985). *Seventh annual report to Congress on the implementation of the Education of the Handicapped Act.* Washington, DC: GPO.

U.S. Department of Education. (1988). *Tenth annual report to Congress on the implementation of the Education of the Handicapped Act.* Washington, DC: GPO.

Wehman, P., & Melia, R. (1985). The job coach: Function in transition and supported employment. *American Rehabilitation, 11*(2), 4–7.

Wehman, P., Moon, M. S., & McCarthy, P. (1986). Transition from school to adulthood for youth with severe handicaps. *Focus on Exceptional Children, 18*(5), 1–12.

Weintraub, F. J., Abeson, A., Ballard, J., & La Vor, M. L. (Eds.). (1976). *Public policy and the education of exceptional children.* Reston, VA: Council for Exceptional Children.

Yanok, J. (1986). Free appropriate public education for handicapped children: Congressional intent and judicial interpretation. *Remedial and Special Education, 7*(2), 49–53.

ADDITIONAL READINGS

Benz, M. R., & Halpern, A. S. (1987). Transition services for secondary students with mild disabilities: A statewide perspective. *Exceptional Children, 53*(6), 507–514.

Bowen, O. R. (1987). The war against AIDS. *Journal of Medical Education, 62*(7), 543–548.

Campbell, P. H., Bellamy, G. T., & Bishop, K. K. (1988). Statewide intervention systems: An overview of the new federal programs for infants and toddlers with handicaps. *Journal of Special Education, 22*(1), 25–40.

Casto, G., & Mastropieri, M. A. (1986). The efficacy of early intervention programs: A meta-analysis. *Exceptional Children, 52*(5), 417–424.

Center, D. B., & McKittrick, S. (1988). Disciplinary removal of special education students. *Focus on Exceptional Children, 20*(2), 1–10.

Chinn, P. C., & Hughes, S. (1987). Representation of minority students in special education classes. *Remedial and Special Education, 8*(4), 41–46.

Henderson, A. T. (1988). Parents are a school's best friends. *Kappan, 70*(2), 148–153.

Rusch, F. R., & Phelps, L. A. (1987). Secondary special education and transition from school to work: A national priority. *Exceptional Children, 53*(6), 487–492.

Warboys, L. M., & Schauffer, C. B. (1986). Legal issues in providing special educational services to handicapped inmates. *Remedial and Special Education, 7*(3), 34–40.

1

Purpose

☐ To assist students in understanding federal legislation.

☐ To assist students in analyzing federal legislation.

Steps

1. Identify a change you would like to make in federal legislation.
2. Develop a written rationale for why the change is important.
3. Draft a proposed amendment to the appropriate federal law.

Analysis

☐ Exchange your ideas for amendments with at least two other students in the course.

☐ Reach agreement with the students on whether your proposed amendment is already covered by federal law.

☐ Review the proposed amendments of the other students and as a group reach agreement on which proposed amendments are most important.

☐ Submit the list of posposed amendments to the instructor to confirm if they are not covered by federal law.

Supporting the Participation of Exceptional Students in Today's Classrooms

Marleen C. Pugach
Caren Wesson
University of Wisconsin—Milwaukee

The legislative accomplishments of the 1970s clearly established as a national priority the value of integrating handicapped and nonhandicapped students. The emergence of this prominent value, with its emphasis on placement in less, rather than more, restrictive settings, meant that the relationship between special education and the general system of education would undergo fundamental change. A special education system formerly characterized by near complete isolation gave way to a reduction in the number of totally segregated schools and classes and, especially for mildly handicapped students, an increase in time spent with nonhandicapped peers.

For all teachers, as well as principals and special education administrators, integration signaled a new and untested challenge to work collegially and cooperatively to support special needs students[1] as they spent more and more time in general classroom environments. The very nature of appropriate interaction between special education and its parent, the general education system, had to be defined because no interactive relationship had existed before. The history of this relationship has been one of how to strike an appropriate balance between two essential goals: (a) the use of special education as an identifiable system for protecting the educational rights of handicapped students and (b) the location of handicapped students in general education classrooms in a way that assures both integration and a high quality of instruction. As this chapter will explain, the relationship continues to evolve nearly two decades after the issue was raised. Today, the question being asked is whether special education needs to have a discrete identity at all. Does education need two branches, general and special, or would unified programs be more advantageous to both students and teachers?

THE LIMITATIONS OF SPECIAL EDUCATION UNDER PL 94-142

Despite the civil rights achievements and philosophical values associated with the enactment of PL 94-142 in 1975, serious limitations quickly became apparent. These concerns had a direct impact on the way special education would be conceptualized in the future. Three major limitations bear mentioning.

The Early Nature of Collaboration

The bond between special education teachers and classroom teachers that had been anticipated after the law was passed never really developed into a mature relationship. Initially, special educators were concerned largely with establishing positive attitudes toward mainstreaming in general, instructing handicapped students in particular, and raising awareness of mainstreaming as a fundamental educational princi-

---

[1] We use the term *special needs students* to refer to a broad class of children including mildly and moderately handicapped students, students receiving special assistance such as Chapter 1 services, and students who are having difficulty achieving success in school. Mildly and moderately handicapped students are students classified as learning disabled, emotionally disturbed, and mildly mentally retarded.

ple. If classroom teachers showed a willingness to accept handicapped students, special educators considered this to be a sign of progress and of a positive relationship.

Legislated requirements also absorbed much of the attention of special educators. For example, they spent much time developing new and stringent procedures associated with (a) referral and identification and (b) the development and implementation of IEPs. Typically, classroom teachers looked to special educators for direction, because they were more knowledgeable about how to meet the legal requirements concerning handicapped students. Although the intent was coordination of actual instruction, coordination of written IEPs was often emphasized more than was instructional support. The actual involvement of classroom teachers in assessment, placement, and instructional development varied widely; in many places their participation was token at best.

As a result, coordinating the programming needed to help classroom teachers accommodate the diverse instructional needs of handicapped students received less attention than did educating classroom teachers in positive attitudes toward handicapped students and the requirements of the law. Special educators spent a great deal of time orienting classroom teachers to the law and the teacher's role in its implementation and little, if any, time actually engaged in collaborative professional work.

With the advent of new forms of service delivery such as consultation, special educators began to ask, "What is the most efficient way of assuring that the classroom teacher has the skills to instruct this particular group of students?" But early attempts at consultation were not consistently successful for two reasons. First, special education teachers needed time for consultation, and in most school districts enough time was not made available (Idol-Maestas & Ritter, 1985). Pull-out programming, which is based on removing students from their home classroom for part of the day, continued to dominate, with all the attendant problems of instructional fragmentation (Allington & Johnston, 1989). Second, classroom teachers were not always comfortable or skilled in using the ideas suggested by special education teachers. The interpersonal dynamics of consultation were often characterized by an attitude of superior knowledge on the part of special educators, rather than by a more collegial approach that might have encouraged mutual planning and implementation of classroom interventions (Johnson, Pugach, & Hammitte, 1988).

The Referral and Identification Process

A second limitation was the nature of mandated referral and identification procedures. Numerous studies indicated the existence of the following problems (Ysseldyke, Thurlow, Graden, Wesson, Algozzine, & Deno, 1983):

☐ The referral process was unwieldy and time consuming, with many tests being given for every child; decisions regarding identification were not based systematically on test results.

☐ Many nonhandicapped students were declared eligible to receive special education.

☐ Inconsistencies existed in the definitions and assessment procedures for learning disabilities.

☐ Once students were referred for special education, the probability was very high that they would be identified and placed; the teacher's decision to initiate a referral seemed almost to assure positive identification.

☐ Classroom teachers were often denied status as full partners, were "talked at" by a round robin of experts, and were not recognized for the experience and ideas they brought to the multidisciplinary team.

These findings raised questions about the legitimacy of such an inconsistent system of referral and identification. Students were required to undergo a labor-intensive process of testing before they could be helped, which delayed the delivery of educational services. Although the original intent of these provisions was to protect students from being inappropriately identified as handicapped (a practice that had often occurred prior to 1975) and to assure that students with handicaps were served in a timely fashion, the inconsistency in identification, especially in the largest category—learning disabilities—posed a serious dilemma. Not only did these studies raise the issue of how credible the categories themselves were; these studies also questioned the credibility of having separate preparation programs for teachers in these categories.

The Availability of Remedial Services

A final limitation involved the availability of remedial services other than special education for students who were unsuccessful in school. Although remedial reading services, funded under Chapter 1 programs existed for students with low achievement levels, often the only realistic means for teachers to obtain small group or individualized help for students was to refer them for special education. Due to the inconsistency in identification practices, some students who needed help received it as a result of being labeled as handicapped while others, whose needs may have been comparable, did not.

The nature of federal funding for special education made problematic the availability of services. Funding arrangements were based on the numbers of students identified as handicapped. School district administrators were required to provide an annual count of the number of handicapped students; more students meant extra funding. Therefore, administrators had an incentive for using and expanding special education. Other remedial services, whose funding typically came out of local, not federal, monies, were less attractive financially. During the years following the enactment of PL 94-142, the number of students labeled as learning disabled rose, and the number of students considered to be in need of remedial reading declined (McGill-Franzen, 1987).

Complicating the reduction in the types of services available to teachers was the increasing diversity of the student population, especially in the nation's urban areas. With more students entering school less prepared for academic work than in the past, teachers quickly became frustrated by the lack of support services. In a sense, special education became the "only game in town." But with time-consuming requirements for admission and restrictions on the kinds of problems it could accommodate, the special education system could not, and was never intended to, meet the needs of the increasing numbers of students who were not doing well in school. New ways of preventing failure in schools, rather than waiting for failure to occur and then helping students, were essential.

REDEFINING THE ROLE OF SPECIAL EDUCATION

These limitations became increasingly apparent to educators in the schools, professors of education, journalists, and government administrators of educational programs. A variety of critical analyses began to appear in special education professional journals supporting, among others, these positions:

- ☐ A complete merger of special and general education that would effectively eliminate special education as a separate entity (Stainback & Stainback, 1984)
- ☐ A series of federally and state-sponsored experimental programs free from the complex regulations associated with PL 94-142 that would encourage creative solutions to the issue of accommodating diverse student needs (Reynolds, Wang & Walberg, 1987)
- ☐ Simultaneous consideration within the education reform movement of problems in special education and in the whole of education as a way of coordinating change (Gartner & Lipsky, 1987)
- ☐ A reconceptualization of the preparation of teachers with emphasis on general education preparation as a prerequisite for special education certification (Pugach & Lilly, 1984)
- ☐ A cautious approach on the part of special education to the whole issue of change in service delivery, lest handicapped students lose completely the protections they had gained in 1975 (Kauffman, Gerber, & Semmel, 1988)

The Regular Education Initiative

The official government position on the issue of how to integrate special and general education, commonly referred to as the Regular Education Initiative, was made public in 1986 with the release of a report by OSERS entitled "Educating Children with Learning Problems: A Shared Responsibility" (Will, 1986). This report summarized the problems with current special education practice and advocated a much more interactive relationship between special and general education. The report emphasized the great numbers of students who were not learning successfully, the failure of the pull-out model of service delivery, the need to move from a failure-oriented to a preventive model of service and support, and the importance of using limited resources as efficiently as possible. This report did not advocate a complete merger between special and general education, but it did stress the need for full partnerships between the two at the school building level and shared responsibility for all students with learning and behavior problems. The appearance of this report signaled recognition of special education's shortcomings and challenged professionals in the field to respond with new and more effective ways of serving students in the schools, especially in preventing school failure.

Despite their differences in how they wished change to be achieved, these critics of special education agreed that the existing special education system was not serving students well and would have to be reconceptualized. As a field, special education had seemed overly concerned with meeting regulations (Lilly, 1988). If the educational needs of students were to be met in the least restrictive environment, concerns for the quality of education would have to dominate. Attention to the diverse student population in schools was needed, along with collegial, rather than expert, models of interaction between special and general education.

LRE: The Second Generation of Challenges

The issue of how to reconfigure special education is proving to be controversial. It raises questions about some of the fundamental assumptions on which special education philosophy and practice have traditionally been based. For example, by suggesting a merger that places responsibility for handicapped students on the general education establishment, special educators worry that handicapped students will not receive the priority they need. The basic controversy is whether those who have not made a prior commitment to special education can be trusted with the responsibility of assuring an appropriate education for handicapped students. By promoting waivers of federal regulations so new approaches to the organization and delivery of services can be tried, the federal structure that has protected special education is open to criticism. Yet proponents of a complete merger believe that integration will not be possible as long as special education exists as a separate system.

Moreover, suggestions that some of the skills considered to be part of the preparation of special education teachers may belong in the preparation of classroom teachers calls into question what makes special education "special." At the same time, an increase in prevention programs may result in fewer students being labeled handicapped, and in fewer jobs being available for special education teachers. Arguments against merger include the fear that it could take a long time and great reform before classroom teachers are actually ready to accommodate diverse students. Yet in many ways, these controversies are a logical extension in the development of the LRE concept, a "second generation" of challenges brought on by the commitment to integration of handicapped and nonhandicapped students.

Early Responses to LRE

As we have seen, when it was first introduced, LRE was met with a disproportionate preoccupation with technical and regulatory compliance. As time passed, concern was elevated to substantive issues regarding the nature of instruction in general education and its adequacy for meeting the needs of diverse students. Once the emphasis turned to instruction and serious professional collaboration, questions regarding the necessity of special education as a separate system quickly began to surface. What had to be addressed was how special education could best fit into the educational system as a whole, not how the whole educational system could respond to special education's regulations. As a support service to assist classroom teachers in meeting the instructional needs of students experiencing difficulty in school, special education was challenged to become an integral part of each school.

Merging special and general education has different implications for students with mild, moderate, and severe handicapping conditions. In Activity 1, page 103, you are asked to plan a debate on the topic, "The merger of special and general education will be detrimental to the education of handicapped students."

Much controversy regarding the future of special education continues, and debate and experimentation with new forms of service delivery have been stimulated. Whether a discrete special education system will continue or will be replaced by a totally merged system is a debatable question. Yet notwithstanding the possible outcome of these discussions, two major issues must be addressed if the lives of students with diverse educational needs in general education classrooms are to be successful: (a) the kinds of professional interactions that should take place between classroom teachers and specialists at the school and classroom level to promote and support optimum instruction for all students, including those with handicapping conditions, and (b) the degree to which traditional instructional methods need changing in order to accommodate the diverse student population adequately. When collaboration and support between all teachers in a building exist and when instruction is optimal, motivating, and responsive to the needs of students, it is rarely necessary to label students and to remove them from general education classrooms. It is to the topics of collaboration and pedagogy, which have implications for mildly, moderately, and severely handicapped students alike, that we now turn.

PROFESSIONAL COLLABORATION

In many ways, professional collaboration means an entirely new kind of interaction between adult professionals in schools, one ideally characterized by mutual respect, support, and the shared solving of classroom problems. Earlier in this chapter we noted that prior to 1975, special education teachers and classroom teachers were not expected to engage in joint instructional planning. Their separate educational responsibilities did not require such relationships. As special education has shifted

A CLASSROOM THAT DOES NOT SUPPORT THE PARTICIPATION OF EXCEPTIONAL STUDENTS

My name is Joe and I have a learning disability. From 10:00 to 10:45 each day I go to a ninth-grade social studies class. The teacher arrives just before the bell each day, and almost everyday we do dittoed worksheets. Some days we fill in maps; some days we fill in the blanks by looking at the chapter in our textbook. About once a week we read from the book aloud. I hate those days because I make lots of mistakes and it makes me feel stupid. We hardly get to talk to each other, and lots of kids make fun of the teacher because the teacher hardly ever teaches and when he does, it's boring. Most students do their work, but there are some who never turn in their assignments. If we have trouble doing the worksheets, we just copy from someone else's paper. Some kids seemed to know all about social studies before taking this class. But everyone is expected to act the same way and learn the same way. If we don't, it's our problem, not the teacher's. The teacher seems to decide that we are just dumb or that we don't try hard enough. It feels like he has given up on us.

☐   ☐   ☐

Is this scenario common in schools?

What do you think about Joe's attitude?

If Joe was on your caseload, what would you tell him about dealing with the social studies class?

What are some adaptive responses to this situation?

What do you do as a special educator with respect to working with this social studies teacher?

---

toward supporting classroom teachers in their attempts to integrate handicapped students, a new set of collaborative skills has become a necessity.

Two new forms of collaborative practice typically provide the framework for these relationships: *consultation* and *informal teaming.* The purpose of these collaborative approaches is to provide timely support to students who are not successful and to maximize the benefits of sharing knowledge between special education teachers and classroom teachers. In consultation, individuals provide assistance directly to other individuals within a school. Typically, special education teachers and school psychologists consult with classroom teachers. In informal teaming (distinguished from mandated multidisciplinary teaming under PL 94-142), a small group of faculty, which often includes a special educator, works with teachers on particular student problems. Informal teams may be known by various names, such as building assistance teams, teacher assistance teams, intervention assistance teams, school appraisal teams, and so on. In both the consultation and teaming

A CLASSROOM THAT SUPPORTS THE PARTICIPATION OF EXCEPTIONAL STUDENTS

My name is Scott and I used to have major problems in school. I was in a class for kids with behavior problems, but now I am in a regular sixth grade, and I think I am doing okay. My old special education teacher still checks in on me now and then, and she and my sixth-grade teacher talk about me all the time. But, it's fine with me because I know they are just looking out for me. My sixth-grade teacher, Mrs. M., always greets me when I come in to class in the morning. She is nice to everyone, but I think she has an extra big smile for me. Mrs. M. is a great teacher.

When we arrive each day, we start out by finishing a brainteaser puzzle worksheet with our assigned partner. So, we have something to do as soon as we get in the door, and we have a chance to be with one of our friends right away, too. Our class is kept very busy with lots of reading and writing all morning, but off and on throughout the morning we get to help each other or do the assignment with some other kids. So I don't feel like I am under all this pressure, which can make me feel crazy, but I do feel like I have a lot to do. I guess I don't mind all the work because there is usually some fun in all the assignments. I like how Mrs. M. teaches.

Now and then I will come to school with a bad attitude because of some junk that happened at home with my Mom or my brothers. They can still make me real angry. Mrs. M. usually knows just by looking at me that I am in bad shape. On these days, she spends some time alone with me while the other kids are doing their brainteasers. She takes me out into the hallway and has me tape record the reasons I am so mad. She says that it's good for me to express myself and then drop it. So she helps me calm down and get started, and I spend about 5 minutes just ranting and raving about what happened at home. After just talking about it, I start to feel better, and I can go back into the classroom and start my work.

---

models, the goal is for all school personnel to work together to develop optimal educational approaches for all students.

For students who are not handicapped but who are experiencing difficulties in school, consultation and/or teaming is directed at preventing the escalation of problems by changing instructional practices in the classroom. When used for this purpose, various forms of collaboration are sometimes known as prereferral interventions because the intent is to improve the student's chances for success before a referral becomes necessary and thus to prevent inappropriate referrals from being initiated. Nevertheless, the term *prereferral intervention* is inappropriate because it implies that collaboration only occurs to prevent a referral. Instead, collaboration should be thought of as an appropriate and beneficial way for all professionals in a school to interact as part of their basic commitment to students.

For students who are clearly identified as having a handicapping condition, collaboration is directed at coordinating instructional planning, accommodating the

Later in the day, Mrs. M. has me listen to what I recorded. I make a list of things that bother me, and then I divide the list up into things I can do something about and things that I can't. We talk about it during recess for a few minutes, and Mrs. M. helps me see some things that I could do differently. Then she has me close my eyes and picture all my worries floating away in a pink cloud. I know it sounds funny, but that is what my teacher did last year. So she told Mrs. M. about it, and it really helps me to keep my self under control. When I used to be mad, I hit people, threw desks, and was totally rude. I couldn't stop myself then, but now I can. I am really glad that Mrs. M. knows how to help me. Sometimes I get angry with her, too, like if I think some test is too hard. She has helped me to know when I am getting angry and how to tell her about it in a calm way. We usually end up compromising. Like one time the science test was too hard. I felt like I wasn't getting any of the answers right, and I just couldn't write down everything I knew about the topic. Mrs. M. let me take the test by talking out the answers instead of writing all the answers down. I got a B and that was fine. She knows how to give a little, and that helps me a lot.

□ □ □

What have been the accommodations made for Scott?

How can you as a special education teacher facilitate these kinds of accommodations in the general classroom?

What would you say to a colleague who said, "Mrs. M. is being too easy on Scott and making too many accommodations?"

student's special needs through adaptation, and providing coordinated instructional support as needed. For example, if handicapped students are instructed in both a special education classroom and general education classroom, the relationship between these two experiences must be coordinated to make sense to the student. Likewise, if handicapped students are phasing out of special education and will be making the transition to a general classroom, they must be prepared to meet expectations in that classroom.

Recently, a third form of collaborative interaction has also developed: *team teaching* between special education and classroom teachers. In these situations, teachers share full responsibility for the same large group of students, and handicapped students are permanent members of the class. In many cases, team teaching has emerged as a grassroots alternative to the frustrations teachers were experiencing over (a) scheduling difficulties associated with pull-out programs and (b) the lack of consistency for students who received their education in multiple settings. Team teaching has the advantage of making both teachers equal in their responsibility for all students. No less important is the fact that differing orientations can contribute to programming that meets the needs of diverse students in the team.

The Collaborative Problem-Solving Process

When collaborative interaction takes place to support students who are not receiving special education services, it is usually initiated by a classroom teacher who is expressing particular concern over an individual student. The teacher and the consultant or team members work together using a four-step problem-solving approach. First, the situation is clarified, or described accurately, to ensure that any classroom interventions developed are responsive to the actual characteristics of the situation; accurate definition also enables teachers to gain some objectivity about the situation. Second, potential interventions are generated, predictions are made about the potential benefits and limitations of various intervention plans, and teachers choose one intervention. Third, a schedule of implementation is developed, with the role of the classroom teacher and any specialists defined clearly. Fourth, a method for evaluating the effectiveness of the intervention is established, along with a timeline for joint review of progress.

For a student who is already receiving special education services, collaboration can occur in two ways. When students are newly identified as handicapped, plans for their integration should be established from the outset. Potential areas of difficulty for the student and needs for special materials, assistance, or adaptations of classroom practice should be identified jointly, with the classroom teacher providing information about the norms, routines, and expectations for student performance and the kinds of adaptations that may work best. The special education teacher can then assist by making adaptations in materials, securing alternative materials, or planning to spend time in the classroom working directly with the handicapped student. A similar set of issues would be raised by special education teachers whose students are beginning to participate in general education classrooms for the first time. The special education teacher in these situations would be gaining important information from the classroom teacher regarding a student's changing needs and potential performance in a particular classroom. When the focus of collaboration is an identified handicapped student, the collaborative relationship should be initiated by the special education teacher. In practice this is a goal to which special educators must consciously aspire.

In a consulting relationship, the interaction can be initiated by a simple verbal request for assistance or by an informal written request. Consultation has the advantage of requiring only the coordination of two people's schedules; therefore, initial and subsequent meetings can be frequent and can vary substantially in length. If consultants have blocks of time available, they can assist with tasks such as observing student behavior, observing teacher-student interaction, or collecting data on student progress.

In informal teaming, a group of people must be assembled; typically, teams meet at regularly scheduled times. One individual usually acts as the team chairperson and is responsible for organizing the agenda, setting the schedule, and making sure that all needed information is available. Informal problem-solving teams vary in their composition from district to district and school to school. Some states mandate informal teaming as a prereferral intervention. Many teaming models include specialists as permanent members, as well as the principal, and perhaps one classroom teacher who is considered highly skilled. Some teams are made up primarily of skilled classroom teachers who invite others to participate as needed (Chalfant, Pysh, & Moultrie, 1979).

Practices That Facilitate or Inhibit Collaboration

In both the consultation and informal teaming approaches to collaboration, certain practices contribute to the development of strong collaborative relationships, and other practices inhibit them. Guidelines for promoting the development of collaborative problem solving include:

1. Learn everything you can from the person you are invited to assist. For special education teachers, this means learning about the operation of the general education classroom; for classroom teachers, this means learning about how to construct individual interventions.
2. Assist, rather than lead, your colleague in clarifying the problem.
3. The teacher who initiates a request for assistance should take charge of the collaborative meeting; do not assume that you have to be the one in charge just because you have been asked to help.
4. Provide guidance, not ready-made answers.
5. Ask other staff members for assistance when you have a problem they can help you solve; do not always be in the position of giving but not receiving advice.
6. When planning informal meetings, the schedule of the classroom teacher should be accommodated as much as possible. Remember, classroom teachers have tight schedules, with responsibility for 25–30 students all day long!
7. Listen to your colleague carefully.
8. Remember that you may routinely use terminology that a colleague trained in a different specialization may not understand; be sensitive to your own language during collaboration, and do not shut out others by using jargon.
9. Develop interventions jointly; if you impose a solution one-sidedly, your colleague may be either unwilling to or unskilled at implementing it.
10. Trust your colleague to be as committed as you are to the needs of the student you are discussing.

One of the most frequent mistakes made in the early stages of collaboration is having specialists communicate the attitude that their expertise is more valuable than that of classroom teachers. Although specialists do have knowledge unique to their field, classroom teachers also possess essential information and skills, particularly in the areas of curriculum and large-group instruction/management. Unfortunately, the early history of consultation tended toward expert posturing and often lacked the fundamental characteristic of mutual respect. When consultants engaged only in giving advice, they communicated to their peers that the "expert" interpretation of the problem was the only valid one and that the interventions they suggested were the only appropriate ones. This attitude seriously devalued the classroom teacher's role and jeopardized the collaborative relationship.

Informal teaming can suffer from the same problem; when multiple specialists serve on a team and each considers his or her own expertise as being most valuable, the classroom teacher's contribution may get lost. Without input from classroom teachers, implementation of coordinated instructional programs is difficult. The danger in assuming an expert posture is that the understanding brought to the situation by the classroom teacher may be treated as less important than that of a specialist, when in reality the classroom teacher has ongoing, consistent knowledge about the student. When the classroom teacher's contributions are not taken seriously, informal teaming loses its essence. It is no longer a forum for supporting *all* teachers.

Informal teaming for purposes of building schoolwide collaboration must be clearly distinguished from team meetings that are required following a formal evaluation for special education. In the former, professionals are working in a preventive mode to accommodate a student's needs within the general education environment. In fact, the original conception of teacher assistance teams was informal teams made up of a core of classroom teachers (Chalfant, Pysh, & Moultrie, 1979). This form of teaming was developed not only to stem the tide of inappropriate referrals but to emphasize that classroom teachers are the source of excellent intervention ideas.

Facilitating Collaborative Relationships

To be successful, consultation and teaming should be thought of as flexible procedures within which exist roles that can be played by many professionals in the schools. Both types of collaborative relationships are facilitated when all members of a school staff are trained to participate in problem solving with their peers. Flexibility in consultation means that a person should be able to both give and receive advice from his or her peers; a teacher may be the consultant or the consultee, depending on the problem at hand. In most schools, unfortunately, specialists are seen exclusively as consultants and classroom teachers exclusively as consultees.

Flexibility in teaming means that the membership of the team should not permanently reside with specialists. A team could instead be made up of a small core including the building principal, one permanent teacher, and the teacher initiating a request for assistance. The core members could make judgments regarding who should be present in the team *on the basis of the problem under consideration*. All specialists would not have to be present at all team meetings; in fact, many meetings might be successful in providing assistance without the help of specialists, thereby reserving their time to work with more intensive problems (Pugach & Johnson, 1988).

> In order to be a good collaborative professional, you are wise to reflect on the reasons you are intending to become a special or general education teacher. Activity 2, page 103, asks you to give thought to this crucial issue.

Collaboration is *not* just a function of special education; that is, it should not occur only between special educators and other teachers in the schools. Collaborative planning and problem solving need to be present in all schools and involve all members of the staff; each member of the staff is a potential source of support and expertise for every other staff member. This is an important issue because there are many types of problems that could benefit from professional collaboration that are not focused on special needs students. Multiple levels of problem solving need to take place: between classroom teachers, between specialists and classroom teachers, and between principals and school faculty. In fact, one of the goals of the current education reform movement continues to be the development of collegial, collaborative professional relationships among all teachers in a building.

If partnerships are to be developed and sustained, all teachers must be willing to see themselves as recipients, as well as givers, of advice. This means that all teachers need a well-developed awareness of their attitudes toward and abilities in teaching. It is only as full partners in the collaborative school staff that all teachers can best contribute to the development and support of successful learning environments for today's diverse population of students.

PEDAGOGY

In a classroom that supports the participation of special needs students, positive attitudes and good relationships are essential but not sufficient. The second major factor required for successful integration is an array of alternative pedagogical (instructional) approaches, or classroom interventions, that can be employed to help increase appropriate behaviors and decrease nonfunctional (disruptive or nonproductive) behaviors. Four categories of interventions merit consideration: self-managed interventions, peer-managed interventions, teacher-managed interventions, and whole-school interventions.

Guidelines for Developing Interventions

Although there is no recipe for a successful intervention, there are some helpful principles. Problem definition is the most crucial step in the whole process. One distinction that is helpful in clarifying the problem is the difference between a skill deficit and a performance deficit. When a student has a *skill deficit,* or an inability to demonstrate the skill, remedial teaching is required. If, however, the student has a *performance deficit,* he or she is capable of demonstrating the skill but lacks the motivation to do so. For example, if a student fails repeatedly to complete assignments, the teacher must determine if the problem is a lack of ability to accomplish the task or a lack of incentive to complete the assignment. Interventions vary significantly for these two problems.

As teachers work to define the problem, they should be using questions such as the following to aid definition. Not every question is relevant to every problem; nevertheless, a simple consideration of each variable is always helpful. This list of questions is only an example. Two teachers working together should compose their own list.

1. What do we wish the student would do that he or she is not doing?
2. What is the student doing that we wish he or she was not doing?
3. When does the behavior occur? Does it happen at a certain time of the day? During certain activities?
4. Does the student have the problem during group activities, independent activities, or small group instruction?
5. Does the problem occur during a particular academic topic or across different topics?
6. Do other children also have this problem? If so, who and how many children? Is there something that needs to be changed for the whole class?
7. Does the student know that the problem exists, or is the student oblivious to the problem? Has the student been directly informed to change his or her behavior?
8. Is the problem related to school behaviors (attention, work completion), social behaviors (peer relationships, self-concept), or academic behaviors (learning new concepts, remembering to apply strategies)?
9. Is it a problem that can be ignored because addressing it may create more of a disruption than the problem itself?
10. Should we discuss this problem with another teacher so that we can get someone else's perspective on it and because talking about it may help us understand the problem more fully?

In addition to considering many variables, teachers should create an intervention that is comparable to the problem in terms of its interference in the school day. The old adage "Don't use a cannon to shoot a fly" summarizes this principle. Teachers should always use the simplest, most direct intervention first rather than developing elaborate intervention plans. For example, directly telling the student to change the behavior is a simple intervention. Elaborate plans may work, but they may not be necessary and may create undue amounts of work for the teacher. Whenever possible, the teacher should opt for a self-management plan. Self-management plans have the advantage of teaching the student independence, rather than dependence on someone else for control of the behavior (Lovitt, 1973).

Teachers should keep some kind of formal or informal data on the problem. The teacher may simply record anecdotally the nature, frequency, duration, and intensity of the behavior, or the teacher may keep a running tally of the number of times the problem occurs. With the data in hand, the teacher can make more accurate decisions about the effectiveness of the intervention. Finally, teachers should concentrate on academic behaviors rather than on social behaviors. For example, if the problem is talking to others during independent work time, the teacher may want to construct an intervention that focuses on work completion rather than on talking. Teachers should emphasize the development of constructive behaviors rather than the elimination of negative behaviors.

Self-Managed Interventions

Self-managed interventions are designed to help students control their own behavior; the students play a primary role in the planning and/or the execution of the intervention. Self-managed interventions should be thought of on a continuum from little student input to total student input and control. Teachers should not expect the student to be totally self-managed overnight but should keep that goal in sight as they modify their instruction.

Self-Managed Data Collection and Evaluation Activities

One very effective way to deal with students' problem behaviors has been to require students to record their own behaviors. For example, a grade-school boy had difficulty controlling his aggression. The teacher asked the boy to record a tally mark each time he hit or kicked another student. The boy stopped being aggressive as he apparently wanted to avoid recording his aberrant behavior.

Many teachers help students increase on-task behavior by simply taping a notecard to the students' desks and telling the students to mark a tally each time they consider their work effort and judge that they have been working. For some students the tally marks must be exchangeable for a special activity. Other students benefit from seeing the tally marks themselves and do not need to have the marks exchanged.

Self-correcting activities are another form of self-monitoring. Students learn more by checking their own work than by having the teacher make the corrections. For example, the self-corrected spelling test is the most effective single technique for improving spelling skills (Graham & Miller, 1979). Students can grade their own math papers, grade their workbook answers, or edit their own written expression work. Students can assign their own grades on certain assignments. Similarly, self-evaluation means that students make judgments about their own behaviors. The evaluation may be elicited through a rating scale or a simple yes/no question such as, Did I have appropriate behavior during the last 30 minutes? Finally, self-managed data collection and evaluation include having students graph their own data on a particular behavior. They may graph their number of tallies of on-task behavior, the number of multiplication facts they answer correctly in 2 minutes, or the number of words they write when doing a written expression assignment. These relatively easy-to-implement strategies may be very effective.

Self-Managed Instruction

Self-managed instruction means the students have some input into decisions regarding how they will be taught. For example, students may have a role in creating contracts. Contracts between the teacher and student usually have two primary components: what the student will do and what the teacher will do. As teachers attempt to encourage students to become more self-reliant, they will often ask them to have some input on one of the two components. Eventually, the student can be in full charge of one of the components, and ultimately the student can devise the entire contract. This is one example of using self-management in a more instructional way. Other self-managed instructional decisions include the following:

- ☐ Students may help devise their own reinforcement programs by providing input on what the reinforcer will be, when it will be earned, how it will be earned, how much of the reinforcer they will get, and/or how the reinforcer can be lost.
- ☐ Students may have input on the schedule of their work completion rather than have the teacher dictate when each assignment will be completed.
- ☐ Students may choose what work will be done. For example, students may choose which problems they will complete from a page in their math books. The teacher may say that they have to do a total of 15 out of the 30 problems on the page, but let each individual student select which ones they will do.
- ☐ Students may decide how they will learn new material. For example, students may select a study strategy for spelling.
- ☐ Students may select their own test items when provided with guidelines about the number and type of items to be answered.

Many students respond favorably when they are given choices. Not only do they learn the material at a faster rate; they also learn to make decisions.

Strategy Training

Strategy training means that the teacher not only teaches the new information to the student but also teaches the student how to learn. There are many strategy training interventions that may be useful to special needs students in a general education classroom. These interventions include the use of mnemonics or keywords to recall detailed information, self-questioning strategies to help students understand the material they are reading, elaboration or restatements of what was read to ensure understanding, and rehearsal of the information to be learned. The underlying goal of these strategies is to help the students stop and think about what they are doing. Many students never need this kind of instruction because they can generate their own ways of learning how to learn. But students who are having difficulty in school can benefit greatly from these types of interventions. The strategy training interventions listed previously are primarily self-managed; although they often require a great deal of initial teacher input.

Mnemonics

Mnemonics is the use of a gimmick to help the student recall detailed information. Some examples of commonly used mnemonics are the name ROY G. BIV to help students remember the colors of the rainbow and the expression "Every good boy deserves fudge" to help music students remember the names of the lines on the treble clef. Teachers can create their own mnemonics for the students as these are needed. One first-grade teacher used the song "Old McDonald Had a Farm" to teach the short vowel sounds to her class. "Old McDonald had an 'a,' eieio, and the 'a' he had sounded like a, eieio...." "Thirty days has September," is another example of a mnemonic. The idea is to provide the student with a simple way to remember the material.

Rehearsal

Rehearsal is another useful strategy. To teach the child to rehearse, the teacher verbally models the rehearsal strategy. For example, "Now, let's see. I want to remember the names of the provinces in Canada. So, I'll practice. Quebec, Saskatchewan, Alberta, etc. I'll say them again." Some children need only a few examples of rehearsal, and then they need a self-management strategy to cue them to use the rehearsal strategy. They may quickly realize that rehearsal means to repeat the new information aloud or say it to themselves in their heads, but they will probably not easily learn when to use the rehearsal strategy. The teacher may help the students set up a self-managed strategy in which they ask themselves if they used the rehearsal strategy to remember the new information just read or reviewed. Rehearsals of the whole class are also helpful.

Keywords

Use of *keywords* is another strategy that teachers should consider. Special needs students may benefit by having a teacher who helps them link important (key) words together (Mastropieri & Scruggs, 1987). Pictures may help the students remember certain concepts. For example, when teaching the history of World War I, a picture of a lion sitting behind a desk will help the students recall the name of the secretary of state, William Jennings Bryan. Bryan and lion rhyme and can easily be linked. Mastropieri and Scruggs also suggest that to help the students recall that the Central Powers were Turkey (T), Austria-Hungary (A), and Germany (G), teachers may use a picture of children playing TAG in Central Park.

Self-Questioning

Another effective strategy is the use of *self-questioning*. This technique is particularly helpful when the student is reading either in a content area or in fiction. There are many variations of this technique, but the basic idea is to have students stop periodically to ask themselves questions about the passage they have just read. The specific questions that students ask themselves depend on the type of passage they are reading. When the passage is fiction, they may ask themselves who, what, where, when, why, and how questions. Expository text calls for questions about the main idea or the supporting details for the argument being made. These questions will help the student to pause and consider what was read. Often the problem with comprehending a passage is not that the student is unable to understand the material but that the student reads in a rote manner without thinking about the content.

Elaboration

Elaboration, another strategy, means that the student summarizes what was read or discussed in his or her own words and relates the information to something already known (Reid, 1988). Typically, the teacher must first model this strategy and then prompt the student to use it overtly and then covertly. This strategy helps the student make sense out of the material.

Student self-managed interventions are highly effective. They help students develop independence (the primary goal of education), and because they are more time efficient, self-managed interventions also free the teacher to work with other students. To summarize, if teachers complete tasks for students that the students are capable of doing themselves, teachers deny students the opportunity to learn from these practice occasions (Lindsley, 1972).

Peer-Managed Interventions

If self-management is not an option, the teacher may want to consider peer-managed interventions—strategies which the other students in the class or students from other classes help implement. Younger, older, and same-age peers may be helpful in many ways. They may record information for the teacher, grade papers, provide motivation, and tutor. Younger peers may be valuable in providing an incentive for reading practice. A student who has difficulty reading will benefit from reading to a younger child. A peer in the classroom may be a collaborator with the teacher and the student of concern. The peer can sit behind a student who gets out of his or her seat too often, and the teacher can then train the helper to record each time the student stays seated for 30 minutes. The peer can also be part of the motivation plan. If the student is in his or her seat for four 30-minute periods, the peer and the student may have 10 minutes of free time together.

Peers can also play a valuable role in the education of severely handicapped students. Severely handicapped students benefit from learning functional skills in a community setting. Given proper guidance, peers can assist by guiding a severely handicapped student through a task. An example is a severely handicapped student who is learning to collate papers, staple them, and stuff them into envelopes. A peer can facilitate this task in a setting such as the school office.

Peer Tutoring

The most common use of peers is *peer tutoring,* which is a very effective intervention for both the tutor and the tutee. One caution is that the tutor must be trained in a specific task to do with the tutee. Simply pairing students together is not effective. Rather, the teacher must first think through exactly what the peer tutor should be doing. One common peer tutoring task is to train tutors to use flashcards with tutees. The flashcards, which can be either for reading or math, are selected for the appropriate level of the tutee and should be skills that the tutor has already mastered. Specific steps for the tutor to follow are taught to the tutor.

The teacher may select the tutor based on a variety of criteria. Often tutors are students who always finish their work quickly and need other tasks to occupy their time. The teacher may select a tutor based on the tutor's needs. The experience of being a tutor can boost the self-esteem of average students.

Peer tutoring is an effective intervention.

Cooperative Learning

Another peer-managed strategy is the use of *cooperative learning* goal structures (Johnson & Johnson, 1987). In a cooperative learning activity, the teacher forms groups of mixed ability and gives each group a common task. All students in each group must have some responsibility for mastering the material. The group can succeed in reaching its goal only if everyone in the group learns the information or completes the task. The teacher may either quiz each student to make sure the material is mastered or have each student complete a written product to ensure mastery. Part of the strength of cooperative learning is that as the students teach each other the material, they become very well versed about the content. People tend to learn more when they talk than when they simply listen or read, and so as they teach, they talk and they learn. In cooperative learning, students not only master the content; they also develop interpersonal skills ranging from making eye contact to resolving conflicts. Teachers monitor the group interactions and intervene to teach social skills. During the processing period following each lesson, teachers emphasize the social skills the students need to learn as well as praise the skills the groups have mastered.

Teacher-Managed Interventions

Some problems that occur as the special needs student is mainstreamed cannot be handled either by self-managed or peer-managed interventions. Sometimes teachers must directly deal with the problem. There are several reasons some problems require direct teacher intervention. First, there is a stigma associated with being a slow learner, and if a student is working on material that was covered by the rest of the class months or years earlier, the student cannot be expected to respond favorably to peer tutoring. The teacher should avoid putting students in such embarrassing situations. Second, the methods necessary for instructing the student are not conducive to self- or peer instruction. Third, the personal attention of the teacher is a powerful, motivating influence. (Many of the interventions discussed previously may also be implemented by the teacher rather than by the students or by a peer.)

Structured Motivational Program

The teacher may need to establish a *structured motivational program.* For example, if swearing in class is the problem, the teacher may want to set up a point system that awards points for appropriate class contributions. If having one student singled out becomes an issue for the class, the teacher may have the student earn the points for a whole class activity. In this situation, other students become confederates in helping the student's behavior improve. The student's input into this process will increase the likelihood of its success.

Content Mastery

Another major category of intervention that the teacher may control is the way in which students demonstrate *content mastery.* For some special needs students in general education classes, the problem is not learning the material or doing the work but accomplishing as many tasks per day as their peers. For the student who works at a slower pace, the teacher may simply assign a portion of the work. Teachers must be clear about what the objective is of the lessons and assignments. If the objective for a math lesson is for the student to demonstrate mastery of multiplication, it may be possible for a student to do that at the pace of 20 problems each day rather than 40. Similarly, the problem may be in the modality through which the student expresses mastery of the content. The teacher needs to have a definite purpose for the lesson or the unit of instruction so acceptable adaptations can be developed. If the purpose is for the students to learn about the culture of South America, a student may demonstrate that mastery by answering questions orally. Taking a written test may be the modality used by the other students, but a written test may be unrelated to the actual objective, which is to learn the content.

Teachers may also need to teach the content using a *different modality.* A common technique for special needs students is the use of tape-recorded passages, whereas other students are expected to read the same material. Some younger students benefit from instruction given in multiple modalities. Instead of just telling the information, teachers also write the information on a handout or on the board. Teachers may also require the student to write the information down, whereas others may only need to hear it once. Writing provides another input modality for the student. Some teachers use texture, smell, taste, and as many modalities as possible to help the students learn. When teaching letter sounds, the teacher may say, "Pretend you're a *s*nake hi*s*sing, *s*melling, and *s*ipping *s*oda on a *s*unny day while you *s*it on a *s*tone by the *s*ea." Students exposed to this kind of multisensory experience are more likely to remember this sound than are students who are simply told, "This makes an 's' sound."

Skills Practice

Special needs students frequently need more opportunities to *practice skills* (Allington & Johnston, 1989). For example, some students only need exposure to new words during reading time; others may need to be reminded about these new words more frequently. A major concern about special needs students is that they seem to learn the new information one day, and the next day they have to learn it all over again. Some students have simply not developed the long-term memory capacity of their peers. These students need to be reminded of the new information again and again during the day. Teachers may help students expand their long-term memory by asking them to repeat information frequently during the day. One simple way to accomplish this is to have a set of flashcards near the doorway, and every time the student exits the classroom the teacher asks for the secret password, which is an example of the new words being learned. Sending information to the family to elicit support in helping the student learn the information is also helpful. Each week a list of words can be sent home, and the student can review the words with a parent or sibling.

Reciprocal Teaching

Techniques necessary for teaching the student new information may also require direct teacher intervention. An example of this type of technique is *reciprocal teaching,* in which the teacher creates a dialogue with a student to help the student learn the information and a strategy for learning (Palincsar, 1986). In reading comprehension, the teacher basically talks to himself or herself and thinks aloud the thoughts the students have as they try to understand what they have read.

Increased Direct Instruction

Other teacher-centered interventions may include *increased direct instruction* of the content being taught. Some students learn new information with minimal exposure, but the special needs student in the general education classroom may have skill deficits that require direct teaching. The basic steps teachers follow in direct instruction are (a) demonstrate the behavior, (b) prompt the student to do the behavior, (c) provide feedback for the student's attempt, and (d) have the student practice the behavior in different settings. This kind of teaching can be applied to many different lessons. When learning to spell, for example, the teacher may say to the student, "The word is castle. We spell it C-A-S-T-L-E. I write it like this." Demonstration on the board or on paper. "Say it aloud with me. Castle; C-A-S-T-L-E. Now you spell it on your paper. Say it aloud as you spell it." When using direct instruction techniques, the teacher assumes that the student is basically naive about the information to be learned. The teacher makes sure the student is ready to learn that particular skill and that the student knows the purpose for the lesson. Social skills often require direct instruction. Many special students need to have the teacher model certain skills, such as appropriate social distance, and then prompt the student and have the student practice the behavior in contrived and natural situations.

Whole-School Interventions

Some schools have systematic procedures for dealing with students who are having difficulty in the general classroom. At one end of these strategies is the use of specialists to assist the instruction of targeted students. Midway are procedures used for an entire class or grade. At the opposite end are interventions used systematically throughout the entire school. Whole-school interventions may include instructional techniques, motivational factors, home-school communication systems, self-esteem–building strategies, and interpersonal relationship–building activities. Teachers and administrators who are supportive of the notion that all children can be educated in the general education setting often work to set up preventive systems and systems that assist the special needs student across the settings in the school building.

Use of Experts

On an individual or small-group basis, experts in the building can be helpful. Speech and language therapists are the experts on improving language development and articulation skills. They not only provide the direct instruction for those students needing their services but also help indirectly by guiding the teacher on language training in the classroom. Similarly, counselors and school psychologists can be useful allies as teachers deal with emotional, learning, and behavior problems.

Other colleagues who may be helpful include physical therapists and occupational therapists. They can help a teacher aid the student in developing the physical skills and dexterity necessary for daily living and vocational pursuits. The school social worker may assist in the fostering of the relationships between school and home and may provide insights into the student's home situation. Administrators can be helpful in providing motivation for students. Some principals reward good behavior, both academic and social, by having the student come to the office and play messenger or announcer. Some principals are effective in evaluating instruction and providing helpful feedback to teachers regarding the positive aspects of their teaching as well as suggestions for change.

In some schools, many or all teachers are trained in peer tutoring, and for portions of the school week all students participate as both tutor and tutee. Similarly, training an entire school staff in cooperative learning is another way to involve all students in peer-mediated interventions.

Home-School Communication

Some schools initiate a consistent home-school communication system in an effort to encourage parents to be more involved in the education of the children and to help keep parents more fully informed about their children's progress. Weekly newsletters may be sent home from the class; a checklist of work accomplished during the week or of social behaviors of the students may be sent home; some schools may have a policy that requires teachers to have some kind of contact with parents at least monthly. An implicit purpose of these structured systems is to create a greater sense of community within the school. Contact means more likely involvement, which means greater learning gains.

Self-Esteem–Building Programs

The climate of the school is an important element in successful efforts to facilitate positive peer relationships. A school with high rates of misbehavior among the general education students is a more difficult building in which to integrate the special needs students. Schools may institute a self-esteem–building theme. A "Like Yourself" campaign in the school can be effective. A peace slogan may also be useful in establishing improved interpersonal relationships. Some schools use a consistent approach to behavior problems. The Good Behavior Game is one popular way of dealing with infractions (Barrish, Saunders, & Wolf, 1969). A student court is another effective system. These strategies are useful not just for special needs students; they are also useful in creating a climate in which teachers can in general respond more effectively because they are freed from being isolated disciplinarians.

The development of intervention plans is a skill that improves with practice. Refer to Activity 3, page 104, for some practice in intervention planning.

SUMMARY THOUGHTS

Collegiality is the word of the day in education. All educators, including specialists, have come to realize that each teacher has strengths and weaknesses and that each must learn how to identify those strengths and weaknesses, use colleagues to the students' full advantage, and trust each other. School staffs need to sit down and talk together to consider how they will systematically serve all students who are having problems in school. A variety of services should be available in each building.

Two trends in whole-school improvement will likely have an impact on how special needs students will be served. One is experimenting with relationships between general and special education as a way of reconsidering how resources should be used. A second is the general reform movement in education, one focus of which is increased autonomy of school staff. The notion of site-based management that facilitates decision making by the personnel within a school contributes to a focus on schoolwide change and schoolwide responsibility for students with problems. Teachers work together to decide about important factors such as the allocation of the money, parent contact, inservice needs, and use of personnel. The idea behind site-based management is that better decisions can be made about schools by those who work in them than by those who do not. These decisions should include how the resources for special needs students are to be allocated.

Part of the challenge of being in education is the ever-changing nature of the job. This is an exciting time in education and one filled with opportunity for change and experimentation. Much of this experimentation will focus on the establishment of collaborative relationships between general educators and special educators. Schools that develop ways of supporting the full participation of special needs students will likely provide models for change. Out of this, new ideas for practice will emerge that can benefit all students.

REFERENCES

Allington, R. L., & Johnston, P. (1989). Coordination, collaboration and consistency: The redesign of compensatory and special education interventions. In R. E. Slavin, N. L. Karweit, & N. A. Madden, (Eds.), *Effective programs for students at risk*. (pp. 320–354). Boston: Allyn & Bacon.

Barrish, H. H., Saunders, M., & Wolf, M. M. (1969). Good behavior game: Effects of individual contingencies for group consequences on disruptive behavior in a classroom. *Journal of Applied Behavior Analysis, 2,* 119–124.

Chalfant, J. C., Pysh, M. V., & Moultrie, R. (1979). Teacher assistance teams: A model for within-building problem solving. *Learning Disability Quarterly, 2*(3), 85–96.

Gartner, A., & Lipsky, D. K. (1987). Beyond special education: Toward a quality system for all students. *Harvard Educational Review, 57,* 367–395.

Graham, S., & Miller, L. (1979). Spelling research and practice: A unified approach. *Focus on Exceptional Children, 12*(2), 1–16.

Idol-Maestas, L., & Ritter, S. (1985). A follow-up study of resource consulting teachers. *Teacher Education and Special Education, 8*(3), 121–131.

Johnson, D. W., & Johnson, R. T. (1987). *Learning together and alone: Cooperation, competition, and individualization.* Englewood Cliffs, NJ: Prentice-Hall.

Johnson, L. J., Pugach, M. C., & Hammitte, D. J. (1988). Barriers to effective special education consultation. *Remedial and Special Education, 9*(6), 41–47.

Kauffman, J. M., Gerber, M. M., & Semmel, M. I. (1988). Arguable assumptions underlying the Regular Education Initiative. *Journal of Learning Disabilities, 21*(1), 6–11.

Lilly, M. S. (1988). The regular education initiative: A force for change in general and special education. *Education and Training in Mental Retardation, 23,* 253–260.

Lindsley, O. (1972). From Skinner to precision teaching: The child knows best. In J. B. Jordan and L. S. Robbins (Eds.), *Let's try doing something else kind of a thing: Behavioral principles and the exceptional child* (pp. 1–13). Reston, VA: Council for Exceptional Children.

Lovitt, T. C. (1973). Self-management projects. *Journal of Learning Disabilities, 6,* 138–150.

Mastropieri, M. A., & Scruggs, T. E. (1987). *Effective instruction for special education.* Boston: Little, Brown/College Hill Press.

McGill-Franzen, A. (1987). Failure to learn to read: Formulating a policy problem. *Reading Research Quarterly, 22,* 475–490.

Palincsar, A. S. (1986). Metacognitive strategy instruction. *Exceptional Children, 53*(2), 118–124.

Pugach, M. C., & Johnson, L. J. (1988). Rethinking the relationship between consultation and collaborative problem solving. *Focus on Exceptional Children, 21*(4), 1–8.

Pugach, M. C., & Lilly, M. C. (1984). Reconceptualizing support services for classroom teachers: Implications for teacher education. *Journal of Teacher Education, 35*(5), 48–55.

Reid, D. K. (1988). *Teaching the learning disabled.* Boston: Allyn & Bacon.

Reynolds, M. C., Wang, M. C., & Walberg, H. J. (1987). The necessary restructuring of special and regular education. *Exceptional Children, 53*(5), 391–398.

Stainback, W., & Stainback, S. (1984). A rationale for the merger of special and regular education. *Exceptional Children, 51*(2), 102–111.

Will, M. C. (1986). Educating students with learning problems: A shared responsibility. *Exceptional Children, 52*(5), 411–415.

Ysseldyke, J. E., Thurlow, M., Graden, J., Wesson, C., Algozzine, B., & Deno, S. (1983). Generalizations from five years of research on assessment and decision-making: The University of Minnesota Institute. *Exceptional Education Quarterly, 4*(1), 75–93.

ADDITIONAL READINGS

Greenwood, G. E., & Parkay, F. W. (1989). *Case studies for teacher decision making.* New York: Random House.

Johnson, D. W., & Johnson, R. T. (1987). *Learning together and alone: Cooperation, competition, and individualization.* Englewood Cliffs, NJ: Prentice-Hall.

Lewis, R. B., & Doorlag, D. H. (1987). *Teaching special students in the mainstream.* Columbus, OH: Merrill.

Lovitt, T. C. (1984). *Tactics for teaching.* Columbus, OH: Merrill.

Pugach, M., & Johnson, L. J. (in press). Meeting diverse needs through professional peer collaboration. In W. Stainback & S. Stainback (Eds.), *Support networks for inclusive schools: Integrated interdependent education.* Baltimore, MD: Brookes.

Zins, J. E., Curtis, M. J., Graden, J. L., & Ponti, C. R. (1987). *Helping students succeed in the regular classroom.* San Francisco: Jossey-Bass.

1

Purpose

☐ To increase your understanding of the implications of merging special education and general education

☐ To help you distinguish the meaning of integration for mild, moderate, and severely handicapped students

Steps

1. Divide the class into "pro" and "con" teams for a debate on the viability of a merger of special education and general education. Prepare for the debate by reading the article by Stainback & Stainback (1984) on the proposed merger of special education and general education and the January 1988 issue of *Journal of Learning Disabilities*.

2. Follow a structured format for the debate, with each side speaking initially for 15 minutes and rebuttals of 10 minutes each following. Initial statements must differentiate among effects of a merger on students with mild, moderate, and severe handicapping conditions.

3. Follow the debate with a general discussion of the issue.

Analysis

☐ As a class, prepare a position statement on the potential merger of special and general education. Include a brief rationale and at least five or six major points to support your position. If you cannot agree on one position as a result of the debate, divide into two groups and prepare two papers.

☐ Ask at least two current special education teachers to respond to your paper(s).

2

Purpose

☐ To clarify your thinking on why you wish to become a special or a general education teacher

☐ To begin thinking about your strengths and weaknesses as a potential partner in a collaborative professional relationship

Steps

1. Write a short paragraph on why you chose special or general education as a field. In particular, address the issue of your commitment to special needs students. How does your statement have to read if you have chosen to be a classroom teacher?

2. Write a short assessment of your interpersonal strengths. How will these be an asset to you when you work with other professionals in a school? Now, write a short assessment of your weaknesses in interpersonal relationships. How will these detract from your effectiveness as a teacher responsible for promoting collegiality and collaboration for the sake of your students? Make a list of steps you can take to improve some of these weaknesses.

Analysis

☐ Share your lists with your classmates to see if there are any common strengths and weaknesses; help each other develop ways of preparing for collaboration.

☐ As a result of your discussions, rewrite or add to the guidelines for facilitating professional collaboration provided in this chapter.

| 3 |

Purpose

☐ The purpose of this activity is to provide an opportunity to practice problem solving using the four steps. Repeated opportunities to work through various case studies will help make the strategies more effective.

☐ You are a fourth-grade teacher, and a girl in your class, Nora, has just been mainstreamed from a class for students with learning disabilities. She seems very shy and reluctant to initiate contact with the other students. She answers other people when they talk to her first, but her responses are just one or two words. She is doing fine on the assignments and tests, but you are concerned with how lonely she appears to be. Given this situation, how would you help Nora?

Steps

1. Discuss the following four tasks with a small group. Remember to follow the four problem-solving steps outlined in the chapter. Brainstorm the possible interventions for (a) through (d), and have one group member record your responses.
   a. Design a self-managed intervention that may help Nora. Feel free to add details to this case study such as the support of Nora's parents, her bus ride to school, and favorite activities that she may like to earn.
   b. Design a peer-managed intervention for Nora. What could the peers do to make Nora feel more comfortable? How many students might this intervention involve? How can this type of intervention be done without making Nora feel foolish?

    c. Design a teacher-managed intervention for Nora. Maybe the teacher can be Nora's first friend. After Nora feels secure and comfortable with the teacher, the teacher can have another student join them, and so slowly Nora can be comfortable with more and more people.

    d. Design a whole-building intervention for students such as Nora. In reality, a whole school would not come up with such an intervention for one student. But suppose that peer relationships were the target for the staff's energies. How might you design a system to improve peer relationships schoolwide?

2. Have the group pick its best intervention for each task (a) through (d).

3. Have the group come to a consensus about which intervention is best for this case and why. Be prepared to turn in your group's discussion notes.

Analysis

☐ How did your group proceed? What process did the group use to address each step?

☐ Did your group work well together? Was there a sense of helpfulness or one-upmanship?

☐ How could your group improve its functioning if you were to do this again?

☐ Share each group's ideas with the whole class. We should not look for one right answer.

5

Students with Complex Health Care Needs

Donna H. Lehr
Boston University

Ever since the enactment of PL 94-142 in 1975, school districts have been opening their doors to students who pose greater and greater challenges to their teachers and administrators. The newest challenge is that of providing education to students with complex health care needs (Sirvis, 1988; Viadero, 1987). There has been a long tradition of providing education to students with chronic illnesses such as diabetes, asthma, spina bifida, sickle cell anemia, hemophilia, cystic fibrosis, and muscular dystrophy (cf. Hobbs, Perrin, & Ireys, 1985; Kleinberg, 1982). But typically when those students' conditions progressed to the point that they needed health care services such as catheterization, respiratory therapy, tube feeding, ventilation, or oxygen, they were hospitalized or remained at home and did not attend school. The school(s) usually made adjustments for their absences or provided home or hospital instruction until, when, or if their conditions improved. Now students are not automatically removed from schools for prolonged periods when they need such health care services. After medical conditions stabilize, students with chronic illnesses or with other complex health care needs requiring specialized skilled care and possibly technological support are coming to today's schools. Such students may require care necessary to assure control of the spread of serious communicable diseases, or they may require apnea monitoring, tube feeding, mechanical or machine suctioning, mechanical ventilation, or oxygen. In general, they require health care that is different and often much more complex than has typically been provided in public school settings.

Kathy is an example of such a child currently attending a public school. Kathy is 8 years old. She was a healthy, normally developing child until the age of 2 when she wandered out of the family's summer cottage and found her way to a lake where she nearly drowned. Kathy was in a coma for 4 weeks. On discharge from the hospital after regaining consciousness, Kathy was no longer able to walk, talk, or eat by herself. Kathy has difficulty swallowing and coughing, processes necessary to deal with food and saliva present in her mouth and throat. Consequently, Kathy cannot eat food by mouth; she instead is fed through a tube that enters directly into her stomach. Because she is unable to deal with the buildup of saliva and mucus in her mouth and throat, especially when she gets a cold, those fluids must frequently be removed for her through the use of a suctioning machine. The machine has a long tube that is inserted into her mouth and into her throat, when necessary, to remove the excessive fluid.

THE EMERGENCE OF THE NEW POPULATION OF STUDENTS

Students like Kathy are being seen in increasing numbers in our schools. But why were they not in our schools before? Their presence can be attributed to a number of factors. Among these are technological advances in medicine, acceptance by many of the principle of normalization, an increase in programs for young children and those with severe handicaps (Lehr & Noonan, 1989), and, in part as a result of the previous factors, an increase of group care of children with communicable diseases in schools.

Medical Technology

Improvements in medical technology have had two consequences for students with complex health care needs. First, children with serious health conditions are living longer than was previously possible. In the past, many children who were born prematurely, with low birth weight, or with congenital birth defects or who were injured after birth did not survive long enough to become students (Lehr & Noonan, 1989). Now, they may survive, but often with continued, sometimes very severe, disabilities. The effort to save all children in distress has resulted in an increase in the number of students with severe handicapping conditions.

Second, equipment to monitor and support these children's lives now exists. Much of this equipment is portable, smaller than in the past, and, in some cases, battery operated. As a result, children are much more mobile than they were. Children previously confined to places with electrical outlets can now move much more freely in their communities; they can attend picnics, participate in playground activities, and get to school in family cars and school buses.

The Principle of Normalization

Changes in public attitudes toward the care of individuals with disabilities also accounts for the increased numbers of individuals with complex health care needs in the schools. In the past, the usual practice was to segregate such individuals from the mainstream of society. In 1972, Wolfensberger put forth a principle of normalization that called for the use of normal environmental routines to obtain the desired outcomes of the individual's most normal behaviors. This principle was put into action through the deinstitutionalization movement and the movement to place individuals with disabilities in the least restrictive environments appropriate to meet their needs. In the field of education, the LRE principle found expression in PL 94-142. Now school districts strive to place all students, including those with complex health care needs, in the least restrictive, most-like-normal environment appropriate for each individual student.

Programs for Young Children and Those with Severe Handicaps

The increase in the population of students with complex health care needs in the schools is also the result of the increase in programs for very young students. PL 94-142 mandated programs for students to age 5 with incentives for students down to age 3. PL 99-457, the 1987 amendments to that law, mandated programs to age 3 in all states receiving federal funds and offered further incentives for providing services to birth. Consequently, the number of programs serving young children with handicapping conditions has increased. This young population of children has been the beneficiary of improved medical technology and consequently contains the children who survive with their birth defects but not without continued disabilities or complex health care needs. PL 94-142 also required school districts to serve *all* students, including those with the most severe handicaps. In this population of students we see the greatest number with accompanying medical needs (Hotte, Monroe, Philbrook, & Scarlata, 1984).

Group Care of Children with Communicable Diseases

Among young children and students with severe handicaps are many who do not have control of body functions and require care such as feeding and toileting or diapering. Group care of children who do not control body functions and who, as all young children do, explore their environment by mouthing things increases risks of transmission of contagious diseases unless careful attention is paid to hygienic care of students. Among the diseases of concern are the common cold, as well as more serious diseases such as cytomegalovirus, hepatitis, herpes, and Human Immunodeficiency Virus (HIV).

HIV was simply not known of prior to 1982. Now, medical experts estimate that by 1992 it will be the leading cause of mental retardation and the fifth leading cause of death in children in this country. Although it has not yet become a frequently encountered situation in the schools, experts expect there will be approximately 3,000 children in this country affected by 1991 (Tolsma, 1988). As the number of students is not large and the disease is not transmitted through casual contact, the public concern over the presence of infected students in the schools and the deadly consequences of infection require careful attention to matters regarding their inclusion in schools.

Definition of the Population

The term *students with complex health care needs,* as used here, describes a specific, yet heterogeneous population of students. This term may include students who are labeled in the literature as (a) having chronic illnesses, (b) being technology dependent, or (c) being medically fragile. The term comes into play when delivery of education and health care services to meet the needs of such students raises new issues for the school district and requires other than the traditional care provided in the schools. I hope that the use of the term is temporary, that after a period of time service delivery will become more usual and not as complex. This is not to say that it will become easy to meet students' needs but that the issues and practices will become less complex to those involved.

Definitions exist for each of the subgroups composing this population. Children with chronic illnesses may have "those conditions such as burns; trauma from physical injuries that are long standing, such as spinal cord injuries or closed head trauma; and conditions more classically defined as *chronic illnesses,* such as asthma, diabetes, cystic fibrosis and cancer" (Kleinberg, 1982, p. 4). They may have "a set of conditions that affects one or more body organs and represents an active disease process. It may last many months or a lifetime" (Kleinberg, 1982, p. 4).

The following definitions of *technology dependent* and/or *medically fragile* children who require continuous special health care stand in contrast to those for children with chronic illnesses, whose need for special health care may be intermittent.

The U.S. Congress, Office of Technology Assessment (1987) defined a child who is technology dependent as "one who needs both a medical device to compensate for the loss of a vital body function and substantial and ongoing nursing care to avert death or further disability" (p. 3). This definition distinguishes among four populations within this group: (a) children who are dependent on mechanical ventilators, (b) children who require nutrition or drugs intravenously, (c) children who need daily mechanical respiratory or nutritional support, and (d) children who are dependent in the long term on mechanical devices/processes such as apnea monitors, renal dialysis, and urinary catheters or colostomy bags.

The Task Force on Technology-Dependent Children (1988) defined a technology-dependent child as one who "is a person from birth through 21 years of age; has a chronic disability; requires the routine use of a specific medical device to compensate for the loss of use of a life sustaining body function; and requires daily, ongoing care or monitoring by trained personnel" (p. vii–1).

SKIP (Sick Kids [Need] Involved People) (1986) defined technology assisted/dependent/medically fragile children as requiring "medical technology . . . [as] the instrument used to compensate for the missing component necessary to sustain life, demanding a complete array of medical management. If the technology, support and services they are receiving are interrupted or denied, the child will, within a short period of time (5 to 15 minutes), experience irreversible damage or death. The technological assistance received by the child is essential to the optimal growth and development and well being of the child and family" (p. 2).

The Council for Exceptional Children (1988) used the term *medically fragile* to identify a population of students who "require specialized technological health care procedures for life support and/or health support during the school day" (p. 1).

Characteristics of Students With Complex Health Care Needs

Students with complex health care needs do not demonstrate a common set of learner characteristics. The group includes students with average or above average intellectual abilities; however, they frequently have other accompanying handicapping conditions such as mental retardation and/or significant neuromotor disabilities (Lehr & Noonan, 1989).

Although students with complex health care needs demonstrate tremendous variability in characteristics, they do share the following needs:

☐ The need to be provided with a free public educational program
☐ The need to be provided with an education in the least restrictive environment
☐ The need to have as a part of their educational plan a health care plan
☐ The need to be treated as a child first, then a student, and not as a patient
☐ The need to interact with other children with and without similar health care needs

BASIC PROFESSIONAL VOCABULARY

The terms used in this area that may be unique are those that relate to the medical conditions of the students or the specialized health care procedures they require.

Apnea monitor is a machine that is attached to an individual to detect cessation in breathing and is used when an individual demonstrates irregularities in respiration.

Catheterization is the process of introducing a tube into the bladder through the urethra for withdrawal of urine and is used when an individual is unable to empty the bladder naturally.

Hepatitis B is a disease characterized by infection and inflammation of the liver. It is transmitted through close personal contact, specifically through blood, saliva, and semen as well as through environmental surfaces (mats, teaching materials).

Herpes is a family of diseases. Two are of concern to people who provide group care for children: herpes simplex oral and herpes simplex genital. Symptoms of the former include fever and bleeding ulcers and cold sores in the area around and in the mouth; symptoms of the latter include ulcers on the genitalia and pain or tenderness in the genital area. Oral herpes is transmitted by saliva or respiratory droplets and genital herpes by direct contact with infected area. There is no cure, but there is relief for symptoms.

HIV (AIDS) affects the individual's ability to fight off infections. It is transmitted by exposure to infected blood through transfusions and needles, through sexual contact with an infected partner, and from infected mothers to infants during the perinatal period (Rogers, 1987).

Suctioning is a procedure used to remove fluid from the mouth, throat, or trachea when the individual is unable to accomplish this on his or her own.

Tube feeding is the process through which food is introduced directly into the stomach through a tube attached to an opening (stoma) in the abdomen (gastronomy) or through a tube inserted via the individual's nose and extended to the stomach (nasogastronomy). Tube feeding is used when the individual is unable to obtain proper nourishment via mouth.

Ventilator is a mechanical device that administers air or oxygen to the lungs and is used when an individual is unable to breathe for him or herself.

ISSUES IN PROVIDING EDUCATION TO STUDENTS WITH COMPLEX HEALTH CARE NEEDS

Because attendance of students with complex health care needs in schools is new, many questions arise regarding how to meet their educational and health related needs for which there are no clear answers. No federal guidelines exist, nor are there comprehensive models demonstrating the best practices. Consequently, program administrators are making difficult case-by-case decisions regarding how to serve such children (Lehr & Noonan, 1989). The issues that administrators are addressing include health care procedures to be performed in schools, responsibility for administering the procedures, preparation for personnel to perform the procedures, the relationship between educational and health care service provision, and student transportation.

Health Care Procedures Performed in Schools

In the past, students requiring such procedures as tube feeding or suctioning were routinely excluded from school. The zero-exclusion principle and the least restrictive principle of PL 94-142 did much to change this automatic placement decision. Nevertheless, considerable variation continues to exist in these decisions. Although children with complex health care needs are not automatically excluded from educational programs, their placement may be in a hospital, at home, in a segregated school, or in a regular school. Some districts' policies are to serve all students with any health care needs, whereas others exclude students requiring oxygen or those with communicable diseases such as HIV (AIDS), hepatitis, or herpes.

Responsibility for Administration of Procedures

Another issue is that of whose responsibility it is to provide the health care procedures. Is it the school district's responsibility, the family's, or other health agencies'? If it is the school's responsibiity, who in the school should perform the procedures? Other issues revolve around the definition of a related service, which is the district's responsibility, and a medical service, which is not.

PL 94-142 specified that a school district must provide related services including "transportation, and such developmental, corrective, and other supportive services . . . as may be required to assist a handicapped child to benefit from special education" (Section 1401[a][17]). Medical services are "services provided by a licensed physician to determine a child's medically related handicapping conditions which results in the child's need for special education and related services" (34 CFR Reg 330.13[b][4].) In *Tatro* v. *Texas,* the U.S. Supreme Court determined that clean intermittent catheterization procedures were the responsibility of the school district as a related service necessary for the students to benefit from special education. In three other cases involving the provision of health care to students, one led to a decision that the necessary procedures were related services and therefore were school district responsibility *(Department of Education, State of Hawaii* v. *Dorr);* in the other two cases, the courts determined that the health care procedures under consideration were more complex than those typically provided in schools and therefore were not the school districts' responsibility *(Detsel* v. *Ambach; Bevin, H.).* Clearly, the courts differ in their opinions about what constitutes a related service and what constitutes a medical service. Consequently, with the exception of the provision of clean intermittent catheterization, responsibility for other procedures is being decided by each school district.

When the district's responsibility to implement procedures has been specified, the next question becomes, Who in the district is responsible? Tremendous variability exists. A student in one school district may be receiving care from a school nurse, while a student in a neighboring district may be cared for by an instructional aide. The primary responsibility for providing school health services to students has traditionally rested on the school nurse. Nurses have responsibility for establishing policy and procedures, with school administration, for emergency procedures, medication administration protocols, safety measures and programs, student/personnel health services, and health education (American Nurses Association, 1983). Nevertheless, some of the students attending today's schools require procedures that are different and sometimes more complex than those routinely provided. One study indicated that school nurses did not feel adequately trained to implement many of the procedures required by students now attending public schools (Hester, Goodwin, & Igoe, 1980).

In addition, nurses are not always available to provide the needed services. Many elementary schools have a school nurse assigned for as little as one-half day per week. Obviously, this is inadequate to meet the needs of a student who has to be tube fed daily or requires suctioning hourly. Consequently, classroom teachers are routinely performing such procedures in their classrooms (Mulligan Ault, Guess, Struth, & Thompson, 1988). Sirvis (1988) pointed out, however, that in most cases even the most skilled special education teacher may be hesitant to provide for students with special health care needs.

Preparation of Personnel for Service Provision

Despite the fact that even school nurses do not feel adequately prepared to implement some of the procedures required by students in today's schools, a nurse, a teacher, or an aide may be responsible for implementing such procedures. The provision of training for those involved in the care of this population of students is receiving careful attention. Decisions involve identification of what training should be provided, who should provide it, and who should be the recipient of the training.

The importance of this topic is punctuated by the emphasis placed on the need for policies regarding training in several organizations' recommendations on serving students with special health care needs. For example, the Task Force on Children with Special Health Care Needs in Iowa (1988) made specific recommendations for both preservice and inservice training of all personnel involved with such children, including teachers, support staff, and even bus drivers.

Student Transportation

Transportation of students to schools becomes another difficult decision for administrators of programs. Some students with special health care needs must come to school attached to their portable life-supporting or life-sustaining equipment. Some must receive immediate care in case of medical emergency. The range of responses to this issue include students being transported by family member, students being transported by ambulance, and students being transported on regular buses. Students are being transported with only the bus driver present or with a nurse present to attend to the needs of the students. In one reported case, a bus driver, who was alone in his accompaniment of the student to and from school, was trained to perform mechanical suctioning in the event of distress on the part of the child (Lehr & Haubrich, 1988).

Combining Education with Care

How the health care procedure relates to education is another issue of concern to individuals providing education to students with complex health care needs. The teacher should view the child first as a child and second as a student—*but not as a patient*. Nevertheless, concern about the child's health care can overshadow educational emphases.

An important part of some students' education may relate specifically to their care needs. It may include instructional priorities related to less resistance or increased participation in their own care. Or it may relate to increased communication regarding care needs. But the students will also have educational needs like those of their peers without health care needs: the need to learn basic skills and knowledge, the need to learn to function as independently as possible, the need to learn to read, write, and do arithmetic. The presence of students with complex health care needs is causing educators to rethink the definition and purposes of education.

Students with communicable diseases pose additional questions regarding the combination of education and care. Educational institutions are not accustomed to providing hygienic care for students; until recently, self-care (toilet training) and self-feeding were prerequisites for admission into schools. Now students who lack control of body functions are in schools, and teachers must pay attention to the care of all students but particularly to those with communicable diseases. Hygienic care procedures must become routine and unobtrusive to assure they do not become the emphasis of, rather than a support to, the educational program.

Staff concern regarding the presence of a student with communicable disease may also interfere with the delivery of education. Staff must be provided with information regarding disease transmission, methods for prevention, and control of spread of diseases when caring for all students. Additionally, maintenance of confidentiality of information and proper education are essential to assure that the child's rights as a citizen are not violated.

As there are no definitive federal or state rules to follow regarding educational service provision to students with special health care needs (Task Force on Technology-Dependent Children, 1988), services to those students are variable and inconsistent (Hobbs et al., 1985). Variations in services are necessary to meet the individual needs of students, but these differences must be based on the needs of students, not on differences in district administrative resources or interest.

POLICIES FOR SERVING STUDENTS
WITH COMPLEX HEALTH CARE NEEDS

The first step in the development of consistency of services may be the development of policies. Several groups and organizations have begun to develop recommendations, guidelines, and/or policies that have the potential for guiding administrators in providing educational services to students with complex health care needs. Policies identified address children with special health care needs in general and with communicable diseases specifically.

Children with Special Health Care Needs

The Council for Exceptional Children's Task Force on Medically Fragile Students (1988) developed specific recommendations that focused on nine basic issues:

1. Determining eligibility for special education services
2. Providing related and noneducation services
3. Assuring equal access to appropriate educational settings in the least restrictive environment
4. Promoting a safe learning environment for all students and professionals
5. Assuring that health care services are delivered by appropriately trained personnel
6. Establishing support systems for staff, students, and families
7. Including appropriate information about students' specialized health care needs in preservice, inservice, and continuing education programs
8. Providing of appropriate and safe transportation
9. Promoting research that assesses current and future service delivery models

For each of these points, the council made suggestions regarding how these can be addressed to assure that each student with specialized health care needs receives an appropriate education program.

Iowa was the first state in the country to adopt a series of policy recommendations for dealing with children with special health care needs in the schools (Task Force on Children With Special Health Care Needs, 1988). The task force's recommendations addressed the need (a) to resolve issues relative to fiscal responsibility, (b) to involve health care professionals in IEP planning, (c) to procure statements by the Department of Education regarding evaluation and assessment practices and transportation needs, (d) to gather position papers on placement decision procedures, service delivery issues including reevaluation timelines, and care management responsibilities; (e) to develop technical assistance and training for those school personnel involved in the delivery of specialized health care for students; and (f) to secure model protocols and instructional materials for use by school nurses and staff responsible for providing health care to students.

Children With Communicable Diseases

A survey of 50 states and the District of Columbia revealed that of the 59% of the states that responded, 70% had policies or guidelines regarding communicable disease in the schools (Lehr & Peppey, 1988). The authors of the survey observed considerable differences, however, in regard to the thoroughness of the guidelines or policies for placement, exclusion, care providing procedures, confidentiality, and case management.

> Do you know whether state or district guidelines or policies exist where you live? Activity 1, page 129, directs you to find that out and, if they exist, assists you in becoming familiar with them.

The American Academy of Pediatrics has developed policies regarding infection control of HIV (AIDS) in schools. Changes in the guidelines reflect changes in our knowledge base regarding the spread of the infection. The 1986 guidelines (American Academy of Pediatrics, 1986) suggested exclusions of children infected

Table 5.1   The Council for Exceptional Children's Policy Statement on Managing Communicable and Contagious Diseases

Controlling the spread of communicable and contagious diseases within the schools has always been a problem faced by educators, the medical profession, and the public. Effective policies and procedures for managing such diseases in the schools have historically been developed by health agencies and implemented by the schools. These policies and procedures were primarily designed to manage acute, temporary conditions rather than chronic conditions which require continuous monitoring and remove children from interaction with other children while the condition is contagious or communicable.

The increased prevalence of chronic communicable diseases such as hepatitis B, cytomegalovirus, herpes simplex virus, and acquired immune deficiency syndrome have raised public and professional concern, necessitating the reassessment of existing school policies and procedures. The Council believes that having a communicable/contagious disease does not in itself result in a need for special education. Further, the Council believes that in developing appropriate policies for managing communicable diseases schools and public health agencies should assure that any such policies and procedures:

    a. Do not exclude the affected child from the receipt of an appropriate education even when circumstances require the temporary removal of the child from contact with other children.
    b. Provide that determination of a nontemporary alteration of a child's educational placement should be done on an individual basis, utilizing an interdisciplinary/interagency approach including the child's physician, public health personnel, the child's parents, and appropriate educational personnel.
    c. Provide that decision involving exceptional children's nontemporary alterations of educational placements or services constitute a change in the child's Individualized Education Program and should thus follow the procedures and protections required.
    d. Recognize that children vary in the degree and manner in which they come into contact with other children and school staff.
    e. Provide education staff with the necessary information, training, and hygienic resources to provide for a safe environment for students and educational staff.
    f. Provide students with appropriate education about communicable diseases and hygienic measures to prevent the spread of such diseases.

with AIDS from preschool settings. The 1988 guidelines (American Academy of Pediatrics, 1988) reflected a modification of these recommendations; they cited the risk of transmission being so remote that there was no reason for exclusion.

The Council for Exceptional Children (1988) has developed a policy statement on managing communicable and contagious diseases in the schools. The policy emphasizes the need for case-by-case decision making, education of students and staff, protection for staff, and collaboration among agencies in policy development. The policy also emphasizes the dynamic nature of the data base, which requires frequent review and revision of any established policies. The full text is shown in Table 5.1.

PROGRAM PRACTICES

Although this area of educational service delivery is relatively new, a number of recommendations regarding programs practices have been developed by those currently working with this population of students. The emphasis here is on those recommendations regarding program planning, development of communication systems, training of involved personnel, and family-centered-care management.

Table 5.1   *continued*

---

g. Provide, where appropriate, carrier children with education about the additional control measures that they can practice to prevent the transmission of the disease.
h. Enable educational personnel who are medically at high risk in regard to certain diseases to work in environments which minimize such risk.
i. Provide educational personnel with adequate protections for such personnel and their families if they are exposed to such diseases through their employment.

The Council believes that special education personnel preparation programs should:

a. Educate students about communicable and contagious diseases and appropriate methods for their management.
b. Counsel students as to how to determine their level of medical risk in relation to certain diseases and the implications of such risk to career choice.

The Council believes that the manner in which policies for managing communicable and contagious diseases are developed and disseminated is critically important to their effective implementation. Therefore the following must be considered integral to any such process:

a. That they be developed through the collaborative efforts of health and education agencies at both the state, provincial and local levels, reflecting state, provincial and local educational, health and legal requirements.
b. That provision is made for frequent review and revision to reflect the ever-increasing knowledge being produced through research, case data reports, and experience.
c. That policies developed be based on reliable identified sources of information and principles endorsed by the medical and educational professions.
d. That such policies be written in content and format to be understandable to a variety of consumers including students, professionals and the public.
e. That policy development and dissemination be a continual process and disassociated from pressures associated with precipitating events.

Source: From *Policies Manual* (pp. 21–23), 1988, Council for Exceptional Children, Reston, VA.

Program Planning

Under the law, all students with needs for special education programs must have IEPs. The same is true for students with special education needs who have complex health care needs. For those students, however, careful attention must be paid to the development of plans that include all of the following:

- ☐ Methods for assuring communication among family, school personnel, and medical providers
- ☐ Development of plans to transition students from hospital or home to school
- ☐ Identification of resources for technical assistance

Table 5.2   Catheterization: IEP (Individual Education Plan) Recommendations

Level 1—Total dependence

Goal: (Self-Help) Maintain healthy urinary status by tolerating catheterization in a cooperative manner.

Objective:

The student's family will provide, on a daily basis, the equipment necessary for catheterization, 100% of time.

The student will remain still in a lying position while the assistant performs catheterization in school at 8:00 A.M. and 12:00 Noon, 100% of the time.

The student will assist in assuming the correct position for catheterization when the assistant indicates it is time for the procedure, 90% of the time.

Level 2—Direction of care

Goal: (Self-Help) Maintain healthy urinary status and obtain maximum level of independence by learning how to direct care.

Objective:

The student's family will provide, on a daily basis, the equipment necessary for catheterization, 100% of time.

The student will identify equipment needed for catheterization 4 out of 5 trials.

The student will be able to verbalize "What comes next?", 4 out of 5 trials.

The student will be able to independently (verbally) direct the step-by-step prescribed procedure to include the collection of materials, cleaning, catheterization and then clean-up, 4 out of 5 trials.

The student will be able to state warning signs and symptoms of problems related to catheterization and answer related, "What if?", questions, 4 out of 5 trials.

Level 3—Independent completion of catheterization

Goal: (Self-Help) Maintain healthy urinary status through the independent completion of catheterization.

Objective:

The student's family will provide, on a daily basis, the equipment necessary for catheterization, 100% of time.

☐ Development of health care and emergency plans
☐ Provision of training and monitoring of education personnel (Caldwell, Todaro, & Gates, in press)

An additional important emphasis is that of including objectives on IEP that specifically relate to students' health care needs. Objectives designed to increase students' tolerance of, participation in, or implementation of the procedures are critical. Examples of such objectives can be viewed in Table 5.2.

The development of health care plans is also an important part of comprehensive planning. Health care plans should include information such as what is to be done, the purpose of the service, the frequency with which the procedures should

---

Table 5.2   *continued*

The student will identify equipment needed for catheterization 4 out of 5 trials.

The student will be able to answer questions about the procedure, i.e., "What comes next?", 4 out of 5 trials.

The student will be able to independently (verbally) direct the step-by-step prescribed procedure for the collection of materials, cleaning, catheterization and then clean-up, 4 out of 5 trials.

The student will be able to independently gather equipment for the procedure, 4 out of 5 trials.

The student will be able to demonstrate on a doll step-by-step procedure for cleaning their hands and their genital area, 4 out of 5 trials. Note: This may be accomplished through the purchase of an inexpensive doll with a hole cut in the genital area.

The student will be able to answer question, "Why are you cleaning your hands? Your genital area?", 4 out of 5 trials.

The student will be able to demonstrate placement of the catheter in the doll, 4 out of 5 trials.

The student will be able to set up for self-catheterization and clean self following the prescribed step-by-step procedure, 4 out of 5 trials.

Male

The student will be able to hold his penis in the correct position, clean himself and identify opening, insert the catheter and follow the prescribed step-by-step procedure, 4 out of 5 trials.

Female

The student will be able to open her labia, clean herself, and identify the urethra, insert the catheter and follow the prescribed step-by-step procedure, 4 out of 5 trials.

The student will be able to independently complete self-catheterization according to the prescribed step-by-step procedure, 10 out of 10 trials.

Student will be able to state warning signs and symptoms of problems related to catheterization and answer related, "What if?", questions, 4 out of 5 trials.

The student will be able to independently complete self-catheterization according to the prescribed step-by-step procedure during monthly observation.

Source: From *Children with special health care needs in schools,* by T.H. Caldwell, 1988, Paper presented at Conference Blue Print for Change, Council for Exceptional Children, Orlando, Florida.

be implemented, under what conditions the physician should be contacted, personnel who should be involved and the training they should receive, how the procedures should be implemented, and the equipment needed (Ferguson, 1988). Specification of procedures to be followed in the case of an emergency is also critical.

Development of Communication Systems

Students with complex health care needs are usually the recipients of services from a number of professionals, representing a number of disciplines, usually located at different geographical locations. For example, a student may attend a school in his or her home community but may be under the primary care of a pediatrician who is located in the nearest large city, 90 miles away. The student may be receiving physical therapy from the school district but may be receiving speech therapy from a private clinic in the home community. The student may also be receiving 6 hours a day of home health nursing services by a nurse who is employed by a private home health care agency. In this scenario, the student, in addition to being involved with care providers (natural or foster family or residential home staff), a teacher, a physical therapist, and two paraprofessional aides in the school, is receiving direct services from three other professionals. With this many individuals involved, communication and coordination become major concerns. How can consistent approaches be developed? How can all participants be informed of critical information?

One important factor is the identification of one person as the communications coordinator who is responsible for monitoring the flow of information to and from the schools. Often this process is carried out by either the parent, school nurse, or teacher. Caldwell, Todaro, and Gates (in press) pointed out that the parent was most often responsible for coordinating information between school and medical professionals. They also pointed out problems with this model when the parent's role as primary liaison was assumed rather than specifically established. This resulted in a lack of routine reporting as well as in selective reporting, with the parent making assumptions about what was important. The same problem may occur when the teacher's or nurse's role is not made explicit. Without effective coordination and transmittal of information, quality care cannot be realized.

A second important factor in effective coordination is communication attitudes and specific skills (Holvoet & Helmstetter, 1989). Communication attitudes such as self-acceptance, acceptance of others, and empathy have a powerful impact on the ways in which information is exchanged (Holvoet & Helmstetter, 1989). Parents who feel that a professional is not accepting of them or their child are not likely to be open in their discussions with that individual. The consequence may be a significant barrier to the necessary exchange of information.

Specific communication skills related to listening, nonverbal communication, and verbal responding are also essential to assure coordinating care (Holvoet & Helmstetter, 1989). Among the skills necessary in these areas are careful, attentive, active listening; careful interpretation of nonverbal messages; and verbal responding such as paraphrasing, summarizing, and clarifying (Holvoet & Helmstetter,

1989). Development and use of these skills result in an increase in the accuracy of exchanged information.

Training of Involved Personnel

Personnel involved in the provision of educational and specialized health care services to students with complex health care needs must be properly prepared. This is essential to assure that students are provided with the best possible services and that risks for liability are reduced. The Iowa State Department of Education (1988) has recommended that preservice training programs for special education teachers include information and training related to the following:

☐ Certification in first aid and cardiopulmonary resuscitation
☐ Physical care, general health and nutrition information, infection control, skin care, elimination and oral hygiene, common childhood diseases
☐ Community resources and how to access them
☐ Team approach to service provision, confidentiality, and dealing with sensitive information
☐ Effective IEP writing for children with special health care needs (p. 7)

The Iowa Department of Education also recognized the need for ongoing training for teachers currently in the field and made recommendations for periodic inservice training on topics similar to those listed here.

An important additional emphasis must be placed on training staff on hygienic care of all students to prevent spread of infection and contagious diseases. Proper handwashing has been identified as the single most important procedure for prevention of spread of infections across people (Silkworth, 1988). Cleaning of diapering surfaces, instructional materials, and eating/feeding equipment is essential and must be practiced by all staff involved in the care of children.

> How prepared are you to handle an emergency or to provide hygienic care for students? Activity 2, page 129, is designed to assist you in assessing your own knowledge and skills.

Recently a number of materials have been developed for use in training personnel working with this population of students. A sampling of these materials and brief descriptions of them appear in Table 5.3.

The need for training regarding HIV infection is critical to assure school professionals are knowledgeable about transmission methods. Knowledge that transmission does not occur through casual contact or through contact with saliva or feces and urine will contribute to the acceptance of students who test positive for HIV infections. Knowledge will also result in school personnel using universal pre-

Table 5.3   Training and Resource Materials

Video Training Tapes

CPR and Emergency Choking Procedures for Infants and Young Children—introduction and review of procedures to prevent and provide emergency treatment. 37 minutes.
Clean Intermittent Catheterization—includes information regarding benefits of and procedures for performing CIC, as well as how to instruct others. 25 minutes.
Home Oxygen for Infants and Young Children—demonstrates use of three commonly used home oxygen systems emphasizing precautions for use. 30 minutes.
Home Tracheostomy Care for Infants and Young Children—reviews physiology of infant airways and procedure for caring for the child with a trache tube. 40 minutes.
Infection Control in Child Care Settings—addresses necessary concerns regarding prevention of spread of contagious diseases in group care settings and provides instruction on effective control techniques. 30 minutes.

These tapes are available from Learner Managed Designs, 2201 K West 25th Street, Lawrence, KS 66046.

Books and Manuals

Larson, G. (Ed.). (1988). *Managing the school age child with a chronic health condition.* Wayzata, MN: DCI Publishing.
    A book designed for all personnel in the schools working with students with chronic health conditions, it includes practical how-to-do information on planning and implementing health care procedures.
California State Department of Education. (1980). *Guidelines and procedures for meeting the specialized physical health care needs of students.* Sacramento: Author.
    A manual that includes specific information on how to implement specialized health care procedures in the schools.
Graff, C., Ault, M., Guess, D., & Taylor, M. (1990). *Health care for students with disabilities.* Baltimore, MD: Brookes.
    A manual designed for teachers to provide them with relevant information regarding health related procedures received by their students.

cautions in caring for all students in the school setting. Table 5.4 includes the recommendations of the American Academy of Pediatrics (1988) regarding care for students with HIV infection in the schools.

Family-Centered Care Management

When he was Surgeon General, C. Everett Koop was a significant leader in heading a campaign calling for the building of community-based (as contrasted with hospital-based) systems of services for students with special health care needs and their families (Gittler, 1988). Strong in his message is the importance of the family as central in each child's life: "The family is the constant whereas the public and private agencies, organizations, institutions and individuals that provided health and other needed services for the child are transitory" (Gittler, 1988, p. 5). The campaign calls for the development of supports to assist families in their natural role as the primary providers for their children. It also calls for the development of systems in which partnerships are formed between professionals and families in all aspects of planning and service provision (Gittler, 1988).

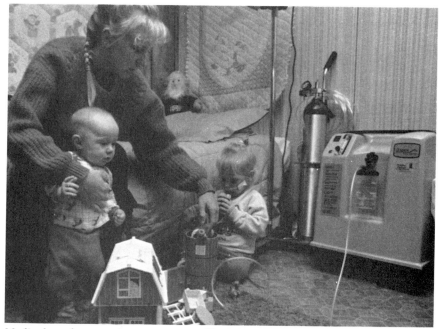

Medical needs are an important part of intervention.

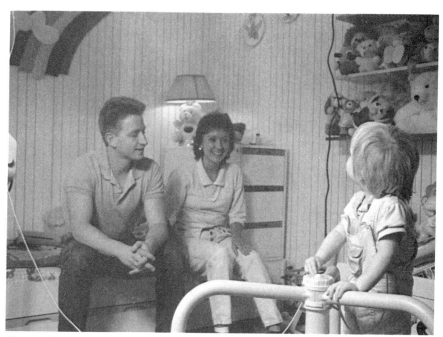

The family is central in special health care needs.

Throughout the country, numerous projects designed to develop the necessary supports for family-centered, community-based care are emerging. These programs are incorporating the following elements:

1. Recognition that the family is the constant in the child's life, whereas the service systems and personnel within those systems fluctuate
2. Facilitation of parent/professional collaboration at levels of health care
3. Sharing of unbiased and complete information with parents about their child's care on an ongoing basis, in an appropriate and supportive manner
4. Implementation of appropriate policies and programs that are comprehensive and provide emotional and financial support to meet the needs of families
5. Recognition of family strengths and individuality and respect for different methods of coping
6. Understanding and incorporation of the developmental needs of infants, children, and adolescents and their families into health care delivery systems
7. Encouragement and facilitation of parent-to-parent support; assurance that the design of health care delivery system is flexible, accessible, and responsive to family needs (Shelton, Jeppson, & Johnson, 1987, p. i)

Only by recognizing that the child is part of a family can educators and other professionals develop comprehensive, effective programming of education and care for children with special health care needs.

Each community differs from others in supports provided for families of children with special health care needs. Activity 3, page 130, directs you in collecting information about what might be available in your area.

Table 5.4   Guidelines for Infection Control in Schools in High-Prevalence Areas

1. HIV-infected children who are old enough to attend school can be admitted freely to all activities, to the extent that their own health permits. The child's physician should have access to consultative expertise to assist in decision making.

2. As all infected children will not necessarily be known to school officials in high-prevalence areas, and because blood is a potential source of contagion, policies and procedures should be developed in advance to handle instances of bleeding. Such policies and procedures should be based upon the understanding that even within an area of high prevalence, the risk of HIV-infection resulting from a single cutaneous exposure to blood from a school-aged child or adolescent with unknown serologic status is minute. Considering such minimal risk, the only mandatory precautionary action should be washing exposed skin with soap and water. Lacerations and other bleeding lesions should be managed in a manner which minimizes direct contact of the caregiver with blood. Schools in high-prevalence areas should provide access to gloves so that individuals who wish to further reduce a minute risk may opt for their use. Under no circumstances should the urgent care of a bleeding child be delayed because gloves are not immediately available.

Source: American Academy of Pediatrics (1988), p. 805. Reprinted with permission.

SUMMARY THOUGHTS

The provision of educational programs in least restrictive environments to students with complex health care needs is a new challenge to public schools. There are as yet many unanswered questions about the best ways to meet these students' educational and health care needs. Focus on this group of students is increasing, but much additional work is necessary. Solutions to these questions and issues are not simple and cannot be solved by the schools alone. Collaborative efforts among educational and medical fields and with families are essential. Dissemination of information and preservice and inservice training of personnel are necessary to guarantee quality programs that combine education and care. It is also necessary to prevent discrimination against students as well as prevent the spread of communicable diseases.

REFERENCES

American Academy of Pediatrics. (1986). School attendance of children and adolescents with Human T Lymphotropic Virus III/Lymphadenopathy–Associated Virus Infection. *Pediatrics, 77*(3), 430–432.

American Academy of Pediatrics. (1988). Pediatric guidelines for infection control of HIV (AIDS) virus in hospitals, medical offices, schools, and other settings. *Pediatrics, 82*(5), 801–807.

American Nurses Association. (1983). *Standards of school nursing practice.* Kansas City, MO: Author.

Bevin, H. In re. *EHLR* 508: 134, 1986.

Caldwell, T. H. (1988). *Children with special health care needs in schools.* Paper presented at Conference Blue Print for Change, Council for Exceptional Children, Orlando, Florida.

Caldwell, T. H., Todaro, A. W., & Gates, A. J. (in press). Special health care needs. In J. L. Bigge (Ed.), *Teaching Individuals with Physical and Multiple Disabilities.* Columbus, OH: Merrill.

Centers for Disease Control. (1985). *What you can do to stop disease in child day care centers.* Atlanta: Department of Health and Human Services.

Council for Exceptional Children. (1988). *Policies manual.* Reston, VA: Author.

Department of Education, State of Hawaii v. *Katherine D. Dorr,* 727, F.2d 809 (9th Cr. 0983).

Detsel v. *Ambach* (ND NY 1986, 1985-86 EHCR DEC, 557:335).

Ferguson, H. (1988). Getting school health services together. Paper presented at TASH Conference, Washington, DC.

Gittler, J. (1988). *Community based service systems for children with special health care needs and their families.* Iowa City: National Maternal and Child Health Resource Center.

Hester, H. K., Goodwin, L. D., & Igoe, J. B. (1980). *The SNAP school nurse survey: Summary of procedures and results.* Washington, DC: U.S. Department of Maternal and Child Health, Project #1846002597A1.

Hobbs, N., Perrin, J. M., & Ireys, H. T. (1985). *Chronically ill children and their families.* San Francisco: Jossey-Bass.

Holvoet, J. F., & Helmstetter, E. (1989). *Medical problems of students with special needs: A guide for educators.* Boston: Little, Brown.

Hotte, E. A., Monroe, H. S., Philbrook, D. L., & Scarlata, R. W. (1984). Programming for persons with profound retardation: A three year retrospective study. *Mental Retardation, 22*(2), 75–78.

Iowa Department of Education Task Force on Children with Special Health Care Needs (1988). *Recommendations: Services for children with special health care needs.* Des Moines, Iowa: Iowa Department of Education.

Kleinberg, S. B. (1982). *Educating the chronically ill child.* Rockville, MD: Aspen.

Larson, G. (Ed.). (1988). *Managing the school age child with chronic health conditions.* Wayzata, MN: DCI Publishing.

Lehr, D. H., & Haubrich, P. (1988). *Service delivery models for students with special health care needs.* Unpublished raw data, University of Wisconsin—Milwaukee.

Lehr, D. H., & Noonan, M. J. (1989). Issues in the education of students with complex health care needs. In F. Brown & D. H. Lehr (Eds.), *Persons with profound Disabilities: Issues & Practices* (pp. 139–160). Baltimore, MD: Brookes.

Lehr, D. H., & Peppey, K. (1988). *Review of communicable disease policies of state departments of education.* Unpublished raw data, University of Wisconsin—Milwaukee.

Mulligan Ault, M., Guess, D., Struth, L., & Thompson, B. (1988). The implementation of health related procedures for classrooms for students with severe multiple impairments. *TASH, 13*(2), 100–109.

P.L. 94-142, Education for All Handicapped Children Act of 1975, 20 U.S.C. 121, (1975).

Rogers, M. F. (1987). Transmission of human immunodeficiency virus infection in the United States. In B. K. Silverman and A. Waddell (Eds.), *Report of the surgeon general's workshop on children with HIV infection and their families* (pp. 17–19). Washington, DC: U.S. Department of Health and Human Services.

Shelton, T.L., Jeppson, E. S., & Johnson, B. H. (1987). *Family-centered care for children with special health care needs.* Washington, DC: Association for the Care of Children's Health.

Silkworth, C.S. (1988). Handwashing techniques. In G. Larson (Ed.), *Managing the school age child with a chronic health condition* (pp. 141–145). Wayzata, MN: DCI Publishing.

Sirvis, B. (1988). Students with special health care needs. *Teaching Exceptional Children, 20*(4), 40–44.

SKIP. (1986). *A skip kid.* Severna Park, MD: Author.

Task Force on Children with Special Health Care Needs. (1988). *Recommendations: Services for children with special health care needs.* Des Moines: Iowa Department of Education.

Task Force on Technology-Dependent Children. (1988). *Fostering home and community-based care for technology dependent children.* Washington, DC: U.S. Department of Health and Human Services.

Tatro v. Texas, 625 F.2d 557 (5th Cir. 1980), 703 F.2d 823 (5th Cir. 1983).

Tolsma, D. (1988). Activities of Centers for Disease Control in AIDS education. *Journal of School Health, 58*(4), 133–136.

U.S. Congress, Office of Technology Assessment. (1987). *Technology dependent children: Hospital v. home care—a technical memorandum* (TA-TM-H-38). Washington, DC: GPO.

Viadero, D. (1987). Medically fragile students pose dilemma for school officials. *Education Week, 1,* 14.

Wolfensberger, W. (1972). *Normalization: The principle of normalization in human services.* Toronto, Canada: National Institute on Mental Retardation.

1

Purpose

☐ To help you determine the existence of policies or guidelines regarding communicable diseases in your state or district

☐ To help you analyze the content of the policy

Steps

1. Contact your state department of education or school district office to request a copy of its guidelines or policies regarding communicable diseases.
2. Review the guidelines.

Analysis

☐ Which contagious diseases are addressed?

☐ Do they address immunizations only?

☐ Do they specify exclusionary criteria? What are they?

☐ Do they specify procedures related to confidentiality of information?

☐ Do they suggest care and handling procedures?

☐ What else is included?

2

Purpose

☐ To help you determine your preparedness to provide care and emergency treatment for students

Steps

1. Answer the following questions.
   a. If a child were choking, I would _____.
   b. If a child has a seizure, I would _____.
   c. If a child fell off the playground equipment and was unconscious, I would _____.
   d. Proper handwashing procedures include _____.
   e. After changing a child's diaper in a group care setting, I should _____.

Analysis

☐ How many could you answer?

☐ How confident are you with your answers?

☐ Could you instruct your instructional support staff or students in what they should do in case of an emergency?

☐ Consider your need for additional training.

☐ If necessary, seek training in basic first aid from a program such as the American Red Cross.

Further References

1. Your local American Red Cross or Epilepsy Society
2. Larson (1988)
3. Centers for Disease Control (1985)

| 3 |

Purpose

☐ To help you determine what types of supports might be available in your area for parents of children with special health care needs

Steps

1. Identify agencies or organizations in your community, such as Children's Hospital, the Association for Retarded Children, United Cerebral Palsy, Hemophiliac Foundation, and SKIP, that serve special needs children.

2. Contact those agencies to determine what services they provide. Use the questions listed in the next section as a guide.

Analysis

☐ Describe the populations served.

☐ Describe the types of services available for children and for their parents.

☐ In what ways do available services meet the specific needs of children with special health care needs?

☐ Where can parents go to obtain services not available in the community?

6

Early Childhood Special Education

Sandra W. Gautt
University of Kansas

EARLY CHILD DEVELOPMENT
TYPICAL PROFILE

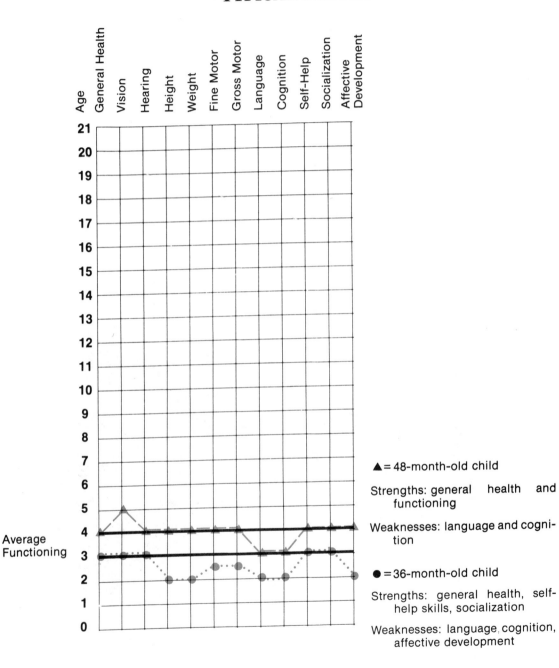

▲ = 48-month-old child

Strengths: general health and functioning

Weaknesses: language and cognition

● = 36-month-old child

Strengths: general health, self-help skills, socialization

Weaknesses: language, cognition, affective development

Early childhood education for young children with handicapping and at-risk conditions is a newly evolving field of special education. Although the importance of the first 6 years of a child's life for establishing the foundation for later development and learning is a universally accepted principle, until recently young children with handicapping and at-risk conditions received few, if any, educational services during this period. Recognition of this new field, its uniqueness, the population served, and the nature and context of intervention services has only recently emerged. The purpose of this chapter is to describe the current status of these elements.

HISTORICAL ROOTS

The historical roots of early childhood special education may be found in the writings of such philosophers as Locke, Rousseau, and Pestalozzi that advocated the importance of experiences during the period of early childhood. Contemporary authors such as Bloom (1964) and White (1975) have emphasized the importance of early environment and experience in a child's life. Further impetus has been provided by findings from empirical studies of the effects of enriched environments and increased stimulation on development (Skeels & Dye, 1939; Kirk, 1958; Gray, Ramsey, & Klaus, 1982; Schweinhart, Berrueta-Clement, Barnett, Epstein, & Weikart, 1985). Yet emergence of a separate and identifiable field within special education has been equally influenced by changes in contemporary society.

Changes have occurred in society's views and values concerning the care, nurturance, and needs of young children, including those with disabilities. During the 1970s, concern for enhancing the educational background of individuals from disadvantaged environments emerged as a part of the War on Poverty. As increasing numbers of women with children entered the workforce during the 1980s, the need for expanded child-care systems became apparent. Both trends sparked renewed interest in the range and quality of experiences provided all young children. The need for services for infants and young children with at-risk and handicapping conditions was further reinforced by increased advances in medical technology and increased advocacy within the field of special education, including passage of legislation such as PL 99-457. Such political, economic, social, and technological changes in society as well as changing views of development, including the importance of environment and of early stimulation, set the conditions for the emergence of programs for young children with at-risk or handicapping conditions.

RATIONALE

Three themes underscore the importance of early childhood education for children with at-risk and handicapping conditions.

☐ Intervention during a period of rapid development has a potentially positive effect on acquisition of more complex skills.

☐ The presence of a handicapping condition or developmental delay affects the family unit.

☐ Early intervention has long-term economic and social benefits.

Impact During a Period of Rapid Development

Intervening during a period in which development and learning are most rapid can make a significant difference in the developmental status of young children. Timing of intervention becomes particularly important when the child runs the risk of missing an opportunity to acquire the competencies and skills required for integration into more complex behaviors or needed to progress to the next stage of development. Some researchers (Clarke & Clarke, 1976) have questioned the concept that failure to intervene early results in "missed opportunities" that cannot be made up by later intervention. Others (Castro & Mastropieri, 1986) have raised questions concerning the validity of the concept "earlier is better." Although the issues raised have not been resolved, children with apparently normal capabilities do appear to compensate for early deprivation (Bricker, 1986), and intervention at least by age 3 does appear to have a significant impact on the developmental status of children with handicaps (Castro & Mastropieri, 1986). Bricker (1986) contended that as a group, the handicapped infant and young child by definition possessed fewer resources with which to compensate. Thus, it seems wise to assume that quality early intervention is required to assist these children in acquiring the adaptive responses that lead to independent functioning. Such a perspective emphasizes the need to intervene early and stresses the need for continuity of intervention.

Impact on the Family Unit

Handicapping and at-risk conditions not only affect the developmental status of the child but impact the entire family unit. Even under ideal circumstances, the parenting role is highly complex. The presence of a handicapping condition or developmental delay within a family member automatically increases the complexity and demands of the parenting role (Beckman-Bell, 1981; Gallagher, Beckman, & Cross, 1983). Intervention can assist parents in establishing effective parenting skills required to manage normally expected caregiving needs and the special needs created by the child's handicapping condition. In reducing the debilitating effects of the handicapping condition and enhancing the child's ability to function independently, intervention further facilitates the parenting role and the individual's integration into the family unit.

Economic and Social Impact

Benefits of early intervention extend beyond the child and family to include the larger society. Economic and social benefits may be derived from decreased dependence on social institutions and increased potential for employment as a result of the child's increased developmental and educational gains. A substantial body of research provides both quantitative and qualitative evidence that early intervention increases the developmental and educational gains for the child which results in the need for fewer or less intense special education and other habilitation services later in life and in increased employability (Smith & Strain, 1988a).

DISTINGUISHING CHARACTERISTICS

Early childhood special education follows strong traditions from the fields of early childhood education, special education, and compensatory education models such as Head Start and Follow-Through. These "parent" fields have shaped current conceptualizations of effective practice. Nevertheless, early childhood education for infants and preschoolers with at-risk or handicapping conditions has its own distinct features. Peterson (1987) identified eight unique characteristics of the field and its programs: (a) a cross-categorical field that addresses a diverse group of children; (b) a blending of the principles, practices, methodology, service delivery models, and values of special education, early childhood education, and compensatory education; (c) an intervention perspective; (d) alternative approaches to delivery of services; (e) the content and procedures of identification and assessment; (f) curricular priorities; (g) models of professional interaction; and (h) the nature and context of parent involvement. Table 6.1 summarizes the distinct features of early childhood special education. Of these characteristics, the diversity of the population served, the underlying philosophy of intervention, and the focus on developmental impact define the character of the field.

Population Diversity

Early childhood special education provides services for an unusually diverse group of children with special needs, often within the same program or classroom setting. The population served in early intervention and early childhood special education programs includes all disabilities, degrees of severity and functioning levels, and ages birth to 5 or 6 years. This cross-categorical field encompasses children with cognitive, physical, and neurological disorders; sensory impairments; and/or severe health or behavior disorders and multiple handicaps. The field also encompasses children who do not have a clearly diagnosable disorder but whose development is delayed or deviant in some way. The broad age range reflects not only the variation evidenced by children across and within the chronological age ranges but different phases of development, infancy, toddler, and preschool.

Philosophy of Intervention

Basic to the philosophy and practices of early childhood special education is the principle that one can impact the process of development. This belief is seen in the emphasis on an intervention perspective and is reflected in the age at which intervention is begun, the ways programs are organized, curricular priorities, and instructional strategies. Basic to this perspective is the belief that through carefully planned interventions, one can change the course of development and the results of deviant or delayed development. Such a perspective implies services that occur as early as possible, are intensive and continuous, consider the needs of the whole child, and focus on the individual needs of each child in the program. The purpose of intervention is to maximize development and to minimize the impact of the handicapping condition on current and later development and the child's interaction with the environment. This perspective distinguishes early childhood special education from the remediation (corrective) or supplemental instruction perspective of traditional special education. It also distinguishes early childhood special education from the enrichment perspective of early childhood education programs for non-handicapped or disadvantaged young children.

Focus on Developmental Impact

Much professional debate in special education has focused on the use of conventional categorical labels (Hobbs, 1975). The diversity of the population, variability of the developmental process, interrelatedness of developmental domains, assess-

Table 6.1 Unique Characteristics of Early Childhood Special Education

- A blend of the principles, practices, teaching methodologies, service delivery methods, and values of special education, early childhood education, and compensatory education

- A cross-categorical field that addresses a diverse group of children with all types of disabilities, all levels of impairment, and ages birth to age 5 or 6

- An intervention rather than enrichment or remediation perspective

- A broad range of alternative approaches for delivering services to infants, preschoolers, and their parents

- Curricular priorities based on the specific development and functional needs of the child

- Identification and assessment content and procedures addressing the unique issues of a young population and the purposes of intervention

- Multidisciplinary input and use of interdisciplinary or transdisciplinary teams to deliver services

- An emphasis on inclusion of parents as team members and commitment to family-focused intervention

- Emphasis on developmental descriptors and impact of handicapping conditions rather than on traditional categorical labels

Source: Adapted from Peterson (1987).

ment limitations, and intervention perspective have prompted professionals in early childhood special education programs to rely less on categorical labels for children. Rather, professionals emphasize assessing and describing the child's current developmental capabilities and developmental difficulties or deviations. Professionals view young children with at-risk or handicapping conditions in terms of the degree of deviation from normal patterns of development, including differences in rate or evidence of distortions in their pattern of development. Concerns are raised when the deviation is significant enough to potentially impact subsequent development or to cause the child to experience a significant handicap in his or her natural environment. Criteria for eligibility for services are not restricted to diagnosis of an underlying categorical condition. Evidence of significant developmental delays not correlated with a confirmed handicapping condition or the presence of conditions that place children at risk for later delays or disruptions in development may be considered in determining eligibility. Thus, emphasis on the child's current developmental capabilities and difficulties as a basis for determining intervention needs differs significantly from determination of an appropriate diagnostic category, resultant label, and categorically oriented service delivery.

> Activity 1, page 167, expands your understanding of the field of early childhood special education by comparing the professional literature in this field with its "parent fields" of special education and early childhood education.

LEGISLATIVE INITIATIVES AND IMPERATIVES

Early federal initiatives in early childhood education, such as Head Start, focused on enriching the experiences of young children from disadvantaged environments. The underlying premise of federal action was to intervene in order to promote optimal development by reducing the impact of poverty. The national scope of this effort brought immediate visibility to a previously invisible population and refocused the nation's attention on young children and their needs. Similarly, legislation played a major role in the development of programs for young children with at-risk and handicapping conditions. Legislative initiatives also reflected the evolution of the field of early childhood special education. Table 6.2 identifies the major legislation and its impact on programs and services.

Three legislative initiatives, PL 90-538, PL 94-142, and PL 99-457, have played critical roles in the establishment and expansion of services and have encouraged best practices in the delivery of these services. Each reflected and was responsive to the issues of service delivery at the time of its passage and has since provided direction for the continued development of effective practices and resolution of service delivery issues.

Table 6.2 Legislation Impacting Early Childhood Special Education

---

PL 90-538 Handicapped Children's Early Education Assistance Act (1968)

Summary

- First legislation to focus exclusively on education of children with handicaps without being attached to another legislative bill

- Development of exemplary model programs for early intervention with preschoolers, infants, or their parents (model demonstration projects)

- Dissemination of effective practices (outreach projects)

- Expansion of current knowledge in the field and identification of critical issues (early childhood research institutes)

Impact

- Model programs during the 20 years history of this program have developed and implemented effective practices reflecting the following aspects of early intervention: identification and assessment, multidisciplinary services, interagency collaboration, family and professional collaboration, inservice training for child-care professionals; service delivery models, transition to public schools; curriculum development and evaluation of child progress, services for infants with special health needs, collaboration between allied health and special education service providers.

- As the needs of the field of early childhood special education have changed, the focus of the demonstration projects has changed to address current or projected issues (cultural diversity, LRE, provision of integrated services, inservice training for early childhood and day care service providers, and services for infants with specific disabilities).

- Through dissemination of proven procedures, models, or components of models, outreach projects have been major contributors to the expansion of quality program and service delivery efforts and interagency and interstate collaboration.

- Research institutes have focused on the long-term investigation of selected aspects of early education for those with handicaps, development and analysis of new information concerning early intervention, and identification of methods for enhancing services.

PL 92-424 Economic Opportunity Act (1972 amendments)

Summary

- Establishment of Head Start and Follow-Through Program designed to assist economically disadvantaged preschool-aged children achieve full potential by attempting to intervene to reduce or prevent the damaging effects of poverty on their development

- Inclusion of children with handicaps through mandating that no less than 10% of the total number of enrollment opportunities in each state be available for handicapped children

Table 6.2   *continued*

Impact

- The national scope of Head Start brought immediate visibility to a population previously "invisible."
- The philosophy of comprehensive services including parents brought a new perspective to the provision of services for young children with handicaps.
- The 1972 amendments to this legislation confirmed a philosophical commitment to serving children with handicaps by mandating Head Start services be extended to such children from low-income families.

PL 94-142 Education for All Handicapped Children Act (1975) and 1983 Amendments

Summary

- Entitlement of a free and appropriate education for all children and youth between the ages of 3 and 21 with services for children under school age dependent on state law or precedence
- Establishment of a preschool incentive grant program to encourage states to provide services to children under school age
- Establishment of the state plan grant program to assist state educational agencies or other appropriate state agencies to plan, develop, and implement a comprehensive service delivery system for the provision of special education and related services to young children, birth through 5 years, with handicaps

Impact

- This legislation provided formal endorsement to early education programs for children under age 5 and a basis for continued expansion of services through the incentive grant program to the states.
- Amendments passed in 1983 extended the initial endorsement down to birth through the state planning grant program and authorized use of funds under the preschool incentive grant program to be used in services for children, birth to age 3.

PL 99-457 Education of the Handicapped Act Amendments of 1986

Summary

- Extension of the provisions of PL 94-142 to all children, ages 3–4 years, by 1990-91 and increase of incentives for services to this age group (Preschool Grants Program [Part B, Section 619])
- Establishment of a discretionary program designed to assist states in planning, developing, and implementing coordinated, comprehensive, multidisciplinary, interagency statewide systems of early intervention services for children, ages birth to 3 years, and their families (Program for Infants and Toddlers with Handicaps [Part H])

Impact

- The intent of previous legislation (PL 94-142) was strengthened by the extension of its provisions including a free and appropriate education to all children 3–4 years of age and by a significant increase in the incentives for services for this age group.
- This legislation established a national policy concerning preschool services for children with handicaps and early intervention.

PL 90-538

Based on the premise that lack of services for young children with disabilities was due to an absence of exemplary models, Congress passed PL 90-538, the Handicapped Children's Early Education Assistance Act, in 1968. The emphasis of the Handicapped Early Children's Early Education Program established by the legislation was to address the need for locally designed ways to serve young children with disabilities, for more specific information on effective programs and techniques, and for distribution of replicable models throughout the nation. More than 500 demonstration projects were funded from 1969 through 1987 (Smith, 1988). Although the initial intent of PL 90-538 was not to establish a wide-scale service delivery system such as Head Start, the legislation has led to the initiation of other related demonstration, training, and dissemination activities nationwide, including state implementation grants, research institutes, state outreach initiatives, and state planning efforts for early intervention. The wealth of program models and data supportive of early intervention has affected and continues to affect the delivery of effective services, public policy, and legislation. The issues raised have stimulated continued growth and debate as well as future research directions in the field.

PL 94-142

Although special education services were required for all students of school age under PL 94-142, implementation of the law for children under school age (ages 3 and 4 years) was dependent on state law and/or precedence. Thus, if state law did not require school programs for handicapped children under school age, local districts were not required to provide such services. Even with this exception, PL 94-142 represented a significant step toward increased service provision for young children with handicapping conditions. This legislation provided formal endorsement to early education programs for children under age 5 and a basis for continued expansion of services through an incentive grant program to the states. Amendments passed in 1983 further supported the development of services by extending the initial endorsement from birth to school age (Weintraub & Ramirez, 1985).

PL 99-457

The education of young children with handicapping conditions or at risk for developmental delays did not become a national priority until the passage of PL 99-457. Development and passage of this legislation reflected a 20-year evolution of public policy on early intervention. Previous legislation supported effective models and technology, training for professionals, endorsement of the concept of early intervention, state planning efforts, and encouragement of the generation of new knowledge through research and development activities. PL 99-457 was a landmark legislation for early intervention as it reflected a national policy of access to services for all handicapped and at-risk children (birth through 5 years of age) and their families.

Passage of PL 99-457 changed both the scope and extent of services for young children with handicaps. Services for preschool children, ages 3 to 5, were expanded, and a new discretionary program was introduced to assist states in developing early intervention services for infants and toddlers (birth through age 2). The Preschool Grants Program (Part B, Section 619) strengthened the intent of PL 94-142 by extending its provisions to all children 3 to 4 years of age by 1990-91. Financial incentives for services for this age group were significantly increased to encourage states to provide services to the remaining unserved preschool children with disabilities.

Programs for Infants and Toddlers with Handicaps (Part H), a new discretionary program under PL 99-457, was designed to assist states in planning, developing, and implementing coordinated, comprehensive, multidisciplinary, interagency statewide systems of early intervention services for children birth through age 2, and their families. Critical features of the program reflected new directions for public policy for special education including (a) the population eligible for services, (b) the range and definition of services, and (c) family-focused individual plans.

Three groups of children, ages birth to 3 years, are eligible for services under this component of the legislation:

☐ Children who are experiencing developmental delays in one or more of the following areas: cognitive, physical, language and speech, psychosocial or self-help skills
☐ Children who have a physical or mental condition that has a high probability of resulting in delay
☐ At state discretion, children who are considered at risk medically or environmentally for substantial developmental delays if early intervention is not provided

The infant or toddler's family may also be viewed as a target for intervention and may receive services that are needed to assist in the development of the child (Weiner & Koppelman, 1987).

Services for each eligible child must include multidisciplinary assessment, an individual family service plan (IFSP), services to meet developmental needs, and case management services. Early intervention services addressing developmental needs may include the following as primary services:

☐ Special education
☐ Speech and language pathology
☐ Audiology
☐ Occupational therapy
☐ Physical therapy
☐ Psychological services
☐ Parent and family training and counseling services
☐ Transition services

☐ Medical services for diagnostic purposes
☐ Health services necessary to enable the child to benefit from other early inter-
    vention services

Coordination and monitoring of the delivery of services required by the child
or family are carried out by case management services. Case management responsibilities extend beyond the services specified in the IFSP to include coordination of
early intervention with other services that the child or family needs or is being provided but that are not required under the legal provisions of the legislation (Weiner
& Koppelman, 1987).

The family-oriented approach mandated by the legislation addresses the
child's needs in the context of the family. The need for intervention is individualized not just for the child but for the family as well. Parental involvement in the
intervention process extends beyond the requirements implemented under PL 94-
142. Although similar in content to an IEP, an IFSP must address the needs of both
the child and the family. Parents are viewed as partners in efforts to intervene
and/or manage the delivery of services for their child. The requirement of the
development and implementation of an IFSP rather than an IEP is designed to
ensure that intervention occurs within the context of the family.

Activity 2, page 168, gives you an opportunity to determine the current status
of legislation and program development in your state.

PERSPECTIVES OF INTERVENTION

Intervention for young children with disabilities may be viewed from a variety of
perspectives. Program elements reflecting the context in which intervention occurs,
the diversity of program models, and service delivery options suggest the diverse
configurations that characterize the delivery of intervention services.

Context of Intervention

Early childhood special education programs differ in relation to whom they serve,
the way in which they deliver services, and the context in which they deliver these
services. Rather than the place-oriented definitions of traditional special education
service delivery or the content-oriented definitions of early childhood education,
Peterson (1987) proposed a process-oriented definition. Such an approach provides
a clearer perspective on intervention for infants and young children by emphasizing
the strategies and activities used to deliver services to young children. Thus, the
context of intervention is defined by addressing issues concerning who, when,
what, where, by whom, with whom, and through whom. The possible options for
each question are presented in Table 6.3. Responses to each of these dimensions

Table 6.3 Early Intervention Service Delivery Decision Matrix

Target of Service (Who)	Beginning Point of Intervention (When)	Services to be Provided (What)	Setting for Intervention Program (Where)	Intervention Agent[a] (By Whom)	Social Context of Services (With Whom)	Agencies Providing Service(s) (Through Whom)
Child	Birth	Case-finding and screening services	Home based	Paraprofessional	Individual program	Public schools
Mother	Infancy	Diagnostic services	Center based	Parent		Private schools
Father	Toddler years	Education program	• classroom • clinic	Teacher	Group program	State/local government agencies
Both parents	Preschool years	Therapy services	Combination home/center	Therapist	• segregated • mainstreamed integrated • reverse mainstreamed	Nonprofit service organizations
Family	Kindergarten	• speech/language • physical • occupational • other special therapies		Social services personnel		
Teacher				Multidisciplinary team		Churches
		Parent education and training		Combination of intervention agents		Profit-making agencies
		Family counseling				Multiagency consortia
		Social services				
		Nutritional services				
		Medical services				
		Transportation				
		Case management				
		Transition services				
		Technical assistance				

[a]Model of interaction can be multidisciplinary, interdisciplinary, or transdisciplinary.

Source Adapted from Peterson (1987).

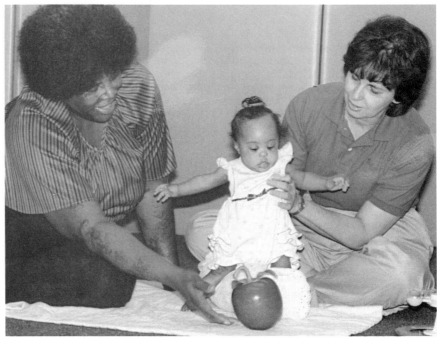

Stimulation for young children from parents and professionals is critical.

define a specific program's configuration and the context in which intervention occurs. Thus, differences among service delivery alternatives can be found on the following dimensions:

- ☐ Who—the primary target of services (child, parents, both)
- ☐ When—at what age intervention will begin
- ☐ What—the types of specific services included in program
- ☐ By whom and how—the types of professional or paraprofessional staff employed to deliver the services and the model of interaction
- ☐ Where—the settings in which services are delivered
- ☐ Through whom—administrative responsibility for delivery services

Diversity of Program Models

As a result of the information gathered from the Handicapped Children's Early Education Program, Head Start, and Follow-Through, early childhood special education has had the unique opportunity to develop systematic and replicable service delivery models prior to the "mandate" for full services. Table 6.4 describes a limited number of the program models that have been developed to serve infants and young children with at-risk and handicapping conditions.

The diversity reflected in these models indicates that options for serving young handicapped or at-risk children are great. Peterson (1987) suggested that this variability or flexibility was necessary for several reasons: the ages, types, and levels of disability and at-risk conditions vary, as do resultant needs of the children served; the geographic characteristics of the areas served differ; and the population needing services and the available resources differ from one community to the next. The resulting diversity found across intervention programs is most evident in the ways in which services are delivered and the environments in which intervention occurs.

Service Delivery Options

Administrative arrangements for delivering services to young children include home-based, center-based, combination center-based and home-based, hospital-based, and technical assistance programs. The optimal model for service delivery depends on family and child characteristics and needs, intensity of services, and geographic characteristics of the service area.

Home-Based Programs

Home-based programs deliver services principally in the child's home, with the parent or primary caregiver acting as the teacher. An interdisciplinary team assesses the child, determines appropriate instructional objectives, and monitors data to determine child progress and instructional effectiveness. The parent is instructed by the team in how to implement specific instructional strategies and activities designed for the child. Delivery of services in the home—the natural environment for the child—enhances generalization of skills and promotes active parental or other family member/caregiver involvement in the child's program. Programs may also provide support for the parent in parenting skills. Problems that must be considered when using this option include interference of the teaching role with parenting, variation in parent interest, follow-through and time commitment due to multiple demands and skill levels, limited opportunities for socialization for the child, and restriction of the range of services that may be provided efficiently. Home-based programs are often provided in rural areas where geographic distances require an excessive amount of time for transportation or where relatively few children require services.

Center-Based Programs

Center-based programs transport children to a center or school for scheduled instruction, which is provided by interdisciplinary team members. Although various patterns of staff interaction have been developed, the trend in early childhood education programs is toward implementation of a transdisciplinary model of intervention. This model allows team members to provide a broader range or greater intensity of services; the model also increases the efficiency of the program's use of staff. Paraprofessionals and parents often assist in the provision of instruction. Cen-

Table 6.4 Program Models for Early Childhood Intervention

Program Title	Target Population	Service Delivery Setting	Program Description
Developmental Therapy Model Rutland Center Atlanta, GA	2–14 years with severe emotional and behavioral disorders	Center based	The goal of this psychoeducational treatment approach is to reduce children's emotional and social difficulties. The curriculum model guides the planning of appropriate sequences of experiences and setting goals for behavior, communication, socialization, and preacademics at five different stages of therapy. When appropriate, children spend part of the day in an "integrated" preschool placement.
ACTT (Activating Children Through Technology) Western Illinois University Macomb, IL	Birth–8 years with moderate to severe handicapping conditions	Home or center based	Computer intervention sessions are designed for individual, small-group, and large-group use in the classroom or home setting. The curriculum is designed to foster control over the environment, promote autonomy, increase opportunities for communication, and develop problem-solving and cognitive skills. The program model includes procedures for the use of microcomputer hardware, software, and adaptive peripherals.
Portage Project Portage, WI	Birth–6 years with multicategorical handicapping conditions	Home based	The Portage model is a structured, data-based individualized home teaching program. Home visitors help parents assess their child's skills in five developmental areas, target emerging skills, define appropriate teaching techniques, and evaluate the child's performance. A classroom/home option is offered to facilitate transition into kindergarten.
SKY*HI Utah State University Logan, UT	Birth–5 years with hearing impairment	Home based	Three components constitute the model: (a) child identification and processing and program management; (b) direct services to families in communication, auditory and language programs and procedures; and (c) ongoing audiological, hearing aid, parent group, and psychological support services. The home visit curriculum is implemented by professional parent advisers through weekly home visits.
EMI (Education for Multihandicapped Infants) Charlottesville, VA	Birth–2 years with physical disabilities	Hospital, home, and center based	The model combines a clinic- and home-based program for infants who are initially seen in the neonatal intensive care unit program. The hospital/center program consists of weekly hour-long individual sessions for the infant and at least one parent supplemented by monthly home visits.

Table 6.4 *continued*

Program Title	Target Population	Service Delivery Setting	Program Description
SEFAM (Supporting Extended Family Members) Seattle, WA	Family members of young children with disabilities	Center based	This program supplements direct services provided for children with handicaps. Services are provided to family members through three components: a fathers program, a siblings program, and a grandparents program. The fathers program is designed to provide fathers of handicapped children ages birth to 5 with information and peer support through twice-monthly meetings. The siblings program consists of quarterly meetings in which siblings, ages 7–12, have opportunities to meet other siblings, develop friendships in the context of social activities, meet to discuss their concerns, and learn more about their siblings' disabilities. Quarterly meetings provide grandparents opportunities to get peer support and to obtain answers to their questions about their grandchildrens' disabilities.
RAPYHT (Retrieval and Acceleration of Promising Young Handicapped and Talented) University of Illinois Urbana, IL	3–6 years with mild and moderate disabilities with potential talent	Center based	Intervention provides special programming to nurture the talent and to promote development of the child's critical thinking skills and creativity. Curriculum materials for home and the focus on critical thinking skills and on special talent areas. These strategies are in addition to the intervention programs provided to meet the other areas of special need.
Hampton University Mainstreaming Model Hampton, VA	23 months–6 years significant developmental delays	Mainstreamed classes	This model is designed to integrate individualized and culturally appropriate educational objectives into the daily classroom routines in mainstreamed settings. The mainstreaming resource teacher serves as a teaching model in the classroom and provides resource services, consultation in team planning sessions, and transition support.
Family Day Care Project Child Care Coordinating Referral Service Ann Arbor, MI	Birth–2 years at-risk and handicapped	Family day care homes	The focus of the project is to train family day care providers to care for children with special needs. After training, children are placed with the providers who receive weekly or bimonthly visits from an early interventionist specialist.

[a]Additional information concerning these programs and other program models may be found in National Dissemination Study Group (1987), National Early Childhood Technical Assistance System (1988), and Jordan, Gallagher, Hutinger, and Karnes (1988).

ter programs provide opportunities for social interactions with both handicapped and nonhandicapped peers through integrated and reverse mainstream settings, facilitate transition into later instructional settings, and offer parents opportunities for interaction with other parents. As the number of families in which both members are employed increases, the center-based model assists in meeting the family's child-care needs as well as the child's developmental and therapeutic needs.

Combination Programs

To counteract the disadvantages of either home- or center-based settings, three alternatives have been developed as ways to deliver services in combination home-based–center-based models: (a) home-based intervention for infants and toddlers followed by center-based intervention at ages 3, 4, or 5; (b) home- or center-based intervention depending on the needs of the child and the family; and (c) center-based intervention augmented by weekly home visits. Each alternative for service delivery increases the flexibility programs have in determining appropriate intervention options based on family and child needs and wishes and reflects the advantages of both service delivery options.

Hospital-Based Programs

Hospital-based programs are offered for infants and chronically ill young children. These programs emphasize the developmental and medical needs of the infant or young child as well as the needs of the family. Intervention programs, which may begin in the neonatal intensive care unit (NICU), are developed and monitored by an interdisciplinary team. Intervention may include supportive services to the family prior to, during, and after birth; medical and developmental intervention; instruction to the family on how to meet the medical and developmental needs of the infant; and transition services that include accessing appropriate services in the community. Developmental progress and medical intervention continue to be monitored through systematic follow-up procedures.

Technical Assistance Programs

Technical assistance programs have grown out of the search for alternatives that meet the requirements of least restrictive environment. As a result, many young children with handicapping conditions are enrolled in traditional day care and early education programs established for their nonhandicapped peers. These programs provide for increased social interaction and facilitation of language and play skills. Through the provision of inservice training and continued consultation, personnel in day care and early education settings are assisted by personnel from early childhood special education programs. Collectively, the professionals work to modify the instructional environment, content, and/or strategies to meet the needs and instructional goals of children integrated into their programs.

Early intervention is helping this preschooler learn language skills.

Activity 3, page 169, expands your understanding of the characteristics of early childhood special education programs and factors that influence specific program configurations.

UNIQUE ASPECTS OF INTERVENTION

Many of the practices and methods utilized in early childhood special education may be found in the fields of special education and early childhood education. Nevertheless, aspects of identification, least restrictive environment, curricular emphases, and family-focused intervention are specific to early childhood special education.

Identification

The initial step in the provision of comprehensive services to young children with handicapping and at-risk conditions is identification—the process that determines whether a child displays a clearly identifiable handicapping or at-risk condition or a significant developmental delay. Child Find, screening, diagnosis, and assessment are part of this identification process.

Because young children in need of special education services are seldom found in a single environment, specific strategies must be used to locate them. To be effective, Child Find activities require collaboration with health care, medical, and social service agencies as well as early education and parenting programs in the community. Specific activities include dissemination of awareness information to parents concerning expected developmental milestones, parent education programs, and developmental screening of preschool-age children in the community. After the child has been located, screening procedures determine whether the child requires more comprehensive evaluation, needs periodic monitoring of development, or is not at risk for developmental delays.

Diagnostic Assessment

Once screening procedures are completed and results indicate the need for further evaluation, a diagnostic assessment and evaluation are conducted by an interdisciplinary team. Diagnostic assessment of young children extends beyond determination of the cause of the difficulties and identification of factors that may influence intervention. A comprehensive interdisciplinary diagnosis includes measures of abilities that remain intact, measures of factors external to the individual such as home environment, determination of the parent-child interaction, and consideration of the impact of the difficulties on the developmental process. This assessment process is the basis for planning the intervention. Assessment is the linkage between the child/family characteristics and needs and the design of effective intervention strategies. Although emphasis in the identification process is on initial assessment as a basis for determining the child's specific level of functioning and identifying information needed for the development of the IEP or IFSP, assessment strategies are ongoing. Ongoing assessment assists in monitoring child progress, the effectiveness of intervention strategies, and the impact on the family system.

Fewell (1983) has pointed to researchers' dissatisfaction with available assessment measures. A number of problems exist with the technical properties of the instruments, nature of test construction, and outcome information obtained for young children with handicapping conditions. Thus, a number of new directions in assessment have emerged in the field of early childhood special education: assessment in a natural environment, arena assessment strategies, and inclusion of a broader range of domains and factors. Observational instruments such as the Carolina Record of Individual Behavior have been developed to assess domains not included on traditional instruments. This instrument assesses such factors as social orientation, response to frustration, initiation, compliance, child-child interactions, and child-adult interactions (Simeonsson, Huntington, Short, & Ware, 1982).

The range and complexity of developmental areas and domains assessed in young handicapped children are clearly beyond the expertise of a single profession. Attempts have been made to facilitate the synthesis of information through assessments in the child's natural environment or arena assessment strategies. In an arena assessment, only the parent and one team member, who functions as the facilitator, interact with the child. The child is required to go through only one combined assessment and to interact with only one new adult; this minimizes fatigue and resistance and enhances the child's ability to perform (Woodruff & McGonigal, 1988). Such an approach also increases the efficiency and accuracy of the assessment. All team members observe the child's reactions and responses in all developmental areas and thus have an opportunity for varied observations. These observations can then be synthesized to determine the child's functioning level, strengths, and needs.

Least Restrictive Environment

The term *least restrictive environment* as traditionally used in education has its basis in the concept of removal from the regular class environment. But as there is no regular class setting at the preschool level, the relationship between LRE and services for children from birth through age 5 is problematic. Clearly, a need exists for the development of integrated services at the preschool level as well as for transition from preschool services. Although the legal relationship of LRE and preschool services has yet to be clarified, the empirical and instructional bases for integrating young handicapped children with their nonhandicapped peers must be considered when implementing LRE (Smith & Strain, 1988b).

Several administrative arrangements have been proposed that can lead to developmentally appropriate integrated services. These include:

☐ Mainstreamed noneducational option: enrollment in appropriate family- or center-based day care or preschool with implementation of the IEP in a different setting
☐ Mainstreamed educational option: enrollment in programs for nonhandicapped children, such as Head Start, in which specialized services are designed to implement the IEP
☐ Reverse mainstream option: enrollment of nonhandicapped children in specialized programs as regular class members and peer models to foster social integration
☐ Enrollment of handicapped children in school-sponsored preschools and kindergartens

Nevertheless, administrative settings do not lead directly to developmentally appropriate programming or significant developmental changes. Program quality in terms of instructional and social integration is the critical factor. Such integration is achieved only when children share an instructional and social environment and when teachers develop specific plans for supporting interaction between handicapped children and their nonhandicapped peers (Strain & Cordisco, 1983).

Curricular Emphases

Four developmental domains—*communication, affective-social, cognitive,* and *sensorimotor*—include the skills and capabilities that children normally acquire

Engaging environments facilitate intellectual and social skills.

during the period prior to age 5. Children with handicapping or at-risk conditions demonstrate delays, deficits, or distortions in one or more of these areas of development as well as in self-help or adaptive behaviors. Thus, these developmental domains are the primary objects of curricular, or instructional, emphases in early childhood special education. The considerable scope of curriculum content derives from the wide range of age and functioning levels of the special education population. For example, cognitive development targets may range from the visual tracking of an object, which reflects early sensorimotor skills, to the more advanced skills required in classification and problem solving. As young children develop, the interrelatedness of development is considerable and influences the design and delivery of instruction. A response such as waving bye-bye extends beyond the motor domain. This single response requires the child to integrate motor, communication, and social skills within a specific environmental context. Specific curricular emphases are dependent on child characteristics and needs and the impact of the handicapping condition on development.

Although a variety of theoretical orientations (cognitive interactionist, behavioral, developmental) underlie the range of curricula found in early childhood special education, two broad perspectives—the developmental and the functional—influence the implementation of curriculum for at-risk and handicapped young children. The developmental perspective assumes (a) that critical developmental changes are hierarchical, predictable, and sequential and (b) that

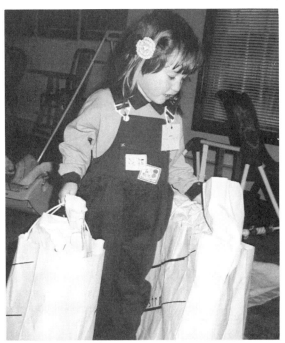

Interesting and fun activities help development in young children.

developmental progress is characterized by the integration and reorganization of previously acquired concepts or skills into more complex elements. Age-related developmental milestones as identified by Gesell or the broader developmental stage orientations of Piaget and Erickson reflect this orientation. Instructional targets are those skills or processes that occur next in the sequence or that are required to encourage movement to the next stage or greater integration of the skill into more complex behavior. The functional approach to curriculum assumes that development comprises the acquisition of skills that will immediately or in the future improve the child's ability to interact with the environment and to become more self-sufficient and independent. Curriculum targets are those skills that are or will be functional for the child in his or her current or next most probable environment.

Decisions concerning the use of a developmental or a functional approach are complex and involve consideration of both criteria for selecting specific curriculum targets. The two perspectives are not in opposition; rather, educators try to teach developmentally appropriate skills within a functional context. For example, fine motor skills requiring manual dexterity may be increased by stringing beads or by lacing or tying a shoe (a functional activity). Decisions concerning the relative emphasis or integration of developmental and functional instructional targets vary according to the child's age, the severity of the handicapping condition, the current and projected impact of the condition on the child's development, and the current and future environmental demands. Both perspectives underlie effective intervention.

PATRICK

Patrick, a 4-year-old with Down syndrome, currently receives early intervention services in a home-based program. The home trainer visits once a week. Patrick's family works with him during the week on a series of activities in the areas of cognitive, language, and fine motor development. He and his family have been in the program for 2 years.

Patrick is about 12 months below age level in his cognitive development. His language development is about 18 months below age level. Although he has a limited vocabulary and articulation difficulties, he evidences a variety of behaviors indicating communicative intent. He manipulates others' hands, pulls the other person, or makes minimal gestures to express his needs and wants. He demonstrates independence in self-help skills such as toileting and feeding but needs help dressing. Patrick primarily engages in solitary play but also enjoys the presence of others and initiates entry into another child's play. He likes to play with puzzles but has difficulty maintaining attention or completing an activity independently.

During the initial IEP conference for the year, Patrick's teacher and parents are discussing projected instructional targets for the next 6 months. Consideration may be given to placement in a mainstreamed kindergarten setting during the next year.

□ □ □

What skills in the areas of cognition, language, motor development, and self-help could be important for Patrick's success in kindergarten?

Family-Focused Intervention

During the 1970s, a dramatic and radical shift occurred in both the philosophy and practice of involving parents in their child's educational program. The advent of PL 94-142 provided the major impetus for inclusion of parents in the educational process. Passage of this legislation officially changed parents' rights and duties from a role as passive observer to a role as educational decision maker and advocate for the child. The emphasis on family-focused intervention found in early childhood special education is an extension of this defined practice.

Early intervention is almost by definition intervention for the family as well as for the child. Parents are in a strategic position to enhance the development of their child in terms of time, contact, and responsibility. Even if they are unable to act as primary direct provider, parents are responsible for securing adequate care. Inclusion of the family in the intervention process is further supported by research literature (Bronfenbrenner, 1974; Lazar & Darlington, 1982) documenting the positive influence of parent participation on child performance and the potential benefits for siblings. Parents provide continuity and consistency to the child's program and opportunities for the child to generalize learning to a natural environment. Acquisition of increased skills and interaction patterns increases parental feelings of satisfaction and competence in their parenting role (Weigerink, Hocutt, Posante-Loro, & Bristol, 1980; Bromwich, 1981).

Initially, parent involvement in early childhood special education settings was achieved through structured formats including observation opportunities, classroom participation, referral assistance, parent education group meetings, parent-mediated instruction, home visits, parent support groups and networks, and counseling. Although programs differed in the range of activities and structure, the following themes represented best practice:

☐ Necessity of a parent needs assessment
☐ Importance of a range of participation options allowing for individualization of parent involvement
☐ Need for consistency of parent involvement
☐ Acceptance of the parent as the primary facilitator of the child's development

A Changing View of the Family

Changing family patterns, economic and societal demands on the family, and the introduction of family systems theory have challenged early intervention professionals to rethink their assumptions regarding parent involvement. Turnbull and Turnbull (1986) encouraged the field to reexamine assumptions regarding parent involvement and consider that not all parents want or have the resources to strive for the idealized role of decision maker, advocate, or teacher. Dramatic societal changes, such as the increased number of single-parent households or the greater likelihood of both parents working outside the home, further influenced the need for reexamination of the traditional models of parent involvement. Professionals realized that they had to be more responsive to parents regarding inclusion of other family members, style and amount of involvement, changing types of involvement and level over time, and options and the right of choice. Such changes led professionals in early childhood special education to support Bronfenbrenner's (1979) argument that the traditional concept of family involvement be replaced with an ecological perspective of intervention. This perspective provided the impetus for two major changes in interactions with families: reconceptualization of the approach to and inclusion of the family in the child's program and recognition that the child was part of a larger social milieu, the family. Not only was the content of involvement reconceptualized; the role of intervention itself was redefined.

As professionals reconceptualized the ways in which they viewed families and the ways in which they interacted with and helped families, a family-focused philosophy of intervention evolved. Current practices are characterized by an increasing awareness that intervention must be designed and implemented within the context of the family (Affleck, McGrade, McQueeney, & Allen, 1982; Bailey et al.,

1986; Dunst, Trivette, & Deal, 1988). Early intervention professionals acknowledge that the unique dependence of the infant or young child on his or her family has made a family focus necessary. Family-focused intervention acknowledges the interrelated functioning of a family and the need to design interventions that take the impact on this functioning into consideration; the family is consulted and involved in decision making, case management, and educational/therapeutic efforts. Table 6.5 identifies the major characteristics of family-focused intervention.

Table 6.5　Elements of Family-Focused Intervention

- Partnership concept

  Parent should have full membership on the multidisciplinary team and share equally in all team decisions. This concept acknowledges that disagreement is typical of group decision making and that options for negotiation of differences, systematic review, and renegotiation must be identified.

- Respect for the autonomy of the parents

  Parents have the right to choose and to determine the course of their own personal and family life including the right to ultimately choose the style of participation and set their own values concerning the level of participation. The professional's role is to support parents in their choices.

- Validation of the parenting role

  The parenting role is validated through recognition of the difference between the professional's role and the role of family members. Expectations and the design of interventions attempt to assure that the teaching role does not interfere with the parenting role. For example, parents teach only those skills that they care about, that are natural to the home environment, and that facilitate family functioning.

- Family-determined needs and priorities

  Family involvement is based on family-determined needs rather than on information and skills professionals believe family members require. Intervention emphasis is to assist families in identifying resources, both real and potential, within the family and community systems that can be utilized to meet these needs.

  Educational intervention is only one of many functions and related needs experienced by families. The more time the family expends on the child, the less time it has for other priorities. Effective family functioning requires a balance across a variety of personal and family goals.

  Family-focused intervention recognizes changing family and individual needs and levels of involvement. Program expectations and design allow for individual differences in levels of interest, skill, comfort, and time available to devote to program activities.

The IFSP

Much of this philosophy and its underlying assumptions has been formalized in the IFSP component of PL 99-457. The IFSP must be written and must include the following elements: (a) the infant's present levels of development based on professionally acceptable objective criteria; (b) family strengths and needs related to enhancing the development of the family's handicapped infant; (c) major outcomes expected to be achieved for the infant and the family; (d) specific intervention services necessary to meet the unique needs of the infant and family; (e) identification of the case manager who will implement the plan and coordinate it with other agencies and persons; and (f) procedures for transition from early intervention into the preschool program as appropriate. The IFSP must be evaluated at least once a year and must be reviewed every 6 months or more often as appropriate (Weiner & Koppelman, 1987). Figure 6.1 depicts a sample individual family service plan.

The outcome of a family-focused model of intervention is to preserve and reinforce the role of families in the intervention process by respecting and responding to their desire for services and incorporating families in the assessment, planning, and evaluation processes. The model's general emphasis is on interaction with and empowerment of families; the model's specific emphasis is on teaching, encouraging, and reinforcing advocacy, problem-solving, and independent decision-making skills (Dunst et al., 1988). The goal of family-focused intervention is to identify and build on family capabilities as a way of strengthening families and facilitating the intervention process for the child. This perspective represents a major theme in early childhood special education.

Guidelines for implementation of family-focused interventions and the refinement of strategies for development of the IFSP will continue to evolve. Activity 4, page 169, provides you an opportunity to determine current perceptions of parents and professionals concerning the IFSP process and family-focused intervention strategies.

INTERAGENCY COLLABORATION

Effective intervention requires input and collaboration from many professional disciplines and agencies that service young children with disabilities and their families. The range and multiplicity of needs within and across children and families transgress the traditional boundaries of the educational, health, community, and social service systems. All systems must be considered when determining appropriate services for meeting the diverse needs of young children and their families. This multidisciplinary view is reinforced in PL 99-457—the IFSP requirement further expands the range of services identified for young children and their families.

Table 6.1 First Steps Pilot Project Individual Family Services Plan

SECTION 1 Identifying Information

1. Child's name:_____
   Last   First   MI

2. Part-H case # __ __ - __ __ - __ __ __

3. Child's date of birth: ____/____/____   4. Child's sex: ☐ male ☐ female
                          mo day yr

5. Mother's name:_____
   Last   First   MI
   _____ ( ) ____-____
   Street   City/County   State   Zip   Phone

6. Father's name:_____
   Last   First   MI
   _____ ( ) ____-____
   Street   City/County   State   Zip   Phone

7. Legal guardian/custodian's name:_____
   Last   First   MI
   _____ ( ) ____-____
   Street   City/County   State   Zip   Phone

8. Case manager's name:_____
   Last   First   MI

9. Case management agency: _____
   _____ ( ) ____-____
   Street   City/County   State   Zip   Phone

10. School District: _____

SECTION 2 Multidisciplinary Evaluation/Staffing

11. Date of staffing: _____/_____/_____
                      mo   day   yr

12. Child's age at evaluation: _____ _____
                               year   month

13. Corrected gestational age at evaluation: _____ _____
                                             year   month

14. Participants in the multidisciplinary evaluation/staffing (use an asterisk to denote participants who did not attend staffing):

Name   Position   Agency
_____
_____
_____
_____
_____
_____
_____
_____
_____
_____
_____

SECTION 3 IFSP Team Meeting

15. Date of meeting: _____

16. Projected date for six month review: _____

17. IFSP team members (use an asterisk to denote team members not present at IFSP meeting):

Name   Position   Agency
_____
_____
_____
_____
_____
_____

Section 4 Functional Development

Describe the child's present level of functional development in the following areas:

18. Cognitive development:
_____
_____
_____
_____
_____

_____
_____
_____
_____
_____
_____
_____

19. Physical development:
_____
_____
_____
_____
_____
_____
_____
_____
_____
_____
_____

Table 6.1 *continued*

20. Psycho-social development:

_____
_____
_____
_____
_____
_____

21. Speech and language development:

_____
_____
_____
_____
_____
_____
_____

22. Self-help skills development:

_____
_____
_____
_____
_____
_____

Section 5 Family Profile

23. Summarize the family's assessment of their strengths and needs as they relate to the enhancement of the development of the child.

Strengths: _____
_____
_____
_____
_____
_____
_____
_____
_____
_____
_____

Needs: _____
_____
_____
_____
_____
_____
_____
_____
_____
_____

Section 6 Child and Family Outcomes

24. Indicate the major outcomes expected for the child and family. State the criteria, procedures for measurement, and timelines that will be used to determine progress. Complete the status column at the six month review, using the following code: 1 - completed, 2 - in progress, 3 - interrupted, 4 - not started, 5 - unavailable, 6 - refused.

Major Outcomes	Criteria	Procedures for measurement	Timelines	Status

Section 7 Early Intervention Services Needed

Intervention Services	Child	Parent/Family
25. Case management services	☐	☐
26. Early identification, screening, and assessment services	☐	
27. Family training, counseling, and home visits	☐	☐
28. Health services	☐	
29. Medical services (only for diagnostic and evaluation purposes)	☐	

Intervention Services	Child	Parent/Family
30. Occupational therapy	☐	
31. Physical therapy	☐	
32. Psychological services	☐	☐
33. Special instruction	☐	
34. Speech pathology	☐	
35. Audiology	☐	

36. Other services needed but not funded by First Steps: _____
_____
_____

Table 6.1   *continued*

Section 8 Intervention Service Narrative

37. For each intervention service identified above, please complete the following. The status column should be completed only at the six month review period, using the following code: 1 - completed, 2 - in progress, 3 - interrupted, 4 - not started, 5 - unavailable, 6 - refused.

Intervention Service	Initiation Date (MM/DD/YY)	Intensity (specify in 15 minute blocks)	Frequency (# of sessions) (please circle)	Duration	Method	Provider	Status
			week / month				
			week / month				
			week / month				
			week / month				
			week / month				
			week / month				
			week / month				
			week / month				
			week / month				
			week / month				
			week / month				
			week / month				

Section 9 Financial Resources

Identify those resources that may be used to support the early intervention services specified in this plan.

38. Medicaid: ☐ yes ☐ no comments: _____

   If yes: DCN # _____

39. CCS: ☐ yes ☐ no comments: _____

   If yes: DCN # _____

40. SSI: ☐ yes ☐ no comments: _____

   If yes: SS # _____

41. Soc.-Sec. Dis.: ☐ yes ☐ no comments: _____

   If yes: SS # _____

42. DMH: ☐ yes ☐ no comments: _____

   If yes: DMH # _____

43. Private insurance: ☐ yes ☐ no

   company name: _____

   policy number: _____

44. Community resources/other: ☐ yes ☐ no comments: _____

   _____
   _____
   _____
   _____

Section 10 Transition Plan

45. Specify those steps needed to support the transition of children who will be exiting First Steps program.

   _____
   _____
   _____
   _____

Section 11 Comments/Remarks

46. _____
   _____
   _____
   _____
   _____
   _____
   _____
   _____
   _____
   _____
   _____

Source: Section of Special Education, Missouri Department of Elementary and Secondary Education, Jefferson City, MO 65101. Reprinted by permission

Characteristics of the service systems themselves and the delivery of services dictate the need for coordination and collaboration in the provision of consistent and effective services. Educational, social, health, and family services for young children with disabilities and their families are spread across several agencies. Each agency has its unique administrative structure, policy and fiscal resources, eligibility requirements, and service priorities. Thus, in order to minimize or avoid duplication or gaps in service, a system with well-defined, highly integrated, and accessible resources is needed. Collaboration may also reduce the complexity of the bureaucracy the family must face in accessing services. Families can be overwhelmed by the number of professionals with whom they must interact. Contradictory information may be given if communication does not occur among service providers. Single intake agencies, lead agency designations, and transdisciplinary models of intervention reflect collaborative efforts that reduce the burden many families feel in understanding the various service systems designed to meet their needs and in relating to multiple professionals. Interdisciplinary and interagency collaboration brings the required service systems into a combined and coordinated effort that addresses the total needs of the child, family, and, in many instances, the community.

Collaboration Strategies

Professionals sensitive to the complexity of the needs of children and families and the problems they face in pulling together services from a variety of resources have responded by developing models of collaboration among disciplines and among agencies. Recognition of the need for effective interagency collaboration can be found at the state and community levels and in the specificity of this requirement in Part H of PL 99-457.

Collaborative efforts have been encouraged and mandated through legislation and agency regulations. State initiatives tend to utilize interagency councils or coordinating councils composed of representatives of the service systems responsible for providing services. The specific responsibilities of the councils include policy review, identification of service needs, duplication and gaps, and planning efforts. Further collaborative efforts occur through interagency agreements for service provision and funding. State implementation grants and state planning grants under the amendments to PL 94-142 encouraged state level planning and collaborative efforts in developing early intervention service systems. These efforts were further reinforced and the nature and scope of collaboration at the state level were expanded with the passage of PL 99-457. With the advent of these policy mandates and actions at the federal and state levels, the reality of integrated service delivery became the challenge of community human service systems. Examples of collaborative efforts and/or models that have been developed include development of community interagency groups to coordinate the components of the service delivery system; joint use of personnel and facilities; and use of uniform procedures, processes, or activities for delivering services.

ELIZABETH

Elizabeth was born with spina bifida, hydrocephalus, and Arnold-Chiari syndrome. She was transferred to a neonatal intensive care unit at 3 hours of age and remained in the NICU and pediatric intensive care unit (PICU) for 5 months. While in the PICU, a tracheostomy was performed to facilitate breathing. On discharge from the PICU, Beth and her family were enrolled in the hospital's early intervention program and have received weekly home visits by a developmental therapist for the past 6 months. She receives speech, physical, and occupational therapy and monitoring of her medical needs through the birth defects clinic at the hospital. The parents take an active role in coordinating the various therapy sessions. Although Beth's initial hospitalization was covered by family's health insurance, her parents are seeking information concerning additional financial resources to assist in meeting her subsequent therapy needs.

□ □ □

What human service systems (health, education, social) and professionals are required to effectively meet Beth's and her family's needs?

Which discipline or professional would be assigned the role of case manager at the IFSP conference? Why did you select that discipline?

Could Beth's parents assume the role of case manager?

Case Management: A Critical Link

Regardless of administrative efforts at the state and community service system levels, the critical aspect of collaboration is the accessibility of services for young children with special needs and their families. Reduction in the problems families face in pulling together services from a variety of disciplines and across agencies should be an outcome of collaborative efforts as well as of the development of a comprehensive service system. Case management provides the critical linkage between families and service systems. This process may be viewed as "a bridge between people and systems...closing the gap between traditional service systems and the needs and rights of the whole person" (Eriksen, 1981, p. 9). Case management provides the mechanism for linking and coordinating segments of the service delivery system to ensure the most comprehensive, efficient, and effective program for meeting the individual's needs. Recognition of the importance of this process is found in its specific inclusion as one of the requirements of the comprehensive service system and component of the IFSP under the provisions of PL 99-457 for early intervention.

Collaboration as an Attitude

Interagency/interdisciplinary collaboration is more than a set of specific mechanisms or procedures, such as delineation of team or agency membership and roles, case management, and formal or informal agreements. Collaboration reflects an attitude of trust, respect, and mutual dependence, shared communication, group decision-making processes, openness, and mutually beneficial interactions. Such collaboration in early intervention extends beyond service systems to include professional-professional interaction and parent-professional interaction. Effective early intervention requires both the formal structures and attitudes underlying collaboration.

SUMMARY THOUGHTS

Political, social, economic, and technological changes in society as well as recognition of the special needs of young children with disabilities and the value of early intervention set the conditions for increased interest in and the development of early childhood education programs for the handicapped. Legislation played a major role in the development and expansion of programs for infants and young children with disabilities. These programs have given rise to early childhood special education as an identifiable and unique field within special education.

Early childhood special education provides services for an unusually diverse group of children with special needs. The population served in early intervention and early childhood special education programs includes all disabilities, degrees of severity and functioning levels, and ages birth to 5 or 6 years. This cross-categorical field encompasses children with cognitive, physical, and neurological disorders; sensory impairments; severe health or behavior disorders; multiple handicaps; or developmental delays that are not clearly diagnosable. The purpose of providing services is to maximize the child's development and to minimize the impact of the handicapping condition on current and later development, the child's interaction with the environment, and the family unit. A variety of settings, service delivery systems, and program models have been developed. Options for delivering services vary in terms of the primary target of services, when services are initiated, the range of services offered, the primary intervention agent, and the settings and social context of services.

Parent involvement has been a critical element of early childhood special education programs. Parents are active participants in the decision-making, case management, and educational/therapeutic processes. Likewise, the family's goals and the way the family functions are important considerations in the intervention process. Input and collaboration from the range of professional disciplines and agencies serving young children and their families are critical to the provision of effective intervention. Due to the range of needs and the diversity and complexity of service systems, interagency collaborative efforts are required to ensure that needed services are provided consistently and appropriately.

PL 99-457 has established a national policy of access to services for young children with at-risk and handicapping conditions and their families. Nevertheless, early childhood special education is still an emerging field. The challenge to the field of special education is to assure continued growth of quality programs and support of research defining the unresolved questions and issues of best practice.

REFERENCES

Affleck, G., McGrade, B. J., McQueeney, M., & Allen, D. (1982). Promise of relationship-focused early intervention in developmental disabilities. *Journal of Special Education, 16*, 413–430.

Bailey, D. B., Simeonsson, R. J., Winton, P. J., Huntington, G. S., Comfort, M., Isbell, P, O'Donnell, K., & Helm, J. (1986). Family-focused intervention: A functional model for planning, implementing and evaluating individualized family services in early intervention. *Journal of the Division for Early Childhood, 10*(2), 156–171.

Beckman-Bell, P. (1981). Child-related stress in families of handicapped children. *Topics in Early Childhood Special Education, 1*(3), 45–53.

Bloom, B. (1964). *Stability and change in human characteristics.* London: Wiley.

Bricker, D. D. (1986). *Early education of at-risk and handicapped infants, toddlers, and preschool children.* Glenview, IL: Scott, Foresman.

Bromwich, R. (1981). *Working with parents and infants.* Baltimore, MD: University Park Press.

Bronfenbrenner, U. (1974). *A report on longitudinal evaluations of preschool programs. Vol. 2: Is early intervention effective?* Washington, DC: Department of Health, Education, and Welfare.

Bronfenbrenner, U. (1979). *The ecology of human development: Experiments by nature and design.* Cambridge, MA: Harvard University Press.

Castro, G., & Mastropieri, M. A. (1986). The efficacy of early intervention programs: A meta-analysis. *Exceptional Children, 52*(5), 417–424.

Clarke, A., & Clarke, A. (1976). *Early experience: Myth and evidence.* New York: Free Press.

Dunst, C., Trivette, C., & Deal, A. (1988). *Enabling and empowering families: Principles and guidelines for practice.* Cambridge, MA: Brookline Books.

Eriksen, K. (1981). *Human services today.* (2nd ed.). Reston, VA: Reston Publishing Co.

Fewell, R. (1983). Assessing handicapped infants. In S. G. Garwood & R. R. Fewell (Eds.), *Educating handicapped infants: Issues in development and intervention* (pp. 257–297). Rockville, MD: Aspen.

Gallagher, J. J., Beckman, P., & Cross, A. H. (1983). Families of handicapped children: Sources of stress and its amelioration. *Exceptional Children, 50*(1), 10–19.

Garland, C., Woodruff, G., & Buck, D. (1988). *Case management.* Reston, VA: Council for Exceptional Children.

Gray, S., Ramsey, B., & Klaus, R. (1982). *From 3 to 20: The early training project.* Baltimore, MD: University Park Press.

Hobbs, N. (Ed.). (1975). *Issues in the classification of children.* San Francisco: Jossey-Bass.

Jordan, J., Gallagher, J. J., Hutinger, P., & Karnes, M. B. (Eds.). (1988). *Early childhood special education: Birth to three.* Reston, VA: Council for Exceptional Children.

Kirk, S. (1958). *Early education of the mentally retarded.* Urbana: University of Illinois Press.

Lazar, I., & Darlington, R. (Eds.). (1982). Lasting effects of early education: A report from the Consortium for Longitudinal Studies. *Monographs of the Society for Research in Child Development, 47*(2–3, Serial No. 195).

McGonigal, M. J., & Garland, C. W. (1988). The individualized family service plan and the early intervention team: Team and family issues and recommended practice. *Infants and Young Children, 1*(1), 10–21.

National Dissemination Study Group. (1987). *Educational programs that work: A collection of proven exemplary educational programs and practices* (13th ed.). Longmont, CO: Sopris West.

National Early Childhood Technical Assistance System. (1988). *1987–88 directory of selected early childhood programs.* Chapel Hill, NC: Author.

Peterson, N. L. (1987). *Early intervention for handicapped and at-risk children.* Denver: Love.

Schweinhart, L. J., Berrueta-Clement, J. R., Barnett, W. S., Epstein, A. S., & Weikart, D. P. (1985). Effects of the Perry Preschool Program on youths through age 19: A summary. *Topics in Early Childhood Special Education, 5*(2), 26–35.

Simeonsson, R., Huntington, G., Short, R., & Ware, W. (1982). The Carolina record of individual behavior: Characteristics of handicapped infants and children. *Topics in Early Childhood Special Education, 2*(2), 114–136.

Skeels, H. M., & Dye, H. B. (1939). A study of the effects of differential stimulation on mentally retarded children. *Proceedings and Addresses of the American Association on Mental Deficiency, 44,* 114–136.

Smith, B. J. (1988). Early intervention public policy: Past, present, and future. In J. Jordan, J. J. Gallagher, P. L. Hutinger, & M. B. Karnes (Eds.), *Early childhood special education: Birth to three* (pp. 213–228). Reston, VA: Council for Exceptional Children.

Smith, B. J., & Strain, P. S. (1988a). *Does early intervention help?* (ERIC Digest No. 455). Reston, VA: ERIC Clearinghouse on Handicapped and Gifted Children.

Smith, B. J., & Strain, P. S. (1988b). Early childhood special education in the next decade: Implementing and expanding P.L. 99-457. *Topics in Early Childhood Special Education, 8,* 37–47.

Strain, P. S., & Cordisco, L. K. (1983). Child characteristics and outcomes related to mainstreaming. In J. Anderson & T. Black (Eds.), *Issues in preschool mainstreaming* (pp. 45–64). Chapel Hill, NC: TADS Publications.

Turnbull, A., & Turnbull, H. (1986). *Families, professionals and exceptionality: A special partnership.* Columbus, OH: Merrill.

Weigerink, R., Hocutt, A., Posante-Loro, R., & Bristol, M. (1980). Parent involvement in early education programs for handicapped children. *New Directions for Exceptional Children, 1,* 67–86.

Weiner, R., & Koppelman, J. (1987). *From birth to 5: Serving the youngest handicapped children.* Alexandria, VA: Capitol.

Weintraub, F. J., & Ramirez, B. A. (1985). *Progress in the education of the handicapped and analysis of P. L. 98-199: The Education of the Handicapped Amendments of 1983.* Reston, VA: Council for Exceptional Children.

White, B. (1975). *The first three years of life.* Englewood Cliffs, NJ: Prentice-Hall.

Woodruff, G., & McGonigal, M. J. (1988). Early intervention team approaches: The transdisciplinary model. In J. Jordan, J. J. Gallagher, P. L. Hutinger, & M. B. Karnes (Eds.), *Early childhood special education: Birth to three* (pp. 163–181). Reston, VA: Council for Exceptional Children.

ADDITIONAL READINGS

Bailey, D. B., & Wolery, M. (1984). *Teaching infants and preschoolers with handicaps.* Columbus, OH: Merrill.

Deberry, J., Ristau, S., & Galland, H. (1984). Parent involvement programs: Local level status and influences. *Journal of the Division for Early Childhood, 8,* 173–185.

Garwood, S. G., Fewell, R. R., & Neisworth, J. T. (1988). Public Law 94-142: You can get there from here! *Topics in Early Childhood Special Education, 8,* 1–11.

Neismith, J. T., & Bagnato, S. J. (1987). *The young exceptional child: Early development and education.* New York: Macmillan.

Purpose

☐ To increase your understanding of the unique features of the field of early childhood special education

☐ To help you become aware of the professional literature that addresses topics of interest to individuals in early childhood special education

Steps

1. Locate the following professional journals from each of the identified fields:

   Early Childhood Special Education

   > *Topics in Early Childhood Special Education*
   >
   > *Journal of Early Intervention (*formerly *Journal of the Division of Early Childhood)*
   >
   > *Infants and Young Children*

   Special Education

   > *Exceptional Children*
   >
   > *Teaching Exceptional Children*

   Early Childhood Education

   > *Child Development*
   >
   > *Young Children*

2. Review the topics covered in each of the journals during the last 2 years.

3. Select one topic, such as assessment, mainstreaming, parent involvement, identification, definitions of exceptionality, service delivery alternatives, or curriculum, to review across the journals. Review one article on the selected topic from at least one journal in each of the three groups of journals.

Analysis

☐ How often were topics and issues specific to early childhood special education addressed in each journal?

☐ Did the journals offer differing views or perspectives on the topic you selected to review?

☐ What was the perspective of the journals from the field of early childhood special education?

2

Purpose

☐ To help you identify your state's statutes on early childhood special education and early intervention

☐ To familiarize you with the current status of program development in your state

Steps

1. Contact the state education agency to identify the person(s) responsible for early childhood special education and Part H early intervention programs.

2. Interview the identified person(s) to determine the level of activity and current status of the following:

   ☐ State laws affecting early childhood special education

   ☐ State agencies responsible for services for children with at-risk or handicapping conditions

   ☐ Eligibility criteria

   ☐ Number of programs in the state and their location

3. Ask where you may obtain a copy or borrow information concerning the official state plan for special education and state education regulations and guidelines for early childhood special education programs.

4. Review the information gathered through the reading in (3) and the interviews in (2) to determine the status of program development in your state.

Analysis

☐ What impact has the passage of PL 99-457 had on state legislation and changes in the provision of services in your state?

☐ Who is eligible for early childhood special education and early intervention services in your state?

☐ What early intervention services for children with handicaps can be delivered as part of the state plan for special education and the comprehensive service plan developed through PL 99-457 Part H activities?

☐ How are services organized and implemented?

☐ What changes do you foresee in the development and/or expansion of programs? What changes would you like to see?

3

Purpose

☐ To familiarize you with early childhood special education programs

☐ To help you identify characteristics of early childhood special education programs

Steps

1. Arrange to observe an early childhood special education program for preschoolers or an early intervention program for infants and toddlers in your community.

2. Use the information in Table 6.4 as a guide for your observation. Record your observations.

3. Interview the director of the program to determine the range of at-risk and handicapping conditions of the children served and the program model and to discuss your observation.

Analysis

☐ Review your observation notes. What additional information did you gain from the interview with the director?

☐ Describe the specific configuration of the program based on your observations and interview.

☐ What would you identify as key characteristics of this program?

4

Purpose

☐ To familiarize you with the IFSP process

☐ To give you an opportunity to interact with parents and professionals to gain their perceptions of the IFSP process

Steps

1. Interview a parent and a professional who have participated in the IFSP process. Determine their perceptions of the process and of what occurred.

     or

2. If appropriate, observe an IFSP conference.

3. Read McGonigal and Garland (1988).

4. Develop a set of guidelines for developing an IFSP that reflects the major elements of family-focused intervention (partnership, family determined needs and priorities, validation of the parenting role, and respect for the autonomy of the parents).

Analysis

☐ The content requirements and underlying assumptions of the process for developing an IFSP have been specified in the legislation. Nevertheless, guidelines for the process are continuing to emerge. Articles like the one by McGonigal and Garland are offering practitioners a beginning point for initiating the process.

☐ Review your observation notes of the IFSP conference or the perceptions of parents and professionals to determine the extent to which they reflect the major elements of family-focused intervention in the development of the IFSP.

7

Parental Involvement

Richard L. Simpson
University of Kansas

Debra Whorton Kamps
Juniper Gardens Children's Project — Kansas City, Kansas

The family is still the most basic institution in our culture and the primary arena in which a child learns to interact with his or her environment. In spite of the rapidly changing composition of families, including increasing numbers of single-parent homes, most children obtain their initial experiences and training through interactions with their parents and siblings. The crucial role of the family, and the parents in particular, applies to all children, both exceptional and nonexceptional. Parents have a primary influence on their children's lives regardless of purported normality or abnormality. Yet although the same basic principles of human and family interaction operate independently of individual differences, an exceptionality can change the ecology of the family and the interactions that take place within it. Because of the significant influence parents have on children and the potential impact of an exceptionality on the parents and the family structure, professionals are becoming increasingly aware of the necessity of involving parents in programming efforts.

Parents and families of exceptional children are also becoming much more involved in their children's educational activities. They now have a strong voice in determining the direction of their offsprings' education and training. This increased level of involvement has resulted in part from professionals acknowledging the importance of parental participation and cooperation. In greater part, however, the current position and role of parents and families have been a consequence of legal, legislative, and political maneuvers. Despite the obvious role parents and families play in the development of their offspring, until recently, limited historical precedent and support existed for involving parents in educational processes affecting their children. Parents were widely denied legitimate involvement in the various decisions associated with habilitation and education of their children. In addition, parents of exceptional children were not effectively trained by the professional community to work with their own children in the home environment. Rather than being considered as colleagues with valued input in the educational planning process, parents were commonly perceived as unqualified for or incapable of applying procedures at home to facilitate the educational, social, or physical development of their children. Even more inequitably, parents were sometimes viewed as the cause of a child's problems and thus in need of intervention themselves.

CHANGES IN PARENTAL INVOLVEMENT

As a result of this legacy, parents were forced to assert their influence by other means, including power groups and legal legislative channels. Through those efforts, they have now been granted significant authority regarding the disposition and education of their handicapped children. Laws have required professionals to accommodate parents and families as a part of the educational team. Interestingly, such involvement has resulted in the discovery by both parents and professionals that home-school cooperative involvement is most frequently associated with maximum pupil progress (Espinosa & Shearer, 1986; Kroth, 1985; Simpson, 1982).

Parents achieved significant gains in two landmark cases—*Pennsylvania Association for Retarded Children* v. *Commonwealth of Pennsylvania*, 334 F. Supp. 279(E.D.Pa., 1971) and *Mills* v. *Board of Education, District of Columbia*, (348 F. Supp. 866(D.D.C.,1972). In the *Pennsylvania* case, suit was brought against the state for failure to provide access to a public education for all retarded children. That lawsuit resulted in a court order for development of educational services for retarded children in the state. The court decreed that these children be educated in a program as similar as possible to that provided nonhandicapped students. In the *Mills* case, parents brought a class action suit against the District of Columbia for failure to provide a publicly supported education for all children. Again, the court ordered that educational opportunity include the handicapped.

In 1975, the Education for All Handicapped Children Act (PL 94-142) was signed into law; it provided for a free and appropriate public education for all handicapped children. It also significantly increased parental authority. This law was an amendment to PL 93-380, the Education of the Handicapped Amendments of 1974, which in turn clarified, expanded, and amended the Elementary and Secondary Education Act of 1965. In 1986, PL 99-457 extended the requirements of PL 94-142 to children ages 3 to 5. The four basic components of enactment—assessment safeguards, due process, guarantee of placement in the least restrictive environment, and an individualized education plan—each provide for parental input and the opportunity for parents and legal custodians to serve as advocates for their own children.

As a result, parental involvement has undergone significant change during the past few years, and parent participation and influence will continue to characterize the services extended to exceptional pupils. Schools and agencies are also increasingly recognizing the individuality of parents and families and thus the need for a variety of services and program options. The majority of these parent-related programs fall within one of five major areas: opportunities for parents and professionals to exchange information; training programs designed to make parents better advocates, consumers, and participants in the educational process; training programs to instruct parents in procedures for managing and tutoring their own children at home; parent counseling, therapy, and consultation services; and parent-coordinated service programs. Table 7.1 presents specific examples of parent and family services and programs within each of these major categories. These elements will be discussed later in the chapter. Each of the elements shown in Table 7.1 is considered necessary to meet the varied needs of parents and families of exceptional children and youth, even though all families may not need all services.

BASIC PROFESSIONAL VOCABULARY

The following terms are defined to familiarize readers with some of the terminology commonly used in parental involvement literature and discussions. These terms are used in other contexts and settings as well, so their understanding has broad application.

Active listening is a technique in which an individual conveys understanding of and interest in what a person is saying through expressions, gestures, reflecting or reiterating statements, and similar means.

Advisory board is a group of knowledgeable individuals, including parents and consumers, who serve as advisers in developing and reviewing services offered by a program. The individuals are typically not employees of the program.

Advocacy refers to parents, family members, or other interested parties representing or acting in support of an exceptional child or youth.

Community service program is one that provides a variety of offerings, including emergency programs, community consultation and education, and counseling and therapy, throughout the locality.

Counseling/therapy is a structured relationship or process through which an individual is helped to feel and behave in a more satisfying way, gain a better understanding of himself or herself, and take positive steps toward dealing with the environment. A counselor or therapist directs this process.

Table 7.1   Parental Involvement and Service Program Components

Major Parent and Family Programs and Services	Examples of Programs and Services Within Each Major Category
Programs and opportunities for parents and professionals to exchange information	Initial conference, parents provided program information, interpretation of diagnostic testing, IEP conference, progress reporting conference, written, phone, and other informal reports of progress
Training programs for parent advocacy	Information on community and school resources; workshops on parent rights and responsibilities, especially under the Education for All Handicapped Childrens Act; training on participation in IEP, progress report, and other conferences; assertiveness training workshops; advocacy training
Training program to instruct parents in procedures for managing and tutoring their own children at home	Training programs on behavior modification, tutoring training, procedures for implementing specific educational/training programs
Parent/family counseling, therapy, and consultation services	Group and individual therapy programs, crisis intervention services, consultation for parents and families experiencing specific problems, conflict resolution activities
Parent coordinated service programs	Parent advisory groups, parent classroom volunteers, parent-to-parent groups

Denial is a defense mechanism operating unconsciously to resolve emotional conflict and anxiety by not recognizing thoughts, feelings, needs, or external reality factors that are consciously unacceptable.

Family dynamics refers to the structures, interactions, patterns, and responses of individuals within a family unit. With a handicapped child, family dynamics may include overcompensation or rejection by some or all members, for example.

Guilt involves feelings of being responsible or at fault for an event or circumstance. Some parents of handicapped children, for instance, feel they are to blame for their child's handicapping condition.

Parent-to-parent group is a program designed to offer parents of handicapped children the opportunity to discuss their feelings about their children. This sharing of similar concerns can be highly beneficial.

Value systems are the underlying motives, goals, and expectations that influence others' (parents' and teachers') actions and philosophy.

PARENTAL NEEDS AND CONCERNS

With enactment of Public Law 94-142, parents were afforded participation rights in their exceptional children's education that public schools never before had to allow. Thus, parents were permitted to be involved in the evaluation and placement process, have access to school records on their children, challenge educational recommendations and procedures prescribed for their children, and participate in planning their children's IEPs. The foundation for this enactment was the recognition that parents and families were necessary associates of professionals who were planning and working on behalf of exceptional children and youth and that parents needed legislative support to allow them to exercise their advocacy role. Thus, PL 94-142 formalized parents' role as contributors and partners in the educational process and endorsed their right to monitor school and agency compliance with legal and legislative mandates.

Professionals' awareness of and compliance with legislative enactments are an important part of facilitating productive parent/family relationships.[1] Development of effective parent-educator programs and rapport also requires educators' awareness of parent and family needs. Although needs vary from individual to individual and family to family, professionals can anticipate several common needs of parents and families of exceptional children and youth, including appropriate educational, vocational, and other direct services for exceptional children and youth; opportunities to communicate with professionals; awareness of exceptional children's family impact; participation, advocacy, and home-setting program application training; and parent and family support programs.

---

[1]For additional information on legislative enactments relating to parents and families, see Turnbull and Turnbull (1978).

Appropriate Direct Services

The need for appropriate direct services (such as school programs and therapy services) is the most basic need of parents and families of exceptional children and adolescents. Although the importance of other parent and family needs should not be underestimated, in most cases these issues will be overshadowed by requests for appropriate programs and services for exceptional family members. That most parent organizations and advocacy groups were originally formed to promote educational and treatment programs for children underscores the significance of this need.

The mother of an elementary-school-age child with mental retardation indicated that on moving to a new community she and the other members of her family were consumed with identifying a school and other appropriate services for her handicapped daughter. She further revealed that only after enrolling her child in a suitable school program and identifying acceptable after-school care were she and other family members able to turn their full attention to other matters.

Opportunities to Communicate with Professionals

Nearly all parents and families of exceptional children and youth want information about their child's exceptionality, including characteristics, causes, educational and intervention options, and prognosis. The most desirable means of disseminating such information is through face-to-face contact; thus, educators must not rely exclusively on telephone and mail communication. Educators and other professionals must recognize parents' and family members' need to discuss their children's educational diagnosis and educational and treatment options. Thus, discussions of children's strengths and weaknesses are important to most parents and families, as are program procedures and specific intervention strategies.

In addition to initial information, most parents and family members want to exchange information with professionals on an ongoing basis. Thus, regularly scheduled progress meetings and reports and opportunities to discuss significant issues are important to nearly all parents and families.

Awareness of Exceptional Children's Family Impact

For parents and families, adjusting to and accommodating a child with handicaps involve a variety of emotional responses and issues. When parents first learn that their child has a handicap, they are vulnerable to a number of strong emotions and also may lack a frame of reference for functioning as parents. Although few individuals are trained to be parents, most have as models their own mothers and fathers, allowing some preconceived notions of the parenting process. Unfortunately, this frame of reference is usually lacking for parents of handicapped children. They understandably may feel unqualified and overwhelmed with that role. Issues such as "What should we do differently with this child?" and "How can I be a good parent to a child like this?" are often raised. In addition, questions such as

"Why did this happen to us?" "How will we explain it to friends and relatives?" and "Will this destroy our marriage and family?" are common.

Helping parents to understand their emotional experiences and to arrive at answers to their questions is not easy, but the process can be facilitated by providing them a forum in which to discuss these issues and by offering appropriate reassurance and information. Such efforts can be extremely helpful to families as they attempt to accommodate a handicapped child and can also provide for greater understanding of responses such as shock, refusal, guilt, anger, disbelief, sorrow, inadequacy, envy, bitterness, and rejection. That some researchers have described parents' reactions to having a handicapped child to parallel reactions to death and dying underscores the importance of assisting parents and family members.

Parents and family members must also be made aware that all elements of a family are interconnected and that events affecting one family member influence others. For example, cancellation of a family's swimming club membership in order to save money for a handicapped child's therapy needs, immoderate child-care demands on siblings of handicapped children that restrict their participation in social activities, and implementation of a behavior management program that negatively affects others (cancellation of a family vacation as a consequence of a handicapped child's failure to reach a goal) all influence entire families. In order to control for problems arising from such circumstances, professionals must assist families with an exceptional child or youth in considering and accommodating each family member, not just the exceptional child.

Participation, Advocacy, and Home-Setting Program Application Training

Parents have been granted significant power to participate in educational decisions and programs for their exceptional children. Unfortunately, few training opportunities are provided to assist them in this role. Thus, parents are often expected to participate in conferences, assist in developing and implementing their child's IEP, extend programs into home and community environments, and generally advocate for their child—all without training. One parent, for instance, noted that when she attended her son's initial IEP meeting she was the only one who was not provided a folder of information and the only person who was unfamiliar with the IEP process. Nonetheless, she was told that she was "an equal partner" in developing the IEP and that her participation was "mandatory." Another set of parents reported that they were asked to assist by applying a home-tutoring program, but they were given virtually no direction in how to do so.

If parents and families are to function at a level commensurate with their assigned rights, they must have appropriate training. Only when parents' need for information in this area is met can they be expected to fully participate in parent-school activities and maximally contribute to their children's development.

Training in this regard also includes assisting parents in learning how to advocate for their children. As noted earlier, parents not only have a legal advocacy right but naturally function in this capacity. In the case of parents and families of exceptional children and youth, advocacy means that they assign their children's interests priority status. Providing parents direction in how to advocate for their children not only satisfies a basic parent and family need but usually enhances parent-school rapport.

Parent and Family Support Programs

The impact an exceptional child or adolescent has on a family is such that some members may want and need support programs and opportunities. A few parents and family members may require in-depth counseling and therapy. Most, however, simply need opportunities to join parent and family support and advocacy groups as well as to interact informally with other families of exceptional children.

RESPONDING TO PARENT AND FAMILY NEEDS THROUGH INDIVIDUALIZATION

Educators and other professionals who work with exceptional children and youth must recognize that their parents and families are unique in terms of interests, time, resources, and motivation. Thus, professionals must not make the error of assuming that all parents and families have the same needs or that their needs can be met in the same way. For example, parents and families do not have the same professional com-

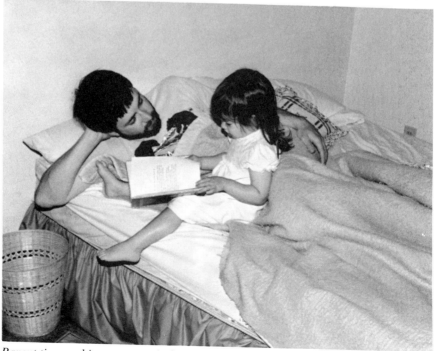

Parent time and interest are vital to child motivation.

munication needs, family impact awareness needs, and family support needs. Some parents and families may in fact reveal an absence of need in certain areas. Similarly, the most effective means for satisfying needs varies from family to family and across time. Thus, professionals must apply individualized parent and family strategies.

Recognition and planning for individual needs require that parents and families be given a range of involvement options. Specifically, parents and families should be encouraged to select a level of involvement that most adequately meets their needs. For some parents and for certain needs, making parents aware of options and procedures may be adequate. Other parents and families may need and want training in carrying out a home management or home tutoring program.

It is important for educators to recognize that levels of involvement are not hierarchical—that is, more involvement is not necessarily better for a particular family. A family's involvement level may also vary over time and differ for various needs. For example, a family going through a divorce or financial exigency may experience different needs and require different levels of involvement than were the case before the crisis.

Identification of parents' and families' needs and appropriate involvement levels is not based on a precise formula. Rather, parent and family preferences and professionals' perception of parent and family needs are used to make such decisions. Thus, educators must consider their perception of parents' and families' needs along with parents' reports and demonstrations of need. Additional considerations include children's age and type of exceptionality (including severity); family makeup and characteristics (such as socioeconomic and cultural factors); community, school, financial, and human resources available to a family; level of family communication and cohesiveness; and family problems related to a child's exceptionality (for example, restriction of family social options because of the severity of a child's handicap). Awareness and sensitivity to parent and family needs are prerequisites to the provision of appropriate services. Such measures are also basic to the establishing and maintaining of rapport and cooperative relationships between educators and families.

METHODS OF BUILDING EFFECTIVE RELATIONSHIPS WITH PARENTS

The numerous and significant needs of parents and families of exceptional children necessitate that professionals develop and demonstrate basic aptitudes and competencies. These elements enable the establishment and maintenance of the relationships necessary for family intervention and conferencing. Included among these basic aptitudes and competencies are use of active listening skills, ability to establish initial trust and rapport, sensitivity to individual value systems, and awareness of family dynamics associated with an exceptionality.

Use of Active Listening Skills

The ability to effectively listen and to communicate this attention to another person is perhaps the most vital attribute of successful conferencing and the primary means for generating information regarding parents' needs. According to Benjamin (1969), the ability to create an acceptable listening environment and to accurately understand parents is so basic a requisite that other conferencing components and procedures are almost totally contingent on this single skill.

Listening is not a passive process. It involves the professional's full attention to manifest verbal messages as well as to the many nonverbal messages and emotions conveyed by body language, pauses, and tone of voice. Listening as a skill is easy to overlook because of its elementary nature, but it is indispensable to any successful conferencing program (Ivey, Ivey, & Simek-Downing, 1987).

Kroth (1985) described the active listener as "one who is actively involved in helping another person identify and clarify his problems, his beliefs, and his value system....Verbally, he/she will reflect back to the parent the feelings he/she hears expressed and may try to reverbalize important and complex statements with 'I hear you saying'...to test his/her perceptions" (p. 38). Kroth also discussed some deterrents to being an effective listener, including strong feelings, fatigue, the use of emotionally laden words, and notetaking.

> Activity 1, page 191, is designed to expand your listening skills. You are asked to use active listening techniques with another person and to observe how people communicate nonverbally.

Ability to Establish Initial Trust and Rapport

The ability to establish and maintain a satisfactory interpersonal relationship is among the most important of all conferencing skills. It lays the groundwork for future cooperation. Research has clearly documented the efficacy of initial rapport-building techniques (Duncan & Fitzgerald, 1969). Without a positive relationship as a base, the professional will not be in an advantageous position to apply his or her specific conferencing and problem-solving techniques. In addition to the professional's knowledge and skill, he or she must "set the stage" for rapport to develop with the parent. This can be done in varying ways, but the essential ingredients include good listening and rapport-building skills. Family conferencing programs appear to be most successful when parents are assured that they are a legitimate and valued resource and that they are working in concert with the professionals in their child's behalf.

Sensitivity to Individual Value Systems

According to Kroth and Simpson (1977), "The importance of assessing your own values or attempting to understand another's values is that ultimately you tend to act on those values you cherish the most" (p. 8). If professionals are to effectively serve children and parents, many of whom come from cultures, backgrounds, and experiences different from their own, they must be able to understand their own value systems and those of the people with whom they interact.

Conflict resolution, information sharing, cooperative planning, and virtually any of the other activities undertaken in parent conferencing are effective only to the extent that parents and professionals understand and respect each other's positions and values. Frequently, conflicts between parents and professionals arise because they fail to understand one another's values and the significance of particular goals and expectations. Rutherford and Edgar (1979) suggested that "when a specific school problem already exists, a misunderstanding between parents and teachers of each other's motives or actions causes the additional problem of interpersonal conflict" (p. 40). The lack of value sensitivity can both increase the probability of conflicts and reduce the potential effectiveness of intervention and conferencing measures.

In one school a teacher asked the parents of an 8-year-old boy to help establish a program aimed at decreasing their child's hyperactivity. But the parents interpreted the target behavior as a reflection of their child's inquisitiveness. Consequently, the parents were unwilling to approve such a program. Not until further efforts led to an understanding of the other's values was a solution negotiated.

> Activity 2, page 191, requires that you complete a self-assessment teacher value form in order to better understand your own values.

Awareness of Family Dynamics Associated with an Exceptionality

The birth or identification of a handicapped child will most likely influence both the parents and the family structure. A variety of difficult questions are bound to arise ("Why did this happen to us?" "How are we going to explain this?"). A number of stages and responses can be anticipated, including shock, mourning, denial, blame, guilt, hostility, and depression. For professionals to effectively work with parents, they must first recognize and gain information about specific impacts of an exceptional child on the family structure.

CONFERENCERS' ACTIVITIES NEEDED FOR EFFECTIVE INVOLVEMENT

In addition to basic conferencing aptitudes and competencies, professionals must be able to employ specific communication and problem-solving strategies or direct parents to agencies that can provide appropriate services (such as respite care and counseling). These strategies and procedures are designed to address parents' and family members' individual needs. As illustrated in Table 7.1, this may be accomplished through skillful attention to the following areas: information exchange; parent advocacy and participation training; training programs to enable parents to work with their own children; counseling, therapy, and consultation; and parent-coordinated programs.

Information Exchange

The effective professional must be able to clearly provide information required by parents and families and to solicit information about the child and family. This informational exchange serves not only to allow sharing of significant facts but also to offer a forum for more informal discussions. The opportunities for parents and families to discuss their feelings and attitudes about having an exceptional child are often as beneficial as the exchange of factual information and data.

Parents and family members should receive assessment and diagnostic data and information on the procedure used for evaluating the child's progress, along with an opportunity to discuss this information and ask questions. If parents have received an interpretation following an evaluation of their child, they probably will still welcome a review of that information after having had an opportunity to reflect on it. Discussion of the educational program prescribed for the child is another opportunity to specify the educational philosophy and approach of the teacher and staff, academic and social remediation programs scheduled for use, auxiliary services to be provided, and parent/family programs available. Finally, parents and families should be apprised of problem-solving alternatives and other resources available to them through the school or community. In all of these exchanges, the atmosphere should readily allow parents to ask questions or bring up problems they have.

Information solicited from parents typically includes their perceptions of the child's need for special class placement or program modifications and whether discrepancies exist between the parents' and professionals' assessment of the problem. Other information sought pertains to the child's developmental history (if not already available); a description of the child's personality, including strengths and weakness, likes and dislikes; school history, including relationships that have historically existed between the parents and school personnel; the parents' expectations for their child and their expectations for the teacher; and social information about the home and family.

> Activity 3, page 192, is a group exercise that allows you to role play an information exchange like that discussed here, incorporating as many of the suggestions as possible. Earlier topics, such as active listening, should also be remembered and utilized.

Parent Advocacy and Participation Training

In addition to the many responsibilities of normal parenting, parents of handicapped children have an additional role to play as advocates for their children. The role of advocate is a demanding one in that it requires a wide breadth of knowledge in several areas: the handicapping condition itself, types of services to best provide for the child's needs (medical, educational, community), where to find those services, and, perhaps most importantly, where to go for help in finding or receiving those services. At a minimum this requires a knowledge of the legal rights of handicapped students and their families.

Rights regarding special education services are written into federal and state regulations. These rights are summarized in the following key terms:

Advocacy—Parents are entitled to have someone represent them at every stage of the IEP. That person may be an attorney, friend, or spokesperson.

Confidentiality of information—With the exception of certain individuals (for example, school officials and teachers with a need to see certain records), no one may see the child's records unless parents give written permission.

Consent—Parents must give written consent before special tests are conducted and before their child is placed in or removed from a special education program.

Evaluation—Parents have a right to a full evaluation of the child's functioning level. If parents disagree with the school's evaluation, they have a right to an independent evaluation. Under certain circumstances, the school may be required to pay for the independent evaluation.

Hearing—If at any point along the way parents do not agree with the way the school is programming for their child, they have the right to request a hearing. This means that they may seek a formal review if they cannot reach an agreement with the school concerning the identification, evaluation, placement, or educational program for the child.

IEP—Parents have a right to participate in the planning of their child's IEP.

Least restrictive environment—Parents have the right to have their child educated with nonhandicapped children to the maximum extent appropriate.

Notice—Before the child is tested or placed in a special education program, parents have a right to be notified of what the school plans to do.

Records—Parents have the right to know what records are kept on their child and a right to see them.

Fortunately, most school districts now incorporate parent rights information into their parent handbooks or dissemination mechanisms. Additional information concerning rights and legal resources is also available from state advocacy and protective services offices and from many parent centers.

Beyond the basic knowledge of legal rights is the need for support in ensuring that these rights are safeguarded and appropriate services are in place. Parents and professionals have made many advances in this area. Currently there exist national advocacy organizations for many handicapping conditions. As previously mentioned, these organizations have been instrumental in initial legislation mandating free, appropriate public education for handicapped children. In addition, advocacy groups continue to impact potential legislation. Examples of national advocacy groups (many with state and local chapters) include:

The Association for Retarded Citizens
The Association for Children with Learning Disabilities
United Federation of the Blind
Epilepsy Foundation of America
Autism Society of America

Parent advocacy services, either singly or at the state and national level, provide a mechanism for ensuring quality programs and support to parents in fulfilling the demands of parenting children with handicapping conditions. With regard to helping parents and families meet their needs in this important area, professionals must be able to direct parents to specific agencies and services and train parents and family members to be more effective consumers of social and educational services, advocates for their children, and participants in educational meetings and activities.

Training Programs to Enable Parents to Work with Their Own Children

Research has confirmed that parents can be effectively trained to perform educational services with their own children (Berkowitz & Graziano, 1972; O'Dell, 1974; Patterson, Chamberlain, & Reid, 1982). Both as agents of behavioral control and as academic tutors, parents have proven to be a valuable resource and a means of extending professional intervention and academic services beyond the classroom environment. Although some parents are unmotivated or inappropriate for this role, many others are highly effective. Training parents to serve in this capacity extends problem-solving efforts into noneducational environments and channels the motivations of parents for involvement and participation.

Under the direction of professionals, parents and family members can provide extensive individualized attention to their child through tutoring programs. Utilizing parents as academic tutors involves them in their child's program and communicates parental concern to the child as well. It allows for positive, structured interactions among the parent, family, and child and provides a mechanism for bridging the gap between home and school environments.

Figure 7.1 is an example of one parent tutoring program, in which the mother of a learning disabled student tutored her child on daily reading assignments. As illustrated, the child's classroom reading performance significantly improved as a function of the parent involvement (Sasso, Hughes, Critchlow, Falcon, & Delquadri, 1980).

Parents have also been trained to use behavior management procedures with their own children in their natural environment. This approach serves to extend the therapeutic influence of professionals beyond the school. In noting the advantages of training parents to use behavior modification procedures, O'Dell (1974) stated

Figure 7.1   Oral Reading Correct/Error Rate with the Parent as Tutor, Using a Daily 10-minute Correction Precedure

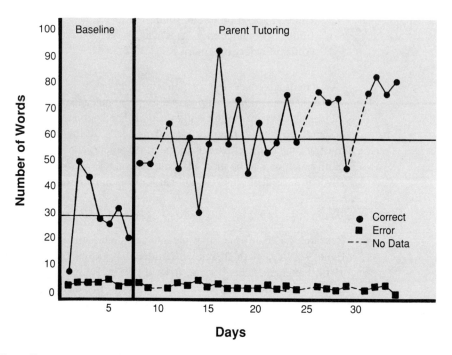

Source: From *The effects of home tutoring procedures on the oral reading rates of learning disabled children,* by G. Sasso, V. Hughs, W. Chritchlow, M. Falcon, and J. Delquadri (1980), Unpublished manuscript, University of Kansas.

that (a) the procedures can be disseminated to individuals lacking knowledge in traditional therapeutic approaches; (b) groups of parents can be trained simultaneously in how to use the system; (c) time requirements for training individuals are relatively brief; (d) the behavioral model allows for more treatment impact than one-to-one treatment approaches do; (e) the approach does not assume pathology (either on the part of the child or parents) as the basis for problem behavior; (f) many child-related problems can be dealt with via a behavioral approach; and (g) the model allows for intervention in the natural environment by individuals who routinely experience the problem.

Use of a daily report card system resulted in significant behavioral and academic improvements by one severely handicapped adolescent. The youth was provided a daily report, which he was required to submit to his parents. The parents, in turn, differentially reinforced their son for his performance. This program, as is the case with many behavior programs in which parents are involved, allowed for coordinated parent-school involvement and ongoing communication. The daily report used in this program is shown in Table 7.2.

Counseling, Therapy, and Consultation

As noted earlier, the vast majority of parents' need for services can be met by educational personnel. Nonetheless, resources must be available to the small percentage that require in-depth attention. For those people, the educator's primary role is to put them in contact with other professionals specifically trained to serve them. Although educational personnel should realize their strengths and capabilities, they must also recognize that some problem areas are outside their expertise.

> Activity 4, page 192, is designed to familiarize you with counseling resources available to parents and families in the community.

Parent-Coordinated Programs

Some parents whose own basic needs and those of their children have been met are able to, and interested in, helping the larger community of handicapped children and their families. They may serve on advisory boards, in community service programs, in parent-to-parent groups, and as volunteers in special classrooms.

The importance of this role is highlighted by noting again that virtually all major changes in policies and services for handicapped children have been effected through the work of parent groups. With the cooperation of professionals, certain parents can be channeled to work collectively at local, state, and national levels to secure more and better services for all handicapped children. Such opportunities

Table 7.2   Example of a Daily Report Card Using Behavior Modification with Parent Involvement

	Daily Report Card				
	Poor		Fair		Excellent
	1	2	3	4	5
Behavior score				4	
Academic work				4	
Compliance					5
Self-control					5
Social interaction					5

Total: 23
Comments: Excellent day
Date: 3-19-88

should be made available to individuals with the time, knowledge, and energy to serve in this way.

SUMMARY THOUGHTS

The importance of parents' and family members' involvement in their handicapped children's education cannot be underestimated. Although federal and state laws now mandate that parents be involved in specific ways, the legislation does not indicate how this is to be done. Parent involvement and educators' roles in it are relatively unexplored areas, but some effective concepts and approaches have emerged in the form of service programs and specific interventions.

Teachers must come to understand parents' needs and concerns. Educators must provide conditions and settings in which parents feel free to express themselves. In so doing, parents gain reassurance and confidence, and educators derive information that helps them better understand and plan for the child's education.

Educators should also acquire a variety of conferencing skills, including active listening, establishing trust and rapport, and understanding their own and the parents' value systems. They must be able to provide specific information and resources and to recognize when parents and families might benefit from the expertise of other professionals to whom they can make referrals.

As specific communication and problem-solving strategies, teachers should be able to train parents in how to be active participants and advocates in their child's educational program, how to most effectively take part in school conferences and meetings, and how to work with their own children toward educational goals. Parents should be familiarized with problem-solving strategies and alternatives and with applicable legislation and school district policies. Importantly, parents should become convinced of the impact they have had and can continue to have on their children's educational futures. This involvement can range from participation in home-school programs using behavior management techniques, to academic tutoring or classroom volunteer work, to serving on advisory boards or community service organizations, to advocating for state and national legislation.

Increased parental input and involvement in planning goals, making decisions, and implementing recommendations appear evident. Indications are that parents will continue as active participants in the development of programs for their children and as primary instigators of needed legislative change. On the local level parental strength will grow through training and dissemination programs as parents become legitimate members of the team that serves their child.

The first and final responsibility for special children rests on the parents' shoulders. But the professional community must support them in this role. Through understanding parent and family needs, establishing a mutually reinforcing working relationship, and individualizing specific interventions, teachers and other professionals can enhance parental involvement as a valuable resource in educating and treating exceptional children.

REFERENCES

Benjamin, A. (1969). *The helping interview.* Boston: Houghton Mifflin.

Berkowitz, B. P., & Graziano, A. M. (1972). Training parents as behavior therapists: A review. *Behavior Research & Therapy, 10,* 297–317.

Duncan, L. W., & Fitzgerald, P. W. (1969). Increasing the parent-child communication through counselor-parent conferences. *Personal & Guidance Journal,* 514–517.

Espinosa, L., & Shearer, M. (1986). Family support in public school programs. In R. Fewell & P. Vadasy (Eds.), *Families of handicapped children* (pp. 253–277). Austin, TX: Pro-Ed.

Ivey, A., Ivey, M., & Simek-Downing, L. (1987). *Counseling and psychotherapy.* Englewood Cliffs, NJ: Prentice-Hall.

Kroth, R. (1985). *Communicating with parents of exceptional children.* Denver: Love.

Kroth, R., & Simpson, R. (1977). *Parent conferences as a teaching strategy.* Denver: Love.

O'Dell, S. (1974). Training parents in behavior modification: A review. *Psychological Bulletin, 81,* 418–433.

Patterson, G., Chamberlain, P., & Reid, J. (1982). A comparative evaluation of a parent-training program. *Behavior Therapy, 13,* 638–650.

Rutherford, R. B., & Edgar, E. (1979). *Teachers and parents: A guide to interaction and cooperation.* Boston: Allyn & Bacon.

Sasso, G. M., Hughes, V. M., Critchlow, W. I., Falcon, M. J., & Delquadri, J. D. (1980). *The effects of home tutoring procedures on the oral reading rates of learning disabled children.* Unpublished manuscript, Juniper Gardens Children's Project, University of Kansas.

Simpson, R. (1982). *Conferencing parents of exceptional children.* Rockville, MD: Aspen.

Turnbull, H. R., & Turnbull, A. P. (1978). *Free appropriate public education: Law and implementation.* Denver: Love.

ADDITIONAL READINGS

Baruth, L., & Burggraf, M. (1979). *Readings in counseling parents of exceptional children.* Guilford, CT: Special Learning Corp.

Becker, W. C. (1971). *Parents are teachers.* Champaign, IL: Research Press.

Ehly, S., Conoley, J., & Rosenthal, D. (1985). *Working with parents of exceptional children.* St. Louis: Times Mirror/Mosby.

Fine, M. (1988). *The second handbook on parent education.* New York: Academic Press.

Schulz, J. (1987). *Parents and professionals in special education.* Boston: Allyn & Bacon.

Stewart, J. C. (1978). *Counseling parents of exceptional children.* Columbus, OH: Merrill.

Turnbull, R., & Turnbull, A. (1985). *Parents speak out: Then and now.* Columbus, OH: Merrill.

Waggonseller, W., & McDowell, R. (1979). *You and your child: A common sense approach to successful parenting.* Champaign, IL: Research Press.

1

Purpose

☐ To familiarize you with the importance of effective listening in parent conferencing

☐ To provide an opportunity to apply active listening skills under simulated conditions

Steps

1. Divide the group into pairs. One member of each pair is to relate a topic of interest while the other person practices "active listening."
2. Reverse the roles of speaker and listener and repeat (1).
3. Repeat the process but practice "nonlistening." Again, reverse the roles.
4. Later, observe friends, family, or children as they express different moods and emotions. Note how their body posture, voice tone, and expressions serve as communication cues.

Analysis

☐ After the "active listening" exercise has been completed, as a group discuss reactions to the two different listening environments.

☐ After observing the manner in which people express emotion and moods, discuss your observations. Note how this information can be of value to the parent conferencer.

2

Purpose

☐ To increase your awareness of your own values and the significance of values in the parent-educator relationship

Steps

1. Complete the accompanying "Are You a Teacher Who..." form (Kroth & Simpson, 1977). First check items in column A that pertain to you.
2. After covering your column A responses, ask a friend or colleague to rate you (using column B).

Analysis

☐ A month or more later, complete column C or have another person rate you to see if changes have occurred.

☐ Discuss as a group the responses—ratings made of you by others and rating changes that occurred over time. Consider the manner in which your values influence the parent-teacher relationship.

<table>
<tr><td>3</td></tr>
</table>

Purpose

☐ To give you an opportunity to exchange information with parents under simulated conditions

Steps

1. Divide up into groups of three, in which one member of each group takes the role of teacher and describes the program in his or her classroom (curriculum, academic and social remediation procedures in use, ancillary services available, parent and family programs, progress reporting procedures, community resources) to a person assuming the role of parent, who in turn asks questions about the program. The third member provides feedback on the information disseminated.
2. Rotate the roles until each member has assumed all roles.

Analysis

☐ Discuss as a triad the effectiveness with which each member was able to disseminate information.
☐ Bring up additional information that might have been shared during the sessions.

<table>
<tr><td>4</td></tr>
</table>

Purpose

☐ To familiarize you with community resources in your area that offer services to parents and families

Steps

1. As a group, develop a list of resources in your community that offer counseling and therapy services for parents and families. Utilize phone books, newspapers, promotion materials, word-of-mouth information, and other sources.
2. Specify the type of service and other information that parents interested in securing services may require (free, contact persons, address, and so on).

Analysis

☐ Discuss means of suggesting to parents that they, family, or children may require therapy or counseling.
☐ As a group, discuss the effectiveness and reputation of each of the resources suggested.
☐ Discuss situations in which the counseling needs of parents and families may be better served by an outside agency than by school personnel.

Learning Disabilities

Steve Graham
Karen R. Harris
Robert Reid
University of Maryland

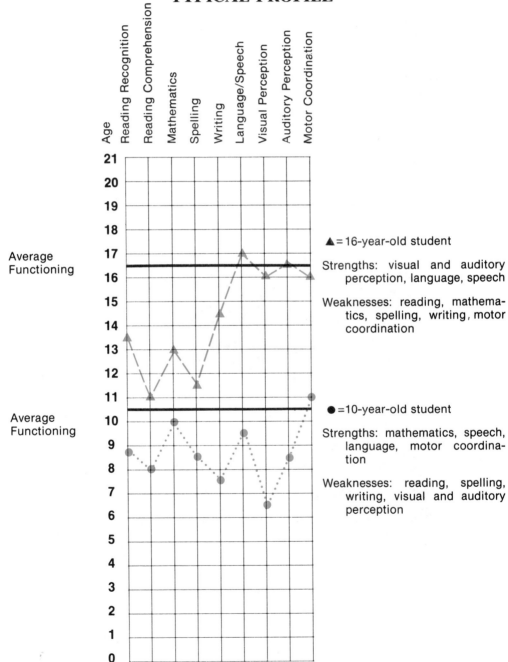

LEARNING DISABILITIES
TYPICAL PROFILE

▲ = 16-year-old student

Strengths: visual and auditory perception, language, speech

Weaknesses: reading, mathematics, spelling, writing, motor coordination

● = 10-year-old student

Strengths: mathematics, speech, language, motor coordination

Weaknesses: reading, spelling, writing, visual and auditory perception

Average Functioning

Average Functioning

Professionals and laypersons have for many years been concerned with the plight of children who evidenced academic and social problems even though they were not necessarily less intelligent than their "normal" counterparts. As early as the beginning of this century, physicians were describing and working with children with average intelligence and good visual acuity who were unable to learn how to read using ordinary instructional methods. During the ensuing years, however, professionals found that many of these children could learn to read using special remedial approaches. Multisensory approaches, such as the Orton-Gillingham and Fernald methods developed during the 1930s and 1940s, that emphasized seeing, hearing, and feeling the letters or words to be learned were particularly useful in helping some of these students learn to read at a level commensurate with their potential.

Because many of these children did not appear to be mentally retarded, emotionally disturbed, physically disabled, environmentally disadvantaged, or sensorially handicapped, they were not eligible for the more traditional special education programs. As a result, parents of children with learning problems sought assistance from a wide variety of professionals, including psychologists, pediatricians, optometrists, speech and language specialists, neurologists, and physical therapists. Not surprisingly, numerous labels were used to describe these children. They were often classified as hyperactive, perceptually handicapped, brain injured, dyslexic, neurologically impaired, and so forth. The overabundance of terminology caused a great deal of confusion among specialists, parents, teachers, and the general public.

THE EMERGENCE OF THE FIELD

Against this backdrop, Samuel Kirk coined the term *learning disabilities* (LD) in a 1963 speech delivered at a conference sponsored by a parent organization. Dr. Kirk's speech had a galvanizing effect: The convention decided to reorganize itself as the Association for Children with Learning Disabilities (ACLD), and the label proposed by Kirk provided a rallying point not only for members of ACLD but for other parents, educators, and legislators as well. Subsequent pressure by these groups, especially parents, at the state and federal levels resulted in the rapid formation of a new field. In 1969, an amendment to the Elementary and Secondary Education Act granted the U.S. Office of Education the authority to establish programs for the learning disabled. During the 1970s and the 1980s, programs for students with learning disabilities became very common in both elementary and secondary schools. In fact, approximately one half of the students presently identified by school systems as handicapped are labeled learning disabled.

In today's schools, most students identified as learning disabled receive the majority of their instruction within the regular classroom environment. Special education services to these students generally involve one or more of the following options. They may participate in a "pull-out" or resource program in which they leave the regular classrooms environment and receive one-to-one or small-group instruction from an educational specialist on basic academic skills, school survival skills, and so forth.

Or special education services may be delivered through a "plug-in" program: The educational specialist provides instructional assistance to students with learning disabilities within the regular classroom. The educational specialist may also provide indirect services to students with learning disabilities by acting as a consultant to the regular classroom teacher. This can include cooperative brainstorming on how to solve a student-related problem or demonstration teaching of a specific procedure that may be particularly promising for a student with learning difficulties.

Because most students with learning disabilities spend the majority of their school day within the regular school environment, considerable attention has recently been focused on how regular educators can accommodate these students. Procedures commonly recommended for promoting accommodation have centered on their academic and social welfare. Recommendations to regular educators for accommodating students with learning disabilities within their classrooms include the use of research-supported practices for teaching academic skills and managing the classroom, systems for individualizing instruction for all students, and techniques for promoting cooperative learning situations involving handicapped and nonhandicapped students.

Although the field of learning disabilities has shown much progress since Samuel Kirk's 1963 speech, this growth has not been without problems. At the field's conception, no precedent existed for program development, and there was a lack of competent professionals, adequate definitional parameters, appropriate conceptualization of intervention processes, and the undergirding of research (Hallahan & Cruickshank, 1973). Many of these problems (particularly issues related to definition and identification) have not yet been resolved. Nonetheless, many important gains have been realized, the most prominent of which is a nationwide commitment to helping those with severe learning difficulties.

Dr. Samuel A. Kirk coined the term "learning disabilities" resulting in the formation of a new field.

CHARACTERISTICS OF CHILDREN AND YOUTH WITH LEARNING DISABILITIES

Definition of Learning Disabilities

Development of the concept of learning disabilities has been heavily influenced by the fields of medicine, psychology, and education. Each of these disciplines, however, describes students with learning disabilities in terms of its own theoretical perspective. As a result, many different definitions have been proposed. Early definitions often stressed neurological factors, whereas more recent definitions have placed greater emphasis on academic constructs. Despite a number of differences, most of the current definitions have six points in common. They define an individual with a learning disability as one who (a) exhibits a significant discrepancy between expected and actual achievement; (b) has difficulty with academic and learning tasks; (c) demonstrates a disorder in one or more of the basic psychological processes; (d) evidences an uneven pattern of growth; (e) has a central nervous system dysfunction; and (f) does not have learning problems that are primarily a result of mental retardation, emotional disturbance, environmental disadvantage, sensory handicaps, or physical disabilities.

The National Advisory Committee Definition

The definition incorporated in PL 94-142 was based on the definition proposed by the National Advisory Committee on Handicapped Children in 1968, which stated that

> specific learning disability means a disorder in one or more of the basic psychological processes involved in understanding or in using language, spoken or written, which may manifest itself in an imperfect ability to listen, think, speak, read, write, spell, or to do mathematical calculations. The term includes such conditions as perceptual handicaps, brain injury, minimal brain dysfunction, dyslexia, and developmental aphasia. The term does not include children who have learning problems which are primarily the result of visual, hearing, or motor handicaps, of mental retardation, of emotional disturbance, or of environmental, cultural, or economic disadvantage.

This definition is significant for two reasons. First, it strongly emphasizes the academic, rather than the neurological, nature of learning disabilities. Second, it stresses the importance of the discrepancy between the student's expected achievement and actual achievement and makes learning disabilities a category of underachievement, albeit underachievement due to disorder in the basic psychological processes.

Nevertheless, this definition has been criticized for four reasons. First, it is both simplistic and ambiguous in stating that a learning disability may manifest itself in an imperfect ability to listen, think, speak, read, write, spell, or do mathematical calculations while not clearly indicating if these processes are impaired, impeded, delayed, or qualitatively different. Second, it does not define the concept of basic psychological processes or the cited disorders.

Third, this definition is exclusive rather than inclusive. It does not include children whose primary problems are a result of mental retardation, emotional disturbance, sensory handicaps, environmental disadvantage, or physical disabilities. This exclusivity is arbitrary and is not based on scientific evidence; it is frequently misinterpreted as indicating that a learning disability cannot occur in conjunction with other handicapping conditions. Nevertheless, research has indicated that children who are deaf or environmentally disadvantaged may exhibit learning problems and that conditions associated with poverty and disadvantage (such as malnutrition and poor health care) may result in learning disabilities (Auxter, 1971; Kappelman, Kaplan, & Ganter, 1969). Our present psychometric procedures, however, are not reliable or valid enough to give clearcut differential diagnosis (Hammill, 1976).

Fourth, and perhaps most seriously, this definition offers relatively few practical guidelines for the identification of individuals with learning disabilities. The guidelines in PL 94-142 indicate that in order to identify an individual as learning disabled, he or she must exhibit a significant discrepancy between expected achievement and actual achievement in one or more areas related to communication skills or mathematical ability. But the prediction of a student's school potential may be subject to considerable error, and the determination of a significant discrepancy between academic achievement and aptitude presents a variety of measurement problems. Furthermore, when a significant discrepancy does exist, determining whether it is due to a learning disability or to other factors can be difficult. Not surprisingly, therefore, overidentification of children as learning disabled is a serious issue facing the field.

The National Joint Committee Definition

In 1981, the National Joint Committee for Learning Disabilities (NJCLD) developed a definition that ameliorated some of the deficiencies of the PL 94-142 definition. The NJCLD definition recognizes the heterogeneity of learning disabled students, recognizes that learning disabilities is a lifelong condition, and states that learning disabilities can occur in the presence of other handicapping conditions. Nevertheless, the NJCLD definition is subject to many of the same criticisms as the PL 94-142 definition; furthermore, it has no legal stature and has not been universally embraced by professionals in the field.

Three major problems make defining learning disabilities a difficult task: (a) because LD as a field is relatively new, there is a sparse data base; (b) the field is multidisciplinary and must include medical, psychological, and educational perspectives; and (c) the theoretical basis for learning disabilities is still developing. The number of students identified as learning disabled has increased dramatically in the past 10 years, perhaps at least partially due to definitional issues. In the 1976-77 school year, 1.79% of the school-age population was identified as learning disabled. By the 1983-84 school year, 4.57% (or 1,811,489 students) of the population between the ages of 3 and 21 was classified as learning disabled. Valid identification of students with learning disabilities is in part dependent on an adequate definition. The eventual development of an adequate definition depends on additional scientific investigation and philosophical inquiry.

A 10-YEAR-OLD WITH LEARNING DISABILITIES

On meeting Sam, many people could not believe he was having difficulty in school. His geniality and streetwise manner suggested a maturity well beyond his 10 years. Strangers were often dazzled by this toothy grin and quick wit.

Despite Sam's verbal resourcefulness and creativity, he lacked even the most rudimentary academic skills. His mastery of math facts, spelling words, or literal information within a written passage was spotty at best. On Monday he might learn a new reading word, but on the following day he would insist he had never seen it.

In the classroom Sam drove his teachers to distraction. He was almost always bewildered by assignments. He frequently asked other students what he was supposed to do and was usually slow at starting a new task or was unable to do it at all. He seemed to be everywhere at once. He couldn't sit still or keep his hands off others. As a result, many of Sam's teachers let him spend a considerable portion of the day playing in the back of the room.

Even though he professed hatred for school, Sam rarely missed a day. He was usually there when the first teachers began to arrive in the morning and was generally one of the last to leave at the end of the day. Before and after school Sam was a teacher's delight. He was courteous, entertaining, and helpful. Once the opening bell rang, however, he often became bossy, stubborn, and irritable.

☐ ☐ ☐

What might have been some of the contributing factors to Sam's academic underachievement?

If you were Sam's teacher, how could you help him stay on task?

Why do you think Sam spent so much time at school?

What kinds of academic and social experiences should Sam receive?

Characteristics of Learning Disabilities

A variety of characteristics have been associated with learning disabilities. The 10 most frequently cited are (a) hyperactivity, (b) perceptual-motor impairments, (c) emotional lability, (d) coordination problems, (e) disorders of attention, (f) impulsivity, (g) disorders of memory and thinking, (h) academic retardation, (i) language deficits, and (j) equivocal neurological signs (Clements, 1966). All of these characteristics, however, have not been substantiated by research, and not all students with learning disabilities exhibit all or even several of these problems. Furthermore, some of these characteristics are associated with other diagnostic classifications—mental retardation, emotional disturbance, and so forth. In essence, students with learning disabilities represent a diversified group who evidence numerous educational and social deficits.

Although some students with learning disabilities have difficulty with only one or two subjects, most of these students have academic problems across scholastic areas. Common reading problems involve difficulties in decoding words and using effective learning strategies to remember information presented in the text. In the early elementary grades, students with learning disabilities are generally only 1 to 2 years behind the norm in reading achievement. By the time they reach junior high school, they may be 3 or more years behind their expected reading level. As students with learning disabilities mature, their reading problems become more severe.

Many students with learning disabilities have severe and persistent writing difficulties as well (Graham, Harris, & Sawyer, 1987). Their written products are inordinately short, poorly organized, and replete with mechanical errors (see Figure 8.1). They are not very knowledgeable about the process of writing and appear to have considerable problems in planning, framing, producing, or revising written text.

Difficulties with mathematics are also very common among students with learning disabilities. They may fail to master basic computation skills such as multiplication or division and experience difficulty in applying the skills they do have

Figure 8.1 Writing Errors

I got afraid when the
lights go out I got afaid
and my mom teld me you
are a babby and I siad
I'm not a babby mom
will why are you afraid of
the lights I Do not know
my Sister and Brother Do not
know want Im talk abought
and Im glad I Do want to
go to School and I want
to my mom is a good mom
and She is afraid of Dog and
Cat the end

in problem-solving situations. Given the difficulties that students with learning disabilities have with basic academic learning skills, it is not surprising that they find content area subjects at the secondary level to be especially problematic.

Students with learning disabilities are also likely candidates for a host of social problems. Although some of these students are socially well adjusted and well liked, many have a tendency to alienate others. They are commonly described as being obstinate, sassy, bossy, stubborn, impulsive, aggressive, and difficult to approach. Their social interactions are likely to be different and less desirable than those of normally achieving children. They are often inept at interpreting the social milieu, are less likely to successfully interpret friendly initiations, and have greater difficulty recognizing and labeling emotions. They frequently generate hostile and competitive statements, and they tend to be less considerate and less able to receive affection. When interacting socially, they have trouble initiating conversations, spend less time looking at others while speaking or listening, and smile less often. Moreover, they usually over-rate their own social status. These social and emotional characteristics may be both the result of and the contributors to the academic problems they experience. Other variables that contribute to learning disabled students' academic and social difficulties include motivational, cognitive, and school-related factors. The relationships among these variables, however, are neither simple nor direct.

Students with learning disabilities are typically anxious, easily frustrated, unwilling to attempt new tasks, and lacking in persistence and effort. This is hardly surprising because they are generally pessimistic about their ability to influence the outcome of a task. They are likely to exhibit an external locus of control, believing that their successes and failures are a result of uncontrollable external factors such as luck. As a result, they may rely on external assistance rather than on their own resources. A lack of motivation or persistence can adversely affect an individual's academic and social competence. Chronic failure can lead to the development of *learned helplessness*—the belief that no matter how hard one tries, failure is inevitable (Licht, 1983). Students who have repeatedly failed educationally and socially may thus be unable to achieve even when success is within their capabilities (Thomas, 1979). Predictably, students with learning disabilities commonly experience low self-esteem and a poor self-concept.

Students with learning disabilities have further been portrayed as exhibiting a variety of information-processing deficits. Visual and auditory perceptual difficulties are more common in learning disabled than in normal children. Substantial evidence indicates that children with learning disabilities have difficulty focusing and maintaining their attention. They often have memory deficits for auditory and visual information and may have difficulty using appropriate and effective strategies for memorization. Both receptive and expressive language problems are common among students with learning disabilities; these difficulties tend to endure over time. Finally, many of these students are impulsive, and they may have trouble gen-

A 16-YEAR-OLD WITH LEARNING DISABILITIES

Greg is 16 years old but is functionally illiterate. Nevertheless, his level of skill development is not an accurate reflection of his cognitive capabilities. Although he cannot read a book like *A Tale of Two Cities,* he is able to comprehend the delicate interaction of the characters and events if he sees the movie of the same title. As a result, Greg spends a great deal of his free time watching television or going to a theater.

Greg plans to drop out of school at the end of the academic year. Although he has had 9 years of special education services, he thinks school has been an empty enterprise that has caused him a great deal of emotional stress. During elementary school, Greg was basically a shy, introspective child. As his academic retardation became more severe, he became the object of ridicule. Once the frustrations of academic and social failure became too much, Greg reacted by striking out at others.

During the school day, Greg spends a lot of time daydreaming and doodling. He often sits in the back of the room, attempting to be as innocuous as possible. He rarely participates actively in class activities and almost always appears to be disorganized and disoriented.

Greg has an older brother, Scott, who is a second-year medical student. His brother never experienced academic difficulties. Greg feels he is as smart as Scott but cannot understand why he does poorly in school.

☐ ☐ ☐

What types of problems will Greg most likely face after he leaves school?

Why has Greg had difficulties in school while his brother did not?

How could someone help Greg participate actively in the classroom?

What could a teacher do to help Greg circumvent his reading problems?

---

erating novel alternatives, obtaining a solution from a given premise, detecting and correcting errors, and critically weighing alternative actions or results.

Activity 1, page 219, helps you understand how children with learning disabilities react to failure in the classroom and with peers.

Academic and social deviance can also be affected by the situational factors a student encounters in school. To illustrate, many handwriting problems appear to be the result of inadequate instruction, not of learning disabilities (Graham & Miller,

1980). Only 1 of every 10 schools requires its teachers to have any kind of handwriting training, and some schools have no formal handwriting program. Furthermore, most teachers feel inadequately prepared to teach handwriting, and they seldom individualize instruction.

BASIC PROFESSIONAL VOCABULARY

Terminology in the area of learning disabilities has been drawn from various disciplines. The most common terms and acronyms follow.

Aphasia is an impairment in the ability to understand or use oral language. It is often associated with an injury or dysfunction of the brain.

Apraxia is an impairment in the ability to perform purposeful motor movements. It is often associated with an abnormality of the central nervous system.

Brain-injured child is a child who before, during, or after birth received an injury or suffered an infection to the brain that impeded normal development.

Council for Learning Disabilities is an organization of professionals who work directly or indirectly with persons with learning disabilities. It was formerly the Division of Children with Learning Disabilities of the Council for Exceptional Children.

Division of Learning Disabilities is a professional organization interested in persons with learning disabilities. It is a division of the Council for Exceptional Children.

Dyslexia is a disorder in which an individual fails to learn to read despite adequate intelligence and proper classroom instruction. It is commonly associated with an injury or dysfunction of the brain.

Emotional lability refers to frequent and unexplainable shifts in a person's mood.

Hyperactivity is a condition involving motor behavior that may be disruptive and unnecessary to the situation at hand.

Impulsivity means making quick and often erroneous responses without considering their consequences.

LD is the acronym for learning disabilities.

Minimal brain dysfunction is a mild neurological abnormality that is accompanied by near-average intelligence and learning problems.

Perseveration refers to difficulty in discontinuing an activity once it has started.

Psychological processes are covert cognitive behaviors that transform and manipulate information.

Soft neurological signs are mild or slight neurological abnormalities that are difficult to detect.

ASSESSING INSTRUCTIONAL NEED

Enactment of Public Law 94-142 gave local school districts a set of procedural policies for identifying, assessing, and providing services to students with learning disabilities. Although variance does exist between school districts, assessment procedures follow a general pattern.

The initial step in providing LD services is to determine who is eligible. A student may become a concern when he or she does not conform to academic or behavioral expectations and is brought to the school's attention through systematic screening or through referral from a teacher, parent, or other interested person.

If the school decides that the student may benefit from special education services, permission to conduct a comprehensive assessment is requested from the parents through a signed letter of consent. If the parents grant permission, a multidisciplinary team evaluates all areas related to the suspected disability. Assessment instruments, administered by trained personnel, must be appropriate, valid, and without cultural or racial bias. The multidisciplinary team must include the student's regular classroom teacher and at least one person qualified to conduct an individual diagnostic evaluation. The evaluation results in a summary document that includes the student's present level of functioning, strengths and weaknesses, and unique learning needs.

Determining the Existence of a Learning Disability

According to federal regulations, the existence of a learning disability is demonstrated by (a) academic underachievement and (b) a severe discrepancy between achievement and intellectual ability in one or more areas related to communication

Individual assessment of instructional needs is appropriate.

skills or mathematical abilities. To further determine the presence of an LD, an evaluation team must observe the student's academic performance in the regular classroom and affirm that the discrepancy is not primarily a result of sensory or motor handicaps, mental retardation, emotional disturbance, or environmental, cultural, or economic disadvantage.

Academic achievement is usually ascertained through standardized tests. Most of these tests provide grade- or age-level scores and are relatively easy to administer. Instruments that provide a measure of the student's present level of functioning and diagnostic information include the Key Math Diagnostic Arithmetic Test—Revised (Connolly, Nachtman, & Pritchett, 1989), the Woodcock Reading Mastery Tests—Revised (Woodcock, 1987), the Woodcock-Johnson Psychoeducational Battery (Woodcock, 1978), and the Kaufman Test of Educational Achievement (Kaufman & Kaufman, 1985).

Intellectual ability is generally determined through administration of an individual, standardized intelligence test. The two most commonly used are the Stanford-Binet (Terman & Merrill, 1973) and the Wechsler Intelligence Scale for Children—Revised (WISC-R) (Wechsler, 1974). Both of these scales rely heavily on verbal skills. The WISC-R, however, has both a performance and a verbal scale.

The federal regulations present several problems, however. First, the guidelines are too vague; they do not clearly state what constitutes a severe discrepancy. Second, determining if the student has received appropriate educational services is extremely difficult; obviously, some children diagnosed as learning disabled are simply educational casualties. Third, labeling a student as learning disabled solely on the basis of scholastic attainment is impractical and unethical. Even though many experts agree that learning disabilities constitutes 3–5% of the population, a much larger percentage could easily be classified as such if professionals were to apply the federal regulations literally. Fourth, the guidelines do not consider social behaviors as relevant indicators of a learning disability.

Instructional Assessment

Once a student is diagnosed as learning disabled, an individualized educational plan delineating annual goals and short-term objectives is developed for the student. The basis on which such a plan is constructed varies from one student to another. Nonetheless, the student's present level of functioning, strengths and weaknesses, and unique learning needs form the foundation for determining educational and related priorities (see Hudson & Graham, 1978). In addition to analyzing the student's performance through formal and informal techniques, the team considers the instructional environment and instructional variables that may inhibit or enhance the student's learning behavior. Chief among these variables are the classroom environment, teachers' attitudes, curricular organization, instructional materials, reinforcement strategies, method of matching student's needs to instruction, and interpersonal relationships with teachers, peers, and others.

After the IEP is operationalized, the student's progress toward the specified annual goals and short-term objectives is evaluated. Without a strong evaluation component, the IEP can become a paper tiger of little practical value. Systematic evaluation enables teachers to ascertain if the IEP is being accomplished and to make adjustments where needed.

Two means for measuring progress on specific objectives are the student's daily work products and the teacher's observations. By noting the time required for a student to complete an instructional task, a teacher can estimate the rate of progress. Accuracy on daily work products indicates the degree of success the student is exhibiting on tasks.

Activity 2, page 219, casts you in the role of an observer and enables you to see the differences and similarities between a child who has learning disabilities and a child who does not.

Observing the number of trials per lesson is another means of assessing a student's progress toward a specific objective. Graphs that indicate the number of trials per lesson often reveal whether the task is appropriately sequenced and presented. A large number of trials per lesson point to the possible need for instructional revision.

Criterion-referenced testing is commonly used to examine a student's performance on a specific behavior. The intermediate steps necessary to complete an objective are delineated, and each step is specified in terms of performance. For example, a criterion-referenced test item might read: When presented a flashcard with the letters "ch," the student will be able to orally produce the "ch" sound.

Another means of reassessing progress toward a specific objective is the use of a data-based system consisting of five essential elements: (a) specification of the objectives in performance terms; (b) collection of baseline data; (c) initiation of instruction; (d) collection of progress data; and (e) appropriate modifications of the IEP. This procedure enables teachers to continually assess the appropriateness of objectives and instruction. *Curriculum-based assessment* (CBA)—the development of such assessment procedures within the context of the local school's curriculum (Mercer, 1987)—allows instruction to be closely tailored to the student's needs because progress is assessed in terms of the student's classroom curriculum. In addition to monitoring progress, CBA can be useful for screening, identification of learning disabilities, and program planning. Nevertheless, as with norm-referenced assessment, issues of reliability and validity must be addressed in the development of CBA procedures.

Evaluation of progress toward annual goals can be determined by examining the data collected on the intermediate short-term objectives. In combination with pre- and poststandardized achievement tests, this informal information indicates the student's rate and amount of educational change.

INTERVENTIONS

Instructional Interventions at the Elementary Level

The primary method used initially to "remediate" a learning disability was the *process approach*. This method assumed that children with learning disabilities suffered from some internal disorder that interfered with their ability to effectively manipulate and utilize sensory information. The process approach also assumed that these children had an inherent disorder in one or more of the basic psychological processes (auditory perception, visual perception, psycholinguistic abilities, and so on). Proponents of this approach supposed that the processes underlying effective academic learning could be specified. Once they were identified, the student could then receive training designed to improve the functioning of the impaired processes. As a result of appropriately applied efforts, academic performance would be enhanced.

Although this approach may have been successful with some children, scientific research failed to validate the general use of process training. Opponents questioned whether tests commonly used to assess psychological processes measured skills that were essential to academic success. Little empirical evidence supported the position that psycholinguistic or perceptual training did in fact improve academic performance (Arter & Jenkins, 1979). Although some teachers still continue to use the process approach when working with students with learning disabilities, its use has been in steady decline, and the procedure may become a historical footnote in the development of the field.

The most frequent school-based interventions used with learning disabled children today involve procedures designed to improve academic performance. Proponents of the *academic method* do not assume that the child is handicapped by internal deficit. They gear instruction toward direct teaching of academic skills. If a child has reading problems, remedial efforts are directed at teaching reading.

Activity 3, page 221, gives you an opportunity to intervene directly to improve a student's spelling vocabulary.

The types of instructional procedures that teachers generally use to teach basic academic skills to students with learning disabilities have been summarized by Graham (1985). He proposed that these remedial techniques could be roughly grouped into three areas. First, teachers can direct and support the actions of students with learning disabilities through the external provisions of the lessons they use and/or design. For example, the teacher may select or construct reading materials that are attractive, well organized, and appropriate. The teacher may also direct the student to set a purpose for reading, consider what the student knows about the assigned passage, make predictions about what the student will read, and/or give an

Selecting attractive reading materials will support students with reading disabilities.

overview of the material prior to reading (Graham & Johnson, 1989). Such teacher-directed provisions are analogous to a heart pacemaker in that the instructional arrangements do some of the work for the student.

Second, teachers can help and encourage students to change existing academic behaviors into more preferred ones. Although some academically related behaviors such as short-term memory appear to be unalterable, personal qualities such as the student's learning strategies, skills, attitudes, and accumulated knowledge can be changed to exert a positive influence on school performance (Graham, 1985). For students with reading problems, for instance, instruction may be aimed at improving their existing skills in decoding words, and they may be taught how to independently use strategies for summarizing what has been read and/or asking and answering questions about important information in the text (Graham & Johnson, 1989). In the case of writing, students may be taught to independently use strategies for generating, framing, planning, and/or revising what they compose (Graham & Harris, 1988). Strategy training represents one of the more promising procedures for affecting the academic performance of students with learning disabilities (Harris, 1982).

In a similar vein, teachers may also be able to modify, at least in part, negative motivational characteristics that many students with learning disabilities exhibit. This can be accomplished by increasing students' personal control over their environment, providing training aimed directly at modifying students' attributions, or involving students in the process of selecting and accomplishing academic and behavioral goals.

Third, peers can be taught to help students with learning disabilities (Graham, 1985). Teachers can employ cooperative learning arrangements designed to promote interaction between students with learning disabilities and academically achieving students. With academic tasks that involve cooperative goal structures, peers can affect the performance of students with learning disabilities by encouraging them to do their best and by offering assistance.

Instructional Interventions at the Secondary Level

Most of the children identified as learning disabled during elementary school enter secondary schools still hampered by their disability. Although the types of instructional options commonly used at the secondary level vary considerably, at least three instructional orientations have been noted: programs with a remedial emphasis, programs with a compensatory emphasis, and programs built around an alternative curriculum (Deshler, 1978).

Programs with a remedial emphasis are basically extensions of the academic methods used with elementary-age students. Because many disabled adolescents still lack the basic academic skills, instructional efforts are geared toward acquiring competency in reading, writing, and mathematics.

Programs with a compensation emphasis teach students how to learn. They are taught strategies or procedures for acquiring information through nontraditional methods. The instructional environment may also be modified. For example, a student may learn how to compensate for a reading disability through auditory information received via taped materials, talking books, and so on.

Programs built around an alternative curriculum are geared toward students for whom the secondary curriculum may be too difficult, irrelevant, or inappropriate. An alternative curriculum affords the youngster with learning problems a curriculum different from the one offered by the public school. Generally, an alternative curriculum stresses functional, life-adjustment skills intended to prepare the student to function in society.

Many students with learning disabilities have behavioral and social difficulties that often become more pronounced during adolescence. Although teachers commonly implement programs designed to improve the classroom behaviors of students with learning disabilities, little attention is directed at improving their interactions with peers.

Placement Options

Most students with learning disabilities receive part or all of their education within the mainstream of the regular school environment. Presently, the resource room concept is the most popular service arrangement for these students. Resource programs provide supportive education services aimed at successfully sustaining and maintaining students within an integrated setting. In an appropriate mainstreaming program, educational planning and programming are an integral part of the process and require that resource program personnel and regular classroom teachers establish effective lines of communication, work together cooperatively, and coordinate their instructional plans.

Because students with learning disabilities have a diverse, unique range of problems, resource room services are not appropriate for every child. Thus, a range of placement options should be available so that the student's individual needs can be matched to services. For example, students with learning disabilities with relatively mild problems may receive direct services from itinerant teachers, whereas children with more severe disabilities may be assigned to self-contained classrooms or special day schools.

Because of the diversity of the learning disabilities population and the large number of students identified as LD, considerable experimentation in the use of different program options has occurred in recent years. One of the most notable options has involved collaborative arrangements between regular classroom teachers and learning disabilities specialists. Emphasis has increased on consultation in which regular educators receive help from special educators in the identification, intervention, and monitoring of student behavior. Use of "plug-in" models has increased; in these, the learning disabilities specialists work with students directly in the regular classroom. Prereferral intervention approaches, in which a school-based consultant team assists regular education teachers prior to referral of a student for learning disabilities services, have also become very popular.

Perhaps the most prominent as well as emotional issue surrounding service delivery for learning disabled students in today's schools is the Regular Education Initiative (REI). The advocates of REI argue that the current categorical system of classification and special education service delivery should be abolished and that a more inclusive general education system that includes the total integration of mildly handicapped students should be implemented (McKinney & Hocutt, 1988). A discussion of all of the basic issues surrounding the REI is beyond the scope of this chapter, but it is worth noting that the regular education system as a whole has been repeatedly criticized and that the REI movement has had little input from those (regular classroom teachers) who will be required to implement the initiative (Keogh, 1988).

Needed Related Services

In addition to learning disabilities specialists, assistance from other professionals in education as well as psychology and medicine may be necessary in order to provide an appropriate education or adequate care for a particular student. To illustrate, a speech pathologist may be called on to provide relevant contributions in the treatment of language problems. A school psychologist may be asked to conduct an individual diagnostic examination during the identification process. A pediatrician may be needed to diagnose and treat physical and physiological problems (metabolic disorders, nutrition, visual or auditory handicaps) that might impair learning. A psychiatrist may prescribe a specific drug to help control the child's behavior.

Preschool Programs

Most children who are classified as learning disabled are identified during their elementary school years; this usually occurs after they have had difficulty with school learning. As a result, most preschool programs for children with learning disabilities are aimed at children who are at risk for later academic failure. Preschool children who are at risk include those who have language disorders and delays, score poorly on tests of cognitive skills, have limited opportunity due to economic deprivation, and/or are burdened by various medical problems.

The basic assumption underlying preschool programs for at-risk students is that if potential learning problems are identified and students receive appropriate services before they encounter difficulty, these problems can be prevented or at least lessened. Three basic curriculum models have been used with young at-risk children (Lerner, 1985). The *whole-child approach* focuses on a variety of enrichment activities for promoting the child's physical, emotional, social, and intellectual growth. The *direct skills instruction model* stresses the teaching of specific preacademic skills. The *cognitive development curriculum* is oriented to the teaching of thinking and problem-solving skills.

Transitional Services

Increasing evidence indicates that students with learning disabilities graduate or leave high school unprepared to succeed in the workplace (Okolo & Sitlington, 1988). As a group, persons with learning disabilities have considerable difficulty obtaining and maintaining employment commensurate with their abilities. In addition, their social lives are often much more restricted than are those of their normally achieving peers. As a result of the difficulties persons with learning disabilities have in making the transition from school to adult life, there has been increased interest in helping these students obtain the skills necessary for socialization, personally fulfilling lives, and the adjustment to either employment or higher education. Nevertheless, many students with learning disabilities are not receiving the necessary services from schools to facilitate the transition to adult life.

Parental Involvement

The instructional process can be greatly enhanced by enlisting the cooperation of the parents of students with learning disabilities. The involvement of parents as "equal partners" in decisions about their child's educational placement and programming is explicitly mandated by PL 94-142. Nevertheless, parents appear to have only a minimal effect on the IEP process.

A sizable percentage of parents do not attend IEP meetings. The most commonly cited barriers to attendance are the scheduling of meetings during normal working hours and the lack of transportation to the meeting site. Attendance is greatest at lower grades and decreases with increased grade level and the time the student has spent in special education. Estimates indicate that more than one third of meetings are not attended by parents. Of those attended, the child's mother is the parent most likely to attend.

Parents who do not attend meetings generally do not take an active role and have little impact on placement and programming decisions. This is partly due to the fact that many parents simply do not realize that they have the right to request specialized services or placement changes. Lack of knowledge of professional jargon, the perception that their input is not desired, and parents' faith in (or, regrettably, fear of) the schools are also cited as factors in low involvement. Schools clearly need to do more to foster parent participation in the IEP process.

Sometimes direct parental involvement in the educational process is beneficial. Parents can be asked to set up a regular time and quiet place for their child to study at home. They can help their youngster practice basic skills such as math facts, monitor the completion of homework, and read to or with their child for a specified period of time each night.

SELECTING AND ADAPTING INSTRUCTIONAL MATERIALS

Providing learning disabled students with appropriate materials is an essential consideration in delivering effective instruction. Too often students with learning disabilities are assigned materials that are too difficult or uninteresting. The first step in selecting appropriate materials for students with learning disabilities is to become familiar with their strengths and weaknesses, and to look for materials that correspond to these constraints. The child's performance on and motivation to use the selected materials should also be considered. If the materials appear to be appropriate, they should be retained. If not, the search should begin again.

Difficulties in Selection

Although most learning disabilities specialists agree with the concept of assigning the "right" materials and monitoring the appropriateness of the student-material match, implementation is another matter. Materials selection is, at best, an educated guess because (a) among the variety of formal and informal techniques for selecting the right materials, few have been properly validated; (b) different techniques for selecting materials often yield conflicting results; (c) recommending performance criteria for a specific technique is difficult because present scoring procedures are questionable; and (d) one section of a material may be more difficult than another. Even though these obstacles are formidable, they are not insurmountable.

Unfortunately, few instructional materials have been developed specifically for students with learning disabilities. Consequently, many learning disabilities specialists adapt available materials to meet the student's special needs. When selecting or adapting materials for a specific student, teachers may wish to consider the following questions:

☐ What specific skills or concepts is the material designed to develop?
☐ Is the material based on sound learning principles? Relevant research findings?
☐ Has the material been probably validated?
☐ How receptive is the student to the proposed material?
☐ Is the material durable? Attractive? Interesting?
☐ Does the material support an ethnic or sexist bias?
☐ How many new concepts are presented in each study unit?
☐ Are ample opportunities provided for review and reinforcement?
☐ Does the material provide for individualization? Evaluation? Self-correction?
☐ How is the content of the material presented? Symbolically? Representationally? Concretely?
☐ Is the material teacher directed? Student directed?
☐ Does use of the material require specific training? Specific preparations?
☐ How is the student expected to interact with the material?
☐ For whom is the material appropriate?
☐ What is the comparative cost of the material?

Methods of Adaptation

On selecting materials that are appropriate, many teachers use only a portion of the adopted series or adapt the material to meet the student's characteristics and individual needs. Common adaptations include (a) breaking the material up into smaller, more manageable sets; (b) inserting additional activities or other materials in order to foster motivation, comprehension, or learning; (c) changing the way in which students receive information (listening instead of reading) and are asked to respond (oral instead of written); and (d) resequencing the material so that it follows the teacher's preferred pattern. Even though the complexity of materials can be altered by rewriting the content at a lower level or by reducing the content load, this is not recommended for two reasons. First, such revisions are very time consuming; second, they may actually make the text more difficult unless the person making the changes is particularly adept at such modifications.

Activity 4, page 222, has you experience the challenges of selecting and modifying instructional materials.

One example of a specific procedure for adapting materials has been presented by Deshler and Graham (1980). They recommended that reading assignments for learning disabled adolescents be tape-recorded in many instances. This would minimize students' reading deficits, allowing them to stay current with class assignments. To ensure that students receive maximum benefits from taped materials, tapes must be adequately organized and presented. Effective use of taped content materials includes:

☐ Decisions about what is to be taped
☐ The use of taped materials to teach text usage and study skills
☐ Effective application of learning principles
☐ The use of a marking system to help students coordinate the tape recording with text materials
☐ Careful consideration of the mechanics of recording
☐ Evaluation of the effectiveness of taped products and the learning that results from using them

TECHNOLOGY APPLICATIONS

The advent of low-cost microcomputer technology in the mid 1970s afforded schools the opportunity of applying computer technology in educational settings. Many believed that microcomputers would revolutionize education for both handicapped and nonhandicapped students. At present, the impact of computers has failed to live up to the advanced billing because of (a) a lack of educational programs for the computer, (b) a relatively small number of computers in the schools, (c) a lack of trained "computer literate" teachers, and (d) a lack of knowledge on how to integrate the computer into the classroom.

Computers are now commonly used for educational instruction and management. Probably the most common instructional use of the computer is for drill and practice, as computers are well suited for this application. Research has shown that some well-designed programs can increase the achievement of students with learning disabilities. Other instructional applications such as word processing and simulations are becoming more prevalent and have promising potential. Computers can also assist in management tasks such as planning, testing, and record keeping. By making such tasks as IEP production less time consuming, computers free teachers for other instructional activities. New technologies such as the videodisc, which can provide interactive instruction through high quality audio and video, hold great promise.

Technology has great potential, but it should not be accepted blindly. The efficacy and appropriateness of technology-based instruction for students with learning disabilities have not been universally demonstrated. Questions about the equity of access and the potentially dehumanizing effects of technology are only now being addressed. Technology is not a panacea; like any educational tool, its effectiveness depends on the knowledge and sensitivity of the user.

MULTICULTURAL CONSIDERATIONS

During the 1980s, the number of students from ethnic minorities enrolled in public schools increased dramatically. The values, language and nuances in language style, attitudes toward education, and problem-solving strategies of ethnic or cultural groups may differ significantly from those of the majority of society. Members of ethnic minorities may suffer from economic deprivation, and poverty can have a negative effect on learning and school achievement. A sizable proportion of children from ethnic minorities also have limited proficiency with English. Although children who speak Spanish as their primary language represent the largest group of these students in our nation's schools, more than 50 different native languages are spoken by children in some urban areas.

Many students who are classified as learning disabled are members of ethnic minorities. There has been a growing concern that children from ethnic minorities are over-represented in classrooms for the learning disabled. The reasons for over-inclusions are extremely complex and are beyond the scope of this chapter. Nevertheless, careful consideration needs to be given to test results, adaptive behavior, classroom performance, and cultural patterns before a child from an ethnic minority is labeled as learning disabled (Sattler, 1988).

In working with students with learning disabilities from varying ethnic groups, teachers should learn as much as possible about the child's culture and guard against inappropriate generalizations, stereotypes, and preconceived notions (Sattler, 1988). The child's primary language or dialect should not be denigrated, and children should be addressed by their right names.

Some ethnic minority children with learning disabilities may participate in a bilingual education program; not all schools have these programs. In bilingual programs, students receive instruction in skill development in the language they understand. At the same time, students receive help in becoming proficient in the use of English.

SUMMARY THOUGHTS

Learning takes place in many settings and across a wide variety of areas. The home, the school, and the community all play a part in promoting the physical, psychological, social-emotional, and academic development of children. Learning disabilities are not just an enigma of our educational system; they are a family and community problem that requires the resources and energy of a diverse group of educational and noneducational personnel.

Furthermore, learning disability is not solely the sphere of children in school. Many adolescents who have failed to acquire basic academic skills need continued support during and after their secondary school experiences. At the same time, at-risk children can be helped through relevant preschool programs to reduce their learning problems. Finally, some persons with learning disabilities may require support and assistance throughout their lives.

REFERENCES

Arter, J., & Jenkins, J. (1979). Differential diagnosis—prescriptive teaching: A critical appraisal. *Review of Educational Research, 49*, 517–556.

Auxter, D. (1971). Learning disabilities among deaf populations. *Exceptional Children, 37*, 573–577.

Clements, S. (1966). *Minimal brain dysfunction in children* (NINDS Monograph No. 3, Public Health Service Bulletin 1415). Washington, DC: U.S. Department of Health, Education, and Welfare.

Connolly, A. J., Nachtman, W., & Pritchett, E. M. (1989). *Key Math Diagnostic Arithmetic Test—Revised.* Circle Pines, MN: American Guidance Service.

Deshler, D. (1978). Issues related to the education of learning disabled adolescents. *Learning Disability Quarterly, 1*, 2–10.

Deshler, D., & Graham, S. (1980). Tape recording educational materials for secondary handicapped student. *Teaching Exceptional Children, 12*, 52–54.

Graham, S. (1985). Teaching basic academic skills to learning disabled students: A model of the teaching-learning process. *Journal of Learning Disabilities, 18*, 528–534.

Graham, S., & Harris, K. R. (1988). Instructional recommendations for teaching writing to exceptional students. *Exceptional Children, 54*, 506–512.

Graham, S., Harris, K. R., & Sawyer, R. (1987). Composition instruction with learning disabled students: Self-instructional strategy training. *Focus on Exceptional Children, 20*, 1–11.

Graham, S., & Johnson, L. (1989). Teaching reading to learning disabled students: A review of research-supported procedures. *Focus on Exceptional Children, 21*, 1–12.

Graham, S., & Miller, L. (1980). Handwriting research practice: A unified approach. *Focus on Exceptional Children, 13*, 1–16.

Hallahan, D., & Cruickshank, W. (1973). *Psychoeducational foundations of learning disabilities.* Englewood Cliffs, NJ: Prentice-Hall.

Hammill, D. (1976). Defining learning disabilities for programmatic purposes. *Academic Therapy, 12*, 29–37.

Harris, K. R. (1982). Cognitive-behavior modification: Application with exceptional students. *Focus on Exceptional Children, 15*, 1–16.

Hudson, F., & Graham, S. (1978). An approach to operationalizing the I.E.P. *Learning Disability Quarterly, 1*, 13–31.

Kappelman, M., Kaplan, E., & Ganter, R. (1969). A study of learning disorders among disadvantaged children. *Journal of Learning Disabilities, 2*, 261–268.

Kaufman, A., & Kaufman, N. (1985). *Kaufman Test of Educational Achievement.* Circle Pines, MN: American Guidance Service.

Keogh, B. (1988). Perspectives on the Regular Education Initiative. *Learning Disabilities Focus, 4*, 3–5.

Landau, E., Epstein, S., & Stone, A. (1978). *The exceptional child through literature.* Englewood Cliffs, NJ: Prentice-Hall.

Lerner, J. (1985). *Learning disabilities: Theories, diagnosis, and teaching strategies* (4th ed.). Boston: Houghton Mifflin.

Licht, B. G. (1983). Cognitive-motivational factors that contribute to the achievement of learning disabled children. *Journal of Learning Disabilities, 16*, 483–490.

McKinney, J., & Hocutt, A. (1988). Policy issues in the evaluation of the Regular Education Initiative. *Learning Disabilities Focus, 4*, 15–23.

Mercer, C. D. (1987). *Students with learning disabilities* (3rd ed.). Columbus, OH: Merrill.

Okolo, C., & Sitlington, P. (1988). Mildly handicapped learners in vocational education: A statewide study. *Journal of Special Education, 22*, 220–230.

Sattler, J. (1988). *Assessment of children* (3rd ed.). San Diego: Author.

Terman, L. M., & Merrill, M. A. (1973). *Stanford-Binet Intelligence Scale.* Boston: Houghton Mifflin.

Thomas, A. (1979). Learned helplessness and expectancy factors: Implications for research in learning disabilities. *Review of Education Research, 49*, 208–221.

Wechsler, D. (1974). *Wechsler Intelligence Scale of Children—Revised.* New York: Psychological Corp.

Woodcock, R. (1978). *Woodcock-Johnson Psychoeducational Battery.* Hingham, MA: Teaching Resources Corp.

Woodcock, R. (1987). *Woodcock Reading Mastery Tests—Revised.* Circle Pines, MN: American Guidance Service.

ADDITIONAL READINGS

Alley, G., & Deshler, D. (1979). *Teaching the learning disabled adolescent: Strategies and methods.* Denver: Love.

Hammill, D., & Bartel, N. (1986). *Teaching students with learning and behavior problems.* Boston: Allyn & Bacon.

Reid, K. (1988). *Teaching the learning disabled: A cognitive developmental approach.* Boston: Allyn & Bacon.

Purpose

☐ To help you identify characteristics of learning disabled children

☐ To increase your familiarity with children's reactions to academic and social failure

Steps

1. Locate Landau, Epstein, and Stone (1978).
2. Read "Gideon: A Boy Who Hates Learning," by Gladys Natchez, beginning on page 6.
3. Answer the following questions:

Analysis

☐ What types of problems did Gideon have?

☐ How did Gideon react to his academic failure?

☐ How did the school react to Gideon's problems?

☐ Can you suggest some different ways of dealing with Gideon's problems?

☐ What were some of the positive things Mrs. Davis did?

☐ In what ways do you think Gideon would change the schools if he could?

Purpose

☐ To assist you in observing a student's performance in the regular classroom

☐ To increase your familiarity with observation techniques

Steps

1. Identify a student who has been labeled as learning disabled.
2. Identify a child in the same classroom who is considered average in achievement and behavior.
3. Arrange for a visit during an academic class period.
4. Take the accompanying recording form and a stopwatch along for the visit.
5. Seat yourself away from the students but not behind the two students you are to observe. Do not interact with the students.
6. Observe both children for 9 minutes during independent seatwork, noting at the end of every 20 seconds whether each student is on task or off task. Look away from the target children from time to time so they do not notice you are observing them specifically.
7. Determine the percentage of time each student is on or off task.

Analysis

☐ What differences did you find in the two observations?

☐ What similarities did you find in the two observations?

☐ What other types of activities could be observed using this method?

☐ Do you think you would have obtained the same results with 10-second versus 20-second intervals?

☐ What different ways can you suggest for observing and collecting this same information?

☐ Why should the performance of the child with learning disabilities be compared to that of another student?

Recording Form

Observer _____ Date _____

First Name
of Student A _____ Setting _____

Behavior
Student B _____ Observed _____

Total Length
of Observation _____

Time (Specify the time interval.)	Behaviors (Record a check [✔] if the student is on task a circle [○] if off task.)	Summary (Determine percentage on task and off task.)

Time Interval

___sec. ___sec. ___sec. ___sec. ___sec. ___sec. ___sec. ___sec.

Student A								
Student B								

___sec. ___sec. ___sec. ___sec. ___sec. ___sec. ___sec. ___sec.

Student A								
Student B								

___sec. ___sec. ___sec. ___sec. ___sec. ___sec. ___sec. ___sec.

Student A								
Student B								

Observations _____
_____
_____
_____

3

Purpose

☐ To consider factors relevant to direct intervention

☐ To increase your familiarity with techniques for improving a student's spelling vocabulary

Steps

1. Identify a student with learning disabilities who has spelling difficulties.

(Procedure 1)

2. Select 10 spelling words that are difficult for the student.
3. Dictate the list to the student to determine his or her ability to spell the words before studying them. Score the paper.
4. Give the student a copy of the same list of words. Ask the student to study the words for 10 minutes.
5. Repeat (3). Score the paper.

(Procedure 2)

6. Select another 10 spelling words of equivalent difficulty.
7. Dictate the list to the student to determine his or her ability to spell the words before studying them.
8. Give the student a copy of the same list of words. For each word, have the student: (a) look at the word and say it; (b) with eyes closed, visualize the word; and (c) cover the word and write it. Repeat each of these steps two times.
9. Repeat (7). Score the paper.

Analysis

☐ Did the student learn to spell more words correctly using procedure 1 or procedure 2?

☐ What do the results of the two procedures indicate about the student's ability to learn new spelling vocabulary?

☐ How could you modify procedure 1 to make it more effective?

☐ How could you modify procedure 2 to make it more effective?

☐ Was the presentation of 10 words too difficult for the student?

4

Purpose

☐ To help you select appropriate materials for a specific student

☐ To increase your familiarity with techniques for selecting appropriate reading materials

Steps

1. Enlist a student at any level to be your subject.

2. Select a book or passage that you estimate to be at the student's instructional level.

3. Isolate a selection of approximately 250 words from the middle of the book or passage.

4. Delete every fifth word in the selection. Do not delete words in the first and last sentence.

5. After deleting every fifth word, retype the selection, replacing each deleted word with a blank of the same length.

6. Instruct the student to fill in the blanks with the exact words he or she judges to be missing.

7. Determine the percentage of the number of correct responses. If the student missed more than 30% of the responses, the book or passage is probably too difficult.

Analysis

☐ What percentage of the responses was correct?

☐ What percentage of the responses would have been correct if synonyms were also counted as right?

☐ Was the book too difficult for the student?

☐ Was the book appropriate for the student?

☐ Could this technique be used with all types of reading materials?

9

Emotional Disturbance

Linda L. Edwards
University of Missouri—Kansas City

Janice De Palma Simpson
Bethany Medical Center — Kansas City, Kansas

EMOTIONAL DISTURBANCE
TYPICAL PROFILE

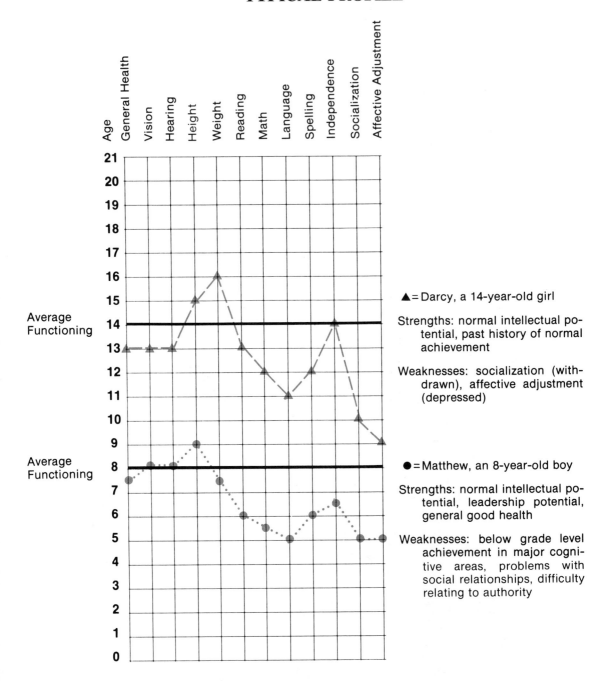

▲ = Darcy, a 14-year-old girl

Strengths: normal intellectual potential, past history of normal achievement

Weaknesses: socialization (withdrawn), affective adjustment (depressed)

● = Matthew, an 8-year-old boy

Strengths: normal intellectual potential, leadership potential, general good health

Weaknesses: below grade level achievement in major cognitive areas, problems with social relationships, difficulty relating to authority

The challenges posed by children and youth with emotional disturbance in educational settings have been present as long as schools have existed; however, special education programs specifically designed for such children are a fairly new phenomenon. In the recent past, many people believed that the conflicts presented by troubled children were the responsibility of those outside the school—namely, the family, the child guidance center, the psychiatrist, or the psychologist. Often disturbed students who required special behavioral and academic assistance to tolerate an educational environment were excluded from school services. When several experimental special education programs were funded in 1961 by the National Institute of Mental Health (NIMH), the idea that teachers could teach children with emotional disturbance was considered somewhat radical (Rhodes & Paul, 1978). Since that time, the role of the teacher as a trained mental health professional has gained increasing acceptance, and public school programs for these students have become a traditional part of the special services offered by school systems.

The impetus for this growth came from several complex, interrelated factors. National attention was focused upon the needs of seriously disturbed children and youth by President John F. Kennedy. In 1963, he was instrumental in designing legislation aimed at combating mental illness and mental retardation by, among other measures, increasing the number of qualified personnel to work with such populations (Reinert, 1980). Later, public school educational services for children with severe disturbance became mandatory after passage of Public Law 94-142, the Education for All Handicapped Children Act of 1975.

As a result of the development of the knowledge base in mental health and the passage of legislation mandating services for students with emotional disturbance, a variety of service delivery models may be found in today's schools. These may include self-contained classrooms, resource rooms, regular classes with support services, alternative programs, and others. Many districts provide support services in addition to special class placement. These services may include individual or group counseling by district social workers, counselors, or psychologists; family support services through individual social work assistance or support groups; parent training sessions; and inservice training for regular education personnel who participate in mainstreaming students with emotional disturbance. Programs for these students are among the most costly in special education due to the large number of support personnel required to provide comprehensive services and the low pupil-teacher ratio necessary to work effectively with the behavioral and academic problems such students present. In addition, fully certified teachers of the emotionally disturbed are at a premium in most states. Consequently, many districts offer only one or two service delivery models due to costs and personnel availability (Rizzo & Zabel, 1988).

Services for students with emotional disturbance provide academic and behavioral support beyond the scope of the regular class. As will be discussed later, these students often exhibit academic deficits and interfering behaviors that require specific interventions in order for them to be able to benefit from school attendance. Teachers trained in emotional disturbance employ a variety of techniques to teach students and train appropriate social behaviors. Often students are able to participate to some degree in regular education when achievement in a subject is within the instructional range of the regular class and when the behavioral responses of the student are tolerable in that environment. The objective of special class placement for students with emotional disturbance is to provide a structured environment that fosters successful academic and behavioral experiences. As students progress through such programs, it is usual to gradually mainstream students in regular classes until special class placements are no longer required. Throughout the mainstreaming process, special education teachers consult with regular class teachers to provide assistance. When students are totally mainstreamed for academics, they are often provided support services such as counseling and monitoring by the special education teacher or by other special educational personnel for a period to assure successful adjustment.

CHARACTERISTICS OF CHILDREN AND YOUTH WITH EMOTIONAL DISTURBANCE

Children and youth with emotional disturbance are a heterogeneous group. Although many display similar behavior patterns, such as anger toward teachers and other adult authority figures or apathetic withdrawal from school situations, the function of the behavior and the reasons for its existence vary widely among individual students (Hallahan & Kauffman, 1978). For one child, an aggressive display of anger may be an attempt to increase status with peers, whereas for another, the same behavior may serve to test the limits of the adult's apparent caring responses. Additionally, the behavior of troubled children is characterized by inconsistency and unpredictability, which are often responses to their chaotic environments. Discussion of characteristics is a difficult task because generalization may lead to oversimplification of the complex problems accompanying emotional disturbance.

As in other categories of exceptionality, the *severity*—extent of variance from "normal" children's behavior patterns—is an essential factor when we consider characteristics of students with emotional disturbance. Definitions of normality in the realm of social-emotional behavior are perhaps more a matter of convention, agreements arrived at between groups of people, than of physical reality such as height or weight (Clarizio & McCoy, 1976). Furthermore, normal emotional development does not imply the absence of problematic behavior. Statistical data from the Berkeley Guidance Study, for example, showed that a large percentage of the normal children studied averaged five or six problems (behaviors such as lying or destructiveness) at any given time during their preschool and elementary years (MacFarlane, Allen, & Honzik, 1954). When considering the characteristics of children who are disturbed, therefore, we might apply criteria developed by Bower (1969) that the problems presented be both *acute* (exist to a marked extent) and *chronic* (exist for a period of time). Bower's research into identification of students

DARCY, A GIRL WITH EMOTIONAL DISTURBANCES

Her teachers have always described Darcy as a quiet, polite student. During her elementary school years, she made average grades and progress, seemed to have playmates, and showed generally acceptable behavior. In sixth grade, her teacher noted that as the year progressed, Darcy participated less often in group activities and daydreamed increasingly. A parent conference before the end of that year revealed that Darcy's parents were having marital difficulties and were considering divorce.

On entering junior high school, Darcy seemed to be constantly preoccupied and isolated from her peer group. Her attempts at academic work were dismal, and she began falling behind. When teachers began to pressure her for academic work, she cut classes. Later in the school year she was more withdrawn and rarely spoke, even when called on by teachers.

After a series of absences from school, Darcy's mother was contacted for a conference. She was surprised to hear of Darcy's excessive absences. Investigation revealed that Darcy had been getting on the school bus but leaving the school grounds as soon as she arrived. She then spent the day wandering in the neighborhood of the school or returning to school and hiding in the restrooms.

☐ ☐ ☐

What possible factors led to Darcy's poor school attendance?

Were there any clues that Darcy might have been experiencing emotional difficulties in elementary school?

What kinds of assistance should school personnel offer Darcy and her family?

---

with emotional disturbance resulted in a description of behavior patterns that has become known as the "educator's definition" of emotional disturbance, has been widely used since its publication, and was adopted for use in PL 94-142. Bower identified five behavior patterns that characterized these students:

☐ Inability to benefit from academic instruction not attributable to intellectual capacity, hearing, or vision problems

☐ Inability to develop and maintain positive interpersonal relationships with peers or adults

☐ Behaviors that are highly inappropriate responses to environmental or social conditions

☐ Wide variations in mood (such as moods of extreme happiness or depression)

☐ Frequent physical complaints or periods of tiredness that have no medical basis.

The behavior patterns noted by Bower may occur in any student in isolated instances; however, when they occur to a marked degree or for a long period of time they are cause for concern.

Another useful conceptualization of the characteristics of children with emotional disturbance was presented by Whelan and Gallagher (1972), who categorized them in terms of behavior excesses and deficits: "Behavior excesses are those actions which the child displays to an inordinate degree—too many tantrums, too many fights. Deficits are behaviors which the child does not exhibit, or does so to a much lesser extent than the norm—too few appropriate social contacts, too few assignments completed" (p. 333). These dimensions can be applied to the disturbed student's academic responses and social-emotional responses, both of which must be considered in a discussion of learner characteristics, although trying to separate one from the other is somewhat artificial.

Academic Achievement Characteristics

A review of the PL 94-142 definition of children with emotional disturbance (which is really a kind of listing of characteristics) indicates that a primary criterion for defining and identifying such children is a deficit in knowledge and skill acquisition that cannot be attributed to intellectual, sensory, or health factors. Emotionally disturbed children are usually underachievers. Even though problem behaviors may prevent them from doing well on standardized tests of any kind, actual academic performance in the classroom generally demonstrates underachievement as a major characteristic. As a general rule, these students have repeatedly failed to be successful in school situations. Whether this failure can be attributed to the interference of problematic behavior (for example, short attention span or energy spent coping with internal or external conflicts rather than academic tasks) or whether the behavior problems are activated by difficulty in learning can become a pointless argument. Both factors are probably in operation, perhaps separately in individual children at first and then simultaneously as a sort of interaction effect, building in severity over time. This kind of overlap of academic underachievement and social-emotional problem behavior may present difficulty for the professional in discriminating between students with mild or moderate learning disabilities and students with emotional disturbance because many individuals in both groups have the two characteristics in common. Again, the most salient features of emotional disturbance are the degree and frequency to which maladaptive behavior is present, but these are not the only features of their exceptionality (Kauffman, 1977).

Research concerning the nature of academic underachievement among children with emotional disturbance shows relatively uniform educational retardation in both reading and arithmetic (Motto & Wilkins, 1968), although in several studies math performance was somewhat more depressed than reading. The few investigators looking at spelling achievement have also reported specific deficits in this basic skill area for these children. In substantiating the correlation between under-achievement and behavior problems, Graubard (1971) found that the more severe the maladjustment of the child (as measured by a behavior rating scale), the greater was the amount of academic retardation in reading.

Children with disturbance are also often deficient in expressive oral language ability. Students with mild or moderate disturbance have been found to have structural language patterns typical of much younger children, such as high usage of sentence fragments and a low occurrence of structures indicating language complexity and facility (Edwards, 1988). We might hypothesize that verbal language as a tool for coping with the environment is frequently by-passed by troubled children who have learned instead to act out negative, hostile feelings or to withdraw entirely from human interaction, both physically and verbally. Children with severe disturbance are characterized by a nearly complete lack of functional expressive language.

Underachievement is a concept that is difficult to define, but it generally means academic performance less than would be expected given an accurate measure of a child's ability to learn (intelligence). Most mild and moderately disturbed children score in the "dull average" or "slow learner" range on individual intelligence tests (Heward & Orlansky, 1980). This lowered intelligence quotient (IQ) might simply be a reflection of the extent to which emotional problems have affected past learning opportunities, but it is nevertheless indicative of the child's ability to perform. Academic achievement is still far short of what might be expected for children with emotional disturbance, even when possible lower potential ability is taken into consideration.

Social and Emotional Characteristics

In the PL 94-142 definition of children with emotional disturbance, the last four criteria or characteristics refer specifically to problems in the social-emotional or affective domain. Such children have great difficulty building satisfactory interpersonal relationships and expressing their feelings appropriately, and they may often seem depressed or have an inordinately large number of fears, pains, or other physical symptoms related to school situations.

The PL 94-142 definition of students with emotional disturbance has frequently been called an "educator's definition" and is intended to help teachers identify such children. Activity 1, page 251, has been designed to help you translate its components into actual learner characteristics. You are asked to be an observer in a special classroom for disturbed students and to identify the presence or absence of the components just discussed.

MATTHEW, A THIRD-GRADE STUDENT

Matthew's records from elementary school reflect a long history of behavior and academic problems. Report cards and parent conference records from kindergarten through the present contain teacher comments substantiating lack of cooperation, poor citizenship skills, and irresponsible behavior.

Test scores indicate that Matthew functions in the normal range intellectually. His classroom academic performance, however, is currently at least 1 year below grade-level expectations. His work is usually carelessly done or incomplete because he spends most of his time seeking inappropriate attention. In class he is generally off task. When the teacher says, "Get out your spelling book," Matthew continues to browse through his math book or goes to the pencil sharpener with four or five pencils in hand. He seems to make a concerted effort to come up with subtly disruptive behaviors.

Matthew has difficulty sharing teacher attention as well. During group reading he reads in a slow, halting manner but enjoys being the center of attention. When the teacher calls on another student to take a turn, Matthew sometimes slams his book shut and pouts, loudly telling the teacher that she never calls on him. When he is doing seatwork, he constantly has his hand in the air. Generally, his questions indicate that he has not read the instructions or attempted to solve the problem himself. When help is given, he fails to listen. Teacher reprimands seem to accelerate the behavior problems rather than reduce them. Matthew seems equally reinforced with negative or positive attention.

On the playground Matthew demands control over any activity in which he is involved, which often results in rejection by peers. Other students are often angry with him and as a result fights frequently break out. Matthew seems to delight in provoking this kind of disruption.

Matthew's teachers, parents, and school administrators are perplexed by these behaviors. The family has two other children, several years older, who attended the same elementary school and had above average school records with no significant behavior problems. The boy's parents are exhausted by his demanding ways and constant behavior problems at school and at home. During their last parent conference, they indicated that they felt powerless to control him.

□ □ □

What kinds of management techniques could be used to deal with Matthew's non-compliant classroom behavior?

What special materials or techniques might be introduced to alleviate Matthew's academic problems?

What part could Matthew's parents play in working with the school to improve his behavior?

What significance might family relationships have to the boy's school performance?

The social-emotional characteristics of learners with emotional disturbance may be generalized as falling into two sets or dimensions—aggressive, acting-out behavior and immature, withdrawn behavior (Hallahan & Kauffman, 1978). These two dimensions are easily translatable into Whelan and Gallagher's (1972) model of behavioral excesses (aggressive, acting out) and deficits (immature, withdrawn).

Aggressive, acting-out behaviors are easy to identify because they are forced on the attention of teachers and other students in an often unpleasant or painful way. The components of aggressive behavior in children have been identified and specified by Quay (1972) and his associates through a factor analytic procedure. These factors include, among others, disobedience, disruptiveness, tantrums, destructiveness toward one's own and other's property, uncooperativeness in group situations, and negativism. The picture that emerges from these descriptors is of a child in frequent conflict with others in the school or classroom, who in turn may react negatively or punitively toward the child. People often reciprocate the behaviors with which they are confronted. An angry child, yelling at the teacher, may get yelled at in return. A withdrawn, nonresponsive child may be ignored or overlooked by the teacher and other students. When examining aggressive (as well as withdrawn) behaviors, we should take a close look at the interaction between the child in conflict and the others in his or her environment, especially because many aggressive behaviors appear to be learned rather than inherent (Bandura, 1973).

Characteristics of the immature, withdrawn child have also been delineated by Quay (1972) and others. These characteristics include shyness, preference for solitary activity, lack of self-confidence, anxiety, and chronic fearfulness, sadness, or depression. Identifying children who have these behaviors is just as important as identifying aggressive students, even though teachers less frequently consider passive, withdrawn children problematic. Extreme forms of withdrawal and immaturity may characterize severe and profound emotional disorders including childhood schizophrenia. Even when present to a milder degree, such patterns, if allowed to persist, may indicate possible future adjustment problems (Kauffman, 1989). An individual child may display both sets of characteristics, being in turn aggressive, withdrawn, and aggressive again.

Any listing of characteristics of children with emotional disturbance must be viewed and used with caution. In addition to the behaviors the child exhibits, factors surrounding them must be carefully evaluated. Clarizio and McCoy (1976) suggested that maladaptive behaviors be looked at in the context of the child's age and development level, sex, culture and subculture, tolerance level of adults associated with the child, and specific setting in which the behavior occurs. Knowledge of a set of characteristics of children with emotional disturbance by itself is not sufficient. The functional implications of those characteristics for any given child can only be understood through the careful collection and analysis of appropriate assessment data.

Eligibility Criteria

The definition of emotional disturbance put forward by Bower (1969) was used as the basis for the definition in PL 94-142 and served as the basis for eligibility criteria set by states and local districts. Nevertheless, application of the definition adopted by the federal government has been quite problematic. The federal definition reads as follows:

> "Seriously emotionally disturbed" is defined as follows: (i) The term means a condition exhibiting one or more of the following characteristics over a long period of time and to a marked degree, which adversely affects educational performance: (a) an inability to learn which cannot be explained by intellectual, sensory, or health factors; (b) an inability to build or maintain satisfactory interpersonal relationships with peers and teachers; (c) inappropriate types of behavior or feelings under normal circumstances; (d) a general pervasive mood of unhappiness or depression; or (e) a tendency to develop physical symptoms or fears associated with personal or school problems. (ii) The term does not include children who are socially maladjusted, unless it is determined that they are seriously emotionally disturbed. (Education of Handicapped Children, *Federal Register,* Section 121a.5, 1977)

Two changes in Bower's original definition were made when the federal definition was written. First, the final sentence in the federal definition, which did not appear in Bower's work, excluded socially maladjusted students. Second, the word *seriously* was added to emotionally disturbed. These changes have been the cause for major concerns (see Kauffman, 1980).

Exclusion of Socially Maladjusted Children

The first issue of concern revolves around the clause stating that students must be found to be seriously emotionally disturbed as opposed to socially maladjusted in order to qualify for special services. Obviously, this becomes a diagnostic problem open to personal opinion and professional judgment. Kauffman stated:

> Perhaps the intent was simply to exclude nonpsychotic adjudicated delinquents. But are we really to believe that the exclusionary clause will not make a bureaucratic nightmare of attempts to provide appropriate education for children whose behavior gets them into serious legal trouble, but who can be ignored on a technicality because there is a mental health expert willing to say that the child's difficulty is not due to disturbed emotions? (p. 524)

The problem presented by the ambiguity of the clause and the multiple interpretations that arise from it are a continuing source for appeals and litigation in addition to presenting identification problems to educators and mental health practitioners.

Addition of "Seriously"

The second major concern as identified by Kauffman is the addition of the adjective "seriously" and its effect on qualification for services. For some years an estimated 2% prevalence of emotional disturbance among children was widely quoted. Many educators think this is a very conservative figure. Bower (1969) found the figure of children needing behavioral intervention during their school years to be nearer 10%. Other recent studies cited figures ranging from 8% to 20%. The law mandating that all identified disturbed students must be served took effect in September 1978. At that time, the Bureau of Education for the Handicapped estimated that using a 2% prevalence figure, only 25% of the children with emotional disturbance were then being served. We might assume that the number of children receiving services would be at or above the conservative 2% prevalence estimate several years after implementation of the federal mandate. Nevertheless, by 1984, the number of children and adolescents who had been formally identified as seriously emotionally disturbed was placed at less than 1% (Smith-Davis, Burke, & Noel, 1984).

Several factors may be involved in the failure of PL 94-142 to dramatically effect the level of services to children with emotional disturbance. First, parents of such children may be reluctant to have their children classified as emotionally disturbed and may insist on other services or problem-solving techniques. Second, schools may be reluctant to identify milder problem behaviors as emotional disturbance because of inadequate funds, space, and trained personnel to provide services for this increased number of students. Federal aid notwithstanding, the financial burden falls to local districts, which are struggling to provide services on tight budgets. The qualifier "seriously emotionally disturbed" may prevent large numbers of children from gaining access to services.

Third, identification brings on a whole gamut of bureaucratic procedures, paperwork, and administrative problems that do not encourage school personnel to seek out new students for special education placement. As a result, probably only the students with the most severe disturbance are singled out, identified, and served. This has ultimately led to a failure to serve the more mildly affected. The law has effectively allowed children in the severe category to be identified because their identification is more obvious, and services are usually demanded not only by parents but also by teachers and administrators because of the disruption these children cause. It is reasonable to assume that the 1% now being served fit this category. But the mildly disturbed population that might respond more quickly to the services, trained teachers, and other specialists the schools can provide is poorly served. A study by Dodge (1976) concluded that children in the moderately to mildly emotionally disturbed category might constitute the most underserved category of all handicapped students.

The definition of emotional disturbance as it appears in PL 94-142 remains subjective, complicating the process of identification with professional and personal judgments and interpretations inherent in the diagnosis of such children. Perhaps no other area of special education requires so much subjective input from multiple sources including parents, teachers, social workers, administrators, and mental health professionals. Other areas of special education appear to have more measurable, systematic, and concrete criteria for identification. Defining and identifying children with emotional disturbance place heavy burdens of judgment on all concerned with the fair, equitable, and constructive application of special education services.

BASIC PROFESSIONAL VOCABULARY

Many of the terms that apply to emotional disturbance are derived from medical origins. Others represent organizations that serve those with emotional problems and needs. A sample of some of the terminology used in this field is listed and briefly defined here.

Attention deficit disorder is characterized by developmentally inappropriate degrees of inattention, impulsiveness, and hyperactivity.

Autism, one of the more severe childhood disturbances, is characterized by bizarre behavior, developmental delays, and extreme isolation. Although now categorized as an exceptionality, the behavioral features of autism are often appropriate for interventions employed with emotionally disturbed students.

BD is the acronym for behavior disorders and as a term has become a synonym for emotional disturbance.

Council for Children with Behavior Disorders is a division of the Council for Exceptional Children. It is composed of professionals interested in working with this population of children.

Diagnostic Statistical Manual of Mental Disorders (3rd ed.—rev.), published by the American Psychiatric Association, serves as a manual of mental disorders and specifies the criteria used in making psychiatric diagnoses.

Medical model refers to an approach to emotional disturbance that views present behaviors as symptoms of an underlying cause.

Pervasive developmental disorders involve distortions of the whole range of psychological functions during childhood development including attention, perception, learning abilities, language, social skills, reality contact, and motor skills.

Positive reinforcement is a rewarding consequence such as praise or food given to encourage appropriate or desired behaviors.

Psychosis, a term of medical origin, refers to a type of severe behavior disorder whose characteristics include loss of reality contact and abnormal acts, thoughts, and feelings.

ASSESSING INSTRUCTIONAL NEED

Comprehensive assessment of students with emotional disturbance is critical to the establishing of an organized, positive learning environment. Perhaps in no other area of special education is it so important to see the total child as a person, class member, family member, and community member. Formal and informal procedures designed to assess intellectual, personality, sensory, academic, and social functioning are crucial to an understanding of the forces affecting the child. A multifaceted assessment with such components requires cooperative efforts by educators, mental health practitioners, and family to produce a comprehensive evaluation that in final form will yield insight into which teaching techniques, materials presentation, and teacher responses will be of maximum benefit to the pupil.

Formal Assessment

Because most students with emotional disturbance exhibit academic retardation, a team of educational personnel including school psychologists, speech-language pathologists, reading specialists, and others may participate in administering standard intellectual and academic measures. The Wechsler Intelligence Scale for Children—Revised (Wechsler, 1974) and the Stanford-Binet Intelligence Scale (Thorndike, Hagen, & Sattler, 1986) are frequently used individual tests that indicate intellectual potential. The Kaufman Assessment Battery for Children (Kaufman & Kaufman, 1983) may be used to assess the intelligence and academic achievement of children. Formal assessment measures of general academic achievement used frequently with emotionally disturbed students include the Woodcock-Johnson Psychoeducational Battery-revised (Woodcock & Johnson, 1989) and the Peabody Individual Achievement Test-revised (Dunn & Markwardt, 1989). These are screening tests that indicate general grade-level functioning in reading, math, spelling, written language, and general information.

Diagnostic tests measuring specific skills in given subject areas provide detailed information on student strengths and weaknesses. Many diagnostic tests are available for assessing skills in reading, mathematics, spoken language, spelling, and perceptual-motor functioning. Classroom Reading Inventory (Silvaroli, 1973), Gray Oral Reading Test (Gray & Robinson, 1967), and Key Math—Revised (Connolly, 1988) are examples of tests often used with students with emotional disturbance because many have problems in reading and math. The Peabody Picture Vocabulary Test—Revised (Dunn & Dunn, 1981), a measure of one feature of receptive language, may be used to evaluate the extent of language delay in some students.

Personality, psychological, and projective testing are assessment areas of unique concern to those working with the emotionally disturbed. Administration and interpretation of projective tests such as the Rorschach (1942) and Thematic Apperception Test (Murray, 1943) require extensive specialized training, which necessitates cooperation with professionals in the mental health field. Many school systems contract with psychiatrists and psychologists for these services. Information resulting from such measures, together with trained clinical judgment, can be used to assist in providing a therapeutic learning environment.

Assessment of behavior may also be aided by rating scales and checklists administered by educational personnel. Rating scales such as the Hahnemann High School Behavior Maturity Scale (Spivak & Swift, 1971), Walker Problem Identification Checklist (H. M. Walker, 1970), Vineland Social Maturity Scale (Doll, 1965), Peterson-Quay Behavior Rating Scale (Quay & Peterson, 1967), Behavior Evaluation Scale (McCarney, Leigh, & Cornbleet, 1983), and Behavior Disorder Identification Scale (Wright, 1988) provide behavioral information that is quantified and may be used as pretest data for comparison at a later date. These scales, when used in conjunction with direct observational data and informal procedures, can yield useful information about the nature of a child's behavior problems.

Ecological assessment (examination of the student and his or her interaction with environments) is a significant aspect of evaluation. Various models have been recommended for a comprehensive ecological assessment. One such model, suggested by Laten and Katz (1975), features a five-phase approach including (a) descriptions of the general environment where problems are prevalent or absent, (b) expectations that exist in problem and nonproblem environments, (c) behavioral descriptions in both environments where problems are present or absent, (d) summary of information gathered, and (e) statement of what goals can reasonably be set for the child in the academic setting. These steps require detailed family and educational histories and observations of behavior in problem-provoking and nonproblem settings to gain specific data about circumstances contributing to appropriate responses.

Informal Assessment

Informal academic assessment is typically the classroom teacher's responsibility. Data from standardized tests, although an essential component of comprehensive evaluation, provide only part of the information for actually working with children in a teaching situation. Teacher-made instruments may be used to informally assess skill areas, subject matter information, and learner preferences. These informal measures have the advantages of simple design, direct teacher involvement, and similarity to the teacher's unique teaching style (Wallace & Larsen, 1978). Information gathered from such instruments provides important specific information. For example, in an informal math assessment, the teacher may observe that in a two-place addition problem the child does not understand carrying from the ones to the tens place, which may be the reason the child scored low in the addition section of a formal test. Furthermore, the teacher may note that the child has a low frustration tolerance when presented with a whole page of math problems. By giving small segments of a math assignment in succession, the student may demonstrate a much higher accuracy rate.

In addition to assessing individual student performance in specific subject or skill areas, Gallagher (1979) cited the following areas that should be assessed as part of the informal evaluation: (a) the student's ability to follow either written or verbal instructions, (b) the student's ability to manage daily school expectations such as organization of work area and to find his or her way through the building, (c) the effect of varying environmental conditions on the student's behavior and academic performance (effects of noise, visual stimuli, presence or absence of teacher, time limits), (d) the effect of positive or negative teacher comments, and (e) those special interests of the student that could be used to motivate him or her. For each of these areas, teachers can design simple assessment techniques specific to their teaching style, classroom environment, and management system. Assessing the student within these contexts provides excellent cues for altering the existing classroom structure and expectations.

Equipped with a comprehensive picture of the students with emotional disturbance drawn from academic, intellectual, ecological, personality, and informal measures, the evaluation team can set realistic goals. Furthermore, goals originating from such an assessment can be effectively used to evaluate the whole child's progress.

INTERVENTIONS

Instructional Interventions

Several theoretical perspectives are currently used in the education of students with emotional disturbance. Kauffman (1989) cited six conceptual models based on Rhodes and Tracy's (1974) work of the early 1970s: (a) behavioral, (b) psychodynamic, (c) psychoeducational, (d) biogenic, (e) ecological, and (f) humanistic. Each of these conceptual models offers a different explanation of human behavior, methods of evaluating and assessing it, and different ways of intervening to help. Adherence to any theory of emotional disturbance may to a large extent determine the teacher's role and responses to the academic and behavioral problems disturbed children exhibit in school settings, although teachers more often use portions of many theories to achieve positive educational experiences.

Behavioral Theory

Behavioral theory assumes that the essence of the problem is the behavior itself and that behavior is a function of the environment (Kauffman, 1989). Behaviorists are primarily concerned with teaching and reinforcing appropriate behaviors and decreasing inappropriate behaviors through interventions that develop more positive and acceptable response patterns. The behaviorist believes all behaviors are observable and measurable, excluding biochemical and physiological processes (Roberts, 1975). Behaviorists also view behavior problems as the result of reinforcement systems that developed negative rather than positive or appropriate behavior patterns. Shea (1978) cited four procedures for applying behavioral theory in the school setting. These procedures require that the teacher (a) observe and define the behavior to be changed, (b) select appropriate reinforcers and apply them at a time selected to intervene in the behavior identified for change, (c) consistently apply intervention techniques based on reinforcement theories, and (d) design and use a system for ongoing monitoring and evaluation of the effectiveness of the intervention program.

Psychodynamic Theory

Psychodynamic theory is based on several theories that derive from Freud's psychoanalytic theory. Basically, this school of thought holds that behavior is determined by the dynamics of the intrapsychic life (Shea, 1978). In Freud's conception, the personality consists of the id, ego, and superego, which interrelate to form the personality and dictate a person's behavior. Educators who subscribe to this theoretical position view their primary goal as being understanding the child and assisting the child in gaining the self-understanding necessary to change personality and behavior. These educators may also be concerned with *etiology* (the historical causes for the problems the child exhibits in the present).

Psychoeducational Theory

Psychoeducational theory focuses on the communication of acceptance to the child and the establishment of a secure and meaningful relationship. Formal educational goals are of secondary importance (Hewett, 1968, pp. 17–18). Walker and Shea (1976) cited the following guidelines for the psychoeducational classroom: (a) developing a mentally healthy climate; (b) accepting the child and his or her pathological condition without reservation; (c) encouraging and assisting the child in learning, beginning at a low enough level and with conditions under which the child can function; (d) assuming the role of the educational therapist who accepts, tolerates, and interprets the child's behavior (p. 7).

Biogenic Theory

Biogenic theory concerns itself with the organic origins and neurophysiological mechanisms of emotional disturbance—for example, metabolic error, genetic factors, biochemical imbalance, and brain dysfunction. This school of thought has some proponents among professionals and parents not only of children with emotional disturbance but also of children with perceptual problems, developmental delays, and learning disabilities. Some of its strongest supporters are those concerned with individuals exhibiting characteristics of autism or schizophrenia. Rimland (1964), a major proponent of biophysical theory, believes that biophysical or organic causes are rejected by many practitioners because of the limitations in current knowledge of human physical and chemical functions. Teacher responses based on this theory emphasize a structured, orderly learning environment with a consistent class routine, detailed sequencing of tasks with repetition until skills are acquired, and reduced stimuli of all kinds to produce an optimum educational environment.

Ecological Theory

Ecological theory is rooted in the relationship between human beings and their surroundings. Contained within this model are theories that consider community psychology and sociology as the origins of individual behavior disorders. Des Jarlais (1972) proposed that mental illness is a breaking of social rules and urged consideration of two factors important in deviant behaviors: (a) the social forces involved in rule following or rule breaking and (b) the relationship between rule enforcers and rule breakers. Educators applying ecological theory are concerned with the impact of environment on the child with emotional disturbance and with how to arrange more therapeutic settings.

Humanistic Theory

Humanistic education was originally identified by Rhodes et al. (1974) as the counter-theory approach derived from the social-political movements of sixties and early seventies which emphasized such ideas as open education, alternative schools and deschooling. Drawing from humanistic psychology, proponents of this approach advocated self direction, self fulfillment and self evaluation for emotionally disturbed pupils. A basic assumption of humanistic education was that "...youngsters will find their own solutions to their problems if they are freed to do so in a loving and supportive environment" (Kauffman, 1989, p. 81).

Successful Teachers

The personal attributes of individuals teaching the emotionally disturbed are critical to success with such students. Investigations of teachers of students with emotional disturbance indicate that several personality traits seem to be good predictors of success with children and job satisfaction. Haring and Phillips (1962) found that successful teachers had (a) a calm manner at all times in the classroom; (b) stable relationships with their students; (c) fairness and a sincere approach to students; (d) a belief that students could develop and improve in the classroom; (e) firm, consistent, and clear application of classroom rules and procedures; and (f) an organized presentation of classroom materials. According to LaVietes (1962), the importance

Motivation is a major challenge for successful teachers.

of the teacher's personality attributes cannot be overemphasized. He cited several attributes as essential: (a) low anxiety about teaching, (b) ability to handle frustration, (c) sensitivity to other people, (d) emotional motivation, (e) strong self-identity, and (f) health/personal adjustment patterns.

Those who choose to teach children with emotional disturbance must not rely on formal training alone in making such a career decision. A good deal of insight is necessary to decide if teaching these kinds of students, who can often challenge the limits of a teacher's tolerance, is an activity that can also provide feelings of accomplishment and satisfaction.

Placement Options

Because of the nature of the population, any discussion of placement for children with emotional disturbance must include a wide variety of plans. These range between the extremes of regular class and residential placement. The evaluation and identification team must consider a comprehensive, total picture of the student in order to make prudent judgments about the most beneficial environment.

Currently, school districts utilize many different placement options. PL 94-142 instructs them to place children in the least restrictive environment in which they can effectively learn. Pursuant to this mandate, schools have been exploring alternatives to the self-contained special education classroom.

Deno (1970) designed a continuum of service delivery systems ranging from least restrictive to most restrictive. This continuum identified general concepts for service design, which have been applied to service delivery systems for the disturbed. Many students can be served within the regular class with support such as social work services, individual counseling, or group counseling. Some schools are beginning to use the "crisis teacher" to assist with management problems of disturbed children in the mainstream. Other districts provide behavior management specialists who design specific programs to help solve regular class problems and also aid special class teachers on an on-call basis.

Instructional support with regular class placement is another option when the problems are mild. Reading and math labs to assist with academic deficiencies are examples of this option. These support classes lessen some of the pressures of academic underachievement through individualized programming, which makes the child easier to handle behaviorally. The resource room is another option for giving academic and behavioral support to disturbed students without totally removing them from the regular curriculum. The resource teacher aids the student and other teaching staff in meeting the student's needs when he or she is not in the special education setting. If students are unable to tolerate the academic and behavioral standards of the regular program, self-contained placement must be considered as the least restrictive environment until they make progress.

At the secondary school level, many districts have developed alternative school programs to serve disturbed and maladjusted students. These programs feature low teacher-pupil ratios, individualized academic programming, specialized subject area instructors, a wide variety of elective subjects, and individual and group counseling. Some schools work cooperatively with community mental health services.

As in any other category of handicap, a segment of the population exhibits such chronic and severe problems that placement options outside public education are necessary to provide beneficial services ranging from short-term crisis intervention to long-term placement. Intensity of treatment needs may dictate that a psychiatric hospital, group psychiatric treatment facility, or residential institution can best meet the child's needs. Whenever services of this type are agreed on to promote the welfare of the child, a professional team must conduct periodic reevaluation of the need for such restrictive placement. At any time a less restrictive environment is recommended, mental health professionals, educators, and family members should make a joint effort to secure proper placement and transition support.

The aim of any continuum of services is to effectively reduce problems that interfere with a child's behavioral and academic success and to move the student to increasingly less restrictive placement. The ultimate goal is independent functioning.

Related Services

As pointed out earlier, children and youth with emotional disturbance do not constitute a homogeneous group. They have a great number of different educational characteristics, including significant underachievement in basic academic areas, perceptual-motor problems, maladaptive behaviors, and language delays. Therefore, related service needs can run the gamut of possible services. Once again, results of the comprehensive evaluation and the informal assessment can help guide decision making in this realm. Often, specialists in remedial reading, speech-language pathologists, and adaptive physical education teachers are integral members of the team that assists in providing services to a child identified as disturbed. In addition, school psychologists and social workers may follow the child closely, coordinating home-school programs, counseling students and parents, and assisting school personnel in behavior management.

Many students in any segment of the continuum of service may be receiving assistance from mental health professionals outside the school system. Private psychologists, psychiatrists, social workers, and family therapists working with the student and family might call on educators to help work with the problems the child presents. Teachers working with children with emotional disturbance may find that professionals outside the school can contribute valuable technical assistance. In many cases, these professionals welcome the opportunity to participate as team members in program planning with parents and school personnel.

Parental Involvement

Diagnosis of the exceptional child can be traumatic for parents and perhaps doubly so for parents of a child suffering from emotional difficulties. Studies indicate that parents of such children often feel great anxiety, guilt, and confusion. They have a need for clear, forthright information about their child's problem. Many times, professionals regard parents of such a child as the cause of the child's problem. This may or may not be the case, but professionals should approach parents as partners and instruments of therapeutic change rather than as the source of the problem.

Parental involvement in special education programs is not only mandated by PL 94-142 but has effectively been shown to be a critical factor in pupil progress. Including parents as essential team members is important from the outset and critical to the receiving of their cooperation and support in working with the child. Parents can offer valuable background information and insight in the evaluation process. Parental support in home-school management programs can mean the difference between success or failure in changing behaviors.

Parent training programs can be of great help in alleviating the problems parents experience in managing their child's behaviors. If they receive some professional training, parents can help by applying management procedures, carrying therapeutic techniques into the natural environment, serving as educational tutors for their children, and extending treatment in similar ways.

SELECTING AND ADAPTING INSTRUCTIONAL MATERIALS

To the casual observer, students in a class for the emotionally disturbed may appear to be working with the same or similar materials in use in regular classrooms in the same building. This is usually true, but a closer inspection will reveal that these materials have been selected and slightly or greatly modified to consider the learning and social-emotional characteristics of these children. Some selection principles for use by the special teacher suggested by Wood (1986) include:

- ☐ Select materials that have intrinsic qualities for catching and holding students' attention. Materials should not need much selling to interest the students.
- ☐ Select materials that address a number of instructional objectives simultaneously instead of only one.
- ☐ Select materials that elicit active, not passive, participation. For example, just listening to a story is not as effective as being asked to create a new ending or to describe characters.
- ☐ Select materials for group activities that can be adapted to the developmental level of each individual student in the group.
- ☐ Select materials that provide a gratifying or successful outcome for each student and that do not depend on the teacher to provide a reward for involvement.

Social Skills Curricula

Teachers of children with emotional disturbance have a unique responsibility: to combine remediation of the student's primary behavioral problems with the provision of basic academic instruction. Educators have become increasingly convinced that such students do not incidentally learn (as normal learners do) such important social skills as self-control. Therefore, in addition to selecting appropriate academic materials, the teacher has a primary responsibility to teach social skills. A large number of commercially available materials provide much needed assistance to the teacher in this endeavor. The following is a representative list of several social skills curricula.

Anderson, J. (1981). *Thinking, changing, rearranging.* Eugene, OR: Timberline Press.

Camp, B. W., & Bash, M. S. (1981). *Think aloud: Increasing social and cognitive skills.* Champaign, IL: Research Press.

Jackson, N. E., Jackson, D. A., & Monroe, C. (1983). *Getting Along with Others: Teaching social effectiveness to children.* Champaign, IL: Research Press.

McGinnis, E., & Goldstein, A. P. (1984). *Skillstreaming the elementary school child: A guide for teaching prosocial skills.* Champaign, IL: Research Press.

Stephens, T. M. (1978). *Social skills in the classroom.* Columbus, OH: Cedars Press.

Walker, H. M., McConnell, S., Holmes, D., Todis, B., Walker, J., & Golden, N. (1983). *The Walker social skills curriculum.* Austin, TX: Pro-ed.

Modeling and role playing are two of the most commonly used methods through which new social skills are taught to emotionally disturbed learners. Table 9.1 is a sample of role-play situations among which a teacher might choose in teaching the skill "Saying 'no' to stay out of trouble" (Jackson, Jackson, & Monroe, 1983).

> Helping students acquire prosocial skills is an important educational intervention for emotionally disturbed children and adolescents. Activity 2, page 253, will help you to become familiar with the various materials available in this domain.

More appropriate and less self-defeating behaviors can also be taught using traditional basic skills materials similar or identical to those used in the regular classroom. Academic and behavioral goals can be incorporated into the same lesson. For example, math number fact acquisition can be taught at the same time the student's propensity to compliment other children is increased; this can be accomplished by using a game format and by reinforcing the student for paying compliments and learning her times tables. Although traditional materials and scope and sequence charts may be used in the special classroom for emotionally disturbed children, methods of using them will vary according to the goals and objectives ascertained for each individual student.

TECHNOLOGY APPLICATIONS

The coming of the age of microcomputer technology in special and regular classroom settings offers an interesting range of possibilities to educators of students

Table 9.1　Sample Social Skills Sequence

Situations Target Behaviors	School Problems (Teacher/Peers)	Neighborhood Problems	Sibling Problems	Parent Problems
Listen carefully	The teacher says anyone who does not clean his desk will not go to recess. A bully tells you to clean his desk for him.	The last time you cut across the neighbor's lawn on your bike, she asked you not to. Your friend wants you to do it with him now.	Your sister asked you to watch her bike while she runs in the store. Some kids come by and ask to ride it around the block just once.	Your mom told you to be home by 6:00. Your friend wants you to go to the store with her. It's 5:45 now.
Treat others nicely	The kids in your class are hiding books and things from the teacher. They want you to join in.	Your friends are all bugging a kid down the street. They want you to join in.	Your little brother just got glasses. Your friend thinks it would be funny to take them and hide them.	You know your mom is looking forward to making pies with the cherries on her tree. Some kids want to eat them now.
Join in with others	Your friends are joking about what they want to do at recess—maybe take a ball from the first-graders. You want to play.	Your friend has asked you to join her club. In order to join, you have to steal something from the drugstore.	Your brother broke his leg while skiing. Your best friend thinks it would be fun to steal his crutches.	You are a member of a ball team. Your mom told you to come right home. Your teammate wants you to go to a game tonight.
Keep a good attitude	Some kids try to get you to throw rocks at the school window. You say "no" and they threaten not to be your friends anymore.	Some kids want you to smoke a cigarette with them. They call you a chicken when you say "no."	Your sister wants you to go to the 7-11 with her and play electronic games. Mom told you to stay home and finish your chores.	Your mom says to babysit your little brother at home. Your pal suggests you bring him along to a ball game. You can't.
Take responsibility for self	Your friend wants you to cut school and meet him at the river to fish.	While playing softball, you break the neighbor's window. Your friends suggest that you say someone else did it.	Your brother suggests that you try some of your dad's whiskey.	Your dad says you have to do yard work every day this week. He's out of town. Your pal suggests you take the day off.
Stay calm and relaxed	Your friends want you to spray paint the school. You say "no," and they call you a sissy.	A kid who always bullies you at school asks you if he can come to your birthday party. Your mom says, "Definitely not!"	You're picnicking at the lake, and your sister suggests that you swim across. She says you're a big chicken if you don't.	Your dad leaves you to babysit your sister while he goes to the store. Your friends ask you to go swimming with them.
Solve problems	The teacher told you the wrong page to study, and you failed the test. A kid says she'll help you change your grade.	Some kids want you to go to a movie with them. You know your mom wouldn't want you to see that movie.	Your mom took your bike away for a week. You're late for school, and your sister suggests that you ride your bike.	You lost the money you had saved to go to a movie. Your friend suggests that you take some from your mom's purse.

Source: From N.E. Jackson, D.A. Jackson, and C. Monroe, 1983, *Getting Along with Others,* p. 155, Champaign, IL: Research Press

with emotional disturbance (Manion, 1986). Currently, activities in this domain fall into three categories: procedures that aid the teacher, such as graphing and charting software; activities that help motivate and keep the troubled student on task; and computer-assisted instruction designed to meet affective and behavioral as well as academic objectives.

Teacher Aids

Microcomputer assistance to the teacher of students with emotional disturbance is provided in several ways. Telecommunication boards such as the B.D. board on Special Net provide a range of information on current topics as well as a method of communicating with other professionals for getting help with specific problems. Test scoring software such as that available for the Woodcock-Johnson Psychoeducational Battery (Woodcock & Johnson, 1989) offers a time-saving alternative to lengthy hand-scoring procedures. Software programs that assist the teacher with a wide array of classroom and IEP management possibilities are becoming increasingly available. For example, one program, the *Discipline Diagnostician* (Warger, Aldinger, & Eavy, 1988), generates a problem analysis and a list of preventive, supportive, and corrective interventions appropriate to specific situations after the user describes the problem in terms of student type, behavior problem exhibited, and

Even children with emotional concerns learn with new technologies.

instructional format during which the problem behavior tends to occur. Listings of a large number of classroom and IEP management programs can be obtained from the Council for Exceptional Children's Center for Special Education Technology Information Exchange.

Charting and graphing software such as *Aimstar* (Hasselbring & Hamlett, 1983) also provide data management assistance for special education teachers. Formal data collection and graphing help the teacher make informed decisions about a student's progress, such as determining when an instructional program is ineffective and what type of change would most likely be beneficial. Charting software makes data collection for 8 or 10 students, each of whom may be on several instructional or behavioral programs, a feasible rather than formidable task.

Motivating Activities

For students with emotional disturbance, motivational deficits are most evident in students' inability to concentrate on tasks for sustained periods of time (Carmen & Kosberg, 1982), which makes drill and practice exercises especially problematic. Several studies have demonstrated that computer-assisted instruction has increased time on task and produced higher levels of learner motivation for such students (Spring & Perry, 1980; Roahrig, 1984). These benefits are attributed to the high level of structure and the orientation toward success built into many computer-based programs in such prosaic areas as word decoding skills, math number facts, and spelling drills. If planned and used wisely to supplement traditional remediation and other behavioral management approaches, computer-assisted instruction can improve student behavior and learning both quantitatively and qualitatively (Manion, 1986).

Objective Specific Programs and Methods of Use

Social development and computer-assisted instruction may appear on the surface to be two mutually exclusive orientations. Nevertheless, microcomputers can be used to create positive interactions among students, to enhance self-esteem, and to develop independence and a sense of competence (Male, 1988). Cooperative learning, which is based on fostering a sense of positive interdependence among members of a learning group, and computer-assisted instruction can be readily combined when appropriate software is selected. Studies have demonstrated that this combination has promoted a higher level of daily achievement and more successful problem solving than did computers paired with either competitive or individualized instruction (Johnson, Johnson, & Stanne, 1986). Examples of software with which this approach might be used include *Our Town Meeting* or *The Other Side* (Snyder, 1988), which build in collective problem solving among students for successful resolution of the tasks presented. When structured appropriately, computer use can foster social and affective gains.

MULTICULTURAL CONSIDERATIONS

Teachers and educational specialists must take into account the unique responses to environment and education among students of various cultural or minority groups. Behavioral and academic expectations for these children may significantly differ from the norm as perceived by school personnel. Children from diverse cultural backgrounds must be assessed carefully and considered within the framework of their community and environment. Academic and intellectual measures must be evaluated to assure that no biases place the child at a disadvantage. A highly individualized, comprehensive evaluation of the child as a learner, family member, and community resident is necessary to evaluate whether the perceived problems are attributable to differences rather than deviance.

SUMMARY THOUGHTS

Although special education for children and youth with emotional disturbance seems to have justified its existence and appears to be assured of continuance, controversy and needs in the field continue to exist. Legislation has created a mandate for the education of all children, regardless of how severely disturbed, on the one hand, and a caution, on the other hand, that a child's best interest be served by placement in the least restrictive environment possible. This produces a triple challenge: implementing programs and training teachers for the severely disturbed; helping and training regular classroom teachers to educate for a wider range of individual differences; and heightening the sensitivity of administrative personnel toward providing a wide range of service options and discriminating which children need which kind of service.

A further complication is the lack of uniformity in identification procedures. What constitutes emotional disturbance is largely a subjective judgment at present. Educators and mental health practitioners must work together to clarify and structure the definition of disturbance and the diagnostic procedures that lead to its identification.

Efforts to educate the regular class student and the community at large about mental health matters must be broadened in scope. Understanding the student with emotional problems will help remove the social stigma that still exists both in and out of the school setting. Such negative attitudes tend to deter these students and their parents from seeking the assistance that educational services might offer.

Attention needs to be directed toward meeting the unique needs of individuals with emotional disturbance both at the preschool and postsecondary age range. Research and practice have demonstrated that intervention at a young age is extremely effective with behavioral problems; the advent of noncategorical early childhood special education programs provides hope that such intervention will be more commonly available. Transition to the world of work for all handicapped students appears to be a focus for the coming decade; attention directed toward this area holds promise for the adolescent with emotional disturbance.

Dealing with these students is a challenge that must involve the total world of the child. No teacher, parent, or therapist can hope to effect change in a vacuum or isolated segment of the child's life. In many instances, the school may be the arena in which the troubled child's problems are first noticed. Educators must become sensitive to the problems students exhibit and must take into account the affective needs of the children they serve.

REFERENCES

American Psychiatric Association. (1987). *Diagnostic and statistical manual of mental disorders* (3rd ed. rev.). Washington, DC: Author.

Bandura, A. (1973). *Aggression: A social learning analysis.* Englewood Cliffs, NJ: Prentice-Hall.

Bower, E. M. (Ed.). (1969). *Early identification of emotionally handicapped children in schools.* Springfield, IL: Thomas.

Carmen, G. O., & Kosberg, B. (1982). Educational technology research: Computer technology and the education of emotionally handicapped children. *Educational Technology, 22*(2), 26–30.

Clarizio, H. F., & McCoy, G. F. (1976). *Behavior disorders in children.* New York: Crowell.

Connolly, A. J. (1988). *Key Math Diagnostic Arithmetic Test—Revised.* Circle Pines, MN: American Guidance Service.

Deno, E. (1970). Special education as developmental capital. *Exceptional Children, 37*(3), 229–237.

Des Jarlais, D. C. (1972). Mental illness as social deviance. In W. C. Rhodes and M. L. Tracy (Eds.). *A study of child variance* (pp. 259–322). Ann Arbor: University of Michigan Press.

Dodge, A. B. (1976). National assessment of the supply and demand of personnel to work with the handicapped. Master's thesis, University of Kansas.

Doll, E. (1965). *Vineland Social Maturity Scale.* Circle Pines, MN: American Guidance Service.

Dunn, L. M., & Dunn, L. M. (1981). *Peabody Picture Vocabulary Test—Revised.* Circle Pines, MN: American Guidance Service.

Dunn, L. M., & Markwardt, F. C. (1989). *Peabody Individual Achievement Test-Revised.* Circle Pines, MN: American Guidance Service.

Education for All Handicapped Children Act. (1977). Washington, DC: Federal Register.

Edwards, L. L. (1988). Educational diagnosis. In P. A. Gallagher (Ed.), *Teaching students with behavior disorders* (pp. 89–101). Denver: Love.

Gallagher, P. A. (Ed.). (1979). *Teaching students with behavior disorders: Techniques for classroom instruction.* Denver: Love.

Graubard, P. S. (1971). Relationship between academic achievement and behavior dimensions. *Exceptional Children, 37,* 755–757.

Gray, W. S., & Robinson, H. M. (Eds.). (1967). *Gray Oral Reading Test.* Indianapolis: Bobbs-Merrill.

Hallahan, D. P., & Kauffman, J. M. (1978). *Exceptional children.* Englewood Cliffs, NJ: Prentice-Hall.

Haring, N. C., & Phillips, E. L. (1962). *Educating emotionally disturbed children.* New York: McGraw-Hill.

Hasselbring, T. S., & Hamlett, C. L. (1983). *Aimstar: Charting and graphing individualized student data in the classroom.* Portland, OR: ASIEP Education.

Heward, W. L., & Orlansky, M. D. (1980). *Exceptional children.* Columbus, OH: Merrill.

Hewett, F. M. (1968). *The emotionally disturbed child in the classroom: A developmental strategy for educating children with maladaptive behavior.* Boston: Allyn & Bacon.

Jackson, N. E., Jackson, D. A., & Monroe, C. (1983). *Getting along with others.* Champaign, IL: Research Press.

Johnson, R., Johnson, D., & Stanne, M. (1986). Computer assisted instruction: A comparison of cooperative, competitive and individualistic goal structures. *American Educational Research Journal, 23*(3), 382–391.

Kauffman, J. M. (1977). *Characteristics of children's behavior disorders.* Columbus, OH: Charles E. Merrill Co.

Kauffman, J. M. (1980). Where special education for disturbed children is going: A personal view. *Exceptional Children, 46,* 522–527.

Kauffman, J. M. (1989). *Characteristics of children's behavior disorders* (4th ed.). Columbus, OH: Merrill.

Kaufman, A., & Kaufman, S. (1983). *Kaufman Assessment Battery for Children.* Circle Pines, MN: American Guidance Service.

Laten, S., & Katz, G. A. (1975). *A theoretical model for assessment of adolescents: The ecological/behavioral approach.* Madison, WI: Madison Public Schools.

LaVietes, R. (1962). The teacher's role in the education of the emotionally disturbed child. *American Journal of Orthopsychiatry, 32*(5), 854–862.

MacFarlane, J., Allen, L., & Honzik, M. (1954). *A developmental study of the behavior problems of normal children between twenty-one months and fourteen years.* Berkeley: University of California Press.

Male, M. (1988). Social development in the computer environment. *Special magic.* Mountainview, CA: Mayfield.

Manion, M. H. (1986). Computers and behavior disordered students: A rationale and review of the literature. *Educational Technology, 26*(7), 20–24.

McCarney, S., Leigh, J., & Cornbleet, J. (1983). *Behavior evaluation scale.* Austin, TX: Pro-Ed.

Motto, J. J., & Wilkins, G. S. (1968). Educational achievement of institutionalized emotionally disturbed children. *Journal of Educational Research, 61,* 218–221.

Murray, H. (1943). *Thematic Apperception Test manual.* Cambridge, MA: Harvard University Press.

Quay, H. C. (1972). Patterns of aggression, withdrawal, and immaturity. In H. C. Quay & J. S. Weery (Eds.), *Psychopathological disorders of childhood* (pp. 234–267). New York: Wiley.

Quay, H. C., & Peterson, D. R. (1967). *Manual for the behavior problem checklist.* Champaign: Children's Research Center, University of Illinois.

Reinert, H. R. (1980). *Children in conflict: Educational strategies for the emotionally disturbed and behaviorally disordered.* St. Louis: Mosby.

Rhodes, W. C., & Paul, J. L. (1978). *Emotionally disturbed and deviant children: New views and approaches.* Englewood Cliffs, NJ: Prentice-Hall.

Rhodes, W. C., & Tracy, M. L. (Eds.). (1974). *A study of child variance. Vol. 1: Conceptual project in emotional disturbance.* Ann Arbor: University of Michigan Press.

Rimland, B. (1964). *Infantile autism.* New York: Appleton-Century-Crofts (Prentice-Hall).

Rizzo, J., & Zabel, R. (1988). *Educating children and adolescents with behavior disorders: An integrative approach.* Boston: Allyn & Bacon.

Roahrig, P. L. (1984). Microcomputers and handicapped children. *Electronic Learning,* November-December, 17–20.

Roberts, T. B. (1975). *Four psychologies applied to education: Freudian-behavioral-humanistic-transpersonal.* Cambridge, MA: Schenkman.

Rorschach, H. (1942). *Psychodiagnostics.* Berne, Switzerland: Verlag Hans Huber.

Shea, T. (1978). *Teaching children and youth with behavior disorders.* St. Louis: Mosby.

Silvaroli, N. J. (1973). *Classroom reading inventory* (2nd ed.). Dubuque, IA: Brown.

Smith-Davis, J., Burke, P. J., & Noel, M. M. (1984). *Personnel to educate the handicapped in America: Supply and demand from a programmatic viewpoint.* College Park: University of Maryland, Department of Special Education, Institute for the Study of Children and Youth.

Snyder, T. (1988). *Our town meeting: A lesson in civic responsibilities.* Cambridge, MA: Snyder.

Spivak, G., & Swift, M. (1971). *Hahnemann High School Behavior Rating Scale.* Philadelphia: Hahnemann Medical College and Hospital.

Spring, C., & Perry, L. (1980). *Computer assisted instruction in word-decoding for educationally handicapped children.* Carmichael, CA: San Juan Unified School District. (ERIC Document Reproduction Service No. ED 201 075).

Thorndike, R. L., Hagen, E. P., & Sattler, J. M. (1986). *Stanford Binet Intelligence Scale* (4th ed.). Chicago: Riverside.

Walker, H. M. (1970). *Walker problem identification checklist.* Los Angeles: Western Psychological Services.

Walker, J. E., & Shea, T. M. (1976). *Behavior modification: A practical approach for educators.* St. Louis: Mosby.

Wallace, G., & Larsen, S. C. (1978). *Educational assessment of learning problems: Testing for teaching.* Boston: Allyn & Bacon.

Warger, C., Aldinger,L., & Eavy, P. (1988). *The discipline diagnostician.* Ann Arbor, MI: Exceptional Innovations.

Wechsler, D. (1974). *Wechsler Intelligence Scale for Children—Revised.* New York: Psychological Corp.

Whelan, R. J., & Gallagher, P. A. (1972). Effective teaching of children with behavior disorders. In N. G. Haring & A. H. Hayden (Eds.), *The improvement of instruction* (pp. 331–357). Seattle: Special Child Publications.

Wood, M. M. (1986). *Developmental therapy in the classroom.* Austin, TX: Pro-Ed.

Woodcock, R., & Johnson, M. B. (1989). *Woodcock-Johnson Psychoeducational Battery.* Allen, TX: DLM Teaching Resources Corp.

Wright, F. (1988). *Behavior disorders identification scale.* Columbia, MO: Hawthorne Educational Services.

ADDITIONAL READINGS

Kauffman, J. M. (1982). *Characteristics of children's behavior disorders.* Columbus, OH: Merrill.

Kerr, M. M., & Nelson, C. M. (1983). *Strategies for managing behavior problems in the classroom.* Columbus, OH: Merrill.

McDowell, R. L., Adamson, G. W., & Wood, F. A. (1982). *Teaching emotionally disturbed children.* Boston: Little, Brown.

Morse, W. C. (1985). *The education and treatment of socio-emotionally impaired children and youth.* Syracuse, NY: Syracuse University Press.

Rizzo, J. V., & Zabel, R. H. (1988). *Educating children and adolescents with behavioral disorders: An integrative approach.* Boston: Allyn & Bacon.

Wood, M. M. (1986). *Developmental therapy in the classroom.* Austin, TX: Pro-Ed.

Zionts, P., & Simpson, R. (1988). *Understanding emotional and behavioral disorders of children and youth.* Austin, TX: Pro-Ed.

1

Purpose

☐ To increase your familiarity with the definition and characteristics of emotional disturbance in children

☐ To help you identify these characteristics as exemplified among actual children.

Steps

1. Locate a special classroom for children with emotional disturbances, and arrange for an observation. Make sure that your timing and purpose have the approval of both the school administrator and the teacher.

2. Allow enough time for the observation so that you can watch each student for about 10 minutes. You may benefit from arranging for time to discuss some of the observations with the teacher afterward.

3. When you go to observe, take the accompanying recording form along. During the observation, write down specific behaviors exhibited by individual students that seem to illustrate the characteristics listed on the left side of the recording form. For example, if you observe student 4 complain loudly about having a sore throat just before a math assignment is due, briefly describe this incident under component 5, "A tendency to develop physical symptoms, pains, or fears associated with personal or school problems."

Analysis

☐ Did you observe an example of each component or learner characteristic in every student?

☐ Which characteristic(s) seems most prevalent among students in this classroom?

☐ Did any of the students not seem to have any of the listed characteristics? If so, how would you account for this?

☐ Do you think your presence as an observer had an effect on the behaviors or actions of the children you observed? Why or why not?

☐ Which student(s) appeared to have the most severe difficulties? Were more characteristics present for this student, or was one characteristic present to a more marked degree?

Recording Form

Definition Components and Learner Characteristics	Students Observed				
	1	2	3	4	5
1. An inability to learn that cannot be explained by intellectual, sensory, or health factors					
2. An inability to build or maintain satisfactory interpersonal relationships with peers and teachers					
3. Inappropriate types of behavior or feelings under normal conditions					
4. A general, pervasive mood of unhappiness or depression					
5. A tendency to develop physical symptoms, pains, or fears associated with personal or school problems					

<table>
<tr><td>2</td></tr>
</table>

Purpose

☐ To increase awareness of the concepts and methods of teaching prosocial skills

☐ To familiarize you with at least two curricular materials in the area of social skills development

Steps

1. Locate any two of the materials listed in this chapter under social skill curricula in an instructional materials center or library.

2. Read the introductory chapters of both materials, answering the following questions:

   • What is the age range considered in the material?

   • What specific methods are employed?

   • What degree of preparation is necessary for the teacher?

   • How is generalization of skills encouraged (for example, homework)?

   • How interesting to students do the materials appear to be?

3. Select one social skill identified by both materials. Compare the ways each material attempts to teach the skill. Identify differences and similarities.

Analysis

☐ Did the two materials offer distinctly different ways of teaching the same social skill?

☐ Which of the approaches do you feel might be more beneficial? Why?

☐ What might you anticipate as some of the difficulties inherent in social skill teaching? What can you identify as advantages to this kind of teaching?

10

Speech and Language Disorders

Mary Ross Moran
University of Kansas

SPEECH AND LANGUAGE DISORDERS
TYPICAL PROFILE

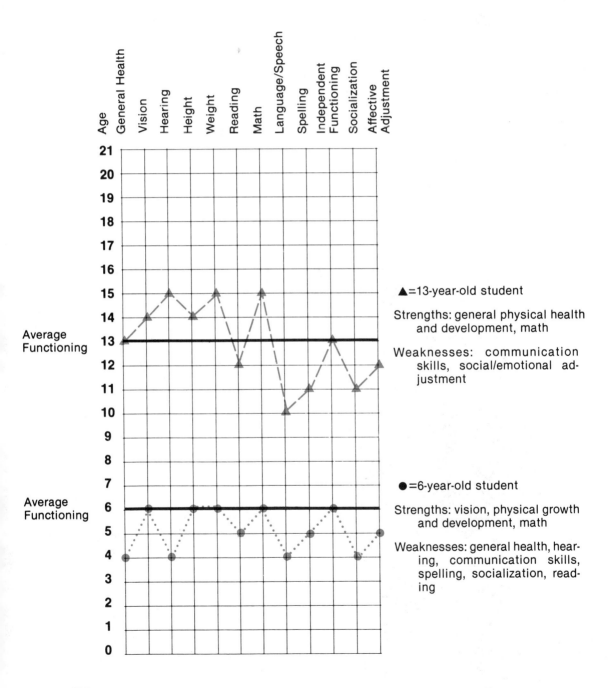

▲=13-year-old student

Strengths: general physical health and development, math

Weaknesses: communication skills, social/emotional adjustment

●=6-year-old student

Strengths: vision, physical growth and development, math

Weaknesses: general health, hearing, communication skills, spelling, socialization, reading

School speech and language programs offer a continuum of services for identification, assessment, individualized planning, and intervention. Resources also include referral to community agencies, parent counseling and training, teacher inservice instruction, and program evaluation. Within this range of services, the role of the speech-language pathologist—the specialist primarily responsible for school communication programs—is expanding under implementation of the federal mandate for students with disabilities. The SLP, once an extra itinerant provider of speech services, is now an essential member of instructional planning teams. This change is the result of three conditions: the integration of learners with more severe communication disorders into public schools, a shift by SLPs from a concern with speech to an emphasis on the cognitive and social aspects of language, and increasing recognition by educators of the essential role of communication competencies.

Depending on the severity of the problem and on whether other handicapping conditions accompany the communication disorder, the SLP's direct clinical-educational management of individualized student programs differs in intensity and delivery setting. The federal requirement for least restrictive placement results in a high proportion of placements in the regular classroom for most of the instructional day.

For this reason, SLPs have become more active as resource persons to school personnel in the regular curriculum. Because studies have shown that school personnel may not know language acquisition milestones and tend to hold unrealistic expectations in regard to language comprehension and expression (Bromley & Cavallaro, 1983), administrators and teachers rely on SLPs to help them appreciate the extent to which learners with communication disorders are challenged by heavily verbal instructions and presentation styles while struggling with the content of academic subject matter. Including SLPs on school screening, assessment, and intervention teams has increased educators' sensitivity to the diversity of language competence and the pervasiveness of speech and language disorders among school-age children.

STRATEGIES FOR SUPPORTING STUDENTS WITH SPEECH/LANGUAGE DISORDERS

Learners' concepts of themselves as communicators develop not only from specific acts of talking and listening but also, to a great extent, from the reactions of others to their communicative attempts. In an example of how reactions can influence competence, Williams (1982) compared a first grader who stutters with one who colors outside the lines. If teachers become concerned when the latter student puts crayon to paper, if they frown or look away when he goes outside a line, if they urge him to be careful, to start over, to try again, the colorer reacts negatively. He begins to tense, become shaky, anxious, frustrated, and embarrassed—all of which will make it harder for him to color readily and spontaneously the next time. Similarly, teachers' reactions to students with communication disorders have the power to restrict communication as well as to foster it.

Students with speech and language problems can be helped to perform socially and academically in a regular classroom when a teacher models communicative interactions and modifies instruction style. For instance, how a teacher deals with communication breakdowns exerts a powerful influence in the classroom. If a teacher shows a willingness to interact with and treat with patience and courtesy students who are unintelligible, dysfluent, or language limited, other students can follow these models for their own interactions with classmates whose communications are disordered.

In their instructional styles, teachers can reduce the heavy verbal comprehension load by limiting directions to one or two steps, giving essential information in short utterances that keep the sentence subject close to the verb, and avoiding indirect commands and either/or statements. They can often show students what to do rather than tell them. To help with expression, teachers can allow students with communication problems extra time to respond, ask them to act out or gesture what they cannot express verbally, and gently encourage them to continue when they initiate communication. Teachers can reduce students' anxiety in group situations by giving them opportunities to answer earlier rather than later when questions are placed to an entire group, to select a correct one-word answer from two or three provided, or to raise a hand when a true statement is made as opposed to a false one. Teachers can forgo requests for a single right answer or specific convergent response in favor of more open-ended questions that permit communicatively limited students to structure the available language in divergent ways. Similar adjustments can minimize conditions that place students on the spot under peer scrutiny and at the same time ensure that those receiving special instruction for speech and language are at all times part of the mainstream class while they are improving their communication skills.

Activity 1, page 283, will give you practice reducing the demands of oral instructions on students with communication disorders.

Special populations who may be limited in the extent to which they can profit from unaided mainstream instruction, such as those whose deafness or physical handicaps preclude speech, must be taught to use visual-gestural languages or communication boards in classrooms. Students with learning disabilities, behavior disorders, and mental retardation often require instructional modifications in materials, pace, volume, and presentation style across the curriculum.

Activity 2, page 283, will help you to understand the techniques for modification of questioning. It will give you practice on how to reduce demands on students with communication disorders.

To serve these groups, regular classroom teachers, special educators, and speech-language pathologists form an educational team, assisted by nurses, psychologists, social workers, and an audiologist or conservationist qualified to evaluate hearing. In addition to professional personnel, parents are sources of information and providers of home interventions. Planning for students with communication disorders requires examining their environments; physical condition; cognitive and emotional development; achievement motivation; social adaptation in home, school, and recreational settings; and, above all, hearing. The scope of intervention services varies with state and district funding practices and the guidelines derived from interpretations of federal regulations.

FEDERAL DETERMINATIONS OF SPEECH/LANGUAGE DISORDERS

Federal regulations governing Public Law 94-142 permit delivery of speech and language services to children in two ways. Those for whom a communication disorder is determined to be a primary handicap can be so classified and served under special education; those whose speech and language problems are secondary to another handicapping condition can be placed on the basis of the primary handicap and can then receive speech and language habilitation as a related service (Van Hattum, 1985).

Federal regulations (*Federal Register,* August 23, 1977), stated under 121a.5, define speech impaired as "a communication disorder, such as stuttering, impaired articulation, a language impairment, or a voice impairment, which adversely affects a child's educational performance." According to these regulations, the related services to which these children are entitled "means transportation and such developmental, corrective, and other supportive services as are required to assist a handicapped child to benefit from special education, and includes speech pathology and audiology, psychological services, physical and occupational therapy, recreation, early identification and assessment of disabilities in children, counseling services, and medical services for diagnostic or evaluation purposes." (See Van Hattum [1985], pp. 96–97, for a list of sources on PL 94-142.)

According to Snyder (1984), although preschool children are labeled with speech and language disorder as a primary handicap, after they enter school and begin to exhibit problems with reading and writing, they are more likely to be classified under the category "specific learning disability" because regulations define it to include reading and writing disorders. In Snyder's view, this practice in effect ignores the foundation role of oral language and masks the prevalence of speech and language disorders in the school-age population. This shift in classification tends to underestimate the numbers of school-age children requiring communication services and may artificially limit the numbers of SLPs and hearing experts hired for assessment and intervention.

CHARACTERISTICS OF CHILDREN AND YOUTH WITH COMMUNICATION DISORDERS

Communication is an interactive cognitive and social process in which a message is conveyed from one person to another. Face-to-face communication occurs by means of speech sounds accompanied by intonation, stresses and pauses, gestures, facial expression, eye contact, posture, and physical distance between interacting parties. For some groups, speech is replaced by a visual-gestural system, such as American Sign Language, but it has no written counterpart. Written English is the only choice for communication at a distance or over time. Of course, communication can occur without a language system of any kind, spoken or manual, as happens when children who know no English enter an American school and readily play with classmates by using nonverbal signs and pantomime.

Previous Definitions of Communication

Past attempts to identify separate speech and language characteristics of children and youth with handicaps have proved counterproductive because they have led to instruction in splinter skills without generalization to real communication situations. Professional persons now view communication as a holistic capacity for using speech and language to learn how the world operates; to receive, analyze, organize, and store information; to share that information with others as filtered through a cultural value system; and to adjust the manner of communication in accord with the prior knowledge, age, social status, and other characteristics of listeners. Although underlying competencies may be identified and labeled for purposes of assessment and instruction, it is the *integration* of those competencies into a seamless whole that comprises competent communication.

Concepts of what constitutes communication disorders have changed in recent years (see Rice's [1986] description of a communicative competence model). In a heterogeneous society such as the United States, children learn a first language within their own cultural community. Cultures differ in standards for what to say and how to say it. So long as children can communicate within that first-language setting, they cannot be said to demonstrate a communication disorder even if their language is substantially different from that of the mainstream culture. This view acknowledges that a discrepancy between mainstream cultural expectations and the way an individual child talks can give a false appearance of a language disorder when the discrepancy is merely a language difference. Therefore, in determining whether individual characteristics constitute a communication disorder, the standard to apply is whether the traits in question reflect the conventions of the speaker's own first-language community, even if these traits differ from school language. Regional or ethnic rule-governed dialects meet first-language community standards and are therefore not linguistically deficient. This model distinguishes language disorders from language differences across cultural subgroups.

A practical referral indicator can be applied by professional persons working with children. A student should be referred for speech and language evaluation if

LISA

Lisa, now 9, was never enrolled in preschool but entered kindergarten at age 5, when she was said to be unintelligible and language delayed. In the course of the year, she kicked her teacher and other students, threw books, and frequently ran out of the classroom when she was asked to complete tasks. Lisa was retained in first grade because she could not label common objects; describe spatial, causal, or temporal relationships; or follow directions for small-group or independent work. During her second year in first grade, her refusals increased to the point that an evaluation team recommended half-day placement in a learning center where management systems brought her behavior under classroom control. By the end of second grade, Lisa had made virtually no progress in the district's adopted phonics-based reading series, but she began to follow directions and complete some tasks.

With a supplementary series based on a word-family approach instead of phonics, Lisa has recently developed a basic sight vocabulary of more than 100 words, and she can now read connected text and join a reading group. Peers in the reading group constitute her first successful social contacts. With intensive articulation therapy, she has reduced her consonant omissions and substitutions, but she still needs both individual and group sessions twice a week. Language therapy focused on concept building also continues in both individual weekly sessions with the SLP and group sessions delivered three times a week in her regular third-grade classroom. The team monitoring her IEP has tied improvements in her speech intelligibility and language comprehension directly to gains in her classroom task behavior. As she begins to demonstrate academic progress, Lisa's status is 3 years behind expectations based on her nonverbal intellectual functioning.

☐ ☐ ☐

What might be the relationship between Lisa's acting-out behavior in class and her unintelligibility and language delay?

Why would the type of reading series adopted in her classroom affect Lisa's ability to profit from reading instruction?

What are some nonverbal ways to provide directions and behavior cues to a student like Lisa who cannot follow verbal instructions?

How could a teacher offer incidental information to Lisa throughout the day to improve her grasp of common concepts about the world?

---

the way the child talks is more noticeable than the content of what the child is saying. That is, if mispronunciations, dysfluencies, unusual pitch, rate, hoarseness, omitted words or word endings, words used in unusual ways, or atypical word sequences call attention to the manner of expression more than to the message, the learner may be demonstrating a communication disorder.

Communication Disorders Versus Communication Differences

Differences that might be due to dialect or to a first language other than Standard American English, although they are not communication disorders, may be indistinguishable from speech or language problems by people without special training. According to Bloodstein (1984), the question to ask is whether the deviation interferes with intelligibility or simply represents nonconformity. Referral for screening is appropriate if concerns emerge because the screening process does not take an undue amount of time from the child's instruction, but it may identify genuine speech or language problems early enough to provide effective interventions before a communication disorder interferes with early schooling. In the case of dialect or first-language differences, screening will not lead to comprehensive evaluation for services under PL 94-142 unless the language difference is accompanied by a covered handicapping condition, but other services may be available under bilingual or other programs to which learners can be referred.

Learners whose communication problems can be classified as disorders rather than differences must next be determined to demonstrate either a primary speech and language problem or one that is secondary to another handicapping condition. Johnston (1988) described the first group as those "who meet the minimal criteria of significant language delay, normal-range performance intelligence quotient (IQ), and adequate peripheral hearing. The key feature of the working definition is, of course, the developmental gap between language and other aspects of growth" (p. 685).

Students may exhibit both speech and language impairments in varied combinations. Speech problems may involve *articulation* (the way sounds are produced), *fluency* (the speech rate and rhythm), or *voice* (the pitch, volume, and quality of speech). Language problems may involve *syntactic structure* (the organization of phrases and clauses), *morphology* (the use of prefixes and suffixes to build words), *semantic content* (concepts and vocabulary), or *pragmatics* (the application of semantics, syntactics, and morphology to interactive communication with differing listeners in varied settings). Pragmatics cuts across both speech and language because it overlaps with social customs; it is the system that makes language form (syntax and morphology) and content (semantics) applicable to life situations.

A problem in any one of these areas may qualify a learner for special services under PL 94-142, but traits usually occur in clusters (Bloodstein, 1984). Speakers with severe articulation problems tend to be out of pattern in language development. Those whose speech is dysfluent may be so reluctant to talk that they fail to engage in the interactive process of attempting patterns so listening adults can provide feedback; this lack of experience is reflected in their language milestones. The following descriptions of specific speech and language disorders, separated for discussion purposes, do not imply that these conditions are likely to occur in isolation. When problems are identified in a specific subsystem, it is the relationship of that impaired component to the whole communication system—and to the whole communicating person—that is important. The relevant question is, How does this breakdown interact with other aspects of the individual's linguistic and social interactions?

Articulation

According to McReynolds (1988), normally developing children of preschool ages may substitute (/t/ for /k/ in *kitten*), add (*suhleep* for *sleep*), omit (*buh* for *bus*), or make other less frequent changes in speech sounds. Mastery of consonant sounds begins about age 2, and between 5 to 8 years most children spontaneously master speech sound production.

Among children with handicapping conditions such as learning disabilities, mental retardation, or behavior disorders, articulation problems persist into school age. Children or youth with cerebral palsy or cleft palate demonstrate articulation disorders as a typical characteristic. For a larger number of school-age children, however, articulation problems are not readily explained. "This subgroup of children constitutes the largest single communicative disorder treated by speech-language pathologists" (McReynolds, 1988, p. 419).

Learning problems associated with articulation errors center on beginning reading and spelling. Because normal consonant mastery may not be complete until age 8, formal reading instruction occurs during the final 2 years of that process; when articulation mastery is delayed or is out of sequence, the entire course of beginning reading throughout grades one through three may take place before readers can pronounce the words presented to them. If reading is taught by a phonics approach, as is usual today, the route to accurate word recognition is through the phonologic system. Students who misperceive individual sounds, cannot reproduce

Articulation disorders require a learner to have special help.

them on demand, and fail to blend separate sounds into words recognizable as part of their oral vocabulary are at a disadvantage in beginning phonics instruction.

Because spelling depends on word-recognition skills—children cannot spell words they cannot recognize—breakdowns in discriminating and producing individual sounds affect both reading and writing of phonetically regular words. Of course, many English words are not phonetically predictable in pronunciation or spelling; learning of irregular sight vocabulary by a whole-word method may not be affected by articulation errors unless the beginning reader is unwilling to pronounce words orally because of self-consciousness about substitutions or distortions.

Children who are unintelligible are readily referred. But behavioral indicators of referral for articulation evaluation include pronunciations perceived as appropriate for chronologically younger children. For example, the common substitution of /w/ for both /r/ and /l/ is worth treating because it could lead peers to ostracize a third grader as using baby talk. Another behavioral implication is that being treated as younger may lead children to adopt social patterns appropriate for earlier developmental stages.

Fluency

Dysfluent speech is characterized by interruptions in the rate or phrasing of speech or production flow. The common behavioral interpretation of dysfluent speech is called *stuttering*. All normally developing children during preschool years demonstrate some degree of nonfluency in the form of word and phrase repetitions or revisions to correct false starts. Such nonfluency differs from early stuttering, which includes not only word and phrase repetitions at higher frequencies but also sound and syllable repetitions and sound prolongations. Children who stutter form a heterogeneous group, but more advanced stuttering is often associated with secondary facial or motor mannerisms in efforts to avoid or hide the vocal blocking. "Children are likely to be diagnosed as stutterers if they exhibit sound and syllable repetitions that contain a minimum of two or three repetitions per unit" or "if their dysfluencies last for 2 seconds or longer. The presence of tension or struggle is...a diagnostic clue" (Wall, 1988, p. 629).

Bloodstein (1984) described a less common type of dysfluency as *cluttering*, which is characterized by very rapid, indistinct speech with some breakdown in word order or unusual uses of words, along with sound or word repetitions and sound prolongations. Bloodstein distinguished cluttering as more diffuse than stuttering; the former is marked by an impression of haste in a pattern of jerky, indistinct speech with hesitations and repetitions, but is not accompanied by the secondary facial or motor symptoms associated with stuttering.

Learning problems emerging from dysfluency center on reluctance to engage in verbal interactions. Lessons dependent on group discussions, oral reports, volunteers answering teacher questions, or similar activities that put an individual speaker on the spot to perform are avoided by students who stutter. Lack of opportunities for oral rehearsal of content in classroom groups may translate into problems in organizing written responses when similar content appears on tests.

Voice

Voice disorders include deviations in pitch, loudness, or quality—any abnormality in tone arising from the vibrations of the vocal cords as modified by the resonating cavities of the vocal tract. Childhood vocal disturbance may be due to structural problems, neurological disorders ranging from vocal fold paralysis to spasticity, vocal abuse such as screaming, or functional causes related to psychoneurosis or faulty learning (Wilson, 1987).

Voice problems carry few implications for specific learning or social behavior, although an unpleasant voice registers as distracting to listeners and may indicate medical or psychological conditions that should be investigated. Voice disturbances may be more likely than other speech problems to be overlooked in school, so that a referral is not made when it is indicated. For example, hoarseness secondary to a cold or ear infection may recur several times during a winter or might last up to 3 weeks, but if hoarseness persists longer, a referral for medical evaluation is in order because chronic hoarse voice can be associated with serious conditions.

Syntax

The organizing principles used in putting words together to form longer units constitute the syntactic system of any language. In English, word order is the major factor. For example, it makes a difference whether a child says, "The dog bit the boy" or "The boy bit the dog." In some other languages, the relationships between the two actors would be expressed by word endings instead of word order. The syntactic demands of English require that children learn to sequence patterns. Because syntactic patterns exist in a limited number, they can be mastered by a specific age—usually around 6 (Johnston, 1988).

Behavioral indicators of syntactic breakdowns may be omissions or failures to match sentence parts in addition to resequencing. Thus, some children delete parts of a verb phrase and say, "He running" instead of "He is running." Others use a pronoun form without matching it to the referent for gender, case, or number and say, "Him go they house" in identifying a picture of a girl walking into her home. Order of occurrence of specific word types may be violated as when children do not reverse the position of the verb in the question "What time lunch is?" or do not state multiple modifiers conventionally, as in "The green big second ball."

Learning problems arise from syntactic disorders because they disrupt comprehension of both subject matter content and oral directions in classrooms. According to Laughton and Hasenstab (1986), inability to grasp complex structures using "who" and "which," or subordinating terms such as "because" or "if," lead to misunderstandings and so occupy learners with trying to grasp what is happening procedurally in class that they are unready to take in information. When production is attempted, utterances limited to base structures do not provide specifics of what the learner means to say and lead to crossed messages. Students who do not form questions conventionally cannot ask for the help they need to clarify instructions or lesson content.

Morphology

A *morpheme* is the smallest unit of meaning in any language. A word always consists of at least one morpheme but contains more than one if the word is plural (book/s), has a past-tense marker (test/ed), or has a prefix (pre/test) or suffix (learn/ing). The study of and application of these word parts to add meaning to base words is called *morphology*.

Up to about age 5, children follow a relatively predictable order of acquisition of inflectional markers for number, tense, possession, and so forth, although markers are often omitted during stages when learners are trying to consolidate several syntactic features simultaneously. Normally developing preschool children overgeneralize markers, as in "We goed home," for example, which indicates that the speaker has internalized the rule for regular past tense. But by school entry, omissions such as "We play yesterday" or redundant markers such as "two shoeses" have typically been corrected, and persistence of such patterns may indicate a problem. Irregular verb forms, however, may not be learned even by achieving children until age 10 or so.

Failures to build words conventionally seldom interfere with meaning as much as do errors in syntax. Because listeners can usually understand intended meaning even if children misapply a marker, learning implications are relatively minor, although children can be penalized socially for nonstandard usage.

Semantics

The semantic system is concerned with meaning, both broadly in terms of concepts about how the world works and narrowly in terms of the number and types of vocabulary words an individual can use. Learning the semantic system of a language permits children to map the reality they perceive through their senses and to talk about objects and relationships when they are not physically available to their senses.

Children do not use words as adults do, so semantic acquisition is a process of discovering more and more features until learners' meanings approach those of adults. In this process, children both overextend and underextend meanings. For example, they may call all furry creatures with four legs and a tail "dog," or, conversely, they may call any dog "a Frisky" if that is the name of their family dog. Children tend to learn first the most general features of a semantic domain and later the more specific or restricted features that distinguish one example from another. Because they learn new words and additional concepts throughout a lifetime, learners can never be said to have mastered the semantic content of a language, although vocabulary norms on standardized tests can estimate whether progress accords with that of a large sample of representative children of the same age.

Indicators for vocabulary problems are usually of two types. In one case, children simply have not learned the names of commonly seen objects, places, or persons; their vocabulary is inadequate to describe their experience. In the second case, known labels cannot be recalled on demand; the learner who has a word-retrieval problem cannot produce the label "book" if a teacher asks "What is this?"

but can point to the correct object if told, "Point to the book." More serious semantic problems are associated with failure to organize incoming information into concepts about the world. This might be indicated by gross misuse of relational terms,
so that, for example, "before" is used when "after" is meant, or "to" is used when
"from" is intended. These small words that hold sentences together—called *function words*—require more abstract learning than do the labels associated with tangible objects (nouns), actions (verbs), or attributes (adjectives and adverbs).

Learning problems associated with inadequate vocabulary pervade all instruction; learners lack basic foundation tools. Word-retrieval problems interfere with
the conduct of oral lessons and with early oral reading because even a recognized
word cannot be pronounced. Inadequate concepts prevent reading comprehension.
Recent findings by reading researchers emphasize the role of prior knowledge in
drawing meaning from reading (Lipson & Wixson, 1986). That is, the reader incorporates new information in a reading passage into the prior schema about the topic.
Children who lack basic classification systems for organizing incoming information
are not prepared to gain from reading; if the concepts of "same" and "different" are
not established, for example, a passage classifying objects on this basis in a third-
grade science text remains meaningless.

Pragmatics

Pragmatics is concerned with the appropriateness for audience and setting of (a) the
way speech and language are delivered (use of facial expressions, eye contact,
physical distance, and so forth); (b) whether the speaker distinguishes shared prior
information from new information in selecting vocabulary and syntax; and (c)
whether the speaker judges the interaction usefully in terms of taking turns, repair-
ing misunderstandings, maintaining a mutual topic, and generally grasping the
needs and intentions of the other party. Pragmatic applications both precede and
supersede other language learning. They precede other language systems because
infants of 6 months or so develop social communication systems by eye contact,
gesture, turn-taking, and topic maintenance before words appear a half year later;
preverbal infants can readily express requests, refusals, greetings, and numerous
other functions (Russel, 1984). Pragmatic systems supersede other language systems because articulation, fluency, voice, syntax, semantics, and morphology have
to function together in appropriate interaction with another speaker/listener before
communication can be said to occur (Laughton & Hasenstab, 1986).

Behavioral indicators that pragmatic competencies are inadequate may be
overt, as when a hearing student grabs others to gain attention instead of calling their
names, says "He hit me" without identifying who "he" is or rudely insists on introducing a new topic in a small group. More subtle indicators may include standing
too close while talking, addressing adult acquaintances by first names, or missing
the indirect request to stop talking when the teacher says, "It's getting noisy in here."
Asking personal questions, initiating conversations in disruptive ways, and missing
jokes or sarcasm are typical reports from teachers of students with disabilities.

ERIC

Eric, age 14, attended preschool for 3 years and appeared to demonstrate readiness for reading and writing along with average intelligence when he entered first grade, although teachers' notes show that he stood out in class because he volunteered irrelevant comments or questions at inappropriate times, interrupted teachers, and was generally loud, boisterous and off-task though neither noncompliant nor aggressive toward other students. Between grades two through four he fell behind peers in all language arts competencies. When his fourth-grade teacher noticed that he was omitting word endings and some verb forms in his speech, did not produce known words on demand, and omitted entire syllables in spelling words he could read, she referred Eric for evaluation. But test comparisons showed he scored just above the oral language and reading discrepancies that would have permitted service delivery under special education; the evaluation team determined that he did not demonstrate a covered handicapping condition. Unable to maintain classwork or homework in fifth grade, Eric was required to drop out of after-school sports programs in which he excelled to make time for daily tutoring provided by his family. A team reevaluated Eric in grade six and determined that he now met discrepancy criteria for learning disabilities services in reading and writing. He also demonstrated a mild central hearing loss, a syntax disorder, and a word-retrieval problem. Eric could not use textbooks in his regular class without one-to-one help, produced fragments and run-ons full of misspelled words when asked to write a paragraph, and had withdrawn from school to the extent of inventing illnesses so he could stay home.

Intensive holistic language instruction delivered by the SLP, the sixth-grade teacher, and the reading specialist allowed Eric to focus for the remainder of the year on a selected 500-word subject-matter and survival vocabulary for concept building, reading, spelling, oral and written sentence formulation, and ultimately, paragraph construction. With preferential classroom seating, class text materials read onto tapes so he could play them repeatedly, intensive training in a learning

Activity 3, page 284, lets you practice an informal procedure for recognizing three subsystems within language as distinct from speech. You will need a tape recorder and a set of action pictures to complete this activity.

Learning implications of pragmatics breakdowns are serious. Many referrals to special education based on classroom disruptions arise from lack of pragmatic skills, as when students talk out or interrupt other speakers. A high proportion of learner frustration in instruction can be traced to inability to read nonverbal signals, to fol-

strategy that taught him to preview and organize class texts to make comprehension more accessible, daily instruction in putting together word strips to form modeled syntactic patterns, and flexible oral question-and-answer sessions to avoid laborious spelling demands, Eric began to improve oral communication and reading.

He was then willing to enter a group social-skills training program centered on pragmatic language competencies and delivered by the SLP and one of the school counselors. With the same type of team instruction in grade seven, he improved to the point that his present eighth-grade program is predominantly in mainstream core classes, with 1 hour a day in resource programs for oral and written language supplementary instruction in addition to a regular remedial English class. As soon as he had an individualized language program during school hours, Eric resumed after-school sports, and he has begun to apply his new social skills to making after-school friends. Eric is doing well but has lost time from intensive language instruction because his was a subtle, difficult-to-identify set of communication problems.

□ □ □

Why would Eric have appeared to teachers to be ready for reading and writing when he had a hearing loss, a syntax problem and a word-retrieval problem?; to what strengths were teachers apparently responding, and how might those assets mask a communication problem?

If Eric could not read textbooks in his regular fourth- and fifth-grade classrooms, how could teachers have modified this task to enable Eric to learn content material even though he was not eligible for special services?

Faced with a choice between a sports program in which Eric excelled or after-school tutoring in basic language competencies of reading and writing in which he constantly failed, what reasoning could a teacher follow to advise his parents?

Why would Eric's cluster of communication problems respond better to a team approach (involving the SLP, the 6th-grade teacher, and the reading specialist) than to individual therapies from the same staff?

---

low indirect commands, or to know when a question is in order. Students who cannot judge the interpersonal and setting contexts so they can adjust according to the status of the listener and the demands of the situation are at a disadvantage in dealing with others. Pragmatic disorders disrupt basic interpersonal human relationships.

BASIC PROFESSIONAL VOCABULARY

Conant (1986) has pointed out the irony that SLP experts on the social appropriateness of language sometimes use in their own professional jargon terms that are offensive to students who demonstrate communication disorders—words such as "defective," "deviant," or "deficient." Furthermore, researchers seeking precision among child language users lack specificity in their use of professional terms. "The apparently straightforward word *disorder,* for example, may be used either to refer to language problems in general or to distinguish delayed from otherwise unusual courses of language development" (p. 136). Arguing that quasi-medical designations are inappropriate to describe interpersonal relationships, Conant asserted that no one member of an interpersonal system can be said to "have" a disorder and that the other partner in the transaction is not to be designated as "normal" in contrast. Nevertheless, because no adequate term exists to express these pragmatic considerations, most practitioners continue to use the term *disorder,* as did Johnston (1988) when she pointed out that "differences in labels usually reflect theoretical emphasis rather than differences in population" (p. 686).

In general, the term *communication* is used to describe interactions between people using speech and language, both of which are subsumed under the term. *Speech* is the realization of language through a sound system, including articulation, fluency, and voice parameters. *Language* is a set of arbitrary symbols used for both thinking and interpersonal transactions.

Subsumed under *language, syntax* and *morphology* describe form; *semantics* and *pragmatics* describe meaning. *Syntax* refers to the form of structures longer than one word; *morphology* refers to the form of a single word. *Semantics* is associated with cognitive meaning—vocabulary and concepts—whereas *pragmatics* refers to the broader functional, social meanings of speech and language acts. Beyond these classification terms, the following terms are useful to teachers in collaborative consultation with speech-language pathologists and audiologists.

Code switching is the ability of a speaker to shift between two or more dialects (Black English to Standard American English) or between formal and informal Standard American English in adjusting to different listeners and settings.

Dialect comprises the rule-governed sound, form, and content variations in a language due to age, race or ethnic group, geography, or other factors that isolate one group of speakers from another; the standard dialect is that used by those holding educational, political, and social status in a language community.

Generalization is the transfer of a learned production or response to untrained items or to another setting.

Grammar is the descriptive or prescriptive rules governing the interactions of word order (syntax) and word form (morphology) in any language.

Referent is the object, idea, or event in the real world symbolized by words.

ASSESSING INSTRUCTIONAL NEED

Although assigning causes of disorders may be necessary for funding purposes, especially in resolving questions of primary or secondary handicap, the search for causality is typically a minor part of a speech and language assessment. The consensus is that most speech and language disorders have no single, identifiable cause but arise from multiple genetic, medical, and environmental conditions (Bloodstein, 1984). A child whose language acquisition is globally delayed is usually identified early by the family and referred for appropriate preschool intervention. But a learner who has a mild hearing loss or who develops some language but follows an atypical sequence and fails to master certain concepts or linguistic patterns is more difficult to identify. Many language problems do not become apparent until children are faced with the demands of academic instruction.

Screening for Identification

Speech or language assessment begins with a developmental history followed by screening to confirm the existence of a speech or language problem. A history uncovers parental reports of ear infections, allergies, or high fevers that raise questions about possible hearing loss during early stages of speech and language acquisition. Comparing language data with motor and social developmental milestones indicates whether problems are associated with global developmental delay, are secondary to another handicapping condition, or are limited to speech and language acquisition. Screening results are used to determine (a) whether referred individuals demonstrate the minimum discrepancies that would permit schools to serve them under PL 94-142 and (b) which speech and language systems require a closer look through more comprehensive evaluation.

Hearing is screened first because speech and language are dependent on intact sensory function. A complete audiometric test is warranted if a student does not pass a screening within a narrow volume range across the pitches at which speech is heard. If there is a history of middle-ear infections, it may be appropriate to refer for further testing even if screening results appear normal. Audiometric screening is performed by an SLP in an ordinary room, but a full audiometric evaluation, if indicated, is administered by an audiologist in a sound-treated room.

Speech and language screening may consist of short versions of standardized tests along with informal conversation with the SLP. Voice screening attempts to distinguish chronic from transient disorders and to identify children who should be referred to a laryngologist, the medical specialist who treats the voice mechanism.

Standardized tests are used to decide whether testees can be considered for special education or related services. In order to qualify for speech and language problems to be treated as a primary handicapping condition, students in most states must demonstrate a specific discrepancy between the current IQs and scores on norm-referenced speech and language tests that compare the testees with a sample national group of the same age. Results of the comparison must show that students are now performing considerably below what would be predicted from nonverbal intellectual level. If, instead, speech and language status accords with other developmental milestones—all below chronological age with the IQ below 70—speech and language delays are considered secondary to mental retardation. Evidence for combinations of speech and language problems secondary to other handicapping conditions such as physical mobility limitations, learning disabilities, or behavior disorders is weighed on a case-by-case basis when the comprehensive evaluation is completed.

Comprehensive Evaluation for Intervention Planning

Examiners adjust comprehensive assessment batteries on the basis of presenting problems. To support an intervention design, speech and language evaluation must describe deviations from expected limits in detail, document the reliability with which they occur, and estimate their severity. Speech and language evaluation employs both published tests and samples of elicited and spontaneous connected language supplemented by informal probes designed by examiners.

Published Tests

Published articulation measures include tests of single-word productions that place each sound or blend in beginning, middle, and final positions as subjects name pictures of common objects. Published stuttering tests include speaking tasks such as imitation or response to questions increasing in demand from one word to formulation of a narrative. Some procedures require reading, and most require conversation between the examiner and the subject.

Published language tests tend to rely on comprehension measures rather than on expression of connected text. They may require pointing responses to pictures or single-word answers to incomplete sentences. Picture vocabulary tests estimate the extent of receptive vocabulary of single words in isolation, and syntax and morphology tests typically demand selection of pictures in response to examiner statements or insertion of missing parts into sentence frames.

Published tests are appropriate to determine the extent of a discrepancy between current status and expectations; tests predict to some extent speakers' ability to function with age and grade peers in a regular classroom. Nevertheless, standardized tests yielding a language age, percentile rank, or standard score are developed primarily to show up differences between testees; the content of these tests does not include some of the most basic speech or language items because most testees would pass those items and the test would not produce the desired variability. Therefore, standardized tests cannot provide the detailed information needed to plan individualized programs.

Contextual Samples

For program planning, examiners collect an audiotaped sample of connected speech and language to study pronunciations, fluency, and voice in context and to evaluate syntax, morphology, and semantics. To examine formulation of syntactic and morphologic structures, the sample is elicited by asking open-ended questions such as, "Tell me about" pets, a favorite vacation, a hobby, or after-school activities. Questions that can be answered yes or no or those that begin with who, what, when, where, why, or how are avoided to increase the likelihood that speakers will form complete utterances rather than fragments.

Puppets and play activities encourage language development and make learning fun.

Pragmatic competencies can be evaluated to some extent with an audiotaped sample, but a videotape is required to assess many pragmatic features. A videotape of spontaneous (as opposed to elicited) speech and language is a valuable source for comparative analysis, especially if it includes interactions with parents and siblings or age peers. Interactions of pragmatic language patterns with other speech and language traits are of diagnostic import, as when speakers react to their unintelligibility, dysfluencies, or limited vocabularies by reducing language interactions and substituting nonverbal signals.

Using one or preferably two audiotaped speech and language samples, examiners can do many types of articulation analyses, ranging from plus-minus scoring of correct productions through identification of substitutions and omissions to detailed phonetic transcriptions that may include not only the targeted sound but also its context. Dysfluencies can be assessed using qualitative data such as descriptions of sound and syllable repetition. Quantitative measures include the percentage of repeated phrases, words, syllables, or sounds per minute; the proportion of each type; and the duration of a single prolongation.

Language analysis from audiotapes or videotapes depends on examiners knowing the context of the connected text. In other words, the language is evaluated in terms of its appropriateness to the other speaker/listener participants, the social constraints of the situation, and the formality or informality of the setting. In a clinic, a language sample of 100 words or more is transcribed and scored according to both qualitative and quantitative measures. In schools, where caseloads are heavy and time constraints severe, only a portion of the sample is typically evaluated for language; analysis may be as informal as completing a checklist and taking notes while listening to the tape several times.

Some parts of the speech evaluation depend on examiner impressions. For example, the SLP checks alignment of the teeth along with tongue and mouth exercises to determine whether the articulators are of normal shape and mobility. The comprehensive voice evaluation focuses on *respiration* (measures of breathing patterns), *phonation* (vocal fold position and vibration), and *resonance* (hypernasality, hyponasality, or denasality). In addition, analysis of pitch range, rate, loudness, and vocal endurance combine with subjective judgments of voice quality to provide a description detailed enough to suggest a treatment plan (Wilson, 1987).

Informal Observations

Informal language impressions are most useful if gathered in the regular classroom, cafeteria, halls, and recreation areas instead of in a testing room. Observations are guided by sets of questions. What is the degree of attention to and compliance with oral directions? When a direction is given, do observed children begin to respond at once or look around to see what others are doing? Is uncompleted work associated with these behaviors? What is the response to and use of questions? Are they used for clarification of tasks? To gain definitions of terms? To request additional information? Do target students volunteer in group discussions? If so, are comments relevant or related to points discussed five minutes earlier? Do referred students initiate conversations with peers at appropriate times and places? How do they respond to such initiatives? To what extent do peer interactions depend on nonverbal signals? Are turn-taking and topic maintenance respected? With such a frame of reference for observation, the SLP and the regular or special teacher can complement the formal evaluation with detailed examples of language use in applied settings.

To make a distinction between language disorder and language difference, two major advantages of informal observation over testing are the opportunity to collect data without the bias enforced by test instruments and the chance to note whether referred students engage in code switching by, for example, using more formal language with teachers than with peers. Naturalistic settings can be varied enough to allow a speaker from a minority culture to select usages from the language repertoire and demonstrate strengths that may not be revealed by tests.

Activity 4, page 285, will allow you to practice an informal observation procedure to recognize applied uses of language.

Similarly, nontest data can be helpful in identifying the compensatory behaviors available to students with varied degrees of speech and language problems. If standard forms of speech or language are not yet established, the way students choose to communicate when free to do so offers valuable predictive data about how those learners may function in a regular curriculum and with mainstream classmates.

INTERVENTIONS

Planning Instruction

Therapists' views of how disorders are organized affect selection of instructional procedures as well as priorities for intervention. For example, according to McReynolds (1988), three theories attempt to account for articulation problems. The *phonologic-disorders model* holds that rule-governed error patterns arise from children's attempts to simplify adult forms that they cannot reproduce. The *perceptual-motor model* proposes that articulation is a matter of cognitive and motor planning, influenced by feedback as speakers move from acquisition to automaticity. The *discrimination model* explains problems as an inability to distinguish one speech sound from another, with experts disagreeing about whether discrimination is based on production or vice versa. SLPs who view articulation problems as based on phonologic rules develop intervention plans differently from those committed to perceptual-motor or discrimination training.

Similarly, when planning language intervention, SLPs who believe in following the sequence of normal acquisition for language therapy develop objectives different from those who follow other theoretical models. Thus, some practitioners choose to work first with those language structures that are developmentally the earliest to appear in most children without disabilities. Others select first the targets that can be considered easier to teach to mastery because they are less complex than other needs or those targets most amenable to patterns or rules. Still others make decisions on social considerations, selecting to work first, for example, on those speech features that make a speaker sound like a chronologically younger child or on those pragmatic language competencies that would help a student be better accepted by adults and peers in mainstream settings.

Placement Options

When speech and/or language impairment is considered a primary handicapping condition under special education, most school districts now attempt to provide services for preschool ages in special developmental programs, although the federal mandate for services to toddler and preschool age groups does not yet require full implementation. Typically, preschool programs are offered for a half day, and they are supplemented by organized instruction for parents designed to help them intervene more effectively at home. Parental intervention programs, traditionally a part of the therapy plan, have recently assumed a more visible role as parents have been enlisted to deliver more intensive programs and keep records of progress. Some preschool programs integrate preschool children with communication disorders with nonhandicapped learners.

Primary school students may be placed in a type of self-contained classroom that has recently become widespread. Many school districts have organized special classes for beginning students with speech and language impairments, often staffed by an SLP and a special educator as team teachers who emphasize a speech and language curriculum throughout the day. Such classes serve as alternatives to kindergarten or first-grade placements, after which students are again evaluated to determine whether they can enter the general curriculum or continue to need special services.

When self-contained classrooms are not established or are not considered to be needed by an individual learner, the next level of services consists of a regular classroom placement supplemented by a pull-out program in which the SLP delivers services in a resource room, usually on a twice-weekly basis, for 30 minutes per session. The same twice-weekly schedule is typically followed if speech and language programs are delivered as related services when the primary handicapping condition is determined to be learning disability, behavior disorder, or mild mental retardation. Programs then provide both special education instruction and speech and language therapy on a pull-out basis. Under this plan, students may spend up to 2 hours a day in a special education resource room in which a learning disabilities teacher or other specialist delivers reading, writing, and/or mathematics individualized lessons; the SLP meets the same students in a separate resource room twice a week for intensive therapy.

The prevailing view is that naturalistic settings are the best context for delivering communication interventions (Rice, 1986), which implies that services should be delivered in regular classrooms. This model requires close collaboration among SLPs, special educators, and regular classroom teachers if appropriate communication emphasis is to be incorporated into lessons across the curriculum for students with varying communication problems.

The extent to which students with communication problems are served in the regular classroom varies with the teacher's priorities, the type of schedule on which the SLP is present in the building, the availability of a paraprofessional assistant to permit small-group instruction, and, above all, the extent to which the SLP has defined with the team and the administration a role that includes consultation time in addition to direct services to children. Traditionally, at a minimum, SLPs have enlisted regular classroom teachers to do carryover activities in order to reinforce intensive pull-out instruction. Some SLPs have provided small-group concept building or vocabulary lessons in regular classrooms. A more central role for the SLP in the regular classroom featuring delivery of services to small groups within that setting has emerged during the years of implementation of PL 94-142.

Holistic Approaches

Recently, holistic language arts approaches that combine oral and written language activities within each lesson have offered another framework for service delivery in regular classrooms. A design for integrated instruction, as presented by Baldwin and Henry (1985), attempts to integrate discrete lessons into a coherent program for learners and a more realistic instructional task for teachers. The distinguishing features of this program are the presentation of listening, oral discussion, reading, spelling, writing, phonics, grammar, and handwriting activities in combined lessons based on content-free scripts and a key vocabulary as opposed to separate basal reading series and traditional spelling and handwriting workbooks. Although the Baldwin and Henry example is based on an alphabetic approach to instruction, with which not all teachers would agree, the format for combining content and structure into daily lessons is applicable to other language approaches. It is too early in the schools' experiences with holistic models to determine effects on learners with moderate to severe communication disorders, but Baldwin and Henry offered reasons to believe that the plan serves the needs of learners with mild communicative problems.

Contributions of Regular Teachers

Whether language arts instruction is traditionally separate or holistic, regular classroom teachers typically add at least two major services for students with speech and language problems: They promote generalization of new speech and language competencies to the classroom, and they collect progress data in the natural setting. In addition to praising students for applying new speech or language patterns in the classroom, teachers aid generalization by creating brief opportunities to rehearse new skills. Asking the SLP and the special education teacher which competencies are being emphasized in a given week gives regular classroom teachers the information they need to reinforce those competencies. For example, students working on relational concepts of behind, between, above, below, and so forth could be asked to follow an arithmetic workbook lesson with a 1-minute session in which they point to specific numerals located behind, between, above, or below others as arranged on the workbook page. Quick extra lessons of this type are powerful when provided with regularity to reinforce more structured lessons by the SLP or special educator.

Maintaining progress data in real settings is one of the greatest needs while students are engaged in speech and language intervention programs. Teachers are in a good position to provide information about how learners are applying new skills. Record keeping can be as simple as slash marks for each spontaneous example of a structure or as detailed as daily charting of 1-minute probes over multiple structures. However informal, such data are helpful in determining the extent to which learners are responding to instruction.

TECHNOLOGY APPLICATIONS

In describing some of the available technology for augmentative communication, Russel (1984) distinguished *unaided systems* requiring no hardware, such as a visual-gestural sign system, fingerspelling, and pantomime, from *aided systems* that rely on electronic hardware, usually a microcomputer. Russel outlined the goals, capabilities, and limitations of aided systems, also known as *communication prostheses*.

The appropriate goal of an aided system, according to Russel, is to serve as a tool to promote and facilitate, rather than replace, other communication modes already in the user's repertoire. For example, if a student has been using a smiling response to indicate "yes" and a frown for "no," there is no gain in insisting that a device that prints the words be substituted. Instead, the focus should be on ways to use an augmentative system to reduce ambiguities in communication methods already in use. Capabilities differ in terms of vocabulary selection, symbol system, means of indication, and overall complexity of steps required to use the aid. Outputs include a visual display employing pictures or printed words, auditory messages using a synthesized voice, or combinations of the three activated by motions ranging from head movement to manual pushbuttons. Slower systems employ scanning and selection of predetermined choices; faster ones are personalized using most frequently needed items. The limitations of these systems include the amount of time it takes to formulate and express a message, the student's attention given to a machine rather than to faces, the stereotyped interactions such systems encourage, and the reliance on many systems that the communicatively impaired user may not master.

Cerebral palsy children are benefiting from new communication technology.

The videodisc promises to overcome reliance on reading skills by providing spoken instruction to accompany high-quality, real-life demonstrations on a television screen. Combined with a microcomputer to give it directions based on student responses, the videodisc gains random access capabilities that permit it to search thousands of frames in less than 3 seconds to locate and display those requested by the user; the disc can also maintain data on student progress. According to Friedman and Hofmeister (1984), who conducted instructional studies, videodiscs accommodate a wide spread of entry levels, permit individual pacing, and decrease the probability of interference from past instruction.

Van Tatenhove (1987) outlined the advantages of early introduction of augmentative devices, pointing out that this practice prevented anticipation and misreading by communication partners. But a recent study of technology applications across school settings revealed that mainstreamed handicapped and nonhandicapped students had a greater variety of microcomputer opportunities available than did students in special education settings; furthermore, the microcomputer use observed was far from the most advanced technology on the market (Cosden, Gerber, Semmel, Goldman, & Semmel, 1987). This study implies that many of the technological advances available in augmentative communication for students with speech and language problems may not yet be available to them in their special education programs.

MULTICULTURAL CONSIDERATIONS

In both preintervention assessment and monitoring of progress through instruction, determining whether speech and language are appropriate is a matter of comparing performance with other speakers in the same culture. The major responsibility is to distinguish difference from disorder. If assessment is conducted in Standard American English using materials based on that dialect only but the testee's first language is Spanish or one of the Black English dialects, a false impression of language status is inevitable. The regulations governing PL 94-142 have attempted to guard against this outcome by stating that assessment must be conducted in the child's native language, which means the language normally used by that person, or in the case of a child, the language normally used by the parents.

Linguistic variations in a heterogeneous society are influenced by geography, ethnic subgroups within larger racial groups, and social class as defined by educational level or occupation. When the language of children and youth is evaluated, age is a factor that accounts for predictable variations. For example, patterns of simplification in sound production ("toof" for "tooth") or word omissions ("He going") constitute the type of rule-governed behavior that can be labeled an age dialect. As children grow older, patterns change. Adolescents develop a local dialect marked by rapidly shifting slang shared by a group of peers for the purpose of keeping adults from knowing what is being said. Elderly grandparents may use more formal structures, such as "It is I" for "It's me." These age dialects are minor variations, however, in contrast to dialect differences based on region or ethnicity or to English variations of speakers whose first language is, for instance, Spanish or Vietnamese.

The dialect taught in schools and printed in books is the standard. This does not in any way imply that the standard dialect holds any *linguistic* superiority; all dialects are equally valid linguistically, but they come to carry social implications based on the identity of those who principally use a given nonstandard dialect. Again, the term *nonstandard* does not imply *substandard*—it describes a difference, not a deficiency.

According to Taylor (1986), culturally different speakers have a linguistic repertoire that always includes formal and informal codes of the first dialect and typically includes more than one dialect—the standard version, a regional or ethnic dialect, and a local variation. The ability to move from one variation to another in response to listener characteristics, setting, and topic is a measure of code switching, a skill to be cultivated for social or work purposes. For example, an African-American child who comes to school speaking one of the Black English dialects learns the American Standard English variation in school; uses it orally with teachers, for reading and writing, and ultimately in the mainstream workplace; but maintains the first dialect for oral use in the home community throughout school years and adult life.

SUMMARY

Any speech or language disorder can isolate students from effective interactions with others because the ability to communicate through spoken and written language is the essence of being human. Inability to communicate thus affects relationships with families, peers, teachers, and society at large. Whether a speech and/or language disorder is the primary presenting problem or secondary to another handicapping condition, the effects on social and academic learning can be severe. Language is a tool for discovering customs, mores, and values as well as a means for interacting with other human beings. Children and youth without adequate communication competencies are at a social and academic disadvantage in the highly verbal classroom, and they face a difficult challenge in attempting literacy.

Laughton and Hasenstab (1986) cited studies showing that more than 50% of children demonstrating speech or language deficits also exhibited some degree of behavior problem (p. 183). Among characteristics they identified were the following: (a) inappropriate motor activity may be a substitute when children or youth cannot say what bothers them; (b) withdrawal occurs when they cannot grasp what is wanted of them; (c) stubbornness and inflexible reactions to events may be means of imposing order on chaotic perceptions; (d) distractibility and impulsivity are associated with inability to use language to organize and reflect on incoming sensory information. Expectations of failure associated with repeated inability to express themselves lead children to compound failures.

Academic problems arise when children misinterpret directions; cannot name common objects, much less master the specific terminology of mathematics or science; cannot process teachers' questions or raise their own queries when they need clarifications; cannot rehearse their recall and integration of facts in class discussions; do not classify or distinguish on the basis of verbal categories; or cannot use language to draw inferences, make conclusions, advance predictions. Above all, speech and language problems interfere with the critical ability to step back from language to study how it works; this metalinguistic ability has been recently identified as central to beginning reading and writing but lacking in students with language disorders (Kamhi, 1987). Academic problems increase as learners move from dependence on drawing content from teachers' oral statements to the need to read for information and to write in order to demonstrate what they have learned. Van Kleek and Schuele (1987) posited that domains of literacy knowledge gained through early language experiences facilitated a smooth transition into later learning of reading as a technical skill.

SLPs and their professional colleagues, although they use differing interventions derived from a variety of theories and models, are increasingly united in opposing the fallacy of viewing speech and language as separate from academic subject matter and skills. Language systems are interdependent during school years, in that oral language acquisition provides the concepts, vocabulary, sentence structure, and social conventions about language that form the basis for literacy, while progress in reading and writing reinforces understandings of the sound, form, and meaning systems of oral language. The concept of oral language as primary with reading and writing as secondary systems constitutes a distortion because data from preschool readers indicate that early reading improves phonological development while early writing reinforces semantic and syntactic oral language progress (Lipson & Wixson, 1986). Identification, assessment, intervention, and monitoring of growth in communication therefore require integrated efforts by families, SLPs, audiologists, and hearing conservationists, along with regular, special, and reading teachers, with the cooperation of administrators who set hiring priorities and organize delivery systems.

REFERENCES

Baldwin, L. S., & Henry, M. K. (1985). Reading and language arts: A design for integrated instruction. In C. S. Simon (Ed.), *Communication skills and classroom success* (pp. 315–337). San Diego: College Hill Press.

Bloodstein, O. (1984). *Speech pathology: An introduction.* Boston: Houghton Mifflin.

Bromley, K. D., & Cavallaro, C. (1983). Teachers' perceptions of language skills necessary for mainstreaming. *Journal of Childhood Communication Disorders, 6,* 100–109.

Conant, S. (1986). The language of language disability. *Journal of Childhood Communication Disorders, 9,* 133–138.

Cosden, M. A., Gerber, M. M., Semmel, D. S., Goldman, S. R., & Semmel, M. I. (1987). Microcomputer use within micro-educational environments. *Exceptional Children, 53,* 399–409.

Friedman, S. G., & Hofmeister, A. M. (1984). Matching technology to content and learners. *Exceptional Children, 51,* 130–134.

Johnston, J. R. (1988). Specific language disorders in the child. In N. J. Lass, L. V. McReynolds, J. L. Northern, & D. E. Yoder (Eds.), *Handbook of speech-language pathology and audiology* (pp. 685–715). Toronto: Decker.

Kamhi, A. (1987). Metalinguistic abilities in language-impaired children. *Topics in Language Disorders,7,* 1–12.

Laughton, J., & Hasenstab, M. S. (1986). *The language learning process.* Rockville, MD: Aspen.

Lipson, M. Y., & Wixson, K. K. (1986). Reading disability research: An interactionist perspective. *Review of Educational Research, 65,* 111–136.

McReynolds, L. V. (1988). Articulation disorders of unknown etiology. In N. J. Lass, L. V. McReynolds, J. L. Northern, & D. E. Yoder (Eds.), *Handbook of speech-language pathology and audiology* (pp. 419–441). Toronto: Decker.

Rice, M. L. (1986). Mismatched premises of competence and intervention. In R. L. Schiefelbusch (Ed.), *Language competence: Assessment and intervention* (pp. 261–280). San Diego: College Hill Press.

Russel, M. (1984). Assessment and intervention issues with the nonspeaking child. Exceptional Children, 51, 64–71.

Synder, L. (1984). Developmental language disorder: Elementary school age. In A. Holland (Ed.), *Language disorders in children* (pp. 129–158). San Diego: College Hill Press.

Taylor, O. L. (1986). *Nature of communication disorders in culturally and linguistically diverse populations.* San Diego: College Hill Press.

Van Hattum, R. J. (1985). *Organization of speech-language services in schools.* San Diego: College Hill Press.

Van Kleek, A., & Schuele, M. (1987). Precursors to literacy: Normal development. *Topics in Language Disorders, 7,* 13–21.

Van Tatenhove, G. M. (1987). Teaching power through augmentative communication. *Journal of Childhood Communication Disorders, 10,* 185–199.

Wall, M. J. (1988). Dysfluency in the child. In N. J. Lass, L. V. McReynolds, J. L. Northern, & D. E. Yoder (Eds.), *Handbook of speech-language pathology and audiology* (pp. 622–639). Toronto: Decker.

Williams, D. E. (1982). Coping with attitudes and beliefs about stuttering. *Journal of Childhood Communication Disorders, 6,* 60–66.

Wilson, D. (1987). *Voice problems of children.* (3rd ed.). Baltimore, MD: Williams & Wilkins.

ADDITIONAL READINGS

Hasenstab, M. S. & Laughton, J. (1982). *Reading, writing, and the exceptional child: A psycho-socio-linguistic approach.* Rockville, MD: Aspen Systems Corporation.

Heath, S. B. (1983). *Ways with words.* Cambridge: Cambridge University Press.

Rice, M. L. (1980). *Cognition to language.* Baltimore: University Park Press.

Wallach, G. P. & Miller, L. (1988). *Language intervention and academic success.* Boston: Little, Brown and Company.

1

Purpose

☐ To practice reducing the demands of oral instructions on students with communication disorders

Steps

1. Select about six workbook pages or teacher-made worksheets that you use from year to year.

2. Write down all the words in the oral directions you typically use to introduce these pages to your students (be honest!).

3. Modify the directions as follows:

   • Separate each instruction into one-step units;
   • Insert a graphic reminder to pause after each step until students have complied;
   • Keep statements under seven words;
   • Maintain temporal order; that is, say, "First take out a pencil; next, open to page 15" instead of saying "Before you open to page 15, take out a pencil."
   • Instead of explaining verbally how to "circle," or "underline," or "match," demonstrate on a chalkboard.

Analysis

☐ Reread on page 274 the first three questions, which refer to student compliance with oral directions.

☐ Conduct a simple comparison experiment in observing the performance of one student identified as having a communication disorder by watching how the student reacts: (a) when you use your typical, unmodified approach to presenting oral directions for a workbook page or worksheet and (b) when you reduce demands by following the above steps.

2

Purpose

☐ To practice modifying questioning techniques to reduce demands on students with communication disorders

Steps

1. Jot down a set of questions you typically use to test comprehension of a concept in a social studies, science or other content lesson.

2. Select two questions that you consider preliminary or relatively easy to answer; reduce them to seven words or fewer, then mark them to ask nonvolunteers early in the questioning session before moving to more complex portions of the lesson.

3. Select two questions that you can change so that responders could choose a one-word answer instead of supplying one. For example, instead of saying, "Name the country in which rain forests are disappearing," ask "Are rain forests disappearing in Chile, Brazil, or Peru?"

4. Rephrase several questions so that you make statements about the content, then say, "I'll say some things about the lesson. Raise your hand if a statement is true." Then call on nonvolunteers by name to respond to individual questions without having to say anything.

5. Rephrase several questions so that more than one correct one-word answer is acceptable to fit into a process. Say, "Tell me one thing to do."

6. Consciously extend wait time after asking a question by using a stopwatch until you can reliably estimate a 5-second wait between the end of your question and encouraging a response or moving on to another student.

Analysis

☐ Reread on page (258) the methods recommended for reducing anxiety in group questioning sessions.

☐ Conduct a simple comparison experiment in observing the performance of one student identified as having a communication disorder by watching how the student reacts: (a) when you use your typical, unmodified approach to asking questions and (b) when you reduce demands by following the above steps.

3

Purpose

☐ To practice an informal procedure for recognizing three subsystems within language (as distinct from speech)

Steps

1. Select a friend's or relative's normally developing child between the ages of three and seven; arrange to meet in a setting familiar to the child.

2. Ask the parent(s) to allow you to tape a sample of the child's language. Tell the parent(s) that you are not qualified to analyze the tape because you are still learning, but offer to let the parent(s) listen to the tape if they wish.

3. Assemble a set of pictures of action scenes appropriate for the age and interests of your subject.

4. After visiting to establish rapport, turn on the tape recorder and ignore it. Show the pictures one at a time and say, "Tell me about this picture." Avoid yes/no and wh-questions.

5. Tape for five minutes, take the child for a brief walk or to get a drink of water, then tape another five minutes.

6. Make up a worksheet with three columns headed *Syntax, Morphology* and *Semantics*.

7. Reread the pages (265-267, & 270) that describe these subsystems.

Analysis

☐ Play the tape twice without taking notes, but listening for examples.

☐ On the third play, write down one conventional (adult) example of each of the following: word order, a morphological ending such as a plural noun or past-tense verb, a vocabulary word used appropriately.

☐ On the fourth play, write down any unconventional word order, overregularized ending, over- or underextended use of a word, substitution of "stuff," "thing," or "junk" for a vocabulary item, or misuse of a word.

4

Purpose

☐ To practice an informal observation procedure to recognize applied uses of language (pragmatics)

Steps

1. Select one student who has been identified by a speech-language pathologist as requiring instruction in Standard American English; note whether you have chosen a child with a language disorder or a language difference due to nationality or ethnic membership.

2. Reread the pages (267-269 & 270) that describe pragmatics, the final nine questions on page (274) which cover interactive language, and the pages that discuss multicultural considerations (279-280).

3. Write down the final nine questions on page (274); from the other pages, add a few similar questions suggested by the descriptions; prepare two copies of the questions and label one *Target* and the other *Contrast*.

4. Arrange to sit in while the target student engages with peers in a small-group activity while the teacher circulates to answer questions.

5. Within the small group, select a second student who has not been identified as demonstrating language disorder or difference.

6. Observe for about 20 minutes.

7. As you see either the Target or Contrast student exhibit any of the behaviors covered in your questions, place a tally mark next to the question.

Analysis

☐ Compare the frequency of requests for clarification, definition, or explanation; count the number of volunteer comments, both relevant and out-
of-place; count initiations of conversations, use of non-verbal signals,
and turn-taking. Judge how the two students may have differed in their
participation in the group on this single occasion, which may or may not
be representative.

☐ Meet with the SLP and the classroom teacher to discuss your perceptions, and discuss how the other professional observers might have perceived the target student differently based on inferences drawn over a
longer time period.

11

Hearing Impairment

Margaret H. Mayer
Northwest School for Hearing Impaired Children — Seattle

HEARING IMPAIRMENTS
TYPICAL PROFILE

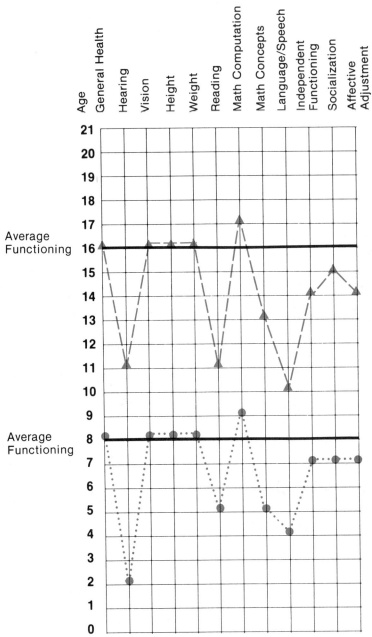

▲ = 16-year-old student

Strengths: general health and physical functioning, math computation, and vocational aptitude

Weaknesses: profound hearing loss, speech and language skills, reading comprehension, math concepts, and personal-social adjustment

● = 8-year-old student

Strengths: general health and physical functioning, fine motor skills, and performance items such as math computation

Weaknesses: severe hearing loss, speech and language skills, reading comprehension, and math concepts

A variety of educational programs are available in today's schools for students with hearing impairment. Although educators of children with hearing impairment agree on the importance of early identification and intervention, controversy still divides them on such topics as the use of sign language and what constitutes the least restrictive environment for students with hearing problems.

The first school serving children with hearing handicaps in the United States, the American Asylum for the Education of Deaf and Dumb (now known as the American School for the Deaf), was established in 1817 in Hartford, Connecticut. Like most of the early programs for deaf children, this residential school relied on the use of sign language for communication and gave little attention to the development of speech and articulation skills. In the mid-19th century, educators became interested in the oral methods used in German schools for the deaf. The Horace Mann School was founded during this period to support oral education for deaf children and became the first day school for deaf students.

Students with hearing impairment have been educated in an array of educational programs since the passage of PL 94-142. Placement is influenced by the student's abilities, parental preference for a specific type of educational approach, and the alternatives offered by the home district. Many students with hearing impairment are able to attend regular program classes in their neighborhood school with little or no special education support. Others spend part of the day in regular program classes and part of it in a resource room setting where they receive additional instruction related to the development of speech, language, and hearing. Those requiring more specialized instruction may be educated primarily in a self-contained class taught by a specially trained teacher. In these settings, students with hearing impairment are selectively mainstreamed with hearing peers for specific classes or activities. In many areas, the traditional state supported, residential "school for the deaf" is still an option.

STUDENTS WITH HEARING IMPAIRMENT IN REGULAR CLASSES

Integrating students with hearing impairment into mainstream classes without hindering their learning requires overcoming common barriers to communication. A few simple steps can facilitate speechreading and enhance the student's participation in class. To optimize speechreading opportunities the child should be seated near the front and center of the class. Teachers should face the class when speaking, being sure not to cover their mouths or turn away from the group. Comments and questions from people in other parts of the room should be repeated by the teacher at the front to assist the student with hearing impairment in following class discussions.

Besides facilitating speechreading, teachers can take other steps to assist children participating in regular classes. The use of clear visual aids such as overhead transparencies, charts, pictures, models, or demonstrations will assist all learners, especially those with hearing difficulties. In lecture format classes in which students take notes for later study, one student can be assigned to share notes with the child with impaired hearing in order to enable him or her to focus visual attention on speechreading rather than on writing. Stating key points of the lesson in at least two different ways, using different vocabulary, may improve the child's comprehension while reinforcing the concept for the entire class. Because children with hearing handicaps may not have extensive vocabularies, it is often helpful to rephrase difficult concepts, using simple sentences.

CHARACTERISTICS OF CHILDREN AND YOUTH WITH HEARING IMPAIRMENT

Children with hearing handicaps represent a heterogeneous group. The effect of hearing dysfunction on individual functioning varies greatly depending on a number of factors: the type and degree of hearing loss, the child's age when the loss occurred, the child's IQ, the ability of the child's family and community to cope with the hearing impairment, and the child's linguistic and educational experiences.

Speech and Language

The most handicapping aspect of hearing impairment is related to the obstacles created in the child's ability to communicate using the language of the community at large. Children whose hearing losses occur before they have the opportunity to develop expressive skills in the language spoken by their families often have difficulty mastering oral language skills. Thus, an 8-year-old child with a profound hearing loss who became handicapped after her second or third birthday may have better speech, language, reading, and writing skills than a classmate with a milder hearing loss that occurred shortly after birth.

The English and speech skills of children with hearing impairment often lag far behind those of their able-bodied peers. Whereas most children are able to use their hearing to learn both the language and speech pattens of their community, children with hearing handicaps must often be taught these skills directly through much painstaking repetition and corrective instruction. These students' speech problems often include the omission or substitution of some sounds, problems with speech intonation and pitch, and difficulties with the normal rate and rhythm of spoken English. Speech may sound nasal, gutteral, or breathy. In general, individuals with mild to moderate hearing losses may have more intelligible speech than do those with severe to profound losses.

In addition to speech and oral articulation impairments, hearing loss can make it difficult for children to learn the vocabulary, structure, and rules of the oral language in their community. Children with hearing impairment usually have limited vocabularies as compared to nonhandicapped students. These students may omit grammatical components of English such as plurals, prepositions, articles (a, the), tenses, and a variety of "little" words or word endings. These children tend to use short and simple sentences and rely often on subject-verb-object word order. Students with hearing impairment may lack an understanding of alternative meanings for words and figurative language. (For example, these students may have trouble with phrases such as "The refrigerator is running" and "I have a run in my stocking.")

Instructional Implications

Because of the language difficulties that can accompany hearing loss, a hearing disability may affect how well a student is able to hear spoken language and other stimuli in the average classroom as well as influence performance in language related subjects such as reading and writing. Standardized achievement test scores reported for students with hearing impairment in the United States lagged significantly behind those of their hearing peers (Allen, 1986). The average level of literacy for individuals with hearing handicaps was reported to be between the third- and fifth-grade levels (Allen, 1986; Trybus & Karchmer, 1977; DiFrancesca, 1972).

The impact of the language difficulties commonly experienced by children with hearing handicaps may extend beyond the expected subject areas of language arts and reading. Classes that rely heavily on students' reading and integrating printed material from texts and that require written products such as essays and reports can also be problematic for deaf children. Likewise, problem solving in so-called language-free subjects such as math and science depend on the use of language to manipulate and communicate concepts.

Social-Emotional Development

The social-emotional development of children with hearing impairment follows the same basic patterns found among nonhandicapped peers. Few differences are noted among very young deaf and hearing children, who often develop friendships based on mutual play interests that are not impeded by their communication differences. With age, however, language becomes an increasingly important facilitator of friendships, socialization, and social-emotional growth. Thus, communication problems can make it more difficult for older children with hearing difficulties to interact and develop close friendships with hearing peers with whom communication is difficult.

Children with hearing impairment must often be directly taught subtle social mores and attitudes that normally hearing children seem to pick up incidentally by overhearing and observing conversations in the world around them. Thus, older students may appear more "naive" or less well socialized than hearing students their age.

Communication difficulties and issues related to parental acceptance of the child's deafness can have a negative impact on the parent-child relationship, which in turn may influence the child's social-emotional development. Families of children with hearing impairment report they must work harder to encourage strong relationships between family members who do not sign and the child who does. Recent efforts of early intervention programs have focused on assisting families in learning to adapt to these challenges and their child's special needs.

DEFINITIONS

The umbrella term *hearing impairment* covers hearing losses of all types, ranging from mild to profound in intensity (see Figure 11.1). A "hearing loss" occurs when something impedes the translation of sound waves into neural impulses, which the brain processes as information. The impairment can result from a variety of factors. Different types of hearing losses are determined by the part of the hearing mechanism where the impairment occurs.

Sound waves travel through the outer ear (which includes the "pinna" on the outside of the head and the auditory canal). When they encounter the eardrum, or tympanic membrane, the soundwaves are conducted mechanically through the three tiny bones of the middle ear—the malleus, the incus, and the stapes. The latter terminates at the inner ear (which includes the cochlea and the semicircular canals), where the sound is translated into neural impulses.

An impairment located in the outer or middle ear, such as an obstruction of the ear canal by hardened earwax, a ruptured eardrum, or fluid in the middle ear that prevents the vibration of the three bones, is called a *conductive hearing loss*. Properly amplified sounds can usually be heard without distortion. This type of impairment rarely results in more than a moderate hearing loss and is often corrected through medical intervention.

If the site of the impairment is in the inner ear, due to damage to the cochlea or the auditory nerve, a *sensorineural hearing loss* occurs. Sound is often distorted in addition to being diminished; thus, even amplified sounds may not be heard clearly.

ELIGIBILITY CRITERIA

Under PL 94-142 children who are "hard of hearing" and those who are "deaf" are eligible for special education services. The distinction between the two categories of hearing impairment is based on the extent to which the child can use hearing to understand speech. Those who are deaf have hearing losses so severe that they can not rely on hearing to process oral language. Hard of hearing children have hearing losses that adversely affect their ability to function in school but are not considered to be deaf. To be eligible for special education, a child's hearing loss must be documented and described through audiological testing (see Figure 11.2). Moreover, the child's language abilities and academic functioning must be evaluated to demonstrate the negative impact of the hearing loss on the child's ability to participate without assistance in a regular school placement.

Communication difficulties pose the biggest challenge when students with hearing impairment participate in regular program classes. Some students may require additional language remediation ranging from assistance in language-related subjects to assistance in devising study skills that help broaden linguistic understanding. Often children who are mainstreamed receive additional educational assistance from itinerant language specialists. These special educators can provide assistance to regular program teachers in meeting the specific educational needs of children with hearing handicaps in their classes. In addition, special educators may provide extra tutoring and instruction aimed at ameliorating language or information deficits in the special child.

Students with limited oral skills may be accompanied by an educational interpreter. Participation in class discussions is difficult for children using interpreters because the interpreted message usually lags a second behind the spoken one. Thus, another student has already answered a question before the student with hearing impairment can even raise his or her hand. These children may feel isolated in mainstream classes because of the difficulty communicating with teachers and other students.

Figure 11.1   Parts of the Ear

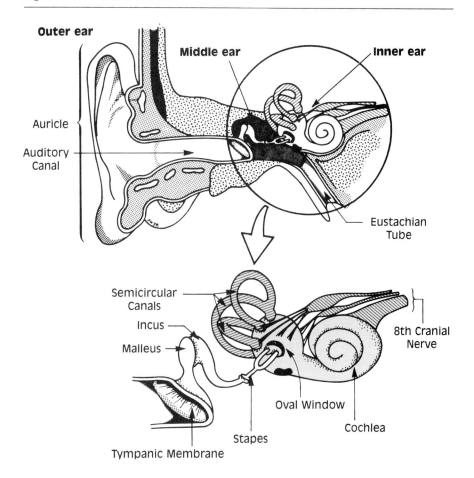

Figure 11.2　Types of Hearing Loss and the Frequency Spectrum of Common Sounds

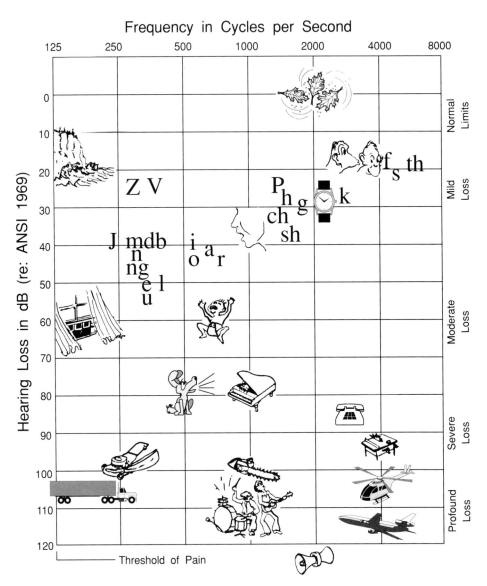

Source: From J.L. Northern and M.P. Downs, 1974, *Hearing Impaired Children,* p.7, Baltimore, MD: Williams & Wilkins.

ELEMENTARY LEVEL STUDENT
WITH HEARING IMPAIRMENT

Bill, a profoundly deaf 7-year-old, lives in a rural suburb of a major city with his parents and older brother. Bill's home district pays his tuition at a private school for students with hearing impairments. There are five other second graders in Bill's self-contained class. Math and spelling are Bill's favorite subjects. He is reading at the mid-first-grade level. Every day he and another student participate in math instruction and recess at a nearby regular school. They are accompanied by the teaching assistant from their class, who interprets for them. Bill reports that mainstream math is hard, but his grades indicate he is being successful.

A year ago Bill had cochlear implant surgery in an effort to give him enough auditory information to help him develop better speech. His parents and teachers report an improvement in his speech and hearing skills since the operation.

Bill communicates primarily through sign language and is sometimes reticent to participate in social activities in which most people do not sign because he finds it hard to follow what is going on. His language structure is a mixture of American Sign Language and English. The school speech pathologist reports that Bill's speech intelligibility is about 50% if he signs and speaks at the same time. Listening to Bill speak, one hears mostly vowel sounds and a few consonants.

Everyone in Bill's immediate family signs. His mother completed an interpreter training program shortly after he entered school full time. She reports that her biggest adjustment has been the extent to which Bill is dependent on her to communicate with the world around him. She must remain at soccer practice to interpret for him, rather than dropping him off. When watching TV or movies, she often feels obligated to interpret for Bill. Sometimes she feels sad that the extended family cannot communicate well enough with Bill to appreciate his delightful personality.

□ □ □

What difficulties might be present in situations like Bill's in which the mainstream school is several miles away from the special school? What effects might this have on the mainstreaming experience?

Why do Bill and the other student with hearing impairment stay for recess at the mainstream school? What steps could the regular program teacher take to make the math class more comfortable for Bill?

How does Bill's hearing impairment place additional demands on his mother? What effects might Bill's hearing loss have on his older brother?

SECONDARY LEVEL CHILD WITH HEARING IMPAIRMENT

Holly is a witty and attractive 15-year-old with a profound hearing loss. A good student, her grades rank in the top third of the junior class at an academically competitive public high school. An educational interpreter is provided for Holly in all her classes, which include drama, honors English, French, chemistry, geometry, and study hall.

Outside of class Holly is an avid swimmer and competes on a community team as well as for her high school. Because she cannot hear the starting gun, her times are often hindered by delayed starts, although at some meets a light signals the start in addition to the gun.

Holly was 3 years old when she contracted meningitis and lost her hearing. Prior to first grade she participated in early intervention programs in which she and her mother both learned total communication skills and other techniques for maintaining her oral abilities. Today Holly has intelligible speech, good speechreading abilities, and excellent English skills. Holly learned to read at age 5 and has been an insatiable reader ever since.

Throughout elementary school, Holly was often the only child with hearing impairment in her community. She says sometimes this distinction was nice because other children were fascinated by her and therefore made an effort to become friends with her. She reports this isolation also made her strong and developed her vocabulary when she had to cope with children who taunted and swore at her.

Today when nearly 70 of the 2,200 students at Holly's school have hearing impairments, some of her close friends are deaf and some are hearing. She admits that it is easier to have more personal conversations with other deaf teenagers. Interacting with hearing peers who do not know her often requires that she take the initiative and be very outgoing.

Holly says the biggest frustration about having a hearing impairment is that hearing people are often afraid of her. When asked what advice she had for hearing teachers receiving mainstream deaf students into their class, Holly replied that the teachers should treat deaf students the same as everyone else. If the student has oral skills, the teacher should try to become familiar with the student's speech so communication does not depend so heavily on the interpreter.

What factors have contributed to Holly's good speech and language skills?

What could educators at Holly's school do to facilitate interaction between hearing students and students with hearing impairments?

BASIC PROFESSIONAL VOCABULARY

Air conduction is the process by which soundwaves travel through the air to the auditory mechanism.

American Sign Language, which is also known as ASL or Ameslan, is a visual-manual or sign language entirely unrelated to English. Originating in the United States, ASL is the language used by the adult deaf population in this country.

Amplification is the use of hearing aids or other electronic devices to make sound stimuli more perceptible to the hearing mechanism.

Auditory training is systematic training to improve the student's use of his or her remaining (residual) hearing.

Aural pertains to the ears or hearing. *Binaural* refers to both ears.

Bone conduction is the transmission of sound through the bones of the skull to the inner ear.

Inner ear is made up of the cochlea and the semicircular canals, the innermost part of the hearing mechanism.

Interpreter is a professional who facilitates communication between hearing and deaf individuals, usually by translating between voiced information and sign language. Oral interpreters mouth the speaker's verbal information to enable the individual with a hearing handicap to speechread the message.

Manual communication mode is communication through a sign language or code expressed by use of the hands.

Middle ear is the part of the ear consisting of the eardrum, the three bones of the hearing mechanism, and the eustachian tube.

Prelingual hearing loss is a hearing impairment that occurs before a child learns oral language.

Speechreading, formerly called "lipreading," is a technique for decoding verbal information using visible movements of the speaker's mouth in conjunction with context and auditory cues.

ASSESSING INSTRUCTIONAL NEED

A thorough assessment battery useful for diagnosis and placement of a child with hearing impairment includes assessment of communication skills, cognitive functioning, academic achievement, and social-emotional adjustment. The selection of testing materials and procedures varies with the type of information needed about the student and the reasons for testing. Children are often assessed using both formal measures, such as standardized tests and curriculum-based tests, and informal measures, such as teacher-made tests and standardized tests used for diagnostic purposes (the student's performance is analyzed but not compared to the scores of a norm group).

Very few standardized tests, such as achievement or IQ tests, are useful for academic planning for children with hearing impairment. Because these tests are designed primarily for hearing children and rarely include children with hearing impairments when test standards or "norms" are developed, the resulting scores are not always valid for the latter group.

Regardless of the tests used, the professionals involved in administering and analyzing test results must be knowledgeable about the impact of hearing impairment on academic, linguistic, cognitive, and social development. This understanding contributes to the accuracy of test results and minimizes the possibility that results will be misinterpreted. For example, someone not sensitive to the reading and language difficulties of many students with hearing impairment may fail to distinguish between a student's actual difficulties in the area of mathematics and problems in understanding the language used in the test. In one case the student requires remedial assistance in math; in the other, the student needs remedial language instruction. It is imperative that a specific skill deficit not be misinterpreted as a knowledge deficit.

Administering tests for children with hearing impairment requires special considerations. Testing should be conducted in the child's communication mode of choice. For some students, the standard verbal presentation is appropriate, although efforts to ensure an environment optimal for speechreading should be made. For other children, the test instructions should be given in the manual or combined oral-manual language the student generally uses for communication. Many researchers recommend that tests be administered individually (Sullivan & Vernon, 1979).

Assessing Communication Skills

Communication includes a number of important components, all of which must be assessed. The child's ability to receive and utilize auditory information must be established by audiological testing. The child's ability to use and understand language, including English, American Sign Language, or any non-English language used in the child's home, must be measured. The child's ability to impart information to others using speech (articulation), a manual sign language or code, and other communication strategies (such as mime or invented signs) must also be examined.

Audiological Assessment

Complete audiological assessment is necessary both to document the child's hearing loss and to prescribe and maintain appropriate amplification. Unlike the hearing screening tests that have been conducted in public schools since 1927 (Northern & Downs, 1974), diagnostic hearing testing is done in a sound-attenuated room, which is usually found in speech and hearing clinics. While seated in the room, the client is asked to signal when he or she hears specific sounds generated by a machine called an *audiometer.* The result of the testing is a chart, or *audiogram,* on which the individual's hearing thresholds are plotted at different frequencies for each ear. The threshold for a particular *frequency* (heard by the client as a tone) is the *intensity* (level of volume measured in decibels) at which the individual hears the tone 50% of the time. Figure 11.3 shows an audiogram for an individual with a moderate to severe hearing loss. The thresholds for the left ear are plotted with an "x," and those for the right ear are shown with an "o."

Additional information about the type of hearing loss is provided when the results of the *air conduction test* described in the preceding paragraph are compared with *bone conduction test*. These are done using a *bone conduction oscillator,* which looks like a headphone strap with a button at the end. The "button" is placed on the bony prominence just behind the ear. In this way the stimulus is presented only to the inner ear. Results for bone conduction testing are plotted on the audiogram using ">" for the right ear and "<" for the left. In Figure 11.3, notice that there is no difference in the results of the bone conduction test and the air conduction test. This indicates a sensorineural hearing loss or one that is due to a malfunc-

Figure 11.3   Audiogram Showing a Binaural Sensorineural Hearing Loss

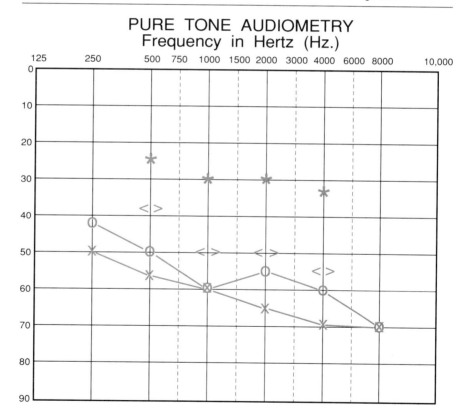

KEY: O — right ear air conduction
      X — left ear air conduction
      > — right ear bone conduction
      < — left ear bone conduction
      * — aided responses

tion in the inner ear. If the bone conduction results were near normal and the air conduction results were not, the hearing loss would most likely be the result of a problem in the middle or outer ear and might be ameliorated medically.

When testing the client's ability to hear when wearing hearing aids, the technician presents auditory stimuli through loud speakers in the sound-attenuated room. Figure 11.3 shows thresholds for "aided" responses with an "*." Comparison of aided and unaided results on pure tone and speech discrimination tests indicates the extent to which a child is benefiting from amplification. Hearing aids must be periodically checked electronically to ensure their proper functioning.

Speech and Language Assessment

Traditionally, speech skills were assessed using such tests as the Photo Articulation Test (Pendergast, Dickey, Selmar, & Soder, 1984), in which articulation is judged according to the child's ability to pronounce sounds while naming pictured objects. More recent trends in both speech assessment and speech instruction have been influenced by the work of Ling (1976), who developed an assessment battery that tests the student's ability to combine the sounds of English at the rates, rhythms, and pitches normally required in connected speech. Results from these tests yield immediate instructional objectives for speech remediation.

Language testing for students with hearing handicaps must examine the child's skills as both sender and receiver of English messages. Testing must also analyze abilities in three major aspects of language: form (how words are put together in sentences), content (vocabulary and meanings of language), and use (the ability to use language appropriately in different contexts and environments). Because most language tests do not assess all these areas of language, professionals must use several different tests in order to accurately determine the language abilities of the child and the appropriate objectives for language instruction.

A student's skill at using language to express ideas and communicate effectively with others is often assessed by a method called "language sampling." This requires an analysis of a predetermined number of the student's verbal (or signed) utterances that have been recorded verbatim. Language sampling provides insight into how well the rules and structure of English have been internalized and can be applied.

> Activity 1, page 315, is designed to help you experience the process of analyzing expressive language.

Cognitive Assessment

Intelligence tests for students with hearing impairment must be carefully selected to avoid those that rely heavily on verbal abilities to measure intellectual functioning.

At least two different performance scales should be used to measure cognitive abilities (Vernon & Brown, 1964). Deaf children are often given the performance subtests of the Wechsler Intelligence Scale for Children—Revised (WISC-R) (Wechsler, 1974), which offers a hearing impaired norming sample (Anderson & Sisco, 1977). This test is sometimes used in conjunction with the Hiskey-Nebraska Test of Learning Aptitude (Hiskey, 1966), which consists of nonverbal subtests. The Leiter International Performance Scale (Leiter, 1948) is another suitable test for hearing impaired students because it requires only nonverbal responses.

Psychologists who administer cognitive assessments should be skilled in the child's communication modality. The use of sign language interpreters to assist nonsigning psychologists administering intelligence tests is discouraged, as it may interfere with the rapport between the examiner and the student (Sullivan & Vernon, 1979) and does not comply with the validity requirements for such tests (Vernon & Brown, 1964).

INTERVENTIONS

Instructional Interventions

The biggest challenge facing educators of children with hearing impairment is that of facilitating the acquisition of speech and language skills. How best to meet this challenge has been the topic for much discussion, investigation, experimentation, and polemic argument throughout the history of education of these children. The variety of communication strategies presently used across the United States reflects this disagreement. (See Quigley & Paul [1984] or Moores [1987] for a more detailed description of these methods.) Two of the most prevalent and influential approaches are the Aural-Oral Method and Total Communication.

Aural-Oral Method

Aural-oral methods are based on the philosophy that children with hearing impairment should learn to use the oral English of the greater community. Advocates of this method believe that this goal will be impeded if the child is allowed to use other means of communication, such as sign language (Simmons-Martin, 1972). Oral education emphasizes the development of normal speech skills through direct and rigorous speech training. The use of appropriate amplification is stressed and augmented by an emphasis on auditory training. This method also relies on the development of speechreading. This skill requires great visual perceptual abilities in order to differentiate between very rapid movements of the lips. Some speech sounds are invisible (like /h/ in "hug"). Many others look alike on the lips and are distinguished from one another only by voicing one and not the other (like /p/ in "Pat" and /b/ in "bat"). Until the early 1970s, aural-oral methods were used to teach nearly all children with hearing impairment who attended day programs and private residential schools (Quigley & Paul, 1984).

Total Communication Method

Total Communication (TC) method was developed in the late 1960s by educators who were dissatisfied with the results of traditional aural-oral instruction. Based on the idea that too little information is transmitted through aural-oral modalities when used alone, TC methods use a manual communication system in addition to speech, speechreading, and audition. Thus, people using TC sign and speak at the same time. By the mid-1970s, 65% of special programs were using Total Communication (Jordan, Gustason, & Rosen, 1976).

A great many manual communication systems are in use in the United States today, and no professional agreement or empirical evidence exists as to which is the

Figure 11.4   The Manual Alphabet

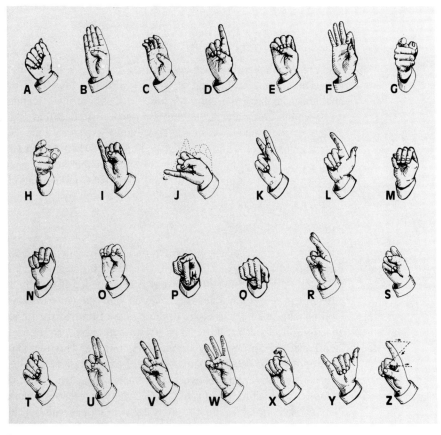

Source: Gallaudet University Division of Public Services, Kendall Green, Washington, DC 20002.

most effectively used in TC. The systems are alike in that they usually represent concepts with signs or specific handshapes and motions. Often signs are borrowed from American Sign Language and are put in English word order. Words can also be *fingerspelled*—spelled out letter by letter using the manual alphabet that assigns each letter a specific hand configuration. Manual systems differ in the degree to which they attempt to represent English. Some (such as Seeing Exact English or Signed English) attempt to provide a direct correspondence of English into a manual code wherein each part of the English sentence, including grammatical markers like word endings such as "-ing" and "-ed," is represented in the signed message as well. Other codes (such as Pigin Signed English) supply a signed accompaniment to spoken English that indicates the content of the oral message without representing the grammar and structure of English.

American Sign Language is an autonomous manual language with its own grammar and structure; ASL is totally unrelated to oral English. In fact, the word order and structure of the two languages are so different that individuals proficient in both languages have difficulty using them simultaneously. In 1969, it was estimated that ASL was used by 75% of the adult deaf community in the United States (Rainer, Altschuler, & Kallman, 1969).

Placement Options

In the years since the passage of PL 94-142, an entire array of educational programs have become available to children with hearing handicaps throughout the United States. Placement options differ according to the amount of time students spend in regular program classes with hearing peers. Alternative educational settings include the following:

☐ *Full-time regular program class:* Many students with hearing impairment successfully participate full time in regular education classes. Depending on need, these students may be assisted in this achievement by the following:
  • Educational interpreter
  • Regular consultation between the regular program teacher and an educator of the hearing impaired
  • In-class tutoring of the student by an itinerant teacher of the hearing impaired
  • Additional speech, language and/or auditory therapy
  • Notetakers
  • Special amplification devices

☐ *Part-time regular education class and part-time special education class:* Students may spend up to half their school day in a resource room to address special education needs and participate in the regular program the remainder of the day. This model requires coordination between the regular education teacher and the special educator. Additional support services, such as speech and language therapy, auditory training, and educational interpreting, may be needed.

☐ *Special class in regular education day school:* Many students attend regular schools for nonhandicapped children that have one or more special classes for special education students. The student spends a majority of the day in the special class but may participate in either:

- *Academic mainstreaming:* The student joins a regular class for one or more academic subjects. Interpreter services are provided as needed.
- *Nonacademic mainstreaming:* The student joins a regular class for activities such as art, library time, or gym.
- *Social mainstreaming:* The student joins regular education children for social activities such as lunch, recess, assemblies, and other all-school activities.

☐ *Separate Day School:* Special schools educate many children with hearing impairment. These settings may be public or private. Mainstreaming opportunities may be limited, but some children are transported to nearby regular education facilities to participate in regular classes.

☐ *Separate residential school:* Large residential facilities have historically been the mainstay of deaf education. Today about 32% of students with hearing impairments in the United States are enrolled in these programs, although 40% of them attend as day students who live at home. Only about 8% of students in these separate school settings participate in any regular program mainstreaming activities (Lowenbraun & Thompson, 1987).

Recently, many educators and advocates for children with hearing impairment have challenged traditional concepts that such a child's least restrictive environment is a neighborhood day program. They contend that self-contained programs serving large numbers of deaf students provide less restrictive environments than do district day schools in which a few special educators address the educational needs of a small number of children with hearing handicaps. Indeed, residential programs can boast that all members of the faculty are familiar with hearing impairment and are skilled at communicating with deaf children. Their students can participate without stigmatization in "normal" school activities such as after-school sports and clubs and without the complications of public school transportation schedules. Students can choose friends from a larger group of peers with hearing impairment than is available in smaller programs. Research on students in these two placements indicate that although students in district day programs score higher on academic measures, students in separate residential programs score higher on social skill and self-esteem measures (Farrugia & Austin, 1980).

Related Services

The related services needed by a child with hearing impairment are outlined during the IEP process. Services can be delivered by a variety of individuals, depending on the child's educational placement. For a student in a self-contained special education class, auditory training, language remediation, and speech therapy may all be provided by the certified teacher of the hearing impaired. For a student who participates in the regular program throughout the day, these services may be provided on a scheduled basis by any one of three different professionals: an audiologist, an itinerant teacher of the hearing impaired, or a communications disorders specialist (CDS). Although children with hearing impairment may have additional conditions requiring occupational therapy or physical therapy, the support services most commonly required to address their special needs include:

> *Speech therapy:* A CDS works with the student to develop articulation skills, including the production of the sounds of spoken English, the use of correct patterns of voice intonation and pitch, and the use of appropriate rates of speaking.
>
> *Language therapy:* A CDS, a language therapist, or a certified teacher of children with hearing impairment may provide language instruction that focuses on expressive and receptive language including grammar, vocabulary, and the appropriate use of language in a variety of settings.
>
> *Auditory training:* A specially trained educator may provide remedial training to improve the student's use of his or her residual hearing. Very young children often need to be taught that sound has meaning and even to notice the presence or absence of sound. In later years goals focus on use of hearing to understand speech and assist in speechreading.
>
> *Counseling:* Many programs help children cope and adapt to a hearing world by providing individual or group counseling as part of the educational

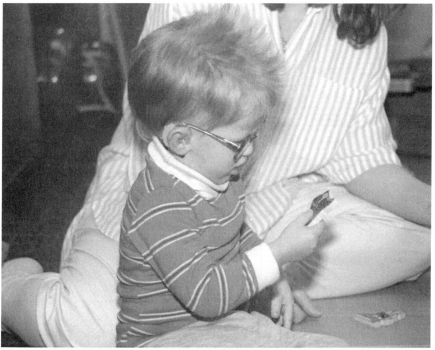

This youngster is learning even though he has both hearing and visual impairments.

program. Objectives can range from interpersonal skill development to problem-solving strategies. These services are most often provided by a school mental health professional (social worker, school psychologist, or nurse) who has appropriate communication skills and a strong background in hearing impairment.

Preschool Programs

Preschools for children with hearing impairment provide normal preschool curricula in addition to activities to stimulate communication skills and address auditory, speech, and language delays. These programs may provide the first opportunity for students to associate with other individuals with hearing handicaps. Preschool may also be the child's introduction to functioning in a group, following basic rules, and sharing materials.

Some preschool programs use a mainstream model in which children with hearing and children with hearing impairment are taught together. This provides the opportunity children with impaired hearing to observe and interact with hearing peers, who inadvertently model age-appropriate language and communication skills.

Often preschool programs include a parent training component through which parents may receive information on available local resources, the educational system, appropriate discipline techniques, communication strategies, and other issues related to hearing impairment.

Transitional Services

Successful transition into new programs as the child's needs change often involves a variety of community professionals and services. Families learning to adjust to the new challenges of having a child with impaired hearing are often assisted by teachers, counselors, or other specialists from local speech and hearing centers or early intervention programs. Sometimes the audiologist, social worker, CDS, or infant program teacher assists the family in gathering the information needed to make initial educational placement and communication training decisions. Later educational interpreters or itinerant teachers of children with impaired hearing may assist in meeting the challenges of transitions between special classes and mainstream programs. A successful move into the regular program often requires coordination, cooperation, and open communication among the special education teacher, the regular program teacher, the interpreter, other support personnel, the student, and the family.

Programs for students with hearing impairment can ease the transition to secondary education, vocational training, or employment by offering career counseling and coursework on vocational skills and independent living. In addition to stressing academic achievement, successful college preparatory training involves instruction on dorm life, responsible social behavior, and problem-solving strategies for coping with the multitude of problems encountered by college students with impaired hearing.

Parental Involvement

Public law requires that parents participate annually in the process of planning their child's educational program. Parents have the right and the responsibility to advocate for the inclusion of special services to be provided by the district. Thus, the law recognizes that the success of intervention efforts is greatly influenced by family background, experience, education, and socioeconomic status (Luterman, 1979).

It is estimated that only 10% of children with hearing handicaps have at least one parent who also has an auditory disability (Rawlings & Jensema, 1977). This means that most parents of deaf children have little or no experience or understanding of their child's disability prior to diagnosis. On learning that their child is hearing impaired, parents often experience the same stages of the grief process associated with adjusting to death or other great loss (shock, denial, anger, depression, and acceptance) (Luterman, 1979). While coping with their own adjustment, as well as that of other family members, parents are faced with the task of learning about the disability, their child's needs, and what to expect in the future. In the midst of all this, parents are expected to begin their careers as advocates for their child.

In response to the needs of parents in this situation, many public and private school programs offer early intervention programs. Professionals assist families in learning new skills to cope with the child's needs, provide information about the disability, and facilitate contact with community services. Professionals also assist the child directly by providing early auditory training and language stimulation, while training parents to enhance the child's language development and communication skills. Some programs also offer individual, family, and group counseling to ease the adjustment process.

Postsecondary Support

Historically, residential schools for the deaf provided vocational training for high school students that enabled them to compete successfully in the job market. Recently, the labor force has required a higher level of skills from its workers, thus encouraging more deaf as well as hearing high school graduates to seek higher education. Today a wider variety of postsecondary educational opportunities are available to students with hearing impairment than ever before. Popular majors include business, manufacturing, fine arts, humanities, public service, and communication (Rawlings & King, 1986).

Students with impaired hearing often require special support services in order to participate in the academic and cultural offerings of postsecondary programs serving the general population. In selecting programs, these students need to match their career goals with the support services and program options offered at each institution. Such services may include accredited classes designed specifically for students with hearing impairment, sign language and voice interpreting services, notetaking, vocational counseling and placement, personal counseling by mental health professionals with a background in hearing impairment, speech and hearing services, communication and sign language training for faculty and students, supervised housing, and social and cultural activities specifically for deaf students.

Postsecondary education is available to students with hearing handicaps in more than 145 local, state, regional, and national programs; these offer training ranging from 1-year certificate programs to doctoral-level education (DeCaro, Karchmer, & Rawlings, 1987). Gallaudet University in Washington D.C. was established in 1864 and remains the only liberal arts university established expressly for the education of students with impaired hearing. The National Technical Training Institute for the Deaf at Rochester Institute of Technology provides vocational and technical education to college students from all over the country. These two institutions serve 41% of all postsecondary deaf students in the United States (DeCaro, Karchmer, & Rawlings, 1987).

SELECTING AND ADAPTING INSTRUCTIONAL MATERIALS

Teachers working with children with hearing impairment must find materials suitable for their students' language levels. This task becomes increasingly challenging for those working with older children who may not have achieved the reading and language skills expected for students in content-oriented classes such as history, geography, and literature. To meet this challenge, teachers often make their own materials to supplement or even replace commercially made instructional products. Teachers must often preteach vocabulary and language concepts necessary to understand the conceptual basis of lessons. Visual aids such as pictures, drawings, diagrams, or brief outlines are commonly used in lessons for these students. Thus, every class teaches both language and the content at hand.

> Activity 2, page 315, provides you with experience making visual aids for lessons.

Commercially produced materials for children with hearing impairment often emphasize language instruction. Students learning English grammar can use programs such as the *Apple Tree series* (Canglia, Cole, Howard, Krohn, & Rice, 1972) or *Lessons in Syntax* (McCarr, 1973). Books such as *The King Who Rained* (Gwynne, 1970) are useful for teaching idioms and other difficult semantic concepts.

Teachers of children with impaired hearing sometimes rewrite printed information in texts using vocabulary and language structures familiar to their students. In this way the students learn to acquire content information from print but are not hindered by their language deficits.

Activity 3, page 316, is designed to help you understand the benefits and drawbacks of rewritten text.

The "Writing Workshop" approach developed for regular education students by Graves (1983) has recently been enthusiastically adopted for use with children with hearing impairment (Kretschmer, 1985). This process involves students in daily writing activities, including sharing, conferencing, revising, editing, and publishing their original written work. Proponents of the approach believe it assists children in developing all their communication skills, verbal/manual as well as written.

TECHNOLOGY APPLICATIONS

Amplification

Improvements in hearing aid technology occur so rapidly that students' hearing aids should be evaluated every few years to ensure they provide the best possible benefit. In the past, hearing aids simply amplified all sound equally. Today they can amplify selected frequencies to more closely match the configuration of an individual's hearing loss.

Many hearing impaired children in schools use FM auditory training units. Teachers in such programs wear a small FM microphone. The student wears a modified hearing aid that incorporates an FM receiver, so she or he hears the teacher's voice directly and clearly regardless of where the teacher is in the room. Although such assistive listening devices have been shown to be very effective, older students are often reluctant to use them for fear of calling undue attention to their hearing loss (Leavitt, 1987).

Cochlear Implants

The cochlear implant is one of the most important technological advances related to hearing impairment in recent years. This new and somewhat controversial procedure is designed to provide a sensation of hearing in individuals with sensorineural hearing losses so profound that they do not benefit from any standard amplification devices. A tiny electronics package is surgically implanted in the deaf person's inner ear or cochlea and is attached to a receiver-stimulator implanted just behind the ear in the base of the skull. The individual wears a microphone and a speech processor that resemble a body-level hearing aid and are attached by a tiny electrical wire leading to a button size electronic transmitter placed over the implant site. Although the resultant sensation is not the same as hearing, it enables the individual to better discriminate speech sounds.

Captioning

Captioned films and television programs make information generally available to the public more accessible to individuals with impaired hearing. Captioned films, videos, and filmstrips are available to educators from Captioned Films for the Deaf in St. Petersburg, Florida.

Television caption decoders display a transcript of television conversation and commentary. A separate decoder box can be attached to an ordinary television for captioning, or a special television can be purchased that displays the captions directly onto the viewing screen.

Telecommunication Devices for the Deaf

Individuals with hearing handicaps can communicate by phone if each party in the conversation has a telecommunication device for the deaf (TDD). A TDD is a small keyboard with an electronic display screen and modem attached. The telephone receiver is placed in the modem, and messages typed onto the keyboard are carried on the phone line to be displayed on the answering party's TDD. Today's market also supplies telephone answering machines that can store messages for retrieval on the TDD display.

Computer Technology

Microcomputers have many applications in educating children with hearing disorders. In addition to the standard use of microcomputers for tutorial drill-and-practice activities, there are special programs available for speech drill, auditory training exercises, sign language instruction, speechreading, and supplemental reading and language instruction.

Computer technology has recently been utilized to transliterate speech onto a printed display screen to enable college students with hearing handicaps to read verbal communications. When offered as an alternative to sign language interpreters in lecture classes, this technology was chosen about half the time (Stuckless, 1983).

Alerting Devices

Many everyday devices have been adapted to better suit the needs of people with hearing handicaps. Doorbells, fire alarms, and alarm clocks can all be installed with flashing lights in addition to auditory signals. For those who can sleep right through their flashing alarm, there are special bed or pillow vibrators to literally shake them out of bed in the morning!

MULTICULTURAL ISSUES

Until recently, students with impaired hearing from non-English-speaking (NES) backgrounds were simply included in special programs for classmates from

English-speaking homes. There was little recognition that children from NES backgrounds might have special academic, social, cultural, and linguistic needs in addition to those posed by their hearing handicap. Such an oversight can damage children's relationships with their families and native cultures, diminish their abilities to acquire English, and contribute to inappropriate educational placement and programming.

Recent surveys of programs serving children with impaired hearing indicate that the number of NES students is on the rise (Delgado, 1981). The ethnic diversity of students in such programs is reported to be 70.3% white, 17.4% black, and 9.4% Hispanic, with all other cultural backgrounds making up the remaining 2.4% (Maestas y Moores & Moores, 1984). The predominant language groups represented are Spanish, Portuguese, Vietnamese, and East Indian languages and dialects (Delgado, 1984).

Research findings indicate that NES children with hearing impairment are more likely to be placed in classes for low functioning or multiply handicapped children (Delgado, 1984). Experts are concerned that this over-representation is the result of culturally biased assessment and culturally insensitive placement and teaching procedures (Figueroa, Delgado, & Ruiz, 1984; Fischgrund, 1984).

Often, the insensitivity of educators to the circumstances of NES families contributes to the tension between school and home, thereby interfering with the provision of services to the child. Many teachers do not realize that NES families may be isolated from community support and struggling to cope with financial deprivation in an alien setting. Parents are often so engrossed in providing for basic family survival that they have little energy remaining to participate in their children's education. Because technological assets such as hearing aids may be uncommon in their home country, parents may not understand the benefits of early amplification for their child (Blackwell & Fischgrund, 1984).

Special educators are beginning to include sociocultural needs in addition to cognitive and linguistic needs when planning IEPs (Fischgrund, 1984). They are recognizing the importance of appropriately trained, ethnically sensitive, bilingual/bicultural support services and assessment for children from NES homes. Cooperation between regular program and special education bilingual/bicultural programs is critical if all children are to receive a meaningful education.

SUMMARY THOUGHTS

Education for students with hearing impairment has changed radically since the establishment of the American Asylum for the Deaf and Dumb in 1817. Many students are now mainstreamed, schools are now more aware of the social-emotional needs of their students with impaired hearing, support services are available through the school if not in it, and improvements in hearing aid technology are occurring at a rapid rate.

Assessment strategies for diagnosis and placement of children with hearing impairment must include assessments of communication skills, academic achievement, cognitive functioning, and social-emotional adjustment. Because very few standardized tests are useful for academic planning with this population, informal testing must supplement this assessment. It is important that professionals who administer tests to these students have the information necessary to differentiate between a skill deficit and a knowledge deficit.

The most important challenge that educators must face in designing instructional interventions for students with hearing impairment is how to facilitate the acquisition of speech and language skills. Two of the most influential approaches for doing so are the Aural-Oral Method and Total Communication. Students may often require related services such as speech therapy and auditory training.

Any program—whether preschool or transitional from one school experience to another—must take into account the entire family of the student with impaired hearing in order to ensure program effectiveness and familial support. Sometimes the family needs direct support in coping with a child whose impairment has just been diagnosed or in helping a child face a new challenge.

As the student prepares for a role in the larger world, he or she must examine present skills in relation to those needed to enter an increasingly more competitive job market. Postsecondary educational opportunities for individuals with hearing impairment are greater now than at any time previously, and many colleges and universities offer additional support services to these students. Likewise, applications of technology to everyday life for the hearing impaired—such as captioned films and television programs and telecommunication devices—are increasing the access those in the nonhearing world and those in the hearing world have to one another.

REFERENCES

Allen, T. E. (1986). Patterns of academic performance among hearing impaired students: 1974 and 1983. In A. N. Schildroth & M. A. Karchmer (Eds.), *Deaf children in America* (pp. 161–206). San Diego: College Hill Press.

Anderson, R. J., & Sisco, F. H. (1977). *Standardization of the WISC-R performance scale for deaf children.* Washington DC: Gallaudet College, Office of Demographic Studies.

Blackwell, P. M., & Fischgrund, J. E. (1984). Issues in the development of culturally responsive programs for deaf students from non-English-speaking homes. In G. L. Delgado (Ed.), *The Hispanic deaf: Issues and challenges for bilingual special education* (pp. 154–166). Washington DC: Gallaudet College Press.

Canglia, J., Cole, N. J., Howard, W., Krohn, E., & Rice, M. (1972). *Apple tree.* Beaverton, OR: Dormac.

DeCaro, J. J., Karchmer, M. A., & Rawlings, B. W. (1987). Postsecondary programs for deaf students at the peak of the rubella bulge. *American Annals of the Deaf, 132*(1), 36–42.

Delgado, G. L. (1981). Hearing impaired children from non-native language homes. *American Annals of the Deaf, 126*(2), 118–121.

Delgado, G. L. (1984). Hearing impaired children from non-native language homes. In S. L. Delgado (Ed.), *The Hispanic deaf: Issues and challenges for bilingual special education* (pp. 28–37). Washington DC: Gallaudet College Press.

DiFrancesca, S. (1972). *Academic achievement test results of a national testing program for hearing impaired students, United States: Spring 1971.* Washington DC: Gallaudet College, Office of Demographic Studies.

Farrugia, D., & Austin, G. (1980). A study of social-emotional adjustment patterns of hearing-impaired students in different educational settings. *American Annals of the Deaf, 125*(5), 535–541.

Figueroa, R. A., Delgado, G. L. & Ruiz, N. T. (1984). Assessment of Hispanic children: Implications for Hispanic hearing impaired children. In G. L. Delgado (Ed.), *The Hispanic deaf:* Issues and challenges for bilingual special education (pp. 124–152). Washington, DC: Gallaudet College Press.

Fischgrund, J. E. (1984). Language intervention for hearing-impaired children from linguistically and culturally diverse backgrounds. In G. L. Delgado (Ed.), *The Hispanic deaf: Issues and challenges for bilingual special education* (pp. 94–145). Washington, DC: Gallaudet College Press.

Graves, D. H. (1983). *Writing: teachers and children at work.* Exeter, N.H.: Heinemann Educational Books.

Gwynne, F. (1970). *The king who rained.* New York: Windmill Books and Dutton.

Hiskey, M. S. (1966). *Hiskey-Nebraska Test of Learning Aptitude.* Lincoln, NE: Union College Press.

Jordan, I., Gustason, G., & Rosen, R. (1976). Current communication trends in programs for the deaf. *American Annals of the Deaf, 121*(6), 527–532.

Kretschmer, R. R. (Ed.). (1985). Learning to write and writing to learn. *The Volta Review, 87*(5), 5–185.

Leavitt, R. J. (1987). Promoting the use of rehabilitation technology. *ASHA, 29,* 28–31.

Leiter, R. (1948). *The Leiter International Performance Scale.* Chicago: Stoelting.

Ling, D. (1976). *Speech and the hearing impaired child: Theory and practice.* Washington, DC: A. G. Bell Association for the Deaf.

Lowenbraun, S., & Thompson, M. (1987). Environments and strategies for learning and teaching. In M. C. Reynolds, H. J. Walberg, & M. C. Wang (Eds.), *Handbook of Special Education Research and Practice. Volume B* (pp. 47–69). Oxford: Pergamon.

Luterman, D. (1979). *Counseling parents of hearing impaired children.* Boston: Little, Brown.

Maestas y Moores, J., & Moores, D. F. (1984). The status of Hispanics in special education. In G. L. Delgado (Ed.), *The Hispanic deaf: Issues and challenges for bilingual special education* (pp. 14–27). Washington, DC: Gallaudet College Press.

McCarr, J. E. (1973). *Lessons in Syntax.* Lake Oswego, OR: Dormac.

Moores, D. (1987). *Educating the deaf.* Boston: Houghton Mifflin.

Northern, J. L., & Downs, M. P. (1974). *Hearing impaired children.* Baltimore, MD: Williams & Wilkins.

Pendergast, K., Dickey, S. E., Selmar, J. W., & Soder, A. L. (1984). *Photo Articulation Test.* Danville, IL: Interstate Publishers & Printers.

Quigley, S. P., & Paul, P. (1984). *Language and deafness.* San Diego: College Hill Press.

Rainer, J., Altshuler, K., & Kallman, F. (Eds.) (1969). *Family and mental health problems in a deaf population.* Springfield, IL: Thomas.

Rawlings, B., & Jensema, C. (1977). *Two studies of the families of hearing impaired children.* Washington, DC: Gallaudet College, Office of Demographic Studies.

Rawlings, B., & King, S. J. (1986). In A. N. Schildroth & M. A. Karchmer (Eds.), *Deaf children in America* (pp. 231–257). Boston: College Hill Press.

Simmons-Martin, A. (1972). Oral-aural procedure: Theoretical basis and rationale. *Volta Review, 74*(9), 541–551.

Stuckless, E. R. (1983). Real-time transliteration of speech into print for hearing impaired students in regular classes. *American Annals of the Deaf, 128*(5), 619–624.

Sullivan, P., & Vernon, M. (1979). Psychological assessment of hearing-impaired children. *School Psychology Digest, 8*(3), 271–290.

Trybus, R., & Karchmer, M. (1977). School achievement status and growth patterns. *American Annals of the Deaf Directory of Programs and Services, 122*(2), 62–69.

Vernon, M., & Brown, D. W. (1964). A guide to psychological tests and testing procedures in the evaluation of deaf and hard of hearing children. *Journal of Speech and Hearing Disorders, 29*(4), 414–423.

Wechsler, D. (1974). *Wechsler Intelligence Scale for Children—Revised.* New York: Psychological Corp.

ADDITIONAL READINGS

Alexander, F. M., & Gannon, J. R. (1984). *Deaf heritage.* Silver Springs, MD: National Association of the Deaf.

Garretson, M. D. (1978). Total communication. *Volta Review, 78*(4), 88–95.

Gustason, G., Pfetzing, D., & Zawolkow, E. (1980). *Signing Exact English*. Los Alamitos, CA: Modern Sign Press.

Lane, H. (1984). *When the mind hears*. New York: Random House.

Lowenbraun, S., Appelman, K., & Callahan, J. (1980). *Teaching the hearing impaired*. Columbus, OH: Merrill.

Markowicz, H. (1977). *American Sign Language: Fact and fancy*. Washington, DC: Gallaudet College.

Mindel, E. D., & Vernon, M. (1971). *They grow in silence*. Silver Springs, MD: National Association of the Deaf.

Moores, D. (1987). *Educating the deaf*. Boston: Houghton Mifflin.

Neisser, A. (1983). *The other side of silence*. New York: Knopf.

Panara, R., & Panara, J. (1981). *Great deaf Americans*. Silver Springs, MD: T. J. Publishers.

1

Purpose

☐ To experience a technique commonly used to examine the language of a student with hearing impairment

☐ To develop a sense of how frequently idioms and words with multiple meanings are used in everyday language

Steps

1. Sample the language of a friend by observing him or her for 10 minutes during a mealtime or other activity involving another person.

2. For the 10 minutes specified, write down everything your subject says exactly the way he or she says it. (For example, "Don't like it" rather than "I don't like it"—if the first is the way it was said.)

3. If the person is speaking rapidly, do not try to get down all the sentences. Instead concentrate on being sure you get complete utterances, even if this means missing the next two or three utterances.

4. If necessary, take notes about the topic of conversation if it is not obvious from the utterances you are writing down.

Analysis

☐ Make a list of all the words in the language sample that have multiple meanings. (For example "baskets" in "I made two baskets.")

☐ Make a second list of all the idioms and slang expressions used in the language sample.

☐ Devise a simple lesson for teaching either multiple word meanings or idioms and slang expressions to someone who is learning English as a second language.

2

Purpose

☐ To practice using visual aids and experiential activities in lesson preparation

Steps

1. Plan a brief lesson about the first Thanksgiving suitable for a grade level you want to teach.

2. Prepare a list of visual aids you can use that will communicate the essential points of the lesson.

3. Make at least one of the aids on the list.

4. Design one experiential activity to communicate the main point of your lesson.

Analysis

☐ How was your lesson planning affected by incorporating the visual aids and an experiential activity?

☐ What are the benefits in using visual aids and experiential activities?

☐ What aspects of the information in the lesson are not available through your visual aids and experiential activity?

3

Purpose

☐ To understand the process of rewriting text for use by students with hearing impairments

Steps

1. Select a paragraph from both a fairy tale and a social studies or history textbook.

2. Rewrite each paragraph using only simple sentences, with subject-verb-object word order and common words.

Analysis

☐ Compare your rewritten paragraphs with the original texts. Which is more interesting to read?

☐ Is the information equally clear in the original and the rewritten paragraphs?

☐ Is one type of text (fiction versus content writing) easier to rewrite than the other?

☐ What are the disadvantages in using rewritten texts?

☐ What are the advantages in using rewritten texts?

12

Visual Impairments

Rosanne K. Silberman
Hunter College—City University of New York

VISUAL IMPAIRMENTS
TYPICAL PROFILE

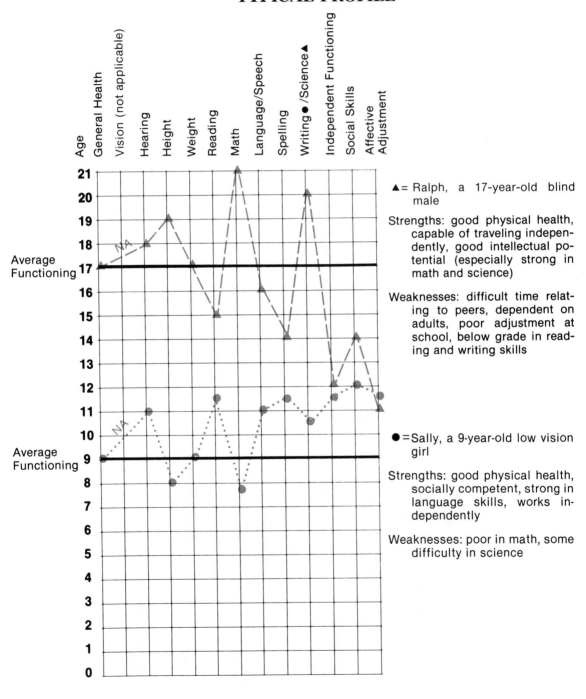

▲ = Ralph, a 17-year-old blind male

Strengths: good physical health, capable of traveling independently, good intellectual potential (especially strong in math and science)

Weaknesses: difficult time relating to peers, dependent on adults, poor adjustment at school, below grade in reading and writing skills

● = Sally, a 9-year-old low vision girl

Strengths: good physical health, socially competent, strong in language skills, works independently

Weaknesses: poor in math, some difficulty in science

Children and youth with visual impairments represent a low percentage of the school age population. About one student in a thousand has a visual impairment and receives additional support services. According to a 1987 annual survey (American Printing House for the Blind, 1988), 43,145 legally blind students are enrolled in school programs. In comparison to surveys of recent years, the total number of students in all categories did not increase; however, the number of children in infant and preschool categories grew, as did those in grades K–12. Of particular significance is that many of these registered students have other disabilities in addition to a visual impairment. As it is sometimes difficult to obtain appropriate educational services, some students with visual impairments and other disabilities are counted in another disability category, such as learning disabilities, physical impairments, or mental retardation. This results in lower and inaccurate statistical counts.

Because of the wide variation in ages and levels of functioning, children and youth with visual impairments are educated today in many different types of service delivery systems. As reported by the American Printing House for the Blind (1988), 83.3% of the population attend public or private nonprofit day school programs, while only 10.4% attend residential school programs. This clearly reflects the impact of PL 94-142 and the increasing emphasis on educating students in the least restrictive environment. An additional 6.4% either attend facilities serving students with multiple disabilities or programs conducted by rehabilitation agencies.

Of the various service delivery models for meeting the needs of children and youth with visual impairments in regular classes, two models—the itinerant teacher model and the resource room model—are extremely effective (both use the team approach). In the *itinerant teacher model,* students with visual impairments attend the same neighborhood school as their peers and siblings and are enrolled in a regular class. A teacher with special training to work with students with visual impairments travels from school to school to assist in modification of materials and to provide instruction in special subjects such as reading braille, reading using low vision aids, and using a computer with voice output. The itinerant teacher also serves as a resource for the classroom teacher and suggests ways in which these students can participate fully in activities with sighted classmates (Silberman, Trief, & Morse, 1988). The time a teacher spends with each student varies according to need, travel time, and caseload. Visits usually last 1 or 2 hours and are made three to four times per week. This model is most common in suburban and rural areas.

In the *resource room model,* most children and youth with visual impairments have to travel away from their neighborhood and attend a school that has a resource room program for all students with visual impairments within a specified area, usually a school district. The students are enrolled in a regular class and receive services from a vision teacher in a specially equipped resource room in the same building. The resource room teacher performs many of the same functions as the itinerant teacher but is always available if a problem arises. The students with visual impairments go to the resource room at scheduled times for assistance. This model is most common in densely populated urban areas. (Other models in which the emphasis is not on accommodation in the regular class will be discussed later in the chapter.)

CHARACTERISTICS OF CHILDREN AND YOUTH WITH VISUAL IMPAIRMENTS

Although visual impairment is a low-prevalence disability affecting only about .1% of the population with handicapping conditions, the characteristics of the population of children and youth with visual impairments vary from individual to individual. Factors such as etiology and age of onset of visual impairments, type and severity of the visual loss, and incidence of additional impairments all have an impact on development and learning. In addition, those children who become visually impaired prior to age 5 usually do not retain visual imagery and are taught concepts differently from those who lose their vision after this age.

Anatomy of the Eye

The eye is a complex organ that receives visual images from the environment and sends them to the brain for interpretation. As light hits an object in a person's field of vision, the light rays are reflected and first pass through the *cornea* (the transparent portion, or window, of the eye). Then the light rays pass through the *aqueous humor,* (the watery liquid behind the cornea) and then the *pupil* (the circular hole in the center of the colored iris). The muscles of the *iris* control the amount of light entering the eye by expanding or contracting the size of the pupil. The light rays then pass through the *lens* (a transparent, elastic structure held in place by suspensory ligaments). From the lens the rays pass through the *vitreous humor* (a jellylike substance that helps the eye maintain its shape) and finally to the *retina* (the inner lining of the eye, which contains optic nerve cells), where the rays come to a point of focus in the normal eye. The retina contains photoreceptors called *cones* or *rods*. The cone cells, located in the macular portion of the retina, are responsible for central vision. These cells, sensitive to color and high levels of illumination, enable one to perform fine detail visual tasks such as reading, seeing distant objects, and discriminating colors. The rods, located in the periphery, are sensitive to movement and low levels of illumination. They are necessary for night vision. The stimulation of the cones and rods by light rays results in the transmission of electrical impulses to the optic nerve and to the occipital lobe of the brain. Damage to any of these structures in the eye results in visual defects (Vaughan, Asbury, & Tabbara, 1989). (See Figure 12.1.)

Causes of Visual Impairments

Refractive errors caused by a defect in the eye's ability to focus light rays directly on the retina can usually be corrected by glasses or contact lenses. Those with severe refractive errors, however, may still be visually impaired after correction.

These conditions include *myopia,* or nearsightedness, in which light rays focus in front of the retina because the eyeball is too long. Students with myopia can usually see near objects clearly, but they have difficulty seeing distant objects. In *hyperopia,* or farsightedness, the eyeball is too short, and light rays come to a point of focus behind the retina. Students with hyperopia are unable to see near objects clearly and have difficulty in such tasks as reading; they are able to see distant objects easily. In *astigmatism,* vision is distorted or blurred at near and far distances because of the unequal curvature of the cornea and the lens.

Other eye conditions found in children may result in severe visual impairments that require intervention by specially trained teachers. These include:

Figure 12.1 Anatomy of the Eye

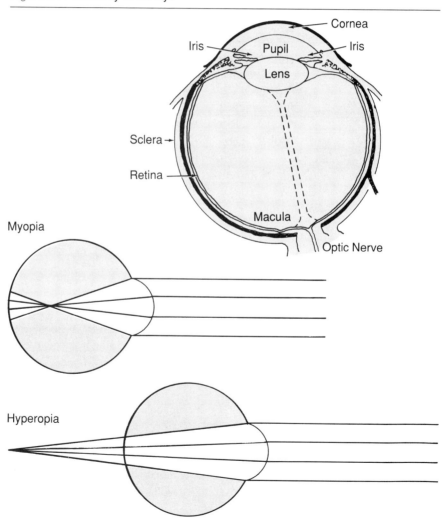

Albinism—This hereditary congenital condition results in reduced or total lack of pigment throughout the body. Ocular albinism, which is more common in males, includes reduced visual acuity, astigmatism, photophobia, and nystagmus (involuntary movement of the eyes).

Amblyopia—This condition results in reduced visual acuity in one eye for which no organic cause is found. Amblyopia may occur when one suppresses the image in one eye to avoid double vision or when the two eyes have unequal refractive errors. This condition must be diagnosed and treated as early as possible in order to prevent permanent visual loss.

Congenital cataracts—This is an opacity or cloudiness of the lens that prevents the passage of light rays to the retina. Images are distorted and hazy. The effect of a cataract on vision varies according to the size, position, and density of the opacity. When the lens is surgically removed, children then need to wear contact lenses, bifocals, or glasses for near and far distances. But even with corrective lenses, many are still severely visually impaired.

Congenital glaucoma—This condition is characterized by an abnormally developed drainage system, which blocks the flow of the aqueous and increases the pressure in the eye and the size of the eyeball (buphthalmus). Glaucoma causes damage to the optic nerve and can lead to permanent visual loss or blindness if not treated medically. Children with this condition should be under continual care by an ophthalmologist. Those who develop glaucoma after the age of 3 exhibit symptoms such as nausea, headache, and pain resulting from the increased ocular pressure. Early medical treatment is essential to avoid visual loss or save the remaining vision.

Nystagmus—This condition refers to involuntary eye movement of one or both eyes. It can be jerky, slow, rotary, or pendular. Nystagmus usually accompanies other ocular disorders. Even though the eyes move, the child sees objects as stationary. Movement may be more apparent when the child is fatigued or stressed.

Optic nerve atrophy—This condition is characterized by damage to the fibers in the optic nerve. Electrical impulses are unable to travel from the retina to the occipital lobe. The extent of the visual impairment depends on the location and severity of the damage. Defects include reduced visual acuity, visual field losses, and color vision difficulties.

Retinitis pigmentosa—This is an inherited condition whose symptoms usually begin to appear during adolescence and result in progressive deterioration of the retina. Retinitis pigmentosa affects the rods first and causes loss of peripheral vision and night blindness. Eventually, the result is tunnel vision or total blindness. This condition is also associated with Usher's syndrome in which an individual is born with congenital deafness and begins to develop retinitis pigmentosa during the teenage years.

Retinopathy of prematurity—This condition develops in premature infants who receive high levels of oxygen in order to survive; it occurs in rare cases in full-term babies. The extent of the condition depends on both the amount of oxygen and the length of time an infant is administered the oxygen. Nevertheless, there are still mysteries as to why some infants administered the same amount for the same length of time develop the retinal scarring while others do not. The severity of the visual impairment may range from moderate myopia to total blindness caused by retinal scarring and complete retinal detachment.

Strabismus—This condition refers to any deviation of the eyes from simultaneously focusing on the same object. Strabismus is caused by lack of fusion due to muscle imbalance. The basic types are *esotropia,* in which an eye turns inward; *exotropia,* in which an eye turns outward; and *hypertropia,* in which one eye deviates upward relative to the other. In order to avoid seeing a double image, the child usually uses the straight eye and suppresses the vision in the other eye. This can result in amblyopia.

Effects of Visual Impairment on Development

Lack of vision resulting in total blindness or low vision affects all areas of development including motor, cognitive, language, and social development. It is critical to understand the consequences of the sensory impairment and the instructional implications that follow.

Motor Development

Young infants with visual impairments begin to exhibit motor delays during the earliest stages of the sensorimotor period of development. Sighted infants lift their heads up to see an interesting spectacle such as a moving mobile or turn their heads to see a face or track a visually interesting moving object. Through repetitive experiences, they are able to develop both head control and rotation, important prerequisite skills for locomotion. Infants with little or no vision lack these ongoing opportunities to develop both head control and rotation and require both touch and sound stimuli to motivate them to reach these milestones (Ferrell, 1986). Furthermore, because of the lack of visual input, infants with visual impairments do not naturally know that objects exist out in the environment; they are therefore not motivated to reach or move toward objects. Until infants with visual impairments learn to connect the sound of an object with its source, they do not move, which further results in locomotor delays (Fraiberg, 1977). Many children and youth with visual impairments also exhibit low muscle tone and poor *proprioception* (sensory awareness of the body's position in space) and as a result have poor posture and faulty gait patterns (Hill, Rosen, Correa, & Langley, 1984).

Concept Development

Children and youth with blindness and severe visual impairments, particularly those who are born blind or who lose their vision early in life, have deficits in their information-gathering system. Without the use of vision, blind children must use their remaining senses to acquire concepts and perceptions. They acquire information in incomplete ways and sometimes reach erroneous conclusions. Hearing provides clues as to distance and direction, but it does not provide any ideas regarding such concrete aspects as size and shape. A child with a visual impairment can hear the sound of a bird and detect its location but cannot determine its physical characteristics. When asked how many legs a bird has, a girl with a severe visual impairment answered, "A dog has four legs; a cat has four legs, but a person has only two legs. A bird is not a person, so it has four legs" (Scott, 1982). The sense of touch is helpful in furthering development of concrete concepts, but some objects are inaccessible to tactual observation. For example, mountains and rivers are too large to be touched as a whole; flies and ants are too small to access directly; and butterflies and spider webs are too fragile to be touched. Other objects such as boiling water or burning wood are dangerous to touch, and those in liquid form, such as mercury, are in containers (Lowenfeld, 1981a). Touch also does not enable the blind person to scan the environment in order to gain knowledge. Only what is reachable at arm's length can be perceived. Thus, a blind student going to a store to shop or to a concert or football game will miss out on the variety of experiences that the sighted student has. He or she is dependent on others to explain and interpret the experience.

Activity 1, page 357, will help you to become more aware of the difficulties blind and low vision students encounter in acquiring concepts dependent on vision. In this activity, you will design specific instructional strategies.

There is no indication that children and youth with visual impairments have any less intelligence than those with sight. Because of the lack of vision, however, concepts acquired during the sensorimotor period, such as object permanence, causality, and means-end relationships, are frequently delayed because the individual with visual impairments must rely on different and less informative modalities for learning about the environment. Without vision, the child does not have numerous and repeated opportunities for imitation and observation. As a result of possible delays in acquiring these concepts, children and youth with visual impairments fall behind their sighted peers in the development of skills acquired during later stages, including conservation and classification (Stephens & Grube, 1982).

Language Development

Blindness or severe visual impairment affects the development of language in infants and young children in several ways. Without the ability to see facial expressions and use eye gaze and gestures such as pointing, children with visual impairments are unable to use these early communication cues with their parents as a means to direct attention, convey messages, and share information. When a parent refers to an object in the environment such as a ball or a shovel, the sighted child shows his or her understanding by gazing at it; the parent will continue to expand the concepts related to the object and thereby help the child to increase his or her vocabulary and linguistic concepts. Parents of children with visual impairments tend only to provide names of objects or requests for objects without any additional enriched information because they receive little or no feedback or indication that the child understands or is even interested. This emphasis on overlabeling thus prevents the child with visual impairments from acquiring increasingly complex language patterns (Andersen, Dunlea, & Kekelis, 1984). Other comparisons between sighted children and children with visual impairments show that the latter ask more questions, change the topic to focus on their own interests, and relate more to adults in communication than to their peers (Anderson et al., 1984).

Realistically, it is necessary for blind children to learn about concepts and objects in the environment that they cannot experience directly. These may include such concepts/objects as the height of trees or buildings, colors, the moon, and the stars. Some children with visual impairments, however, inappropriately overuse verbal descriptions that are based on the visual impressions of others. The term *verbalism* (Cutsforth, 1951; Harley, 1963; Warren, 1984) refers to the usage of language that has no meaning for the blind individual because it is not based on concrete experience. Two examples of a blind child using verbalisms with visual attributes are descriptions of the "sun shining on the white blanket of snow" and "squirrels flying through the trees."

Social Development

Because the development of social skills is highly dependent on vision, children with visual impairments differ from their sighted peers in several ways. As indicated earlier, a child with little or no vision is unable to rely on visual signals such as eye gaze and smiling by parents, siblings, and peers in social exchanges with him or her. Without being able to imitate these behaviors, the child with visual impairments is also unable to return these cues, and his or her social interactions are limited and sometimes misinterpreted (Fraiberg, 1977; Warren, 1984). This can cause negative attitudes toward the child and result in his or her becoming socially isolated. As the child with a visual impairment gets older, the lack of facial expressions and other nonverbal cues tends to signal to sighted persons a message of uninterest or apathy. How others react to and interact with the child with a visual impairment clearly affect his or her ability to develop a positive self-concept, a sense of independence, and opportunities for further experiences to develop social competence (Sacks & Reardon, 1989).

Without vision, it is difficult to initiate and maintain social contact. With just a glance, a sighted child can greet a classmate, show interest, and know when it is

A BLIND CHILD

Doug is a 9-year-old boy who has light perception and can distinguish light from dark. He has been blind since birth, and he lives with his parents and one younger sister on the 11th floor of an apartment building in a large city. He is somewhat chubby, but well groomed, and has a pleasant appearance. Occasionally, when he is either intensely involved in an activity or unoccupied, he tends to rock back and forth in his seat.

Doug's parents are very warm and supportive of his being with sighted peers. Since nursery school, he has always attended mainstreamed programs and has not participated in any activities with other children with visual impairments outside of school. He plays mainly with his younger sister and does not utilize any community programs for exercise and physical fitness. At home, he spend a great deal of time using his computer with voice output and sitting in front of the television. As a result of his blindness, he walks somewhat slowly and with a wide gait, particularly when going from room to room and on the steps of his new school. He is unable to go by himself from his apartment downstairs to meet the school bus outside of the building.

Doug is in the fourth grade and attends a resource room program for learners with visual impairments in his school for 1 hour each day. His resource room teacher communicates frequently with his regular classroom teacher and observes him in class with his sighted peers. Sometimes she team teaches with the regular teacher during group lessons.

Doug reads Grade 2 braille and is on or above grade level in almost all of his subjects, including reading, social studies, math, and science. He is slightly below grade level in spelling. He did well on a braille form of the Stanford Achievement Test given to his classmates. But with his increased workload in fourth grade he is

appropriate to take turns or respond to the attention of another individual. A blind or low vision child, however, has difficulty monitoring the attention of peers; the child does not always know if someone is talking directly to him or her or when a classmate joins or leaves him or her. As a result, this child may initiate conversation when no one is near. Sometimes young blind or low vision children use physical contact such as a tap on the arm in place of eye contact in their social exchanges, a behavior that may hinder friendship because some sighted children do not want to be touched (Kekelis & Sacks, 1988).

In the area of play, young blind and low vision children tend to spend less time playing with toys appropriately than do sighted children; instead, they tend to play with toys in a stereotypic manner such as mouthing or banging them (Parsons, 1986). Their attention span with toys is also brief; they prefer to leave toys in order to interact with adults. The play behavior of some young children with visual

beginning to find it difficult to keep up with all his reading because braille is much slower than print. He uses his braillewriter to take his spelling tests and write stories in Grade 2 braille. As Grade 2 braille uses many contractions, he is unaware of how some words are actually spelled and tends to rely on phonics. He uses mental arithmetic for most of his mathematics. He has not yet mastered the Nemeth code. Doug's teacher writes his homework assignments for him in a notebook, and his mother reads them to him. He does not have his own system for keeping track of assignments and deadlines. Socially, because of Doug's lack of vision, he is unable to interpret nonverbal cues and relate to what is happening in the environment. He tends to call out answers and ask inappropriate questions in order to be included in class discussions. As a result of this behavior, classmates ignore him unless they are working on a joint school project.

□ □ □

What are some goals for Doug that will help him to increase his orientation and mobility skills both at home and at school?

Identify some effective ways that the resource room teacher can help Doug increase his listening skills.

What are some social skills strategies that the resource room and classroom teachers can use to help Doug gain the acceptance of his peers?

Based on Doug's level of functioning in spelling and mathematics, give some specific suggestions for increasing his skills.

Suggest a solution that will enable Doug to independently keep track of his homework assignments.

impairments also lacks creativity and imagination and focuses on their own interests, which further hampers the establishment of social relationships (Kekelis & Sacks, 1988).

Some social skills that are learned naturally through visual imitation need to be taught specifically to children with visual impairments, particularly with the current emphasis in schools on normalization and integration. These skills include looking at the person who is speaking, standing up straight with head up, positioning one's body at a certain distance from a peer or teacher, initiating conversations, joining a group, and learning to be a good listener and share in the conversation. Appearance, grooming, and current styles of dressing are also important in relation to furthering social skills.

Some children and youth with visual impairments exhibit repetitive forms of physical activity such as rocking, head turning, and eye pressing. These self-stimu-

AN ADOLESCENT WITH LOW VISION

Nancy is a 16-year-old adolescent with low vision. She can see objects up to 5 inches away, and she wears thick spectacle lenses. She has been severely visually impaired since birth, but she recently lost more vision, making it impossible for her to see the board. She lives at home with her parents in a suburban town. She is average looking and neat in appearance. She dresses in clothes purchased by her mother that are somewhat out of style in comparison to what her peers are wearing. She does not wear makeup.

Nancy has no siblings, and because of her visual difficulties, her parents are overprotective and prefer that she spend time with her peers in her own home. Nancy has one best friend, and she sometimes invites friends over for small parties and sleepovers. Nancy wants to be physically fit like her teenage friends. There is a YWCA 2 miles from her home, and Nancy wants to go by bus with her friends to participate in the swimming program there on Saturdays. But her parents are afraid that she will miss her stop if she is alone for part of the trip.

Nancy is a junior in the local high school. An itinerant teacher trained to work with learners with visual impairments comes to the school three times a week for 1 hour. Nancy, a bright academic student, plans to go to college. She performs successfully in almost all of her academic subjects but has difficulty in her required mathematics course because she is unable to see the graphs and equations in the text and can no longer read her own writing. The State Commission for the Blind has just provided Nancy with a closed circuit television system that will be placed in the library along with the computer with voice output. In addition, she just had a low-vision evaluation, and the low vision specialist gave her a telescopic lens for looking at the blackboard as well as other distance objects. Nancy has not tried this optical aid yet in school. To reduce some of the visual demands placed on Nancy, her itinerant teacher orders many of her textbooks and leisure reading material on tape from various sources. So far, Nancy has not had any experience using peers as readers.

---

latory behaviors or mannerisms are socially inappropriate, and although they may begin as patterns occuring during stress or intense involvement, they become habits. With behavior modification and contracts mutually made by the student and the teacher, these behaviors are frequently reduced and omitted altogether.

BASIC PROFESSIONAL VOCABULARY

Eligibility for Social Security and disability benefits, rehabilitation services, and tax exemptions are based on legal definitions of blindness. The definitions are also used as criteria for providing educational services and specialized aids and materials for children and youth with visual impairments. The legal definitions provide no

In preparation for the home economics course she will take during the second semester of this year, Nancy and the itinerant teacher went to the home economics room and met with the teacher to determine what modifications would be necessary in order for Nancy to use the dials on the oven, find tools in the unstructured drawers, and work on highly reflective surfaces that produce glare. Nancy also expressed interest in learning how to do simple sewing repairs that will help her to be independent when she goes away to college.

☐ ☐ ☐

What strategies can the itinerant teacher use to help improve Nancy's appearance so that she looks more socially appropriate for her age?

What skills can the orientation and mobility instructor teach to Nancy that will enable her to use her vision more efficiently and help her to travel more independently?

Suggest ways that the itinerant teacher can help Nancy to accept and use her new telescopic aid.

What technological devices can Nancy use to increase her visual efficiency in reading and writing mathematics problems?

In order to reduce Nancy's dependency on the itinerant teacher, what resources can she contact to obtain her own educational and recreational materials?

What role can the school personnel play, in cooperation with the itinerant teacher, in helping Nancy to obtain the assistance of peers as readers?

Based on the difficulties that have been identified in the home economics room, suggest environmental modifications that will enable Nancy to participate fully in the home economics class.

---

indication of how a person uses his or her vision. Two students could have the same visual acuity and function differently in home and school environments. For example, one may be able to read the regular print in a book, whereas the other may require enlargement. Important legal definitions include:

Legal Blindness
   A. Central visual acuity for distance vision of 20/200 or less in the better eye with correction. This means that if a person wearing glasses or contact lenses has 20/200 vision, he or she can see an object at 20 feet that a person with normal vision can see from a distance of 200 feet away.

B. A person can also be considered legally blind if the visual acuity is greater than 20/200 and the visual field is restricted to 20 degrees or less. A person with a normal visual field can look straight ahead at a target and see objects within a range of 180 degrees without shifting his or her head or eyes. If a child has normal visual acuity and has a field of vision of 20 degrees, he or she can see fine detail, but only what a sighted person can see peering through a narrow tunnel. This child has poor peripheral vision.

Partially seeing

This refers to those who have a visual acuity greater than 20/200 but not greater than 20/70 in the better eye with correction. This term is outdated and is not currently used by practitioners in the field.

Educators, realizing the limitations of the preceding legal definitions, have developed more meaningful functional definitions, which are now incorporated into federal and state laws (Scholl, 1986). These terms aid in placement, curriculum planning, and instruction. The most commonly used terms follow.

Blind refers to those who have only light perception without projection or to those who are totally without the sense of vision (Faye, 1970). Educationally, the blind child learns through tactile and auditory materials (Caton, 1981).

Low vision refers to those who have a significant visual handicap but also have significant usable vision. Educationally, the term refers to those who are still severely visually impaired after correction but who may increase visual functioning through the use of optical aids, nonoptical aids, environmental modifications, and/or techniques (Corn, 1980). It is critical *not* to refer to this low vision population as "blind" (Barraga, 1983).

Ophthalmologist is a physician (M.D.) who specializes in diagnosis and treatment of defects and diseases of the eye. He or she can perform surgery and prescribe drugs and glasses.

Optician is a technician who grinds lenses, fits them into frames, and adjusts frames to the wearer.

Optometrist is a licensed doctor of optometry (O.D.) who specializes in measurement of refractive errors of the eye and prescribes glasses or contact lenses to correct these refractive errors. Those specializing in low vision prescribe optical aids such as telescopic lenses.

Visual efficiency is "the degree to which the student can perform specific visual tasks with ease, comfort, and minimum time. Visual efficiency is unique to each child and cannot be measured or predicted clinically with any accuracy by medical, psychological, or educational personnel" (Barraga, 1983, p. 25).

Visual functioning is how people use whatever vision they have. Some children and youth have limited visual capacity and are extremely visually oriented. Others with similar visual potential are not responsive to visual stimuli and act as if they are blind and unable to see anything (Barraga, 1983).

Visual impairment refers to a measured loss of any of the visual functions such as acuity, visual field, color vision, or binocular vision (Barraga, 1983). In practice, the term *visually impaired* has begun to be synonymous with "visually handicapped."

Visually handicapped describes a child with a visual impairment that even after correction adversely affects the child's educational performance (PL 94-142). This term is widely used to denote the total group of children who have impairments in the structure or functioning of the eye and require special educational provisions. Recently practitioners have begun to substitute the term *visually impaired* for visually handicapped.

ASSESSING INSTRUCTIONAL NEED

When children and youth with visual impairments are being assessed, it is essential for the specially trained teacher of this population to be involved in the selection of the formal and informal tests to be administered. Placement and educational decisions should be made by this special teacher and other members of the transdisciplinary team, which consists of the classroom teacher, orientation and mobility (O&M) instructor, the school psychologist, the parents, and the speech and language therapist, occupational therapist, and physical therapist when necessary.

Educational assessment used for the purposes of placement and instructional decisions should be comprehensive, broad-based, and ongoing. No single assessment tool should be used alone. Of primary importance is the determination of the prognosis of the visual impairments, the presence of additional disabilities, and the cultural values, attitudes, and preferences of the family. Components of a comprehensive assessment for learners with visual impairments include functional vision; intelligence and cognitive development; psychomotor skills; academic achievement in all areas but especially in concept development, braille or print reading, and listening skills; social interaction and recreation and leisure skills; functional living skills, including daily living skills, orientation and mobility, and community and vocational skills (Scholl, 1986).

The use of test norms for sighted students is not always appropriate for those with visual impairments. Many instruments contain subtests or items that are dependent on vision; these should be deleted or modified by additional explanations. If a student is given additional time to complete a test, answers the questions verbally, or has the items read by the examiner, the results cannot be interpreted in the intended manner. Such modifications in the testing procedures reduce the validity of the test. Therefore, test scores by themselves should not be used as a basis for making educational decisions regarding learners with visual impairments. Nevertheless, a normed test might be warranted if the results show the student's specific strengths and weaknesses and overall performance in comparison with other sighted students in the class. The vision teacher's role is to explain and interpret incorrect or inadequate responses by the learner that are specifically related to the lack of vision.

It has been difficult to develop normed tests that have been standardized on the population of children and youth with visual impairments. Because of the low prevalence of the disability and the variation in types of visual loss, visual functioning, age of onset of disability, educational placements, and geographical distribution, few reliable and valid instruments exist.

Criterion-referenced tests are appropriate informal means of assessing learners with visual impairments. Because these instruments are not standardized, administration procedures can be modified to meet the needs of a student with little or no usable vision. The teacher can employ a wide variety of testing materials as well as varied time limits. These types of assessment tools are helpful in determining achievement levels and the effectiveness of specific instructional strategies.

Other methods of informal assessment include the use of teacher-made checklists, interviews, and direct observation. The latter, more than any other type of assessment, provides information on how successfully the learner with the visual impairment is performing academically and interacting socially with peers in the regular classroom.

Following are a few suggested assessment instruments developed specifically for use with children and youth with visual impairments. Although normative data are lacking in most of them, they can be helpful in program planning. More comprehensive lists can be found in Scholl (1986), Silberman (1986), and Swallow (1981).

Functional Vision

The Program to Develop Efficiency in Visual Functioning (Barraga & Morris, 1980) consists of criterion-referenced assessment tasks on functional visual skills from the beginning stage of visual development to the visual reading stage. It also contains an instructional program of 150 lesson plans to use following assessment. Appropriate scales for assessing functional vision in learners with multiple impairments have been developed by Smith and Cote (1982) and Langley (1980).

Early Childhood/Multiply Handicapped

The Reynell Zinkin Scales (Reynell, 1981) and the Oregon Project for Visually Impaired and Blind Infants and Preschoolers (Brown, Simmons, & Methvin, 1979) are developmental scales designed for use with preschool children with visual impairments. The Callier-Azusa Scales are intended to be used with children with dual sensory impairments (Stillman, 1979). A section that focuses specifically on communication skills was developed recently (Stillman, 1984).

Concept Development and Readiness Skills

The Boehm Test of Basic Concepts has a tactile version in which simple geometric forms are used to assess specific concepts, including those focusing on directionality, which are important prerequisite skills for mobility (Caton, 1976). The Peabody Mobility Scales (Harley, Wood, & Merbler, 1981), a criterion-referenced instrument, assesses concept development, including body image, spatial relations, and left-right discrimination. It also assesses sound localization and tactual and olfactory discrimination. The Mangold Developmental Program of Tactile Perception and Braille Letter Recognition (Mangold, 1977) is helpful in both assessing and teaching braille readiness skills.

Academic Content Areas

Adapted versions of several commercial achievement tests widely used in public schools to assess sighted children are available in braille and large print. These include the Stanford Reading Achievement Tests on a variety of levels, the Stanford Diagnostic Reading Test, and the Iowa Test of Basic Skills. The adapted version of the Key Math Diagnostic Arithmetic Test is available in braille. These and other adapted versions are published by the American Printing House for the Blind, and teachers of learners with visual impairments should contact APH to determine if a particular test used in their school is available in braille or large print. Excellent teacher-made checklists have been developed to focus on unique academic needs, such as listening abilities, using the braillewriter, slate and stylus, and script writing (Swallow, Mangold, & Mangold, 1978). These informal instruments are helpful in assessing critical skills and in developing appropriate intervention strategies.

Adaptive Behaviors

While no instrument designed specifically for individuals with visual impairments can be recommended, both the Vineland Adaptive Behavior Scales and AAMD Adaptive Behavior Scales provide important information on the student's ability to function within domestic, community, vocational and recreational domains. Skills that measure readiness for transition into the adult world can be assessed.

It is not within the realm of this chapter to further discuss assessment instruments developed for other populations; however, it is important to note that with a few modifications some of these instruments are being used successfully with children and youth with visual impairments. It is the responsibility of the entire team to select a battery of assessment tools that is appropriate for each learner and which provides valuable input for making appropriate placement and program planning decisions.

INTERVENTIONS

Instructional Interventions

Children and youth with visual impairments have unique needs that require special methods in instruction. Lowenfeld (1981b) identified several important principles for teaching strategies, including:

1. *Concreteness*—Whenever possible, provide real objects for blind and low vision students to manipulate in order to obtain information regarding shape,

size, weight, hardness, surface qualities, pliability, and temperature. Sometimes models can be used, but students must be made aware that the information provided is incomplete or distorted in some way.

2. *Unified experiences*—The unit plan of instruction enables blind and low vision students to assimilate and organize separate impressions into a meaningful and unified experience. By going to actual field sites, students can learn all the component parts and develop concepts that sighted children and youth learn by casual glances. For example, by going to a supermarket students can learn about the organization of stock on shelves, display of goods, labeling, and pricing of items. In addition, academic subjects such as reading, spelling, and arithmetic can be taught in relation to this unit on the supermarket.

3. *Learning by doing*—Blind and low vision children need many opportunities to learn how to do things for themselves. Although training may take longer because of the inability to imitate, emphasis should be on providing as little assistance as possible so that they can develop confidence and independence.

Children and youth with visual impairments also require specific instruction in curriculum areas beyond what is needed by their sighted classmates. Following are some of the subjects that should be taught by specially trained teachers.

Braille

Braille is a tactual system for reading and writing that is used by those who are blind or who have too little vision to be able to use print as a communication tool. It was developed in 1829 by Louis Braille, a Frenchman who was himself blind. Braille consists of embossed characters using various combinations of raised dots in a braille cell, which is two dots wide and three dots high (see Figure 12.2). In Grade 1 braille, each character stands for a letter, and words are spelled just as they are in print. In Grade 2 braille, words and parts of words are contracted in order to save space and increase the reading rate. For example, in Grade 2 braille, when the letter "e" stands alone it means the word "every." One character is used instead of five. Grade 2 braille is used from the start in kindergarten or first grade to teach children to read and write. Grade 2 braille is complex to learn, and one of its major disadvantages is that there is often no relationship between the braille symbols and the actual spelling of the word. For example, when a braille reader (tactually) sees the letter "x" standing alone, it refers to the word "it"; when the letters standing alone are "xf," the word is "itself." Thus, the blind child in a regular class learning to read has a more difficult time than his or her sighted peers. The child is expected to read material based on a particular curricular approach rather than on the varying levels of difficulty of the particular words in braille. In addition, braille readers have more difficulty learning to spell accurately because they encounter most words in a contracted form. It is extremely important for teachers to require these students to spell words in their entirety as well as in their Grade 2 contracted form.

As already indicated, young students write in braille at the same time as they learn to read it. They first use the *braillewriter.* They are introduced to the *slate and stylus* when they are proficient in reading braille and using the braillewriter and have sufficient manual dexterity. This usually occurs in fourth or fifth grade.

The specially trained teacher of learners with visual impairments is responsible for providing braille reading and writing instruction. Because braille is such a critically important tool, adequate time should be allocated for the student to develop competence. The itinerant or resource room teacher also transcribes material into braille for a braille student and translates his or her written work back into print so that the student can keep up with sighted peers and be evaluated appropriately by the regular classroom teacher. As the student gets older, he or she relies more and more on technological devices (described elsewhere) for obtaining print and/or braille output.

An excellent program for teaching braille readiness skills is the Mangold Developmental Program of Tactile Perception and Braille Letter Recognition (Mangold, 1977). The skills emphasized include tracking skills, coordinated and independent use of the hands for reading, left-right and top-bottom orientation, and introduction of the braille alphabet characters. Another valuable resource is the reading series *Patterns* (Caton, Pester, & Bradley, 1983), which is designed specifically for blind primary grade readers. The stories have an experiential base that is not dependent on visual clues, and the vocabulary is related to the complexity of the braille characters. Simple contractions are taught first and repeated in a variety of words.

Students need to learn other braille codes in order to gain access to print materials. These include the Nemeth Code for reading and writing mathematics and scientific notations, a music code, and various foreign language codes.

Figure 12.2 **Braille Alphabet**

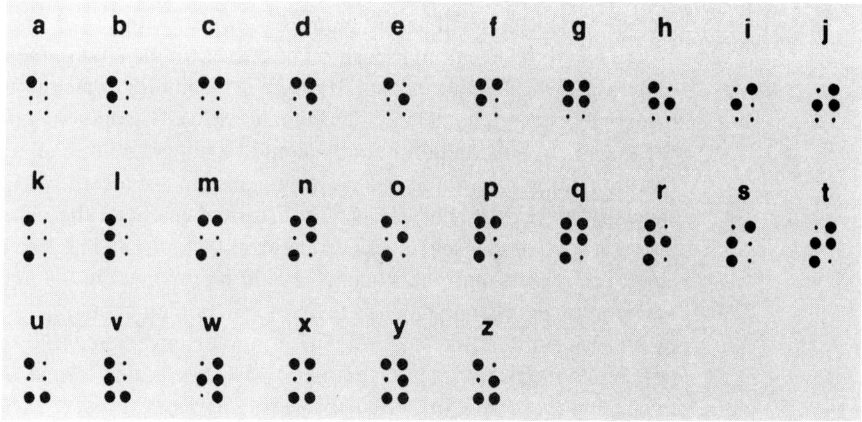

Listening Skills

Because children and youth with visual impairments are dependent on their auditory channel for most of their learning, they need to develop efficient listening skills in a systematized way. Contrary to popular opinion, they are not necessarily better listeners just because they do not see. Regardless of the degree of visual loss, as most students get older, they obtain more and more information through recorded books, magazines, face-to-face readers, and technological devices with synthesized speech output.

The specially trained teacher must incorporate listening skills into every aspect of the student's education. Young children with visual impairments need to learn skills such as awareness, identification, and localization of sounds; discrimination, vocalization, and interpretation of sound patterns; and ability to follow simple directions. Skills needed by older learners with visual impairments include listening for specific purposes, such as critical analysis and selection of the main idea; auditory memory, including recall of important facts; use of formatting cues; and selective listening in which distracting sounds are screened out (Harley, Truan, & Sanford, 1987; Heinze, 1986). Several listening programs with training components have been developed specifically for learners with visual impairments (Alber, 1974; Leach, 1973; Stocker, 1973; Swallow & Conner, 1982).

The resources most commonly used for borrowing recorded materials are Recordings for the Blind (educational texts) and regional branch libraries of the National Library Service for the Blind and Physically Handicapped of the Library of Congress (recreational reading material). APH also produces recorded texts and operates a computerized catalog system of volunteer and commercially produced recorded as well as braille and large type materials. Many of these materials are disseminated through state and regional Instructional Materials Resource Centers for the Blind.

Orientation and Mobility

Orientation and mobility (O & M) are important related services that should be included in the educational program for learners with visual impairments. *Orientation* refers to the location or position of oneself in the environment and in relation to objects within the environment. *Mobility* is the ability to move safely and efficiently from one place to another (Hill & Ponder, 1976). Orientation and mobility are interdependent, and instruction in both should be integrated into all areas of the curriculum from infancy to adulthood. A team consisting of a certified O&M specialist, the specially trained teacher of visually impaired learners, the classroom teacher, the physical education teacher, the occupational therapist and physical therapist (if available), the parents, and the students should be involved in the assessment and intervention process. Each student's level of functioning should be assessed in the areas of sensory skills, concept development, motor development, environmental awareness of landmarks and clues, community awareness, and formal O&M skills in order to develop short- and long-term goals (Hill, Rosen, Correa, & Langley, 1984).

One example of a realistic orientation goal in the area of sensory skills for students with visual impairments is to use visual cues such as the light from the window to find the braillewriter on the shelf. A goal in concept development might be to locate the water fountain two doors to the right of the cafeteria or the clothing hook that is second from the end. Goals related to motor development might be to reduce the shuffling patterns and wide gait that are common in children with visual impairments. A goal related to environmental awareness might be to use auditory clues such as the sound of the typewriters to locate the principal's office in the school or the textured wall as a landmark for locating the gym.

In Activity 2, page 357, you will become aware of the importance of systematic use of landmarks and clues by children and youth with visual impairments as they travel. You will have an opportunity to design and use a planned route in a familiar environment.

Frequently O&M specialists are not available to instruct children and youth with visual impairments. Consequently, the responsibility of teaching precane skills falls on the specially trained teacher who has taken at least one O&M course. Descriptions, techniques, and illustrations for instruction are found in books by Hill and Ponder (1976) and Allen, Griffith, and Shaw (1977).

Sighted guide techniques: Formal mobility instruction usually begins with teaching sighted guide techniques. The student with visual impairments grasps a sighted person's arm just above the elbow and walks about one-half step behind the guide. By using kinesthetic awareness, the student can follow the movements of the guide's body and move safely from place to place, around obstacles, through narrow passageways, and up and down stairs.

Protective techniques: These are used mainly in familiar indoor environments to detect objects such as support beams or door frames that are encountered at either the waist or upper parts of the body. When protecting the upper body, the student extends an arm in front of the body at shoulder level and parallel to the floor, with the palm outward. When protecting the lower body, the student extends an arm down and forward toward the midline of the body, with the palm inward.

Trailing: This technique enables the student to establish and maintain a straight line of travel and to locate specific objects along the trailing surface, such as a counter or a wall. The student stands a comfortable distance from the trailing surface, extends an arm forward at hip level, and establishes contact with the outside of the little and ring fingers (Kappan, 1981).

Cane skills: O&M specialists should teach formal cane skills. The most popular type of cane used for independent travel is the long cane, made of aluminum with a rubber grip, nylon tip, and a crook. The length of the cane varies according to the user's height, stride, and speed of reaction time (Hill, 1986). The cane enables children and youth to travel independently throughout the building, as well as to and from familiar and unfamiliar places, such as the school and local store. The traveler sweeps the cane lightly in an arc while walking to gather information about the path ahead. When used correctly, the cane enables the traveler to detect obstacles such as curbs, stairs, doors, and holes. The cane also detects changes in the texture of the travel surface, such as carpet to tile or wood and grass to concrete (Heward & Orlansky, 1988). The greatest disadvantage of the long cane is that it offers no protection from suspended objects such as tree branches (Hill, 1986). Because of the cane's overall value, younger children in elementary school are being taught to use a cane with increasing frequency.

Dog guides: Less than 2% of persons with visual impairments use dog guides for independent travel. Prospective users must be older than 16 and have no useful travel vision. In addition, dog guide users must be in excellent health and willing to take care of the dog. Dog guides wear a special harness that serves as a signal that they are at work. They are trained to obey such commands such as walk faster, walk slower, turn right, sit down, and fetch a dropped object. They stop at street corners, know when it is unsafe to cross the street, and go around obstacles. Blind users need good orientation skills as they must direct the dogs. Blind individuals attend an accredited training school for a period of 4 weeks, where they undergo intensive training with the dogs in order to travel together safely and effectively. Dog guides and users are matched on such factors as size, personality, strength, and agility.

Electronic travel aids: There are several electronic travel devices that can be used along with or in place of a long cane. These use sonar waves or laser beams to detect obstacles in the environment. Such aids give tactile or auditory signals to travelers that indicate the direction and distance of obstacles from their bodies. The major advantage of these aids is that they alert travelers to hazards at head level, such as hanging branches, drop-offs, or holes below. Hill (1986) presented detailed descriptions of the four most widely used aids: the Laser Cane, the Sonicguide (a spectacle-mounted device), the Mowat Sensor (a lightweight hand-held device), and the Russell Pathsounder (a chest-mounted device supported by a neck strap). Disadvantages of these devices are the high cost and intensive training needed to use most of them effectively. Research is being conducted to assess their value for learners with multiple impairments, including both visual and auditory disabilities, in helping them to increase their awareness of the environment.

Visual Efficiency

Children and youth with visual impairments can learn to use their vision more efficiently through a variety of instructional approaches provided by specially trained teachers, O&M instructors, and low vision specialists. Without training and actually "learning to see," low vision students may be unable to use their vision to derive meaningful information.

Educators first need to know the etiology of a student's visual loss, the relevant educational implications of the disability, and the prognosis in order to plan effective intervention programs. Second, specialists in the field should administer criterion-referenced checklists and informal instruments to assess the student's current level of visual functioning. The information obtained will indicate how the student uses his or her vision in ordinary activities such as daily living, academics, physical education, social interaction, and orientation and mobility. Even someone who sees only hand movements can benefit from a functional vision assessment, as results will indicate how that person uses vision to determine shapes, colors, contrast, and light cues (Roessing, 1982).

Ophthalmologists and optometrists who specialize in low vision help many children and youth with visual impairments to see better by prescribing optical aids for specific activities. For example, a telescope, either hand-held or inserted into spectacles, may enable a student to see the blackboard, find a friend's house number, or see the pins and score when bowling with his sighted friends. A magnifier, placed directly on the page or inserted into glasses, may enable a student to read regular print books in school, a menu at a restaurant, or price tags on clothing in a store. Students need a great deal of encouragement, practice, and reinforcement when they are learning to use these aids. Some students, especially teenagers, reject optical aids because they feel conspicuous and weird. But when students become convinced of the value of aids in assisting them to see many more objects and events in the environment, they use them willingly whenever the need arises.

Teachers of young children with visual impairments and of students who have additional disabilities are responsible for including visual stimulation activities in the curriculum. Some specific skills are fixating on objects, tracking or following moving objects, shifting gaze from one object to another, and reaching for objects using vision. It is important to teach these skills as part of the child's normal activities throughout the day. For example, a young child can be taught to look at the brightly colored spoon before he or she is fed or to choose between juice or milk at snack time by shifting his or her visual gaze from one to the other in order to make a selection. An excellent resource is *Look at Me* (Smith & Cote, 1982).

Teachers of students with visual impairments in elementary and secondary school are responsible for providing ongoing training in the use of vision. They should assist students in selecting appropriate seats in each classroom for optimum view of the blackboard and for minimization of glare, determining suitable print size in each subject area, and improving tracking skills in reading and interpreting maps. Even though low vision students cannot harm their eyes by using them, they do experience visual fatigue after performing visual tasks for a certain period of time. The teacher should balance the day's schedule by rotating activities requiring vision with those involving auditory and motor channels. Teachers should also help students select appropriate lighting. Some prefer dim light, whereas others need bright light for visual tasks.

Although helping students utilize their vision to the highest degree possible is important, so is recognizing that some low vision students find it more efficient to use visual and tactual modes in combination. For example, a student may use an optical aid to read limited amounts of print material but rely on braille for required reading and notetaking. Teachers need to explore a variety of methods and use "everything that works."

Social and Recreational Skills

Children and youth with visual impairments need to develop specific social skills that their sighted peers learn through visual observation. Specific curriculum areas should include such simple social skills as initiating a greeting through verbal or gestural means, maintaining a sighted peer's interest through facial expressions, and learning appropriate body positions, gestures, and hand signals (Hatlen & Curry, 1987). In addition, because of their inability to utilize nonverbal cues, these students need to learn how to refrain from interrupting other people and to stay on a topic when they are conversing with their sighted peers. Structured practice sessions are essential, and a variety of tape-recorded role-playing situations might be helpful. Furthermore, because these students cannot observe current fashion trends, teachers of this population need to spend time with individual students in or out of school focusing on sensitive areas such as appearance, hygiene, dress, and makeup. Sacks, Kekelis, and Gaylord-Ross (1988) presented excellent suggestions for increasing social interaction skills in young children with visual impairments. The guidance department of the school can also promote social interaction skills by setting up peer tutoring or buddy systems for nonacademic subjects. If a student with visual impairments spends time with a classmate, a friendship may develop.

Students with visual impairments are able to function in a wide variety of community recreational activities. The itinerant teacher or resource room teacher should discover the interests of these students and of their families and encourage them to join small clubs in which it is easy to identify voices and interact socially. Once other teachers in the school are aware of adaptations such as guide ropes, brightly colored markings, beepers, audible balls, and sighted guides, students with visual impairments can participate along with their sighted peers. Physical activities enjoyed by individuals with little or no vision include swimming, track, cross-country skiing, bowling, and fishing. These individuals may also enjoy card games, chess, checkers, and other board games with braille and enlarged print adaptations.

Career Education

Career education for children and youth with visual impairments should begin early and continue throughout their schooling. For these students to learn about the wide variety of available employment opportunities, make informed choices about their suitability, and be aware of the technological devices and adaptations that can make various jobs possible, specially trained teachers and vocational rehabilitation counselors must provide this ongoing training (Hatlen & Curry, 1987).

Even though learners with visual impairments may graduate from high school and even college with a good academic background, many have poor work habits, such as tardiness, disorganization, and inappropriate work-related social skills, and are therefore unprepared for the world of work (Hatlen & Curry, 1987).

The career education program developed by Brolin (1983) is appropriate for students with visual impairments. It consists of four general phases. In the first phase, *awareness,* students with visual impairments study different types of jobs and are directly exposed to them through as many concrete experiences as possible. This enables them to learn about the actual tasks that people perform at work, which cannot be learned sufficiently through reading materials alone. Students with visual impairments have to be directly exposed from the beginning. Great benefit can be derived from introducing them to employed individuals with visual impairments who can describe what they do on their jobs and serve as successful role models. Good habits such as being punctual, following directions, and maintaining an attractive appearance are taught during this phase. In the next phase, *exploration,* which overlaps the first one, students continue to visit work settings that address different skills and interests. Opportunities for job-shadowing (following an employee during work) are arranged.

The third phase, *preparation,* takes place in secondary school. In this phase, specialists help students with visual impairments to focus on appropriate academic and vocational tracks in school. The specially trained teacher provides teachers of vocational subjects with strategies or suggestions for modifying the work environment or the equipment used in the class to enable students with visual impairments to participate. In preparation for the final phase, *participation,* supported work experiences in the community help students develop self-confidence and good work habits and attitudes. When they are ready, students obtain part-time jobs after school, on weekends, or during the summer in which supervision is provided on a continuing basis. Joint meetings with the student, teacher, and employer assess the individual's strengths and weaknesses and ultimately help him or her to take a place in the workforce.

Independent Living Skills

Children and youth with visual impairments need structured, task-analyzed instruction in daily living skills from infancy to adulthood. Unlike sighted children, they are often unable to learn how to eat, dress, and groom themselves, care for their clothing, prepare food, and perform other domestic tasks by observing and imitating their parents, siblings, and peers. They also need to learn other adaptive techniques such as money management, shopping, use of the telephone, and minor household maintenance. As these skills are critical to independent living, they cannot be overlooked and should be taught using a team approach, with the parents as active participants whenever possible. Swallow and Huebner (1987) and the American Foundation for the Blind (AFB) (1974) have published curriculum guides with many practical suggestions.

Placement Options

As indicated earlier in this chapter, most children and youth with visual impairments attend regular public school. Students with additional impairments, however, may require more supportive environments. There are several other options for their placement.

Special Class

In this setting, students spend most of the day in a special class in a public school with a trained teacher of learners with visual impairments. Regardless of functioning level, these students should be provided with opportunities to interact with their nondisabled peers on a daily basis in integrated activities such as physical education, music, art, assembly programs, and lunch.

Special Day Schools

Some students attend special day schools, such as those that serve only students whose major disability is visual. The staff members are specifically trained to work with this population. Other students attend schools that serve children and youth with a variety of multiple impairments. For example, a student with both visual and severe motoric impairments may attend a school sponsored by United Cerebral Palsy in which intensive physical and occupational therapies are provided. In this type of program model, an itinerant teacher visits the student several times each week to focus on unique needs related to his or her visual impairments. These students should have integrated experiences with nondisabled peers.

Residential Schools

Students at residential schools live on campus and have immediate access to specially trained personnel, educational materials, and technological aids to meet their unique needs (Tuttle, 1986). Although most students at these schools have additional disabilities such as hearing loss, physical impairment, or mental retardation, some academically oriented students also go there because appropriate services are not available in the areas in which they live. Some families also prefer this placement option because in these programs their children can partake in extracurricular activities and receive more individualized instruction. Many students leave the campus for part of the day to attend integrated classes at the local elementary or secondary school. The residential school also provides short-term intensive instruction on weekends or during summers for mainstreamed students who need to develop specialized skills. These may include orientation and mobility, utilization of technological devices, independent living skills, and vocational training. Placement options should be flexible, and students should be transferred from one setting to another as different needs arise.

Related Services

Children and youth with visual impairments require related services in orientation and mobility and adaptive physical education to help with motor and physical fitness skills. Students with additional impairments may need physical, occupational, or speech therapy. As part of the assessment process, the transdisciplinary team determines which related services are necessary and ensures that they are provided.

Preschool Programs

The importance of early intervention programming for infants and preschoolers with visual impairments cannot be overemphasized. Programs for infants and young children under 3 years of age are either home based or center based. In the home-based model, the specially trained teacher visits the home several times a month and works with the family and the child to ensure healthy development in motor, language, concept, and social areas. For example, the teacher shows the parents how they can use everyday objects in the home to help the child explore the environment.

In one type of center-based model, infants, young children, and preschoolers may attend an integrated program in a regular nursery school with sighted peers. An itinerant teacher visits several times a week, providing support to the regular teacher and other staff and working directly with the child. An alternative placement is a self-contained class in an agency or public school. Staff members usually include the specially trained teacher, an O&M instructor (when available), a physical or occupational therapist, and a speech therapist to facilitate oral-motor development. Parental involvement is encouraged and even required in many of these programs. In some, social workers are available to conduct support groups for the parents. *Reach Out and Teach* (Ferrell, 1985) is an excellent resource on preschool children with visual impairments. The program consists of training manuals and slide and audio cassette presentations that can be used by professionals or parents.

Transitional Services

Transition for youths with visual impairments is a comprehensive process encompassing ongoing development of skills from infancy through adulthood and a wide array of services that facilitate movement from school to the adult world. Components of the process include planning and arranging for services for community living and employment options as well as ensuring the availability of opportunities for recreation and leisure with sighted individuals. The process should also include making provisions for health care and other social and support services, such as transportation (Covert & Fredericks, 1987).

Parents and families play a critical role in the transition process. In order to make informed decisions, they must be provided with accurate information on their child's abilities, limitations, and realistic goals as well as on the range of options and services available. In planning for the future, their preferences must be considered as well as those of the student.

A formal individualized transition plan (ITP) should be developed at least four years prior to a student's graduation from the school system. Even though the ITP may be part of the IEP, the goals of the former must focus specifically on the functional skills needed for working and living independently in adulthood. The key to success of the ITP is close collaboration between the school personnel who are responsible for training and job procurement and the adult agency providers who will offer support and follow-up during the student's adult life. The goals, which should be reviewed and modified annually, become a part of the individual's individual written rehabilitation plan if or when the person is served by vocational rehabilitation or an adult community service agency.

Providing coordinated, comprehensive transition services for students with visual impairments requires a sharing of responsibility and resources among agencies at all levels and among families, local service providers, and consumers (Wehman, Moon, Everson, Wood, & Barcus, 1988). Some states have designated a "lead agency" to coordinate services so that individuals do not fall through the cracks. There is a need for greater collaboration between state departments of education and rehabilitation services for the blind. Simpson, Huebner, and Roberts (1985) and Wehman et al. (1988) have presented models for developing collaborative plans at the local level.

Historically, many young adults who were blind and not college bound were placed in segregated work settings such as sheltered workshops. Recently, intensive efforts have been made to employ these individuals in a variety of work experiences in the community. In addition, residential schools are preparing students for independent living by setting up semi-independent family-type residences on and off campus. Sacks, Hatlen, and Pruett (1988) have provided professionals in the field of vision with inservice training in specific transition skills for assisting adolescents and young adults.

Preparing students with visual impairments to be independent in their living skills and employable in the marketplace is a major goal of the educational system. Instruction in independent living skills, social interaction, and career education is particularly important in preparing students with visual impairments for adult life. Regardless of whether they go to college or directly into some type of work experience, a commitment to the inclusion of these content areas in their educational programs will enable all students with visual impairments, regardless of their functioning level, to acquire the skills they need to function independently in the world.

Parental Involvement

As mandated by PL 94-142, parental involvement is an integral part of every step of a child's education. Parents are key decision makers regarding referral, identification, placement, programming, and evaluation. Teachers of children and youth with visual impairments need parents as their partners in working together toward common goals. Parents, given meaningful explanations, can help professionals follow through on instructional programs for their child at home, resulting in increasing the likelihood for generalization of skills. For example, students will learn to hold their heads up and face people who are speaking to them if both the teachers and parents encourage them to do so.

The National Association for Parents of Visually Impaired Children, an active organization that holds conferences and publishes a newsletter, provides a wonderful vehicle for parents to share common concerns. The majority of its members are parents; however, membership is open to anyone concerned with children and youth with visual impairments.

SELECTING AND ADAPTING INSTRUCTIONAL MATERIALS

Selecting and adapting appropriate instructional materials for children and youth with visual impairments are essential for effective educational programming. A large variety of educational materials are available, including visual, tactual, and auditory aids. But they are not panaceas and cannot substitute for vision. For example, giving a low vision student a large print book does not assure that the student will read any more efficiently than with a regular sized print book, with or without optical aids. Specific materials must be selected by the trained teacher of learners with visual impairments, the parents, and the student, based on such factors as level of functioning, needs, age, and short- and long-term goals (Cartwright, Cartwright, and Ward, 1989).

Visual Aids

Many low vision children and youth benefit from simple nonoptical aids that help them to use their vision more efficiently. These aids require no training to use and are particularly helpful in seeing print images with greater ease and reducing visual fatigue. Some of the more common visual nonoptical aids include the following:

Bookstands—Bookstands make it possible to raise, angle, and/or bring the print closer to the student's eyes. They reduce postural fatigue caused by bending over to get close to the printed material on the desk.
Felt tip pens—These pens come in varying widths and produce a dark, bold letter or diagram. Black ink is usually preferred.
Acetate—Yellow acetate placed over the printed page darkens the print and heightens the contrast of the background paper.
Large print textbooks—Large print refers to letters that are 14–30 point high. Books and other written materials can be put into large print by photo

enlarging standard type, resetting standard type in large sizes, or using a computer software program that enables the printer to produce large type. Large print is helpful for students who cannot read regular print at close distances even with an optical aid. Some students need large print materials only for subjects such as mathematics and science in which numerical equations are difficult to read. The spacing, boldness of letters, and paper color and quality are also related to the ease with which a student can read. Sometimes reading is less efficient because the reader can see only small parts of words or phrases at a time. Other disadvantages of large type books are their lack of color, their size, and their reduced availability once the student leaves school (Todd, 1986).

Lamps with rheostats—Light sources with variable intensities and positions enable the student to increase or decrease the illumination and adjust the angle of light in each room, depending on the lighting conditions. It is important for each student to determine the levels of lighting that enable him or her to see most comfortably and efficiently.

The Perkins Brailler for typing braille on paper.

The slate and stylus is used for taking notes.

Tactual Aids

Children and youth who are blind rely on tactual aids for much of their learning. Some learners with low vision can use tactual aids in combination with visual and auditory aids. Some of the more commonly used tactual aids include the following:

> *Braille books*—Braille books and readiness materials are produced by volunteers, paid transcribers, computers, commercial publishers, and APH. It is extremely important for blind learners to learn braille, have direct access to a braille text, and be able to read along with their sighted peers in the regular class.
>
> *Braillewriter*—A braillewriter is a machine for typing braille on paper. The machine has six keys, which correspond to one of the six dots in the braille cell, a space bar, a back spacer, and a line spacer. This device serves as the major writing tool for the blind student in elementary school. It is slowly being replaced by more advanced technological equipment, such as the combination of a computer, voice output, and braille printer for the secondary level student.
>
> *Slate and stylus*—This tool is used mainly by blind students for taking notes. The slate is a metal frame with openings through which braille dots are punched with a pointed stylus. The student embosses the dots from right to left and then turns the slate or the paper over to read the raised dots.
>
> *The Sewell Kit*—This kit consists of a rubber covered board on which acetate or paper is placed. The teacher and the blind student can produce raised

lines on the acetate or paper with a pen or pointed object. The Sewell Kit is used to draw tactual representations of letters, geometric shapes, simple charts, and line diagrams.

Tactile graphics kit—The tools in this kit produce various types of textured lines and shapes that can be used for drawing graphs and maps for social studies and O&M.

Tactual maps and globes—These materials have raised surfaces and different textures for teaching skills related to geography and map reading. A variety of tactual maps and globes are available from several sources; teachers can also adapt regular ones with the use of puff paint, yarn, or a sewing tracing wheel.

Abacus—This is a device modeled after the Japanese soroban for doing numerical calculations. It has felt backing so that the beads do not slip.

Braille measuring devices—Embossed markings on such devices as a ruler, compass, protractor, slide rule, and tape enable a blind student to participate in mathematics activities with sighted peers.

Templates and writing guides—These guides are made of cardboard, plastic, or metal, and their open rectangular forms enable blind students to write within specific boundaries. They are primarily used for writing signatures and checks.

Activity 3, page 358, will help you to become aware of the importance of concrete, hands-on learning experiences for students with visual impairments. You will have an opportunity to adapt a print representation from a textbook.

Auditory Aids

Auditory aids are used in combination with tactile and/or visual aids by children and youth with little or no vision. Some of the more commonly used aids (other than technological devices discussed in another section) are the following:

Cassette tape recorders—Students with visual impairments use the recorder to take notes, record homework, record test answers, and listen to assignments and recorded texts. Some recorders have the capacity for increasing or reducing the rate of listening without changing the pitch, which is known as *compressed speech*.

Recorded books—Books recorded on tapes and/or records are sometimes referred to as talking books (Todd, 1986). Many are produced under the talking book program of the Library of Congress, which receives public funding to produce and record books. These materials are distributed free of charge by regional libraries to children, youth, and adults with visual impairments and to others who are unable to read regular print.

Resources

The visual, tactual, and auditory aids listed above can be obtained from a variety of sources. Teachers should contact relevant agencies and obtain comprehensive catalogues and price lists in order to select appropriate adapted materials. Some important resources are the following:

> *American Foundation for the Blind,* a national nonprofit organization located in New York City, promotes the development of educational and rehabilitative services from infancy through adulthood for individuals with visual impairments. AFB publishes books, monographs, and a journal and operates a reference library on blindness and a technology center. Some of its other services include conducting research and manufacturing and selling special aids and appliances.
>
> *American Printing House for the Blind,* a national nonprofit agency located in Louisville, Kentucky, is the largest publishing house in the world for learners who are blind. APH produces materials in various media and manufactures educational aids for students with visual impairments. APH maintains a computerized, centralized catalog of volunteer and commercially produced braille, recorded, and large type textbooks that enables teachers to obtain materials for their students as quickly as possible.
>
> *Federal Quota Program,* to which all legally blind students enrolled in educational facilities below college level are entitled, is administered by APH. Each year Congress allocates an appropriation to APH that schools and agencies can then use to purchase adapted educational texts, equipment, and instructional aids produced by APH for all registered students. The amount of the per capita allotment varies from year to year, but it is usually about $100.
>
> *Recordings for the Blind,* a nonprofit agency located in Princeton, New Jersey, produces recorded texts for students in educational programs.
>
> *Howe Press,* a nonprofit agency located at the Perkins School for the Blind in Watertown, Massachusetts, manufactures such devices as the Perkins Braillewriter, tactile graphics kit, and tactual and low vision aids.

TECHNOLOGY APPLICATIONS

In recent years, new devices made possible by technological advances have had a great impact on the educational and vocational opportunities afforded to children and youth with visual impairments. Some of these new devices can be used by themselves to access information, whereas others coexist with computers. Following are examples and descriptions of some of the equipment that has made the lives of this population so much richer and has enabled students with visual impairments to gain knowledge more efficiently and work together with their sighted peers.

Synthetic Speech

Synthetic speech is the computerized production of phonemes into words based on a variety of programming formats (Todd, 1986). Available as either hardware or software, synthetic speech devices give students with visual impairments direct access to information through voice output. Voice synthesizers vary in such factors as intelligibility of speech, control of speaking rate, pitch, and cost. Most of them are easy to understand and require little training to use. Synthetic speech is used in such commonplace items as calculators, clocks, thermometers, and scales. Its most valuable use is in providing voice output for information entered into a computer. Students can also rely on voice output devices for direct feedback when they type papers on the computer. By hearing what they have written, they can use the synthesizer as a word processing tool and make modifications without depending on the assistance of a sighted person. One major limitation of synthetic speech is that it cannot translate graphics into speech.

Reading Devices

The Xerox/Kurzweil Personal Reader is a computer-based device that converts printed material into synthetic speech. Any book, journal, clearly typed letter, or memo is placed on the machine face down; a scanner then moves across the page one line at a time and converts the written words into spoken words. The reader can change the speed and tone of the voice and have words spelled out letter by letter. Thus, a student with little or no usable vision can do research for a school project by directly accessing printed texts. The Kurzweil Personal Reader also has a portable model with a hand-held scanner that the reader can use in a variety of locations.

Optacon is a small electronic device that converts print into vibrating tactual images. The optacon consists of a miniature camera, electronics section, and a tactile array of 100 vibrating pins. As the reader moves the miniature camera across a line of print with one hand, he or she simultaneously feels the vibrating image of the print letter on the index finger of the other hand, which is resting on the tactile array. For example, as the camera moves across an upper case L, the reader feels one vertical line and one horizontal line moving beneath his or her finger. Even after much training and practice, the reading rate of an optacon user is still slow; nevertheless, this skill gives blind students immediate access to print and enables them to participate in a wide range of activities that would not have been possible without relying on a sighted reader or on braille transcription. For example, users are able to read their own typewritten mail privately; identify labels on packages and cans; read recipes, song titles, and lyrics on tapes or records; and read computer printouts independently.

Braille Printer

A braille printer reproduces information stored in a computer's memory in braille. This equipment enables the sighted teacher to input tests and other material into the computer and print them on a regular printer and on a braille printer. The latter procedure requires a Grade 2 translation program, which sends a message from the computer to the braille printer to emboss in Grade 2 braille. Thus, both sighted and blind students can have the material for use in and out of the classroom at the same time. This invention has also greatly reduced the production time for braille textbooks needed each year by blind students in integrated school programs.

Paperless Braille

The term *paperless braille* refers to equipment that stores information on a cassette tape, on a disk, or in a microcomputer and presents it tactually on a playback unit with a braille display strip ranging from 20 to 40 braille cells at one time. Blind students can use this device for various purposes. For example, they can use it to take braille notes in class and retrieve them at a later time; to create a paper in braille and edit it, or to link the unit with a microcomputer and access information by means of a braille display instead of a monitor or voice output. Finally, using a paperless braille unit in combination with a microcomputer, printer, braille printer, and speech synthesizer, students can choose from the following options to input and retrieve information: braille input and output, braille input with print output, print input with braille output, or speech output of the printed text. Because of their outstanding value, these paperless braille units are being purchased and distributed to more and more secondary-age students through state education departments, commissions for the blind, and rehabilitation agencies.

Closed Circuit Television System

This valuable system gives many students with severe visual impairments access to regular sized print materials. By moving a page of print placed on a sliding table under a camera with an adjustable zoom lens, the user can see the material enlarged on a television monitor. Individual adjustment can be made in the size, contrast, and brightness of the images. In addition, the student can choose to read black letters on a white background or white letters on a black background. Besides being able to read text materials, students can see and correct their own written work. The system can also be hooked up to a computer to provide for enlarged screen output. In addition to cost, the greatest disadvantage of this system as a primary mode of reading is that it is not portable. Usually the system is housed in a special place, such as the resource room or library (Heward & Orlansky, 1988).

Braille Notetaking Devices

There are several notetaking devices that allow individuals to take notes in braille and review them using a speech synthesizer. These devices are small, lightweight, and comparatively inexpensive and can be interfaced with computers, printers, and braille printers.

MULTICULTURAL CONSIDERATIONS

In recent years, attention has been focused on the need for teachers to be aware of and sensitive to the diverse multicultural needs of children and youth in the school setting (Scholl, 1986). Unfortunately, very little data exist on statistics related to the cultural variations in students with visual impairments. But members of ethnic minority groups are probably more likely to have visual impairments because, for example, inadequate prenatal care and the high incidence of premature births in disadvantaged women from ethnic minority backgrounds may contribute to a greater percentage of visual impairments in their offspring (Kirchner & Peterson, 1981).

Even though there is a paucity of literature on the specific cultural concerns related to families of students with visual impairments, implications can be drawn from broader sources. The most frequent teacher variable relating to student success is respect for individuals and their cultural backgrounds (Plata, 1982). If teachers regard their students as individuals and are knowledgeable about their cultural background and ethnic values, teachers are in a better position to make appropriate instructional decisions. Teachers sometimes complain that parents are not motivated to reinforce lessons at home. But it may be that the teacher's goals for the student with the visual impairments differ from the preferences of the family and from its cultural norms. For example, the mother may resist any attempts on the part of the teacher to encourage independence and "letting go" of her child (Correa, 1989). Because the family always provides the child with a sighted guide, they are likely to question the value of the teacher's emphasis on the development of O&M skills. Members of certain ethnic minority groups may not be willing to use low vision aids because they are stigmatizing. In some cultures, fathers may not allow their sons to wear glasses because to do so is not considered masculine (Correa & Keif, 1987). Because many minority cultures are patriarchal, the father must approve all educational decisions, but the teacher usually communicates only with the mother, an older sibling, or perhaps a member of the extended family (Correa, 1987; Falicov, 1982; Trankina, 1983).

The language barrier is a major consideration in working with children and their families from diverse language backgrounds. Because they do not speak the parents' native language, teachers are frequently unable to gather important information from the families that is critical to the education of their children. The teacher might not be able to find out how the child uses vision at home and whether he or she wears glasses. Parents with limited proficiency in English are unable to interpret the findings from ophthalmological and low vision evaluations. This prevents them from contributing fully to their child's development. Furthermore, caretaking is usually the major responsibility of the ethnic minority mother. If she cannot communicate with the teacher, the mother may object to the teacher's "hands-on" intervention with the child.

The ability of the teacher to greet the parents and make a few comments regarding their child in the parents' native language shows respect for the culture of the family, facilitates the establishment of trust and rapport, and greatly increases the likelihood of greater parental involvement in the education of their child

(Linares, 1983). Volunteers from the community or other team members in the school can help to develop survival vocabularies. Silberman and Correa (1989) presented suggestions for learning words and phrases as well as provided examples in Spanish that related to the needs of students with multiple impairments. This model can be replicated in other languages. Suggestions to parents about their child should always be translated into their native language.

In the area of assessment, students with a visual impairment and limited English proficiency are at a double disadvantage. A child with only a visual impairment can answer test questions verbally rather than writing or brailling the answers, but a student with limited English proficiency has difficulty doing so. Even if paper and pencil assessment materials are available in the student's native language, they are probably not available in large print or braille (Correa & Keif, 1987). Finally, although a picture test can be enlarged, the objects and concepts may appear abstract and unfamiliar to students with visual impairments because of the lack of concrete visual experience. Moreover, these students may not be able to verbally describe what is happening in the picture because those objects and concepts are unknown in the student's family culture (Woo, 1988). Therefore, the transdisciplinary team must reflect the collaborative efforts of the bilingual teacher, the itinerant or resource room teacher, the orientation and mobility specialist, the school psychologist or diagnostician, the classroom teacher, and the parents.

In the area of curriculum, multicultural needs of learners with visual impairments must also be considered. For example, when teaching food preparation to students from Asian- or Hispanic-American backgrounds, using ethnic dishes commonly prepared in their homes as the basis for instruction would be more relevant (Correa & Keif, 1987). Students would be more motivated, and they could generalize their newly acquired cooking skills to competence in cooking at home.

SUMMARY THOUGHTS

Although children and youth with visual impairments represent only a small percentage of the population, their wide variation in ages and levels of functioning require a range of services to help them reach their full educational potential. Assessment strategies must take into account the vision bias built into many test norms, and interventions should attend to social as well as conceptual development. Of the many principles on which instructional interventions can be based, three bear repeating: concreteness—providing students with visual impairments with real objects; unified experiences—providing students with multidimensional, real-world experiences so that what they learn in the classroom can be integrated with what they must know to function in the real world; and learning by doing—giving students as little assistance as possible so that they may learn how to do things for themselves. Finally, in addition to providing such services as early intervention and transition, the education system must continue to develop sensitivity to the diverse multicultural needs of the students in its charge so that instructional decisions are culturally appropriate as well as effective.

REFERENCES

Alber, M. B. (1974). *Listening: A curriculum guide for teachers of visually impaired students*. Springfield: Illinois Office of Education.

Allen, W., Griffith, A., & Shaw, C. (1977). *Orientation and mobility: Behavioral objectives for teaching older adventitiously blinded individuals*. New York: New York Infirmary Center for Independent Living.

American Foundation for the Blind. (1974). *A step-by-step guide to personal management for blind persons*. New York: Author.

American Printing House for the Blind. (1988). *Distribution of January, 1987, quota registration by school, grades, and reading media*. Louisville, KY: Author.

Andersen, E. S., Dunlea, A., & Kekelis, L. S. (1984). Blind children's language development: Resolving some differences. *Journal of Child Language, 11*, 645–664.

Barraga, N. (1983). *Visual handicaps and learning* (rev. ed.). Austin, TX: Exceptional Resources.

Barraga, N., & Morris, J. (1980). *Program to develop efficiency in visual functioning*. Louisville, KY: American Printing House for the Blind.

Brolin, D. E. (1983). *Life-centered career education: A competency based program* (rev. ed.). Reston, VA: Council for Exceptional Children.

Brown, D., Simmons, V., & Methvin, J. (1979). *The Oregon project for visually impaired and blind preschool children*. Medford, OR: Jackson County Education Service District.

Cartwright, G. P., Cartwright, C. A., & Ward, M. E. (1989). *Educating special learners* (3rd ed.). Belmont, CA: Wadsworth.

Caton, H. (1976). *Tactile Test of Basic Concepts*. Louisville, KY: American Printing House for the Blind.

Caton, H. R. (1981). Visual impairments. In A. E. Blackhurst & W. H. Burdine (Eds.), *An introduction to special education* (pp. 235–280). Boston: Little, Brown.

Caton, H. R., Pester, E., & Bradley, E. J. (1983). *Patterns: The primary braille reading program*. Louisville, KY: American Printing House for the Blind.

Corn, A. (1980). *Development and assessment of an in-service training program for teachers of the visually handicapped: Optical aids in the classroom*. Unpublished doctoral dissertation, Teachers College, Columbia University.

Correa, V. (1987). Working with Hispanic parents of visually impaired children: Cultural implications. *Journal of Visual Impairment and Blindness, 81*(6), 260–264.

Correa, V. (1989). Involving culturally diverse families in the educational process. In S. H. Fradd & M. J. Weismantel (Eds.), *Meeting the needs of culturally and linguistically different students: Handbook for educators* (pp. 130–144). Boston: College Hill Publication/Little, Brown.

Correa, V., & Keif, E. (1987). Ethnic minority visually impaired students and clients: Implications for education and rehabilitation. In *AER Yearbook of the Association for Education and Rehabilitation of the Blind and Visually Impaired, 4*, 33–39.

Covert, A., and Fredericks, B. (Eds.). (1987). *Transition for persons with deaf-blindness and other profound handicaps*. Monmouth, OR: Teaching Resource Publications.

Cutsforth, T. (1951). *The blind in school and society* (2nd ed.). New York: American Foundation for the Blind.

Falicov, C. (1982). Mexican families. In M. McGoldrich, J. Pearce, & J. Giordano (Eds.), *Ethnicity and family therapy*. New York: Guilford Press.

Faye, E. E. (1970). *The low-vision patient*. New York: Grune & Stratton.

Ferrell, K. A. (1985). *Reach out and teach*. New York: American Foundation for the Blind.

Ferrell, K. A. (1986). Infancy and early childhood. In G. T. Scholl (Ed.), *Foundations of education for blind and visually handicapped children and youth* (pp. 119–136). New York: American Foundation for the Blind.

Fraiberg, S. (1977). *Insights from the blind: Comparative studies of blind and sighted infants*. New York: Basic Books.

Harley, R. K. (1963). *Verbalism among blind children*. New York: American Foundation for the Blind.

Harley, R. K., Truan, M., & Sanford, L. (1987). *Communication skills for visually impaired learners.* Springfield, IL: Charles C. Thomas.

Harley, R. K., Wood, T. A., & Merbler, J. B. (1981). *Peabody Mobility Scales.* Chicago: Stoelting.

Hatlen, P., & Curry, S. (1987). In support of specialized programs for blind and visually impaired children: The impact of vision loss on learning. *Journal of Visual Impairment and Blindness, 81,* 7–13.

Heinze, T. (1986). Communication skills. In G. T. Scholl (Ed.), *Foundations of education for blind and visually handicapped children and youth* (pp. 301–314). New York: American Foundation for the Blind.

Heward, W. L., & Orlansky, M. D. (1988). *Exceptional children* (3rd ed.). Columbus, OH: Merrill.

Hill, E. W. (1986). Orientation and mobility. In G. T. Scholl (Ed.), *Foundations of education for blind and visually handicapped children and youth* (pp. 315–340). New York: American Foundation for the Blind.

Hill, E. W., & Ponder, P. (1976). *Orientation and mobility techniques: A guide for the practitioner.* New York: American Foundation for the Blind.

Hill, E., Rosen, S., Correa, V., & Langley, B. (1984). Preschool orientation and mobility: An expanded definition. *Education of the Visually Handicapped, 16*(2), 58–72.

Kappan, D. L. (1981). Orientation and mobility. In G. Napier, D. Kappan, & D. W. Tuttle, *Handbook for teachers of the visually handicapped* (pp. 45-56). Louisville, KY: American Printing House for the Blind.

Kekelis, L., & Sacks, S., (1988). *Mainstreaming visually children into regular education programs: The effects of visual impairment on children's interactions with peers.* San Francisco: San Francisco State University.

Kirchner, C., & Peterson, R. (1981). Estimates of race-ethnic groups in the United States visually impaired and blind population. *Journal of Visual Impairment and Blindness, 75,* 73–76.

Langley, M. B. (1980). *Assessment of multihandicapped, visually impaired children.* Chicago: Stoelting.

Leach, F. (1973). *Listen and think adapted tape lesson series for developing and improving listening comprehension and thinking skills.* Louisville, KY: American Printing House for the Blind.

Linares, N. (1983). Management of communicatively handicapped Hispanic American children. In D. R. Omark & J. G. Erickson (Eds.), *The bilingual exceptional child* (pp. 145–162). San Diego: College Hill Press.

Lowenfeld, B. (1981a). Effects of blindness on the cognitive functions of children. In B. Lowenfeld, *Berthold Lowenfeld on blindness and blind people* (pp. 67–78). New York: American Foundation for the Blind.

Lowenfeld, B. (1981b). The child who is blind. In B. Lowenfeld, *Berthold Lowenfeld on blindness and blind people* (pp. 29–37). New York: American Foundation for the Blind.

Mangold, S. S. (1977). *The Mangold developmental program of tactile perception and braille letter recognition.* Castro Valley, CA: Exceptional Teaching Aids.

Parsons, S. (1986). Function of play in low vision children (Part 2): Emerging patterns of behavior. *Journal of Visual Impairment and Blindness, 80,* 777–784.

Plata, M. (1982). *Assessment, placement, and programming of bilingual exceptional pupils: A practical approach.* Reston, VA: ERIC Clearing House on Handicapped and Gifted Children, Council for Exceptional Children.

Reynell, J. (1981). *Reynell Zinkin Scales: Developmental scales for young visually handicapped children.* Windsor, England: NFER-Nelson Publishing.

Roessing, L. J. (1982). Functional vision criterion-referenced checklists. In S. S. Mangold (Ed.), *A teacher's guide to educational needs of blind and visually handicapped children* (pp. 35–52). New York: American Foundation for the Blind.

Sacks, S., Hatlen, P., and Pruett, K. (1988). *Summer Transition Project, Office of Special Education and Rehabilitation Services Administration.* San Francisco: San Francisco State College.

Sacks, S., Kekelis, L., & Gaylord-Ross, R. (Eds.). (1988). *The social development of visually impaired students.* San Francisco: San Francisco State College.

Sacks, S., & Reardon, M. (1989). Maximizing social integration for visually handicapped students: Applications and practice. In R. Gaylord Ross (Ed.), *Integration strategies for students with handicaps* (pp. 77–104). Baltimore, MD: Paul H. Brookes Publishing Co.

Scholl, G. T. (1986). What does it mean to be blind? In G. T. Scholl (Ed.), *Foundations of education for blind and visually handicapped children and youth* (pp. 23–34). New York: American Foundation for the Blind.

Scott, E. (1982). *Your visually impaired student: A guide for teachers.* Baltimore, MD: University Park Press.

Silberman, R. K. (1986). Severe multiple handicaps. In G. T. Scholl (Ed.), *Foundations of education for blind and visually handicapped children and youth* (pp. 145–164). New York: American Foundation for the Blind.

Silberman, R. K., and Correa, V. (1989). Spanish survival words and phrases for professionals who work with bilingual severely/multiply handicapped students and their families. *Division for Physically Handicapped Journal, 10* (2), 57–66.

Silberman, R. K., Trief, E., & Morse, A. R. (1988, May-June). Parent perspectives: What if your child has a visual impairment? *Exceptional Parent,* 40–45.

Simpson, F., Huebner, K., & Roberts, F. R. (1985). *Transitions from school to work: Collaborative planning (training model).* New York: American Foundation for the Blind.

Smith, A. J., & Cote, K. S. (1982). *Look at me: A resource manual for the development of residual vision in multiply impaired children.* Philadelphia: Pennsylvania College of Optometry.

Stephens, B., & Grube, C. (1982). Development of Piagetian reasoning in congenitally blind children. *Journal of Visual Impairment and Blindness, 76*(5), 133–143.

Stillman, R. (1979). *Callier-Azusa Scale.* Dallas: Callier Center for Communication Disorders.

Stillman, R. (1984). *Callier-Azusa Scale: Form H.* Dallas: Callier Center for Communication Disorders.

Stocker, C. (1973). *Listening for the visually impaired: A teaching manual.* Springfield, IL: Charles C. Thomas.

Swallow, R. M. (1981). Fifty assessment instruments commonly used with blind and partially seeing individuals. *Journal of Visual Impairment and Blindness, 75*(2), 65–72.

Swallow, R. M., & Conner, A. (1982). Aural reading. In S. S. Mangold (Ed.), *A teacher's guide to special education needs of blind and visually handicapped children* (pp. 119–135). New York: American Foundation for the Blind.

Swallow, R., & Huebner, K. (1987). *How to thrive, not just survive.* New York: American Foundation for the Blind.

Swallow, R., Mangold, S., & Mangold, P. (1978). *Informal assessment of the visually impaired.* New York: American Foundation for the Blind.

Todd, J. (1986). Resources, media and technology. In G. T. Scholl (Ed.), *Foundations of education for blind and visually handicapped children and youth* (pp. 285–300). New York: American Foundation for the Blind.

Trankina, F. J. (1983). Clinical issues and techniques in working with Hispanic children and their families. In G. J. Powell (ed.), *The psychosocial development of minority group children* (pp. 307–329). New York: Brunnel/Mazel.

Tuttle, D. (1986). Educational programming. In G. T. Scholl (Ed.), *Foundations of education for blind and visually handicapped children and youth* (pp. 239–254). New York: American Foundation for the Blind.

Vaughan, D., Asbury, T., & Tabbara, K. F. (1989). *General ophthalmology* (12th ed.). San Mateo, CA: Appleton & Lange.

Warren, D. (1984). *Blindness and early childhood development* (2nd ed.). New York: American Foundation for the Blind.

Wehman, P., Moon, M. S., Everson, J. M., Wood, W., and Barcus, J. M. (1988). *Transition from school to work: New challenges for youth with severe disabilities.* Baltimore, MD: Paul H. Brookes Publishing Co.

Woo, J. (1988). *Handbook on the assessment of East Asian students.* New York: Hunter College of CUNY, Department of Special Education, Training Program for Teachers of Handicapped Children of Asian Origin.

1

Purpose

☐ To alert you to the use of visual imagery in children's reading materials

☐ To assist you in developing structured lesson plans to teach visual concepts

Steps

1. Select a children's textbook or storybook.
2. Identify and list at least 10 instances in the book in which the meaning of the concept is dependent on vision.
3. From this list, select one item and prepare a detailed written step-by-step procedure on how you would teach the specific concept to a blind student.
4. Select another item on the list, and repeat (3) for a low vision student.

Analysis

☐ What is your impression of the frequency of visually oriented concepts in children's books?

☐ What difficulties did you encounter in modifying your instructional technique for a blind student and for a low vision student?

☐ Would the step-by-step procedure require you to conduct activities, provide materials, or spend extensive time beyond what is feasible in the regular class?

☐ Which member of the team is responsible for ensuring that the student with visual impairments acquires these concepts?

2

Purpose

☐ To assist you in identifying landmarks and clues to facilitate travel in a familiar environment

☐ To help you verify the usefulness of landmarks and clues in traveling a specific route

Steps

1. Select a school building.
2. Choose a specific classroom, and record all the landmarks and clues that would be useful to a blind or low vision student traveling from that classroom to another room on the same floor.
3. Become familiar with your list of clues.
4. Using a blindfold and the landmarks and clues you learned in (3), travel the route. Be sure to have a peer accompany you for your safety.

5. Review the success of your travel, and revise your list of landmarks and clues as necessary.

Analysis

☐ How many senses were involved in the landmarks and clues you identified?

☐ Did you rely on certain senses more than on others?

☐ What problems did you encounter in relying on your landmarks and clues?

☐ What problems might have occurred if the hallways were unusually noisy and filled with students?

3

Purpose

☐ To stress the importance of adapting learning materials so that they can be directly accessed by blind or low vision students

☐ To help you modify materials into a variety of useful media for blind and low vision students

Steps

1. Select a graph, chart, diagram, or map from a print textbook.
2. Construct a tactual representation for use with a student who is blind.
3. Construct a tactual/visual representation for use with a student with low vision.
4. Develop a set of questions to determine whether the representations constructed in (3) and (4) worked.
5. If at all possible, incorporate your representations and questions in a lesson with a blind or low vision student.

Analysis

☐ What modifications did you make, if any, to simplify the representations?

☐ What difficulties did you encounter in making the representation tactual or tactual/visual?

☐ If you were to redo your representation, what other modifications or materials would you use?

☐ If you were able to use your representation with an actual student, was the student able to successfully interpret the material and answer your questions?

13

Physical Disabilities

Linda K. Gleckel
Richard J. Lee
State University College at Buffalo

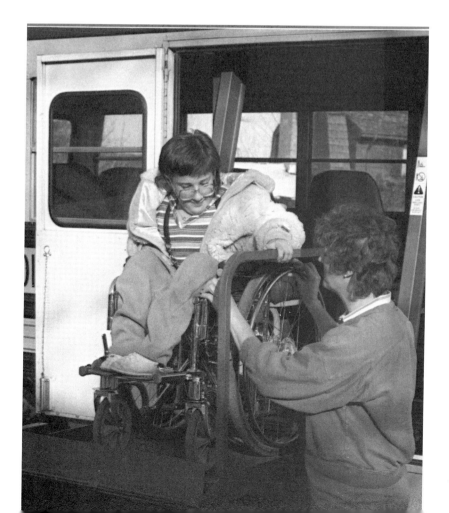

PHYSICAL DISABILITIES
TYPICAL PROFILE

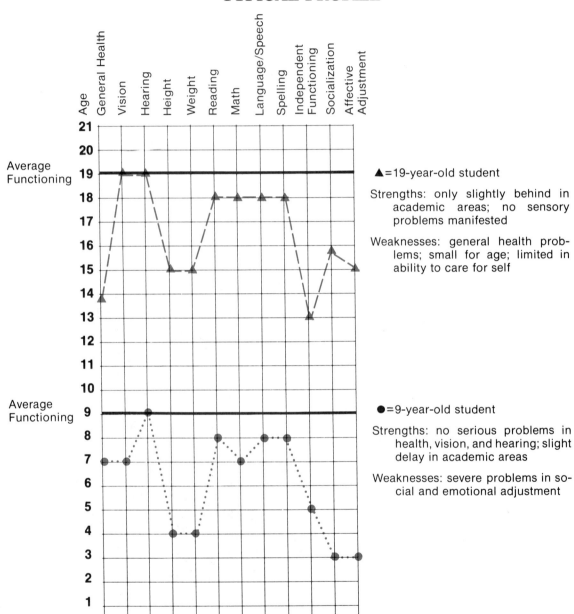

Average Functioning (at 19)

▲=19-year-old student

Strengths: only slightly behind in academic areas; no sensory problems manifested

Weaknesses: general health problems; small for age; limited in ability to care for self

Average Functioning (at 9)

●=9-year-old student

Strengths: no serious problems in health, vision, and hearing; slight delay in academic areas

Weaknesses: severe problems in social and emotional adjustment

I awake like everyone else.
My brain becomes active and my muscles control my direction.
But, still; things are different.

I shower and dress, like everyone else.
I eat breakfast in the morning
just like every other person in the world.
But, still; things are different.

I am confronted by the problems
all people face. Where should I go next?
What should I do now? Who am I?
But, still; things are different.

I have the same needs as everyone else.
The need to be accepted as a person.
The need to be loved for what and who I am,
not pitied for what I am not.
But, still; things are different.

I like the same things everyone else does.
The warmth of a summer's day, the excitement of
a new discovery, the touch of another.
But, still; things are different.

I am not that different from you.
I have days that are better than others.
I have days that are worse than most.
But, because of prejudice and ignorance;
Things are different.

Howard Benns (1985)

Individuals with physical disabilities are defined as those who have nonsensory physical impairments or health impairments that interfere to a significant degree with their academic performance. Special education provisions for individuals with disabilities should include modifications of the environment, the use of adaptive equipment, and special transportation arrangements necessary to facilitate the education of individuals with disabilities in regular educational settings. Educational agencies and schools must provide the services that will encourage and assist individuals with disabilities to achieve to their maximum capacity.

A team approach for delivering such services as physical, occupational, and/or speech therapy is utilized in many settings. The transdisciplinary approach, one of many team approaches employed in special education programs, appears to be very successful in meeting the needs of individuals with physical disabilities. In this cooperative arrangement, members of the team work closely together to assess needs, identify goals, and implement programs so that identified goals (such as goals related to communication, appropriate positioning, and mobility) can be pursued throughout the day in all settings.

For years, schools and educational agencies provided two justifications for isolating students with physical disabilities from their nondisabled peers. First, integration of students with disabilities might have a negative effect on their nondisabled peers. Second, individuals with disabilities could not be successful in regular classes because of the physical demands that would be placed on them. Neither justification has stood the test of scrutiny. Nonhandicapped peers are generally not negatively affected by the presence of individuals with disabilities (Esposito & Reed, 1986). Many individuals with disabilities have normal intellectual functioning and, with the aid of specialized equipment, can function successfully in regular programs.

The passage of PL 94-142, the Education for All Handicapped Children Act, created a greater awareness of the discriminatory nature of earlier practices and provided support for services that would allow individuals with physical disabilities to be educated in more normalized settings. The least restrictive environment mandate requires that based on their particular educational needs individuals with disabilities be educated in programs that are most similar to those attended by their nondisabled peers. The placement decision is predicated on each student's learning abilities, not solely on the diagnosed disabling condition.

Since the passage of PL 94-142, many improvements have been observed. But much remains to be accomplished in order to fully realize the mission of this major civil rights legislation. Continued vigilance and ongoing advocacy are essential to assure full compliance.

PREVALENCE

Because physical disabilities are generally not isolated conditions, accurately determining their prevalence is difficult. Often the primary disability is accompanied by associated conditions, and the individual is then viewed as a person with multiple disabilities. Connor, Scandary, and Tulloch (1988) provided additional reasons for the difficulty in computing the prevalence rates for this group: "The physiological and functional problems are complex and their handicaps may be temporary, intermittent, chronic, progressive, or terminal." (p. 7)

The actual number of students identified as physically disabled is less than the numbers of students identified as mentally retarded, learning disabled, or emotionally disturbed. According to the U.S. Department of Education (1987), the number of individuals with orthopedic disabilities, ages 3 to 21, served in special education programs is 58,835 for 1984-1985. The number of individuals with health impairments, ages 3 to 21, served in special education programs is 69,118. The total population of individuals with physical disabilities (127,953) represents approximately 0.31% of all students receiving special education services in today's schools.

CHARACTERISTICS OF CHILDREN AND YOUTH WITH PHYSICAL DISABILITIES

Physical disfigurement, mobility limitations, chronic pain, use of orthoses/prostheses or other necessary medical/therapeutic equipment, physical dependency on others, life-threatening medical episodes, and communication difficulties are characteristics that elicit negative responses from nondisabled individuals. These negative responses may create certain unique adjustment problems with which individuals with disabilities will have to cope (Connor et al., 1988).

Although individuals with physical disabilities usually have distinct physiological and physical management differences from their nondisabled peers, they have the same needs, desires, and interests. Above all, they want to be treated with the same dignity afforded nondisabled individuals. An initial step in achieving acceptance as an individual is to become known as a person first and not to be identified by the type of disability one has. The American Association on Mental Deficiency, now known as the American Association on Mental Retardation, has adopted the following policy: "It is therefore, the policy of this Association to clear away all archaic stigmatizing, dehumanizing and syntactically incorrect usage of labels and replace these with appropriate socially valued references that emphasize the humanity and individuality of our consumer constituency whenever possible" (California Department of Health, 1977). Adoption of this policy reflects appropriate recognition of individuals with disabilities. A person should be identified as an individual who has a specific disability and not, for example, as a "CP" (cerebral palsy) or an "MD" (muscular dystrophy).

Identification of an appropriate descriptor has plagued this population for many years. Terms such as "crippled," "deformed," and "handicapped" have frequently been used to describe individuals with physiological differences. Each of these terms promotes a notion of inability, restriction, and difference. There may not be a perfect descriptor, but the more acceptable, noninflammatory term seems to be "disability" (DeFelice, 1986). A disability is a dysfunction that results from an impairment. It differs from the commonly used term *handicap,* which refers to an actual or perceived limitation (Hardman, Drew, & Egan, 1984). Individuals with physical disabilities dislike the implication that they are unable to function. With current rehabilitation technology, many barriers have been removed. Individuals with physical disabilities are now able to function in many situations once thought to be impossible.

As a rule, the only common element among individuals with physical disabilities is the existence of some interference with normal motor functioning. Such disabilities may be progressive or nonprogressive, intermittent or chronic, terminal or not terminal, persistently painful or intermittently painful.

Children with physical disabilities have a diverse range of motor characteristics. Accurate observation of these characteristics is necessary to select appropriate assessment instruments. In Activity 1, page 387, you are instructed to observe a child with physical disabilities and record information about ability levels.

Physical disabilities are most commonly classified according to their etiologies (causes). The three major causal classifications are *neurologic* conditions, which are disabilities caused by damage to or incomplete development of the brain or spinal cord; *orthopedic* conditions, which are caused by damage to, disease of, or lack of development of bones, muscles, or joints of the body; and *health* conditions, which are caused by acute or chronic disease.

Neurologic Conditions

Cerebral Palsy

Cerebral palsy is a neurologic condition characterized by abnormal movement or motor dysfunction caused by damage to the brain (Harryman, 1986). The alteration or interruption of motor function is its distinguishing characteristic. Cerebral palsy can occur during gestation (prenatally); during the birth process (perinatally); or in the wake of an accident, a disease, or an injury (postnatally) (Harryman, 1986).

The extent of cerebral palsy can range from mild to severe disability. Individuals with *mild* involvement are usually ambulatory, have good verbal skills, and generally are average or above average in intelligence. Fine motor coordination is usually impaired. Individuals with *moderate* involvement may or may not need assistance in walking. Their ability to speak intelligibly and use both fine and gross motor coordination may be affected. Individuals with *severe* involvement are usually wheelchair users. Often they lack verbal communication skills and need the assistance of augmentative communication devices. Fine and gross motor skills are severely impaired.

In addition to degree of severity, cerebral palsy may be classified according to *physiological type* (spasticity, athetosis, ataxia, rigidity, tremor, hypotonia, or mixed) and *topography* (limb involvement) (Bleck, 1982a). Terms that identify limb involvement include monoplegia, hemiplegia, paraplegia, triplegia, quadriplegia, diplegia, or double hemiplegia. (See "Basic Professional Vocabulary" for definitions.)

Associated disorders of cerebral palsy include sensory impairments, convulsive disorders, mental retardation, communication disorders, and learning disabilities. An individual may have any one or several of these associated disorders.

Epilepsy

Epilepsy is a disorder of the central nervous system characterized by recurring explosive discharges of electrical activity that cause episodic periods of unconsciousness or psychic dysfunction (Wolraich, 1984). These episodic periods are referred to as *seizures*. Because some individuals with physical disabilities have experienced brain damage, epilepsy is a common associated disorder. The most frequent types of seizures that individuals with epilepsy experience are grand mal, petit mal, psychomotor, and Jacksonian. On occasion, some individuals may exhibit more than one type of seizure.

RACHEL, AN INDIVIDUAL WITH CEREBRAL PALSY

Rachel is a 13-year-old who has moderate spastic quadriplegic cerebral palsy. She is able to walk for limited periods, but because of fatigue and muscle spasms, Rachel frequently uses an electronically powered wheelchair for mobility. She is able to speak; however, her verbal communication is slow and sometimes difficult to understand. She often uses an electronic communicative device to clarify what she has said. Because Rachel has limited fine motor coordination and finds writing difficult, she uses a modified tape recorder to record information. To facilitate the preparation of written assignments, Rachel uses a computer to complete her assigned academic projects. Her vision and hearing are normal. Although in the past, Rachel had occasional grand mal seizures, they are generally controlled by medication; she has not had a seizure for 10 months. Rachel attends a regular middle school in her neighborhood and is on grade level in all academic subjects with her nondisabled classmates.

What environmental modifications in the classroom might be made to ensure Rachel's full participation in activities?

Are there any special health care considerations that should be made because of Rachel's physical condition?

Can you anticipate necessary modifications that must be made when testing Rachel to better determine her level of understanding of academic material?

During a *grand mal* seizure, an individual usually loses consciousness and has major convulsions. A *petit mal* seizure is a very subtle momentary loss of consciousness that is frequently undetected. During a *psychomotor* seizure, the individual does not lose consciousness but may behave in unusual ways such as staring, running, screaming, or crying. A *Jacksonian* seizure is a localized spasm confined to one part of the body or one group of muscles. Medication is used frequently to treat epilepsy, and although medication is not always successful in totally eliminating seizure activity, it usually helps to decrease the severity or frequency of the seizures.

Teachers and other school personnel should remain calm and in control when an individual is having a seizure. This will minimize the development of fearful reactions on the part of other students and will help promote a better understanding of epilepsy. Because the management of epileptic seizures generally entails following simple, passive procedures, individuals with epilepsy should not be denied the right to function in regular school situations. (For information regarding first aid for epileptic seizures, contact the Epilepsy Foundation of America.)

Spina Bifida

Spina bifida is a defect in the closure of the bony spinal canal (Bleck, 1982c). This defect may result in the protrusion of the spinal cord or its coverings through the opening. There are several variations of this condition; the most severe type is myelomeningocele, in which both the spinal cord and its coverings protrude through the spinal opening. The resulting trauma to the spinal cord may cause varying degrees of paralysis in the trunk and lower extremities. Lack of bowel and bladder control are associated with myelomeningocele. Some individuals may incur the loss of sensation (touch, temperature, pressure, and pain), which will require careful physical management.

Individuals with myelomeningocele may also have hydrocephalus, a condition characterized by an increased volume of cerebral-spinal fluid within the cranium (Bleck, 1982c). A shunting operation is generally performed to enable the cerebral-spinal fluid to be diverted successfully to other parts of the body where it can be absorbed. If this procedure is not implemented in a timely fashion, the individual will experience brain damage, become mentally retarded, and may eventually die.

The intellectual abilities of many individuals with spina bifida may not be affected. With necessary support services provided by the school, individuals with spina bifida should be included in regular school activities.

Orthopedic Conditions

Juvenile Rheumatoid Arthritis

Juvenile rheumatoid arthritis is a condition characterized by recurring inflammation of the joints of the body that causes swelling, stiffness, pain, and possible permanent deformity (Miller, 1982). Symptoms fluctuate frequently and are more pronounced during certain periods. During these periods, because of the motoric inhibitions and severe pain caused by the arthritis, depression and anger may be evidenced. Permanent orthopedic deformities may result from the prolonged swelling and stiffness of the joints.

Most individuals with juvenile rheumatoid arthritis can benefit from education in regular education settings with only modest modifications in instructional requirements and materials. Empathy for an individual's reactions associated with severe crisis periods will further facilitate successful integration.

Legg-Calve-Perthes

Legg-Calve-Perthes is a degenerative flattening of the head of the femur (thigh bone) caused by disruption of the blood supply to this area (Nagel, 1982). The bone tissue is destroyed, which causes muscle spasms, limping, and severe pain. This condition rarely is in evidence in children younger than 3 years of age and occurs more frequently in males. Several treatment procedures are available including traction, casting, use of special leg braces, operative procedures, or a combination of these to allow regeneration of the head of the femur. During the regeneration process, which takes approximately 2 years, modifications must be made so that the individual avoids placing weight on the affected area.

Although many physically disabling conditions are permanent, Legg-Calve-Perthes is temporary. Special educational services required may include home or hospital instruction or provision of special transportation (for example, bus with hydraulic lift) to transport the individual who is wearing a leg brace or cast to school.

Limb Deficiencies

A limb deficiency is the absence or loss of all or part of an arm(s) or a leg(s) (Brooks, 1983). A congenital limb deficiency is present at birth; an acquired limb deficiency results from disease or accident sometime after birth. An acquired limb deficiency may also be referred to as an amputation.

Frequently, an individual with a limb deficiency is fitted with a *prosthesis*—an artificial limb developed to compensate for the deficiency. The use of a prosthesis is highly individual. Some people, particularly those with upper extremity losses, prefer not to use a prosthesis because they have learned to function successfully without it. For them, the artificial limb is cumbersome and prohibitive rather than facilitative.

Individuals with amputations generally have normal intellectual capabilities. Therefore, such individuals function successfully in regular class settings. Careful counseling and guidance can help prevent the psychosocial difficulties amputees may experience because of the insensitivity of their curious and uninformed classmates.

Muscular Dystrophy

Although there are several different types of muscular dystrophy, the most common and most severe is pseudohypertrophic dystrophy of Duchenne (Bleck, 1982b). Duchenne dystrophy is a gradual, progressive degeneration and wasting of the voluntary muscles. Muscle tissue is displaced by fatty, connective tissue, which often causes a false enlargement (pseudohypertrophy) of the affected area. Consequently, obesity is frequently observed in individuals with Duchenne dystrophy. This type of muscular dystrophy is hereditary and sex linked because it is attached to the x-chromosome. The mother is the carrier; half of her sons will have the condition, and half of her daughters will become carriers of the affected gene. Due to the progressive nature of the degeneration and wasting (generally starting on the dorsiflexors of the foot), the child will initially need to be braced to remain ambulatory but will eventually require the use of a wheelchair. Death caused by cardiac and pulmonary complications resulting from the weakened condition generally occurs during the late teens or early adulthood.

Individuals with Duchenne dystrophy usually have average intelligence and therefore should be encouraged and enabled to remain in regular school programs. During the latter stages of Duchenne dystrophy, hospitalization or prolonged absences may be frequent due to the individual's increased susceptibility to illness. Therefore, adjustments in the school program will be necessary to accommodate the unique needs of the individual with Duchenne dystrophy.

J. J., AN INDIVIDUAL WITH MUSCULAR DYSTROPHY

J. J. is an 8-year-old who has Duchenne muscular dystrophy. J. J. is able to walk, but his gait is slow and deliberate and he falls frequently. J. J. is aware of the progressive nature of his condition and frequently asks questions concerning his future.

J. J. attends regular elementary school and is on grade level with his nondisabled classmates. School officials are beginning to question whether J. J.'s safety can be assured in this placement. They believe that a school specifically designed for individuals with physical disabilities might better meet J. J.'s changing physical needs. J. J.'s parents would like him to remain in the present situation.

□ □ □

Do you think that J. J. should remain in his current situation?

What necessary modifications need to be made in any school J. J. would attend?

What benefits might J. J. receive by remaining in the present situation?

If J. J. is transferred, do you think the new placement would be the least restrictive for him? Why?

Should J. J. be consulted before the decision is made?

Osteogenesis Imperfecta

Osteogenesis imperfecta is a condition associated with defective collagen fibers of the bone that cause the bones to be weak and brittle (Bleck, 1982d). Minor traumas, ordinary stresses of walking, or position changes can easily cause bone fractures.

Because of the fragile nature of the bones, physical activity must be limited. Care in moving and handling are necessary considerations in the individual's physical management. Individuals with osteogenesis imperfecta are usually of normal intelligence and with necessary equipment needed for mobility should function well in regular school programs. Because of long periods of hospitalization due to multiple fractures and slow healing, special accommodations such as hospital and home instruction will be necessary to prevent interruptions in the individual's educational program.

Health Conditions

Whereas the neurologic and orthopedic categories are composed of conditions characterized by some variation of motor functioning, the area of other health conditions includes those that generally do not directly affect movement or motor coordination but do affect general health or stamina. For example, individuals with asthma, sickle cell anemia, cystic fibrosis, juvenile diabetes mellitus, or cardiac conditions may not require special education services because these conditions, unless unusually severe, generally do not affect an individual's ability to learn, speak, or walk. Students with health conditions, however, may require minimal modifications of educational programming, such as adapted physical education, to function optimally in regular classroom settings. Knowledge of medication requirements and overt symptoms, as well as precautions to prevent fatigue in these students, must be taken by regular educators in order to enhance each student's ability to function successfully in school.

Furthermore, many individuals with health conditions are medically fragile or technologically dependent and have special medical needs as well as special educational needs (Sirvis, 1988). Many of the conditions that did not exist several years ago may ultimately have a significant impact on special education and the delivery of necessary services.

Learner Characteristics

Disabilities, especially physical disabilities, impose three serious limitations on learning. The first is the limitation in the ability to process information. In some instances, individuals with physical disabilities resulting from brain damage have cognitive deficits such as learning disabilities or mental retardation. These associated disabilities generally result in difficulties with attention, memory, and thinking skills.

The second is the limitation on the ability to receive information through the senses. Sensory impairments (limitations in or total absence of vision or hearing, for example) are frequently encountered by individuals who have experienced brain damage. Individuals deprived of sensory input are less efficient learners.

The third limitation is on the range and nature of interpersonal and environmental interactions. The world of an individual who is born with a disability is different from that of the child who is not disabled. For children who lack the motor coordination to voluntarily explore their surroundings, the environment is "physically removed." Typical children are able to interact with the environment at an early age by reaching out, touching, feeling, and eventually grasping and manipulating objects. Later, crawling and walking allow children to further explore the physical characteristics of their worlds as well as actively interact with objects and people in their surroundings. By contrast, lack of control over voluntary movements may deprive children with disabilities of these early learning experiences. Furthermore, these limitations in voluntary exploration may result in frustration and reduced motivation.

Intellectual Characteristics

Individuals whose conditions affect only motor functioning should reflect the full range of cognitive abilities represented in the nondisabled population. Indeed, some individuals who have disabilities characterized only by neuromuscular difficulties (such as orthopedic disabilities, cerebral palsy, spina bifida) may even function within the "gifted" range of intellectual ability.

But if an individual with a physical disability experiences associated disabilities (such as visual/hearing impairment, seizures, mental retardation), his or her ability to receive and process information becomes more difficult. Therefore, the type or degree of the primary physical disability is not the only determinant of the potential for learning. The type and degree of associated disabilities may present equally limiting obstacles to the acquisition and mastery of information.

Given the potential difficulties in learning that individuals with physical disabilities face, early intervention programs must be designed to stimulate learning, promote healthy parent-child relationships, and develop positive self-concepts in these youngsters. Even a bright child who fails to perceive himself or herself as capable, who lacks motivation and support of parents, or who fails to interact with the environment will function far below his or her potential capabilities. Parents and caregivers of children with disabilities need assistance as early as possible to set appropriate expectations for, provide quality stimulating environments for, and develop appropriate ways of interacting with their children.

Cerebral palsy children have special motor and coordination concerns.

Physical/Motor Characteristics

Individuals with physical disabilities frequently experience difficulty in mobility as a result of poor muscle coordination, abnormal movement patterns, muscle paralysis or weakness, or absent body parts. All or any of these problems may necessitate the use of wheelchairs, orthoses, crutches, or other devices to facilitate mobility. Problems related to poor gross and fine motor skills may affect areas other than mobility as well.

Communication

Precise control and coordination of the muscles in the oral area, normal functioning of the vocal tract, and effective respiratory patterns are requisites for the production of intelligible speech (Shane, 1979). Difficulties in these areas interfere with an individual's ability to imitate or effectively produce speech sounds and result in unintelligible speech or complete lack of speech. Poor communication skills affect not only an individual's ability to make choices, give information, and make requests but may also interfere with the establishment of social relationships (Peterson, 1987). Individuals who cannot speak may be excellent candidates for augmentative systems of communication such as a graphic display (picture or word board) or a computer with synthetic speech output.

Activities of Daily Living

Many activities of daily living (eating, dressing, toileting, grooming) are dependent on gross motor, fine motor, and perceptual-motor skills. Individuals lacking the necessary physical or cognitive skills to perform daily living tasks independently may benefit from the use of the "principle of partial participation" (Baumgart et al., 1982). This principle allows individuals with disabilities to perform parts of tasks independently while receiving partial or full physical assistance on task components that may be impossible even with extensive instruction. Partial participation enables individuals with severe physical limitations to remain actively engaged in meaningful activities.

In the development of eating skills, therapeutic feeding techniques (feeding with the assistance of a trained adult) may be required to promote more effective eating patterns in individuals who lack voluntary control over the oral mechanism. Self-feeding skills are developed using appropriate foods, adaptive equipment to promote appropriate positions for eating, modified eating utensils, and specific training procedures.

An area of particular concern relative to activities of daily living is toileting. Because muscle weakness or paralysis of the lower extremities may be associated with incontinence (lack of bowel and bladder control), approaches designed to address this problem include surgical diversions, the use of catheters and urinary appliances, and systematic instruction of bowel and bladder management techniques. Major objectives in this area include the improvement of an individual's

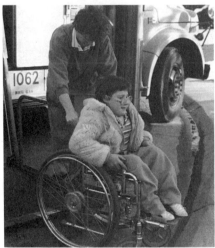

This child does not have any intellectual handicaps.

health through the reduction of bladder and urinary infections, the elimination of rashes and sores frequently encountered by individuals with reduced sensation in their lower extremities, and development of effective toileting skills. These improvements result in increased personal hygiene, enhanced self-concept, greater social acceptability, and increased independence.

Activities related to dressing and personal hygiene present fewer difficulties for individuals with limited fine and gross motor control when modified clothing and adaptive devices to promote independence are utilized. *Task analysis,* the process of breaking activities into their component parts, assists the individual with a physical disability in identifying those subtasks that prevent independent task completion. In many instances, modification or mastery of a subtask or adaptation of materials promotes more independent functioning (Finnie, 1975).

Emotional Development

Children growing up with physical disabilities have unique experiences that have a profound impact on their emotional development. Intense pain, life-threatening episodes accompanied by hospitalizations, and other medical interventions may affect their general disposition, personality characteristics, and, ultimately, their educational performance. Physical dependence may contribute to a state of passivity called "learned helplessness" (Seligman, 1975).

Children who are terminally ill due to conditions such as muscular dystrophy, as well as their families, may need special professional attention. Depression, aggression, and withdrawal are common behaviors among individuals who are anticipating or experiencing serious losses. These feelings and behaviors need to be understood and addressed by competent professionals and sympathetic and caring friends and family members.

Individuals who acquire physical disabilities through accident or injury may experience a deep sense of loss as a result of losing a body part, an ability they once had, or an active lifestyle. Expression of grief, adjustment to the acquired disability, and modifications of life goals are additional stresses with which individuals with acquired disabilities must cope (Wright, 1983).

Social Development

Because individuals with physical disabilities typically have characteristics that do not conform with society's standards for physical attractiveness, they may experience problems with being accepted or have difficulty believing that they are accepted by their nondisabled peers. The physical disfigurement that accompanies some disabilities together with undesirable social characteristics such as incontinence, drooling, and seizure activity can have negative effects on the establishment of positive relationships. Furthermore, devices to facilitate mobility, life-sustaining equipment, and prosthetic aids may interfere with the development of positive images and result in rejection by peers.

"Invisible" disabilities also have an impact on an individual's social development as well. Individuals with health impairments not visible to the observer may behave differently from their peers. A teenager with diabetes who abstains from eating "junk food" at the local "hangout" on a Friday night or an adolescent with a cardiac condition who "sits out" a game of touch football may be stigmatized for behaviors that are not considered "normal."

Worse yet is the situation created when the individual with diabetes violates a diet to "fit in" or when the individual with a heart condition becomes overly fatigued attempting to behave like the rest of the guys on the basketball court. The need to behave "normally" may jeopardize the health of an individual with a health impairment or create a life-threatening situation. The desire to engage in typical behavior paired with the concern for preserving one's general health and well-being can place undue stress on individuals with disabilities.

BASIC PROFESSIONAL VOCABULARY

The special terminology used in the area of physical disabilities is extensive and medical in orientation. Although each disability has descriptors unique to itself, this section is limited to those terms that are applicable to numerous disabilities. (For more detailed explanations of basic terminology, see Batshaw and Perret [1986], Bleck and Nagel [1982], Orelove and Sobsey [1987], and Umbreit [1983].)

Adaptive equipment is equipment developed to assist in the physical management of individuals with physical disabilities.

Augmentative communication systems are assistive devices and/or symbol systems that enhance the communication ability of individuals who have limited verbal communication skills.

Cerebral palsy terminology can be divided into two classifications: physiological and topographical. Physiological terms include *ataxia*—impaired balance and coordination; *athetosis*—fluctuating muscle tone resulting in gross, variable movement; *atonia (hypotonia)*—lack of muscle tone (floppiness); *mixed*—more than one type of cerebral palsy existing concurrently; *rigidity*—state of continuous tension of the muscles; *spasticity*—abnormally high muscle tension; and *tremor*—fine, rhythmical movement (shakiness).

Topographical terms include *diplegia*—involvement of all four limbs but more involvement of lower limbs; *double hemiplegia*—involvement of all four limbs but more involvement of upper limbs (this is rare); *hemiplegia*—involvement of one side of the body; *involvement*—limited control or movement of a limb or limbs; *monoplegia*—involvement of one limb; *paraplegia*—involvement of lower limbs; *quadriplegia*—involvement of all limbs and the trunk; and *triplegia*—involvement of three limbs.

Congenital means present at birth.

Occupational therapy emphasizes work-related and self-help skills designed to assist an individual with fine motor control for optimal functioning.

Orthosis is an appliance used to support, correct, or align a physical deformity; a brace.

Paralysis is the loss of power or sensation in a part of the body caused by disease or injury.

Perinatal means occurring at the time of birth (during the birth process).

Physical therapy is the manipulation, massage, and exercise of body parts to assist an individual with motor control for optimal functioning.

Postnatal means occurring after birth.

Prenatal means occurring during gestation (prior to birth).

Prosthesis is an artificial limb used to replace a missing limb.

Transdisciplinary approach is the sharing of expertise and responsibilities among team members who are involved in the assessment process and the development of the educational program.

ASSESSING INSTRUCTIONAL NEED

The limited ability to speak and the limited motor abilities of some individuals with physical disabilities present unique difficulties in the assessment process. Traditional assessment instruments with standard response modes have contributed to the potentially unfair educational evaluation of individuals with physical disabilities. Traditional assessment techniques penalize individuals with physical disabilities in two ways. First, most assessment protocols focus principally on physical actions (such as reaching and grasping and manipulating objects) and on communication skills to demonstrate cognitive abilities. Almost by definition, children with physical disabilities cannot perform as well on these tasks as their nondisabled peers can. Therefore, children with physical disabilities are at risk of being seen as intellectually slow or "delayed" because they cannot demonstrate motoric responses to protocol questions or tasks.

Second, because other protocol items are dependent on verbal responses to questions asked by the examiner, children who are unable to speak or have incomprehensible speech are also at risk of being viewed as intellectually retarded when in fact they may fully understand but be unable to convey (express) that understanding. Because of the inadequacy of the assessment techniques used with this population, educational misdiagnoses and misplacements have been common. The range of skills and abilities found among individuals with different types of physical disabilities have presented real challenges to test developers.

Given the limitations of traditional means of assessment, information must be provided by members of the transdisciplinary team. Team members, through their daily observations and contact with individuals with disabilities, can provide invaluable information regarding the true abilities of individuals with physical disabilities not uncovered during artificially structured testing sessions.

Information relative to the following areas should be gathered and shared by the transdisciplinary team prior to developing programs for individuals with physical disabilities:

1. Physical/motor abilities: the impact of physical disability relative to its effect upon
   a. Fine motor control
   b. Gross motor control
   c. Abnormal postures
   d. Need for orthotic devices
2. Medical information
   a. Chronic illness (such as seizures or arthritis)
   b. Acute illness (such as Legg-Calve-Perthes)
   c. Medications (and their side effects)
   d. General health (such as stamina)
   e. Medical contraindications (activities that should be avoided)
3. Sensory abilities
   a. Visual
   b. Hearing
   c. Tactile
4. Academic skills
   a. Reading
   b. Mathematics
   c. Writing
5. Communication abilities
   a. Language
      (1) Receptive
      (2) Expressive
   b. Speech
   c. Need for an augmentative system
6. Social skills

7. Positioning necessary for optimal functioning
8. Appropriate positioning of materials for active engagement
9. Adaptive equipment necessary

Careful attention must be given to assure that acceptable, alternative strategies are implemented and multiple assessments are conducted to provide more valid and accurate assessment information. Specific accommodations to compensate for individuals' limited response modes must be incorporated into every aspect of the assessment process to ensure fairness.

INTERVENTIONS

The unique characteristics and varying physical, social-emotional, and educational needs of individuals with physical disabilities present a challenge for the teacher/interventionist responsible for educational programming. No one approach may be used successfully with all individuals who are physically disabled, but several features of quality interventions should be addressed. These include instructional interventions (individualization), placement options (least restrictive environment), related services, preschool programs, transitional services, and parental involvement.

Instructional Interventions

PL 94-142 requires that an IEP be developed for each student with special needs from 5 through 21 years of age. The IEP assures that the unique physical, social-emotional, and learning needs of each student will be addressed through (a) appropriate multiple assessments to determine student needs, (b) identification of individualized education goals and objectives, and (c) implementation of individualized curriculum and learning activities based on the stated objectives for each student.

More recently, PL 99-457, the Education of Handicapped Act Amendments of 1986, instituted a new federal preschool program that extended the rights and protections of PL 94-142 to all 3- to 5-year-old children with special needs. Therefore, states applying for these funds must develop IEPs for all children with special needs beginning at age 3. Furthermore, if appropriate and desired, special instruction will be provided for their parents as well.

Placement Options

A critical issue facing schools with regard to programming for children with physical disabilities is the availability of appropriate program and placement options for meeting the diverse needs of this population. Schools must be committed to the principle of least restrictive environment as the foundation for their district's philosophy, policies, and practices regarding the education of children with disabilities. Given the legal and moral right of every child to a free, appropriate education in the least restrictive environment, there can be no question of a school district's responsibility to advocate for and provide a continuum of services that ensures these rights.

The principle of LRE assumes that individuals with physical disabilities will be educated in regular classrooms with their nondisabled peers unless it can be demonstrated that the unique needs of the student require more individual attention and/or services than can be made available in a regular class setting. LRE requires that individuals with physical disabilities be educated in an appropriate placement within an educational setting that allows maximum integration with their nondisabled peers. Tremendous technological strides made in recent years have maximized the potential for students with physical disabilities to function effectively in integrated settings. Although segregated placements may be least restrictive settings for some students with multiple or severe disabilities, segregated settings are not necessarily appropriate for the majority of students with disabilities. To the contrary, individuals with physical disabilities generally have the greatest potential for successful integration when reasonable accommodations are made for their individual needs in typical settings.

Able-bodied persons are not aware of accessibility needs of individuals with physical disablties. Activity 2, page 389, asks you to survey a school, classroom, or public building in order to identify hazards that might limit or prohibit use of the facility by persons with physical disabilities.

The final decision about the actual placement of an individual with a physical disability depends on which facilities are accessible. Physical accessibility deals with the elimination of architectural barriers (stairs, heavy doors, narrow lavatory stalls) that confront individuals with physical disabilities. An entire set of standards for making buildings accessible has been developed by the American National Standards Institute (1986) and has been adopted by the federal government and many municipalities to make new and renovated buildings accessible.

Because of the need for medical treatment and related services, a greater proportion of students with physical disabilities require hospital and homebound instruction than do other individuals with special needs. These options should be used only as long as appropriate and, as needs change, the student should be placed into a less restrictive setting at the earliest possible opportunity. Hospital and homebound instruction should be used when the primary objective for the student is medical in nature.

Related Services

Because of the complex nature of physically disabling conditions, a transdisciplinary model of service delivery is gaining increased acceptance and is being implemented to ensure optimal learning, promote independent functioning in all areas, and increase the likelihood that a student's potential will be realized (Orelove & Sobsey, 1987). A transdisciplinary model is characterized by a sharing of the expertise and specific responsibilities (roles) that have traditionally been associated exclusively with particular professional disciplines. The teacher, other members of the professional team, and, if appropriate, the parents/caregivers learn to design and implement programs across several areas that particular therapists have historically addressed in isolated settings. For example, the speech language pathologist traditionally worked on individual communication goals in the speech therapy room, perhaps three times a week for 30-minute periods. Given that communication occurs throughout the day in all environments, the transdisciplinary approach requires that other members of the team develop skills in incorporating communication goals into daily activities and in pursuing these goals throughout the day in meaningful ways (for example, communicating "hello" when entering the classroom or communicating "more" to request more milk during lunch).

The transdisciplinary team is composed of individuals who cooperate in the evaluation of a student's needs, the formulation of objectives, and the implementation of a program to address the assessed needs of the student. Potential team members and brief descriptions of major roles are identified in Table 13.1.

In many settings, the teacher assumes primary responsibility for the implementation of programs designed by the transdisciplinary team. Therapists typically maintain active roles, sharing their expertise with other members of the team and working with them to integrate therapy goals into the classroom routine. Therapists work directly with students for part of the day and supervise other staff members who pursue therapy goals within other aspects of the program. This collaborative effort allows students to practice specific behaviors at appropriate times throughout the day, which maximizes their functioning in all areas at school and at home.

Preschool Programs

In addition to the New Federal Preschool Program, PL 99-457 articulated a new federal early intervention program for all infants and toddlers with disabilities from birth through 2 years of age. Appropriate early intervention services are to be made available by states within 5 years of their application for federal funds. This legislation acknowledges and supports the importance of initiating interventions as soon as possible to provide assistance to the child and his or her parents. Goals of early intervention efforts include medical and surgical services, parent involvement and education, and provision of related services to reduce the effects of secondary disabilities. Interventions for infants and young children are home based (interventionist visits child's home), center based (child is brought to a center), or a combination of both.

Some parents may be unprepared to cope with the additional stresses of caregiving that children with physical disabilities present. Therefore, it is not only essential but mandatory under PL 99-457 that early intervention programs include working with parents as well as intervening directly with children. Even though many parents provide excellent prenatal care for their unborn child, a number of risk factors may result in the abnormal development of the fetus in a relatively small number of pregnancies. Some children are born with disabilities due to prenatal maternal substance abuse or poor prenatal care and nutrition; some born to

Table 13.1   Members of Transdisciplinary Teams and Their Roles

Team Member	Expertise	Major Roles
Teacher/interventionist	Cognitive, social-emotional development, designing & implementing instructional programs	To communicate and collaborate with other members of the team to design, implement, and continually evaluate programs for individuals with physical disabilities
Physical therapist	Fine and gross motor skills, ambulation/ mobility training	To analyze motor abilities of individuals with physical disabilities[a]
Occupational therapist	Fine and gross motor skills, perceptual-motor skills, activities of daily living (self-help skills)	To select, design, and construct adaptive equipment and instructional aids
		To position students to prevent deformities, promote comfort, and facilitate independent movement
		To develop students' daily living skills
Speech-language pathologist or Communication specialist	Speech and language development, augmentative communication Therapeutic feeding techniques	To develop appropriate communication programs for individuals who are nonspeaking or who have limited communication ability
		To implement speech and language therapy in the classroom
		To design and work with others to implement therapeutic feeding programs
Parent/caregiver	Parenting	To provide for total needs of child at home
		To implement goals of other team members in nonschool settings
Student/client	Knowledge of own needs	To provide input, if appropriate, relative to programming in all areas
Others: Medical personnel, counselor, psychologist, social worker, nurse	Based on training and background	To provide assistance to meet the total intellectual, physical, medical, vocational, and social-emotional needs of an individual with physical disabilities

[a]Roles of OT and PT generally overlap.

teenage mothers may be low birth weight babies who are biologically or environmentally at risk; in other instances, child abuse may be the cause of physical and neurologic disabilities during early childhood. All of these problems stem from parent behavior, frequently the result of inadequate information or poor coping skills. Therefore, any efforts that may have a positive impact on better prenatal care and caregiving skills are vital.

Transitional Services

Whenever an individual "graduates" from one educational setting to another or from the school to the community, a transition has taken place. The success of a transition is dependent on cooperative planning efforts to prepare individuals with disabilities to function effectively in the "new" setting.

For transitions between two educational placements (such as from a preschool special education program to an elementary school special education program or from a preschool special education program to a regular kindergarten program), the sending teacher, the receiving teacher, and the family must work together to assess the student's changing needs. Family participation regarding placement decisions will facilitate necessary adjustments between schools and home and reduce the stress that these changes may present.

When individuals with physical disabilities are no longer eligible for educational services, advance planning and collaboration are essential to prepare them to make successful transitions into the community. Individuals may be prepared for future work through training programs such as vocational and career education, work-study experiences, and vocational rehabilitation counseling.

Parental Involvement

Because parents are generally the "experts" regarding their children's capabilities, quality programs establish effective partnerships with parents. Such partnerships seek parental assistance in the development of appropriate objectives for their children and in the effective implementation of their children's programs throughout the year. Both PL 94-142 and PL 99-457 empowered parents to participate in the development of the IEP. Furthermore, PL 99-457 required that not only the needs of the young child be identified but that the needs of the family be addressed through the development of the Individualized Family Service Plans as well.

SELECTING AND ADAPTING INSTRUCTIONAL MATERIALS

For individuals with physical disabilities to participate actively in educational, social, recreational/leisure, vocational, and domestic activities, appropriate materials must be developed and selected that promote participation in these activities. Materials must be adapted to overcome the limitations imposed by the particular disability. Many commercially made materials are appropriately designed for use with individuals with physical disabilities. Other materials may need to be modified to accommodate the special requirements of an individual.

In Activity 3, page 392, you are to observe a child with an orthopedic disability performing a motor task in a classroom setting and devise an assistive aid.

When an individual with a disability is unable to complete a task, the instructor must modify the methods and materials in use. By using task analysis and creative problem solving, the instructor may be able to adapt or design materials that enable the individual to complete the task successfully (see Table 13.2). For example, an individual may not be able to put on his or her jacket independently because of the fine motor requirement for zipping. Attaching a larger object to the zipper tab may allow the individual to successfully manipulate the zipper and complete the task independently. Another solution may be to select clothing with velcro fasteners, which also permit greater independence (Bigge, 1982).

Several criteria must be met to ensure that instructional materials facilitate active participation and task completion. These criteria include (a) functionality, (b) match between the motor requirements of the activity and the motor ability of the individual, (c) durability, and (d) age appropriateness.

Functionality

Functionality refers to the degree to which instructional materials allow individuals to operate effectively in activities of daily living. Such materials should be typical for the activity. If standard materials must be modified or new materials developed, they should approximate to the greatest degree possible the material or device that would typically be used by nondisabled individuals.

Match Between Activity and Individual

Because individuals with disabilities have difficulty with gross and fine motor control, materials should be designed with physical features that will enhance the individual's ability to grasp, manipulate, or operate the device. Individuals who have limited strength or who fatigue easily require lightweight and portable aids. Features such as the size of graphics, amount of detail presented, and the use of color may have to be taken into account for individuals with visual impairment or difficulty with visual perceptual skills. For individuals with limb deficiencies, successful participation in activities may require both modification of the activity as well as specially designed instructional materials to promote independent functioning.

Durability

Instructional aids utilized by individuals with disabilities must be durable. They must be constructed to withstand accidental falls, spills, and extensive physical manipulation. Durability of instructional aids may be enhanced by using strong materials, laminating surfaces, and providing for stability of the aid in general use.

Age Appropriateness

Age appropriateness requires that materials be designed or selected with the chronological age of the user in mind. Even though many materials appear to be appropriate relative to an individual's physical and cognitive abilities, these materials should be used only if they are typically used by nondisabled individuals of the same chronological age.

Table 13.2   Examples of Adapted Materials

Environment	Adaptation	Purpose
Education	Book holder	Maintains book in an open position
	Extended levers on tape recorder controls	Allows student to use tape recorder to complete assignments orally
Self-help	Suction cups on bottom of plate	Provides stability by preventing plate from sliding on table surface
	Spoon with swivel handle	Allows individual to reposition food without spillage
Domestic	Flap switch attached to blender	Promotes independent operation of blender
	Substitute knee control for foot pedal on sewing machine	Allows student with below the knee amputation to operate sewing machine
Recreation/leisure	Tricycle with extended back support and velcro straps on foot pedals	Allows child to ride tricycle independently
Vocational	Keyguard for typewriter or computer keyboard	Prevents fingers from hitting more than one key simultaneously

TECHNOLOGY APPLICATIONS

Technology has had a significant effect on the quality of life enjoyed by many people, especially people with physical disabilities. Technological advances have promoted independent functioning of individuals with physical disabilities in a variety of ways. Mobility has been facilitated through the use of well-designed, motorized wheelchairs and other vehicles. Individuals who are nonspeaking may enhance their communication abilities through the use of microprocessor-based communication aids. Many of these devices have synthetic speech output and are flexible and adaptable so they can be reprogrammed as the communication needs of the individual change. If an individual has voluntary control over any one body movement, no matter how small, an appropriate system can be designed to enable that individual to communicate and to exercise control over the environment (Shane & Bashir, 1980). Expanded keyboards and other inputting devices have been designed for individuals with limited fine motor coordination who want to use computers for word processing and data base management. Advancements in robotics and computer-controlled environments continue to allow more independent functioning for many individuals with physical disabilities who prefer to live independently in the community.

SUMMARY THOUGHTS

The effects of physical disabilities manifest themselves in many ways. Some individuals have conditions that affect only their ability to move in a smooth and coordinated fashion. Individuals with associated secondary problems experience sensory impairment, seizure disorders, learning disabilities, mental retardation, or multiple disabilities that affect more than their ability to move effectively.

Valid and reliable assessment of and effective programming for individuals with physical disabilities necessitate involvement and cooperation of all members of a transdisciplinary team. Elimination of architectural barriers, modification of instructional materials, application of technological advances, and use of adaptive equipment enhance individuals' ability to function effectively in least restrictive environments with their nondisabled peers. Until prejudice, stereotypes, and discrimination are eliminated, individuals with disabilities will be prevented from enjoying the full range of rights and privileges to which they are entitled.

REFERENCES

American National Standards Institute. (1986). *American National Standard for Buildings and Facilities—Providing Accessibility and Usability for Physically Handicapped People.* NY: Author, A-117.1.

Batshaw, M. L., & Perret, Y. M. (1986). *Children with handicaps: A medical primer.* (2nd ed.). Baltimore, MD: Brookes.

Baumgart, D., Brown, L., Pumpian, I., Nisbet, J., Sweet, M., Messina, R., & Schroeder, J. (1982). The principle of partial participation and individualized adaptations in education programs for severely handicapped students. *Journal of the Association for the Severely Handicapped, 7*(2), 17–27.

Benns, H. (1985). Untitled, unpublished poem. Buffalo, NY.

Bigge, J. L. (1982). *Teaching individuals with physical and multiple disabilities* (2nd ed.). Columbus, OH: Merrill.

Bleck, E. E. (1982a). Cerebral palsy. In E. E. Bleck & D. A. Nagel (Eds.), *Physically handicapped children: A medical atlas for teachers* (2nd ed.) (pp. 59–132). New York: Grune & Stratton.

Bleck, E. E. (1982b). Muscular dystrophy—Duchenne type. In E. E. Bleck & D. A. Nagel (Eds.), *Physically handicapped children: A medical atlas for teachers* (2nd ed.) (pp. 385–394). New York: Grune & Stratton.

Bleck, E. E. (1982c). Myelomeningocele, meningocele, and spina bifida. In E. E. Bleck & D. A. Nagel (Eds.), *Physically handicapped children: A medical atlas for teachers* (2nd ed.) (pp. 345–362). New York: Grune & Stratton.

Bleck, E. E. (1982d). Osteogenesis imperfecta. In E. E. Bleck & D. A. Nagel (Eds.), *Physically handicapped children: A medical atlas for teachers* (2nd ed.) (pp. 405–412). New York: Grune & Stratton.

Bleck, E. E., and Nagel, D. A. (Eds.). (1982). *Physically handicapped children: A medical atlas for teachers* (2nd ed.). New York: Grune & Stratton.

Brooks, M. B. (1983). Limb deficiencies. In J. Umbreit (Ed.), *Physical disabilities and health impairments: An introduction* (pp. 93–107). Columbus, OH: Merrill.

California Department of Health (1977). *Management Briefs, 3*(2).

Connor, F. P., Scandary, J., & Tulloch, D. (1988). Education of physically handicapped and health impaired individuals: A commitment to the future. *Division of the Physically Handicapped Journal, 10*(1), 5–24.

DeFelice, R. J. (1986, November 8). A crippled child grows up. *Newsweek,* p. 13.

Esposito, B. G., & Reed, T. M. (1986). The effects of contact with handicapped persons on young children's attitude. *Exceptional Children, 53,* 224–229.

Finnie, N. R. (1975). *Handling the young cerebral palsied child at home* (2nd ed.). New York: Dutton.

Hardman, J. L., Drew, C. J., & Egan, M. W. (1984). *Human exceptionality: Society, school and family.* Boston: Allyn & Bacon.

Harryman, S. E. (1986). Cerebral palsy. In M. L. Batshaw & Y. M. Perret, *Children with handicaps: A medical primer* (2nd ed.) (pp. 299–323). Baltimore, MD: Brookes.

Miller, J. J. (1982). Juvenile rheumatoid arthritis. In E. E. Bleck & D. A. Nagel (Eds.), *Physically handicapped children: A medical atlas for teachers* (2nd ed.) (pp. 423–430). New York: Grune & Stratton.

Nagel, D. A. (1982). Temporary orthopedic disabilities in children. In E. E. Bleck & D. A. Nagel (Eds.), *Physically handicapped children: A medical atlas for teachers* (2nd ed.) (pp. 395–403). New York: Grune & Stratton.

Orelove, F. P., and Sobsey, D. (1987). *Educating children with multiple disabilities: A transdisciplinary approach.* Baltimore, MD: Brookes.

Peterson, N. L. (1987). *Early intervention for handicapped and at-risk children: An introduction to early childhood special education.* Denver: Love.

Seligman, M. E. P. (1975). *Helplessness: On depression, development, and death.* New York: Freeman.

Shane, H. (1979, May). Decision making in early augmentative communication system use. Paper presented at the meeting of the Early Intervention Conference, Sturbridge, Massachusetts.

Shane, H., & Bashir, A. (1980). Election criteria for determining candidacy for an augmentative communication system: Preliminary considerations. *Journal of Speech and Hearing Disorders, 45,* 408–414.

Sirvis, B. (1988). Students with special health care needs. *Teaching Exceptional Children, 20*(4), 40–44.

Umbreit, J. (Ed.). (1983). *Physical disabilities and health impairments: An introduction.* Columbus, OH: Merrill.

U.S. Department of Education (1987). *Ninth annual report to Congress on the implementation of the Education of the Handicapped Act.* Washington, DC: GPO.

Wolraich, M. L. (1984). Seizure disorders. In J. A. Blackman (Ed.), *Medical aspects of developmental disabilities in children birth to three* (pp. 297–323). Rockville, MD: Aspen.

Wright, B. (1983). *Physical disability—a psychological approach* (2nd ed.). New York: Harper & Row.

ADDITIONAL READINGS

Bigler, E. (Ed.). (1990). *Traumatic brain injury.* Austin, TX: Pro-Ed.

Bleck, E. (1987). *Orthopaedic management in cerebral palsy.* Philadelphia, PA: Mac Keith Press.

Bobath, B. (1985). *Abnormal postural reflex activity caused by brain lesions* (3rd ed.). Rockville, MD: Aspen.

Brotherson, M. J., Goldfarb, L., Summers, J. A., & Turnbull, A. (1986). *Meeting the challenge of disability or chronic illness—a family guide.* Baltimore, MD: Brookes.

Brown, A. (1987). *Active games for children with movement problems.* Wolfeboro, NH: Teachers College Press.

Connor, F., Siepp, J., & Williamson, G. (1978). *Program guide for infants and toddlers with neuromotor and other developmental disabilities.* Wolfeboro, NH: Teachers College Press.

Cotta, H., Friedmann, L., Heipertz, W. Koester, G., Marquardt, E., Puhl, W., Rompe, G., & tum Suden-Weickmann, A. (1987). *Orthopedics.* Rockville, MD: Aspen.

Flynn, J. (1986). *Coming to terms with disabilities—a compilation of vocabulary relating to visible and non-visible disabilities.* Albany, NY.

Fraser, B., Hensinger, R., & Phelps, J. (1987). *Physical management of multiple handicaps—a professional's guide.* Baltimore, MD: Brookes.

Garwood, S., & Sheehan, R. (1989). *Designing a comprehensive early intervention system.* Austin, TX: Pro-Ed.

Hanson, M., & Lynch, E. (1989). *Early intervention—implementing child and family services for infants and toddlers who are at-risk or disabled.* Austin, TX: Pro-Ed.

Liebman, M. (1986). *Neuroanatomy made easy and understandable* (3rd ed.). Rockville, MD: Aspen.

Lindsay, J., Ounst, C., & Richards, P. (1988). *Temporal lobe epilepsy.* Philadelphia, PA: Mac Keith Press.

Strickland, B., & Turnbull, A. (1990). *Developing and implementing individualized education programs* (3rd ed.). Columbus, OH: Merrill.

Williamson, G., & Szczepanski, M. (1987). *Children with spina bifida—early intervention and preschool programming.* Baltimore, MD: Brookes.

Zimmerman, J. (1988). *Goals and objectives for developing normal movement patterns.* Rockville, MD: Aspen.

Purpose

☐ To help you identify characteristics of a child with physical disabilities

☐ To increase your awareness of potential modifications necessary for an accurate assessment of the child's abilities

Steps

1. Identify a child with physical disabilities.
2. Arrange to observe the child in a home or school setting for 30 minutes.
3. Record your observations on the accompanying form.
4. At the end of the observation period, check the appropriate column on the right side of the recording form to reflect potential modifications of an assessment procedure.

Analysis

☐ Based on your knowledge of assessment procedures, which of the child's demonstrated disabilities could most seriously affect the results of an evaluation?

☐ What are the child's major ability areas?

☐ Could the child's abilities be used to circumvent his or her disabilities? How could this be done?

Characteristics of a Child with Physical Disabilities

Name _____   Date of Observation _____

Student's Name _____   Setting_____

Student's Age _____

	Modification Required	
Observe:	Yes	No
1. Gross Motor Skill _____ _____ _____ _____ _____	____	____
2. Fine Motor Skill (Speed and Accuracy) _____ _____ _____ _____	____	____
3. Mode/Level of Communication_____ _____ _____ _____	____	____
4. Interaction with Others: Adults_____ _____ Children _____ _____	____	____
5. Variety and Attention to Tasks _____ _____ _____ _____		

Comments on any special equipment the child used, adaptations initiated by the child, general level of physical independence, etc. _____
_____
_____
_____
_____
_____
_____

2

Purpose

☐ To increase your awareness of architectural barriers in typical buildings.

☐ To provide you with experience in evaluating the accessibility of buildings and facilities for individuals in wheelchairs.

Steps

1. Select a building or classroom to survey, and make the necessary arrangements to do so.

2. Assemble survey materials—the accompanying checklist (pages 390–391) and a tape measure.

3. Consult the checklist and survey appropriate areas, recording your answers as you go along.

Analysis

☐ What areas are not accessible to individuals in wheelchairs?

☐ What hazards exist?

☐ What simple modifications can be made to eliminate barriers or hazards?

☐ What major construction modifications are necessary for total accessibility?

CHECKLIST

Architectural Barriers and Environmental Hazards

Name _____   Date _____

Area(s) or Building Surveyed _____

		Yes	No
A. *Entrances/Exits*			
1. Is at least one primary entrance to the building usable by individuals in wheelchairs?		___	___
2. Do ramps have a slope no greater than a 1' rise in 12'?		___	___
B. *Doors and Doorways*			
1. Do doors have a clear opening of no less than 32" wide when open?		___	___
2. Are doors operable with minimal strength or pressure?		___	___
3. Do doors close slowly enough for use by persons who are disabled?		___	___
4. Are door handles easily manipulated?		___	___
C. *Stairs and Steps*			
1. Are handrails at appropriate heights for users?		___	___
2. Do handrails extend at least 18" beyond the top and bottom of steps? (necessary distance for individuals using crutches to adjust crutch balance)		___	___
3. Do steps each rise 7" or less?		___	___
4. Do steps have a nonslip surface?		___	___
D. *Floors*			
1. Are all floors on each story at a common level or connected by ramps or elevators?		___	___
2. Do floors have a nonslip surface?		___	___
E. *Restrooms*			
1. Do toilet rooms have a turning space of 60" x 60" to allow use by individuals in wheelchairs?		___	___
2. Do toilet rooms have at least one stall that is accessible...			
a. door at least 32" wide that opens out?		___	___
b. stall size at least 3' x 5'?		___	___
c. grab bars on each side at appropriate height and parallel to floor?		___	___
d. paper roll at reachable distance?		___	___
3. Are lavatories accessible to individuals in wheelchairs...			
a. mounted 30" from floor to accommodate wheelchair arms?		___	___
b. water controls easily activated and mounted close to front?		___	___
c. towel dispenser mounted no higher than 40" from floor?		___	___

F. *Water Fountains*
   1. Are water spouts no higher than 36" from floor?   ____ ____
   2. Do fountains have up-front spouts and controls?   ____ ____

G. *Public Telephones* (if applicable)
   1. Can individuals with physical disablities get into phone area? (large booth without accordion doors or wall mounted)   ____ ____
   2. Is height of dial (buttons) 48" or less from floor?   ____ ____
   3. Is coin slot 48" or less from floor?   ____ ____

H. *Elevators* (if applicable)
   1. Are elevators available in buildings of more than one story?   ____ ____
   2. Is cab at least 5' x 5'?   ____ ____
   3. Are controls 48" or less from floor?   ____ ____
   4. Are buttons easy to push or touch-sensitive?   ____ ____

I. *Classroom Accessibility* (if applicable)
   1. Is classroom door at least 32" wide when open?   ____ ____
   2. Is threshold low enough for a wheelchair to pass over easily?   ____ ____
   3. Are desks arranged so aisles are at least 36" wide?   ____ ____
   4. Is there a turning space at least 5' x 5' at front and back of room?   ____ ____
   5. Are bookshelves and chalkboards no higher than 36" from the floor?   ____ ____
   6. Are grab bars present in at least one chalkboard area?   ____ ____
   7. Is there a desk or table area to accommodate a wheelchair?   ____ ____
   8. Are sinks, work areas, and other special areas accessible to students with disabilities?   ____ ____
   9. Is the classroom area safe from potential hazards...
      a. floor free from small objects and litter?   ____ ____
      b. no sharp corners and protruding objects?   ____ ____
      c. nonslip floor surfaces?   ____ ____

┌─────────┐
│   3   │
└─────────┘

Purpose

☐ To promote your skill in observing and recording sequential motor movements of someone who has an orthopedic disability

☐ To challenge your ability to create an original assistive device to overcome a specific motor problem

Steps

1. Identify a child with an orthopedic disability that includes limited upper extremity control.

2. Arrange to observe the child while he or she attempts to complete a task in order to determine what specific problem exists.

3. During the observation, record information about motor abilities on the accompanying form.

4. Likewise, record information on motor problems.

Analysis

☐ Analyze your observation data as to successful movements and where motor performance failed. (Question why the motor problems occurred. Grasp? Lost postural control? Could not cross midline of body?)

☐ Consider more than one possible solution.

☐ Experiment with potential solutions.

☐ Determine the "best" solution.

(optional)

☐ Instruct the child in how to use the assistive device or method.

☐ Observe the child and make modifications if necessary.

Developing An Assistive Device

Name _____   Date _____

Child's Name _____   Setting_____

Statement of the problem: _____

_____

_____

Motor Abilities   Motor Problems

1.   1.

2.   2.

3.   3.

4.   4.

Why did motor problem occur? _____

_____

_____

_____

Possible solutions:

1.

2.

3.

"Best" solution:

Materials needed for "best" solution: _____

_____

_____

Steps in instructing the child to use the device:

1.

2.

3.

4.

5.

6.

Mental Retardation

Roland K. Yoshida
Queens College—City University of New York

MENTAL RETARDATION
TYPICAL PROFILE

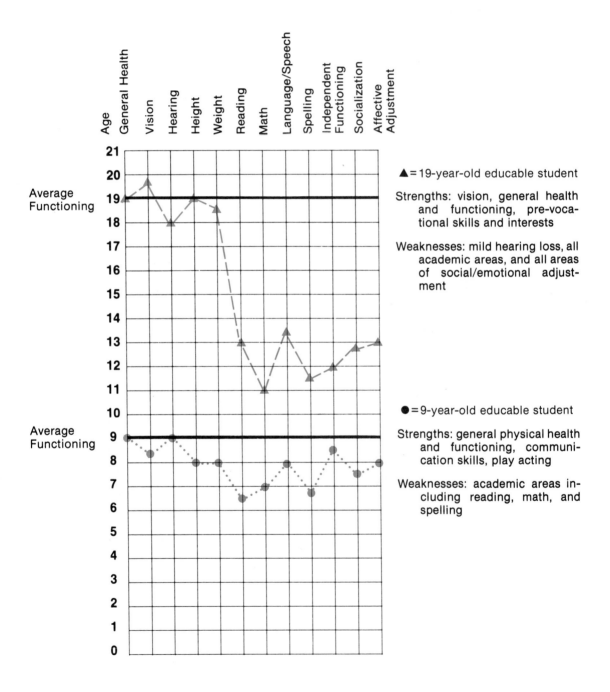

▲ = 19-year-old educable student

Strengths: vision, general health and functioning, pre-vocational skills and interests

Weaknesses: mild hearing loss, all academic areas, and all areas of social/emotional adjustment

● = 9-year-old educable student

Strengths: general physical health and functioning, communication skills, play acting

Weaknesses: academic areas including reading, math, and spelling

What image comes to mind when you hear the words *mental retardation*? If you are like most Americans, you probably think about someone who looks different from most other people, such as a person with Down syndrome. You may think about a person who cannot speak, read, and write well. You may remember friends who have to care for their grown children because they are unable to live by themselves. You may think of some television show or motion picture that portrays the lives of persons with mental retardation, such as the Bennie Stolwitz character on "LA Law," NBC's popular drama.

Although each of these images holds a grain of truth, making generalizations about a large number of persons is dangerous. For example, the most common error is to believe that most persons with mental retardation are severely or profoundly handicapped. This degree of retardation is found in less than 5% of all persons classified as mentally retarded. Another misconception is that persons with retardation cannot live independently in the community. Some do and live productive lives as taxpaying citizens with families. In short, no stereotype of persons with mental retardation accurately and fully describes this group. Rather, the skills and behaviors exhibited by these persons are as diverse as those found in the so-called normal population.

The key to relationships with persons with mental retardation is a short but oftentimes forgotten list of principles that should be your credo. Keep these principles in mind as you wrestle with the issues discussed in this chapter.

1. Every person has value.
2. Every person should be treated with dignity and respect.
3. Every person is capable of growth and learning through community experiences.
4. Every person should experience life in the most natural settings.
5. Every person has the right to be the primary decision maker in his or her life and carries the responsibility for the direction it takes.
6. Every person is protected by the full weight of the Constitution and its amendments (Rucker, 1987, p. 125).

HISTORY OF EDUCATION OF PERSONS WITH MENTAL RETARDATION

The early efforts in educating persons with mental retardation began in the early 1800s with the hope that any person could be taught. Itard (1774–1838) worked for 5 years with the "wild boy of Aveyron," a young boy found in the woods who was capable of making only animal-like sounds. He introduced the boy to daily lessons of handling objects and naming them. (These activities are similar to what we now do in early childhood education programs.) His goal was to improve the wild boy's speech. Although his efforts did not fully succeed, they stimulated interest in others for developing instructional methods for children with learning problems.

Seguin (1812–1880), one of Itard's student teachers, believed that in order to cure persons with retardation, they should be given the benefits of education. He established one of the first publicly supported schools for children with severe mental retardation. Seguin eventually emigrated to the United States and in 1876 helped form the organization that is now known as the American Association on Mental Retardation (AAMR) (formerly, the American Association on Mental Deficiency). He was elected the first president of the organization.

Itard's and Seguin's contributions to the field of mental retardation cannot be overstated. They advanced the philosophy that a structured educational experience should be available to persons with mental retardation. Their instructional techniques were forerunners of Montessori methods and of the diagnostic-prescriptive process, one approach for developing individualized educational programs. Although these pioneers did not serve many children, they set the foundation for the principle that persons with mental retardation can learn with the benefit of good instruction.

The Eugenics Movement

In the early 1900s, this positive attitude gave way to an era in which the rights of persons with mental retardation were generally curtailed. Basically, the idea that mental retardation was primarily genetically transmitted took hold. For example, Goddard (1912) presented the case of Martin Kallikak, a revolutionary soldier. Kallikak fathered an illegitimate son by a girl who was thought to be mentally retarded. The descendants of that union were found to have high rates of criminality. In contrast, descendants of his wife generally achieved high status positions as doctors, lawyers, and educators. Goddard concluded that if persons with mental retardation continued to reproduce, their offspring would pose a grave threat to social order. One way to control reproduction was to sterilize these individuals in the hope that the number of persons with retardation would eventually be reduced. In some states, sterilizations were performed on persons said to be mentally retarded without their consent. Such sterilizations were performed even into the 1970s.

During the same period, institutions were established in areas away from population centers to serve persons with severe mental retardation. Although the original mission of many of these institutions was similar to that of Itard and Seguin (that is, treatment and rehabilitation), the institutions soon espoused goals consistent with a tenet of the eugenics movement—that is, protect society from the negative influences of persons with mental retardation. Institutions provided basic medical care but did very little in providing persons under their care with the most rudimentary self-help skills such as grooming. In general, evidence accumulated that persons placed in institutions were not developing as well as those living at home or in the community. With the discovery that several institutions were unfit places to live (Blatt & Kaplan, 1966), pressure mounted to dismantle institutions and place their residents in settings as close as possible to those of persons in the community in the hope that persons with mental retardation would have the opportunity to model "typical or normal" behaviors. This way of thinking was known as *normalization.*

Special Class Placements

A parallel development occurred with persons with mild retardation. As education was more widely offered, educators became concerned about students who were unable to keep up with most of the children in school. One solution for handling this situation was to remove these students from the elementary and secondary programs and to provide them with alternative curricula. The motives for advocating this approach ranged from protecting "normal" learners from "misfits" (which was advocated by Louis Terman, who introduced the Stanford-Binet Intelligence Test in America) to helping slow learners develop their capabilities to the fullest. Regardless of the motives, special programs emphasized preparing slow learning students for the workplace rather than presenting them with the increasingly verbal and abstract academic curriculum. The number of students enrolled in these programs rose from 23,000 in 1922 to more than 400,000 by 1963. (MacMillan [1982] presented an excellent discussion of these historical trends.)

These programs were mostly grounded in the sincere belief that more meaningful subject matter was being presented to persons with mild mental retardation than would have been presented in the regular academic program. Educators also thought that these students were being protected from continual failure and rejection by peers in the academic program. An extensive series of studies, known as the efficiency studies, sought to determine the effectiveness of segregating students into these programs as opposed to leaving them in regular programs. According to these studies, children with mild retardation assigned to regular classes generally did better in academic achievement than did those in special classes; the results for social adjustment and postschool adjustment were varied. The results did not show a consistent advantage of special class placement. Coupled with overwhelming evidence of the disproportionate numbers of minority students in these classes, educators increasingly questioned the policy of supporting special classes for persons with mild retardation. Many articles were written on the subject, but Dunn's article (1968) seemed to catalyze the profession to consider mainstreaming (the principle of placing exceptional children in regular classrooms with special assistance, if necessary) as the preferred approach for educating children with mild retardation.

Mainstreaming

Parent organizations such as the National Association of Retarded Citizens provided political support for changes in how children with mental retardation were to be educated. The PL 94-142 requirement of the least restrictive environment provided a legal foundation for efforts to provide noninstitutional placements for persons with severe mental retardation and to mainstream students when they attend school. (Roos [1983] presented a concise history of activism by parents of persons with mental retardation.)

We are currently in an era in which the positive principle of providing an appropriate education for persons with mental retardation guides our thinking. But the enlightened policy of today may change back to the restrictive policies of the early to mid-1950s. Professionals such as yourselves must believe in the principle that all persons can learn and, if possible, be part of their communities. By doing so, you support the thinking that resulted in the types of programs currently available to persons with mental retardation.

Negative Labeling

You have probably noticed that I use the term *persons with mental retardation.* Since 1960, professionals have become more sensitive in how they refer to persons with mental retardation. This change is part of the whole movement to reduce the negative impact of being labeled with mental retardation.

Until the 1950s, the professional literature used harsh terms such as "moron," "imbecile," and "idiot." The authors of the major intelligence tests, Wechsler (1949) and Terman and Merrill (1960), referred to persons with IQs below 70 as mental defectives. Research articles in the *American Journal on Mental Deficiency* used the term *retardate.* These terms became part of the layperson's speech. For example, a recent episode of "LA Law" showed attorney Arnie Becker referring to Bernie Stolwitz, a person with mental retardation, as a moron. Many professionals even find more neutral terms—the educable mentally retarded (EMR), the trainable mentally retarded (TMR), and the severely and profoundly mentally retarded (SPMR) (see MacMillan, 1982)—to be unacceptable because they imply an all-encompassing condition. The descriptor "mentally retarded" becomes the only way in which we think of the person. As a result, we come to assume that the person is incapable of doing much. The preferred terminology is the one used in this chapter—person with mental retardation. This term suggests that mental retardation is one of many qualities, albeit an important one. Professionals must remember to be careful in referring to children and adults with mental retardation. Some labels have evident negative meanings, whereas others are more subtle in communicating a negative meaning.

CHARACTERISTICS OF CHILDREN AND YOUTH WITH MENTAL RETARDATION

When children are born, we initially identify them by their names, sex, ethnic origin, hair color, and other physical characteristics. Our common reaction to the row of newborns in the maternity ward is to exclaim how cute and lovable each of those babies is. We are happy for the parents that their babies are healthy and have a wonderful future.

For a few babies, their futures are not so bright. They may experience physical, emotional, and learning problems as they grow. Several questions arise. What are the problems? Are they severe enough that the children should be labeled with a handicapping condition such as mental retardation? Do these children need special services to help them succeed?

In 1959, a group of professionals from the American Association on Mental Deficiency (now the American Association on Mental Retardation) produced what has become the basis for the most widely accepted definition of mental retardation. Its most recent version, published in 1983, is as follows: "Mental retardation refers to significantly subaverage general intellectual functioning resulting in or associated with concurrent impairments in adaptive behavior and manifested during the developmental period" (Grossman, 1983, p. 11).

PL 94-142 used the AAMR definition and added a phrase that emphasized mental retardation's effects on a child's educational performance. This difference was probably the result of the law's focus on the education of children and adolescents until age 21. The AAMR definition implies that mental retardation can exist in the adult population but that adults with mental retardation must have been labeled during the developmental period that AAMR defines as 18 years or younger. The inclusion of the developmental period criterion helps to distinguish mental retardation from other conditions found in adulthood that are manifested by low intellectual functioning or maladaptive behavior.

Intelligence Tests

Intellectual functioning basically refers to intelligence as measured by an individually administered intelligence test. The most commonly used tests are the Wechsler Intelligence Scale for Children—Revised (Wechsler, 1974) and the Stanford-Binet Intelligence Scale, Fourth Edition (Thorndike, Hagen, & Sattler, 1986). The WISC-R yields a deviation intelligence quotient through which an individual's score relative to others of similar chronological age can be compared; the Stanford-Binet produces a composite score (CS) that is interpreted like an IQ. An IQ of 100 means that student's standing is at the very middle of the group, half of the group having higher scores and half having lower ones. The standard deviation (the measure of how different the scores are from one another) of the WISC-R and Stanford-Binet are 15 and 16, respectively. An IQ of 70 is 2 standard deviations below the mean on the WISC-R, which means that in a group of 100 students (normally distributed), approximately 2 students score at or below this IQ and 98 score above this level. The AAMR recommends using IQ levels of below 70 on the WISC-R and CS below 68 on the Stanford-Binet as the criterion for "significantly subaverage general intellectual functioning." These levels may vary usually higher depending upon state definitions.

The AAMR further divides the IQ/CS range into four levels, mild, moderate, severe, and profound. The standard deviations and range of IQ/CS for successive levels of mental retardation are as follows: mild (SD = –2.01 to –3.00; IQ = 69–55; CS = 67–52), moderate (SD = –3.01 to –4.00, IQ = 54–40; CS = 51–36), severe (SD = –4.01 to –5.00, IQ = 39–25; CS = 35–20), and profound (SD = below –5.00, IQ = below 25; CS = below 20).

Adaptive Behavior

Adaptive behavior means the extent to which children meet the expectations for personal independence and social responsibilities for their age and cultural group (Grossman, 1983). Grossman (1983) presented the following list of adaptive behaviors:

During infancy and early childhood in:
1. Sensory-motor skills development
2. Communication skills (including speech and language)
3. Self-help skills
4. Socialization (development of ability to interact with others)

During childhood and early adolescence in:
5. Application of basic academic skills in daily life activities
6. Application of appropriate reasoning and judgment in mastery of the environment
7. Social skills (participation in group activities and interpersonal relationships)

During late adolescence and adult life in:
8. Vocational and social responsibilities and performances (p. 25)

Let us add real life examples to this list. When you get up in the morning, what do you do to prepare yourself for the day? You probably take a shower, brush your teeth, comb your hair, dress yourself, and make breakfast (if you did not press the snooze alarm). How about making change, taking public transportation, buying food, making dinner, or doing the laundry? These surprisingly simple tasks are adaptive behaviors that some children and adults are unable to perform. Depending on the children's ages, the inability to do these tasks could result in an assessment to determine whether mental retardation is present.

Prevalence

This brief discussion of the definition may lead you to conclude that determining which persons should be classified with mental retardation is a straightforward matter. As you know by now in your daily experience, life is never this tidy. Table 14.1 presents the *prevalence* (the number of persons at a given point in time) of children in special education and the number with mental retardation. California has the most children in special education because it is the largest state in terms of children in school. Now compare the number of children with mental retardation in California and Florida. The numbers are nearly the same, but California has more than twice the number of students in special education than Florida does. Yet only 7.11% of California's special education children are labeled with mental retardation in comparison to 14.65% of Florida's. Five states labeled more than 20% of their students with mental retardation: Ohio, 25.64%; Massachusetts, 21.33%; Indiana, 21.13%; Pennsylvania, 20.86%; and North Carolina, 20.58%. Four labeled less than 10%: New Jersey, 4.48%; California, 7.11%; Texas, 9.45%; and New York, 9.72%.

How do we account for these disparities? First, the AAMR and PL 94-142 definitions are sufficiently general, which allow states considerable latitude in defining mental retardation. For example, a state with an IQ cutoff of 85 has a different number of children eligible for the mental retardation label than does a state with a 70 cutoff. Second, professionals may prefer to attach a less derogatory label to some children. Surveys have documented the dramatic rise in the number of children labeled with learning disabilities and the corresponding decrease in the number of children labeled with mental retardation. Such practices may be tolerated in some states and not in others. Third, some states, such as California, have suspended the use of intelligence tests as the basis for determining intellectual functioning because courts have ruled that intelligence tests are biased against certain ethnic groups. Fourth, children's adaptive behavior must be judged in reference to the children's cultural group (Grossman, 1983).

What happens when children seem to be experiencing problems in school, such as not getting along with peers or teachers, but appear to be like most of the children in their neighborhood? For example, you talk with your fellow teachers about particular students with diverse ethnic backgrounds who were referred for assessment. The teachers are convinced that these children should be labeled mentally retarded. The children's parents may be puzzled by the use of the mental retardation label because their children are able to go to school on their own, shop at the store, and talk like the other children in the neighhborhood. The difference in teach-

Table 14.1   Prevalence of Children with Mental Retardation, 1986-87[a]

States	Number of Students in Special Education	Number of Students with Mental Retardation	Percentage of Special Education Students with Mental Retardation
California	391,217	27,798	7.11
Florida	181,651	26,615	14.65
Illinois	248,169	31,683	12.77
Indiana	105,978	22,398	21.13
Massachusetts	143,636	30,644	21.33
Michigan	161,446	22,717	14.07
New Jersey	172,018	7,713	4.48
New York	292,981	28,480	9.72
North Carolina	109,214	22,476	20.58
Ohio	199,211	51,083	25.64
Pennsylvania	203,258	42,405	20.86
Texas	301,222	28,479	9.45
Virginia	103,727	14,528	14.01

[a]For states with more than 100,000 students enrolled in special education.

Source: U.S. Department of Education (1988, p. B-3).

ers' and parents' attributions illustrates the need for you to be sensitive to how different cultural backgrounds may affect the perception of social competence.

This short discussion does not list all the reasons for the variation in percentages from state to state. Although there is a professional and legal definition of mental retardation, that definition may take many different forms in practice depending upon the state/community and can change over time.

> Activity 1, page 421, asks you to find out if people in your community have different conceptions about whom should be classified with mental retardation. These conceptions will influence the decision-making process in your school district when assessing children.

Educable Mentally Retarded

Public schools have usually called children with mild retardation *educable mentally retarded*. Until the 1970s, a common generalization held that most children with mild retardation were not identified until they were in school and did not retain the label of mental retardation once they graduated from school. This view of mild retardation led to the popular image in the 1960s of the "6 hour retarded child"—the child who was retarded during the school day but not in the commu-

Educable mentally retarded children have fun like all other children.

nity. Nevertheless, Forness and Polloway (1987) found that many children labeled EMR had multiple disabilities and required services beyond those provided in classroom programs.

What led to the change in characteristics of children labeled with mild retardation? First, Dunn (1968), among others, raised doubts about whether stigmatizing students with a negative label was worth the costs given the lack of clear advantages with special class placement. Second, the disproportionate number of minority group members labeled mentally retarded led to court cases that focused on the issue of whether the labeling process, specifically the use of intelligence tests, was discriminatory. In an early response to this issue, California declassified several thousand EMR students by lowering the IQ cutoff to 70. Thus, children with IQs above 70 were no longer considered EMR. The intent of this action was to remove from special education students who were thought to have erroneously been labeled by the use of a biased assessment instrument. Unfortunately, the state did not consider whether these students were receiving an appropriate program. Third, and coincidentally, the AAMR lowered the IQ ceiling for mental retardation status from 85 to 70. This change significantly reduced the number of students who could be labeled as mentally retarded. Fourth, studies demonstrated that some students with moderate levels of retardation were enrolled in classes for the EMR.

Research concerning the current composition of EMR classes is in its infancy. Most current research in mental retardation focuses on persons with more severe levels of retardation. We do know that recently labeled students with mild retardation are more likely to exhibit behavioral and emotional problems than their non-handicapped peers are (Polloway & Smith, 1988). We can speculate that if more currently enrolled students in EMR classrooms show moderate levels of retardation, teachers should expect these students to need intensive instruction in oral language and social skills development.

Teachers should also be concerned with the motivation of children with mild retardation to complete tasks correctly. When children with mental retardation succeed, they tend to believe that luck played a major part. They attribute their lack of ability to do the task as the cause of failure. Children not labeled with retardation attribute success primarily to their ability and secondarily to their effort; they usually blame the difficulty of the task for failure. Thus, children with mental retardation generally have little confidence in themselves in performing tasks.

Trainable Mentally Retarded

Children with moderate retardation—about 6% of those labeled with mental retardation—are placed in classes for the trainable mentally retarded. The concept of TMR derives from the belief that these children cannot learn academic skills but can be trained to recognize important words such as stop and exit, to identify the denominations of coins and make change for a dollar bill, and to perform repetitive tasks such as sweeping floors. Many of these children are identified before entering school because this level of retardation is usually associated with some physical problem. Before PL 94-142, many persons with moderate retardation were placed in institutions or in no program at all. Most are now enrolled in public schools. Although some persons with moderate retardation can become self-supporting, most will require some degree of supervision during their lifetimes.

Severely/Profoundly Mentally Retarded

The remaining 5% of persons with mental retardation are at the severe and profound level. At SPMR levels, most of the persons with retardation also have serious physical conditions ranging from central nervous system impairment to cerebral palsy, blindness, and deafness. (MacMillan [1982] provided an overview of the physical and genetic causes of retardation.) These children are identified early in life and may require extensive medical attention. Children with severe retardation are able to acquire self-help skills and perhaps work in shelter workshops under close supervision. These children are more frequently enrolled in public schools than in the past, although they are in separate classes or special schools. But children with profound retardation are nonambulatory (unable to walk) and quite often show stereotypical behaviors such as rocking and self-mutilation behaviors such as biting body parts. These children are able to learn some self-help skills and through carefully developed programs are able to reduce stereotypical behaviors. Nevertheless, most of these children require close supervision with a considerable amount of medical attention.

BASIC PROFESSIONAL VOCABULARY

In addition to terms that have or will be introduced in this chapter, the following are often used when discussing persons with mental retardation. This list is not exhaustive.

Criterion referent refers to assessment instruments or tasks designed to compare the performance of an individual against a set standard. The individual's performance is judged on mastering the task and is not compared in relation to performance of a norm group. Teachers frequently use this form of evaluation when they measure whether students have accomplished the goals of the IEP.

Cultural familial was a term generally used before 1970 to describe persons with mild retardation who showed no obvious physical disabilities associated with retardation but whose family had a history of retardation. The direct cause of retardation could not be determined.

Developmental disabilities, such as defined by PL 95-602, refers to mental or physical impairments likely to be permanent, developed before a person reaches age 22, and resulting in limitations in several areas of independent functioning.

Environment in its broadest sense means the physical, cultural, and social conditions that influence the life of an individual or group. *Nurture* has been used as a synonymous term in the psychological literature. Specific examples of environmental influences are poverty, nutrition, and classroom instruction. Environment is currently thought to be a substantial contributor to the development of persons with mental retardation.

Heredity refers to the genetically inherited qualities of individuals. *Nature* is a substitute term. In the past, psychologists believed that heredity primarily governed the developmental process. Thus, a person's intelligence was viewed as fixed—genetically predetermined at conception and unchangeable.

Norm referent refers to assessment instruments designed to compare the performance of an individual against the levels of performance of a sample of persons on the same test. The intelligence tests discussed in this chapter are examples of this form of assessment.

Norms denote the average performance of a sample of persons on a test. This use of the term is often confused with the incorrect interpretation of "norm" to mean what we believe should be the levels of performance.

Standardized tests are those for which uniform procedures are followed during administration. Deviations from these procedures may compromise the integrity of the results. The tests specifically mentioned in this chapter are standardized.

ASSESSING INSTRUCTIONAL NEED

The first component in the definition of mental retardation is intellectual functioning. What does this term mean? Ask five of your friends what they mean by intelligence. You will probably discover that they can tell you what people do to appear intelligent but cannot tell you exactly what intelligence is. According to MacMillan (1982), three definitional themes of intelligence appear often in the literature: (a) the capacity to learn, (b the totality of knowledge acquired, and (c) the adaptability of the individual, particularly to new situations. But no definition has received total support among psychologists, educators, or members of the community.

How do we go about measuring a concept that engenders disagreement about what it is? Intelligence testing belongs to a long evolutionary process that owes its origins to Binet and Simon in the early 1900s. Paris school authorities presented them with the problem of devising a method for predicting the extent to which students would be successful in school. Those students who scored poorly on these tests would be removed from the regular schools and placed in special schools.

Binet and Simon based their tests on school content. Their tests were found to have *predictive validity*—that is, those students who scored poorly on their tests were rated by teachers to be "dull" students and those with higher scores to be "bright." The tests were also *reliable*—that is, students tended to get similar scores on repeated testing. Thus, confidence grew that these tests measured those children who could profit from instruction in school.

Stanford-Binet Intelligence Scale

These tests were imported to the United States and were modified into the Stanford-Binet Intelligence Scale. (Sattler [1988] provided an extensive history of developing currently used intelligence tests.) The Stanford-Binet can be used for children from age 2 through adults. It is organized into 15 subtests that basically measure verbal reasoning, abstract/visual reading, quantitative reasoning, and short-term memory. The examiner attempts to establish a *basal level* at which the questions are challenging to the child but can be answered. Questioning proceeds until the child is unable to answer any of the questions at a particular level; the level at which this occurs is called the *ceiling*. Credit is given for each correct response. The *raw score* (total number correct) in each subtest is converted into a *scale score* that represents the relative standing of the scores against the scores of a group of similarly aged peers. These scale scores are then used to calculate the composite score.

Wechsler Scales

The Wechsler scales are organized differently from the Stanford-Binet. The 12 subtests are divided into two major sections. Each section contains 5 subtests and 1 optional subtest. The verbal section includes the subtests of information, similarities, arithmetic, vocabulary, comprehension, and digit span (optional). The performance section is composed of picture completion, picture arrangement, block design, object assembly, coding, and mazes (optional). Items are ordered from easy to difficult. The similarities subtest, for example, asks the respondent how X and Y are alike. The picture completion subtest represents a picture of an object such as a brush with its bristles missing; the respondent points out what is missing. The number correct from each subtest is transformed into scores from a table and totaled for a verbal, performance, and full-scale score. These scores are then converted to IQs.

Problematic Nature of Intelligence Tests

In interpreting an IQ, you must exercise some caution. First, even though the Stanford-Binet and Wechsler tests are carefully constructed, they are not perfectly reliable. An IQ of 68 on the WISC-R really represents a band of IQ in which approximately two thirds of the time the verbal IQ could range from 65 to 73. A range of 59 to 77 is needed to be confident 99% of the time that an IQ is included in this range. The test manuals recommend that an examiner consider the entire testing behavior of the child and not rely exclusively on the test score.

Second, investigators have found that IQs fluctuate over time for individual children. Some of the change may be attributable to the reliability of the test. Change may also occur because children have been exposed to a good home or school environment. Whatever the cause, an IQ at a given time should not be considered a permanent representation of children's intelligence. Thus, children are now periodically tested as part of PL 94-142 requirements to determine whether the classification of mental retardation remains appropriate.

The more controversial issue regarding intelligence testing focuses on the disproportionate number of minority children classified as mentally retarded, especially at the mild level. Critics charge that the content of the tests discriminates against children from non-middle-class, nonwhite cultural backgrounds. Attempts have been made to develop culture-fair tests or to use tests such as the Raven Progressive Matrices that replace verbal items with seemingly abstract figures judged to be culture free. These tests have failed to close the gap in scores between children of different social classes or ethnic groups. As a result, California has forbidden the use of intelligence tests as currently constructed for the purposes of assessing children for a classification of mentally retarded. The question remains, What is an alternative testing procedure when intellectual functioning is part of the definition of mental retardation? For states other than California, tests such as the Stanford-Binet and the WISC-R are still acceptable.

Assessing Adaptive Behavior

Adaptive behavior is the complementary component in the definition of mental retardation. It is not a new concept. Major historical figures in the field used terms such as "social competency" and "adaptability to the environment" to describe behaviors now associated with adaptive behavior. For example, Itard wrote that his most famous student's "knowledge was limited to four things, sleeping, eating, doing nothing and running about in the field" (Itard, 1962, p. 12).

Itard's statement is an anecdotal record of a child's behavior. His way of describing the child's behavior is similar to how teachers often keep notes about children. Another method for gathering adaptive behavior data is an interview in which persons who have frequent contact with a particular child, such as parents, siblings, or other caregivers, talk about what a child can or cannot do.

These methods lack some very important qualities of assessment. If the word *standardization* comes to mind, you are on the right track. The most important question is, What behaviors should we assess? The success of students in school and in the community depends on the performance of so many behaviors. Without a standardized set of questions, one person may focus on whether children can dress, feed, and groom themselves, whereas another person may only ask about the children's aggressive behavior.

Adaptive Behavior Scales

The AAMR has supported the development of two versions of the Adaptive Behavior Scale, one for persons with severe/profound retardation (Nihara, Foster, Shellhaas, & Leland, 1974) and one for children with mild/moderate retardation (Lambert, Windmiller, Tharinger, & Cole, 1981). The version for the more severely retarded was developed with persons between 3 and 69 years residing in institutions. The test sampled areas of personal independence (eating, toileting, and grooming; self-expression), social maladaption (hitting others, and talking disrespectfully to adult authority), and personal maladaption (hugging, kissing, and touching inappropriately). The public school version sampled similar behaviors but focused on children who typically were enrolled in school between the second and sixth grades (7 to 13 years). This version also tapped important behaviors such as community self-sufficiency (going to a store and buying things, using the telephone, and taking public transportation); and personal-social responsibility (working independently in the classroom, participating appropriately in group activities, and taking responsibility for one's actions). Other frequently used instruments are the Adaptive Behavior Inventory for Children (Mercer & Lewis, 1978), the Balthazar Scales of Adaptive Behavior (Balthazar, 1976), and the Vineland Social Maturity Scale (Doll, 1953). Whichever one you use, be sure to check whether the instrument was standardized with persons who were similar in age and characteristics with those you will be assessing.

Activity 2, page 421, asks you to familiarize yourself with the instruments and procedures used in the assessment process.

Assessment for Instruction

The foregoing instruments are primarily used for determining the eligibility of students for the label of mental retardation. These instruments must be supplemented in order to help teachers plan IEPs for individual students. The focus of assessment for instruction is how well children perform specific skills and under what conditions.

Children are taught in classrooms that are complex social settings. Put yourself in the learner's position, and think about your educational experiences. Do you think you learn better in one-to-one situations or in large groups? Were there times when instructors presented materials that were too difficult or too easy for you? If you are like most learners, you have examples to answer these questions. The crucial point is that learning does not take place in isolation. Poor achievement is not just the learner's fault. Teachers must take the initiative in carefully assessing a student's level of achievement and optimal learning settings so that the learner receives appropriate lessons.

You may have heard the phrase *the ecology of the classroom,* which means the ways in which teachers and children behave toward one another and how the organization of the classroom affects their relationships. Here is an example of looking at the ecology of the classroom. You generally find that teachers are involved with students through a lesson presentation or through participation in a give and take with their students. At other times, students work alone in doing follow-up exercises, which are sometimes called seatwork. Instruction and seatwork can be found in large classes or in small ones, such as resource rooms for children with disabilities. What happens to children with disabilities in these different settings? According to research, the rate of paying attention to the lesson is highest with teacher instruction in the resource room, followed by teacher instruction in the large classroom, seatwork in the resource room, and seatwork in the large classroom (Friedman, Cancelli, & Yoshida, 1988). Teacher involvement is most important in keeping students on task. Even a smaller group size cannot overcome the problems of leaving students to work independently. (For other investigation into the ecology of the classroom, see Berliner [1983], Doyle [1986], and Greenwood et al. [1984].)

The selection of learning materials is particularly important.

Another important factor in successful learning is the appropriateness of materials to children's ability levels. Rather than rely on tests that may not sample the skills being taught in a particular classroom, teachers use the instructional materials in their classrooms as the basis for test items when assessing children. For example, basal readers at the first and second grades have reading passages that range in grade-level difficulty from 1.2 to 3.5; in the intermediate grades, the range is even greater.

INTERVENTIONS

The assessment process should yield information about children's levels of retardation, the skills they have mastered, and the optimal ways of presenting new material to them. The next steps in the instructional process are to (a) plan lessons, (b) present the lessons to the students, (c) monitor the performance of the students, and (d) evaluate whether the lessons were successful and the reasons for their effectiveness.

In terms of planning lessons, what goals do you want your students to achieve? On a month-to-month or year-by-year basis, you should consult your school districts' curriculum guides. The guides present expectations for the type of behaviors typically mastered at a specific age by persons with different levels of retardation. For example, by age 12, most persons with mild retardation are expected to read simple sentences aloud, whereas persons with moderate retardation are expected to read single words such as "stop" and "exit." For persons with severe/profound retardation, recognizing the meaning of everyday symbols such as red-yellow-green street signals may be difficult at best. But you should be aware that sometimes children at a particular level of retardation may transcend the expectations believed to be appropriate for them.

Community Living and Employment Goals

But what do you eventually want to accomplish with children with mental retardation by the time they leave school? The overriding aim is to create experiences that enhance the chances for persons with mental retardation to develop the behaviors for increasing their levels of independent living—that is, situations in which adult supervision is limited or completely eliminated.

Although more research needs to be done, many adults with mild retardation achieve satisfactory adjustment in the community (Zetlin, 1988). Many hold jobs, make friends, marry, and have children. Nevertheless, recent research does draw attention to adjustment problems for persons with mild retardation such as getting along with others, maintaining employment, and experiencing personal frustration with the quality of their lives (Sullivan, Vitello, & Foster, 1988; Zetlin & Hosseini, 1989). Many require considerable support during trying periods from parents, siblings, friends, and social service agencies.

Adults with more severe levels of retardation still require some form of support from social services agencies when they are being placed in the community. According to Taylor (1987), however, many community placements (nursing homes, community intermediate care facilities) often duplicate the philosophy of the institutions—that is, large groups of persons should be kept together so that they can be given care. These placements are unnatural and dehumanizing. Persons with severe retardation should be served in a home in which a family lives. The family can be the child's own natural family, a foster family, or a small number of persons with mental retardation who are able to live as a supportive unit. Although research is in its infancy concerning the effectiveness of these placements, Taylor, Biklen, and Knoll (1987) presented several examples of how family placements could be created and sustained.

Similarly, professionals have begun to change their outlook about the employment opportunities for persons with more severe degrees of retardation who have not succeeded in the workplace with workers without disabilities. A frequently used option has been the sheltered workshop in which persons with disabilities work in a protective environment on projects under contract to a public or private education or vocational rehabilitation agency. These workers are usually paid a subsidized subminimum wage. The sheltered workshop, however, limits the opportunities for persons with mental retardation to experience and succeed in the typical workplace. An alternative is supported employment, which is a generic term covering the supported jobs, enclave, mobile crew, benchwork, and supported competitive employment models. Under these models, persons with severe retardation are employed with supervision in jobs that provide regular opportunities to interact with nondisabled persons. For example, in the competitive employment model, a public agency, typically a department of rehabilitation, hires persons for the position of job coaches. The job coaches help their clients to find a job in the community, to learn specific job skills on site, to monitor their progress and teach new skills, and to continually provide feedback to clients and employers about the clients' performance (see Wehman and Kregel [1985] for more details about the role). Job coaches are available as long as needed. Studies have begun to show the relative cost/benefit advantages to supported employment (Noble & Conley, 1987).

Given the goals of community living and employment in integrated settings, assessing functional skills is important when designing an educational program for persons with mental retardation. These are the skills necessary for living with minimal supervision in the community and, for persons with severe retardation, in a family unit. These skills are usually categorized under five headings (Dever, 1989)—personal maintenance and development (daily living skills such as feeding, grooming); homemaking and community life (housekeeping, money management); leisure; travel; and vocational (seeking and holding jobs). To become gainfully employed, persons with retardation must be able to fill out applications, follow directions, get along with fellow workers, tell time, and drive or use public transportation, among other skills. The educational program is geared to ensuring that these skills are mastered by graduation.

As an exercise for yourself, go to your local McDonald's and ask for a job application. List what reading, writing, and arithmetic skills are required for high school students to correctly fill out the application. Those are the functional skills that must be taught. As an aside, you have engaged in what educational psychologists call task analysis. Now follow the same procedure for determining what it takes for a person with severe retardation to live in a family unit. You can consult the adaptive behavior instruments listed in the previous section and your schools' curriculum guides for these skills. As an additional resource, Alter and Gottlieb (1987) listed almost 100 different curricula that have been developed for a wide range of skills and levels of retardation.

Applied Behavioral Analysis

Once you know what to teach, what are some good ways for presenting your lesson? One widely accepted approach is called applied behavior analysis (ABA), although it is also known as behavioral technology, operant conditioning, behavior modification, and contingency management. Basically, teachers select a behavior they would like to increase, introduce a stimulus, reinforce desired responses, and record the frequency of the behavior's occurrence. This approach requires teachers to be highly disciplined in precisely defining what behavior to increase, determining what is reinforcing to students, and keeping good records about progress. Repp (1983) presented a detailed text on implementing ABA. According to Repp, ABA's major advantages are that the educational interventions are based on direct observation of what happens in classrooms and are individualized. By continually record-ing behavior, teachers quickly know when their interventions are succeeding.

The way in which you use ABA will be greatly influenced by the extent to which your students have mastered specific skills. When learning a completely new skill, you are engaging students in the *acquisition* phase of learning. You will proba-bly demonstrate the skill and ask students to try performing the skill. Every attempt to perform a behavior is known as a *trial*. It may happen that students can partially do the desirable behavior. In these cases, you will reinforce behaviors that approxi-mate the desired ones; you are shaping behavior by continually reinforcing succes-sive approximations. Once the desired behavior is present, the students should prac-tice it until they reach a predetermined mastery level, such as 90% of attempts. Corrective feedback is provided for incorrect responses; positive reinforcement is given constantly. In the next stage, *maintenance,* teachers periodically determine whether the desired behavior is being performed. Reinforcement at this stage is intermittent; correct responses are reinforced according to an unpredictable sched-ule. For example, you might reinforce students' smiles once after four trials and after eight trials the next time. In the final stage, *generalization,* the behavior is correctly demonstrated not only in the setting in which it was learned (for example, special education classroom) but also in another place such as the home or playground.

Motivation of Students

Besides planning instruction for developing functional skills, teachers must also be aware of the motivational background of persons with mental retardation. We have pointed out that children with mental retardation attribute the causes of their success and failure differently than do unlabeled children. Most children referred in school for mental retardation status have repeated one or more grades. Children with more severe levels of retardation have been isolated from others or have rarely been given the opportunities to succeed. If these experiences persist, the ultimate result is a devalua-tion of the sense of self-worth and the development of a sense of incompetence.

Teachers have to be sensitive in working with students who avoid trying new tasks but not confuse encouragement with providing accurate feedback. Teachers often experience learning situations in which students are unable to give a correct response after many trials. Teachers typically tell students that "they did fine" or that "they did okay." This form of feedback communicates an unclear message. Does "doing fine" or "okay" imply having made correct responses? Teachers may compliment the students for their efforts but cannot make vague statements that may be interpreted as reinforcement for incorrect responses.

Lehr and Meyen (1982) presented a set of questions that teachers could apply to evaluate the appropriateness of their lesson planning (this compendium is an edited version of the original list).

1. Is the activity meaningful and functional? Is the skill used in a situation as close as possible to the way it would be utilized in real life?

2. Can the student do the activity independently? Is it within his or her ability range and experiential background?

3. Does the activity really require use of the skill or reinforcement of the important concept? Make sure the activity reinforces the skills and not just the skills of cutting, pasting, copying, and so on.

4. Does the activity require too many other skills in addition to the one being emphasized? Are any of the secondary skills too difficult?

5. Will the activity engage the student in independent work for a sufficient time? Will it take too long to complete?

6. Is the activity reasonably interesting, attractive, and varied?

7. Can the activity be done quietly if other instruction is taking place in the classroom?

8. Are materials available in sufficient quantities for the particular classroom situation?

Technology Applied to Instruction

These questions can also be applied when deciding the use of technological advances, in particular, the microcomputer, with persons with mental retardation. Although the microcomputer presents great potential for presenting instruction (Bennett & Maher, 1984; Johnson, Maddux, & Candler, 1986), having microcomputers in the classroom does not in itself create a productive learning environment. Teachers must know the skills they want their students to learn and whether the microcomputer software presents the instruction in the desired way. Cosden (1988) found that special education teachers had positive feelings about the instructional potential of the microcomputer, but most had only rudimentary skills in using this technology. They could use packaged software, but they could not use the microcomputer for word processing or program or modify existing software. Such limited skills reduced the possible benefits of using the microcomputer. It was not surprising that drill and practice were the frequently mentioned instructional activity in special education classrooms. Yet Vacc (1987) found that adolescents with mild mental retardation increased their writing skills when using word processing.

In order to exploit the potential of microcomputers, special education teachers need to become more familiar with the advanced skills needed to manipulate this technology. Software does exist for drill and practice and word processing. But to meet the needs of persons with mental retardation, teachers will have to develop their own software or make modifications to published ones. As teachers evaluate the goals of their instructional programs, what skills do persons with retardation require to successfully use computer technology in their daily living? For example, teachers could develop a simulation of how a cash register is used at the local fast foods outlet. The number keypad could be color coded for specific food items, and the monitor could display the item name and price. Regardless of our fascination with this technology, teachers must remember that microcomputers are valuable only insofar as they help meet the goals of instruction.

18-YEAR-OLD GIRL WITH MODERATE
LEVEL OF MENTAL RETARDATION

Sally is 18 years old and, while she reads at the third grade level, may be considered an overachiever by some. Certainly, she is performing at the expectation of her parents and neighborhood adult friends. Sally has Down syndrome and has spent her entire educational history in special classes. She is an only child and has benefited greatly from her parents' instruction.

When Sally was two years old, her mother was instrumental in organizing a cooperative preschool among parents of preschool handicapped children. Four years later, her parents joined with other parents in encouraging the local school board to establish a program for young children with mental retardation. The district was already sponsoring a class for children with mental retardation, but the age range for students was 7-13 years.

Sally's father operates a dry cleaning establishment. Sally has always spent considerable time at the cleaners. Her parents began very early to teach her colors, how to differentiate fabrics, and to hang garments on racks. Because of this training, she has become extremely proficient at sorting clothing for dry cleaning. She has excellent social skills and, under supervision, works effectively at the counter in preparing orders for pickup and delivery.

Her teachers have consistently been cooperative in working with her parents in coordinating school activities with other activities. For the last two years Sally has worked as an assistant to the director of volunteers in a local hospital. Her responsibilities have primarily consisted of distributing newspapers, stationery, and other items to patients. The teacher suggested the idea of the additional work experience.

Responsibilities of School Personnel

In addition to fulfilling their instructional mission, teachers are part of a professional team that provides various services. PL 94-142 mandated that a multidisciplinary team perform the evaluation to determine whether children should be labeled and provided services. Special education teachers may be called on to observe the children's classroom and playground behavior in order to make placement and instructional decisions. For children with severe levels of retardation, these assessments may occur in hospital settings when they are of preschool age.

Persons at all levels of retardation often have other disabilities that require related services (specialized interventions beyond those provided by teachers). Doctors and nurses may be needed to supervise a wide range of tasks associated with the health of persons with mental retardation including prescribing and administering medications, attaching and removing medical devices such as feeding tubes, and recommending levels of physical activity. Physical therapists may assist

He felt Sally needed experience working with people (other than her parents) in authority positions. The hospital job was selected because it placed value on her duties and offered an environment different from the cleaning establishment. She wears a volunteer's uniform and adheres to the same rules as do all volunteers.

Although Sally will continue to live at home in the near future, she does have the capacity to live in a group situation or with other young adults. Her parents are aware of Sally's capabilities but are cautious about giving her too much independence. They do not want her to experience failure and, thus, feel that the transition to a more independent living situation should be approached slowly. But they are realistic in knowing that she will continue to need support, some supervision, and guidance as an adult. Their goal is to create a situation that will assure her the opportunity to live a somewhat normal life—earning at least part of her own support, living apart from her family but maintaining family relationships.

□ □ □

Why did the vignette suggest that Sally might be an overachiever? What do you think has been the primary contributor to Sally's successful performance?

What might be another work experience which Sally could perform and which would further her development?

What kinds of experiences might Sally be missing?

If Sally were to move into an apartment with another young adult, what do you believe would be the five most important skills she should have developed as a prerequisite in making this move?

---

children with mental retardation through prescribed exercises to gain strength, flexibility, and coordination in using their muscle systems. Occupational therapists may try to develop ways in which children can maximally use available body movement and control to do daily activities. One example is placing a dowel on a head band perpendicular to the forehead. Children with head movement can then touch pictures or strike typewriter keys in order to communicate. School psychologists may help teachers plan instructional programs, especially those using ABA techniques. Social workers may contribute by acting as primary liaisons with parents in helping them develop supportive home environments.

Parental Participation

In addition to school or related services personnel, parents are an integral part of the team. Parents should be kept informed about their children's progress and the types of interventions being used in the instructional setting (Fish, in press). At the same time, the needs of all family members must be identified and met to the extent possible. According to Turnbull (1988), we must move beyond parental involvement to family support. She suggested that in order to best serve children with mental retardation families "must remain intact over time, meet the developmental needs of the child over time, and develop the kinds of relationships that remain resilient and vital over time" (p. 263).

SUMMARY THOUGHTS

Many professionals and laypersons have by their activism continually challenged society's perceptions about persons with mental retardation. The most profound result of this activism is the legal mandate that all children are entitled to an appropriate education. Herein lies the newest challenge—to determine what is an appropriate education for each person with mental retardation regardless of severity.

The consciousness of the field is currently focused on children and adults with moderate, severe, and profound mental retardation. According to Taylor (1987) and others, the family is the preferred living unit for persons with mental retardation. The family can be composed of natural parents, foster parents, or other persons with mental retardation. The family provides an opportunity for the personal and intimate relationships missing from the institution or intermediate care facility. Program developers must create new ways of placing children, supporting the family in integrating these children into the family, monitoring their progress, and determining the efficacy of these placements.

Teachers of the more severely mentally retarded must master skills that go beyond the traditional pedagogical role but are intimately intertwined with it. With the mandate to provide services to infants and preschool children with disabilities (PL 99-457), teachers will work with children with mental retardation who have serious physical conditions. These teachers will have to become familiar with medical procedures, not necessarily to administer them but to recognize situations that may require immediate medical attention. Teachers will probably need to learn ways in which to work with families of persons with mental retardation. These skills will probably be the most difficult to learn and use because schools do not have an enviable record of developing working relationships with parents.

The concerns for persons with severe mental retardation have overshadowed the problems confronting persons with mild mental retardation. MacMillan (1988) raised the question of whether these children were being adequately served. A different group of persons with mild mental retardation is now in school because of the lowering of the IQ criterion for mental retardation. This group shows problems that require related services. The profession must investigate the learning and behavioral characteristics of these children in order to develop appropriate instructional goals and strategies for them.

These challenges are a tall order for the field of mental retardation. We have hurdled the barrier of the right to an education, but the question remains as to what constitutes a quality education. We must be tenacious enough to find solutions so that persons with mental retardation will have the best opportunities to live quality lives.

REFERENCES

Alter, M., and Gottlieb, J. (1987). Educating for social skills. In J. Gottlieb & B.W. Gottlieb (Eds.), *Advances in special education: A research annual* (vol. 6, pp. 1–61). Greenwich, CT: JAI Press.

Balthazar, E. E. (1976). *Balthazar Scales of Adaptive Behavior.* Palo Alto, CA: Consulting Psychologists Press.

Bennett, R. E., & Maher, C. A. (Eds.). (1984). Microcomputers and exceptional children. *Special Services in the Schools, 1*(1), 1–113.

Berliner, D. C. (1983). Developing conceptions of classroom environments: Some light on the T in the classroom studies of ATI. *Educational Psychologist, 18,* 1–13.

Blatt, B., & Kaplan, F. (1966). *Christmas in purgatory.* Boston: Allyn & Bacon.

Cosden, M. A. (1988). Microcomputer instruction and perceptions of effectiveness by special and regular education elementary school teachers. *Journal of Special Education, 22,* 242–253.

Dever, R. B. (1989). A taxonomy of community living skills. *Exceptional Children, 55,* 395–404.

Doll, E. A. (1953). *Measurement of social competence: A manual for the Vineland School Maturity Scale.* Minneapolis: Educational Publishers.

Doyle, W. (1986). Classroom organization and management. In M.C. Wittrock (Ed.), *Handbook of research on teaching* (3rd ed.) (pp. 392–431). New York: Macmillan.

Dunn, L. M. (1968). Special education for the mildly retarded: Is much of it justifiable? *Exceptional Children, 35,* 5–22.

Fish, M. C. (in press). Best practices in family-school relationships. In A. Thomas & J. Grimes (Eds.), *Best practices in school psychology.* Kent, OH: National Association of School Psychologists.

Forness, S. R., & Polloway, E. A. (1987). Physical and psychiatric diagnoses of pupils with mild mental retardation currently being referred for related services. *Education and Training in Mental Retardation, 22,* 221–228.

Friedman, D. L., Cancelli, A. A., & Yoshida, R. K. (1988). Academic engagement of elementary school children with learning disabilities. *Journal of School Psychology, 25,* 327–340.

Goddard, H. H. (1912). *The Kallikak family: A study in the heredity of feeblemindedness.* New York: Macmillan.

Greenwood, C. R., Dinwiddie, G., Terry, B., Wade, L., Stanley, S. O., Thibadeau, S. & Delquadri, J.C. (1984). Teacher-versus-peer-mediated instruction: An ecobehavioral analysis of achievement outcomes. *Journal of Applied Behavior Analysis, 17,* 521–538.

Grossman, H. J. (Ed.). (1983). *Manual on terminology and classification in mental retardation.* Washington, DC: American Association on Mental Deficiency.

Itard, J.M.G. (1962). *The wild boy of Aveyron.* New York: Appleton-Century-Crofts.

Johnson, D. L., Maddux, C. D., & Candler, A. C. (1986). Computers in the special education classroom. *Computers in the Schools, 3*(3-4), 1–194.

Lambert, N., Windmiller, M., Tharinger, D., & Cole, L. (1981). *ABS: AAMD Adaptive Behavior Scale, school edition: Administration and instructional planning manual.* Monterey, CA: Publishers Test Service.

Lehr, D. H., & Meyen, E. L. (1982). Mental retardation. In E.L. Meyen (Ed.), *Exceptional children in today's schools: An alternative resource book* (pp. 413–451). Denver: Love.

MacMillan, D. L. (1982). *Mental retardation in school and society* (2nd ed.). Boston: Little, Brown.

MacMillan, D. L. (1988). Issues in mild mental retardation. *Education and Training in Mental Retardation, 23,* 273–284.

Mercer, J. R., & Lewis, J. F. (1978). *System of multicultural pluralistic assessment.* New York: Psychological Corp.

Mitchell, J. V., Jr. (Ed.) (1985). *The ninth mental measurements yearbook* (Vols. 1-2). Lincoln, NE: The Buros Institute of Mental Measurements of The University of Nebraska-Lincoln.

Nihara, K., Foster, R., Shellhaas, M., & Leland, H. (1974). *AAMD Adaptive Behavior Scale* (rev. ed.). Washington, DC: American Association on Mental Deficiency.

Noble, J. H., & Conley, R. W. (1987). Accumulating evidence on the benefits and costs of supported and transitional employment for persons with severe disabilities. *JASH, 12,* 163–174.

Polloway, E. A., & Smith, J. D. (1988). Current status of the mild mental retardation construct: Identification, placement, and programs. In M.C. Wang, M.C. Reynolds, & H.J. Walberg (Eds.), *Handbook of special education: Research and practice, Vol. 2, Mildly handicapped conditions* (pp. 7–22). New York: Pergamon.

Repp, A. C. (1983). *Teaching the mentally retarded.* Englewood Cliffs, NJ: Prentice-Hall.

Roos, P. R. (1983). Advocate groups. In J.L. Matson & J.A. Mulick (Eds.), *Handbook of mental retardation* (pp. 25–35). New York: Pergamon.

Rucker, L. (1987). A difference you can see: One example of services to persons with severe mental retardation in the community. In S.J. Taylor, D. Biklen, & J. Knoll (Eds.), *Community integration for people with severe disabilities* (pp. 109–125). New York: Teachers College Press.

Sattler, J. M. (1988). *Assessment of children* (3rd ed.). San Diego: Author.

Sullivan, C. A. C., Vitello, S. J., & Foster, W. (1988). Adaptive behavior of adults with mental retardation in a group home: An intensive case study. *Education and Training in Mental Retardation, 23,* 76–81.

Taylor, S. J. (1987). Continuum traps. In S. J. Taylor, D. Biklen, & J. Knoll (Eds.), *Community integration for people with severe disabilities* (pp. 25–35). New York: Teachers College Press.

Taylor, S. J., Biklen, D., & Knoll, J. (Eds.) (1987). *Community integration for people with severe disabilities.* New York: Teachers College Press.

Terman, L. M., & Merrill, M. A. (1960). *Stanford-Binet Intelligence Scale.* Boston: Houghton Mifflin.

Thorndike, R. L., Hagen, E. P., & Sattler, J. M. (1986). *The Stanford-Binet Intelligence Scale, fourth edition.* Chicago: Riverside.

Turnbull, A. P. (1988). The challenge of providing comprehensive support to families. *Education and Training in Mental Retardation, 23,* 261–272.

U.S. Department of Education. (1988). *Tenth annual report to Congress on the implementation of the Education of the Handicapped Act.* Washington, DC: GPO.

Vacc, N. N. (1987). Word processor versus handwriting: A comparative study of writing samples produced by mildly mentally handicapped students. *Exceptional Children, 54,* 156–165.

Wechsler, D. (1949). *Manual for the Wechsler Intelligence Scale for Children.* New York: Psychological Corp.

Wechsler, D. (1974). *Wechsler Intelligence Scale for Children—Revised.* New York: Psychological Corp.

Wehman, P., & Kregel, J. (1985). A supported work approach to competitive employment of individuals with moderate and severe handicaps. *JASH, 10,* 3–11.

Zetlin, A. (1988). Adult development of mildly retarded students: Implications for educational programs. In M.C. Wang, M.C. Reynolds, & H.J. Walberg (Eds.), *Handbook of special education: Research and practice, vol. 2. Mildly handicapped conditions* (pp. 77–90). New York: Pergamon.

Zetlin, A. G., & Hosseini, A. (1989). Six postschool case studies of mildly learning handicapped young adults. *Exceptional Children, 55,* 405–411.

ADDITIONAL READINGS

Bellamy, G. T., Rhodes, L. E., Mank, D. M., & Albin, J. M. (1988). *Supported employment.* Baltimore, MD: Brookes.

Cartledge, G., & Milburn, J. F. (1986). *Teaching social skills to children: Innovative approaches* (2nd ed.). New York: Pergamon.

Lakin, K. C., & Bruininks, R. H. (Eds.). (1985). *Strategies for achieving community integration of developmentally disabled citizens.* Baltimore, MD: Brookes.

Paine, S. C., Radicchi, J., Rosellini, L. C., Deutchman, L., & Darch, C.B. (1983). *Structuring your classroom for academic success.* Champaign, IL: Research Press.

Purpose

☐ To identify the extent to which adults have accurate information about persons with mental retardation

Steps

1. Ask five adults who are not school district employees to describe the physical characteristics of persons with mental retardation. Ask them whether these persons are able to live on their own, to read and write, to hold a job, and to have friends. Ask them what experiences lead them to this knowledge.

2. Repeat these questions with a group of elementary or secondary level teachers who do not teach special education.

Analysis

☐ How different and similar to one another are their characterizations of persons with mental retardation?

☐ Compare your respondents' answers to the descriptions presented in this chapter and in the readings suggested at the end of the chapter. How informed are these adults about some of the most basic facts about mental retardation?

☐ Does your respondents' level of knowledge have positive or negative consequences for persons with mental retardation? Describe the consequences. If they are good, how can you enhance your respondents' understanding? If they are bad, how can you change respondents' conceptions?

Purpose

☐ To familiarize you with the kinds of assessment information that are gathered in the process of determining whether children should be given the label of mental retardation

☐ To critically observe and evaluate the conduct of the testing session and the interpretation of the students' performance

Steps

1. Identify two children (if possible, one child who is a member of a minority group) who have been referred for special education evaluation and who are thought to be children with mental retardation.

2. List the instruments used to test the child, and later look up in *The Ninth Mental Measurements Yearbook* (Mitchell, 1985) the validity and reliability of each test.

3. Get permission from the school psychologist and your principal to observe the individualized testing of these children.

4. During the testing session, take notes about how the school psychologist presented the test to the children and their responses to the questions.

5. After testing is completed, ask the school psychologist to show you the test protocols (the sheets on which the students' responses are recorded), and ask how the students' test performances were interpreted.

Analysis

☐ Were the tests used in the assessment process valid and reliable? If not, ask why they were used in these cases.

☐ Were the school psychologist and the children comfortable during the testing session? Did the children seem to understand the instructions, and were they able to respond to the questions?

☐ How were the results of the test interpreted? Did the school psychologist discuss the students' IQs and performance on the adaptive behavior instrument? What was the final decision?

☐ How useful is the information from these tests for helping you develop an instructional program for these students?

15

Severe Handicaps

Donna H. Lehr
Boston University

SEVERE MULTIPLE HANDICAPS
TYPICAL PROFILE

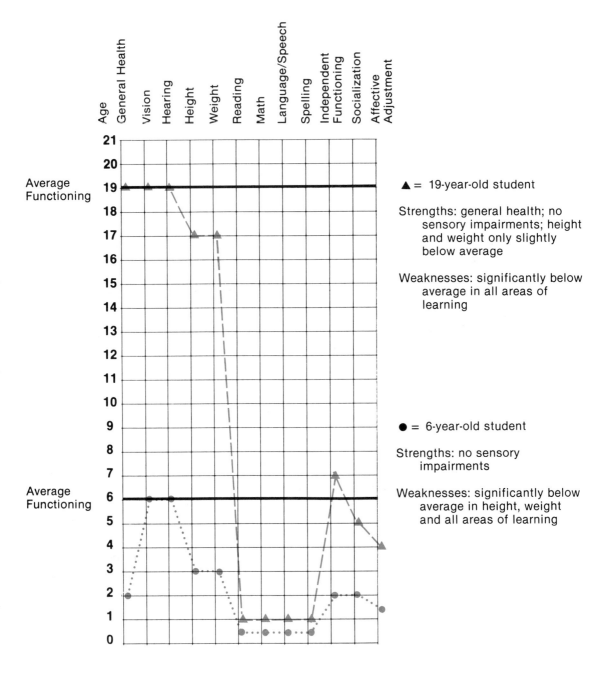

Average Functioning

Average Functioning

▲ = 19-year-old student

Strengths: general health; no sensory impairments; height and weight only slightly below average

Weaknesses: significantly below average in all areas of learning

● = 6-year-old student

Strengths: no sensory impairments

Weaknesses: significantly below average in height, weight and all areas of learning

The education of students with severe handicaps has probably seen the greatest changes in the years since the enactment of PL 94-142. This is the population of students who were routinely excluded from educational programs before PL 94-142. When attempting to enroll their children in school, parents were told there were no school programs for children such as theirs. Since the federal mandate, programs and support for research and program development for this complex population of students have increased.

The consequence has been the development of many new ideas regarding just how students with severe handicaps learn. Because of the urgent need for information, many procedures considered to be best practices have been implemented and subsequently have been found to be the best practices for the time but not for the long run. For example, educators initially believed that specially designed schools for students with severe handicaps in which they were provided with highly specialized adaptive equipment and barrier-free environments would maximize learning. But segregation from students without handicaps has proven inadequate to prepare students with severe handicaps for life in adult integrated environments (Brown, Ford, Nisbet, Sweet, Donnellan, & Gruenewald, 1983). Effective functioning in barrier-free and specialized environments bears little resemblance to the nonschool environments found in the community at large. Skills learned while cooking in specially adapted kitchens do not transfer to home kitchens. To correct this, programs are now moving to models with increasingly greater integration. Students are now attending schools with their nonhandicapped peers in some cases in neighboring rooms and in other cases in the same rooms.

The full continuum of placements continues to exist. Although the benefits of integration for students with and without handicaps has long been acknowledged, segregated placements continue. Consequently, students can be found receiving education in each of the following locations:

Family homes
Institutional schools
Segregated schools
Segregated classes in integrated schools
Segregated classes with lunch and recess integration
Segregated classes with speciality class integration in regular classes

Parents and professionals have also changed their ideas of best practice relative to curriculum for students with severe handicaps. Early programs simply borrowed curricular models from other areas of education, particularly preschool programs. Because students with severe handicaps were considered to be functioning at very low developmental levels, they were taught curriculum designed for very young nonhandicapped students. But implementation of this developmental model did not lead to development of skills useful to students as they interacted with their environments. Instead, research has led to the development of a functional curricular model in which students are taught skills that are critical for functioning in naturally encountered environments. An essential component of this model is the use of naturally encountered materials for instruction and instruction of students in the locations in which the critical skills are to be demonstrated.

The rapid emergence of new ideas has resulted in tremendous diversity in practices. Students can be observed in a full range of settings and involved in a variety of curricular approaches. Many students are participating in functional community-referenced and community-based instruction, whereas many other students with severe handicapping conditions are receiving instruction based on normal development despite the presence of severe handicapping conditions.

CHARACTERISTICS OF CHILDREN AND YOUTH WITH SEVERE HANDICAPS

Students with severe handicaps demonstrate wide differences in their abilities that are not merely a function of their age difference. At the same time, they are similar in that they demonstrate some of the characteristics commonly found in individuals considered to have severe handicaps. These include motor impairments, communication deficits, cognitive delays, demonstration of inappropriate or bizarre behavior, and inappropriate speech or repetitions. Less obvious problems include slower rates of responding, slower rates of acquisition of new information, difficulty generalizing information, difficulty discriminating, and difficulty applying information and skills learned in one setting to a new setting.

A student may show all the characteristics of a handicapping condition or few of them. Students labeled severely handicapped may have sensory impairments, physical abnormalities, crippling conditions, or bizarre behavior repertoires, but "in spite of this heterogeneity in characteristics...severely handicapped students share the fact that each, in some way, exhibits significantly discrepant behavior and demands intensive and sustained intervention from the educational community" (Wilcox, 1979, pp. 140–141). Formal definitions of students with severe handicaps reveal many variations.

As with other areas, no one definition is agreeable to everyone. Consequently, students enrolled in programs for students with severe handicaps vary, not only due to the heterogeneity of the population itself but also due to the lack of a generally agreed upon definition. The definition developed by the Bureau of Education for the Handicapped (U.S. Office of Education, 1974) is as follows:

> A severely handicapped child is one who because of the intensity of physical, mental or emotional problems, or a combination of such problems, needs educational, social, psychological, and medical services beyond those which have been offered by traditional regular and special education programs, in order to maximize his full potential for useful and meaningful participation in society and for self-fulfillment. Such children are those classified as seriously emotionally disturbed (schizophrenic and autistic), profoundly and severely mentally retarded, and those with two or more serious handicapping conditions such as the mentally retarded deaf and the mentally retarded blind.

CHAD

Chad is now 6 years old. Shortly after birth he was placed with foster parents by his biological parents, who were advised that he should be institutionalized. He has profound retardation, cerebral palsy, and a respiratory disorder. His foster parents watch the slow but steady progress he makes. Chad is now able to remove food from a spoon by closing his lips around the spoon while his parents hold it. They are beginning to teach him to hold the spoon as it is brought close to his mouth, as his teacher recommended.

His teacher is helping him sit unsupported for increasingly longer periods of time while he plays with his favorite toy, a Nerf airplane. He seems to enjoy the toy, possibly because it is bright, light, and easy to hold.

Chad's prognosis for walking is questionable. Chad has just recently learned to roll and is being encouraged to do so to get from place to place. He does not always get there because he is easily distracted, but the physical therapists have instructed the instructional aids and teacher in the classroom to make sure that he is encouraged to get places by himself as often as possible.

Chad does not speak, but he does make some needs and wants known through crying and smiling. The instructional staff is working on teaching him to shake his head yes and no in response to questions.

Chad is a student who might be described as having severe handicaps.

What are some reasons for involving Chad's family in teaching him eating skills?

What role might a physical therapist play in Chad's program?

When are some logical times to teach Chad to shake his head yes and no in response to questions?

Such severely handicapped children may possess severe language and/or perceptual-cognitive deprivations, and evidence a number of abnormal behaviors including: failure to attend to even the most pronounced social stimuli, self-mutilation, self-stimulation, manifestation of durable and intense temper tantrums, and the absence of even the most rudimentary form of verbal control, and may also have an extremely fragile physiological condition (pp. 2–3)

The Association for Persons with Severe Handicaps (TASH), an international organization of parents and professionals that has as one of its goals the dissemination of information regarding the education of students with severe handicaps, has defined the target population as

persons with severe handicaps who have been traditionally labelled as severely intellectually disabled. These people include individuals of all ages who require extensive ongoing support in more than one major life activity in order to participate in integrated community settings and to enjoy a quality of life that is available to citizens with fewer or no disabilities. Support may be required for life activities such as mobility, communication, self-care and learning, as necessary for independent living, employment and self-sufficiency. (TASH, 1988, p. 7)

In addition to the variety of definitions, several different terms are being used to describe this population of individuals: severely and profoundly retarded, severely and profoundly handicapped, severely multiply handicapped. Often these terms are used synonymously; at other times they are used to designate a specific subgroup of individuals.

BASIC PROFESSIONAL VOCABULARY

A number of terms and organizations are frequently part of the discussions among people involved with students with severe handicaps in the schools. A sampling of these follows.

Community-based instruction refers to instruction on skills necessary for community functioning that is delivered in the natural community setting.

Community-referenced instruction refers to instructional goals that are prioritized on the basis of their importance relative to a student's functioning in the natural environments found in the community at large.

Ecological assessment is the process used to identify the specific skills needed by any individual to function in particular naturally encountered domestic, vocational, recreational, and community environments.

Functional curriculum is a curriculum model that prioritizes instruction based on those skills that are critical to independent functioning in adult integrated community environments.

Functional domains are the domains of living in which adults typically function, including domestic, vocational, recreational/leisure, and community.

Integrated therapy is the delivery of related services, such as occupational therapy, physical therapy, and speech therapy, into students' usual daily activities. Integrated therapy contrasts *isolated therapy* in which students are "pulled out" of their classrooms to receive therapy.

ASSESSING INSTRUCTIONAL NEED

One of the greatest challenges for those involved in education of students with severe handicaps is that of determining appropriate goals and objectives for instruction. The ultimate aim is for all students to function as independently as possible. A variety of skills may be required to attain this goal. Considering the serious learning problems of students with severe handicaps, instructional time must be efficiently used to teach just those skills considered essential. The challenge is in determining which skills are essential and whether those skills are present or absent in individual children.

ROBIN

Robin is 19 years old. She lives at home with her mother and her 17-year-old brother. She has moderate to severe retardation but no specific motor impairments. Robin attends her neighborhood high school and is assigned to a homeroom with her nonhandicapped peers. She is an assistant in the school store.

Even though Robin is able to talk, understanding what she is saying is sometimes difficult. Consequently, Robin communicates with others through the use of gestures and through pictures of important requests of assistance and food. She keeps these pictures in a wallet and shows them as needed.

Robin gets frustrated easily if she cannot be understood and sometimes grabs others out of frustration. When she works in the school store she is accompanied by instructional aids who have learned from the teacher specific things to do when Robin has difficulty.

Robin is at school only about 25% of the school day. The rest of the time she works in a department store. There she is learning to remove clothes from boxes and to place them on hangers. Her teacher accompanies her to the job 3 days a week, and an instructional aid accompanies Robin the other days.

□ □ □

What benefits might Robin derive from being assigned to a regular classroom?

Why do you think she works in the store? What are the benefits from the community placement?

What types of pictures do you think might be important ones to include in her wallet? What things might be considered critical to request?

For nonhandicapped students, much information exists regarding the skills to teach in school and the sequence in which these skills should be taught. This information is based on studies of normally developing children and youth. The skill sequence is reflected in curriculum guides and curriculum-referenced assessment, which are used by teachers to determine students' performance and the skills that should be included in their instructional program. But using these assessment instruments with students with severe handicaps gives rise to several problems in that (a) many children with handicaps lack even the most basic skills included in the tests; (b) the tests assume a normal course of development, which may not characterize children with severe handicaps; and (c) the skills included are assumed to be necessary for functioning independently, whereas in actuality the child may be able to reach the same end through entirely different means (for example, footwear can be either loafers or sneakers, but sneakers entail the harder task of tying shoelaces). A set of curricular assessment procedures appropriate for students with severe handicaps should result in identification of instructional targets in all areas that are essential to the student's functioning and should be sensitive enough to detect subtle changes in skill acquisition.

Assessment Practices

Assessment practices vary greatly. Some teachers begin instruction without adequately assessing the learners. Others utilize one of the limited number of assessment tools designed for students with disabilities which are adaptable to students with severe handicaps. Some of the most frequently used assessments and a brief description of each appear in Table 15.1. These instruments have the advantage of being ready-made and in some cases have been shown to be valid and/or reliable. But none of the instruments meets all of the specified requirements. Consequently, several other strategies are recommended to assure appropriate assessment of students with severe handicaps.

By far, however, the most valid method of assessing skills appropriate for instruction is that of the ecological assessment strategy (Brown, Branston, Hamre-Nietupski, Pumpian, Certo, & Gruenewald, 1979). In using this strategy, teachers identify current and subsequent environments in which an individual is or will be functioning and then identify the subenvironments, activities and skills that are needed for the individual to function in those settings. An example is provided in Table 15.2. The needed skills are then compared to the student's current repertoire of skills. Those not demonstrated by the student become the instructional priorities. Although the ecological assessment process is difficult and time consuming, its validity makes it the preferred method; it is the most effective method of identifying for each individual student those skills that person is going to need to function in society.

Actually doing an ecological assessment may be the best way to understand its importance to program planning. Activity 1, page 447, is designed to assist you in accomplishing one.

Another method of assessment is that of direct observation and recording of behavior. This strategy is used for two purposes. First, it may be used to validate and provide more specific information regarding data collected via other assessment strategies. That is, a direct observational assessment of a student may reveal that the student does not feed himself or herself. A teacher may then develop a task analysis to identify the steps involved in eating and may then observe the student to determine which steps the student performs and which he or she does not. Because student performance often varies on a day-to-day basis, observation may cover several days, and the data may be analyzed for trends. That way, rather than making judgments about the student based on the one day of observation, the assessor evaluates consistency or inconsistency over time. This method also enables program

Table 15.1   Assessment Instruments for Students with Severe Handicaps

Instrument (Source)	Domains Assessed											Unique Areas Assessed	Target Population
	Independent Functioning	Physical/Motor Development	Language Development	Numerical Concepts	Home Living Skills	Vocational Skills	Socialization	Self-Help Skills	Self-Directed Behavior	Recreation/Play	Cognition		
AAMD Adaptive Behavior Scales (Nihira, Foster, Shellhaas, & Leland, 1974)	X	X	X	X	X	X	X	X	X			Economic activity, maladaptive behaviors	Children and adults with mental retardation
Balthazar Scale of Adaptive Behavior (1971, 1973)	X		X				X	X	X	X		Response to instructors	Children and adults with severe handicaps
Callier-Azusa Scale (Stillman, 1978)		X	X		X		X					Direction following, perceptual abilities	Deaf-blind
Camelot Behavioral Checklist (Foster, 1974)		X	X	X	X	X	X	X				Responsibility, independent travel	Individuals with moderate to severe handicaps
Developmental Pinpoints (Cohen, Gross, & Haring, 1976)		X	X				X	X	X		X		Children, birth to 6 years
Portage Guide to Early Education (Bluma, Shearer, Frohman, & Hillard, 1976)		X	X				X	X		X			Individuals, developmental age 0 to 6 years
Scales of Independent Behavior (Bruininks, Woodcock, Weatherman, & Hill, 1984)	X	X	X	X	X	X	X	X					
TARC (Sailor & Mix, 1976)		X	X				X	X					Individuals with moderate to severe handicaps
Vineland Social Maturity Scale (Sparrow, Balla, & Chicchetti, 1984)		X	X			X	X	X	X				Children and adults with retardation who are institutionalized

planners to detect subtle changes in performance. When the student begins to demonstrate more of the skills related to independent feeding, those skills will be noted on the data sheet and will appear as an increase in the slope of the graph on the trend line on the graph.

Most effective instruction occurs as a result of the use of multiple methods of assessment. Standard tests combined with ecological assessment provide the teacher with much critical information regarding instructional priorities. Data collected from ongoing direct observation serve to guide the teacher in determining the student progress on stated priorities.

INTERVENTIONS

Students with severe handicaps are probably the most difficult group of individuals to teach. The multiplicity of their handicapping conditions poses a tremendous challenge to those involved in their education. It is sometimes said that nonhandicapped children learn in spite of their education. Although this may be an exaggera-

Table 15.2   Ecological Assessment of a Fast Food Restaurant

Domain	Environment	Subenvironment	Activities
Community	McDonald's 76th & Oklahoma Avenue Milwaukee, WI	Parking lot	Walk to door Walk safely in lot
		Entrance/exit	Open doors Enter/exit restaurant
		Counter/ ordering area	Wait in line Make selection Order food Pay for food Wait for order Carry tray or bag
		Eating area	Locate empty table or booth Sit Eat Clear table of trash Throw trash in receptacle
		Bathroom	Use toilet Wash hands Comb hair

Source: Prepared by Julia DeCicco.

tion, many nonhandicapped students do learn a great deal without the benefit of direct instruction. The more severely handicapped the individual, the less this incidental learning is likely to take place. Skills are not often learned without direct instruction, and skills learned in one setting with one teacher are rarely demonstrated automatically in another setting or with another person. Thus, teachers must carefully prioritize skills, deliberately arrange for learning to occur, and apply the most effective teaching strategies to assure acquisition and generalization of skills.

Among the number of questions to be considered by those responsible for educational programs for students with severe handicaps are:

1. What is most important to teach?
2. How shall these skills be taught?
3. Where shall the students be taught?
4. When should students be taught?
5. Who should do the teaching?

Instructional Interventions

Determining appropriate content of an educational program for students with severe handicaps is a continuing challenge for teachers of such programs. Some assessment instruments and curriculum guides are available, but they are limited in number. Many existing instruments are specific to a singular curricular area or are not specially designed for this population.

Given that (a) acquisition of skills is difficult and slow, (b) instructional time is extremely limited (school hours may be 5 days a week, 6 hours a day, but actual instructional time is brief), (c) there is no validated list of essential skills for development of independent living, and (d) no certain rules govern the sequence in which skills should be taught, teachers constantly face the problem of determining for themselves the most essential or functional skills to teach and in what order. The available assessment tools can be used as guides in identifying the specific instructional skills or targets, but in so doing, teachers of students with severe handicaps must ask, "Is this a skill that is (or will be) frequently needed?" or "Is this skill critical for survival?" If the responses to such questions are no, the teacher may question why the skill is included in the curriculum. Time must not be spent teaching skills that are infrequently used in everyday interactions with the environment or not critical for the student's survival.

Sailor, Goetz, Anderson, Hunt, and Gee (1988) emphasized the importance of selecting skills and teaching to meet the following criteria:

1. A skill to be learned has immediate *utility* for the student; it either produces something useful for the student or is part of a broader skill that does so.
2. A skill has *desirability* for the student; it produces something for the student that would likely be chosen by the student if an appropriate choice situation were arranged.

3. A skill is acquired in a *social* context; its acquisition is the product of interactions with more than a single (care-giving) person.
4. A skill is acquired in the *actual, physical contexts* in which the skill will ultimately be requested of the student.
5. A skill has *practicality* for the student; the skill is likely to be needed and practiced with some reasonable frequency.
6. A skill is *appropriate* to the student's age; it will facilitate the student's increasing movement into less dependent and more integrated circumstances.
7. A skill is *adaptable;* its cluster of topographical boundaries are sufficiently diffuse to enable the student to respond to the needs of different stimulus configurations (situations) with appropriate adaptations, including different exemplars of materials where needed. (pp. 68–69)

When one thinks about skills often taught to students with severe handicaps and asks questions regarding the importance of those skills, some are found to be nonessential to functioning. Activity 2, page 448, is designed to assist you in determining the functionality of specific skills.

Programs for students with severe handicaps typically include instruction in the basic domains of living, including domestic, vocational, recreational, and community functioning. Skills within these areas may include teaching a student to talk and use manual signing or a form of augmented communication such as a communication board; to roll, walk, or use a wheelchair; to swallow, hold a spoon, zip a zipper, toilet independently; to respond to others' requests; to play with toys or assemble objects; or to shop, make a bed, or fold clothes.

Task Analysis

Once the relevant skills have been identified, they are analyzed to identify subskills on which to begin instruction. This involves a process referred to as *task analysis*. Task analysis can be defined as "the process of isolating, describing, and sequencing (as necessary) all the necessary subtasks which, when the child has mastered them, will enable him to perform the objective" (Bateman, 1971, p. 33). Such a process is essential to identify the units of instruction the student can acquire. Examples of two frequently used types of task analysis are presented in Table 15.3. Using an *easy-to-hard* sequence, the teacher can begin instruction on the simplest step and move on to more difficult ones as the previous steps are accomplished. In the *series-of-steps* sequence, the instructor can teach the child to perform just the first step or just the last step and then gradually require that more steps be performed in the proper sequence.

In either of these procedures, if the student is having difficulty learning a skill, one possible way of facilitating acquisition is by further breaking down the skill into simpler, easier, or smaller steps. This is illustrated in Table 15.4.

Table 15.3   Examples of Two Types of Task Analysis

Easy-to-Hard Analysis

1. Dresses self with oversized t-shirt

2. Dresses self with appropriately sized t-shirt

3. Dresses self in front-opening shirt with velcro fasteners

4. Dresses self in front-opening shirt with oversized buttons, buttonholes

5. Dresses self in front-opening shirt with regularly sized buttons, buttonholes

Series-of-Steps Analysis

1. Grasps bottom of top layer of t-shirt

2. Raises t-shirt above head

3. Pulls t-shirt over head

4. Pulls t-shirt opening around head to neck

5. Places one arm in sleeve

6. Places other arm in sleeve

7. Grasps bottom of shirt

8. Pulls shirt down around trunk

Table 15.4   Breakout of Series of Steps

1. Grasps bottom of top layer of t-shirt

2. Raises t-shirt above head

3. Pulls t-shirt over head

4. Pulls t-shirt opening around head to neck

5. Places one arm in sleeve

6. Places other arm in sleeve

7. Grasps bottom of shirt

8. Pulls shirt down around trunk

    a. Grasps bottom of shirt with opposite arm

    b. Bends arm to be placed in sleeve

    c. Moves arm under shirt

    d. Finds armhole with hand

    e. Extends arm, pushing hand through armhole

Two ways of developing task analyses are logical, developed by thinking through the process, and empirical, developed by actually performing the task and recording the steps observed. In Activity 3, page 449, you may try either method.

Instructional Staff

Because of the many and complex needs of students with severe handicaps, teams of parents and professionals must work together to plan, implement, and evaluate educational programs for each student. Critical members of the team include the student's teacher(s) and family members as well as the student's occupational, physical, and speech therapists. All members of the team are vital to the student's development; only through careful coordination of efforts will the student receive a comprehensive, cohesive educational program.

Instructional Methodology

After the skill priorities have been identified, teachers and other program planners must decide what types of instructional materials they will use, what type of instructions will be provided to assure demonstration of desired responses, and what will be done to assure certain responses are or are not repeated. Again, given the difficulty students with severe handicaps have in acquiring, maintaining, and generating skills, very careful attention must be paid to decisions about instructional methodology.

Substantial evidence indicates that students may learn certain skills with materials used in instruction but that they subsequently may not be able to demonstrate those same skills with new materials. For example, students may learn to order a hamburger from a teacher-made menu but may not be able to do the same with a restaurant menu. Or they may be able to stack blocks but not stack dishes in the cabinet. Again, the students' difficulty with generalization emerges.

Naturally encountered materials. Teachers are increasingly realizing this problem and the importance of using naturally encountered materials for instruction. The use of silverware to teach sorting skills is preferred over the use of wooden triangles, squares, and circles. The use of a child's own clothes is preferable to the use of dressing dolls as is the use of real money over purple dittoed or cardboard money. In this way students do not have to transfer skills from the instructional materials to the real materials; they are taught initially with the natural materials.

Type of instructions. The selection of appropriate materials alone is not sufficient to assure skills acquisition. Very careful attention must also be paid to the type of instructions provided to students. The typical techniques of verbal directions are not often effective with students with severe handicaps. A considerable amount of research is devoted to determining the most effective cues and prompts (such as gestures and physical assistance) to use to occasion specific responses from students with severe handicaps (Snell, 1987).

These prompts are hierarchical—that is, they are used in a least-to-most order. When teaching a student to feed himself or herself, the instructor may first place the bowl with the spoon in front of the student. If after a short period of time the student does not pick up the spoon, the instructor may try to get that desired response by providing an indirect verbal cue of "It's time to eat" or a gestural cue of pointing to the spoon. If that does not work, the instructor may touch the student's elbow, gently moving it toward the spoon. If all else fails, the instructor may provide full physical assistance and place the student's hands on the spoon, place his or her hand over the student's, and bring the spoon to the student's mouth. Even though different prompts and different hierarchical orders have emerged from the literature, all stress the importance of using the least amount of assistance necessary to get the behavior going and the importance of fading the assistance to the least obtrusive and most natural prompts possible to assure maintenance of behavior beyond the instructional period.

Behavioral technology.   Behavioral technology provides a fairly clear set of rules governing procedures for changing behaviors. One of the basic principles is that a response followed by the delivery of a reinforcer will serve to strengthen that response. With students with severe handicaps, however, identification of effective reinforcers is often difficult. Things we usually think of as reinforcing are not necessarily reinforcing for students with severe handicaps (Green, Reid, White, Harford, Brittain, & Gardner, 1988). Many students without handicaps enjoy free time to play with their favorite toys or games, and they may work hard to earn that privilege. Many students with severe handicaps lack the skills necessary to play with toys independently; thus, such an activity may not be rewarding. Whereas for most of us food is a very effective reinforcer, many students with severe handicaps have physical disabilities that affect their ability to chew and swallow. For such children eating is unpleasant and food does not function as a positive reinforcer. Snell (1988) suggested four procedures for determining effective reinforcers: (a) direct questioning, (b) asking of familiar others and verification of their answers via the other methods suggested, (c) observation of students in natural settings, and (d) structured observation of students with potential reinforcers.

Students with severe handicaps frequently demonstrate excessive behaviors. Traditionally, program planners specifically targeted many of these behaviors as instructional priorities and selected intervention strategies to eliminate or reduce the frequency of these behaviors. These strategies frequently included the use of aversive procedures as punishment to decrease the behaviors. For example, a program plan for a student might have included placing a student in restraints if he or she threw objects in the room or placing a student in a "time-out" booth following a temper tantrum.

Use of such aversive practices is decreasing for several reasons. First, the use of such aversive procedures is not considered humane or typical. That is, these procedures are not typically used with other nonhandicapped students and therefore may be dehumanizing or demoralizing. Second, teaching functional alternatives as compared to decreasing inappropriate behavior has demonstrated advantages (Durand & Kishi, 1987; Horner & Billingsley, 1988; Santarcangelo, Dyer, & Luce, 1987). By analyzing the function of maladaptive behavior, program planners can determine what purpose those behaviors serve for individual students (Gast & Wolery, 1987). For example, a student may demonstrate tantrum behavior each time she or he is at mealtime and each time is removed from the table. After analyzing the situation, a teacher determines that the student probably did not want to eat and the tantrum served to get her or him out of the situation. As an alternative, teachers show the student how to indicate through gestures when she or he does not want to eat. The consequence may be a decrease in temper tantrums and a corresponding increase in the use of gesture. Storey and Kennedy (1988) summarized this more positive approach as including "(1) understanding the functional significance of the behavior; (2) strategies for developing alternative communication modes; (3) alternative activities which are more functional; and (4) using procedures which lessen the undesirableness of difficult activities" (p. 11).

The advantages of positive interventions should be obvious. Most importantly, positive intervention is constructive and teaches the student what to do rather than what not to do. Additionally, it is more likely to lead to intervention strategies that are nonaversive and facilitate generalization and maintenance of reductions in maladaptive behavior (Snell, 1988).

Generalization.   Once again, concern about generalization and maintenance of skills requires that teachers select the most natural, most likely to be generalized reinforcers and provide them as infrequently as possible. Stokes & Osnes (1988) emphasized the need for adherence to the principle of least restrictive intervention to guide initial instruction and generalization training.

Instructional Timelines

Teachers of students with severe handicaps have several choices regarding when to teach. They can follow traditional methods for scheduling in the classroom and can teach skills during specified times, or they can teach the student to make requests when the student has a need. For example, they can teach students to hold their heads erect during "gross motor time," or they can work to strengthen students' neck muscles during snack preparation time when they can watch other students stir milk into instant pudding. One time is clearly more logical than the other. Teaching skills at times when they are needed rather than when they are scheduled to be taught is clearly a more sensible approach. Evidence suggests that learning is greatly facilitated through an approach that serves to integrate learning into natural routines of the student's day (Goetz, Gee, & Sailor, 1985; Helmstetter & Guess, 1987).

Placement Options

Two "where to teach" questions are relevant when educating students with severe handicaps. One relates to the least restrictiveness of the setting and the second to the naturalness of the setting.

As with all exceptionalities, advocates for students with severe handicaps recommend that this group of students be educated in the least restrictive environment appropriate. Considerable evidence exists supporting the benefits of integration for both those students with and without severe handicaps (Brinker, 1985; Voeltz, 1980, 1982). Until recently, however, the ultimate goal has been placement of students with severe handicaps into separate classes on regular school campuses with integration of the students into specialty classes such as music, art, and physical education. Although this model has resulted in many more opportunities for interactions than did separate schools, even more interaction is possible when students with severe handicaps have the regular class as their primary placement. This model is appearing in increasing numbers throughout the country.

Although students with severe handicaps may be assigned to regular classes, these students do not necessarily receive the same instruction as do students without handicapping conditions. Nor are students with severe handicaps "dumped" into the regular class without appropriate instructional supports. Learning characteristics of students with severe handicaps are such that they require different instructional content and more structured educational interventions if they are to develop the skills necessary to function as adults in integrated community environments. Consequently, although the students may be assigned to the regular classroom, they may be receiving parallel instruction or complementary instruction to the instruction occurring in the regular classroom. For example, during math time the regular fourth grade classroom teacher may be providing instruction to the entire class. The students with severe handicaps may also be receiving instruction in the same room, but instead of working on multiplication problems they may be working with an instructional aid on figuring out whether they have enough dollar bills to purchase lunch at McDonalds, where they will go later in the day. Or while the rest of the class is working on building models of the solar system, students with severe handicaps may be learning to use a proper grasp to remove covers from the paint jars the other students are using for their model. Because change is often slow, students are currently being provided with service in all points on the continuum, although there continues to be an excessive number of students still receiving education in segregated environments (Danielson & Bellamy, 1988).

A second "where to teach" issue relates to the naturalness of the setting in which instruction takes place. To maximize skill development and minimize the need to teach for generalization, instructors teach students with severe handicaps skills in the setting in which they will use the skills. If a student needs to learn how to shop in a grocery store, instruction should not take place in a classroom; it should occur in several stores to facilitate generalization across settings. If a student needs to learn how to order food at a fast food restaurant, rather than practicing how to place an order in the classroom, the skill should be taught in restaurants. If a student needs to learn how to clean a house for an eventual job with a cleaning service, the student should be provided with instruction in a variety of community homes.

Because the goal is adult community functioning, as students increase in age they spend more time in the community and less time in school. Figure 15.1 presents a diagram of a suggested proportional amount of time students should spend in the environments of classroom, school, and community as a function of age. For younger students, the school is their community.

Related Services

In addition to receiving instructions from special education teachers and aids, many students with severe handicaps have communication and motor difficulties and

Figure 15.1 **Proposed Proportional Time of Instruction in Classroom, Nonclassroom Within the School, and Community Settings**

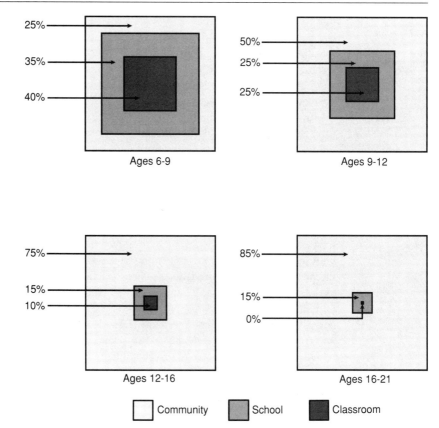

Source: Sailor et al. (1986, p. 253). Reprinted with permission.

receive services from speech, occupational, and/or physical therapists. Traditionally those services were provided through a so-called pull-out program in which students were taken from their classrooms to a therapy room to receive treatment designed to increase their communication skills or to improve their motor functioning. For students with severe handicaps, this approach received considerable criticism (Nietupski, Schuetz, & Ockwood, 1980). Students often learned to demonstrate the desired skills in the isolated therapy rooms but had difficulty transferring those skills to the more natural setting of the school classroom or community at large. The pull-out approach delivered infrequent, episodic treatment and allowed few opportunities for teachers and therapists to learn about each other's instructional priorities and practices. But integrated therapy is now being used to provide services in the setting in which the student needs to learn skills. The therapist works closely with the teacher to demonstrate, monitor, and instruct the teacher how to implement therapy goals on an ongoing basis throughout the day.

Preschool Programs

Life span questions regarding education for students with handicaps include when we should begin and how long we should go. The amendments to PL 94-142 have mandated programs for students with handicaps in all states down to age 3 and have provided incentives for programs to serve children younger than that. Early intervention is clearly effective in preventing or reducing secondary handicapping conditions and in facilitating development. In addition to having direct benefits for children, early intervention provides parents the necessary support during the very critical and stressful early years of their child's life.

Transitional Services

Under PL 94-142, public schools are responsible for providing education to students until age 21. After that time, although individuals continue to learn past that age, educational service provision is not guaranteed. Consequently, tremendous variability exists in communities in terms of available postsecondary educational or vocational training programs.

SELECTING AND ADAPTING INSTRUCTIONAL MATERIALS

Materials used to instruct students with severe handicaps range from the very commonplace to the highly technological. Among the commonplace materials are those that students naturally encounter in their day-to-day interactions in the functional environments of life. These include dishes, items on grocery store shelves, sinks, and all other materials that students may encounter in community training sites. Even though commercially available kits include pictures or models of materials that might be used to simulate instruction the real, natural materials are most effective for instruction.

Due to the physical limitations of many students in this population, however, specialized equipment and adaptations may be needed to assist the students in accomplishing activities of daily living. Such adaptations may include those necessary for mobility; for communication; for domestic, vocational, and recreational purposes; and for environmental control.

Mobility and positioning aids may include wheelchairs, crutches, leg braces, prone standers, all of which assist students in developing motor control or actually moving about their environments (see Figure 15.2). The use of this type of equipment is prescribed by individual students' physicians and adapted by their physical therapists.

Many students with severe handicaps are able to communicate effectively through speech, but others, either as a result of physical disabilities or cognitive delays or a combination of the two, require assistance through communication aids.

Figure 15.2   Mobility and Positioning Aids

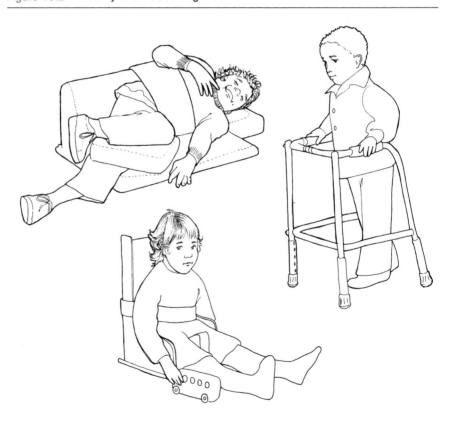

These may include the use of photographs arranged on a wallet picture holder. To communicate a need or want, the student points to the picture of the item he or she desires. This "low-tech" aid can be contrasted with a "high-tech" device such as a Touch Talker with Minispeak—a keyboard on which symbols, letters, words, or pictures are placed. On activation of the keyboard through touch, light pointer, eyebrow wrinkle, or level, a word or entire message is transmitted through a voice synthesizer.

Devices to assist individuals in activities of daily living are limited only by our ability to create them. Many are commercially available through medical supply companies and serve to aid individuals in holding cups, buttoning, pouring, and so on. Others are simple adaptations made by teachers, parents, and therapists as they learn about the student. Some effective teacher-made devices are illustrated in Figure 15.3. Many require the use of simple-to-make switches that enable the student to activate the toy or machine through an easy-to-operate switch.

Figure 15.3   Teacher-made devices

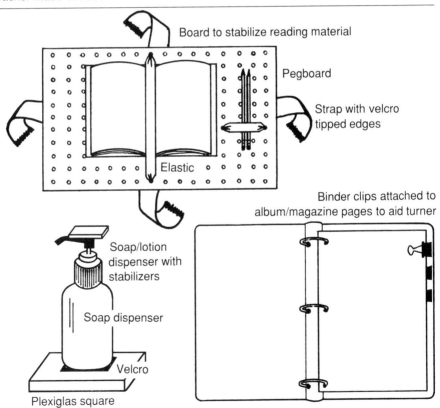

Source: Contributed by Karen Clemens.

SUMMARY THOUGHTS

Students with severe handicaps are a very diverse population of individuals who present complex learning problems. Because learning is so difficult for these students, very careful attention must be paid to the selection of instructional priorities, intervention strategies, and program placements. To assure that students learn the skills necessary for functioning as independently as possible in adult integrated community environments, instruction must focus on teaching functional skills in a wide range of integrated settings in which those skills will ultimately be required.

REFERENCES

Balthazar, E. E. (1971). *Balthazar Scales of Adaptive Behavior.* Champaign, IL: Research Press.

Balthazar, E. E. (1973). *Balthazar Scales of Adaptive Behavior II.* Palo Alto, CA: Consulting Psychologists Press.

Bateman, B. D. (1971). *The essentials of teaching.* San Rafael, CA: Dimensions Publishing.

Bluma, S. M., Shearer, M. S., Frohman, A. H., & Hillard, J. M. (1976). *Portage guide to early education.* Portage, WI: CESA 12.

Brinker, R. (1985). Interactions between severely mentally retarded students and other students in integrated and segregated public school settings. *American Journal of Mental Deficiency, 89*(6), 587–594.

Brown, L., Branston, M. B., Hamre-Nietupski, S., Pumpian, I., Certo, N., & Gruenewald, L. (1979). A strategy for generating chronological age-appropriate and functional curricular content for severely handicapped adolescents and young adults. *Journal of Special Education, 13*(1), 81–90.

Brown, L., Ford, A., Nisbet, J., Sweet, M., Donnellan, A., & Gruenewald, L. (1983). Opportunities available when severely handicapped students attend chronological age appropriate regular schools. *Journal of the Association for Persons with Severe Handicaps, 8*(1), 16–24.

Bruininks, R. H., Woodcock, R. W., Weatherman, R. F., & Hill, B. K. (1984). *Scales of Independent Behavior: Woodcock-Johnson psychoeducational battery, part four.* Allen, TX: DLM Teaching Resources.

Cohen, M. A., Gross, P. J., & Haring, N. G. (1976). Developmental pinpoints. In N. G. Haring & L. J. Brown (Eds.), *Teaching the severely handicapped.* New York: Grune & Stratton.

Danielson, L. C., & Bellamy, G. T. (1988). *State variation in placement of children with handicaps in segregated environments.* Unpublished manuscript, U.S. Office of Special Education Programs, Washington, DC.

Durand, V. M., & Kishi, G. (1987). Reducing severe behavior problems among persons with dual sensory impairments: An evaluation of a technical assistance model. *Journal of the Association for Persons with Severe Handicaps, 12*(1), 2–20.

Foster, R. (1974). *Camelot Behavioral Checklist.* Lawrence, KS: Camelot Behavioral Systems.

Gast, D. L., & Wolery, M. (1987). Severe maladaptive behaviors. In M. E. Snell (Ed.), *Systematic instruction of persons with severe handicaps* (3rd ed.) (pp. 300–332). Columbus, OH: Merrill.

Goetz, L., Gee, K., & Sailor, W. (1985). Using a behavior chain interrupted strategy to teach communication skills to students with severe disabilities. *Journal of The Association for Persons with Severe Handicaps, 10*(1), 21–30.

Green, C. W., Reid, D. H., White, L. K., Halford, R. C., Brittain, D. P., & Gardner, S. M. (1988). Identifying reinforcers for persons with profound handicaps: Staff opinion versus systematic assessment of preferences. *Journal of Applied Behavior Analysis, 21*(1), 31–44.

Helmstetter, E., & Guess, D. (1987). Application of the Individualized Curriculum Sequencing Model to learners with severe sensory impairments. In L. Goetz, D. Guess, & K. Stremel Campbell (Eds.), *Innovative program design for individuals with dual sensory impairments* (pp. 255–282). Baltimore, MD: Brookes.

Horner, R. H., & Billingsley, F. F. (1988). The effect of competing behavior on the generalization and maintenance of adaptive behavior in applied settings. In R. H. Horner, G. Dunlap, & R. L. Koegel (Eds.), *Generalization and maintenance: Lifestyle changes in applied settings* (pp. 197–220). Baltimore, MD: Brookes.

Nietupski, J., Scheutz, G., & Ockwood, L. (1980). The delivery of communication therapy services to severely handicapped students: A plan for change. *Journal of the Association for the Severely Handicapped, 5,* 13–23.

Nihira, K., Foster, R., Shellhaas, M., & Leland, H. (1974). *AAMD Adaptive Behavior Scales.* Washington, D.C.: American Association on Mental Deficiency.

Sailor, W., Goetz, L., Anderson, J., Hunt, K., & Gee, K. (1988). Research on community intensive instruction as a model for building functional, generalized skills. In R. H. Horner, G. Dunlap, & R. L. Koegel (Eds.), *Generalization and maintenance: Lifestyle changes in applied settings* (pp. 67–98). Baltimore, MD: Brookes.

Sailor, W., Halvorsen, A., Anderson, J., Goetz, L., Gee, K., Doering, K., & Hunt, P. (1986). Community intensive instruction. In R. H. Horner, L. H., Meyer, & H. D. Fredericks (Eds.), *Education of learners with severe handicaps: Exemplary service strategies* (p. 253). Baltimore, MD: Brookes.

Sailor, W., & Mix, B. J. (1976). The TARC assessment system. Lawrence, KS: H & H Enterprises.

Santarcangelo, S., Dyer, K., & Luce, S. C. (1987). Generalized reduction of disruptive behavior in unsupervised settings through specific toy training. *Journal of the Association for Persons with Severe Handicaps, 12*(1), 38–44.

Snell, M. E. (1987). *Systematic instruction of persons with severe handicaps* (3rd ed.). Columbus, OH: Merrill.

Snell, M. E. (1988). Curriculum and methodology for individuals with severe disabilities. *Education and Training in Mental Retardation, 23*(4), 302–314.

Sparrow, S. S., Balla, D. A., & Cicchetti, D. V. (1984). *Vineland Adaptive Behavior Scales.* Circle Pines, MN: American Guidance Service.

Stillman, R. (1978). *Callier-Azusa Scale—Revised.* Dallas: Callier Center for Communication Disorders.

Stokes, T. F., & Osnes, P. G. (1988). The developing applied technology of generalization and maintenance. In R. H. Horner, G. Dunkip, & R. L. Koegel (Eds.), *Generalization and maintenance* (pp. 5–20). Baltimore, MD: Brookes.

Storey, K., & Kennedy, C. (1988). A look at recent *TASH* articles on positive programming for behavior problems. *TASH Newsletter, 14*(8), p. 11.

TASH. (1988, April). Definition of the people TASH serves. *TASH Newsletter, 14*(4), p. 7.

U.S. Office of Education. (1974). *Definition of severely handicapped children.* Washington, DC: Bureau of Education for the Handicapped.

Voeltz, L. M. (1980). Children's attitudes toward handicapped peers. *American Journal of Mental Deficiency, 84,* 455–464.

Voeltz, L. M. (1982). Effects of structured interactions with severely handicapped peers on children's attitudes. *American Journal of Mental Deficiency, 86,* 380–390.

Wilcox, B. (1979). Severe/profound handicapping conditions: Administrative considerations. In M. S. Lilly (Ed.), *Children with exceptional needs* (pp. 139–145). New York: Holt, Rinehart & Winston.

ADDITIONAL READINGS

Brown, F., & Lehr, D. H. (Eds.). (1989). *Persons with profound disabilities: Issues and practices.* Baltimore, MD: Brookes.

Falvey, M. A. (1989). *Community-based curriculum.* Baltimore, MD: Brookes.

Orelove, F., & Sobsey, D. (1987). *Educating children with multiple disabilities.* Baltimore, MD: Brookes.

1

Purpose

☐ To help you further understand the ecological assessment strategy used to identify functional skills to teach students with severe handicaps

Steps

1. Identify a community recreational environment you frequent. Record it on the form that follows.
2. Identify and record all the subenvironments.
3. List all the activities that you do in one of the subenvironments.

Environment: _____

Subenvironments:

_____
_____
_____
_____
_____

Activities performed in one subenvironment:

Subenvironment: _____

Activities	**Adaptations**
_____	_____
_____	_____
_____	_____
_____	_____
_____	_____
_____	_____
_____	_____
_____	_____
_____	_____

Analysis

☐ Now that you have thought about all the locations encountered in an environment, and the activities engaged in one of those locations, think about the specific skills necessary to accomplish and one task.

☐ Consider the modifications that might be necessary to enable a student who is unable to speak to participate in the activity.

☐ Does this process lead to the identification of things to teach a student?

```
┌─────────────┐
│     2       │
└─────────────┘
```

Purpose

☐ To assist you in determining if particular skills are functional and therefore should be considered priority objectives for students with severe handicaps

Steps

1. For each of the skills in the following list ask the question, If the student could not demonstrate the skill would someone else have to do it for him or her? Those yielding answers of yes are functional skills. For example: If a student could not put together a three piece puzzle, would someone else have to do it? No, unless you are a parent or teacher who needs to put the puzzle away. But in nonschool settings putting together three-piece puzzles is not a frequently needed skill.

Skill	**Functional?** (yes or no)	**Justification**
Putting pegs in a pegboard	_____	_____
Putting on shoes	_____	_____
Naming colors	_____	_____
Saying the ABCs	_____	_____
Crossing the street	_____	_____
Making a sandwich	_____	_____
Baking a cake	_____	_____

2. For each item justify your answer.

Analysis

☐ Have you identified skills that will continue to be critical as the child reaches adulthood?

☐ Have you identified skills that are critical even when the child is in nonschool environments? Sometimes we teach skills that are important "school skills" but have no relevance to life outside of school.

<table>
<tr><td>3</td></tr>
</table>

Purpose

☐ To help you better understand the process of task analysis

Steps

1. Identify a task such as making a bed or a hero sandwich.
2. Think through the process of actually performing the task.
3. List all the major steps involved in accomplishing the task.

Analysis

☐ Are all the specified steps necessary?

☐ Break down the steps even further. What additional steps could you add?

☐ Could the same task be accomplished by a different process?

Gifted and Talented Students

Reva Jenkins-Friedman
University of Kansas

M. Elizabeth Nielsen
University of New Mexico

GIFTEDNESS
TYPICAL PROFILE

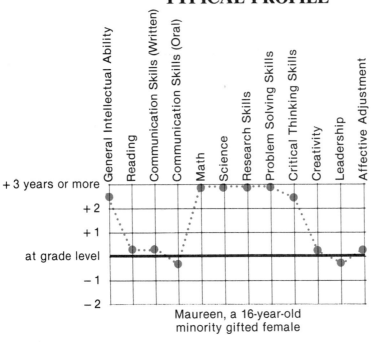

Maureen, a 16-year-old
minority gifted female

Strengths: math,
science, research
skills, critical
thinking, problem
solving

Weaknesses:
none; all abilities at
or above grade
level

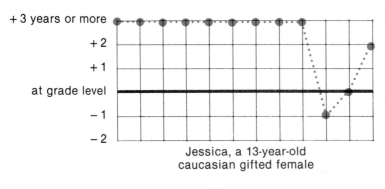

Jessica, a 13-year-old
caucasian gifted female

Strengths: all
academic areas,
research and
critical thinking
skills, affective
adjustment

Weaknesses:
no academic
weaknesses;
relatively low in
creative thinking,
average leadership
ability

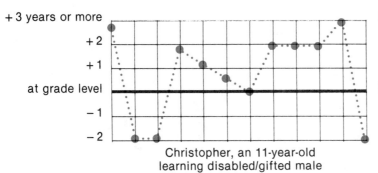

Christopher, an 11-year-old
learning disabled/gifted male

Strengths: critical
thinking, problem
solving, leadership,
creativity, oral
communication

Weaknesses:
reading, written
communication,
affective
adjustment issues
related to learning
problems

Date: September 15   Time: Noon

Place: Teachers' lounge, Anywhere Elementary School

A conversation begins among a fifth and a sixth grade classroom teacher, the gifted/talented (G/T) education facilitator, and the school counselor:

Fifth grade teacher, Mr. Longman: Frankly, I was surprised when you told me that Chris is gifted. He is so disruptive in class, especially during language arts activities. His math achievement scores are quite high, but his daily grades are low because he seldom finishes his work. How can he be excused to go to the resource room to do those creative activities with you?

Gifted education facilitator, Mr. Thomas: Well, we need to keep in mind that Chris is gifted and mildly learning disabled. You know that Chris is new to the program, so the learning disabilities teacher and I are still working out the best ways to remediate his learning problems while continuing to challenge him in his strength areas! Frankly, I could use your help—maybe the three of us could put our heads together.

Sixth grade teacher, Ms. Hill: Hmm. Makes me think of Jessica, our sixth grade science fair winner last year. Now, she was a much more "typical" gifted student as far as I'm concerned. Always handed in her work, neat and on time. Really seemed to enjoy learning. My biggest problem was helping her find her interests—she liked everything! She was popular, too. By the way, how is she doing in seventh grade?

Gifted education facilitator, Mr. Thomas: She certainly goes for the independence! And now she has more of a peer group of bright kids—she says they make it o.k. to be smart. Why, the year's just started and she's already planning her next science fair project. It's hard to get her to do any of the program's interest exploration activities, even in subjects she usually likes. She's finally becoming more assertive, too.

Counselor, Mrs. Perez: I wish that were the case with my niece Maureen! Y'know, I was shocked when she qualified for the Math Talent Search—she's so quiet about her abilities. She has won full scholarships to the Talent Search Program for the past two years and I think she should broaden her horizons by going to a good university. Unfortunately, her parents worry mostly about finding her a good husband after high school graduation.

The issues surfacing in the foregoing conversation illustrate recurring questions faced by educators dealing with bright students. What is giftedness? How easily can it be detected? Is gifted education programming a need or a reward for good work? To what extent should gifted students' needs be met through the general education program? Can a student have learning problems and still be gifted? To what degree does cultural background influence demonstrations of exceptional ability?

ACCOMMODATING THE NEEDS OF GIFTED AND TALENTED STUDENTS

Although history documents that exceptionally able individuals have existed throughout recorded times, systematic provisions for nurturing, supporting, and challenging G/T youngsters are a relatively recent feature of 20th-century public education.

According to the *1987 State of the States: Gifted and Talented Education Report* (Houseman, 1987), 25 states and Guam mandate services for G/T students, and 22 states and Puerto Rico support discretionary (permissive) programs.

Requiring educators who work with G/T students to complete specialized training is becoming more widespread. Twenty-two states now require or encourage teachers to become certified to work with bright students, with another seven states developing policies and procedures. Programs range from 9 to 36 credit hours, with 12 credits being the most frequent option (Boyle & Laurent, 1987). In most states the certificate is available only on the graduate level.

Why is there such variability across the states? Most important to keep in mind is that G/T education was excluded from PL 94-142. Thus, some states have simply added gifted education to their special education mandates, whereas in other states, policies have evolved more slowly and have not paralleled special education regulations. The benefit of these differences is that programming tends to be tailored to local resources and educational philosophies; the liability is a lack of consistency over times and across districts.

The "home" for G/T education services varies with local policy. In states where gifted education is mandated, services tend to be located in departments of special education. But, even in these states, IEPs are not always required (only 15 states and Puerto Rico require IEPs). Unlike other special education students, due process rights for G/T students are endorsed by less than half of the states. Twenty-four states and Puerto Rico specifically exclude gifted students from the right to a due process hearing for identification or services (Houseman, 1987). Nevertheless, overall public awareness of these students' special needs and the potential benefits to society of investing in programs for students with exceptional abilities continues to increase.

Program Models

The regular classroom is the key environment for most bright students, who in a typical week spend only 2.5–5 hours receiving special services out of the classroom (Boyle & Laurent, 1987; Houseman, 1987. Classroom teachers are key features of G/T students' education and therefore need to be involved in modifying the standard curriculum to challenge students in accordance with their abilities.

The most popular model for delivering special education services to able learners is the pull-out, or resource room, program. Gifted education teachers are more likely to be itinerant or to travel among several schools. Self-contained classrooms, magnet schools, or school-within-a-school models are program options in 30 states (Boyle & Laurent, 1987).

At the middle school level, students' interests and abilities become more specialized; thus, programming options tend to be more individualized. Special courses, acceleration alternatives, and extracurricular programs, coordinated by a consulting teacher, are prevalent. Students may elect to take credit-bearing or non-credit seminars, to enroll in honors or advanced placement sections of regular courses, or even to develop "gifted" options within regular classes.

If there is a cooperative arrangement with a local junior college or university, students may test out of the regular high school curriculum and enroll in courses for college credit. Working with practicing professionals in the community through mentorships is another approach popular with adolescents.

Statewide or national programs such as Future Problem Solving, Odyssey of the Mind, Governor's Honors Programs, and the Talent Search or Talent Identification Programs offer bright students the challenge of engaging in national "think tank" competitions or joining (usually for a summer) a supportive yet challenging intellectual community housed at a well-known university. Nevertheless, these options are generally considered to be "extracurricular," supplementing rather than substituting for a program more integrated with general education offerings.

THE CHALLENGE

Educating exceptionally able individuals poses unique challenges for school personnel. First, unlike other exceptional students, G/T students are usually identified because they outperform their peers, not because they are experiencing learning difficulties. This means that G/T students' special education programs need to emphasize strengths rather than weaknesses.

Second, successful programming for bright students should result in making their "condition" more pronounced, widening rather than narrowing differences between these students and their average-ability peers. If anything, effective programs increase able students' needs for services instead of reducing the "presenting condition"—exceptional ability.

Third, G/T students are identified on the basis of their potential to perform at extraordinary levels in the future; their education is aimed at enhancing accomplishments as adults. Results of specialized programming are therefore difficult to predict and do not lend themselves to evaluation on the basis of paper and pencil tests. An emphasis on potential also implies an increased reliance on the judgment of educators, parents, and the identified students to ascertain if "truly gifted and talented" students are being served appropriately.

Beliefs and Expectations

As in every other area of exceptionality, folklore has produced a collection of beliefs that filters people's understanding of giftedness and influences choices for meeting the needs to this special population. As you read this chapter and complete suggested activities, consider your beliefs and expectations as an educator dealing with G/T students in your classroom. To help you begin the process, we have listed in Table 16.1 several beliefs that undermine or increase the effectiveness of gifted education programs.

In Activity 1, page 491, you are asked to collect and examine definitions of giftedness and opinions about programming and to begin a file of anecdotal information on giftedness-in-action.

TABLE 16.1   Beliefs About Gifted/Talented Students

Beliefs That Undermine Gifted/Talented Programming	Beliefs That Support Gifted/Talented Programming
Gifted children can make it on their own.	Gifted students need support to realize their potentials.
Individualizing instruction will take care of gifted students' educational needs.	Gifted students' education needs to go beyond the standard curriculum; teaching methods need to complement students' learning styles and thinking abilities.
Programming for gifted children is undemocratic.	Equality of opportunity means that students have the right to a free and appropriate education, rather than the same opportunity for all students.
Gifted students are good at everything.	Giftedness is many-sided and tends to become specialized.
Being gifted is for "life."	Giftedness is developmental; it changes, can emerge, or can disappear over time.
Gifted education happens only in special programs.	Gifted education needs to happen in all educational settings.
Exceptional ability is easy to identify.	Many gifted students are unrecognized, particularly if they have other handicapping conditions; teachers need to be adept "talent scouts."

DEFINING GIFTS AND TALENTS: A HISTORY OF THE FIELD

For the past 4,000 years, there has been tremendous progress in the ways in which giftedness has been conceptualized, identified, and supported: from the divinity to the ordinary, from the neurotic to the normal, from the inexplicable to the highly understandable and measurable. Perhaps more than any other field, conceptualizations of exceptional ability have mirrored the combined force of four factors: values, research, public policy, and history.

In the overview of the field that follows, you will see the interplay of these factors in defining, recognizing, and understanding giftedness. For purposes of analyzing the forces shaping current definitions and beliefs about giftedness, the study of gifted and talented individuals is divided into three periods: prescientific, psychometric, and legislative. Each has added new dimensions to our understanding or giftedness; each has left a legacy that continues to influence current research, theories, and beliefs about exceptional ability.

Prescientific Era

This era extended from about 2200 B.C. to about A.D. 1850 (in Europe). This period was typified by two powerful misconceptions that continue to influence current beliefs about giftedness. The first, *transcendent abilities,* originated in Greek society; this misconception held that genius was an immeasurable quality inspired either by the gods and the muses or by demons.

According to this belief, gifted behavior happened only through divine inspiration. The individual was merely a channel for creative energy flowing from an unexplainable source. The logical extension of this misconception was that creative potential could not be assessed, nurtured, or suppressed. Therefore special provisions for G/T students were unnecessary.

The second misconception, *immoderate use,* originated in the work of the early psychologists, who believed that immoderate use of the nervous system's energy would result in neurosis. Included in their descriptions of immoderate use were many of the behaviors commonly associated with giftedness and creativity. Immoderate use has lingered on in the belief that expressions of outstanding intellect are accompanied by physical weakness and a neurotic personality. Unfortunately, the image of genius linked to emotional imbalance continues in the popular press and is often echoed even by bright youngsters and their parents (Grinder, 1985; Sicherman, 1981).

These legacies from the prescientific era have partially shaped modern society's ambivalent attitude toward exceptionally able children.

Psychometric Era

The psychometric period, which began in the last quarter of the 19th century and continued through the 1960s, was marked by the invention of psychological measurement and its use in measuring intelligence and studying highly intelligent persons. The social climate of the time established the belief that all people, whatever their intellectual aptitudes, should have a fair chance to develop whatever talents they might have. The key issue was how to make schooling a diverse population both efficient and cost effective. Testing seemed to offer the answer.

Psychologists of this era in Great Britain (Galton), Germany (Stern), France (Binet and Simon), and the United States (Cattell and Terman) shaped research directions in assessing intellectual potential. Although a relative latecomer to this group, Terman in particular developed much of the current knowledge base for G/T child education in this century.

First, Terman designed and conducted the most extensive study of gifted persons to date. Using the Stanford-Binet Intelligence Scale (his revision of the Binet-Simon Intelligence Test) Terman identified more than 1,500 highly gifted youngsters whose scores were 140 or greater. Terman and his research associates collected data on their physical health, family life and background, and emotional development.

Follow-up studies of Terman's subjects continue to this day (Oden, 1968; Sears, 1977; Sears & Barbee, 1977; Terman, 1925; Terman & Oden, 1947, 1959). Results of this seminal work have provided a common set of characteristics and developmental patterns of gifted children, dispelled many genius equals neurosis myths about gifted persons, fostered more positive attitudes toward bright children, and opened the door for special programming to nurture the talents and abilities of G/T youngsters.

Second, based on his theories about the development of intelligence, Terman established a way—the IQ—to calculate a person's aptitude for performing cognitive tasks. His probability tables, indicating the likelihood of an individual obtaining a given intelligence test score, offered an easy method for determining what proportion of a population should be considered as gifted (Grinder, 1985). For example, educational decision makers still rely on "Terman's 2%" and expect that approximately 2% of all school children in the United States will score 132 or greater on an individually administered intelligence test. Thus, educators often use an IQ score of 132 as a cutoff score for students being screened for gifted education programming (Boyle & Laurent, 1987; Houseman, 1987).

Research during the psychometric era also expanded conceptions of giftedness to include sets of talents not measured by intelligence tests. For example, creativity as an aspect of giftedness was introduced through Guilford's pioneering work in expanding the number of measurable factors composing the human intellect and throughout Torrance's development of the Torrance Tests of Creative Thinking.

The successful launching by the Soviet Union of the Sputnik I satellite in 1957 seriously damaged America's self-image as a world leader in science and technology. Public education was blamed. Massive amounts of public and private funds were channeled into "crash courses in pursuit of excellence" (Tannenbaum, 1975). College-level courses, acceleration programs, and honors programs were some of the options created to challenge America's brightest youth. There was a pervasive public climate that emphasized mobilizing talents, particularly in service to society.

Impacts of This Period

The legacy of the psychometric era is mixed. First, the testing movement has led to the still-popular practice of defining giftedness solely in terms of intelligence test scores. This is especially controversial, given the lack of a unified theory of intelligence. Criticisms that tests fail to take into account many factors that seem to influence adult achievement—such as creative thinking, inventiveness, perseverance, and concentration—and concerns about the appropriateness of existing intelligence tests for minority populations are common.

Second, although there was a flurry of public activity following *Sputnik,* very few comprehensive programs resulted. Efforts tended to be spotty and uncoordinated. G/T education was considered a luxury or an "add-on" to the standard program. This notion continues to threaten programs' security.

Third, the national talent search programs of the late 1950s and early 1960s failed, in the main, to identify students with high potential whose cultural differences, poverty, low socioeconomic status, or geographic isolation depressed standardized assessments of intellectual aptitude. The civil rights movement of the 1960s fueled charges of discriminatory assessment practices, which were leveled in particular against IQ testing. The number of G/T education programs declined rapidly during the 1960s.

More positively, the era's research into the nature of intelligence has resulted in reducing much of the bias that characterized earlier labeling methods. New theories of intelligence reflect additional abilities included in the broadened conceptions of giftedness introduced in this period. For example, creativity was introduced as an aspect of giftedness in the 1950s through the pioneering work of J. P. Guilford and E. Paul Torrance. More recently, Robert Sternberg (1986), a Yale psychologist, has constructed a theory of intelligence that specifically includes creativity.

Identifying exceptional potential is much more accessible to school personnel. Culture-fair assessment practices and alternatives to standardized testing are integral to many states' identification guidelines. State plans and comprehensive programming—even the recommended scope and sequence of curriculum objectives for gifted learners—continue to reduce the image of G/T education as the icing on the curriculum cake (Tannenbaum, 1975).

Legislative Period

Current interest in special education for G/T students stems from a comprehensive national survey of programs and needs conducted in 1971 (Marland, 1972). The survey known as the Marland Report, indicated that only a small percentage of G/T children were receiving any special education services. Based on this report, the first federal definition of giftedness was adopted, the Office of Gifted and Talented (OGT) was created, and the federally funded National/State Leadership Training Institute on the Gifted and the Talented was established to provide training, technical assistance, information dissemination, and continuing education for interested professionals.

Most of the states based their definitions of giftedness on the one espoused by the Marland Report. Including abilities beyond general intellectual potential further legitimized a broader conception of giftedness which comprised creativity, leadership, specific academic aptitudes, and the visual and performing arts.

Adopting the definition as the cornerstone of states' plans was foundational for building special education programs that respected the multidimensional nature of giftedness. The definition's acknowledgment of the need for specially trained personnel to work with G/T students spawned many teacher preparation programs.

Although direct support (OGT) was subsequently eliminated during the Reagan administration, the 100th Congress reinstated the office and provided funding for teacher preparation, programs for students, technical assistance to school districts, and programs to strengthen the work of state educational agencies. For the first time, funds were earmarked to establish a national center for research and development in the education of gifted and talented children.

In addition to its emphasis on identifying and educating students who tend not to be recognized by traditional assessment procedures, the newest federal definition, excerpted from the Jacob K. Javits Gifted and Talented Students Education Act of 1988, continues to support an expanded conception of giftedness:

> The term 'gifted and talented students' means children and youth who give evidence of high performance capability in areas such as intellectual, creative, artistic, or leadership capacity, or in specific academic fields, and who require services or activities not ordinarily provided by the school in order to fully develop such capabilities. (Elementary and Secondary Education Conference Report, 1988, p. 114)

Impacts of This Period

Although this era is in its infancy, its effects are already visible. The numbers of organizations sponsoring conferences for educators and parents of bright children, special publications, and research-based articles have grown dramatically since 1980. Mandates have resulted in increased awareness of the rights of G/T students to an appropriate education in the least restrictive environment (which may not be the general education classroom). There is increased pressure on school personnel to be more accountable regarding the methods used to identify and work with bright students.

Unfortunately, codifying definitions through legislation may remove some of the field's needed flexibility to reshape conceptions of giftedness to respond to future societal needs. Definitions of exceptional ability and the nature and directions of programs will need to maintain their close connections to cultural values, research, and history if public policies are to remain relevant to the needs of this special population.

Finally, special education for G/T students is not yet universally accepted in the United States, caught as it is between the demands of equal education for all and individualizing programs required to fit children's needs. The realization is growing that gifted children have educational needs; nevertheless, educators have to consider the influences from the past that can make G/T programming the stepchild of special education.

> How can we measure the sonata unwritten, the curative drug undiscovered, the absence of political insight? They are the difference between what we are and what we could be as a society" (Gallagher, 1975, p. 9).

BASIC PROFESSIONAL VOCABULARY

Acceleration is "any administrative practice designed to move the student through school more rapidly than usual. Acceleration includes such practices as early admission, grade-skipping, advanced placement, telescoping of grade levels, credit by examination, etc." (Ward, 1975, p. 65).

Compacting or telescoping curriculum is the compressing of a standard amount of coursework into an abbreviated amount of time. This is accomplished by moving more rapidly through the material, by demonstrating mastery through pretesting, or by reducing the amount of time spent on guided practice of new information. Compacting "buys" time for independent projects, research, and so on.

Creativity is a nonlinear mental process that ultimately produces unique ideas, solutions, or inventions. Creativity includes the ability to sense problems, generate many ideas, perceive different approaches to a problem, embellish on ideas, and put ideas together in relevant, unique ways. Creativity is relative in that a solution can be original for its developer or someone else at a particular time even if it might not be judged as unique later.

Critical thinking which is often used synonymously with the term *higher level thinking* is a mental process involving assimilating, analyzing, and restructuring information to reach conclusions, solve problems, or create new ideas. Critical thinking includes the ability to recognize assumptions, draw inferences, make deductions, interpret data, and evaluate ideas or projected outcomes.

Differentiated instruction comprises "educational experiences uniquely or predominantly suited to the distinguishing behavioral processes of intellectually superior people and to the adult roles they typically assume as leaders and innovators. When successfully arranged to involve the capacities and needs of the gifted, the experience is beyond the reach of and not appropriate to the capacities and needs of persons not exceptionally endowed with potential for learning and productive or creative behavior" (Ward, 1975, p. 65).

Enrichment refers to practices, intended to increase the depth or breadth of the gifted student's learning experiences. [Enrichment] may include special assignments, independent study, individual projects, small group work, and other adaptations of routine school processes" (Ward, 1975, p. 65).

G/T: frequently used abbreviation or acronym, standing for the term "gifted and talented." This acronym is used throughout the chapter.

VARIABILITY OF BEHAVIOR AMONG BRIGHT YOUTHS

Maureen, a junior in high school, attends a predominantly Hispanic school in the Southwest. She comes from a large family that includes both parents, three siblings, grandparents, and numerous aunts, uncles, and cousins.

Throughout her elementary years, Maureen was an extremely well-behaved, quiet student. Her shyness prevented her from asking questions in class, and she rarely contributed to discussions, preferring to listen rather than to speak. She has always worked hard to do well in school and to please her teachers. Maureen's elementary and midschool grades were always average or slightly above. Yearly achievement test scores consistently placed her reading and written language scores within the normal range for her given grade level. Her achievement scores in mathematics during those years fluctuated between the 80th and 93rd percentiles.

When Maureen was in the eighth grade, her school counselor received information from the Rocky Mountain division of the National Talent Search Program. After reviewing all students' past achievement scores, the counselor identified a group of students whom he felt might benefit from screening for the program, including Maureen.

Maureen took the SAT with the other students. The results of her testing surprised everyone. Her mathematics score was in the top 3% of eight graders taking the test. Maureen was invited to attend Talent Search sponsored summer programs, with scholarship support.

Her scores also drew the attention of Maureen's teachers and the school counselor. These instructors encouraged Maureen to consider being screened for the school district's gifted program. After initial reluctance by both Maureen and her parents, Maureen was tested and easily qualified to join the program.

Jessica is an intellectually gifted eight grader. Her parents, divorced since Jessica was a toddler, have a friendly relationship. Jessica and her older sister alternate weeks at each parent's home.

Jessica's mother claims that Jessica was gifted "since birth," that she walked and talked extremely early. She taught herself to read at age 3 and developed a rudimentary multiplication system before entering kindergarten.

Jessica was screened for the gifted program early in her kindergarten year. Because her intelligence test scores were the highest in the district and Jessica was so mature emotionally, the school psychologist recommended that she "skip" to second grade. Her parents protested, saying that they preferred for Jessica to learn to relate to her nongifted peers as well as to grow cognitively.

Throughout elementary school, Jessica's program was modified to fit her unusual learning needs. One of the greatest challenges her teachers found in working with Jessica was her delight in learning. Interested in everything and highly able to understand complex information, Jessica tended to devour available information on any topic rather than studying a topic in depth.

Now that Jessica has entered seventh grade, she moves among classes with a group of similarly gifted and talented youngsters. For the first time, Jessica has an intellectual peer group and a group of supportive teachers who combine teaching high level thinking skills with advanced academic content. Also for the first time, Jessica, always competitive about her work, is finding that she is not the best at everything. She is beginning to express some anxiety about being less than perfect in her schoolwork. Her teachers are concerned that Jessica is concentrating too much effort on finding the "right" answer instead of using her vast store of information to speculate about possibilities.

Christopher is a gifted/learning disabled fifth grader. Within the past year, Christopher's school experience has changed greatly. Previously, he had participated only in standard elementary school classes. During kindergarten and first grade, he was more active and restless than his classmates, displaying a seemingly insatiable curiosity. He also had an unusual ability to understand and talk about abstract, complex concepts such as time, distance, and ecology. His teachers believed that he was one of the brightest students in his classes.

By fourth grade, Chris's classroom behavior had become problematic. He had discovered that math was easy, fun, and a way to earn praise from teachers. He had also discovered that learning to read was nearly impossible, although he was able to hide this from his previous teachers by becoming the class clown, delighting when his classmates laughed at his antics. His restlessness and continual questions disrupted learning activities and frustrated the teacher.

No longer able to pretend that he could read, Christopher rapidly grew to hate all language arts–related assignments. His written work had missing words, atrocious handwriting, and spelling based on a system that only Chris understood. At home he began referring to himself as "dumb," refusing to complete any homework except math.

Wondering if he had a learning problem, Christopher's teacher recommended him for testing by the special education diagnostician. Because they had become increasingly worried about Chris's deteriorating academic performance and self-image, his parents were most willing to have him evaluated. Christopher was tested by a special education diagnostician during the summer following his fourth grade year. He was identified as possessing exceptional learning abilities as well as some learning problems.

☐ ☐ ☐

List each youngster's G/T characteristics.

Which ones are more likely to be perceived positively?

Negatively?

What might you say to Christopher's teacher that could help him to understand Chris's behavior as gifted?

What behaviors might prevent a teacher from noticing Maureen's abilities?

Which of Jessica's characteristics will present special challenges to her teachers?

Mentorship/internship is a program option or arrangement that provides a G/T student with an extended opportunity to learn from a community person with special skills by working with that person. Mentorship is often used for developing networks, role models, and career awareness.

National Association for Gifted Children (NAGC) in Circle Pines, Minnesota, is the largest G/T child advocacy organization in this country. The NAGC's single focus is the support of G/T youths and their significant others. The association publishes the journal *Gifted Child Quarterly*.

Pull-out/resource room program is a program arrangement wherein G/T students leave their home classroom for part of the school day or week to participate in educational activities designed to address their identified special needs. The program is generally managed by a teacher trained to work with G/T children.

The Association for the Gifted (TAG), in Reston, Virginia, is a division of the Council for Exceptional Children. TAG is devoted to encouraging and supporting advocacy, program development, and professional preparation for educators of G/T students. TAG publishes the *Journal for the Education of the Gifted*.

Talent Search or Talent Identification Program is a nationwide program to identify and develop the abilities of academically talented midschool and high school students. High-performing youth are encouraged to take the Scholastic Aptitude Test (SAT) in seventh or eighth grade. High scorers are invited to take part in fast-paced programs at host universities.

CHARACTERISTICS OF GIFTED AND TALENTED CHILDREN AND YOUTH

Generalizing about G/T children is extremely difficult because, like any group of children, they have traits in common and individual traits that make each child unique.

Researchers primarily employ two methods to create lists of traits common to gifted and talented children. One method is to start by identifying a group of G/T children using very stringent criteria and then to uncover the characteristics shared by most of the group. Terman's longitudinal studies typify this approach. The other method is to generate a list of adults whose adult accomplishments are outstanding and then investigate their common qualities. The Goertzels are well known for their analyses of the biographies of eminent historical and contemporary individuals (1962, 1978). A more recent example of such a study is Bloom and his associates' (1985) case histories of 120 individuals who had attained world class status between the ages of 17 and 35 in athletics (tennis or diving), the fine arts (piano performance or sculpture), or cognitive/intellectual fields (research neurology or pure mathematics).

Both types of research provide the field of gifted education with characteristics common to many G/T youths. Table 16.2 lists 17 of those traits, categorized as either cognitive or affective. Each characteristic is followed by examples of related positive and negative behaviors teachers might see in classrooms.

Teachers and parents need to understand that the wide range of G/T behaviors can support or thwart the continued development of these children's abilities. Often G/T students experience special stresses because they have very high levels of cognitive development but their affective needs and physical growth patterns are similar to their average agemates. The environment plays an important role in determining the "gifted" behaviors that are accepted, rewarded, or punished. Most G/T students are successful, but they need understanding and guidance to reduce the likelihood of school problems (Barbe & Renzulli, 1975). Students will respond in ways that signal exceptional ability when there are opportunities and support to do so.

ASSESSING INSTRUCTIONAL NEED

Identifying G/T students is the first step in a plan to assess instructional needs and to develop relevant options. Because students are identified on the basis of potential for future performance, separating labeling from providing services is important. Thus, if a student is screened but not placed in a gifted program, educators are *not* making a definitive judgment about the youngster's (lack of) potential; the decision is that *at this* time, the student's needs are being met through the standard education program. Thus, because services rather than students, are labeled, if a district has to choose between an identification system that is effective or one that is efficient, effectiveness is the better choice (Swassing, 1985). Although this could result in occasionally misidentifying a student as gifted, it is a more appropriate "mistake" to make because the alternative is to incorrectly exclude bright students from receiving services.

Classroom teachers have the greatest opportunity to observe students and so their input is extremely important at each step of the process. Identification generally covers three groups of activities.

Step 1: Clarification of Goals

In this step a district's planning committee reviews state guidelines, develops local program philosophy and goal statements, and adopts a working definition of gifted/talented. In states where this is an option, grade levels, numbers of children to be served, and types of abilities to be included in the program are decided. Procedures for including special needs populations should be a key part of the district's plan. Assessment procedures and tests need to be chosen.

The planning committee is responsible for disseminating the information to teachers and conducting inservice sessions with faculty to ensure awareness and understanding of the nature of the program and its target group.

Classroom teachers' involvement is crucial to the success of any program for bright learners. Teachers need to understand and accept that needs of G/T students

TABLE 16.2   Characteristics of the Gifted and Talented Child

Affective Characteristic	+ Positive Manifestations of the Characteristic − Negative Manifestations of the Characteristic
Has an advanced sense of right and wrong; is concerned about ethical issues	+ Holds high standards for personal behavior; is able to discuss philosophical topics typically reserved for older students; understands the consequences of his or her actions − Challenges actions considered to be "unfair;" overly critical, eventually becoming a perfectionist; avoids or argues against rules.
Is willing to take risks to achieve a goal or find answers; is adventurous	+ Is not afraid of failure; is willing to chance being wrong in order to find a solution or prove an idea − Makes random guesses without facts or evidence
Possesses unusual insight	+ Makes inferences from nonverbal clues; easily sees how to get task accomplished; can "read between the lines" to see underlying issues − Jumps to conclusions; uses insight to control or manipulate; does not let anyone "get away with anything"
Has high energy levels	+ Is enthusiastic; is willing to work long and hard on projects and assignments − Often exhausts teachers, parents, and less energetic persons
Has a long attention span and superior ability to focus on a topic	+ Is able to become absorbed in learning or in areas of interest. − Refuses to change focus and pursue other necessary activities; resents interruptions
Possesses an advanced, mature sense of humor	+ Enjoys life; sees the humorous side of tasks and problems, relieves tension through humor; enhances writing with puns and so on − Is the "class clown;" uses humor to put down classmates and self; uses humor to avoid issues, assignments, and problems
Is independent and autonomous	+ Begins tasks without urging; sets own goals; requires little teacher direction; plans ways to accomplish tasks − Is extremely stubborn; believes that his or her way is the only way to do something; resists authority
Is unusually sensitive and empathetic	+ Exhibits a caring attitude toward others; relates well to older peers and adults − Is easily hurt by criticism; worries excessively about the opinions and feelings of others

TABLE 16.2 *continued*

Cognitive Characteristic	+ Positive Manifestations of the Characteristic − Negative Manifestations of the Characteristic
Displays a high level of curiosity; wants to know "why" and "how"	+ Is willing to ask questions and seek answers; is excited by new ideas and activities − Challenges and often refuses to accept ready-made answers; seems always to be asking "why?"
Pursues logical answers and solutions, applies logic when evaluating self and others	+ Recognizes cause and effect; sees consequences of action; is good at critical thinking and problem solving − Challenges statements seen as being illogical or unsubstantiated by facts
Is flexible in thinking, is capable of seeing things from an unusual perspective	+ Adds different ideas to discussions; stimulates others to think differently − Always seems to be going in a different or opposite direction than expected or desired
Is able to generate original and unique ideas, solutions, and answers	+ Brings creativity into the classroom; approaches assignments in creative ways − Is critical of the more stereotypic ideas of others
Is developmentally advanced in language and reading	+ Uses large vocabulary in discussions and written work, reads voraciously and above grade level; is willing to give ideas and opinions in class discussions − Uses vocabulary in arguments to show superiority or to manipulate; uses reading to avoid undesirable activities; dominates conversations and discussions
Is extremely generalized, has a variety of interests	+ Enjoys sharing interests; readily investigates new topics; commits energy to multiple interests − Is fragmented and unable to focus long on any one topic; quickly loses interest in topics or activities
Has extremely specialized interests	+ Is able to accelerate in and commit great energy to a specialized interest − Pursues one interest only; is bored with and uninterested in any other topic
Understands complex, abstract concepts, sees how ideas fit together, sees the relationship among ideas, topics, and content areas	+ Progresses rapidly in advanced subjects; has superior understanding of subject matter; easily transfers knowledge from one discipline to another − Rebels against learning small pieces of information; becomes frustrated by classmates' more simplistic perceptions
Learns and retains basic information easily	+ Tests well; moves rapidly through course material − Becomes bored with the rate at which general classes present material; hates drill-and-practice activities

extend beyond the classroom. Recognizing those needs is a hallmark of an effective teacher, not an indicator of an inadequate teacher. Involving classroom teachers in developing options is essential to the building of a bridge between the standard and gifted education programs and to the enhancing of collaboration between their teachers.

Step 2: Referral/Screening

The key purpose of this step is to find a pool of program candidates. Information collected at this stage needs to be useful for later planning (Frasier, 1980; Swassing, 1985). Standardized test scores, school records, and nominations from students, peers, parents, and teachers are possible channels for referrals of program candidates (Feldhusen, 1979; Hagen, 1980). In an ongoing program, the district might target key transitional years (for example, primary to intermediate) for referrals. Some districts conduct the process at designated times of the year; others accept referrals throughout the year.

When the group of candidates has been established, screening begins. Decisions on what data to collect should focus on adding useful information about a child's abilities and should be related to the district's definition of giftedness. Including a range of information from the objective (for example, achievement tests) to the subjective (for example, teacher checklists and evaluations of student products) ensures that students whose test scores might not reflect their abilities accurately will continue to be included in the process. Common assessments include creativity, intelligence, and achievement tests; districts might add tests of problem-solving abilities or assessments of critical thinking.

Checklists of gifted students' characteristics are a popular screening method for identifying talent. The most widely used teacher checklists are based on the *Scales for Rating the Behavioral Characteristics of Superior Students* (Renzulli, Smith, White, Callahan, and Hartman, 1976). Its 10 scales present an extensive list of characteristics identified by research in a variety of talent areas: intellect, motivation, leadership, creativity, the arts, and communication.

Teachers using characteristics checklists to identify high potential must remember, however, that not all gifted children possess all characteristics. Matches between any child and characteristics common to gifted and talented students is only one indicator of giftedness. Teachers should also keep in mind that these characteristics can be demonstrated in positive and negative ways.

Step 3: Placement Decisions

Once the data are assembled and compiled, usually one person or one small committee analyzes students' profiles and recommends placement. In the instance of a "borderline" case, some districts recommend a trial placement and a review of the student's performance within a designated time. Others collect additional information—for example, interviewing the student. Still others defer placement and recommend a review of the student's progress at the end of the quarter or school year.

Again, classroom teacher input is important at this stage of the identification

DEVELOPING AN INDIVIDUALIZED PROGRAM

The WISC-R intelligence test given to Christopher as part of his diagnostic testing indicated superior ability to think at complex levels, manipulate materials, and comprehend ideas. His performance score was 138, clearly in the superior range. In contrast, his verbal score of 103 indicated average ability to understand written material, retain information, use vocabulary, and solve verbal problems. Christopher's total, or full scale, intelligence test score was 122.

Fortunately, the diagnostician recognized the indicators of a gifted/learning disabled child: a wide discrepancy between scores, one score in the superior range, and reading and language problems (such as the ones reported by Chris's teacher). Further testing was conducted to discover Christopher's specific strengths and weaknesses.

At the beginning of Christopher's fifth-grade year, a planning meeting was held. It was attended by Chris's parents, his classroom teacher, the learning disabilities teacher, the G/T teacher, the school counselor, his special education diagnostician, and the school principal. After discussing test results and options, the participants agreed that Chris's special learning needs could best be met through a cooperative effort among the learning disabilities, G/T, and classroom teachers, with the school counselor serving as a consultant.

process. Relevant anecdotal information can support placing a student on a trial basis or providing enrichment materials and monitoring the student's progress in the classroom.

Instructional Needs

After a placement decision has been made, instructional needs should be assessed. Feldhusen and Robinson (1986, p. 156) identify 12 general considerations for G/T students:

1. Maximum achievement of basic skills and concepts
2. Learning activities at appropriate level and pace
3. Experience in creative thinking and problem solving
4. Development of convergent abilities, especially in logical deduction and convergent problem solving
5. Stimulation of imagery, imagination, spatial abilities
6. Development of self-awareness and acceptance of own capacities, interests, and needs
7. Stimulation to pursue higher level goals and aspirations
8. Exposure to a variety of fields of study, art, professions, and occupations
9. Development of independence, self-direction, and discipline in learning

10. Experience in relating intellectually, artistically, and effectively with other gifted, creative, and talented students
11. A large fund of information about diverse topics
12. Access and stimulation to reading

Many of the items from this list fit within the standard curriculum. Choosing particular emphases for a student's program depends on the student's needs, abilities, interests, and program resources.

> Activity 2, page 492, will allow you to experience observation skills for identifying G/T behaviors.

INTERVENTIONS

Instructional/Interventions

In previous decades, programming for G/T students was structured either to accelerate or to enrich. Experts now recommend more comprehensive, eclectic programming that provides opportunities for enrichment, acceleration, and extension of learning beyond the classroom (Feldhusen, 1982; Renzulli & Reis, 1986; Treffinger, 1986). According to Ward, eminent theorist and author of the seminal book *Educating the Gifted: An Axiomatic Approach* (1961) a program of services for G/T students should comprise a pattern of provisions within the total range of school activities which is designed to meet the distinguishable needs and abilities of intellectually superior and talented children. Single or scattered provisions such as advanced placement or early admission to first grade do not alone constitute a *program* (1975), p. 66). Table 16.3 lists program options available within the standard school program, beyond the standard school program and through extracurricular opportunities.

Because most G/T students spend the majority of their school week in general education classrooms, the standard school programs are a vital component of their education. Classroom teachers can accommodate these children by (a) determining the instructional level for each student, (b) creating flexible ability groups for academic subjects and projects, (c) individualizing assignments and activities, and (d) then making modifications in the standard curriculum. Compacting or compressing the curriculum through testing out or self-paced work creates needed classroom time for special projects and activities that extend the curriculum. In addition to these options, many G/T students attend pull-out or resource room programs, while others enroll in full-time, self-contained programs. The gifted program teacher is a useful resource for enrichment ideas and materials that complement the standard curriculum.

Midschool and high school students benefit from participating in specialized academic classes, honors classes, and advanced placement courses. All are options within the standard school program. Grade skipping, enrolling in multiple grade-level classes, testing out of basic courses, and entering the next school level early are successful accelerative options. These students often have opportunities to work with mentors, expand their career knowledge through internships, and participate in seminars on advanced subjects or special topical interests. A variety of extracurricular programs listed in Table 16.3 can also address these students' cognitive and affective needs.

National programs are available within many local school systems. The Future

Table 16.3 Program Options

Options	Elementary	Midschool	High School
Within standard school programs			
Modification of curricular content, process, products, and materials	X	X	X
Ability grouping within classroom	X	X	X
Individualization	X	X	X
Independent study	X	X	X
Curriculum compacting/telescoping	X	X	X
Honors courses		X	X
Advanced Placement courses			X
Specialized courses		X	X
Multiple grade-level classes	X	X	X
Grade skipping	X	X	X
Testing out of courses		X	X
Early entrance	X	X	X
Beyond standard school programs			
Pull-out programs or resource rooms	X	X	X
Full-time, self-contained classes for gifted/talented	X		
Concurrent enrollment	X	X	X
Mentorships/internships		X	X
Seminars		X	X
Within extracurricular settings			
Cultural experiences	X	X	X
Educational field trips	X	X	X
Correspondence courses		X	X
Governor's schools			X
Residential summer programs	X	X	X
Nonresidential summer, Saturday, and after-school programs	X	X	X

Problem Solving Program features small groups of students developing hypothetical solutions to real-world problems such as pollution or child abuse. In the Odyssey of the Mind program, student teams invent and construct tangible solutions to given problems, such as building a weight-bearing bridge with popsicle sticks. Both programs are designed to help students develop skills that can be generalized solving to life's problems. The Junior Great Books program teaches students critical thinking skills through in-depth discussions and analyses of classic literature.

Guidelines for Evaluating Options

The selection of the best combination of programming options should take into account all aspects of a youngster's learning experience (Passow, 1986). A single adaptation or addition to the general school program is not sufficient. The varied abilities and concomitant needs of G/T youths require that responsible, comprehensive programming includes many options.

When choosing program options for particular students, consider the following questions:

What constitutes the general education curricula for the G/T child?
What specialized curriculum opportunities are needed to develop and nurture the child's special abilities and talents?
What subliminal attitudes of teachers, administrators, parents, and the community are influencing the beliefs and expectations of the G/T student?
What nonschool curricula (for example, family, culture, media) are a part of the child's education, and how might these be used to the child's benefit?

Parents in particular are a key influence on the development of giftedness.

Parental Involvement

Understanding parents' perspectives and concerns and working systematically to build a collaborative relationship with parents can provide a solid foundation for educating bright students. Collaboration reduces the possibility of the child being caught between conflicting loyalties. If problems arise, communication is facilitated through a positive working partnership.

Particularly in the early months following a child's identification as gifted, parents report an overwhelming sense of responsibility to "do right by" their gifted child. This might include fears regarding their adequacy to raise a gifted child or guilt feelings that they might be neglecting their child's growth. Parents sometimes compensate for their feelings by placing excessive demands on themselves and their children, which can negatively affect family relationships, their children's self-esteem, and their children's performance in school. Some parents make the gifted child the focal point of the family, which can lead to inappropriate comparisons among the other children, particularly if they are not identified as gifted (Peterson, 1977). Parents from culturally different backgrounds or whose bright children have other handicapping conditions have additional considerations affecting the way they support their child's exceptional abilities.

Promoting Positive Relationships

Different types of assistance and the way in which they are offered can either promote dependency or promote self-sustaining behavior. Three principles for working with parents of bright students can help them to become partners with classroom teachers in educating the gifted child they share (Dunst & Trivette, 1987):

1. *Offer assistance that is reciprocal.* By definition, accepting aid puts parents in a "one-down" position. Because parents of gifted children tend to act in a "take charge" manner, they are likely to be uncomfortable with a help-seeking role. Recognizing parents' abilities and asking them to share relevant expertise are ways to reduce perceived indebtedness. Parents can share information about their child's abilities, serve as mentors, clarify any cultural differences, and provide input about the gifted program by giving feedback on outcomes observed at home.

2. *Promote parents' natural resources and networks.* Because parents of gifted students tend to feel isolated, especially when the child is newly identified, the teacher is wise to enhance a sense of community rather than to encourage parents to replace resources and networks with professional services. The regular classroom program and the gifted program are important sources of support for children and their parents. Encouraging parents to attend information sessions and support group meetings, clearly communicating the child's program to parents, and ensuring that some goals will be carried out in the regular classroom will help parents to maintain their familiar networks and to build new ones as needed.

3. *Convey a sense of cooperation and joint responsibility for meeting needs and solving problems.* Participatory decision making characterizes this principle. Involving parents as partners with an equal stake in developing, evaluating, and selecting choices for their child will help parents feel valued and a key part of their child's education. Parents can help develop and select programming options, authorize their child's participation in the program, and assume responsibility for some learning activities.

SELECTING AND ADAPTING INSTRUCTIONAL MATERIALS

Matching materials to student strengths, learning patterns, and interests are the hallmarks of effective instruction for all learners, including G/T students. A few adaptations can ensure that G/T learners' needs are supported through the standard education program as well as special education services. Bruner (1966) introduced four aspects of instruction that could be useful guides for selecting or adapting materials:

1. *Stimulation or an opportunity for growth.* Stimulation includes varying cognitive input by increasing the abstractness or complexity of information. Provid-

ing "raw data" that students analyze to uncover underlying principles and assumptions or using higher level questioning strategies is an effective method for stimulating G/T students.

2. *An attitude of play.* Inventing activities, encouraging intellectual risk-taking, and infusing instruction with humor when appropriate diminish the emphasis on the kind of "one right answer" thinking that represses creative ideas.

3. *Identification with positive role models.* Using biographies or other media profiling the lives and work of eminent individuals is a powerful technique for encouraging bright students, who tend to relate more to mental then chronological peers (for example, see the Equity Institute, 1985).

4. *Freedom from excessive drive and anxiety.* This is especially important for bright students, who often face achievement issues. Alleviating pressure to perform and accomplish ultimately comes through a positive self-concept based on clear self-knowledge and self-acceptance. The general education classroom is a key environment for helping students develop realistic self-perceptions and expectations.

Adapting the Standard Curriculum

The most useful starting point for selecting topics to target for modification is the district's general curriculum guide. First, it is board approved, state of the art, familiar, and accepted. No special permissions are needed to focus on particular topics. Second, the guide provides a common "language" for addressing G/T student needs: the same curriculum areas in which all students are educated. Third, by focusing on the content objectives around which the standard curriculum is organized, process skills are taught in meaningful context rather than in isolation, which can aid in the transfer of learning. Developing interest-based, special projects or individualized units of instruction is thus made relevant to the student's total program of instruction (VanTassel-Baska, Feldhusen, Seeley, Wheatly, Silverman, & Foster, 1988).

Some general education curriculum series are introducing possible modifications for teachers to use with gifted learners. A recent example is the 1989 Houghton-Mifflin reading series; its "challenge activities" use an accepted gifted education programming model to extend its reading materials (Renzulli & Reis, 1986). Activities are based on the stories in the series. They develop student interests, enhance high level process skills, and provide opportunities for students to produce advanced level projects. Figure 16.1 shows sample activities to extend the curriculum for Chris and Jessica.

Selecting Supplementary Materials

The four principles outlined by Bruner are useful guidelines for evaluating possible supplementary materials. Keep in mind that many of the materials available through the gifted program teacher are good for all students, regardless of their intellectual abilities. Giftedness is in the response to curriculum.

Therefore, teachers must keep in mind the range of competent responses to curricular input. Students whose cognitive reactions to activities demonstrate complex thinking, such as hypothesizing, evaluating alternatives, and investigating problems from many different avenues, are providing clues to the types of materials that would be effective to challenge their abilities.

The COMETS series (Noyce, V. 1, 1984; Smith, Molitor, Nelson, & Matthews, V. 2, 1984) embodies the principles presented in this section. Activities stimulate students' interest and provide opportunities for students to act as scientists. Profiles, interviews with scientists in related fields, can be used in concert with the topical modules. The brief biographies in *Profiles* include extension activities and questions that help students apply the information to their lives and future career choices. Figure 16.2 contains suggestions for supplementing Maureen's science education.

Using the guidelines outlined in the section, become a curriculum evaluator. Activity 3 page 492, shows you how.

Affective Considerations

A key aspect of modifying instruction for G/T learners involves the classroom climate. The most dynamic enrichment materials will be ineffective unless environmental conditions reduce the likelihood of behavior problems commonly associated with exceptionally bright students:

1. Not listening to others and interrupting other students' verbal responses
2. Being argumentative and/or refusing to comply with requests perceived as unreasonable or trivial
3. Excessively criticizing, teasing, or being bossy
4. Displaying a high energy level that results in "perpetual motion" and disorganized work habits (Whitmore, 1979)

Apart from curriculum-based causes such as boredom, a G/T child's lack of social comfort and competence with chronological peers or social norms that devalue expressions of outstanding intellect can induce that child to act out in order to gain acceptance in the general education classroom. The patterns described in the preceding list can represent the child's own efforts to reduce (self-perceived) excessively high performance expectations.

Delisle, Whitmore, and Ambrose (1987) pointed out that teachers could shape students' emotional and behavioral reactions to school. They listed four teacher behaviors, identified by research on teacher-student interactions and student achievement (Rosenshine & Furst, 1971), that could promote positive relationships with G/T students. Table 16.4 specifies these behaviors.

Figure 16.1   An Activity for Christopher

Become a Set Designer

Begin this project by reading ''Best Friends'' on pages 304–320 of **Explorations.**

These books or others like them will help you as you do this project:
Create Your Own Stage Sets by Terry Thomas (Prentice-Hall, 1985).
Stage Scenery: Its Construction and Rigging by A. S. Gillette and J. Michael Gillette (Harper, 1981).

In order to complete this project, you will need:
Pencils
Paper
Graph Paper

You may use many different materials for building a set or a model of a set.

Step 5:   Sketch Your Ideas
Now make some rough sketches of your ideas for sets and drops. You may begin by sketching the set that the audience will see most. You may want to read an art book or ask an art teacher for advice on how to draw sets in perspective, such as the following.

Step 6:   Plan for Help
Now that you know exactly what flats, drops, and props you need, consider what kind of help you may need from other people. How many workers are needed to build and paint the sets and gather the props? How many stagehands will be needed during the play to change sets, move props, and so on?

Make a list of the jobs that need to be done and decide how many helpers you will need. If you have too many stagehands, they may get in each other's way. Be sure not to plan for more helpers than you really need.

Step 7:   Explain Your Design
After you have completed all the other steps, meet with the director of the play. Show the director your sketches scene by scene. Explain how each set can be changed quickly.

Building the Set

If you are not actually going to build the set you designed, you may wish to make a finished drawing of each scene or a model of each scene. Your model can have movable parts. These drawings or models will be a good record of how much you have learned about set design.

If your set design is going to be used for a play, you have a lot to do! You should have your sets finished, complete with props, in time for several rehearsals before the performance.

You can organize the building of your sets by following six steps.

1. List all the materials and props you will need to complete the set. You may already have most of them. Make a ''wish list'' of the things you still need and post it in a place where many people will see it. If there is a bulletin board in the lobby of your school, for example, that would be a good place. Be sure to include your name and telephone number or room number. Make it clear which items you will return.

SCHOOL NOTICES

Wish List for 5th Grade Play

couch
chair   We will return
desk   these things in
desk chair   good condition
roll of butcher paper
green latex paint
Name ———
Room number ———
Thank You !

Figure 16.1 *continued* An Activity for Jessica

Become a Storyteller

Begin this project by reading "Sevek's First Scenario" on pages 54–61 of **Pageants.**

These books will help you as you do this project:
Handbook for Storytellers by C. Bauer (American Library Association, 1977).
Mime by Kay Hamblin (Doubleday, 1986).
Storytelling: A Triad in the Arts by G. Herman (Creative Learning Press, 1986).

In order to become a storyteller, you will need:
Paper
Pens or pencils

You may also want to use:
Musical instruments
Puppets
Costumes

Step 8: Improve your storytelling by working on specific storytelling techniques. Three techniques are explained on the pages that follow.

Techniques for Vocal Variety and Fluency As a way of trying different voices, use this call and echo chant with a friend. Choose a character voice to use. Your friend must echo both your words and your voice.

You: Chick-a-boom, chick-a-boom.
Friend: Chick-a-boom, chick-a-boom.
You: Chick-a-boom, chick-a-boom
Friend: Chick-a-boom, chick-a-boom.
You: Chick-a-rocka, chick-a-rocka, chick-a-rocka, chick-a-rocka, chick-a-boom.
Friend: Chick-a-rocka, chick-a-rocka, chick-a-rocka, chick-a-rocka, chick-a-boom.

You and your friend can take turns leading the echo chant, using different character voices — slow or quick, high or low, loud or soft, firm or light, and so on. You can change **pitch** (high or low), **rhythm** (patterns of beats), **volume** (loud or soft), **inflection** (patterns of rising and falling tones that create meaning and accents), and **quality** (raspy, thin, smooth, deep, and so on). These contrasts will help your listeners to identify different characters in the story. Try to develop some different voices.

Find a percussion instrument, such as a drum, kalimba (thumb piano), or xylophone. Explore the different sounds you can produce. Then brainstorm possible uses for sound effects in stories. For example, you might use a glissando, running the mallet the length of the xylophone, when a magic event occurs.

Try out your different voices as you use the instrument. Do you have to adapt your voices in order to be heard clearly? Try chanting the title of a story with a percussion instrument as a rhythmic

6 Pageants, Challenge Projects

accompaniment. You can use this chant technique to capture your audience's attention when you begin to tell a story.

Practice calls and call-and-echo chants. Magic words and chants can be used with audience response as an echo. Practice simple calls such as "All ab-o-a-rd," stretching out the vowel sounds. If you want the audience to echo you, say, "Now echo me." Does your story have a place for magic words or for chants?

Take a simple song such as "I've Been Working on the Railroad," and change the words to fit the story you are telling. Try to sing the song in a character's voice. How would a little elf sing it, or a giant, or Cinderella, or John Henry? Create your own song and music for the story.

To improve your fluency, play **Pass the Story** with your friends. Use a stick or wooden spoon to show whose turn it is. The first person, holding the stick or spoon, begins a story. That person then passes the stick or spoon to the next person, who adds a sentence or two to the story. Continue passing the object and adding to the story. Strive for fluency of ideas. If you go blank, repeat the previous idea and build on that.

Techniques for Movement Variety Stand in front of a mirror and try to mime walking through mud, climbing a ladder, feeling a wall, opening a door, holding objects, and so on. Think about how these movements and others can be used in your story.

To develop a variety of gestures and voices, play the theatre game **Wave Craze** with your friends. Make a circle. The first person waves to a second person and says *hi* or *hello* or some other greeting. The second student repeats the greeting, trying to copy the gesture and voice exactly. Then this second student greets a third student, using a totally different gesture and voice style. Continue this way around the circle, with each person mimicking the previous player and then creating a new gesture and voice for the next player to mimic.

Another game to help develop character gestures and voices is **King of the Land.** This is a theater game played in a circle. One person enters the circle and announces, "I am King (or Queen) of this land." The person repeats the statement several times while walking around the inside of the circle and making eye contact with other players. The "King" or "Queen" should use confident, regal movements and practice making eye contact.

Then another player moves into the center of the circle and says, "Excuse me. There must be some mistake. I am King (or Queen) of this land." This new player now creates a regal walk and repeats the sentence several times while the first player rejoins the circle.

This game can be played with many other characters, such as clowns, goblins, detectives, and any others you want to try. Create each character through body stance (posture), and movements, as well as voice.

Techniques for the Performance It's natural to be nervous when you perform before your audience. A little stage fright is often a helpful ingredient for a public performance or speech. It may actually help to make the performer alert to the environment and aware of the audience's needs.

Pageants, Challenge Projects 7

Challenge Projects for the Gifted Reader © 1989. Used with permission by Houghton Mifflin Company.

Managing Instructional Modifications

"Buying time" for enrichment or extension activities is a key concern of general classroom teachers. Experts recommend simple procedures such as allowing students to take the end-of-unit test *before* the unit is taught. Teachers can thereby determine the extent of a student's mastery of new content. Students might attend only those class sessions introducing new or unmastered information. The additional time could be used for extension activities relating to the content. Those listed in the teacher's guide are often a good starting point. Again, the gifted program teacher can be a helpful source for ideas and materials.

Providing incentives such as extra credit or time in a high interest activity center reduces perceptions of variations from the standard curriculum as punishment for demonstrations of giftedness. Opportunities for G/T students to participate constructively in the classroom will enhance the educational climate for all students.

Figure 16.2   Enrichment activities for Maureen

Sharon and Karan Baucom

by Carole Spinharney and Ruth Noyce

KANSAS CITY, KANSAS -- Back in the 1950's, two little black girls were growing up in an average Kansas City home. Like a lot of little girls at the time, one of the identical twin sisters wanted to be a nurse, but it was just about that time when Sharon and Karan Baucom began to show they weren't going to think like all the other little girls in the neighborhood.

When Karan Baucom told her dad she wanted to be a nurse he said, "Why don't you be a doctor?" When she replied she had never seen a black lady doctor, he undauntedly told her she could be the first. And since little girls usually believe what daddys tell them, Karan knew she could become a doctor when she grew up.

Sharon Baucom-Copeland remembers the road to doctorhood a bit differently -- she irreverently insists that Karan got the idea because she liked the candy pills in a toy doctor's kit they got from the Salvation Army when they were kids. Sharon says she can't remember when she made the decision to be a physician -- "I just always wanted to be one."

What makes the story of the Baucom twins different from a lot of childhood dreams is that, against the odds of being female and black (which were pretty big odds at the time), they did it. Today Dr. Karan Baucom and Dr. Sharon Baucom, 25 years old, are both second year resident physicians at the University of Kansas Medical Center.

Karan is specializing in obstetrics and gynecology, and Sharon is a family practice resident. A younger brother, Baron, a student at Meharry Medical College, plans to become a surgeon. The three eventually will start a group practice of Baucom "docs" in Kansas City or Topeka.

The twins enrolled at K. U. in 1968. They were roommates, but not competitors, in college. Both worked hard enough to get accepted to medical school. They received their M. D.'s in the first graduating class from the University of Missouri-Kansas City Medical School in 1974.

"So many people told us it was impossible," said Karan, "that it made us determined to do it." There were a lot of "no's" from blacks, she said, because the twins were both black and female, but their mother and father were always behind them.

Karan resents the assumption made by some people that a black professional can't be an average person, but must be some kind of exception. "We need

*This article was released to the press from the University of Kansas Medial Center Public Relations Office in 1976. It was written by Carole Spinharney.

TECHNOLOGY APPLICATIONS

Computer education is no longer an exotic curricular addendum but an integral part of the standard curriculum. Curriculum for gifted students must incorporate these technological advances (VanTassel-Baska et al., 1988). Gifted students need to be sophisticated consumers as well as producers of technology. Accessing advanced knowledge, exploring ideas , conducting research, and even producing new technologies are activities for which gifted students must be prepared.

Gifted Students as Consumers of Technology

The vast amount of new knowledge generated on a daily basis requires students and teachers to become skilled in managing and assimilating information rapidly and affectively. Breakthroughs in technology during the past 20 years have expedited this process and have created a society of information/technology users.

Figure 16.2   *continued*

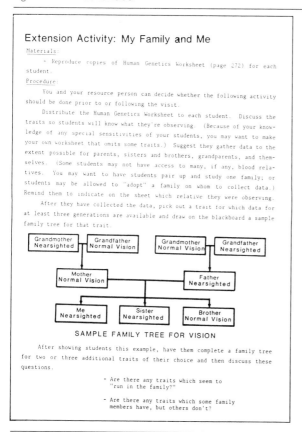

Extension Activity: My Family and Me

Materials:
- Reproduce copies of Human Genetics Worksheet (page 272) for each student.

Procedure:
You and your resource person can decide whether the following activity should be done prior to or following the visit.

Distribute the Human Genetics Worksheet to each student. Discuss the traits so students will know what they're observing. (Because of your knowledge of any special sensitivities of your students, you may want to make your own worksheet that omits some traits.) Suggest they gather data to the extent possible for parents, sisters and brothers, grandparents, and themselves. (Some students may not have access to many, if any, blood relatives. You may want to have students pair up and study one family; or students may be allowed to "adopt" a family on whom to collect data.) Remind them to indicate on the sheet which relative they were observing.

After they have collected the data, pick out a trait for which data for at least three generations are available and draw on the blackboard a sample family tree for that trait.

SAMPLE FAMILY TREE FOR VISION

After showing students this example, have them complete a family tree for two or three additional traits of their choice and then discuss these questions.

- Are there any traits which seem to "run in the family?"

- Are there any traits which some family members have, but others don't?

Source: Smith et al (1984).

Table 16.4 Structuring the Classroom for Success

Teacher Behavior	Description	Teacher Applications
Variability	"Richness" of varied classroom materials and activities	• Make use of learning centers, manipulative materials, computers, independent and sample group projects
	Varied instructional methods	• Provide direct instruction, group discussion, independent/small/large group instruction, peer tutoring, use of media
Use of student ideas	Ability to communicate acceptance of student ideas and integrate them in learning situations	• Acknowledge student ideas by repeating/reflecting student statements • Modify student ideas by rephrasing and conceptualizing • Apply the idea to an inference or as a logical analysis of a problem • Compare the idea to previous student or teacher ideas • Encourage peer reflection, discussion or student ideas
Types of questions	Close-ended, "low-level" (convergent) questions versus open-ended, "high-level" (divergent) questions	• Develop divergent questions that allow analytical thought to occur
Probing	Teacher response to student answers	• Ask further, clarifying questions about student answers that elicit a more comprehensive answer including interrelationships and generalizations

[a]The Complete list of operational definitions of teacher variables that affect student achievement can be found in Rosenshine and Furst (1971).

Source: Delisle, Whitmore, and Ambrose (1987)

Future studies predict that by the end of the 1990s most schools will have ready access to at least six major information technologies: hand-held (lap) computers, microcomputers, mainframe computers, computer networks, mass telecommunications, and interactive videodiscs (Dede, Bowman, & Kierstead, 1982). Table 16.5 illustrates how general classroom teachers, as well as gifted child educators, can help able learners to apply these six technologies both within and beyond the standard school curriculum.

Gifted Students as Producers of Technology

Using the information technologies described in Table 16.5 places gifted students in the position of sophisticated technology *consumers.* Gifted and talented students are also more likely than any other group of learners to become our society's future technology *producers.* Thus, present and future education must equip bright stu-

Table 16.5   Potential Uses of Information Technologies by Gifted Students

Technology	Uses Within Standard Curriculum	Uses Beyond Standard Curriculum
Hand-held (lap) computer	• To individualize and accelerate learning • To do word processing, data management, and temporary storage • To move students rapidly through the basic curriculum	• To immediately record information obtained in libraries, interviews, conferences, and so on • To temporarily store information for use in advanced research and projects
Microcomputer	• To practice and review basic skills briefly and rapidly • To develop critical thinking, problem-solving, and decision-making skills when appropriate software is used • To create and rapidly edit written material through use of word processing • To reduce students' anxiety over written assignments through word processing features such as spelling and grammar checks	• To store, retrieve, manage, and analyze vast amounts of information for special projects and research • To enhance creativity through use of special music, drawing, or desktop publishing software • To learn basic programming skills • To integrate word processing, data bases, and spreadsheets
Mainframe computer	• To conduct on-line searches for library materials • To access and search national and international data banks	• To expand students' knowledge base • To access, where possible, university or business mainframe data courses
Computer network system	• To connect students with network users at other school systems or buildings	• To communicate beyond the classroom and the home • To reduce restrictions imposed by distance • To enable itinerant teachers to communicate with G/T students • To collect special research and project information by surveying network bulletin boards
Telecommunication	(Until this technology makes its way to the classroom, use will be only beyond the standard curriculum.)	• To access televised, interactive instruction • To establish easy, rapid communication between students and professionals • To connect groups of G/T students with a mentor
Interactive video	• To individualize and accelerate learning by enabling students to control the pace and direction of knowledge acquisition • To provide opportunities to learn and use decision-making skills	• To practice higher level decision-making and problem-solving skills when more advanced interactive videos are utilized

dents with the skills necessary to generate technological change. This can be accomplished by training gifted and talented children in the skills directly related to specific technologies and by teaching students generic problem-solving and inquiry skills applicable to a variety of technologies.

Skills training related to specific technologies is best achieved through two approaches. First, teachers can stimulate student interest in technology by creating opportunities for students to use simple, readily available audiovisual materials such as filmstrip, slide, opaque and overhead projectors, tape recorders, and video equipment.

Second, showing students directly how to incorporate simple technological tools into individual and group project reports will alert students to the potential use of these tools in future work. These experiences will student enhance readiness to develop more sophisticated skills in the complex technologies.

Learning general problem-solving skills will enhance creative and critical thinking abilities and equip gifted and talented students with strategies they can transfer in solving real-world problems and developing new technologies. Involving gifted students in technology and futures-oriented learning centers, instructional units, and independent study projects (for example, transportation of the past and future) will also help these students to become producers of future technologies.

Applying Technology

Modifying both the standard curriculum and the gifted program curriculum to offer students training in technological consumption and production requires that educators become more oriented toward the future. Involving gifted students in futures-type activities will help them to understand that the future does not "just happen" but is the result of specific actions. Given research indicating that gifted students are more likely than others to be concerned about the future, these students must learn that they have some control of their own futures and that of humankind (George & Gallagher, 1978; Landau, 1979; Torrance, Bruch, & Goolsby, 1976; Wooddell, Fletcher, & Dixon, 1985).

MULTICULTURAL AND AT-RISK POPULATIONS

In its early days, the field of gifted education focused its attention on those children whose "presenting condition" was most severe—that is, on youngsters whose giftedness was most apparent. By the last 1960s, however, educators, researchers, and the community were voicing a concern for underrepresented G/T populations. This concern resulted in the Marland Report's recommendation that schools locate and serve their minority G/T students. Yet it was not until the 1980s that the field truly committed itself to meeting the needs of children and youth whose giftedness was "at risk."

Across the nation, school systems are beginning to identify and serve these special populations of G/T students. Research in this area is expanding. Conferences are focusing on underserved G/T learners, and special issues of two of the field's key journals have focused on the topic (Gallagher, 1987; Jenkins-Friedman, 1987). The federal government has exhibited some willingness to fund these efforts. The most recently enacted legislation specifically targets support for G/T students who might not be identified through traditional assessment methods (Elementary and Secondary Education Conference Report, 1988).

Economic circumstances, cultural differences, handicapping conditions, geography, and stereotypic beliefs about atypical persons are factors that can mask giftedness and therefore place children at risk for failing to fulfill their potential. Others may have learning, behavioral, and/or physical problems that mask manifestations of extraordinary abilities. Societal attitudes toward certain groups, such as very young children and females, make identifying and programming more difficult to implement effectively.

Typically, students in the at-risk categories are seldom referred for screening as G/T program candidates. Even if these students are assessed for giftedness, standard identification methods often fail to reveal their true potential. Their academic deficits are often more obvious than their strengths, which directs attention to remedial efforts and neglects their G/T needs. Table 16.6 presents eight types of G/T students whose abilities are often unnoticed and unmet. Educational risk factors for each group are outlined as are recommendations for intervention.

Because these children's home environments and school experiences can be quite diverse, risk factors and recommendations should be viewed as general guidelines rather than as specific directives for particular individuals. Heightening educator, parent, and community awareness to the varieties and profiles of at-risk G/T students can dissipate many misconceptions and negative beliefs about these special needs learners and increase the effectiveness of the referral process.

Multidimensional Programming for At-Risk Gifted and Talented Children

Approaches to identifying giftedness in at-risk populations should be multidimensional. Testing in combination with other measures such as classroom observations can help educators locate "hidden" giftedness more effectively. For example, student products such as art work or stories told orally can be collected and analyzed. Teacher rating scales that focus on the characteristics of particular special needs populations can improve the referral process and give clues about student needs (Exceptional Student Education, 1988; Jenkins-Friedman, Bransky, & Murphy, 1986).

All programming recommendations regarding at-risk populations reinforce the importance of considering the child's total learning environment, which includes the subliminal and nonschool curricula affecting these population's education. Efforts must be made to address these children's exceptional abilities even as their basic curricula are modified and remediation is provided. Special education programming should utilize strengths to remediate deficits. Educational goals should include those typical of most G/T programs (for example, critical thinking, problem solving, creative thinking, independence, and self-esteem). Ultimately, educators must reduce the negative impact of the factors that place special needs G/T students at risk and instead to support these youngsters to develop their exceptional abilities fully.

Developing the IEP

As emphasized throughout this chapter, meeting the educational needs of G/T learners requires that educators match programs and curricula to students' varied characteristics, strengths, weaknesses, interests, and learning styles. Developing IEPs for able learners formalizes and summarizes modifications in the standard educational program to support these students' continued growth.

According to Treffinger (1979), "The basic principle in planning the IEP for gifted, talented, and creative students should be that, rather than a detailed prescription of each activity for the student's program, the IEP should be a flexible contract

Table 16.6   At-Risk Gifted and Talented Children

At-Risk Population	Factors Placing Giftedness At-Risk	Intervention Recommendations
Low Socioeconomic Gifted	Lack of stimulating or enriched home environment due to economic factors; low personal and/or family commitment to education; family sees school as an adversary; low self-concepts; poor school attendance	Build upon nonacademic strengths (e.g. creativity or psychomotor); provide highly enriching activities and programs; motivate through warm, safe, creative environment; use older disadvantaged children to serve as role models and peer tutors for younger ones; provide scholarships to special programs; provide adult mentors from similar backgrounds.
Culturally Different Gifted (e.g., Blacks, Hispanics, Asians, Native Americans)	Giftedness often manifested in non-traditional ways; some cultures define "giftedness" differently than the majority culture; negative attitudes toward testing interfere with identification; language barrier (also see "low socioeconomic gifted")	Identify using observation data and nomination forms based on culture-specific characteristics; have at-large minority community nominate potentially gifted youth; use SOMPA adjustments for IQ scores where appropriate; incorporate multicultural awareness into programs; capitalize on cultural strengths; provide broadening and enriching programs; provide adult role models and mentors from same cultural background.
Geographically Disadvantaged Gifted (children from rural or inner city settings)	Community resists change, accepting the status quo; highly trained staff (e.g., counselors, teachers, administrators) often leave or avoid the area; small community populations mean fewer libraries, course offerings and lack of local funds for gifted programs (also see "low socioeconomic gifted")	Use community pride to build programs; expose students to local mentors; have adjacent districts combine resources, teachers, etc.; use technology to establish communication between students and "outside world."
Communication and/or Learning Disabled Gifted (CD/gifted, LD gifted)	Giftedness masked by disability; poor self-concept and peer relations; unable to take in and process information accurately; uneven cognitive development; educational service often focuses only on remediation, scarcity of teachers knowledgeable about handicapping condition and about giftedness	Utilize strengths to remediate deficits; use interests to motivate; have high expectations for success; teach creative problem-solving skills to deal with weaknesses; develop social and leadership skills; seek role models with similar disabilities; teach compensation and coping skills; utilize latest technology; use a multisensory, experiental teaching approach; vary assignments to utilize strengths; individualize.

for services to the student" (p. 54). This key principle translates into several guidelines for developing such IEPs:

1. Focus on ways to build on the student's strengths rather than emphasizing remediation of weaknesses.
2. Take student interests into account.

Table 16.6   At-Risk Gifted and Talented Children

At-Risk Population	Factors Placing Giftedness At-Risk	Intervention Recommendations
Physically Disabled Gifted (e.g., hearing impaired/ gifted, visually impaired/ gifted, gifted children with spinal cord injury, with cerebral palsy, or with muscular dystrophy)	Giftedness masked by disability; poor self-concept; disability prevents adequate intake and output of information; educational provisions address disability only; uneven cognitive and performance development; scarcity of teachers knowledgeable about handicapping condition and about giftedness; limited career choices	Have high expectation for success; teach creative problem-solving skills to deal with disability; develop social and leadership skills; seek role models with similar disabilities; avoid overprotection; teach coping and compensation skills; utilize latest technology, use a multisensory, experiential teaching approach.
Behaviorally Disabled Gifted (underachievers, BD/gifted)	Giftedness masked by disability; poor self-concept and peer relations; low motivation for academics; behavior interests with ability to take in information; developmental delays; feelings of rejection and anger; poor study habits; failure to complete assignments; school phobia; lack of self-confidence and persistence	Utilize strengths to remediate deficits; use interests to motivate; provide challenging, stimulating environment; have high expectations for success; teach a variety of problem-solving methods; encourage family involvement in program; involve child in decision making and goal setting; create a warm, affectionate environment; help child develop leadership/social skills.
Young Gifted (early childhood, preschool, and kindergarten age children)	Uneven development complicates identification; immature bodies impede expressions of giftedness; can lose enthusiasm for learning if not challenged early; teachers are often not trained in early childhood and education of the gifted; lack of local or federal money for special programs	Identify as early as possible; look to parents for indications of giftedness; provide opportunities for family involvement in program; individualize instruction when possible; provide opportunities to learn with other young gifted children; create flexible, stimulating, child-centered programs; teach academic skills when the child is ready, but do not force this learning.
Gifted Girls	Family, school, cultural, and societal stereotypic beliefs about ability, careers, etc., sex bias in textbooks; few professional female role models; fear of estrangement from peers; fear of failure or success	Avoid overprotection; hold high academic expectations; provide opportunities to be independent and to develop self-confidence; maintain equity in academic and career counseling; have equal expectations for females and males; create female support groups; provide female role models and mentors.

Figure 16.3　An IEP for Maureen

INDIVIDUALIZED EDUCATIONAL PLAN

Name: Maureen

Demographic Data:

Age: 16 years, 3 months　　　　Grade: 10th grade

Gender: Female　　Family: Two-parent family, Oldest of four children
　　　　　　　　　　　　　　Maternal grandmother lives with family
　　　　　　　　　　　　　　Father employed, mother is homemaker

Present Level of Performance:
Intellectual Ability: Wechsler Intelligence Scale for Children
　　Revised. Full scale - 126(superior range); Verbal score - 118
　　(High average, bright range); Performance score - 130 (very
　　superior range)
Academic Ability: Iowa Test of Basic Skills,
　　Reading - 80th percentile
　　Mathematics - 99th percentile
Creativity: No creativity test given
Classroom Performance: Two to three grade levels above in
　　mathematics; all other subjects at or above grade level
Learning styles: enjoys quiet activities; prefers to work alone
　　when assignments or projects are graded, otherwise likes
　　to work in small groups; prefers a lecture and application
　　approach to math classes; dislikes discussion in language
　　arts courses.
Teacher Rating Scales:
　　Motivation: Extremely high
　　Creativity: Average
　　Leadership: Average
　　Learning: Well above average in mathematics, slightly above
　　　　average in language arts, all other subjects above
　　　　class average
Interests: mathematics, science, visual arts, dance, music
Affective: Very quiet; sets high standards for self; works hard to
　　satisfy parents, teachers, and self; although wants to fit
　　well with peers, is willing to "be different" when necessary

Long Term Goals:
1. Will maintain accelerated mathematics pace, taking and completing one
　　Advanced Program mathematics course this year (AP Calculus course).
2. Will use research, critical thinking, and problem solving skills to
　　design and conduct a scientific research project (Science Research course).
3. Will develop career awareness skills (Mentorship Program).
4. Will demonstrate effective leadership skills (Seminar course).
5. Will demonstrate discussion skills related to topics of interest.
　　(Seminar course).

Objectives:
1. After selecting a science research topic appropriate for an advanced
　　science experiment, Maureen will review the literature to discover
　　what is known and what is being investigated about the topic (see Goal 2).
2. After investigating the advantages and disadvantages of a selected
　　medical advancement, Maureen will contribute to a debate on the issue
　　presented as a lunchtime event for interested high school students(see
　　Goals 4 and 5).

General Plan for Instructional Services(including the person responsible
　　　　　　　　　　　　　　　　　　　for a specific activity):
1. Maureen will use the Science Indexes at the local university's
　　science library to conduct a literature search related to her science
　　research topic (see Objective 1). Responsible person: Teacher of
　　Science Research course.
2. Working with a small group of students in the Seminar class, Maureen
　　will participate in a debate on the ethical issues (pro and con)
　　related to some recent medical advancement. Note: Maureen can
　　select: a) to be one of the debaters; b) to help organize and advertise
　　the debate; and/or c) to provide background and information to support
　　either side of the debate (see Objective 2). Responsible person: Gifted
　　program seminar teacher.

Service Delivery:

Gifted Education Service: Will participate in a one-hour daily seminar
　　for gifted students and in an after-school mentorship program.
Acceleration of Standard Curriculum: Will take an Advanced Placement
　　Course (10th grade - Calculus) and a science research course
　　restricted to selected students.

(Note: Maureen attended Purdue University's residential summer program
for Talent Search Students; see permanent records for SAT scores.)

Evaluation of Student's Progress:

All high school courses receive standard grades, including the seminar
　　course; the after school mentorship, while monitored by the teacher
　　of the gifted, is an ungraded experience.

3. Consider how the student's learning can best be enriched and accelerated.
4. Present opportunities for the student to develop independence.
5. Coordinate the student's total learning experience (school, home, and community).

Maureen's IEP (Figure 16.3) illustrates concerns outlined in this chapter.

Activity 4, page 493, will help you to simulate a real IEP. You might want to create it for Christopher.

SUMMARY THOUGHTS

The focus of education for the gifted and talented represents something of an anomaly in special education. Whereas special education for students with handicaps intends to correct a deficit, special education for G/T students intends to heighten the presenting symptom—giftedness. Despite this difference, G/T students are similar to other students in special education in that they represent a diverse group whose identification is not clear-cut. Indeed, because G/T students can be just as disruptive in a classroom as other special students, regular classroom teachers are sometimes not easily convinced that the student who is argumentative, does not listen to others, challenges authority, and criticizes "humdrum" activities may be displaying signs of giftedness.

Because most G/T students get their education in regular classrooms, classroom teachers' involvement is critical to the educational success of these students. Accommodation of G/T students requires identification of appropriate instructional levels, flexibility in creating study groups and projects, individualization of assignments and activities, and modification of the standard curriculum. Indeed, giftedness shows itself in response to curriculum.

Instructional interventions, including the provision of incentives such as extra credit or time in a high interest activity center, can be greatly aided by the use of technology. G/T students are more likely than any other group to be the future producers of technology, so early familiarity with computers and the problem-solving and decision-making skills needed to use them effectively are an educational must for G/T students.

REFERENCES

Barbe, W. B. & Renzulli, J. S. (1975). Historical development. In W. B. Barbe & J. S. Renzulli (Eds.), *Psychology and education of the gifted* (2nd ed.) (pp 3-5). NY: Irvington Publishers.

Bloom, B. S. (Ed.). (1985). *Developing talent in young people.* New York: Ballentine.

Boyle, J., & Laurent, C. (1987). A survey of the states' efforts in gifted education. Unpublished report, University of Wisconsin—Stevens Point.

Bruner, J. (1966). *Toward a theory of instruction.* Boston: Belknap Harvard University Press.

Dede, C., Bowman, J., & Fierstead, F. (1982). Communications technologies and education: The coming transformation. In H. F. Didsbury (Ed.), *Communication and the future.* Bethesda, MD: World Future . pp. 174–182.

Delisle, J. R., Whitmore, J.R., & Ambrose, R. P. (1987). Preventing discipline problems with gifted students. *Teaching Exceptional Children.* Summer, 32–38.

Dunst, C. J., & Trivette, C. M. (1987). Enabling and empowering families: Conceptual and intervention issues. *School Psychology Review, 16,* 443–456.

Elementary and Secondary Education Conference Report (1988). Report 100-567, to accompany H.R.5.

Equity Institute (1985). *American women in science biographies.* Bethesda, MD: Author.

Exceptional Student Education. (1988). Unpublished instrument, pilot program for underachieving gifted students. Broward County, FL.

Feldhusen, J. F. (1979). *G/T identification procedure.* Unpublished materials. Purdue University, West Lafayette, Indiana.

Feldhusen, J. F. (1982). Meeting the needs of the gifted through differentiated programming. *Gifted Child Quarterly. 26.* 37–41.

Feldhusen, J. F., & Robinson, A. (1986). The Purdue secondary model for gifted and talented youth. In J. S. Renzulli (Ed.), *Systems and models for developing programs for the gifted and talented* (pp. 153–179). Mansfield Center, CT: Creative Learning Press.

Frasier, M. M. (1980). Screening and identification of gifted students. In J. B. Jordan & J. A. Grossi (Eds.), *An administrative handbook and developing programs for the gifted and talented* (pp. 48–55), Reston, VA: Council for Exceptional Children.

Gallagher, J. J. (1975). *Teaching the gifted child* (2nd ed.). Boston: Allyn & Bacon.

Gallagher, J. J. (Ed.). (1987). Underserved populations of gifted students [Special Issue]. *Journal for the Education of the Gifted. 10*(3).

George, P., & Gallagher, J. J. (1978). Children's thoughts about the future: A comparison of gifted and nongifted students. *Journal for the Education of the Gifted. 2,* (1) 33–42.

Goertzel, M. G., Goertzel, V., & Goertzel, T. G. (1978). *Three hundred eminent personalities.* Boston: Little, Brown.

Goertzel, V., & Goertzel, M. G. (1962). *Cradles of eminence.* Boston: Little, Brown.

Grinder, R. E. (1985). The gifted in our midst: By their divine deeds, neuroses, and mental test scores we have known them. In F. D. Horowitz & M. O'Brien (Eds), *The gifted and talented: Developmental perspectives* (pp. 5–36). Hyattsville, MD: American Psychological Association.

Hagen, E. (1980). *Identification of the gifted.* New York: Teachers College Press.

Houseman, W. (1987). *The 1987 state of the states gifted and talented education report.* Topeka, KS: Council of State Directors of Programs for the Gifted.

Jenkins-Friedman, R. (Ed.). (1987). Special populations of gifted students [special focus issue]. *Gifted Child Quarterly, 31*(4).

Jenkins-Friedman, R., Bransky, T. S., & Murphy, D. L. (1986). *Empowering gifted behavior scale.* Unpublished instrument, University of Kansas.

Landau, E. (1979). The young person's institute for the promotion of science. In J. J. Gallagher (Ed.), *Gifted children: Reaching their potential* (pp. 105-109). Jerusalem: Kolleck & Sons.

Marland, S. (1972). *Education of the gifted and talented.* Report to the Subcommittee on Education, Committee on Labor and Public Welfare, U. S. Senate. Washington, DC: GPO.

Noyce, R. (Ed.). (1984). *COMETS profiles* (Vol. 1). Washington, DC: National Science Teachers Foundation.

Oden, M. H. (1968). The fulfillment of promise: 40-year follow-up of the Terman gifted group. *Genetic Psychology Monographs, 77,* 3-93.

Passow, A. H. (1986). *The four curricula for G/C/T students* (videotape). Mobile, AL; G/C/T.

Peterson, D. (1977). The heterogeneously gifted family. *Gifted Child Quarterly, 20* (3), p. 396–398.

Renzulli, J. S. (1989). *Challenge projects* (Level L: Explorations, Level N: Pageants). Boston: Houghton Mifflin.

Renzulli, J. S., & Reis, S. M. (1986). The enrichment triad/revolving door model: A schoolwide plan for the development of creative productivity. In J. S. Renzulli (Ed.), *Systems and models for developing programs for the gifted and talented* (pp. 216-266). Mansfield Center, CT: Creative Learning Press.

Renzulli, J. S., Smith, L. H., White, A. J., Callahan, C. M., & Hartman, R. K. (1976). *Scales for rating the behavioral characteristics of superior students.* Mansfield Center, CT: Creative Learning Press.

Rosenshine, B. V., & Furst, N. (1971). Research in teacher performance criteria. In B. Othaniel Smith (Ed.), *Research in teacher education* (pp. 44-54). Englewood Cliffs, NJ: Prentice-Hall.

Sears, P. S., & Barbee, A. H. (1977). Career and life satisfactions among Terman's gifted women. In J. C. Stanley, W. C. George, & C. H. Solano (Ed.), *The gifted and the creative: A fifty-year perspective* (pp. 28-65). Baltimore, MD: Johns Hopkins University Press.

Sears, R. R. (1977). Sources of life satisfaction of the Terman gifted men. *American Psychologist, 32,* 119-128.

Sicherman, B. (1981). The paradox of prudence: Mental health in the gilded age. In A. Scull (Ed.), *Madhouses, mad-doctors, and madmen: The social history of psychiatry in the Victorian era* (pp. 218-240). Philadelphia: University of Pennsylvania Press.

Smith, W. S., Molitor, L. L., Nelson, B. J., & Matthews, C. E., (1984). *COMETS science* (Vol. 2). Washington, DC: National Science Teachers Association.

Sternberg, R. J. (1986). A triarchic theory of intellectual giftedness. In R. J. Sternberg & J. E. Davidson (Eds.), *Conceptions of giftedness* (pp. 223-243). New York Cambridge University Press.

Swassing, R. H. (1985). Identification, assessment, and individualization. In R. H. Swassing (Ed.), *Teaching gifted children and adolescents* (pp. 26-58). Columbus, OH: Merrill.

Tannenbaum, A. J. (1975). A background and forward glance at the gifted. In W. B. Barbe & J. S. Renzulli (Eds.), *Psychology and education of the gifted* (2nd ed.). (pp. 21-30). NY: Irvington Publishers.

Terman, L. M. (1925). Mental and physical traits of a thousand gifted children. In L. M. Terman (Ed.), *Genetic studies of genius* (Vol. 1).Stanford, CA: Stanford University Press.

Terman, L. M., & Oden, M. H. (1947). The gifted child grows up. In L. M. Terman (Ed.), *Genetic studies of genius* (Vol. 4). Stanford, CA: Stanford University Press.

Terman, L. M., & Oden, M. H. (1959). The gifted group at mid-life: Thirty-five year's follow-up of the superior child. In L. M. Terman (Ed.), *Genetic studies of genius* (Vol. 5). Stanford, CA: Stanford University Press.

Torrance, E. P., Bruch, K., & Goolsby, T. (1976). Gifted children study the future. In J. Gibson & P. Channels (Eds.), *Gifted children: Looking to their future* (pp. 182-204). London: Latimer.

Treffinger, D. J. (1979). Individualized education program plans for gifted, talented, and creative students. In S. M. Butterfield, S. N. Kaplan, M. Meeker, J. S. Renzulli, L. H. Smith, & D. J. Treffinger (Eds.), *Developing IEPs for the gifted/talented.* (pp. 51–69). Ventura, CA: National/State Leadership Training Institute for Gifted Talented.

Treffinger, D. J. (1986). Fostering effective, independent learning through individualized programming In J. S. Renzulli (Ed.), *Systems and models for developing programs for the gifted and talented* (pp. 429-460). Mansfield Center, CT: Creative Learning Press.

VanTassel-Baska, J., Feldhusen, J. F., Seeley, K., Wheatly, G., Silverman, L., & Foster, W. H. (1988) *Comprehensive curriculum for gifted learners.* Boston: Allyn & Bacon

Ward, V. S. (1975). Basic concepts. In W. B. Barbe & J. S. Renzulli (Eds.), *Psychology and education of the gifted* (2nd ed.) (pp. 61-71). NY: Irvington Publishers.

Whitmore, J. R. (1979). Disciplining and the mentally gifted child. *Roeper Review, 2,* 42-46.

Wooddell, G. D., Fletcher, G. H., & Dixon, T. E. (1985). Futures study for the adolescent gifted: A curriculum evaluation. *Journal for the Education of the Gifted, 5* 24-33.

ADDITIONAL READINGS

Butterfield, S. M., Kaplan, S. N., Meeker, M., Renzulli, J. S., Smith, L. H., & Treffinger, D. J. (Eds.). (1979), *Developing IEPs for the gifted/talented.* Ventura, CA: National/State Leadership, Training Institute for the Gifted/Talented.

Costa, A. L. (Ed.) (1985). *Developing minds: A resource book for teaching thinking.* Alexandria, VA: Association for Supervision and Curriculum Development.

Feldman, D. H., & Goldsmith, L. T. (1986). *Nature's gambit: Child prodigies and the development of human potential.* New York: Basic Books.

Fine, M. J. (in press) (Ed.). *Collaborative involvement with parents of exceptional children.* Brandon, VT: Clinical Psychology Press.

Hayden, T. L. (1980). *One child.* New York: Putnam.

Horn, R. E. (1977). *The guide to simulations/games for education and training* (3rd). Cranford, NJ: Didactic Systems.

Horowitz, F. D., & O'Brien, M. (Eds.). (1985). *The gifted and talented: Developmental perspectives.* Hyattsville, MD: American Psychology Association.

Karnes, F. A., & Collins, E. C. (Eds) (1984). *Handbook of Instructional resources and references for teaching the gifted* (2nd ed.). Boston: Allyn & Bacon.

Kerr, B. A. (1985). *Smart girls, gifted women.* Columbus, OH: Ohio Psychology Publishing Co.

Renzulli, J. S., & Stoddard, E. (Eds.). (1980). *Under one cover: Gifted and talented education in perspective.* Reston, VA: ERIC Clearinghouse on Handicapped and Gifted Children.

Rossiter, M. W. (1982). *Women scientists in America: Struggles and strategies to 1940.* Baltimore, MD: Johns Hopkins University Press.

Sanders, N. M. (1966). *Classroom questions: What kinds?* New York: Harper & Row.

Sternberg, R. J., & Davidson, J. E. (Eds.). (1986). *Conceptions of giftedness.* New York: Cambridge University Press.

Stewart, E. D., & Dean, M. H. (1980). *The almost whole-earth catalog of process oriented enrichment materials.* Mansfield Center, CT: Creative Learning Press.

1

Purpose

☐ To help you develop a definition of giftedness

☐ To enable you to understand programming for bright students and to help you to become alert to giftedness-in-action.

Steps

1. Think of an individual whom you consider to be gifted. Write down the qualities that distinguish this person from others of average ability.

2. Find at least five people to interview, preferably of different ages and walks of life. Ask each to define giftedness.

3. Read the article reprinted from *The Wall Street Journal* and list the G/T characteristics Matthew demonstrated. Scan print media for similar stories and develop a file.

Come to Think of It, Elbows Don't Look Much Like Elbows Either

By DALE MAZER
Special to THE WALL STREET JOURNAL

Dinosaurs are all the rage with kids these days, so American Home Products Corp. figured it had a sure thing when it introduced Chef Boyardee's Dinosaurs Pasta Shapes last year. But the company underestimated how picky kids can be.

Not about pasta, but about dinosaurs.

What's One Claw?

The problem was that kindergarteners can tell the difference between a tyrannosaurus and an allosaurus at a glance. On the off chance that you can't, the distinction is in the fingers: A tyrannosaurus arm has two claws, but the arm of an allosaurus has three.

Somehow, neither the in-house artist at American Home Products nor his supervisors knew this. The result: The original label on the Pasta Shapes can purported to show a tyrannosaurus—but with three claws on each arm.

Before long, children were up in arms over the extra digit, and about 20 complained to the company. Corrina Burkholder of Ephrata, Pa., for instance, wrote a letter in March on behalf of her son, Matthew, then three years old, after he kept insisting that the label was wrong. "For a couple of months, he kept saying he was right, and we kept ignoring him," she recalls. Finally, Matthew's parents resolved the issue by taking the boy to a dinosaur exhibit at a museum in Philadelphia. Then Mrs. Burkholder wrote the letter.

Cutting Off a Finger

But after the complaints came in, the company checked with the New York Museum of Natural History. And last summer it amputated the extra digit—and sent letters and coupons for free Dinosaurs Pasta Shapes to the children who had written.

1/5/89

Reprinted by permission of *The Wall Street Journal,* Dow Jones & Company (© 1989).

Analysis

☐ Categorize the respondents' beliefs along a continuum from supporting of to opposition to gifted education programming.

☐ Think of yourself as a newly identified gifted student. How might you feel about these opinions? In what ways might they affect your attitudes?

☐ Sort the beliefs and definitions according to their historical origin. How many can you attribute to the influence of the prescientific era? The psychometric era? The legislative era? What does this tell you about the influences of these eras on modern American thought?

☐ Think of ways you could incorporate articles from the media into your classroom teaching. Make a plan for yourself to encourage student's abilities.

2

Purpose

☐ To help you develop observation skills for identifying G/T behavior.

Steps

1. Make all of the characteristics list from Table 16.2 into an observation guide, using the following format:

   Child's Name _____ Date of Observation_____

   Characteristic 1:

   > Related positive behaviors
   >
   > Related negative behaviors

2. Pick a child to observe at least five times each, preferably during his/her time in a G/T program **and** in the regular classroom. You will need to arrange this with the G/T and classroom teachers. Keep separate checklists for each setting.

3. Observe the child's behavior, being careful to be as unintrusive as possible. As the child demonstrates a behavior related to a characteristic, make a check mark.

4. After your last observation, total the checks for each behavior.

Analysis

☐ Analyze the child's behavior patterns. What characteristics were displayed most often? Were the behaviors predominantly negative or positive?

☐ In what ways did the child's behavior change in the two settings?

☐ How did others relate to the child in the two settings? Which behaviors were valued in each setting?

☐ Use your experiences to write a brief guide to screening children for giftedness.

3

Purpose

☐ To help you to analyze elements in standard curricula

☐ To enable you to identify topics for modification or extension for G/T learners

Steps

1. Review the chapter's section on modifying and adapting materials, and make a list of desirable G/T curriculum attributes.

2. Borrow several standard textbooks or use ones with which you are already familiar to analyze each textbook's attributes.

3. Review your evaluations. Identify units or topics that you believe would work well with G/T learners and topics that would need to be modified.

4. If you can arrange it, teach a lesson from the first group. Meet with a G/T teacher and develop a plan to modify a lesson from the second group, and teach it to the same group of learners (preferably a mixed ability group).

Analysis

☐ What were the most prevalent features of the standard curriculum? According to your analysis, how much of it was appropriate for G/T students? How much would have to be modified?

☐ What were the results of the lessons? How accurate were your evaluations? In what ways did students of varying abilities respond to the lessons?

☐ Think about what you learned from the experience. Make a personal list of suggestions to use when you evaluate curricula and teach G/T students.

| 4 |

Purpose

☐ To help you to apply the IEP information in this chapter to a simulated "real world" problem

Steps

1. Review the IEP at the end of the chapter.

2. Read the goals and related activities. Select a goal and brainstorm 3–5 additional activities that you, as the child's classroom teacher, could do with that student.

3. Think of some ways to evaluate the student's work **besides** tests.

Analysis

☐ What teaching and management skills would you need to make your plan work?

☐ Based on the information provided about "your" student, what would be the biggest challenges to making your plan work? What could you do to help the student overcome these challenges successfully?

☐ What qualities do you have that would make you an effective teacher of bright learners? What would you need to modify?

17

Exceptional Children In Tomorrow's Schools

Judy Smith-Davis
Information Services Consultant

"The Need to Know" for tomorrow's children.

The point at which one body of water or air flows into another is characterized by extreme turbulence. Figuratively, the same is true whenever social and economic systems undergo a dramatic transformation. The 20th century is concluding in just such a period of transition as the United States passes from the industrial to the postindustrial era, from the modern to the postmodern period, and from the status quo to a new age whose dimensions may be anticipated but not completely understood.

To envision the education of exceptional children in this new age, it is necessary to speculate on the nature of tomorrow's schools and therefore to examine the political, social, and economic issues that are likely to influence education during the period of transition and thereafter. In doing so, this chapter recalls what has unfolded thus far in the education of exceptional children, evaluates the current turbulence and mutability for indications of things to come, and views change as an enabling factor that will liberate teachers, schools, and communities to shape the future of education in positive ways.

DIVERSITY IN THE SCHOOLS

Students with disabilities, along with many other students in today's schools, may be described as "difficult to teach" because they are not likely to learn automatically with typical instruction and because they collectively and individually represent greater diversity than is found in the typical classroom. Until the 20th century, such children were generally excluded from the public schools.

As Skrtic (1988) pointed out, the education of students who are difficult to teach has been an issue for most of this century. Starting in the first decade, waves of immigrants, compulsory attendance laws, and other changes began to bring greater numbers of more diverse students to the schools. An eventual response to greater diversity was the special class, which became fairly widespread from the 1930s to the 1950s. In 1954, the Supreme Court's decision in *Brown* v. *Board of Education,* 347 US 483, 1954, which desegregated the schools, was a major minority challenge to the principle of exclusion. Exclusionary practices have been progressively restricted since that time (Howsam, 1983), not only in the schools but in society at large.

In the 1960s, the civil rights movement raised questions as to whether the special class and special school interfered with equal access to education. In response, the mainstream model emerged, and efforts began to return students with mild to moderate disabilities to the general education classroom, aided by resource services from special education (Skrtic, 1988). The 1970s witnessed the deinstitutionalization of children with severe handicaps, their return to their home communities, and the quest to move their education from centers to classrooms in public school buildings. By the 1980s, the evolving issue was whether special education for students with mild to moderate disabilities should cease to exist and be merged with general education. To actualize such a proposal would require a complete restructuring of the ways that schools are organized, operated, and administered (Skrtic, 1987).

Viewpoints and policies concerning the education of students with disabilities (and other students who bring increasing diversity into the school population) have centered on issues of *where* and *why*. As a result of this focus, all children have gained the right to a free, appropriate public education in the least restrictive environment commensurate to their instructional needs.

The only factor that now impedes greater access to the mainstream by students with disabilities and other types of variance is the capacity of general education to respond with effective instruction to the diversity of needs, learning styles, and other characteristics of children who are not typical. Therefore, in the future we may expect to see the focus move from questions of *where* students are placed (instructional setting) and *why* (rights) to fundamental issues of *what* and *how* to teach students who are difficult to teach (curriculum, instruction, methods, materials, options, alternatives, instructional roles, and relationships). In this situation, special educators should have important responsibilities that cross the educational spectrum.

Activity 1, page 511, asks you to ponder what special education might look like in the 21st century.

FISCAL SIGNALS

While schools and society were becoming more inclusive, the economy and fiscal strength of the United States were fluctuating. Following economic expansion in the 1920s, the Great Depression of the 1930s, and the 40-year industrial and economic surge after World War II, this country found itself in diminished fiscal circumstances in the late 1980s. The federal deficit now exceeds the total of all former debt in the nation's history, and prolonged difficulties exist in managing the change to a postindustrial economy. These and other features of the American financial base have become major public policy issues, and the solutions that are enacted will distinctly influence the nature of tomorrow's schools.

As decision makers grapple with declining resources, several signals are already appearing. One of these signals is the growing emphasis on cost/benefits among taxpayers, policy makers, and governments, all of whom want to invest scarce dollars wisely in programs that bring results. As budgets go down and/or taxes go up, the accountability and performance outcomes of education and human services will become paramount in decisions about allocating funds. Therefore, evidence of effectiveness of education for exceptional students will become more politically influential than it has been in the past (Brandl, 1983).

Concern with cost/benefits increases the probability that the effectiveness of instruction in terms of student outcomes will be the overriding issue. The demonstration of effectiveness will bring not only direct benefits to exceptional children but will probably become the major factor that enables continuing public and political support of many goals advanced for the integration of exceptional individuals in our society.

Another signal emerging from fiscal constraints stems from mounting pressures from a multiplicity of special interest groups, each demanding a greater share of the nation's diminishing resources. As these demands become more unrealistic, society may indeed shift from a concern with special interests and individual rights to a concern with the common good (Stedman, 1983). As this occurs, perhaps special educators and other advocates from many disciplines and services will join in a greater spirit of cooperation and a larger effort in behalf of the many children who are at risk of failing to learn in school and succeed in life.

TRENDS AMONG CHILDREN AND YOUTH

Between 1987 and 1997, the numbers of children ages 5 to 13 in the United States will increase by 10 percent and the population of youth ages 14 to 17 will increase by 4 percent; during the previous ten years (1977 to 1987), the population aged 5 to 24 decreased (National Center for Education Statistics, 1988). The social, economic, and cultural changes occurring within the school-age population are already significant and will doubtless become more prominent as this age group expands.

Nearly 30% of the school-age population and about 33% of preschool children are members of minority groups (American Association of Colleges for Teacher Education, 1988). Among these, the number of language minority students is expected to increase by 33% by the year 2000; between 1980 and the end of the century, the U.S. population of Spanish-speaking people alone is projected to grow by about 48% and include 22 million people (Yates, 1987).

The poverty line for a family of three is $9,000 per year (Kondracke, 1989). In 1984, the Congressional Budget Office reported that approximately 22% of all children under the age of 17 lived in poverty. This number is increasing (Yates, 1987). As of 1988, 45% of black children and 15% of white children were classified as poor (Kondracke, 1989).

In addition to poverty, a variety of other serious problems affect American children and youth, among them changes in family structure, delinquency, substance abuse, teenage pregnancy, homelessness, dropping out of school, adolescent suicide, high rates of youth unemployment, child abuse and neglect, undernourishment, and the various health and adjustment problems that accompany these conditions. Clearly, the diversity of the school population is increasing, and more and more students are at risk of school failure and other vulnerabilities because of social and domestic conditions that interfere with learning. Many of these students are "simply not clear about what their lives are for and what is worth working for" (Singer, 1972, p. 32). Within this context, students with disabilities represent only a portion of a large and growing group of children and youth who have special needs and who are "difficult to teach."

Although the educational community has not yet fully determined how to respond to these needs, a sense of urgency prevails. The implications are strong for all disciplines and services concerned with children's education, health, and welfare to work together in unified ways, not only to help these children now but to prevent these conditions from multiplying in the future. As these changes take place, the skills, knowledge, and values of special educators will become crucial. Ultimately, special education may be able to reposition itself in a more integrated manner with other service systems without losing its identity, integrity, or effectiveness (Stedman, 1983).

In addition, teachers will probably become even more important in the lives of students. Students today judge the excellence of teachers according to how much they encourage individual participation, give students individual attention, have high expectations of students, interact with them informally, and show caring for students (Louis Harris & Associates, 1988). Students who are living through negative experiences are deeply in need of these kinds of interactions. In many cases, their teachers may be the only persons who can offer them.

Young Children

Of all young people who are at risk, none are more vulnerable than infants, toddlers, and preschool children, as the following data show (National Center for Clinical Infant Programs, 1988):

☐ Every year, about 3.7 million babies are born in the United States. Approximately 25% are born to families living in poverty.

☐ The percentage of low-income children ages 6 months to 5 years who are at risk of brain damage due to elevated levels of lead in their blood is nine times that of upper-middle-income children.

☐ Almost 250,000 babies born each year weigh less than 5½ pounds; of these, more than 43,000 weigh less than 3½ pounds. Low birth weight and prematurity are associated with multiple risks, including a greater likelihood of some degree of mental retardation or other disabling condition.

☐ In 1983 alone, nearly 20% (738,000) of all infants were born to single mothers, more than a fivefold increase since 1950. The birthrate for unmarried black teenagers is almost four times that for white unmarried teenagers.

☐ A teenaged mother is more likely than an older mother to bear a low birth weight baby or a baby with a disability. Mothers with less than a high school diploma are half again as likely to have an unintended pregnancy as are mothers who complete high school.

☐ Between 100,000 and 150,000 (3 to 5%) of babies are born with congenital defects that will lead to mental retardation; 1 to 2% of babies are born with another identifiable disability.

☐ Between 1,500 and 2,000 American infants are born each year with fetal alcohol syndrome, which is a cluster of congenital defects, including nervous system dysfunction, known to be caused by the mother's heavy drinking during pregnancy. For every child with identified fetal alcohol syndrome, there are several others who have been affected during pregnancy but lack the full set of characteristics required for the diagnosis at birth.

☐ Smoking during pregnancy has a demonstrable effect on birth weight of the child. Smoking and drinking have been found to be much higher among mothers of low socioeconomic status, including those who are unmarried.

☐ Although there are no national statistics on babies born to drug-abusing mothers, a 1977 study of known births in seven major cities showed that mothers who used heroin or methadone gave birth to 1,980 babies in those cities alone in that year.

☐ Infants and toddlers age 3 and under represent only 22% of all children, yet they account for 30% of the 800,000 reported cases of child abuse each year and for an even higher percentage of fatalities caused by abuse. Infants and toddlers with handicaps are more likely to be abused.

☐ Approximately 70% of all infants and toddlers who are in out-of-home care by nonrelatives are in family day care. More than 70% of family day care centers are unregulated, and 19% of family day care providers have an eighth-grade education or less.

☐ Of all children born in 1983, 45% will have parents who divorce, and 59% will live at some time in a single-parent home.

These facts suggest an increase in the numbers of children who will manifest disabilities or other problems that place them at risk of school failure. The particular vulnerabilities of many of these children will bring new dimensions of diversity and special needs to the school population. Because experiences and opportunities in the first 5 years of life are very important to later development, and because of the rising incidence of deprivation and trauma among young children, some educational leaders are urging that early prevention programs be made widely available (see Urban Superintendents Network, 1987; Hoffman, 1989).

Schools cannot work alone to modify the effects of complex social conditions that debilitate so many children, but schools are central places where children congregate and are often the sites of other community activities as well. If educational, health, and human services are brought into closer alignment by the magnitude of their shared challenges, many agencies might offer clusters of services for parents and children in the school building or on the school grounds before, during, and after school hours.

Schools and teachers may also find themselves joined by the community in efforts to reverse current trends. When confronted by mounting social and educational problems and "more will than wallet" in the public sector, the future may indeed inspire the kinds of community action being urged in the public media: "Every business, church, civic group, social organization, government office, and country club in America should be encouraged to tutor kids, adopt schools, fund settlement houses, staff recreation centers, and otherwise rescue the rescuable" (Kondracke, 1989, p. 20).

Adolescents

The difficulties of children and youth in postmodern society are also expressed in the outcomes of public education. In 1987, nearly 3,800 American teenagers dropped out of school every day (Urban Superintendents Network, 1987). Approximately 14% of white students, 25% of black students, and more than 50% of Hispanic students drop out before completing high school. These individuals have the highest rate of children born out of wedlock (Yates, 1987), and unemployment among youth, most particularly black youth, reached unprecedented proportions in the 1980s.

In a U.S. Department of Education follow-up of students who were high school sophomores in 1980 (Pallas & Verdugo, 1986), the dropout rates for students with disabilities ranged from a low of approximately 19% for students with orthopedic handicaps to a high of approximately 37% for students with learning disabilities. Among exceptional students, "those who are mildly handicapped and capable of being mainstreamed are at the greatest risk of dropping out" (Lichtenstein, 1988, p. 13).

In the late 1960s and early 1970s, one response to the growing diversity among students was an expansion of the curriculum of many high schools to include courses about the popular culture, which sometimes superseded more rigorous basic and academic courses. The response in the 1980s was to raise graduation requirements, introduce competency testing, and return to a more academically oriented curriculum. Neither of these options, however, may be the answer for students who have disabilities or for others who are difficult to teach. It is suspected that "the failure to address the needs of individual students in both regular and special classrooms has resulted in lower achievement and less than acceptable adult outcomes of many leaving the school system" (Bodner, Clark, & Mellard, 1987, p. 50).

To make education more relevant for the diversity of students, and to curb the dropout rate, tomorrow's high schools will probably offer alternative, functional curricula and skills instruction that will benefit the large proportion of students who are at risk as well as adolescents with disabilities. As this occurs, teachers may create linkages with many resources and sites outside the school building that can be useful as instructional alternatives, extensions, and options and that bridge the boundaries among school, work, community living, cultural and social relationships, and postsecondary opportunities. Thus, community-based instruction may become an integral concept of the secondary learning agenda, and schools may "become more of a concept and less of a place" (Ishler, 1988).

In the future, the boundaries must diminish between high school and adult continuing and vocational opportunities for persons with disabilities. The need for greater interaction and continuity is already clear. For example, preliminary findings of SRI International's national study of the status of former special education students a year after they graduated (Viadero, 1989) showed that fewer than 50% of those with mental retardation, multiple handicaps, or deaf-blindness were involved in postsecondary education, were employed, were participating in on-the-job training, or were married and raising children (about 80% of graduates who were deaf, hard of hearing, learning disabled, or speech impaired were involved in these pursuits). As a group, only 15% of graduates with disabilities were taking postsecondary courses (as contrasted with more than 50% of youth without disabilities) in the first 2 years after completing high school.

These findings emphasize the need for greater attention to the adult needs of persons with disabilities and greater consideration for their lifelong learning opportunities. In the future, special educators are likely to be employed in and work more closely with vocational rehabilitation and other adult community services in order to support increasing independence for adults with special needs. Another task, both now and in the future, will be to publicize and communicate to business, industry, postsecondary education, and the public the performance and achievement of persons with disabilities so that growing numbers of employers will recognize the benefits of training and employing these valuable, dependable, and productive workers.

Postsecondary education opportunities for persons with disabilities have been gradually expanding since the late 1970s. Many colleges and universities have worked to remove attitudinal, architectural, and communications barriers in order that more students with disabilities may enter and successfully complete degree programs (Stedman, 1983). The high schools may therefore incorporate learning strategies, individualization, and adaptations that will enable more disabled and at-risk persons to achieve the goal of higher education.

CHANGING THE SCHOOLS

The potentials for fundamental changes in the ways schools are operated, managed, and administered are evident in many of the directions that have been advanced for school reform. Beginning with the report of the National Commission on Excellence in Education (1983), a large number of studies and statements have recommended changes intended to improve American education. Although the earlier reports did not generally examine instruction for students who were disabled, at risk, difficult to teach, or dropping out of school, these concerns became much more prominent in the late 1980s.

Activity 2, page 511, helps you to gain more information on the school reform movement.

In addition to spotlighting the diverse and troubled student population, the later school reform literature has emphasized the status, rights, responsibilities, preparation, and potential roles of teachers; the conditions of the schools that influence teaching and learning; and the importance of change initiated at the local level, in the school building, and in the classroom. Some of these new directions for teachers' leadership, decision making, and professionalism are reflected in the following composites of recommendations selected from the reports of the Carnegie Forum on Education and the Economy (Branscomb, 1986), the Holmes Group (Lanier, 1986), the National Education Association (1986), and the National Governors' Association (Alexander, 1986). Each of these organizations has set forth recommendations, and all are working to actualize them.

☐ Teachers should have strong roles in school management, decision making, and goal setting and should be accountable for achieving agreed-on standards of performance.

☐ The teaching professions should be restructured to enable differentiated staffing patterns, with rewards at various career stages.

☐ More and better resources should be available to teachers in the form of materials and support staff, teachers' noninstructional duties should be minimized, and their working conditions and the climate of the schools should be enhanced.

☐ The bureaucratic structure of school management should give way to a more collegial system in which teachers and principals can decide what services to try in their own buildings.

☐ Teacher education should become stronger, more integrated, and more in line with the intellectual and social realities of the profession.

☐ A national board for professional teaching standards should be created, and future teacher salaries should increase markedly in relation to the higher standards for training, certification, and performance.

As the field begins to work with ideas like these, it becomes clear that teachers can and should act as full partners in education and that they can bring rich varieties of knowledge, experience, and sensitivity to improvements that will make education responsive and meaningful for all students. One example of the new teacher leadership is the High School Futures Planning Consortium, a network of 26 schools. Teams from each school have learned strategic planning techniques for analyzing societal trends and anticipating their consequences for the schools. Their work is leading to changes in the curriculum, instruction, technology, and organization of these schools, and a distinct feature is more close involvement of students in their own learning (O'Neil, 1988). Other examples are the Team Approach to Better Schools and the Learning Laboratory initiative of the National Education Association, which are based on the belief that effective reform must be defined and designed by teachers working at the local level with their administrators (Futrell, 1989). Other teacher-led, building-based efforts are occurring, many of them involving community leaders, higher education, related services, and others who are concerned with the education, health, and welfare of children and youth.

The emphasis on teacher leadership is also creating new roles and career options for teachers, including those of mentorship, lead teacher with administrative responsibilities, consulting teacher, cooperating teacher, team teacher, member of teacher assistance teams, and member of schoolwide planning teams. Teachers will likely have greater influence on the content and formats of texts and learning materials produced by commercial publishers and will have new opportunities for classroom research and development of instructional methods and materials (Osborn & Stein, 1987).

As teachers take more responsibility for the schools, education may become more child based and less bureaucratic. Genuine improvements are more likely to occur when change starts at the school level because efforts are naturally directed toward the specific contexts and problems exhibited by a school and its students.

Teachers have always made a difference in the lives of children, but in tomorrow's schools teachers may become instruments of change not only for students but for the whole course of education in their communities and beyond. The key to effective schools "lies in the people who populate particular schools at particular times and their interactions with these organizations. The search for excellence in schools is the search for excellence in people" (Clark, Lotto, & Astuto, 1984, p. 50).

BUSINESS AND INDUSTRY

An interesting development has been the participation of business and industry in recommendations for school reform, primarily with the goal of increasing the skills of students who move into the workforce so that the United States may become more competitive with international markets (Yates, 1987). The private sector reports difficulties in finding qualified workers with sufficient preparation in the basic skills and often appears to express the view that education should be brought into the service of economic and technological development and production (Stedman, 1983).

Although much discussion has dealt with the schools' responsibility to business, there are signs that in the future the emphasis may shift more to business's and industry's responsibilities to the schools. School/business partnerships are succeeding in many parts of the country in efforts not only to improve the labor force but to provide instructional resources, bring about communitywide cooperation to decrease the isolation of the schools, and help schools develop good management practices (McLaughlin, Bennett, & Verity, 1988). These partnerships also strengthen political support and advocacy for the schools. As teachers and employers work together more closely, they can also be expected to strengthen the linkages necessary for fuller employment opportunities for people with disabilities.

The technological future is also a very promising joint interest of business, industry, and education. Many technologies that will support normalization, adaptation, mobility, control over the environment, and alternative learning among persons with disabilities are emerging from industry and space science. Although these technologies are still in their infancy, the many advancements being researched and developed include electronic self-help devices, computer programs based on stimulus control techniques, adaptations for using transportation and household appliances, electronic communication systems for persons with speech or hearing impairments, electronic braille devices, microprocessors combined with artificial organs for sensory compensation, artificial vision, voice synthesizers, mediating microprocessors to increase control of artificial limbs, keyboard emulators, combination aids and switch controls to increase the use of industrial and office equipment, speech decoders for speech recognition, robotoid devices programmed with artificial intelligence, and the integration of various technologies to create more powerful adaptations (Behrmann, 1984; Colbourn, 1984; Kimbler, 1984; LeBlanc, Hoko, Aangeenbrug, & Etzel, 1985). In the future, the schools can be expected to make more substantive applications of such current technologies as computer-assisted and computer-managed instruction, instructional television, videodiscs, and combinations of computer and video technologies. Besides enhancing the learning and lifestyles of individuals with disabilities, the technologies of the future will extend education in many directions and into many locations, including the home, and thereby increase vocational options and opportunities for lifelong learning.

SUMMARY THOUGHTS

The turbulence in society, economic structures, industry, education, and other spheres in the late 20th century is a harbinger of change, challenges, and opportunities. For education, the ways schools are organized, operated, and managed will change in major ways (see Table 17.1). As these changes take shape, the major imperative is that planning be unified and comprehensive across all of education, rather than fragmented and piecemeal. The signs point to a much greater interdisciplinary, total community effort to address the common good. Within this effort, special education and other services may be repositioned in ways that make them more integrated with, and strategic to, the overall educational enterprise in the new age.

Increasing numbers of at-risk and difficult-to-teach students will bring about greater creativity in options, alternatives, and opportunities for individualization and student-centered programming, and these changes will benefit students with disabilities in important ways. As the schools address diversity more effectively, the importance of teachers will also be elevated. Teachers will be more crucial in the lives of children, and they will be able to exert leadership as schools and districts work toward greater effectiveness, efficiency, and relevance. As their leadership grows, teachers will have greater status, new roles and responsibilities, more recognition, greater career and salary enhancements, more support, and better working conditions.

Accordingly, more will be expected in terms of cost/benefits, accountability, and performance outcomes. Schools will have to demonstrate the effectiveness of education, particularly that of students with disabilities whose school performance is perhaps more tied to their success in life than that of other students. To achieve the best outcomes also means raising expectations about the capacities and potentials of students with disabilities.

The movement through the current turbulence toward the new age in education will offer some of the most exciting and exacting experiences that teachers have ever experienced. Although much remains to be solved, developed, and consolidated, teachers already have the responsibility for ensuring that their instruction measures up to the current state of the art. For both the present and the future, "play school is out. Schooling is a profession. The law requires that practice in the schools measure up to the art of what has been demonstrated by the profession to be possible. What is done must be calculated to be effective" (Gilhool, Laski, & Gold, 1987, p. 5).

Table 17.1   Features That May Characterize Special Education in the 21st Century

- Special education will reposition itself with other service systems to take leadership in helping all educators to provide effective instruction to the increasingly diverse and "difficult to teach" school population.

- Schools will become more student centered, and more meaningful individualization will take place, which will enable more students with disabilities to succeed in the integrated mainstream.

- Special educators will engage in much more team work and decision making. Students with disabilities will receive instruction and services from interdisciplinary teams of professionals who work and plan together.

- Expanded curricular options will be available across education, with significant enhancements in functional curricula and alternatives at the secondary level. This, too, will enable students with disabilities to participate more fully in the mainstream.

- All teachers will have a greater variety of instructional methods and strategies within their repertoires and will therefore be better equipped to meet individual needs and respond to diversity in the classroom.

- Schools and teachers will be responsible for greater accountability and evidence of effectiveness in the form of student performance outcomes. School effectiveness will become a very public issue in communities.

- The use of electronic communication and information technologies, and of distance education, will be widespread, and students with disabilities will be particular beneficiaries. Many new adaptive technologies will be perfected and marketed to assist people with disabilities in compensating for, and fully functioning in spite of, physical, sensory, or cognitive disabilities.

- Schools will become centers of multidisciplinary activity, with clusters of services on or near the school grounds. Students will take part in a variety of services as part of their school programs.

- Education for all students will extend into the community. Community-based education will be part of the program of each student with a disability, with involvement and participation from various sectors. School will become "more of a concept and less of a place."

- Vocational and career education will also change as the nature of the workplace changes. Many students will be prepared for careers in which they can work at offices within their homes. Thus, employment will also become "more of a concept and less of a place."

REFERENCES

Alexander, L. (Chairperson, Governors' Task Forces on Education). (1986). *Time for results: The governors' 1991 report on education.* Washington, DC: National Governors' Association.

American Association of Colleges for Teacher Education. (1988). *Teacher education pipeline: Schools, colleges, and departments of education enrollments by race and ethnicity.* Washington, DC: Author.

Behrmann, M. (1984). *Handbook of microcomputers in special education.* San Diego: College Hill Press.

Bodner, J. R., Clark, G. M., & Mellard, D. F. (1987). *State graduation policies and program practices related to high school special education programs: A national study.* Lawrence: University of Kansas, Department of Special Education.

Brandl, J. (1983). The effectiveness of special education: A survey. *Policy Studies Review, 2*(1), 227–232.

Branscomb, L. M. (Chairperson, Task Force on Teaching as a Profession). (1986). *A nation prepared: Teachers for the 21st century.* Hyattsville, MD: Carnegie Forum on Education and the Economy.

Clark, D. L., Lotto, L. S., & Astuto, T. A. (1984). Effective schools and school improvement: A comparative analysis of two lines of inquiry. *Educational Administration Quarterly, 20*(3), 41–68.

Colbourn, M. J. (1984). Expert systems: Their potential roles within education. In National Association of State Directors of Special Education. *Proceedings: First special education technology research and development symposium.* Washington, DC: National Association of State Directors of Special Education.

Futrell, J. H. (1989). NEA undergirds bottom-up change. *The School Administrator, 46*(2), 64.

Gilhool, T. F., Laski, F. J., & Gold, S. F. (1987). A legal duty to provide effective schooling. *Counterpoint, 8*(2), 5.

Hoffman, D. (1989, January 20). George Bush: Campaign promises. *Washington Post,* p. A29.

Howsam, R. B. (1983). Public education: A system to meet its needs. *Policy Studies Review, 2*(1), 85–108.

Ishler, R. E. (1988, August 9). Looking ahead to education needs in 2000. *Austin American Statesman,* p. C3.

Kimbler, D. K. (1984). Robots and special education: The robot as extension of self. In National Association of State Directors of Special Education, *Proceedings: First special education technology research and development symposium,* (pp. 93–107). Washington, DC: National Association of State Directors of Special Education.

Kondracke, M. M. (1989, February 6). The two Black America's. *The New Republic,* pp. 17–20.

Lanier, J. E. (Chairperson, The Holmes Group). (1986). *Tomorrow's teachers: A report of the Holmes Group.* East Lansing, MI: Holmes Group.

LeBlanc, J. J., Hoko, J. A., Aangeenbrug, M. H., & Etzel, B. C. (1985). Microcomputers and stimulus control: From the laboratory to the classroom. *Journal of Special Education Technology, 7*(1), 23–30.

Lichtenstein, S. (1988). Dropouts: A secondary special education perspective. *Counterpoint, 8*(3), 13.

Louis Harris & Associates. (1988). *The Metropolitan Life survey of the American teacher, 1988.* New York: Metropolitan Life Insurance Co.

McLaughlin, A., Bennett, W. J., & Verity, C. W. (1988). *Building a quality workforce.* Washington, DC: Joint Initiative of the U.S. Departments of Labor, Education, and Commerce.

National Center for Clinical Infant Programs. (1988). *Infants can't wait: The numbers.* Washington, DC: Author.

National Center for Education Statistics (1988, July). *Pocket projections.* Washington, DC: U.S. Department of Education.

National Commission on Excellence in Education. (1983). *A nation at risk: The imperative for educational reform.* Washington, DC: GPO.

National Education Association. (1986).*The learning workplace: The conditions and resources of teaching.* Washington, DC: Author.

O'Neil, J. (1988). Unlocking the secrets of the future: ASCD consortium plans for the 21st century. *ASCD Update, 30*(6), 1, 6.

Osborne, J., & Stein, M. (1987). The best in basals for all students. *Counterpoint, 8*(2), 5.

Pallas, A., & Verdugo, R. (1986). *Measuring the high school dropout problem.* Washington, DC: U.S. Department of Education.

Singer, B. D. (1972). The future-focused role image. In A. Toffler (Ed.), *Learning for tomorrow: The role of the future in education* (pp. 19–32). New York: Random House.

Skrtic, T. M. (1987). *An organizational analysis of special education reform.* Lawrence: University of Kansas, Department of Special Education.

Stedman, D. J. (1983). How can special education be coordinated with other service systems? *Policy Studies Review, 2*(1), 113–130.

Urban Superintendents Network. (1987). *Dealing with dropouts: The urban superintendents' call to action.* Washington, DC: U.S. Department of Education, Office of Educational Research and Improvement.

Viadero, D. (1989). Seven of ten handicapped graduates found "productive." *Education Week, 8*(32), 6.

Yates, J. R. (1987). Current and emerging forces impacting special education, Part I. *Counterpoint, 8*(4), 4–6.

ADDITIONAL READINGS

Algozzine, B., & Korinek, L. (1985). Where is special education for students with high prevalence handicaps going? *Exceptional Children, 51*(5), 388–394.

Apter, S. J. (1982). *Troubled children: Troubled systems.* New York: Pergamon.

American Federation of Teachers. (1986). *The revolution that is long overdue: Looking toward the future of teaching and learning.* Washington, DC: Author.

Armstrong, J., Anderson, B., Odden, A., & Huddle, G. (1986). *Maintaining the momentum for educational reform.* Denver: Education Commission of the States.

Barton, L., & Tomlinson, S. (Eds.) (1984). *Special education and social interests.* New York: Nichols.

Carnegie Foundation for the Advancement of Teaching. (1988). *The condition of teaching: A state by state analysis, 1988.* Lawrenceville, NJ: University Press.

Commission on Minority Participation in Education and American Life. (1988). *One-third of a nation.* Washington, DC: American Council on Education and Education Commission of the States.

Committee for Economic Development. (1985). *Investing in our children: Business and the public schools.* New York: Author.

Council of Chief State School Officers Study Commission. (1986). *Education and the economy.* Washington, DC: Author.

Council for Exceptional Children. (1986). *Proceedings of the CEC invitational symposium on the future of special education.* Reston, VA: Author.

Dixon, V. (Chairperson, CEC Ad Hoc Committee on Children Not Presently Served). (1988). *Final report of the ad hoc committee on children not presently served.* Reston, VA: Council for Exceptional Children.

Educational Development Center, Inc. (1985). *Improving our schools: Thirty-three studies that inform local action.* Newton, MA: Author.

Kozol, J. (1986). *Illiterate America.* New York: Doubleday.

National Association of State Directors of Special Education. (1984). *Proceedings: First special education technology research and development symposium.* Washington, DC: Author.

National Center for Education Statistics. (1988). *The condition of education, 1988.* Washington, DC: U.S. Department of Education.

National Coalition of Advocates for Students. (1985). *Barriers to excellence: Our children at risk.* Boston: Author.

National School Boards Association. (1986). *Rewarding excellence: Teacher compensation and incentive plans.* Alexandria, VA: Author.

Office of Technology Assessment, U.S. Congress. (1988). *Power on! New tools for teaching and learning.* Washington, DC: GPO.

Patterson, J. L., Purkey, S. C., & Parker, J. V. (1986). *Productive school systems for a nonrational world.* Alexandria, VA: Association for Supervision and Curriculum Development.

Reynolds, M. C., Brandl, J., & Copeland, W. C. (1983). Symposium on public policy and educating handicapped persons. *Policy Studies Review, 2*(1), 1–263.

Sarason, S. B., & Doris, J. (1979). *Educational handicap, public policy, and social history.* New York: Free Press.

Schaffarzick, J., & Sykes, G. (Eds.). *Value conflicts and curriculum issues.* Berkeley, CA: McCutchan.

Shepard, L. A. (1987). The new push for excellence: Widening the schism between regular and special education. *Exceptional Children, 53*(4), 327–329.

Skrtic, T. M. (1988). The crisis in special education knowledge. In E. L. Meyen & T. M. Skrtic (Eds.), *Introduction to exceptional children and youth: Traditional, emerging, and alternative perspectives* (pp. 416–447). Denver: Love.

Urban Institute. (1986). *America's children: Who cares?* Washington, DC: Urban Institute Press.

U.S. Department of Education. (1986). *What works: Research about teaching and learning.* Washington, DC: GPO.

U.S. Department of Education. (1987). *Schools that work: Educating disadvantaged children.* Washington, DC: GPO.

1

Purpose

☐ To help you determine the likelihood that special education will change in the upcoming decades

☐ To help you determine the impact that changes in special education may have on the overall educational enterprise in America's schools

Steps

1. Turn to Table 17.1.

2. Use items from this list, plus other factors you might add, to create a chart that shows your estimation of:

   • The current status of the public schools with regard to these factors
   • Barriers that would make it difficult for changes to be enacted in the schools
   • Conditions, events, or actions that might facilitate such changes in the schools
   • What teachers and principals could do to bring about such changes
   • The impact such changes would have on overall education, the way schools are organized, the way instruction is delivered, the way children learn, and other characteristics of schools as they exist today

Analysis

☐ How likely or unlikely is it that changes in special education suggested by this chapter (or by other sources) will occur?

☐ How do changes suggested for special education also indicate changes in education as a whole?

☐ How long did past changes take to materialize? How were they accomplished? How well did they work?

☐ What can you, as a future teacher, do to help bring about constructive changes in the education of exceptional students?

2

Purpose

☐ To help you gain more information on the current school reform movement

☐ To stimulate your thinking on the potential effects of specific reforms on education for exceptional students

Steps

1. Use the reference list and suggested readings at the end of this chapter as a starting point for making a bibliography of school reform reports. Include a note on how many of them are available from your college, university, or departmental library.

2. Read the daily newspaper and popular magazines with an eye toward articles on school problems and school reform in your local area and in the nation. Start a file or scrapbook of such articles.

3. Choose a topic for further study, and make sure it is precise enough to pursue in some depth. Among the topics you might select are education of students with mild disabilities in the general education classroom, preparation of teachers at the master's degree level only, career ladders for teachers, the shortage of qualified personnel for special education as well as for several other instructional areas in education, raising graduation standards and requirements for all students, or competency-based testing of public school students.

4. In reviewing your topic, consider how the school reform measure you have chosen would influence education for exceptional children. Also consider whether exceptional children are included in or excluded from consideration in the school reform measure.

Analysis

☐ What is the potential impact of current school reform recommendations on education for exceptional students?

☐ Do school reform recommendations tend to encompass or ignore education for an increasingly diverse student population?

☐ Would school reform recommendations be likely to increase or decrease the quality of the teaching force?

☐ What are your own recommendations on ways to improve education?

Glossary

ability grouping Combining students in separate instructional arrangements based on their achievement in an area of study (e.g., math or reading).

acceleration An approach in gifted education in which a student completes more than one school grade each year. Practices such as early admission, grade-skipping, advanced placement, telescoping of grade levels in upgraded situations, and credit by examination are some examples.

accommodation, eye Adjustment of the eye by changing the shape of the lens to allow a person to see clearly at different focal lengths.

active listening A technique in which an individual conveys understanding of, and interest in, what a person is saying, through expressions, gestures, reflecting or reiterating statements, and similar means.

adaptive behavior An individual's ability to meet standards set by society and his or her cultural group. The American Association on Mental Deficiency considers three areas of performance in assessing adaptive behavior: maturation, learning, and social adjustment.

adaptive equipment Devices developed to assist in the physical management of individuals with physical disabilities.

adaptive physical education Physical education programs designed to meet the specific needs of handicapped children and youth.

adventitious Acquired after birth through accident or illness, as contrasted with congenital (present at birth).

adventitious deafness A condition in which a person born with normal hearing sensitivity loses hearing as a result of accident or disease.

advocacy Efforts by parents and professionals to establish or to improve services for exceptional children and youth. Self-advocacy describes efforts made by the individual who will benefit from the results of advocacy.

age norms Standards based on the average performance of individuals in specific age groups.

agraphia Inability or loss of ability to write.

air conduction The process whereby sound waves travel through the air to the auditory mechanism.

albinism An inherited condition that results in a deficiency of pigment in the skin, hair, and iris of the eye. The condition causes the eyes to appear pinkish

and in most cases is accompanied by sensitive and defective vision.

ambiopia Double vision.

American Sign Language Also known as ASL or Ameslan, a visual-manual or sign language entirely unrelated to English. ASL is the language used most often by the adult deaf population in the United States, where it originated.

amniocentesis A procedure applied during pregnancy to identify certain genetic disorders in the fetus.

anecdotal method A procedure for recording and analyzing observations of child behavior; narrative description.

aniridia Failure of the iris of the eye to develop fully.

annual goals Activities or achievements to be completed or attained within a year. Annual goals for handicapped children must be stated in individualized education programs (IEPs), as directed in Public Law 94-142.

anoxia Lack of oxygen. If this occurs, brain damage may result.

aphasia Impairment in the ability to understand or use oral language; often associated with an injury or dysfunction of the brain.

apnea monitor A machine that is attached to an individual to detect cessation in breathing and is used when an individual demonstrates irregularities in respiration.

apraxia A condition involving difficulty with voluntary, or purposeful, muscular movement with no evidence of motor impairment.

aqueous humor The fluid that fills the front chamber of the eye, in front of the crystalline lens.

architectural barrier An environmental obstruction that prevents handicapped persons from using facilities. Examples include stairs, narrow hallways, and conventional restrooms.

articulation Speech sound production by modification of the stream of voiced and unvoiced breath, usually through movements of the jaws, lips, tongue, and soft palate.

asphyxia Deprivation of oxygen, as in smoke suffocation or drowning. If the deprivation is prolonged, the person may go into a coma, with accompanying brain injury or death.

asthma A chronic respiratory condition in which the individual has episodes of difficulty in breathing. Emotional factors can contribute to asthmatic conditions.

astigmatism An eye condition involving a refractive error in which rays from one point of an object are not brought to a single focus because of a difference in the degree of refraction in the different meridians of the eye; causes blurred visual images.

ataxia A form of cerebral palsy characterized by lack of muscle coordination; contributes to problems in balance and position.

athetosis A form of cerebral palsy characterized by involuntary, jerky movements of the extremities, as a result of fluctuating muscle tone.

atonia Also known as hypotonia; lack of muscle tone.

at risk Often used to describe students with potential for experiencing some problem or deficiency.

attention deficit disorder A condition characterized by developmentally inappropriate degrees of inattention, impulsiveness, and hyperactivity.

audiogram A graph of hearing threshold levels as measured by an audiometer and plotted for different pure tone frequencies for each ear.

audiometer An instrument that measures hearing sensitivity and acuity. The measurement of hearing loss is recorded in terms of decibels, units of hearing loss, or as a percentage of normal hearing sensitivity.

auditory training Systematic training to improve an individual's use of remaining (residual) hearing.

augmentative communication systems Assistive devices and symbol systems that enhance the communication ability of individuals who have limited verbal communication skills.

aural Pertaining to the ears and hearing. Binaural refers to both ears.

autism A severe childhood disturbance characterized by bizarre behavior, developmental delays, and extreme isolation. Although it is now categorized as an exceptionality under "Other Health Impaired," the behavioral features are often appropriate for interventions employed with students who have emotional disturbance.

baseline Beginning observations as a foundation for measurement prior to intervention or treatment; a beginning point for comparison of treatment effects.

BD An abbreviation for behavior disorder. Behavior disorder has become a synonym for emotional disturbance.

behavior modification Shaping behavior to minimize or eliminate negative behaviors and to emphasize and reinforce positive behaviors, through control of a learning environment with planned and systematic application of the principles of learning.

bilingual Having proficiency in two languages. Frequently used with reference to children who attend schools in which English is the standard language but who speak another language at home.

blind Having only light perception without projection or being totally without the sense of vision. Educationally, the blind child learns through tactile and auditory materials. (*See also* legal blindness.)

bone conduction Transmission of sound through the bones of the skull to the inner ear.

braille A system of six raised dots used to present a code that can be read through the sense of touch.

brain-injured child One who before, during, or after birth has received an injury or suffered an infection to the brain that impedes normal development.

cataract A condition causing opacity of the lens of the eye, resulting in visual limitation or blindness. Surgical removal of the lens is the most frequently used method of restoring or improving sight. Cataracts occur much more often among adults than among children; in children the condition may occur as a results of rubella (one form of measles).

catheter A narrow tube of rubber, plastic, metal, or glass, which can be inserted into the body to empty the bladder or kidneys, by a method known as catheterization.

catheterization The process of introducing a tube into the bladder through the urethra for withdrawal of urine and is used when an individual is unable to empty the bladder naturally.

CEC Abbreviation for the Council for Exceptional Children.

central nervous system (CNS) The brain and spinal cord.

cerebral palsy (CP) An abnormal alteration of human movement or motor function arising from a defect, injury, or disease of the tissues of the central nervous system. Three main types are usually described — spastic, athetoid, and ataxic.

Child Find An organized effort to identify all handicapped children in need of special services.

children with chronic illnesses A term used in classifying children with diseases that may last for months or a lifetime. Examples include asthma, diabetes, cancer, and cystic fibrosis.

class action A legal procedure carried out on behalf of a particular person to benefit all others with similar problems.

class size A factor in many state laws, regulating the number of handicapped students to be served by one teacher; also expressed as pupil-teacher ratio.

cleft palate A condition characterized by an opening in the roof of the mouth, involving the hard or soft palate, or both, and often extending through the upper lip. Causes nasal speech, certain articulation problems, and sometimes additional physical problems.

Cleft palate usually is treated by surgery and speech therapy.

code-switching A speaker's ability to shift between two or more dialects (Black English to Standard American English) or between formal and informal Standard American English in adjusting to different listeners and settings.

cognition The understanding of information.

collaboration A process of interaction and cooperation among professional educators to provide support for students. The focus tends to be on problem solving and may be designed to assist students with or without special needs.

communication skills The many ways of transferring thought from one person to another through speech, written words, and bodily gestures.

community-based instruction Teaching the skills necessary for community functioning in the natural community setting.

community-referenced instruction Instructional goals that are prioritized on the basis of their importance relative to a student's functioning in the natural environments found in the community-at-large.

community service program A variety of offerings, including emergency programs, community consultation and education, and counseling and therapy, throughout the locality.

complex health care needs A term used to describe children with chronic illnesses. (*See also* children with chronic illnesses.)

compulsory attendance Federal and state laws requiring children to attend school.

conduct disorder One of the classifications of behavior disorder in Quay's dimensional classification system; describes individuals who have aggressive and other negative behaviors (e.g., boisterous, bullying).

conductive hearing loss A form of hearing loss characterized by obstruction along the sound conduction pathway leading to the inner ear. This form of hearing loss is the most preventable and treatable.

congenital Describes the presence of a condition or characteristics in an individual at birth but not limited to hereditary factors. Examples are congenital deafness and congenital heart defects. In contrast, adventitious conditions are acquired after birth.

consent Permission from parents to evaluate a child or to place a child in a program. PL 94-142 contains specific provisions regarding consent.

consulting teachers Specially trained instructors who consult with teachers and other instructional personnel involved in educational programs for exceptional children. Their roles differ from those of itinerant teachers in that consulting teachers do not provide direct services to handicapped children and youth except when demonstrating a technique as part of the consultation.

convergent production Seeking one solution or answer to a problem or question.

cornea The clear, transparent, outer coat of the eyeball forming the covering of the aqueous chamber.

Council for Learning Disabilities (CLD) An organization of professionals who work directly or indirectly with persons who have learning disabilities. Formerly the Division of Children with Learning Disabilities of the Council for Exceptional Children.

counseling therapy A structured relationship or process through which an individual is helped to feel and behave in a more satisfying way, gain a better understanding of himself or herself, and take positive steps toward dealing with the environment through information, reactions, and stimulation. A counselor or therapist directs this process.

criterion-referenced test A measure to ascertain an individual's performance compared to a set criterion. The person is evaluated on his or her own performance and not in comparison to others.

cultural-familial Describes a condition in which an individual is diagnosed as having mental retardation without evidence of cerebral pathology, but having a family history of intellectual subnormality and cultural deprivation.

cystic fibrosis (CF) The most common, and usually fatal, hereditary disease of childhood; affects most body organs, particularly the lungs and pancreas. Abnormal mucus secretions obstruct bodily functions, especially the ability to clear the lungs, which results in excessive coughing.

deaf (deafness) A condition in which the sense of hearing is so lacking or drastically reduced as to prohibit normal functioning and the auditory sense is not the primary means by which speech and language are learned.

decibel (db) A unit of hearing or audition; extent of hearing is expressed as the number of decibels necessary for the person to hear pure tones above the baseline used to measure normal hearing.

defense mechanisms An individual's coping processes to facilitate approach or avoidance behaviors.

deficit A level of performance that is less than expected for an individual.

deinstitutionalization The practice of placing handicapped persons in community programs rather than large residential facilities. Large numbers of people have been removed from institutions and placed in more appropriate community environments.

denial A defense mechanism operating unconsciously to resolve emotional conflict and anxiety by not recognizing thoughts, feelings, needs, or external reality factors that are consciously unacceptable.

dependence The tendency to rely on someone else for assistance in decision making, personal care, and other areas of need.

deregulation A process employed to reduce the restrictiveness of regulations governing the implementation of laws.

developmental disability A condition that originates in childhood and results in a significant handicap for the individual, such as mental retardation, cerebral palsy, epilepsy, and conditions associated with neurological damage.

diabetes A metabolic disorder in which the body is unable to properly utilize carbohydrates in the diet because of failure of the pancreas to secrete an adequate supply of insulin, or failure of the insulin secreted to function properly in the digestive process, resulting in an abnormal concentration of sugar in the blood and urine. Symptoms are excessive thirst, excessive urination, weight loss, slow healing of cuts and bruises, pain in joints, and drowsiness.

dialect Rule-governed sound, form, and content variations in a language as a result of age, race or ethnic group, geography, or other factors that isolate one group of speakers from another; the standard dialect is that used by those of the prevailing group.

differential reinforcement Providing rewards for behavior in the presence of one stimulus situation and not reinforcing in the presence of other stimulus conditions.

diplegia Paralysis of the body in which both sides are affected; a result of injury to both hemispheres of the brain.

disability A functional limitation resulting from a condition (e.g., a paraplegic would have a disability because of the inability to use the lower part of the body).

discrimination learning The ability to differentiate relevant cues and dimensions.

dispute settlement The outcome of methods used to resolve disagreements between parents (or parent surrogates) and school officials. Conferences, mediation, and hearings may be involved.

divergent production Generating many solutions to a problem.

diversity A term used to refer to the range of individual differences among students in a classroom or school. The contributors to the range of differences may include cultural backgrounds of students, learning styles, or instructional needs related to disabilities.

Down syndrome A clinical type of mental retardation resulting from a specific abnormal chromosomal arrangement. Most individuals with Down syndrome have intelligence in the moderate range of retardation.

DSM-III-R *The Diagnostic and Statistical Manual of Mental Disorders* (third edition - revised) published by the American Psychiatric Association; it serves as a manual of mental disorders and criteria used in making psychiatric diagnoses.

due process In an educational context, refers to procedures and policies established to ensure equal educational opportunities for all children. PL 94-142 contains due process procedures specific to handicapped children.

dysfunction Partial disturbance, impairment, or abnormality in a particular bodily activity.

dyslexia A serious reading disability in which an individual fails to learn to read despite adequate intelligence and proper classroom instruction; commonly associated with an injury or dysfunction of the brain.

echolalia A speech condition characterized by involuntary repetition of words, syllables, or sounds spoken by others, as if echoing them; a common characteristic of severe retardation.

ecological assessment The process used to identify the specific skills an individual needs to function in domestic, vocational, recreational, and community environments.

electroencephalogram (EEG) A mechanical tracing made by an electroencephalograph that depicts electrical output of brain waves. An EEG is useful in studying seizures accompanying brain injuries, epilepsy, etc.

eligibility Criteria to determine who does and who does not qualify for a specified program.

emotional lability Frequent and unexplainable shifts in a person's mood.

endogenous Originating from within rather than outside of (exogenous) a person.

enrichment An approach in teaching talented or gifted pupils whereby curricular activities or experiences are expanded into greater depth of understanding and application than those of a regular class. May include resource reading, creative projects, community application, special assignments, small group work and other adaptations of routine school processes.

epilepsy A chronic condition of the central nervous system, characterized by periodic seizures accompanied by convulsions of the muscles and, with the more severe attacks, loss of consciousness.

equal protection The principle set forth in the Fourteenth Amendment that guarantees the same rights and benefits to all citizens with respect to government, unless the withholding of rights and benefits has a justifiable reason — e.g., an epileptic person with regular seizures may not be allowed a driver's license and certain other rights, to protect others.

etiology The cause of a disorder, disease, or handicapping condition.

exceptional children Those whose performance in school-related behaviors varies from the norm to the extent that special instruction, assistance, and/or equipment are required. Children may be classified as exceptional because of intellectual, physical, behavioral, or sensory reasons. The term also is used to describe gifted children.

excess costs Extra costs incurred in educating a handicapped child. For example, if the average per-pupil cost for educating a nonhandicapped child is $1,800 per year and the average per-pupil cost for educating a handicapped child is $2,800 per year, the excess cost is $1,000.

exogenous Originating from external rather than internal (endogenous) causes.

family dynamics Refers to the structures, interactions, patterns, and responses of individuals within a family unit. With a handicapped child, family dynamics may include overcompensation or rejection by some or all members, for example.

fetal alcohol syndrome (FAS) A condition found in some infants of alcoholic women, marked by low birth weight, retardation, cardiac and physical defects.

field of vision The entire area one can see without shifting the gaze; in visually impaired individuals a reduction in field of vision can be considered a handicapping condition.

flow-through funds Those that are mandated to local districts by federal laws but are required to be distributed by the state education agency (SEA). Also called pass-through funds.

fluency 1. Uninterrupted smoothness and rapidity, as in reading or speaking. 2. In Guilford's structure of the intellect, the factors in creative thinking that represent the quality and the number of ideas produced.

foster home A living environment other than one with the parents, in which a child may be placed for rearing, usually by a family or welfare agency.

fragile-X syndrome A recently identified chromosomal disorder associated with mental retardation.

free appropriate public education (FAPE) Used in PL 94-142 to mean special education and related services that are provided at public expense, meet requirements of the state education agency, and conform to the individualized education program (IEP) requirement of PL 94-142.

functional Nonorganic; without known organic cause.

functional curriculum The model of curriculum that prioritizes instruction based on skills that are critical to independent functioning in adult integrated community environments.

functional domains The domains of living in which adults typically live, including domestic, vocational, recreation/leisure, and community.

galactosemia The condition characterized by an inborn error in the metabolism of carbohydrates. Mental retardation is one effect, as is visual impairment.

generalization (of learning) The process of forming a conclusion based on or inferred from a number of specific facts or instances. Lack of ability to generalize learning to situations other than that in which the learning occurred is characteristic of children with reduced intelligence.

grade level The placement of a child in the school program: students typically enter first grade at age 6 and progress one grade per year.

grammar Descriptive or prescriptive rules governing the interactions of word order (syntax) and word form (morphology) in any language.

grand mal A severe form of epileptic seizure involving loss of consciousness and extreme convulsions.

group home A form of alternative living arrangement in which individuals with retardation and multiple handicaps live in a community setting rather than in an institution.

guilt Feelings of being responsible or at fault for an event or circumstance. Some parents of handicapped children, for instance, feel they are to blame for their child's handicapping condition.

habilitation The process of improving an individual's performance in a broad range of skills and abilities. Often used in reference to services provided to persons with severe handicaps to prepare them for employment opportunities.

handicap The consequence of a disability when it causes an individual to function measurably lower than typical individuals intellectually, emotionally, or physically, to an extent that special programs and services are needed. This term does not include gifted individuals as does the term "exceptionality."

handicapism A term referring to prejudice, stereotyping, and discrimination against persons with disabilities.

hearing loss (impairment) A deficiency in the ability to hear. May range from a mild loss to a total lack of hearing ability (deafness). At the level of severe loss, defined as 70-90 dB, measured on an audiometer, hearing impaired individuals require extensive training in communication methods.

hemiplegia (hemiparesis) Paralysis of the arm and leg on one side of the body. The latter term implies lesser severity.

hemophilia A condition, usually hereditary, characterized by failure of the blood to clot following an injury. Profuse bleeding, internal as well as external, occurs from even slight injuries. Found primarily in males, because of hereditary determination factors. An individual with this affliction is called a hemophiliac.

hepatitis B A disease characterized by infection and inflammation of the liver. It is transmitted through close personal contact, specifically through blood, saliva, and semen as well as through environmental surfaces (mats, teaching materials).

herpes A family of diseases. Two are of concern to people who provide group care for children: herpes simplex oral and herpes simplex genital. Symptoms of the former include fever and bleeding ulcers and cold sores in the area around and in the mouth; symptoms of the latter include ulcers on the genitalia and pain or tenderness in the genital area. Oral herpes is transmitted by saliva or respiratory droplets and genital herpes by direct contact with the infected area. There is no cure, but there is relief for symptoms.

hertz (Hz) A unit of measurement of frequency, or vibrations per second of sound waves.

heterarchy Vertical orderings on a comparable level; no one entity is on top of everything; in contrast to hierarchy.

HIV (AIDS) HIV affects the individual's ability to fight off infections. It is transmitted by exposure to infected blood through transfusions and needles, through sexual contact with an infected partner, and from infected mothers to infants during the perinatal period.

hologram An image created by a dynamic process of interaction and differentiation.

homebound instruction Teaching provided by specially trained instructors to students who are unable to attend school. Homebound instruction usually is provided on a short-term basis.

hydrocephalus (hydrocephaly) A condition of excess cerebrospinal fluid accumulation in the cranial cavity, causing undue pressure on the brain and resulting in an enlarged head. Referred to sometimes as "waterhead." Now, surgical procedures such as shunting are used to reduce fluid pressure and head enlargement. If unchecked, the condition usually causes mental retardation.

hyperactive Describes behavior characterized by abnormal, excessive activity or movement that may interfere with a child's learning and cause considerable problems in managing behavior.

hyperopia Farsightedness; poor vision at close range, because of shortened eyeball from back to front so the light rays tend to focus behind the retina. Hyperopia most often is corrected by using convex lenses, which bend the rays so they will focus on the retina.

IEU An abbreviation for intermediate education unit. Several states have educational units that comprise several districts or counties. These units also may be referred to as intermediate districts or cooperative, multicommunity, or county units.

IHE An abbreviation for institutions of higher education. Frequently used in referring to private or public colleges and universities.

immaturity A state of being not as fully developed as normally would be expected in physical, mental, or emotional capacities. Opposite of maturity.

impulsivity The act of making quick and often erroneous responses without considering the conse-quences of the action.

incidence As applied to exceptional children, incidence refers to the number of individuals who at some time in their lives might be considered exceptional.

individualized curriculum sequencing (ICS) approach A remedial intervention used with students who have severe and multiple disabilities, following the most logical order of learning for a given child.

individualized education program (IEP) A requirement of PL 94-142 stipulating that a written education plan must be developed and maintained for each handicapped child. The IEP must include a statement of the child's current level of educational performance, annual goals, short-term instructional objectives, specific services to be provided, dates services are to be provided, and criteria for evaluation.

inner ear Made up of the cochlea and the semicircular canals, the innermost part of the hearing mechanism.

integrated therapy The delivery of related services such as occupational therapy, physical therapy, and speech therapy by incorporating therapeutic interventions into students' usual daily activities. Contrasted with the isolated therapy model, in which students receive specific therapy in one area.

integration In the context of special education, refers to the placement of handicapped children in educational programs also serving nonhandicapped children.

interdisciplinary The collective efforts of individuals from several disciplines in assessing and/or planning a program for an individual. An interdisciplinary team might include, for example, a teacher, psychologist, physician, and social worker.

interpreter A professional who facilitates communication between hearing and deaf individuals, usually by translating between voiced information and sign language. Oral interpreters mouth the speaker's verbal information to enable the hearing handicapped individual to speechread the message.

intrapsychic approach Also termed "psychoanalytic approach;" seeks to understand etiology through examining inner turmoil reflected by observable behaviors.

iris The colored portion of the eye, which contracts or expands involuntarily depending upon the amount of light entering it. The iris functions similarly to the shutter of a camera.

itinerant teachers Those who are trained to provide direct services to handicapped children and youth. They do not operate a classroom but visit handicapped children and youth assigned to regular classes. They also consult with regular classroom teachers.

language A system of words or symbols and the rules for putting them together to form a method of communication among a group of individuals.

LD An acronym for learning disabilities.

LEA An abbreviation for local education agency.

least restrictive environment The educational milieu that is as much as possible like that of students in the "mainstream" school environment, without detracting from the learning and growth of the student with a handicap.

legal blindness The level of visual impairment at which eligibility for special consideration, services, or funding is set. Defined as 20/200 in the better eye after correction or vision that does not exceed 20° in the visual field.

lens (of eye) The transparent component of the eye between the posterior chamber and the vitreous body that functions in focusing light rays and images on the retina.

Lesch-Nyhan syndrome An inborn error of metabolism, characterized by retardation and negative behaviors.

life-space interview A procedure in which a trained professional helps a child work out responses to situations; one aspect of the psychoeducational approach to emotional disturbance.

longitudinal study Research that follows a case or situation over a considerable time, usually a number of years.

low-incidence handicap A classification of impairments that are few in number in relation to other handicaps of the general population (e.g., those involving vision, hearing, or orthopedic impairments).

low vision Educationally, refers to severe visual impairment after correction but with the potential to increase visual functioning through optical aids, nonoptical aids, environmental modifications, and specific techniques.

machine suctioning A process involving a machine with a long tube that is inserted into a person's mouth and throat, when necessary, to remove excessive fluid.

macula The small area near the center of the retina, responsible for detailed vision.

mainstreaming The practice of educating exceptional children in regular educational settings. Generally involves placement in regular classrooms and providing support services when necessary. Used most often with students who have mild handicaps.

mandate A requirement that specific tasks or steps are to be carried out (i.e., federal and state laws mandating that educational services be provided to all handicapped children and youth).

manual communication A system sometimes used by deaf individuals employing sign language or a code expressed primarily through the hands.

manually-coded English (MCE) A communication option for deaf individuals; combines American sign language vocabulary with some pragmatic English structures; fingerspelling supplements ASL signs.

medical model One approach to emotional disturbance, viewing present behaviors as symptoms of an underlying cause.

medically fragile Children requiring specialized health care procedures for life and/or health support in order to attend school.

meningitis Inflammation of the membranes that surround the brain and spinal cord.

meningocele A sac-like membranous pouch that protrudes through an opening in the skull or spinal column; the sac contains cerebrospinal fluid but no spinal nerves. Often occurs in conjunction with spina bifida.

mental age The level of intellectual functioning based on the average for individuals of the same chronological age.

mental retardation A broadly used term that refers to significantly subaverage general intellectual functioning manifested during the developmental period and existing concurrently with impairment in adaptive behavior. At present, definitions indicate a person having an IQ of 70 or less and showing impairment in adaptation or social ability.

metacognition Refers to self-knowledge about how one learns and the regulation of one's own cognition.

microcephalus (microcephaly) A condition in which the head size is small because of an inherited defect that causes reduced brain size and severe mental retardation.

middle ear The part of the ear consisting of the eardrum, the three bones of the hearing mechanism, and the eustachian tube.

minimal brain dysfunction (MBD) A term referring to children of near average, average, or above average intelligence who show learning or behavior disorders as a result of diagnosed or suspected deviations in functions of the central nervous system. The preferred term at present is learning disability.

mobility The process of moving about safely and effectively within the environment. An especially important ability for blind persons, who must coordinate mental orientation and physical locomotion to achieve safe, effective movement. Mobility aids such as canes, guide dogs, sighted guides, or electronic devices help them move about.

modeling A teaching technique in which the teacher performs a desired behavior and encourages the pupil to try the same behavior, using the teacher's demonstrated behavior as an example.

monitoring Activities conducted to ensure that particular requirements or procedures are carried out. For example, states may establish monitoring procedures to determine the degree to which local districts fulfill the IEP requirements of PL 94-142.

monoplegia Paralysis involving one limb.

morphology The form of a single word, in language. A morpheme is the smallest unit of language that has meaning.

multifactorially inherited disorders Conditions resulting from the combined effects of genetic and environmental components.

multihandicaps Concomitant impairments, the combination of which causes problems in learning.

muscular dystrophy (MD) A hereditary disorder that causes loss of vitality and progressive deterioration of the body as a result of atrophy, or the replacement of muscle tissue with fatty tissue.

myelomeningocele *See* meningomyelocele.

myofunctional therapy The training of tongue movements to aid speech production.

myopia (nearsightedness) Condition in which distance vision is poor, usually because of a lengthened diameter of the eyeball from front to back, causing the image to come in focus at a point in front of the retina. Myopia usually is corrected by eyeglasses having a concave lens.

native language The language an individual uses most naturally and learned first.

neonatal Refers to time between the onset of labor and 6 weeks following birth.

neurologically impaired or **handicapped** Pertaining to any of a number of conditions resulting from injury or malformation of the central nervous system. Conditions such as cerebral palsy, epilepsy, and the Strauss syndrome are examples.

NIMH Acronym for the National Institute of Mental Health.

nondiscriminatory testing The use of assessment instruments that allow the individual being tested to perform maximally on those skills or behaviors being assessed. A test discriminates against an individual when the norms are inappropriate, the content does not relate to the individual's cultural background, the examinee does not understand the language of the test items or of the person administering the test, or when sensory problems interfere with performance.

norm A standard based on the performance of a representative group with which the performance of others on similar tasks can be compared.

norm-referenced tests Instruments used to ascertain an individual's performance compared to others' performance on the same instrument.

normalization An ideology that has been emphasized as a principle of human service; addresses and provision of patterns of life for the handicapped that are as close as possible to those of members of society in general. This principle has received particular support in reference to improving services for persons with mental retardation.

nystagmus Continuous, involuntary movement of the eyeball; usually affects both eyes and is associated with visual impairment.

occupational therapy Engaging individuals or groups in activities designed to enhance their physical, social, psychological, and cognitive development. A major service provided by most rehabilitation centers.

ophthalmologist A physician (M.D.) specializing in diagnosis and treatment of defects and diseases of the eye who can perform surgery, prescribe drugs, and determine the proper lenses.

optic nerve The cranial nerve that carries nerve impulses of sight to the brain.

optician A technician who grinds lenses, fits them into frames, and adjusts frames to the wearer.

optometrist A licensed doctor of optometry (O.D.) who specializes in measurement of refractive errors of the eye and prescribes glasses or contact lenses to correct these errors. Those specializing in low vision prescribe optical aids such as telescopic lenses.

oral Pertaining to, surrounding, or done by the mouth, as in speech.

organic Refers to factors within the body, particularly the central nervous system, that can cause a handicapping condition.

orthopedic handicap A disabling condition caused by physical impairments, especially those related to the bones, joints, and muscles.

orthosis An appliance used to support, correct, or allign a physical deformity; a brace.

osteogenesis imperfecta A condition characterized by defective development of bone tissue.

otitis media Inflammation of the middle ear, possibly accompanied by pain, fever, interference with hearing, and vertigo. The condition can result in conductive hearing loss or impairment.

pacing Regulating the rate at which material is presented to a student according to how rapidly he or she can learn it.

paralysis Loss of voluntary movement or sensation in a part of the body; caused by disease or injury.

paraplegia A person trained as an assistant to a professionally qualified teacher. Some states have certification requirements for paraprofessionals.

parent-to-parent group A program designed to allow parents of handicapped children the opportunity to discuss their feelings about their children, which can be highly beneficial.

partially seeing Having visual acuity greater than 20/20 but not greater than 20/70 in the better eye with correction; this term is no longer used by practitioners in the field.

peer tutoring An instructional approach involving the pairing of students to help each other. Teachers will guide the tutoring by assisting the tutors on techniques and ensuring that the objectives of the tutoring session are understood.

perceptual disorders Difficulties or deficiencies in using the sense of sight, touch, smell, taste, or hearing to correctly recognize the various objects or situations within the environment. This type of disorder may become apparent in a student's poor performance in activities such as drawing, writing, and recognizing forms, sizes, or shapes.

perinatal Refers to the general time period shortly before, during, or immediately after birth.

peripheral vision Perception of objects, color, or motion by portions of the eye other than the macula. The images perceived are at the extreme edges of the visual field.

Perthes (Legg-Calve-Perthes) disease Degeneration of the growth center of the thigh bone; intervention can reverse its effects.

pervasive developmental disorders Distortions in the whole range of psychological functions during childhood development including attention, perception, learning abilities, language, social skills, reality contact, and motor skills.

petit mal A mild form of seizure occurring in epileptic conditions; characterized by dizziness and momentary lapse of consciousness.

phenylketonuria (PKU) A hereditary condition in which the absence of an enzyme essential for digesting protein affects the metabolism of the body and results in a gradual buildup of toxic substances in the blood and urine of infants having this condition. Interferes with normal development and function of the brain and is possibly the most widely known abnormality of metabolism that causes mental retardation.

phonology The concept relating to the production and comprehension of speech sounds. Phonemes comprise the sound categories.

physical therapy Manipulation, massage, and exercise of body parts to assist an individual with motor control for optimal functioning.

postnatal Occurring after birth.

poverty line An economic index used to identify individuals and families living in poverty. In 1989 a family of three whose annual income was $9,000 or less was considered to be living below the poverty line.

precision teaching A systematic procedure of continuous and direct recording of behavior, espoused by Ogden Lindsley and others. Precision teaching employs the techniques of behavior modification and task analysis for management of instruction and behavior.

prenatal Occurring during gestation; prior to birth.

prevalance As applied to exceptional children, the

number of exceptional children who exist at the present time.

projective technique A relatively unstructured method used to study and diagnose certain problems of personality. A product or response (such as a drawing, interpretation of a picture, or completion of a sentence) is secured from an individual and analyzed in an effort to gain an understanding of the total personality.

prosthesis An artificial body part.

protective safeguards Procedures established to ensure that the rights of the individual are protected.

psychoanalytic approach *See* intrapsychic approach.

psychological processes Covert cognitive behaviors that transform and manipulate information.

psychomotor seizure An epileptic activity in which the individual appears to be conscious during the attack but behaves in an unusual or bizarre way, after which he or she does not remember what happened during the episode. Some indications of psychomotor seizure may be chewing, lip smacking, ringing in ears, abdominal pains, dizziness.

psychosis A term of medical origin, referring to a type of severe behavior disorder. Characteristics include loss of reality contact and abnormal acts, thoughts, and feelings.

Public Law 93-380 Educational Amendments of 1974, passed August 21, 1974.

Public Law 93-516 An amendment passed by Congress broadening the application of Section 504 of the Rehabilitation Act of 1973 to include educational services.

Public Law 94-142 The Education for All Handicapped Children Act of 1975.

Public Law 99-457 Amended and reauthorized the Education for All Handicapped Children Act and appropriated more monies for preschool intervention; also provided specific guidelines, including those for the individualized family service plan (IFSP).

pupil (of eye) the contractible opening in the center of the iris of the eye, through which light enters.

quadriplegia Paralysis involving all four limbs.

referent An object, idea, or event in the real world symbolized by words.

rehabilitation Literally, restoration. Most often used in reference to physical problems.

reinforcement Any consequence of behavior that increases the probability of that behavior being repeated in the future.

remediation Correction of a deficiency. Often used in reference to correction of academic deficits (e.g., problems in reading).

resource room A program option involving placement

of a student in a regular class plus assignment to a special teacher for remedial or supplemental instruction. The special teacher may be referred to as a resource teacher, and the room in which special instruction is offered is referred to as a resource room.

respiratory therapist A specialist trained to assist individuals in breathing through technical devices and/or special procedures and practices.

retina The innermost component of the eye, which contains sensitive nerve fibers that connect to the optic nerve to produce sight. Retinal detachment is the loosening or pulling away of the retina from its normal position in the eye. In children, this condition usually is caused by accidents and may start with a slight loss of vision that might progress to almost complete blindness.

retrolental fibroplasia (retinopathy of prematurity) A disease of the eyes that results from excessive oxygen while a baby is in an incubator. The condition causes a retinal overgrowth that limits vision. The disease was common among premature babies of the 1940s but was drastically reduced in incidence until recent years, when medicine began to save very small infants.

rigidity State of continuous tension of the muscles; seen in some types of cerebral palsy.

rubeola The "old-fashioned" 10-day measles, or red measles, which is accompanied by a red rash and fever. The disease can be prevented with vaccine, and is far less threatening to the unborn fetus than is rubella.

schizophrenia A severe mental disorder characterized by a fragmented personality involving fantasies, illusions, delusions, and, in general, being out of touch with reality.

school social work services School social workers provide a major communication link between school staff and families. Casework services include assistance in interpreting evaluation reports and making recommendations. In some districts social workers chair child-study committees. They are a major resource for special educators working with community agencies.

screening Abbreviated testing procedures by a variety of disciplines conducted on a large scale to locate children requiring more detailed testing or specialized teaching.

SEA An abbreviation for state education agency, the department in state government with primary responsibility for public school education.

Section 504 Refers to Section 504 of the Rehabilitation Act of 1973. Contains requirements designed to guarantee the civil rights of persons with handicaps.

self-contained class A program in which pupils with similar needs and skills are assigned and taught by the same teacher throughout the school day.

self-managed data collection and evaluation activities An approach used in collaboration among professional educators in assisting students which involves requiring students to record their own behavior.

self-managed instruction An instructional approach allowing students themselves to have input into decisions regarding how they will be taught.

self-managed interventions Interventions designed to help students control their own behavior. Students play a primary role in the planning and/or execution of the intervention.

semantics The study of the significance or meaning of words.

sensorineural (sensory-neural) hearing loss A condition involving impairment in the inner ear or the central nervous system. Also referred to as neural or nerve deafness.

sheltered workshop A facility that offers individuals who are not able to work in competitive employment an opportunity to work in a controlled environment at their level of functioning.

shunt (shunting) A technique involving implantation of a tube to drain or provide a bypass for excess cerebrospinal fluid, as in hydrocephalus.

sickle cell anemia A condition of the blood in which the red cells assume a crescent shape and do not funtion properly in carrying oxygen. The condition is genetic and largely limited to the black race. It results in low vitality, pain, sloughing of blood cells, interference with cerebral nutrition and, if severe enough, may cause mental retardation or death.

soft neurological signs Mild or slight neurological abnormalities that are difficult to detect.

spastic Refers to muscular incoordination resulting from muscle spasms, opposing contractions of muscles, and paralytic effects. Also denotes one form of cerebral palsy having the above characteristics.

special class A program option for exceptional children involving assignment of children with similar instructional needs to a class taught by a certified special teacher. Special classes sometimes are referred to as self-contained classes.

special education A broad term covering programs and services for children who deviate physically, mentally, or emotionally from the normal to an extent that they require unique learning experiences, techniques, or materials in order to be maintained in the regular classroom, and specialized classes and programs if the problems are more severe. As defined by PL 94-142, specifically designed instruction, at no cost to the parent, to meet the unique needs of a child with handicaps, including classroom instruction, physical education, home instruction, and instruction in hospitals and institutions.

special-purpose school A term frequently applied to

schools that serve only exceptional children. Such schools may offer programs for one or more types of exceptional children. Sometimes called special schools.

special teacher A teacher certified to teach exceptional children. Historically the term has been applied primarily to teachers of self-contained classes for exceptional children. Currently the term is applied to certified teachers assigned to teach exceptional children.

speech The realization of language through a sound system, including articulation, fluency, and voice parameters.

speech-language pathologist A trained specialist who works with students who have articulation, fluency, voice, and/or language problems. Therapy services may be provided in individual therapy sessions, group therapy sessions, or, in many cases, through consultation with the student's regular classroom teacher.

speechreading Formerly called ''lipreading,'' a technique for decoding verbal information using visible movements of the speaker's mouth in conjunction with context and auditory cues.

spina bifida A congenital malformation of the spine characterized by lack of closure of the vertebral column, which often allows protrusion of the spinal cord into a sac at the base of the spine. The degree of severity may vary, but this condition often causes paralysis of the lower extremities, changes in tactile and thermal sensations, and a lack of bowel and bladder control. Whenever possible, surgery is performed at an early age to reduce the handicapping effects. Spina bifida frequently is associated with hydrocephalus and a reduction of intelligence.

standard deviation A measure of expressing the variability of a set of scores or attributes. Small standard deviations mean the scores are distributed close to the mean; large standard deviations mean the scores are spread over a wider range.

standardized tests Tests for which norms and specific directions for administration are available.

state aid Funds from the state treasury allocated to local districts. Most states provide extra funds to local districts to help cover the additional costs incurred in educating exceptional children.

state institutions Residential programs supported by public tax sources; most states operate institutions for persons with mental retardation and emotional/behavioral problems.

state plan A stipulation of Public Law 94-142 requiring state departments of education to submit a planned program for implementation and administration of the law, following the guidelines for content and structure.

stereotyped behavior Seemingly purposeless motor activity or body posturing. Seen commonly in persons with severe disabilities.

stimulus Any object or happening that excites a response from an organism.

strabismus A condition in which a person's eyes cross as a result of weakness of one or more of the eye muscles; prevents the eyes from focusing on the same object simultaneously.

strategy training An instructional approach where the teacher not only teaches new information to the student, but also teaches the student how to learn.

structure-of-intellect Guilford's model, used extensively in gifted education.

stuttering Slang term for dysfluency; speech characterized by blocking, hesitation, or repetition of single sounds, words, and sometimes sentences.

suctioning A procedure used to remove fluid from the mouth, throat, or trachea when the individual is unable to accomplish this on his or her own.

support services Special services provided to exceptional children beyond their basic educational program. May include speech-language therapy, occupational therapy, physical therapy, music therapy, tutoring, and psychological services.

surrogate parent A person other than an individual's natural parent who has legal responsibility for the person's welfare.

syntax (or **grammar**) The linguistic rules of word order for meaningful sentences; rules governing sentence structure and word/phrase sequence.

Tay-Sachs disease A condition characterized by a defect in the metabolism of fats. Leads to blindness, paralysis, convulsions, and mental retardation.

technology dependent A child who needs a medical device to compensate for the loss of a vital body function. Such children include those requiring nutrition or drugs intravenously, children who are ventilator dependent or children dependent on devices such as renal dialysis or apnea monitors.

telescoping An instructional option in gifted education that involves covering the same amount of material in less than the usual amount of time.

teratogens Outside agents or conditions that cause malformations in developing embryos.

therapeutic recreation A form of treatment that employs leisure activities of a mildly physical nature as corrective measures.

time-out A behavior management technique that eliminates possible reinforcing events for undesirable behaviors for a given time. For example, a child may be moved from classmates to a corner of the room.

total communication A system of expressive/receptive language in which manual signs and fingerspelling are combined with speech, speechreading, and listening in the way deemed most beneficial to a hearing impaired individual.

transdisciplinary approach Involves sharing expertise and responsibilities among team members who are involved in the assessment process and development of the educational program.

trauma Generally, a physical or psychological blow.

tremor Rhythmical movement or shaking; often associated with cerebral palsy.

triplegia Paralysis involving three limbs.

tube feeding The process through which food is introduced directly into the stomach through a tube attached to an opening (stoma) in the abdomen (gastronomy) or through a tube inserted via the individual's nose and extended to the stomach (nasogastronomy). Tube feeding is used when the individual is unable to obtain proper nourishment via mouth.

Turner's syndrome An inherited disorder affecting the chromosome that determines sex characteristics, resulting in retarded mental, physical, and sexual development.

underachiever An individual who does not perform at a level expected for his or her age and ability level.

value system The underlying motives, goals, and expectations that influence others' actions and philosophy.

ventilator A mechanical device that administers air or oxygen to the lungs and is used when an individual is unable to breathe for him or herself.

visual efficiency The degree to which one can perform specific visual tasks with ease, comfort, and minimum time; cannot be measured or predicted clinically with any accuracy by medical, psychological, or educational personnel.

visual functioning How people use whatever vision they have. Some children and youth have limited visual capacity and are still extremely visually oriented; others with similar visual potential are not responsive to visual stimuli at all.

visual impairment A measured loss of any of the visual functions such as acuity, visual fields, color vision, or binocular vision.

vitreous humor The fluid in the back chamber of the eye that fills the space between the retina and the lens.

vocational education Educational programs designed to prepare individuals for employment.

vocational rehabilitation The service of providing diagnosis, guidance, training, physical restoration, and placement to disabled persons for the purpose of preparing them for and involving them in employment that helps them to live with greater independence. The preferred term is now rehabilitation services.

VSTM Acronym for very short-term memory.

work-study programs The teaching of vocational skills combined with actual on-the-job experience.

world view A shared pattern of basic beliefs and assumptions about the nature of the world and how it works.

Author Index

Subject Index